# The Quest for Justice

## Readings in Political Ethics

**THIRD EDITION**

EDITED BY

**Leslie G. Rubin**
**Charles T. Rubin**

**GINN PRESS**

160 Gould Street
Needham Heights, MA 02194

10 9 8 7 6 5 4 3 2 1

 **GINN PRESS**

ISBN 0–536–58152-5

BA 7110

160 Gould Street/Needham Heights, MA 02194
Simon & Schuster Higher Education Publishing Group

# Copyright Acknowledgements

This book is dedicated to Robert H. Horwitz.

# Contents

# Selection from *The Republic*

## *Plato (ca. 427–ca. 348 B.C.)*

*With some reason, it has been said that Western philosophy is a series of footnotes to Plato, for even those thinkers who would like to escape from Plato's concepts and methods find themselves struggling with his ideas and producing footnotes of their own. This student of Socrates and teacher of Aristotle wrote at least 29 dialogues upon widely varied themes, probably the most famous of which is* The Republic. *We consider* The Republic *an apt opening for this collection, because its most obvious theme is the quest for the meaning and value of justice. The excerpt presented here is part of a discussion between Socrates ("I") and a young man named Glaucon ("he"), who was Plato's brother. Socrates paints a picture of the enterprise of education commonly called "the allegory of the cave," in elaboration of the astounding assertion that the only happy city is one in which philosophers rule as kings and kings adequately philosophize.*

*Try to picture the scene as Socrates describes it to Glaucon. (It can be helpful to picture a theater with perpetually running movies.) What does Socrates mean by suggesting that the cave-dwellers are "like us"? Are we like those cave dwellers? What happens to people who leave the cave? What happens after they return? Would you return, if you had the chance to leave?*

### BOOK VII

"Next, then," I said, "make an image of our nature in its education and want of education, likening it to a condition of the following kind. See human beings as though they were in an underground cave-like dwelling with its entrance, a long one, open to the light across the whole width of the cave. They are in it from childhood with their legs and necks in bonds so that they are fixed, seeing only in front of them, unable because of the bond to turn their heads all the way around. Their light is from a fire burning far above and behind them. Between the fire and the prisoners there is a road above, along which see a wall, built like the partitions puppet-handlers set in front of the human beings and over which they show the puppets."

"I see," he said.

"Then also see along this wall human beings carrying all sorts of artifacts, which project above the wall, and statues of men and other animals wrought from stone, wood, and every kind of material; as is to be expected, some of the carriers utter sounds while others are silent."

"It's a strange image," he said, "and strange prisoners you're telling of."

"They're like us," I said. "For in the first place, do you suppose such men would have seen anything of themselves and one another other than the shadows cast by the fire on the side of the cave facing them?"

"How could they," he said, "if they had been compelled to keep their heads motionless throughout life?"

*1*

"And what about the things that are carried by? Isn't it the same with them?"

"Of course."

"If they were able to discuss things with one another, don't you believe they would hold that they are naming these things going by before them that they see?"

"Necessarily."

"And what if the prison also had an echo from the side facing them? Whenever one of the men passing by happens to utter a sound, do you suppose they would believe that anything other than the passing shadow was uttering the sound?"

"No, by Zeus," he said. "I don't."

"Then most certainly," I said, "such men would hold that the truth is nothing other than the shadows of artificial things."

"Most necessarily," he said.

"Now consider," I said, "what their release and healing from bonds and folly would be like if something of this sort were by nature to happen to them. Take a man who is released and suddenly compelled to stand up, to turn his neck around, to walk and look up toward the light; and who, moreover, in doing all this is in pain and, because he is dazzled, is unable to make out those things whose shadows he saw before. What do you suppose he'd say if someone were to tell him that before he saw silly nothings, while now, because he is somewhat nearer to what *is* and more turned toward beings, he sees more correctly; and, in particular, showing him each of the things that pass by, were to compel the man to answer his questions about what they are? Don't you suppose he'd be at a loss and believe that what was seen before is truer than what is now shown?"

"Yes," he said, "by far."

"And, if he compelled him to look at the light itself, would his eyes hurt and would he flee, turning away to those things that he is able to make out and hold them to be really clearer than what is being shown?"

"So he would," he said.

"And if," I said, "someone dragged him away from there by force along the rough, steep, upward way and didn't let him go before he had dragged him out into the light of the sun, wouldn't he be distressed and annoyed at being so dragged? And when he came to the light, wouldn't he have his eyes full of its beam and be unable to see even one of the things now said to be true?"

"No, he wouldn't," he said, "at least not right away."

"Then I suppose he'd have to get accustomed, if he were going to see what's up above. At first he'd most easily make out the shadows; and after that the phantoms of the human beings and the other things in water; and, later, the things themselves. And from there he could turn to beholding the things in heaven and heaven itself, more easily at night—looking at the light of the stars and the moon—than by day—looking at the sun and sunlight."

"Of course."

"Then finally I suppose he would be able to make out the sun—not its appearances in water or some alien place, but the sun itself by itself in its own region—and see what it's like."

"Necessarily," he said.

"And after that he would already be in a position to conclude about it that this is the source of the seasons and the years, and is the steward of all things in the visible place, and is in a certain way the cause of all those things he and his companions had been seeing."

"It's plain," he said, "that this would be his next step."

"What then? When he recalled his first home and the wisdom there, and his fellow prisoners in that time, don't you suppose he would consider himself happy for the change and pity the others?"

"Quite so."

"And if in that time there were among them any honors, praises, and prizes for the man who is sharpest at making out the things that go by, and most remembers which of them are accustomed to pass before, which after, and which at the same time as others, and who is thereby most able to divine what is going to come, in your opinion would he be desirous of them and envy those who are honored and hold power among these men? Or, rather, would he be affected as Homer says and want very much 'to be on the soil, a serf to another man, to a portionless man,' and to undergo anything whatsoever rather than to opine those things and live that way?"

"Yes," he said, "I suppose he would prefer to undergo everything rather than live that way."

"Now reflect on this too," I said. "If such a man were to come down again and sit in the same seat, on coming suddenly from the sun wouldn't his eyes get infected with darkness?"

"Very much so," he said.

"And if he once more had to compete with those perpetual prisoners in forming judgments about those shadows while his vision was still dim, before his eyes had recovered, and if the time needed for getting accustomed were not at all short, wouldn't he be the source of laughter, and wouldn't it be said of him that he went up and came back with his eyes corrupted, and that it's not even worth trying to go up? And if they were somehow able to get their hands on and kill the man who attempts to release and lead up, wouldn't they kill him?"

"No doubt about it," he said. . . .

# "Lycurgus"

## Plutarch (ca. A.D. 45–ca. 120)

*In addition to taking part in politics and composing essays and dialogues on various moral and philosophical topics, Plutarch, a Greek living under the Roman Empire, wrote many historical-biographical essays on famous political actors of Greece and Rome, showing the parallel developments of the two great civilizations. This selection from his* Lives of the Noble Grecians and Romans, *an account of the political accomplishments of Lycurgus (probably seventh century B.C.), provokes questions about the founding of regimes, questions that recur throughout the study of politics, both ancient and modern. President Harry Truman is said to have referred to Plutarch's* Lives *for guidance in understanding enigmatic political figures he encountered.*

*Consider the extensive ramifications that a revolution—a sweeping change of the political order—can have on all aspects of life. What is Lycurgus, the founder who conceives and directs such changes, trying to do to or for his people? What accounts for his reported success? How does the Spartan way of life compare with ours? What is admirable about Lycurgus or his regime? What might be the flaws of this "philosophic state"?*

There is so much uncertainty in the accounts which historians have left us of Lycurgus, the lawgiver of Sparta, that scarcely anything is asserted by one of them which is not called into question or contradicted by the rest. Their sentiments are quite different as to the family he came of, the voyages he undertook, the place and manner of his death, but most of all when they speak of the laws he made and the commonwealth which he founded. They cannot, by any means, be brought to an agreement as to the very age in which he lived; for some of them say that he flourished in the time of Iphitus, and that they two jointly contrived the ordinance for the cessation of arms during the solemnity of the Olympic games. Of this opinion was Aristotle; and for confirmation of it, he alleges an inscription upon one of the copper quoits used in those sports, upon which the name of Lycurgus continued uneffaced to his time. But Eratosthenes and Apollodorus and other chronologers, computing the time by the successions of the Spartan kings, pretend to demonstrate that he was much more ancient than the institution of the Olympic games. Timaeus conjectures that there were two of this name, and in diverse times, but that the one of them being much more famous than the other, men gave to him the glory of the exploits of both; the elder of the two, according to him, was not long after Homer; and some are so particular as to say that he had seen him. But that he was of great antiquity may be gathered from a passage in Xenophon, where he makes him contemporary with the Heraclidae. By descent, indeed, the very last kings of Sparta were Heraclidae too; but he seems in that place to speak of the first and more immediate successors of Hercules. But notwithstanding this confusion and obscurity, we shall endeavour to compose the history of his life, adhering to those statements which are least contradicted, and depending upon those authors who are most worthy of credit.

The poet Simonides will have it that Lycurgus was the son of Prytanis, and not of Eunomus; but in this opinion he is singular, for all the rest deduce the genealogy of them both as follows—

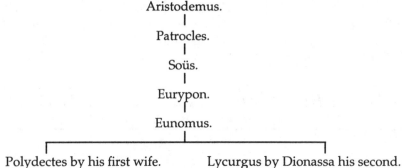

Aristodemus.

Patrocles.

Soüs.

Eurypon.

Eunomus.

Polydectes by his first wife.          Lycurgus by Dionassa his second.

Dieuchidas says he was the sixth from Patrocles and the eleventh from Hercules. Be this as it will, Soüs certainly was the most renowned of all his ancestors, under whose conduct the Spartans made slaves of the Helots, and added to their dominions, by conquest, a good part of Arcadia. There goes a story of this king Soüs, that, being besieged by the Clitorians in a dry and stony place so that he could come at no water, he was at last constrained to agree with them upon these terms, that he would restore to them all his conquests, provided that himself and all his men should drink of the nearest spring. After the usual oaths and ratifications, he called his soldiers together, and offered to him that would forbear drinking, his kingdom for a reward; and when not a man of them was able to forbear, in short, when they had all drunk their fill, at last comes King Soüs himself to the spring, and, having sprinkled his face only, without swallowing one drop, marches off in the face of his enemies, refusing to yield up his conquests, because himself and all his men had not, according to the articles, drunk of their water.

Although he was justly had in admiration on this account, yet his family was not surnamed from him, but from his son Eurypon (of whom they were called Eurypontids); the reason of which was that Eurypon relaxed the rigor of the monarchy, seeking favor and popularity with the many. They, after this first step, grew bolder; and the succeeding kings partly incurred hatred with their people by trying to use force, or, for popularity's sake and through weakness, gave way; and anarchy and confusion long prevailed in Sparta, causing, moreover, the death of the father of Lycurgus. For as he was endeavoring to quell a riot, he was stabbed with a butcher's knife, and left the title of king to his eldest son, Polydectes.

He, too, dying soon after, the right of succession (as every one thought) rested in Lycurgus; and reign he did, until it was found that the queen, his sister-in-law, was with child; upon which he immediately declared that the kingdom belonged to her issue, provided it were male, and that he himself exercised the regal jurisdiction only as his guardian; the Spartan name for which office is *prodicus*. Soon after, an overture was made to him by the queen, that she would herself in some way destroy the infant, upon condition that he would marry her when he came to the crown. Abhorring the woman's wickedness, he nevertheless did not reject her proposal, but, making show of closing with her, despatched the messenger with thanks and expressions of joy, but dissuaded her earnestly from procuring herself to miscarry, which would impair her health, if not endanger her life; he himself, he said, would see to it, that the child, as soon as born, should be taken out of the way. By such artifices having drawn on the woman to the time of her lying-in, as soon as he heard that she was in labour, he sent persons to be by and observe all that passed, with orders that if it were a girl they should deliver it to the women, but if a boy, should bring it to him wheresoever he were, and whatsoever doing. It fell out that when he was at supper with the principal magistrates the queen was brought to bed of a boy, who was soon after presented to him as he was at the table; he, taking him into his arms, said to those about him, "Men of Sparta, here is a king born unto us;" this said, he laid him down in the king's place, and named him Charilaus, that is, the joy of the people; because that all were transported with joy and with wonder at his noble and just spirit. His reign had lasted only eight months, but he was honored on other accounts by the citizens, and there were more who obeyed him because of his eminent virtues, than because he was regent to the king and had the royal power in his hands. Some, however, envied and sought to impede his growing influence while he was still young; chiefly the kindred and friends of the queen-mother, who pretended to have been dealt with injuriously. Her brother Leonidas, in a warm debate which fell out betwixt him and Lycurgus, went so far as to tell him to his face that he was well assured that ere long he should see him king; suggesting suspicions and preparing the way for an accusation of him, as though he had made away with his nephew, if the child should chance to fail, though by a natural death. Words of the like import were designedly cast abroad by the queen-mother and her adherents.

Troubled at this, and not knowing what it might come to, he thought it his wisest course to avoid their envy by a voluntary exile, and to travel from place to place until his nephew came to marriageable years, and, by having a son, had secured the succession; setting sail, therefore, with this resolution, he first arrived at Crete, where, having considered their several forms of government, and got an acquaintance with the principal men amongst them, some of their laws he very much approved of, and resolved to make use of them in his own country; a good part he rejected as useless. Among the persons there the most renowned for their learning and their wisdom in state matters was one Thales, whom Lycurgus, by importunities and assurances of friendship, persuaded to go over to Lacedaemon; where, though by his outward appearance and his own profession he seemed to be no other than a lyric poet, in reality he performed the part of one of the ablest lawgivers in the world. The very songs which he composed were exhortations to obedience and concord, and the very measure and cadence of the verse, conveying impressions of order and tranquillity, had so great an influence on the minds of the listeners, that they were insensibly softened and civilized, insomuch that they renounced their private feuds and animosities, and were reunited in a common admiration of virtue. So that it may truly be said that Thales prepared the way for the discipline introduced by Lycurgus.

From Crete he sailed to Asia, with design, as is said, to examine the difference betwixt the manners and rules of life of the Cretans, which were very sober and temperate, and those of the Ionians, a people of sumptuous and delicate habits, and so to form a judgment; just as physicians do by comparing healthy and diseased bodies. Here he had the first sight of Homer's works, in the hands, we may suppose, of the posterity of Creophylus; and, having observed that the few loose expressions and actions of ill example which are to be found in his poems were much outweighed by serious lessons of state and rules of morality, he set himself eagerly to transcribe and digest them into order, as thinking they would be of good use in his own country. They had, indeed, already obtained some slight repute among the Greeks, and scattered portions, as chance conveyed them, were in the hands of individuals; but Lycurgus first made them really known.

The Egyptians say that he took a voyage into Egypt, and that, being much taken with their way of separating the soldiery from the rest of the nation, he transferred it from them to Sparta, a removal from contact with those employed in low and mechanical occupations giving high refinement and beauty to the state. Some Greek writers also record this. But as for his voyages into Spain, Africa and the Indies, and his conferences there with the Gymnosophists, the whole relation, as far as I can find, rests on the single credit of the Spartan Aristocrates, the son of Hipparchus.

Lycurgus was much missed at Sparta, and often sent for, "for kings indeed we have," they said, "who wear the marks and assume the titles of royalty, but as for the qualities of their minds, they have nothing by which they are to be distinguished from their subjects"; adding, that in him alone was the true foundation of sovereignty to be seen, a nature made to rule, and a genius to gain obedience. Nor were the kings themselves averse to see him back, for they looked upon his presence as a bulwark against the insolencies of the people.

Things being in this posture at his return, he applied himself, without loss of time, to a thorough reformation and resolved to change the whole face of the commonwealth; for what could a few particular laws and a partial alteratic   avail? He must act as wise physicians do, in the case of one who labors under a complication of diseases, by force of medicines reduce and exhaust him, change his whole temperament, and then set him upon a totally new regimen of diet. Having thus projected things, away he goes to Delphi to consult Apollo there; which having done, and offered his sacrifice, he returned with that renowned oracle, in which he is called beloved of God, and rather God than man; that his prayers were heard, that his laws should be the best, and the commonwealth which observed them the most famous in the world. Encouraged by these things, he set himself to bring over to his side the leading men of Sparta, exhorting them to give him a helping hand in his great undertaking; he broke it first to his particular friends, and then by degrees gained others, and animated them all to put his design in execution. When things were ripe for action, he gave orders to thirty of the principal men of Sparta to be ready armed at the market-place by break of day, to the end that he might strike a terror into the opposite party. Hermippus hath set down the names of twenty of the most eminent of them; but the name of him whom Lycurgus most confided in, and who was of most use to him, both in making his laws and putting them in execution was Arthmiadas. Things growing to a tumult, King Charilaus, apprehending that it was a conspiracy against his person, took sanctuary in the temple of Minerva of the Brazen House; but, being soon after undeceived, and having taken an oath of them that they had no designs against him, he quitted his refuge, and himself also entered into the confederacy with them; of so gentle and flexible a disposition he was, to which Archelaus, his brother-king, alluded, when, hearing him extolled for his goodness, he said, "Who can say he is anything but good? He is so even to the bad."

Amongst the many changes and alterations which Lycurgus made, the first and of greatest importance was the establishment of the senate, which, having a power equal to the kings' in matters of great consequence, and, as Plato expresses it, allaying and qualifying the fiery genius of the royal office, gave steadiness and safety to the commonwealth. For the state, which before had no firm basis to stand upon, but leaned one while towards an absolute monarchy, when the kings had the upper hand, and another while towards a pure democracy, when the people had the better, found in this establishment of the senate a central weight, like ballast in a ship, which always kept things in a just equilibrium; the twenty-eight always adhering to the kings so far as to resist democracy, and, on the other hand, supporting the people against the establishment of absolute monarchy. As for the determinate number of twenty-eight, Aristotle states, that it so fell out because two of the original associates, for want of courage, fell off from the enterprise; but Sphaerus assures us that there were but twenty-eight of the confederates at first; perhaps there is some mystery in the number, which consists of seven multiplied by four, and is the first of perfect numbers after six, being, as that is, equal to all its parts. For my part, I believe Lycurgus fixed upon the number of twenty-eight, that, the two kings being reckoned amongst them, they might be thirty in all. So eagerly set was he upon this establishment, that he took the trouble to obtain an oracle about it from Delphi, the Rhetra, which runs thus: "After that you have built a temple to Jupiter Hellanius, and to Minerva Hellania, and after that you have *phyle'd* the people into *phyles*, and *obe'd* them into *obes*, you shall establish a council of thirty elders, the leaders included, and shall, from time to time, *apellazein* the people betwixt Babyca and Cnacion, there propound and put to the vote. The commons have the final voice and decision." By *phyles* and *obes* are meant the divisions of the people; by the *leaders*, the two kings; *apellazein*, referring  to the Pythian Apollo, signifies to assemble; Babyca and Cnacion they now call Cenus; Aristotle says Cnacion is a river, and Babyca a bridge. Betwixt this Babyca and Cnacion, their assemblies were held, for they had no council-house or building to meet in. Lycurgus was of opinion that ornaments were so far from advantaging them in their counsels, that they were rather an hindrance, by diverting their attention from the business before them to statues and pictures, and roofs curiously fretted, the usual embellishments of such places amongst the other Greeks. The people then being thus assembled in the open air, it was not allowed to any one of their order to give his advice, but only either to ratify or reject what should be propounded to them by the king or senate. But because it fell out afterwards that the people, by adding or omitting words, distorted and perverted the sense of propositions, Kings Polydorus and Theopompus inserted into the Rhetra, or grand covenant, the following clause: "That if the people decide crookedly, it should be lawful for the elders and leaders to dissolve;" that is to say, refuse ratification, and dismiss the people as depravers and perverters of their counsel. It passed among the people, by their management, as being equally authentic with the rest of the Rhetra, as appears by these verses of Tyrtaeus,—

> These oracles they from Apollo heard,
> And brought from Pytho home the perfect word:
> The heaven-appointed kings, who love the land,
> Shall foremost in the nation's council stand;
> The elders next to them; the commons last;
> Let a straight *Rhetra* among all be passed.

Although Lycurgus had, in this manner, used all the qualifications possible in the constitution of his commonwealth, yet those who succeeded him found the oligarchical element still too strong and dominant, and, to check its high temper and its violence, put, as Plato says, a bit in its mouth, which was the power of the ephori, established an hundred and thirty years after the death of Lycurgus. Elatus and his colleagues were the first who had this dignity conferred upon them, in the reign of king Theopompus, who, when his queen upbraided him one day that he would leave the regal power to his children less than he had received it from his ancestors, said, in answer, "No, greater; for it will last longer." For, indeed, their prerogative being thus reduced within reasonable bounds, the Spartan kings were at once freed from all further jealousies and consequent danger, and never experienced the calamities of their neighbors at Messene and Argos, who, by maintaining their prerogative too strictly, for want of yielding a little to the populace, lost it all.

Indeed, whosoever shall look at the sedition and misgovernment which befell these bordering nations to whom they were as near related in blood as situation, will find in them the best reason to admire the wisdom and foresight of Lycurgus. For these three states, in their first rise, were equal, or, if there were any odds, they lay on the side of the Messenians and Argives, who, in the first allotment, were thought to have been luckier than the Spartans; yet was their happiness of but small continuance, partly the tyrannical temper of their kings and partly the ungovernableness of the people quickly bringing upon them such disorders, and so complete an overthrow of all existing institutions, as clearly to show how truly divine a blessing the Spartans had had in that wise lawgiver who gave their government its happy balance and temper. But of this I shall say more in its due place.

After the creation of the thirty senators, his next task, and, indeed, the most hazardous he ever undertook, was the making a new division of their lands. For there was an extreme inequality amongst them, and their state was overloaded with a multitude of indigent and necessitous persons, while its whole wealth had centered upon a very few. To the end, therefore, that he might expel from the state arrogance and envy, luxury and crime, and those yet more inveterate diseases of want and superfluity, he obtained of them to renounce their properties, and to consent to a new division of the land, and that they should live all together on an equal footing; merit to be their only road to eminence, and the disgrace of evil, and credit of worthy acts, their one measure of difference between man and man.

Upon their consent to these proposals, proceeding at once to put them into execution, he divided the country of Laconia in general into thirty thousand equal shares, and the part attached to the city of Sparta into nine thousand; these he distributed among the Spartans, as he did the others to the country citizens. Some authors say that he made but six thousand lots for the citizens of Sparta, and that King Polydorus added three thousand more. Others say that Polydorus doubled the number Lycurgus had made, which, according to them, was but four thousand five hundred. A lot was so much as to yield, one year with another, about seventy bushels of grain for the master of the family, and twelve for his wife, with a suitable proportion of oil and wine. And this he thought sufficient to keep their bodies in good health and strength; superfluities they were better without. It is reported, that, as he returned from a journey shortly after the division of the lands, in harvest time the ground being newly reaped, seeing the stacks all standing equal and alike, he smiled, and said to those about him, "Methinks all Laconia looks like one family estate just divided among a number of brothers."

Not contented with this, he resolved to make a division of their movables too, that there might be no odious distinction or inequality left amongst them; but finding that it would be very dangerous to go about it openly, he took another course, and defeated their avarice by the following stratagem: he commanded that all gold and silver coin should be called in, and that only a sort of money made of iron should be current, a great weight and quantity of which was very little worth; so that to lay up twenty or thirty pounds there was required a pretty large closet, and, to remove it, nothing less than a yoke of oxen. With the diffusion of this money, at once a number of vices were banished from Lacedaemon; for who would rob another of such a coin? Who would unjustly detain or take by force, or accept as a bribe, a thing which it was not easy to hide, nor a credit to have, nor indeed of any use to cut in pieces? For when it was just red hot, they quenched it in vinegar, and by that means spoilt it, and made it almost incapable of being worked.

In the next place, he declared an outlawry of all needless and superfluous arts; but here he might almost have spared his proclamation; for they of themselves would have gone after the gold and silver, the money which remained being not so proper payment for curious work; for, being of iron, it was scarcely portable, neither, if they should take the pains to export it, would it pass amongst the other Greeks, who ridiculed it. So there was now no more means of purchasing foreign goods and small wares; merchants sent no shiploads into Laconian ports; no rhetoric-master, no itinerant fortune-teller, no harlot-monger, or gold or silversmith, engraver, or jeweller, set foot in a country which had no money; so that luxury, deprived little by little of that which fed and fomented it, wasted to nothing and died away of itself. For the rich had no advantage here over the poor, as their wealth and abundance had no road to come abroad by but were shut up at home doing nothing. And in this way they became excellent artists in common, necessary things; bedsteads, chairs, and tables, and such like staple utensils in a family, were admirably well made there; their cup, particularly, was very much in fashion, and eagerly bought up by soldiers, as Critias reports; for its color was such as to prevent water, drunk upon necessity and disagreeable to look at, from being noticed; and the shape of it was such that the mud stuck to the sides, so that only the purer part came to the drinker's mouth. For this, also, they had to thank their lawgiver, who, by relieving the artisans of the trouble of making useless things, set them to show their skill in giving beauty to those of daily and indispensable use.

The third and most masterly stroke of this great lawgiver, by which he struck a yet more effectual blow against luxury and the desire of riches, was the ordinance he made, that they should all eat in common, of the same bread and same meat, and of kinds that were specified, and should not spend their lives at home, laid on costly couches at splendid tables, delivering themselves up into the hands of their tradesmen and cooks, to fatten them in corners, like greedy brutes, and to ruin not their minds only but their very bodies, which, enfeebled by indulgence and excess, would stand in need of long sleep, warm bathing, freedom from work, and, in a word, of as much care and attendance as if they were continually sick. It was certainly an extraordinary thing to have brought about such a result as this, but a greater yet to have taken away from wealth, as Theophrastus observes, not merely the property of being coveted, but its very nature of being wealth. For the rich, being obliged to go to the same table with the poor, could not make use of or enjoy their abundance, nor so much as please their vanity by looking at or displaying it. So that the common proverb, that Plutus, the god of riches, is blind, was nowhere in all the world literally verified but in Sparta. There, indeed, he was not only blind, but like a picture, without either life or motion. Nor were they allowed to take food at home first, and then attend the public tables, for every one had an eye upon those who did not eat and drink like the rest, and reproached them with being dainty and effeminate.

This last ordinance in particular exasperated the wealthier men. They collected in a body against Lycurgus, and from ill words came to throwing stones, so that at length he was forced to run out of the market-place, and make to sanctuary to save his life; by good-hap he outran all excepting one Alcander, a young man otherwise not ill-accomplished, but hasty and violent, who came up so close to him, that, when he turned to see who was near him, he struck him upon the face with his stick, and put out one of his eyes. Lycurgus, so far from being daunted and discouraged by this accident, stopped short, and showed his disfigured face and eye beat out to his countrymen; they, dismayed and ashamed at the sight, delivered Alcander into his hands to be punished, and escorted him home, with expressions of great concern for his ill usage. Lycurgus, having thanked them for their care of his person, dismissed them all, excepting only Alcander; and, taking him with him into his house, neither did nor said anything severely to him, but, dismissing those whose place it was, bade Alcander to wait upon him at table. The young man, who was of an ingenuous temper, without murmuring did as he was commanded; and, being thus admitted to live with Lycurgus, he had an opportunity to observe in him, besides his gentleness and calmness of temper, an extraordinary sobriety and an indefatigable industry, and so, from an enemy became one of his most zealous admirers, and told his friends and relations that Lycurgus was not that morose and ill-natured man they had formerly taken him for, but the one mild and gentle character of the world. And thus did Lycurgus, for chastisement of his fault, make of a wild and passionate young man one of the discreetest citizens of Sparta.

In memory of this accident, Lycurgus built a temple to Minerva, surnamed Optiletis; *optilus* being the Doric of these parts for *ophthalmus*, the eye. Some authors, however, of whom Dioscorides is one (who wrote a treatise on the commonwealth of Sparta), say that he was wounded, indeed, but did not lose his eye with the blow; and that he built the temple in gratitude for the cure. Be this as it will, certain it is, that, after this misadventure, the Lacedaemonians made it a rule never to carry so much as a staff into their public assemblies.

But to return to their public repasts;—these had several names in Greek; the Cretans called them *andria*, because the men only came to them. The Lacedaemonians called them *phiditia*, that is, by changing *l* into *d*, the same as *philitia*, love feasts, because that, by eating and drinking together, they had opportunity of making friends. Or perhaps from *phido*, parsimony, because they were so many schools of sobriety; or perhaps the first letter is an addition, and the word at first was *editia*, from *edode*, eating. They met by companies of fifteen, more or less, and each of them stood bound to bring in monthly a bushel of meal, eight gallons of wine, five pounds of cheese, two pounds and a half of figs, and some very small sum of money to buy flesh or fish with. Besides this, when any of them made sacrifice to the gods, they always sent a dole to the common hall; and, likewise, when any of them had been hunting, he sent thither a part of the venison he had killed; for these two occasions were the only excuses allowed for supping at home. The custom of eating together was observed strictly for a great while afterwards; insomuch that king Agis himself, after having vanquished the Athenians, sending for his commons at his return home, because he desired to eat privately with his queen, was refused them by the polemarchs; which refusal when he resented so much as to omit next day the sacrifice due for a war happily ended, they made him pay a fine.

They used to send their children to these tables as to schools of temperance; here they were instructed in state affairs by listening to experienced statesmen; here they learnt to converse with pleasantry, to make jests without scurrility, and take them without ill humor. In this point of good breeding, the Lacedaemonians excelled particularly, but if any man were uneasy under it, upon the least hint given, there was no more to be said to him. It was customary also for the eldest man in the company to say to each of them, as they came in, "Through this" (pointing to the door), "no words go out." When any one had a desire to be admitted into any of these little societies, he was to go through the following probation, each man in the company took a little ball of soft bread, which they were to throw into a deep basin, which a waiter carried round upon his head; those that liked the person to be chosen dropped their ball into the basin without altering its figure, and those who disliked him pressed it betwixt their fingers, and made it flat; and this signified as much as a negative voice. And if there were but one of these flattened pieces in the basin, the suitor was rejected, so desirous were they that all the members of the company should be agreeable to each other. The basin was called *caddichus*, and the rejected candidate had a name thence derived. Their most famous dish was the black broth, which was so much valued that the elderly men fed only upon that, leaving what flesh there was to the younger.

They say that a certain king of Pontus, having heard much of this black broth of theirs, sent for a Lacedaemonian cook on purpose to make him some, but had no sooner tasted it than he found it extremely bad, which the cook observing, told him, "Sir, to make this broth relish, you should have bathed yourself first in the river Eurotas."

After drinking moderately, every man went to his home without lights, for the use of them was, on all occasions, forbid, to the end that they might accustom themselves to march boldly in the dark. Such was the common fashion of their meals.

Lycurgus would never reduce his laws into writing; nay, there is a Rhetra expressly to forbid it. For he thought that the most material points, and such as most directly tended to the public welfare, being imprinted on the hearts of their youth by a good discipline, would be sure to remain, and would find a stronger security, than any compulsion would be, in the principles of action formed in them by their best lawgiver, education. And as for things of lesser importance, as pecuniary contracts, and such like, the forms of which have to be changed as occasion requires, he thought it the best way to prescribe no positive rule or inviolable usage in such cases, willing that their manner and form should be altered according to the circumstances of time, and determinations of men of sound judgment. Every end and object of law and enactment it was his design education should effect.

One, then, of the Rhetras was, that their laws should not be written; another is particularly levelled against luxury and expensiveness, for by it it was ordained that the ceilings of their houses should only be wrought by the axe, and their gates and doors smoothed only by the saw. Epaminondas's famous dictum about his own table, that "Treason and a dinner like this do not keep company together," may be said to have been anticipated by Lycurgus. Luxury and a house of this kind could not well be companions. For a man might have a less than ordinary share of sense that would furnish such plain and common rooms with silver-footed couches and purple coverlets and gold and silver plate. Doubtless he had good reason to think that they would proportion their beds to their houses, and their coverlets to their beds, and the rest of their goods and furniture to these. It is reported that king Leotychides, the first of that name, was so little used to the sight of any other kind of work, that, being entertained at Corinth in a stately room, he was much surprised to see the timber and ceiling so finely carved and panelled, and asked his host whether the trees grew so in his country.

A third ordinance of Rhetra was, that they should not make war often, or long, with the same enemy, lest that they should train and instruct them in war, by habituating them to defend themselves. And this is what Agesilaus was much blamed for, a long time after; it being thought, that, by his continual incursions into Boeotia, he made the Thebans a match for the Lacedaemonians; and therefore Antalcidas, seeing him wounded one day, said to him, that he was very well paid for taking such pains to make the Thebans good soldiers, whether they would or no. These laws were called the Rhetras, to intimate that they were divine sanctions and revelations.

In order to the good education of their youth (which, as I said before, he thought the most important and noblest work of a lawgiver), he went so far back as to take into consideration their very conception and birth, by regulating their marriages. For Aristotle is wrong in saying, that, after he had tried all ways to reduce the women to more modesty and sobriety, he was at last forced to leave them as they were, because that, in the absence of their husbands, who spent the best part of their lives in the wars, their wives, whom they were obliged to leave absolute mistresses at home, took great liberties and assumed the superiority; and were treated with overmuch respect and called by the title of lady or queen. The truth is, he took in their case, also, all the care that was possible; he ordered the maidens to exercise themselves with wrestling, running, throwing the quoit, and casting the dart, to the end that the fruit they conceived might, in strong and healthy bodies, take firmer root and find better growth, and withal that they, with this greater vigor, might be the more able to undergo the pains of child-bearing. And to the end he might take away their over-great tenderness and fear of exposure to the air, and all acquired womanishness, he ordered that the young women should go naked in the processions, as well as the young men, and dance, too, in that condition, at certain solemn feasts, singing certain songs, whilst the young men stood around, seeing and hearing them. On these occasions, they now and then made, by jests, a befitting reflection upon those who had misbehaved themselves in the wars; and again sang encomiums upon those who had done any gallant action, and by these means inspired the younger sort with an emulation of their glory. Those that were thus commended went away proud, elated, and gratified with their honor among the maidens; and those who were rallied were as sensibly touched with it as if they had been formally reprimanded; and so much the more, because the kings and the elders, as well as the rest of the city, saw and heard all that passed. Nor was there any thing shameful in this nakedness of the young women; modesty attended them, and all wantonness was excluded. It taught them simplicity and a care for good health, and gave them some taste of higher feelings, admitted as they thus were to the field of noble action and glory. Hence it was natural for them to think and speak as Gorgo, for example, the wife of Leonidas, is said to have done, when some foreign lady, as it would seem, told her that the women of Lacedaemon were the only women in the world who could rule men; "With good reason," she said, "for we are the only women who bring forth men."

These public processions of the maidens, and their appearing naked in their exercises and dancings, were incitements to marriage, operating upon the young with the rigor and certainty, as Plato says, of love, if not of mathematics. But besides all this, to promote it yet more effectually, those who continued bachelors were in a degree disfranchised by law; for they were excluded from the sight of those public processions in which the young men and maidens danced naked, and, in winter-time, the officers compelled them to march naked themselves round the marketplace, singing as they went a certain song to their own disgrace, that they justly suffered this punishment for disobeying the laws. Moreover, they were denied that respect and observance which the younger men paid their elders; and no man, for example, found fault with what was said to Dercyllidas, though so eminent a commander; upon whose approach one day, a young man, instead of rising, retained his seat, remarking, "No child of yours will make room for me."

In their marriages, the husband carried off his bride by a sort of force; nor were their brides ever small and of tender years, but in their full bloom and ripeness. After this, she who superintended the wedding comes and clips the hair of the bride close round her head, dresses her up in man's clothes, and leaves her upon a mattress in the dark; afterwards comes the bridegroom, in his everyday clothes, sober and composed, as having supped at the common table, and, entering privately into the room where the bride lies, unties her virgin zone, and takes her to himself; and, after staying some time together, he returns composedly to his own apartment, to sleep as usual with the other young men. And so he continues to do, spending his days, and, indeed, his nights with them, visiting his bride in fear and shame, and with circumspection, when he thought he should not be observed; she, also, on her part, using her wit to help and find favorable opportunities for their meeting, when company was out of the way. In this manner they lived a long time, insomuch that they sometimes had children by their wives before ever they saw their faces by daylight. Their interviews, being thus difficult and rare, served not only for continual exercise of their self-control, but brought them together with their bodies healthy and vigorous, and their affections fresh and lively, unsated and undulled by easy access and long continuance with each other; while their partings were always early enough to leave behind unextinguished in each of them some remainder fire of longing and mutual delight. After guarding marriage with this modesty and reserve, he was equally careful to banish empty and womanish jealousy. For this object, excluding all licentious disorders, he made it, nevertheless, honorable for men to give the use of their wives to those whom they should think fit, that so they might have children by them; ridiculing those in whose opinion such favors are so unfit for participation as to fight and shed blood and go to war about it. Lycurgus allowed a man who was advanced in years and had a young wife to recommend some virtuous and approved young man, that she might have a child by him, who might inherit the good qualities of the father, and be a son to himself. On the other side, an honest man who had love for a married woman upon account of her modesty and the well-favoredness of her children, might, without formality, beg her company of her husband, that he might raise, as it were, from this plot of good ground, worthy and well-allied children for himself. And indeed, Lycurgus was of a persuasion that children were not so much the property of their parents as of the whole commonwealth, and, therefore, would not have his citizens begot by the first comers, but by the best men that could be found; the laws of other nations seemed to him very absurd and inconsistent, where people would be so solicitous for their dogs and horses as to exert interest and to pay money to procure fine breeding, and yet kept their wives shut up, to be made mothers only by themselves, who might be foolish, infirm, or diseased; as if it were not apparent that children of a bad breed would prove their bad qualities first upon those who kept and were rearing them, and well-born children, in like manner, their good qualities. These regulations, founded on natural and social grounds, were certainly so far from that scandalous liberty which was afterwards charged upon their women, that they knew not what adultery meant. It is told, for instance, of Geradas, a very ancient Spartan, that, being asked by a stranger what punishment their law had appointed for adulterers, he answered, "There are no adulterers in our country." "But," replied the stranger, "suppose there were?" "Then," answered he, "the offender would have to give the plaintiff a bull with a neck so long as that he might drink from the top of Taygetus of the Eurotas river below it." The man, surprised at this, said, "Why, 'tis impossible to find such a bull." Geradas smilingly replied, "'Tis as possible as to find an adulterer in Sparta." So much I had to say of their marriages.

Nor was it in the power of the father to dispose of the child as he thought fit; he was obliged to carry it before certain triers at a place called Lesche; these were some of the elders of the tribe to which the child belonged; their business it was carefully to view the infant, and, if they found it stout and well-made, they gave order for its rearing, and allotted to it one of the nine thousand shares of land above mentioned for its maintenance, but, if they found it puny and ill-shaped, ordered it to be taken to what was called the Apothetae, a sort of chasm under Taygetus; as thinking it neither for the good of the child itself, nor for the public interest, that it should be brought up, if it did not, from the very outset, appear made to be healthy and vigorous. Upon the same account, the women did not bathe the newborn children with water, as is the custom in all other countries, but with wine, to prove the temper and complexion of their bodies; from a notion they had that epileptic and weakly children faint and waste away upon their being thus bathed, while, on the contrary, those of a strong and vigorous habit acquire firmness and get a temper by it, like steel. There was much care and art, too, used by the nurses; they had no swaddling bands; the children grew up free and unconstrained in limb and form, and not dainty and fanciful about their food; not afraid in the dark, or of being left alone; without any peevishness or ill humor, or crying. Upon this account, Spartan nurses were often bought up, or hired by people of other countries; and it is recorded that she who suckled Alcibiades was a Spartan; who, however, if fortunate in his nurse, was not so in his preceptor; his guardian, Pericles, as Plato tells us, chose a servant for that office called Zopyrus, no better than any common slave.

Lycurgus was of another mind; he would not have masters bought out of the market for his young Spartans, nor such as should sell their pains; nor was it lawful, indeed, for the father himself to breed up the children after his own fancy; but as soon as they were seven years old they were to be enrolled in certain companies and classes, where they all lived under the same order and discipline, doing their exercises and taking their play together. Of these, he who showed the most conduct and courage was made captain; they had their eyes always upon him, obeyed his orders, and underwent patiently whatsoever punishment he inflicted; so that the whole course of their education was one continued exercise of a ready and perfect obedience. The old men, too, were spectators of their performances, and often raised quarrels and disputes among them, to have a good opportunity of finding out their different characters, and of seeing which would be valiant, which a coward, when they should come to more dangerous encounters. Reading and writing they gave them, just enough to serve their turn; their chief care was to make them good subjects, and to teach them to endure pain and conquer in battle. To this end, as they grew in years, their discipline was proportionably increased; their heads were close-clipped, they were accustomed to go barefoot, and for the most part to play naked.

After they were twelve years old, they were no longer allowed to wear any undergarments; they had one coat to serve them a year; their bodies were hard and dry, with but little acquaintance of baths and unguents; these human indulgences they were allowed only on some few particular days in the year. They lodged together in little bands upon beds made of the rushes which grew by the banks of the river Eurotas, which they were to break off with their hands without a knife; if it were winter, they mingled some thistledown with their rushes, which it was thought had the property of giving warmth. By the time they were come to this age, there was not any of the more hopeful boys who had not a lover to bear him company. The old men, too, had an eye upon them, coming often to the grounds to hear and see them contend either in wit or strength with one another, and this as seriously and with as much concern as if they were their fathers, their tutors, or their magistrates; so that there scarcely was any time or place without someone present to put them in mind of their duty, and punish them if they had neglected it.

Besides all this, there was always one of the best and honestest men in the city appointed to undertake the charge and governance of them; he again arranged them into their several bands, and set over each of them for their captain the most temperate and boldest of those they called Irens, who were usually twenty years old, two years out of the boys; and the eldest of the boys, again, were Mell-Irens, as much as to say, who would shortly be men. This young man, therefore, was their captain when they fought, and their master at home, using them for the offices of his house; sending the oldest of them to fetch wood, and the weaker and less able, to gather salads and herbs, and these they must either go without or steal; which they did by creeping into the gardens, or conveying themselves cunningly and closely into the eating-houses; if they were taken in the fact, they were whipped without mercy, for thieving so ill and awkwardly. They stole, too, all other meat they could lay their hands on, looking out and watching all opportunities, when people were asleep or more careless than usual. If they were caught, they were not only punished with whipping, but hunger, too, being reduced to their ordinary allowance, which was but very slender, and so contrived on purpose, that they might set about to help themselves, and be forced to exercise their energy and address. This was the principal design of their hard fare; there was another not inconsiderable, that they might grow taller; for the vital spirits, not being overburdened and oppressed by too great a quantity of nourishment, which necessarily discharges itself into thickness and breadth, do, by their natural lightness, rise; and the body, giving and yielding because it is pliant, grows in height. The same thing seems, also, to conduce to beauty of shape; a dry and lean habit is a better subject for nature's configuration, which the gross and over-fed are too heavy to submit to properly. Just as we find that women who take physic whilst they are with child, bear leaner and smaller but better-shaped and prettier children; the material they come of having been more pliable and easily moulded. The reason, however, I leave others to determine.

To return from whence we have digressed. So seriously did the Lacedaemonian children go about their stealing, that a youth, having stolen a young fox and hid it under his coat, suffered it to tear out his very bowels with its teeth and claws, and died upon the place, rather than let it be seen. What is practised to this very day in Lacedaemon is enough to gain credit to this story, for I myself have seen several of the youths endure whipping to death at the foot of the altar of Diana surnamed Orthia.

The Iren, or undermaster, used to stay a little with them after supper, and one of them he bade to sing a song, to another he put a question which required an advised and deliberate answer; for example, Who was the best man in the city? What he thought of such an action of such a man? They used them thus early to pass a right judgment upon persons and things, and to inform themselves of the abilities or defects of their countrymen. If they had not an answer ready to the question Who was a good or who an ill-reputed citizen, they were looked upon as of a dull and careless disposition, and to have little or no sense of virtue and honour; besides this, they were to give a good reason for what they said, and in as few words and as comprehensive as might be; he that failed of this, or answered not to the purpose, had his thumb bit by the master. Sometimes the Iren did this in the presence of the old men and magistrates, that they might see whether he punished them justly and in due measure or not; and when he did amiss, they would not reprove him before the boys, but, when they were gone, he was called to an account and underwent correction, if he had run far into either of the extremes of indulgence or severity.

Their lovers and favorers, too, had a share in the young boy's honor or disgrace; and there goes a story that one of them was fined by the magistrate, because the lad whom he loved cried out effeminately as he was fighting. And though this sort of love was so approved among them, that the most virtuous matrons would make professions of it to young girls, yet rivalry did not exist, and if several men's fancies met in one person, it was rather the beginning of an intimate friendship, whilst they all jointly conspired to render the object of their affection as accomplished as possible.

They taught them, also, to speak with a natural and graceful raillery, and to comprehend much matter of thought in few words. For Lycurgus, who ordered, as we saw, that a great piece of money should be but of an inconsiderable value, on the contrary would allow no discourse to be current which did not contain in few words a great deal of useful and curious sense; children in Sparta, by habit of long silence, came to give just and sententious answers; for, indeed, as loose and incontinent lovers are seldom fathers of many children, so loose and incontinent talkers seldom originate many sensible words. King Agis, when some Athenian laughed at their short swords, and said that the jugglers on the stage swallowed them with ease, answered him, "We find them long enough to reach our enemies with;" and as their swords were short and sharp, so, it seems to me, were their sayings. They reach the point and arrest the attention of the hearers better than any. Lycurgus himself seems to have been short and sententious, if we may trust the anecdotes of him; as appears by his answer to one who by all means would set up a democracy in Lacedaemon. "Begin, friend," said he, "and set it up in your family." Another asked him why he allowed of such mean and trivial sacrifices to the gods. He replied, "That we may always have something to offer to them." Being asked what sort of martial exercises or combats he approved of, he answered, "All sorts, except that in which you stretch out your hands." Similar answers, addressed to his countrymen by letter, are ascribed to him; as, being consulted how they might best oppose an invasion of their enemies, he returned this answer, "By continuing poor, and not coveting each man to be greater than his fellow." Being consulted again whether it were requisite to enclose the city with a wall, he sent them word, "The city is well fortified which hath a wall of men instead of brick." But whether these letters are counterfeit or not is not easy to determine.

Of their dislike to talkativeness, the following apophthegms are evidence. King Leonidas said to one who held him in discourse upon some useful matter, but not in due time and place, "Much to the purpose, Sir, elsewhere." King Charilaus, the nephew of Lycurgus, being asked why his uncle had made so few laws, answered, "Men of few words require but few laws." When one blamed Hecataeus the sophist because that, being invited to the public table, he had not spoken one word all supper-time, Archidamidas answered in his vindication, "He who knows how to speak, knows also when."

The sharp and yet not ungraceful retorts which I mentioned may be instanced as follows. Demaratus, being asked in a troublesome manner by an importunate fellow, Who was the best man in Lacedaemon? answered at last, "He, Sir, that is the least like you." Some, in company where Agis was, much extolled the Eleans for their just and honorable management of the Olympic games; "Indeed," said Agis, "they are highly to be commended if they can do justice one day in five years." Theopompus answered a stranger who talked much of his affection to the Lacedaemonians, and said that his countrymen called him Philolacon (a lover of the Lacedaemonians), that it had been more for his honor if they had called him Philopolites (a lover of his own countrymen). And Plistoanax, the son of Pausanias, when an orator of Athens said the Lacedaemonians had no learning, told him, "You say true, Sir; we alone of all the Greeks have learned none of your bad qualities." One asked Archidamidas what number there might be of the Spartans, he answered, "Enough, Sir, to keep out wicked men."

We may see their character, too, in their very jests. For they did not throw them out at random, but the very wit of them was grounded upon something or other worth thinking about. For instance, one, being asked to go hear a man who exactly counterfeited the voice of a nightingale, answered, "Sir, I have heard the nightingale itself." Another, having read the following inscription upon a tomb,

> Seeking to quench a cruel tyranny,
> They, at Selinus, did in battle, die,

said, it served them right; for instead of trying to quench the tyranny, they should have let it burn out. A lad, being offered some game-cocks that would die upon the spot, said that he cared not for cocks that would die, but for such that would live and kill others. Another, seeing people easing themselves on seats, said, "God forbid I should sit where I could not get up to salute my elders." In short, their answers were so sententious and pertinent, that one said well that intellectual much more truly than athletic exercise was the Spartan characteristic.

Nor was their instruction in music and verse less carefully attended to than their habits of grace and good breeding in conversation. And their very songs had a life and spirit in them that inflamed and possessed men's minds with an enthusiasm and ardor for action; the style of them was plain and without affectation; the subject always serious and moral; most usually, it was in praise of such men as had died in defence of their country, or in derision of those that had been cowards; the former they declared happy and glorified; the life of the latter they described as most miserable and abject. There were also vaunts of what they would do, and boasts of what they had done, varying with the various ages, as, for example, they had three choirs in their solemn festivals, the first of the old men, the second of the young men, and the last of the children; the old men began thus:

> We once were young, and brave and strong;

the young men answered them, singing,

> And we're so now, come on and try;

the children came last and said,

> But we'll be strongest by and by.

Indeed, if we will take the pains to consider their compositions, some of which were still extant in our days, and the airs on the flute to which they marched when going to battle, we shall find that Terpander and Pindar had reason to say that music and valor were allied. The first says of Lacedaemon—

> The spear and song in her do meet,
> And Justice walks about her street;

And Pindar—

> Councils of wise elders here,
> And the young men's conquering spear,
> And dance, and song, and joy appear;

both describing the Spartans as no less musical than warlike; in the words of one of their own poets—

> With the iron stern and sharp
> Comes the playing on the harp.

For, indeed, before they engaged in battle, the king first did sacrifice to the Muses, in all likelihood to put them in mind of the manner of their education, and of the judgment that would be passed upon their actions, and thereby to animate them to the performance of exploits that should deserve a record. At such times, too, the Lacedaemonians abated a little the severity of their manners in favor of their young men, suffering them to curl and adorn their hair, and to have costly arms, and fine clothes; and were well pleased to see them, like proud horses, neighing and pressing to the course. And therefore, as soon as they came to be well-grown, they took a great deal of care of their hair, to have it parted and trimmed, especially against a day of battle, pursuant to a saying recorded of their lawgiver, that a large head of hair added beauty to a good face, and terror to an ugly one.

When they were in the field, their exercises were generally more moderate, their fare not so hard, nor so strict a hand held over them by their officers, so that they were the only people in the world to whom war gave repose. When their army was drawn up in battle array, and the enemy near, the king sacrificed a goat, commanded the soldiers to set their garlands upon their heads, and the pipers to play the tune of the hymn to Castor, and himself began the paean of advance. It was at once a magnificent and a terrible sight to see them march on to the tune of their flutes, without any disorder in their ranks, any discomposure in their minds or change in their countenance, calmly and cheerfully moving with the music to the deadly fight. Men, in this temper, were not likely to be possessed with fear or any transport of fury, but with the deliberate valor of hope and assurance, as if some divinity were attending and conducting them. The king had always about his person someone who had been crowned in the Olympic games; and upon this account a Lacedaemonian is said to have refused a considerable present, which was offered to him upon condition that he would not come into the lists; and when he had with much to-do thrown his antagonist, some of the spectators saying to him, "And now, Sir Lacedaemonian, what are you the better for your victory?" he answered smiling, "I shall fight next the king." After they had routed an enemy, they pursued him till they were well assured of the victory, and then they sounded a retreat, thinking it base and unworthy of a Grecian people to cut men in pieces, who had given up and abandoned all resistance. This manner of dealing with their enemies did not only show magnanimity, but was politic too; for, knowing that they killed only those who made resistance, and gave quarter to the rest, men generally thought it their best way to consult their safety by flight.

Hippias the sophist says that Lycurgus himself was a great soldier and an experienced commander. Philostephanus attributes to him the first division of the cavalry into troops of fifties in a square body; but Demetrius the Phalerian says quite the contrary, and that he made all his laws in a continued peace. And, indeed, the Olympic holy truce, or cessation of arms, that was procured by his means and management, inclines me to think him a kind-natured man, and one that loved quietness and peace. Notwithstanding all this, Hermippus tells us that he had no hand in the ordinance, that Iphitus made it, and Lycurgus came only as a spectator, and that by mere accident too. Being there, he heard as it were a man's voice behind him, blaming and wondering at him that he did not encourage his countrymen to resort to the assembly, and, turning about and seeing no man, concluded that it was a voice from heaven, and upon this immediately went to Iphitus, and assisted him in ordering the ceremonies of that feast, which, by his means, were better established, and with more repute than before.

To return to the Lacedaemonians. Their discipline continued still after they were full-grown men. No one was allowed to live after his own fancy; but the city was a sort of camp, in which every man had his share of provisions and business set out, and looked upon himself not so much born to serve his own ends as the interest of his country. Therefore, if they were commanded nothing else, they went to see the boys perform their exercises, to teach them something useful or to learn it themselves of those who knew better. And, indeed, one of the greatest and highest blessings Lycurgus procured his people was the abundance of leisure, which proceeded from his forbidding to them the exercise of any mean and mechanical trade. Of the money-making that depends on troublesome going about and seeing people and doing business, they had no need at all in a state where wealth obtained no honor or respect. The Helots tilled their ground for them, and paid them yearly in kind the appointed quantity, without any trouble of theirs. To this purpose there goes a story of a Lacedaemonian who, happening to be at Athens when the courts were sitting, was told of a citizen that had been fined for living an idle life, and was being escorted home in much distress of mind by his condoling friends; the Lacedaemonian was much surprised at it, and desired his friend to show him the man who was condemned for living like a freeman. So much beneath them did they esteem the frivolous devotion of time and attention to the mechanical arts and to money-making.

It need not be said, that, upon the prohibition of gold and silver, all lawsuits immediately ceased, for there was now neither avarice nor poverty amongst them, but equality, where every one's wants were supplied, and independence, because those wants were so small. All their time, except when they were in the field, was taken up by the choral dances and the festivals, in hunting, and in attendance on the exercise-grounds and the places of public conversation. Those who were under thirty years of age were not allowed to go into the market-place, but had the necessaries of their family supplied by the care of their relations and lovers; nor was it for the credit of elderly men to be seen too often in the market-place; it was esteemed more suitable for them to frequent the exercise-grounds and places of conversation, where they spent their leisure rationally in conversation, not on money-making and market-prices, but for the most part in passing judgment on some action worth considering; extolling the good, and censuring those who were otherwise, and that in a light and sportive manner, conveying, without too much gravity, lessons of advice and improvement. Nor was Lycurgus himself unduly austere; it was he who dedicated, says Sosibius, the little statue of Laughter. Mirth, introduced seasonably at their suppers and places of common entertainment, was to serve as a sort of sweetmeat to accompany their strict and hard life. To conclude, he bred up his citizens in such a way that they neither would nor could live by themselves; they were to make themselves one with the public good, and, clustering like bees around their commander, be by their zeal and public spirit carried all but out of themselves, and devoted wholly to their country. What their sentiments were will better appear by a few of their sayings. Paedaretus, not being admitted into the list of the three hundred, returned home with a joyful face, well pleased to find that there were in Sparta three hundred better men than himself. And Polycratidas, being sent with some other ambassadors to the lieutenants of the king of Persia, being asked by them whether they came in a private or in a public character, answered, "In a public, if we succeed; if not, in a private character." Argileonis, asking some who came from Amphipolis if her son Brasidas died courageously and as became a Spartan, on their beginning to praise him to a high degree, and saying there was not such another left in Sparta, answered, "Do not say so; Brasidas was a good and brave man, but there are in Sparta many better than he."

The senate, as I said before, consisted of those who were Lycurgus's chief aiders and assistants in his plans. The vacancies he ordered to be supplied out of the best and most deserving men past sixty years old, and we need not wonder if there was much striving for it; for what more glorious competition could there be amongst men, than one in which it was not contested who was swiftest among the swift or strongest of the strong, but who of many wise and good was wisest and best, and fittest to be intrusted for ever after, as the reward of his merits, with the supreme authority of the commonwealth, and with power over the lives, franchises, and highest interests of all his countrymen? The manner of their election was as follows: the people being called together, some selected persons were locked up in a room near the place of election, so contrived that they could neither see nor be seen, but could only hear the noise of the assembly without; for they decided this, as most other affairs of moment, by the shouts of the people. This done, the competitors were not brought in and presented all together, but one after another by lot, and passed in order through the assembly without speaking a word. Those who were locked up had writing-tables with them, in which they recorded and marked each shout by its loudness, without knowing in favor of which candidate each of them was made, but merely that they came first, second, third, and so forth. He who was found to have the most and loudest acclamations was declared senator duly elected. Upon this he had a garland set upon his head, and went in procession to all the temples to give thanks to the gods; a great number of young men followed him with applauses, and women, also, singing verses in his honor, and extolling the virtue and happiness of his life. As he went round the city in this manner, each of his relations and friends set a table before him, saying, "The city honors you with this banquet;" but he, instead of accepting, passed round to the common table where he formerly used to eat, and was served as before, excepting that now he had a second allowance, which he took and put by. By the time supper was ended, the women who were of kin to him had come about the door; and he, beckoning to her whom he most esteemed, presented to her the portion he had saved, saying, that it had been a mark of esteem to him, and was so now to her; upon which she was triumphantly waited upon home by the women.

Touching burials, Lycurgus made very wise regulations; for, first of all, to cut off all superstition, he allowed them to bury their dead within the city,  and even round about their temples, to the end that their youth might be accustomed to such spectacles, and not be afraid to see a dead body, or imagine that to touch a corpse or to tread upon a grave would defile a man. In the next place, he commanded them to put nothing into the ground with them, except, if they pleased, a few olive leaves, and the scarlet cloth that they were wrapped in. He would not suffer the names to be inscribed, except only of men who fell in the wars, or women who died in a sacred office. The time, too, appointed for mourning, was very short, eleven days; on the twelfth, they were to do sacrifice to Ceres, and leave it off; so that we may see, that as he cut off all superfluity, so in things necessary there was nothing so small and trivial which did not express some homage of virtue or scorn of vice. He filled Lacedaemon all through with proofs and examples of good conduct; with the constant sight of which from their youth up, the people would hardly fail to be gradually formed and advanced in virtue.

And this was the reason why he forbade them to travel abroad, and go about acquainting themselves with foreign rules of morality, the habits of ill-educated people, and different views of government. Withal he banished from Lacedaemon all strangers who could not give a very good reason for their coming thither; not because he was afraid lest they should inform themselves of and imitate his manner of government (as Thucydides says), or learn anything to their good; but rather lest they should introduce something contrary to good manners. With strange people, strange words must be admitted; these novelties produce novelties in thought; and on these follow views and feelings whose discordant character destroys the harmony of the state. He was as careful to save his city from the infection of foreign bad habits, as men usually are to prevent the introduction of a pestilence.

Hitherto I, for my part, see no sign of injustice or want of equity in the laws of Lycurgus, though some who admit them to be well contrived to make good soldiers, pronounce them defective in point of justice. The Cryptia, perhaps (if it were one of Lycurgus's ordinances, as Aristotle says it was), gave both him and Plato, too, this opinion alike of the lawgiver and his government. By this ordinance, the magistrates despatched privately some of the ablest of the young men into the country, from time to time, armed only with their daggers, and taking a little necessary provision with them; in the daytime, they hid themselves in out-of-the-way places, and there lay close, but, in the night, issued out into the highways, and killed all the Helots they could light upon; sometimes they set upon them by day, as they were at work in the fields, and murdered them. As, also, Thucydides, in his history of the Peloponnesian War, tells us, that a good number of them, after being singled out for their bravery by the Spartans, garlanded, as enfranchised persons, and led about to all the temples in token of honors, shortly after disappeared all of a sudden, being about the number of two thousand; and no man either then or since could give an account how they came by their deaths. And Aristotle, in particular, adds, that the ephori, so soon as they were entered into their office, used to declare war against them, that they might be massacred without a breach of religion. It is confessed, on all hands, that the Spartans dealt with them very hardly; for it was a common thing to force them to drink to excess, and to lead them in that condition into their public halls, that the children might see what a sight a drunken man is; they made them to dance low dances, and sing ridiculous songs, forbidding them expressly to meddle with any of a better kind. And, accordingly, when the Thebans made their invasion into Laconia, and took a great number of the Helots, they could by no means persuade them to sing the verses of Terpander, Alcman, or Spendon, "For," said they, "the masters do not like it." So that it was truly observed by one, that in Sparta he who was free was most so, and he that was a slave there, the greatest slave in the world. For my part, I am of opinion that these outrages and cruelties began to be exercised in Sparta at a later time, especially after the great earthquake, when the Helots made a general insurrection, and, joining with the Messenians, laid the country waste, and brought the greatest danger upon the city. For I cannot persuade myself to ascribe to Lycurgus so wicked and barbarous a course, judging of him from the gentleness of his disposition and justice upon all other occasions; to which the oracle also testified.

When he perceived that his more important institutions had taken root in the minds of his countrymen, that custom had rendered them familiar and easy, that his commonwealth was now grown up and able to go alone, then, as, Plato somewhere tells us, the Maker of the world, when first he saw it existing and beginning its motion, felt joy, even so Lycurgus, viewing with joy and satisfaction the greatness and beauty of his political structure, now fairly at work and in motion, conceived the thought to make it immortal too, and, as far as human forecast could reach, to deliver it down unchangeable to posterity. He called an extraordinary assembly of all the people, and told them that he now thought every thing reasonably well established, both for the happiness and the virtue of the state; but that there was one thing still behind, of the greatest importance, which he thought not fit to impart until he had consulted the oracle; in the meantime, his desire was that they would observe the laws without any the least alteration until his return, and then he would do as the god should direct him. They all consented readily, and bade him hasten his journey; but, before he departed, he administered an oath to the two kings, the senate, and the whole commons, to abide by and maintain the established form of polity until Lycurgus should be come back. This done, he set out for Delphi, and, having sacrificed to Apollo, asked him whether the laws he had established were good, and sufficient for a people's happiness and virtue. The oracle answered that the laws were excellent, and that the people, while it observed them, should live in the height of renown. Lycurgus took the oracle in writing, and sent it over to Sparta; and, having sacrificed the second time to Apollo, and taken leave of his friends and his son, he resolved that the Spartans should not be released from the oath they had taken, and that he would, of his own act, close his life where he was. He was now about that age in which life was still tolerable, and yet might be quitted without regret. Everything, moreover, about him was in a sufficiently prosperous condition. He, therefore, made an end of himself by a total abstinence from food; thinking it a stateman's duty to make his very death, if possible, an act of service to the state,  and even in the end of his life to give some example of virtue and effect some useful purpose. He would, on the one hand, crown and consummate his own happiness by a death suitable to so honorable a life, and, on the other would secure to his countrymen the enjoyment of the advantages he had spent his life in obtaining for them, since they had solemnly sworn the maintenance of his institutions until his return. Nor was he deceived in his expectations, for the city of Lacedaemon continued the chief city of all Greece for the space of five hundred years, in strict observance of Lycurgus's laws; in all which time there was no manner of alteration made, during the reign of fourteen kings, down to the time of Agis, the son of Archidamus. For the new creation of the ephori, though thought to be in favor of the people, was so far from diminishing, that it very much heightened, the aristocratical character of the government.

In the time of Agis, gold and silver first flowed into Sparta, and with them all those mischiefs which attend the immoderate desire of riches. Lysander promoted this disorder; for, by bringing in rich spoils from the wars, although himself incorrupt, he yet by this means filled his country with avarice and luxury, and subverted the laws and ordinances of Lycurgus; so long as which were in force, the aspect presented by Sparta was rather that of a rule of life followed by one wise and temperate man, than of the political government of a nation. And as the poets feign of Hercules, that, with his lion's skin and his club, he went over the world, punishing lawless and cruel tyrants, so may it be said of the Lacedaemonians, that, with a common staff and a coarse coat, they gained the willing and joyful obedience of Greece, through whose whole extent they suppressed unjust usurpations and despotisms, arbitrated in war, and composed civil dissensions; and this often without so much as taking down one buckler, but barely by sending some one single deputy to whose direction all at once submitted, like bees swarming and taking their places around their prince. Such a fund of order and equity, enough and to spare for others, existed in their state.

And therefore I cannot but wonder at those who say that the Spartans were good subjects, but bad governors, and for proof of it allege a saying of king Theopompus, who, when one said that Sparta held up so long because their kings could command so well, replied, "Nay, rather because the people know so well how to obey." For people do not obey, unless rulers know how to command; obedience is a lesson taught by commanders. A true leader himself creates the obedience of his own followers; as it is the last attainment in the art of riding to make a horse gentle and tractable, so is it of the science of government, to inspire men with a willingness to obey. The Lacedaemonians inspired men not with a mere willingness, but with an absolute desire, to be their subjects. For they did not send petitions to them for ships or money, or a supply of armed men, but only for a Spartan commander; and, having obtained one, used him with honor and reverence; so the Sicilians behaved to Gylippus, the Chalcidians to Brasidas, and all the Greeks in Asia to Lysander, Callicratidas, and Agesilaus; they styled them the composers and chasteners of each people or prince they were sent to, and had their eyes always fixed upon the city of Sparta itself, as the perfect model of good manners and wise government. The rest seemed as scholars, they the masters of Greece; and to this Stratonicus pleasantly alluded, when in jest he pretended to make a law that the Athenians should conduct religious processions and the mysteries, the Eleans should preside at the Olympic games, and, if either did amiss, the Lacedaemonians be beaten. Antisthenes, too, one of the scholars of Socrates, said, in earnest, of the Thebans, when they were elated by their victory at Leuctra, that they looked like schoolboys who had beaten their master.

However, it was not the design of Lycurgus that his city should govern a great many others; he thought rather that the happiness of a state, as a private man, consisted chiefly in the exercise of virtue, and in the concord of the inhabitants; his aim, therefore, in all his arrangements, was to make and keep them free-minded, self-dependent, and temperate. And therefore all those who have written well on politics, as Plato, Diogenes and Zeno, have taken Lycurgus for their model, leaving behind them, however, mere projects and words; whereas Lycurgus was the author, not in writing but in reality, of a government which none else could so much as copy; and while men in general have treated the individual philosophic character as unattainable, he, by the example of a complete philosophic state, raised himself high above all other lawgivers of Greece. And so Aristotle says they did him less honor at Lacedaemon after his death than he deserved, although he has a temple there, and they offer sacrifices yearly to him as to a god.

It is reported that when his bones were brought home to Sparta his tomb was struck with lightning; an accident which befell no eminent person but himself, and Euripides, who was buried at Arethusa in Macedonia; and it may serve that poet's admirers as a testimony in his favor, that he had in this the same fate with that holy man and favorite of the gods. Some say Lycurgus died in Cirrha. Apollothemis says, after he had come to Elis; Timaeus and Aristoxenus, that he ended his life in Crete; Aristoxenus adds that his tomb is shown by the Cretans in the district of Pergamus, near the strangers' road. He left an only son, Antiorus, on whose death without issue, his family became extinct. But his relations and friends kept up an annual commemoration of him down to a long time after; and the days of the meeting were called Lycurgides. Aristocrates, the son of Hipparchus, says that he died in Crete, and that his Cretan friends, in accordance with his own request, when they had burned his body, scattered the ashes into the sea; for fear lest, if his relics should be transported to Lacedaemon, the people might pretend to be released from their oaths, and make innovations in the government. Thus much may suffice for the life and actions of Lycurgus.

# Selections from *The War of the Peloponnesians and the Athenians*

## *Thucydides (ca. 460–ca. 400 B.C.)*

*Thucydides was an Athenian general for a short period during the long Peloponnesian War (431-404 B.C.), though, as a result of a serious defeat, he was exiled from Athens for twenty years. He records and comments on the war up to 411. The first reading from his history is Thucydides' version of the oration delivered by the most famous Athenian statesman, Pericles, at the mass funeral for those who died in the first year of the war; the second, the debate between military representatives of Athens and the leaders of the Melians, occurs in 416, during the period of truce in the midst of the war (421-415 B.C.). This truce is made at a point of Athenian dominance, but after the hostilities are renewed, the Spartan alliance eventually forces Athenian capitulation.*

*Consider the vision of Athens that Pericles presents in contrast to its enemy. Do you recognize in Pericles' remarks the Sparta of Plutarch's "Lycurgus"? Which understanding of freedom and happiness, that of Athens or that of Sparta, is better for human beings? Why? In reading the Melian Dialogue, compare Pericles' statements about the greatness of Athens and its democracy with this example of Athenian military action. Do you see a connection or a disjunction between the principles of Athenian life and the actions the city takes toward foreign cities? The Athenians and Melians present two stark alternatives concerning the place of justice and the use of force in politics. Is either of them right, and in what respects?*

### THE FUNERAL ORATION OF PERICLES

34.    During this winter, the Athenians used of the law their fathers and made a burial, at the public expense, of those who had first died in this war, in the following manner. After they made a tent, they laid out the bones of the departed three days before; and each one brought to his own relative whatever funeral offering he might desire. While the funeral procession took place, carts conveyed coffins of cypress wood, one for each tribe; wherein were the bones of each according to his tribe. One empty bier was also carried and spread in honor of the unseen, who could not be discovered on the battlefield to be taken up. Whoever wished, both villagers and strangers, joined in the procession. Their female relatives were also present at the burial to lament. Then, they laid them in the public sepulcher, which was in the most beautiful suburb of the city and in which they always buried those who have died in the wars (except, at least, those who fell at Marathon; for them, because they judged their virtue to be magnificent, they made a burial on the spot). After they had covered them with earth, a man was chosen by the city, who in mind seemed to be not unintelligent and in worthiness was first, to speak over them a fitting praise. After this, they went away. In this manner, did they bury their dead. Throughout the whole of the war,

whenever it might befall them to do so, they used the law. Over these who were first buried, Pericles, son of Xanthippus, was chosen to speak. When he took the opportunity and advanced from the sepulcher up to a platform, which had been made at some height so that he might be heard over as great a part of the crowd as possible, he said the following.

35.     "The many, because of those who have already spoken in this place, praise the man who introduced this speech into the law, as though it is noble that a speech should be publicly delivered over those who are buried as a consequence of our wars. It would seem to be sufficient to me that, when men have become good in deed, they should have their honors also displayed in deed—as even now you see in the case of this burial, which is prepared at the public expense. The virtues of many should not be hazarded on one man, who is entrusted to speak well or ill of them. For it is difficult to speak in a measured fashion on a subject where the opinion of the truth is scarcely even secure. For the hearer, who knows the deeds and is well disposed toward the doers, might perhaps believe them to be somewhat deficiently evidenced compared with what he both wishes and knows. But the hearer, who is ignorant of them, might believe that they were very excessive, because of his envy, if he should hear anything surpassing his own nature. For praises spoken of others are only endured up to the point where each one also thinks that he might also be sufficient to do some of what he has heard. What exceeds their own capacity, men at once envy and mistrust. However, since these things have seemed to our ancestors to be so noble, I also ought to follow the law and endeavor to meet by chance the wishes and opinions of each of you, as far as possible.

36.     "I will begin with our progenitors first. For it is just, and at the same time becoming, that on such an occasion this honor be paid to their memory. For they continuously inhabited the country in successive generations and bequeathed a free city to posterity, because of their virtue, up to this very time. Therefore, those ancestors are worthy of praise; and still more worthy of it are our own fathers. For in addition to what they inherited, they acquired a great empire, such as we possess, and not without labor left it to us of the present time. The larger part of it we, who are still in existence and very much in the prime condition of our lives, have increased in power. Likewise, we have prepared the city in every way to be most self-sufficient both for peace and for war. As for our deeds in wars, by which every possession was gained, if either we ourselves or our fathers defended the city somewhat spiritedly against the attacks made on us by a barbarian or Greek enemy, I do not wish to permit myself to speak at length on things known to you. By what practices we came upon these things, and by what regime and from what ways the city became so great, these things first I am going to evidence to you; and afterwards I shall praise them. I believe that on the present occasion they would not be inappropriately mentioned. It is also expedient for the whole society, as well as for both villagers and strangers, to listen to them.

37.     "For we use a regime that does not emulate the laws of our neighbors. We are ourselves more an example to some than imitators of others. In name, because it is not administered for the few but for the many, it is called a democracy. Therein, according to the laws, all partake of equality with regard to their private differences. According to public worth, as each man has a good reputation for something, he is also honored by the community not more from partial considerations than from virtue. A worthy man, who is able to do the city any good at all, has never been prevented from participating in public life by his poverty and obscurity. We also have political freedom both with respect to the community and with regard to mutual suspicion in our daily practices. Therefore, we are not angry at our neighbor if he should do something only for the purpose of pleasure, even though it is not harmless, because we would have pain added to vexation in our countenances. While in private matters we associate without personal offense, in public matters we do not transgress the laws because of fear. We listen to those who are from time to time in office and to the laws. And most of all, we listen to the laws that are enacted for the profit of those who are done injustice and that are unwritten and bring acknowledged disgrace on those who break them.

38.     "In truth, we have also provided for our minds the most numerous recreations from our labors by instituting games and sacrifices throughout the whole year and by maintaining magnificent private establishments, from which the daily gratification relieves us of the pain. Due to the greatness of our city everything from every land is imported into it. It befalls us that the good things, which are produced here, offer us no more personal enjoyment than those from the rest of humanity.

39.     "In our training for war, we also differ from our adversaries in the following respects. We throw our city open in common and not even sometimes do we expel strangers nor constrain anyone from either learning or observing our practice. Any of our enemies might see it, because it is not kept in secret, and derive profit from it. For we trust not to stratagems and deception more than to our own courage in the deeds. As for the training of our children, while our adversaries are young, straightway they strive for manliness by laborious exercise. Although we have an easy way of life, we advance no less equal to the task against dangers. There is proof of this because the Lacedaemonians never march against our land by themselves, but with all their allies together. However, we for the most part attack the country of our neighbors, and with no difficulty we conquer them, when we are doing battle alone in an alien land against those who are defending their own households. No enemy ever yet chanced to encounter our massive force because we pay attention to our navy at the same time as we send our troops by land for many purposes. But wherever they might have engaged with any part of it, if they should conquer some of us, they boast that we were all repulsed by them. When they have been defeated, they say that they had the worse from all of us. And yet, if with an easy spirit rather than with laborious practice, and with a manliness not from the laws more than from our natural ways, we are willing to face danger, we have the advantage of not being distressed beforehand from the impending grief and we appear, when we go against them, no less daring than those who are always toiling. Therefore, our city is worthy of admiration both in these respects and in still others.

40.     "For we both love beauty in good measure [*Met' euteleias*, also "with economy" or "for good purpose,"] and we philosophize without softness. We use our wealth rather for opportunity of deed than for boastfulness of speech; and poverty is nothing disgraceful for someone to confess in speech, but not to escape it in deed is very disgraceful. Again, the same individuals can attend to household as well as to political affairs; others, who have turned to deeds, are not deficient in understanding the political things. For we alone believe the man who takes no part in these things not merely inactive, but useless. We ourselves either judge or, at any rate, reflect correctly on our actions because we do not believe that the speeches are harmful to the deeds. But we believe that it is more harmful not to have been instructed by speech beforehand than to go after what is required in deed alone. For we surely have this characteristic so surpassingly that we are both most daring and most calculating in what we will take in hand. To other men, ignorance brings boldness and calculation brings hesitation. But the best men would be judged justly with respect to their souls, who understand most clearly the terrible and pleasant things and are not turned away from dangers because of them.

        "As regards virtue, we are also opposite to the many because we acquire friends not by being treated well, but by doing them favors. For the one who does the favor is more secure because he can preserve the good will that is owed to him by the one on whom he has conferred it. But he who owes it in return feels his virtue more dimly because he knows that he owes his virtue not to a favor, but to a debt. Therefore, we alone fearlessly profit anyone not more from calculations of expediency than from trust in our liberality.

41.     "Taken together, I say that as a whole the city is a school of Greece and that individually, it seems to me, the same man among us would produce a self-sufficient body for the most varied forms of action and with the most graceful versatility. That this is not a boastful display of speeches for the present occasion more than a truthful account of deeds, the very power of the city, which we have acquired by these ways, signifies. For it is the only city at the present time

that, when brought to the test, is superior to the hearsay reports of it. And it is the only one that neither brings indignation to the attacking enemy for suffering evil at the hands of such opponents as us nor censure to the subject for not being ruled by worthy men. We shall be admired both by the present and future generations for having presented our power with great evidence and by no means indeed without proof. For we have, in addition, no need either of Homer to praise us, nor anyone else who might delight us for the moment by his verses, because the truth would harm the poets' conjecture of our deeds. We shall be admired for having compelled every sea and land to become accessible to our daring and for having established everywhere everlasting testimonies both of evil and of good. It was for such a city, then, that these men, who acted justly and nobly lest they be deprived of it, met their end in battle. Therefore, it is right for everyone of those left behind to toil in its behalf.

42.     "For this reason, indeed, it is that I have enlarged on the characteristics of the city. For I have taught a lesson that the struggle is not for an equal object in our case, as in the case of men who have none of these advantages in a like degree. Moreover, I have clearly established by evidence the eulogy of these men, over whom I am now speaking. Now, the greatest points of it have been mentioned. For while I have sung the praises of the city, the virtues of these men have been adorned. Not many of the Greeks are there whose speech, like the speech about these here, would appear to be equally balanced with their deeds. Again, the catastrophic end of these men now seems to me to evidence their manly virtue as a first disclosure and a final confirmation.

"For even in the case of the men here who were in other respects inferior, they became just by putting forward a good and manly appearance against their enemies in their fatherland's behalf. For they obscured evil by good because they profited the common good more than they harmed it by their private offenses. Of these men, neither were any of them cowardly by honoring first the continued enjoyment of his wealth, nor were others made hesitant from danger through the hope, springing from his poverty, that he might yet escape it and grow rich. Since they grasped that revenge on their adversaries was more important [*Potheinoteran*, literally "more to be desired or longed for"] than these things, and at the same time believed this to be the noblest of dangers, they wished amidst it to be avenged on their enemies. They aimed at those advantages both by committing to hope the uncertainty of success and by deeming it worthy to have trusted in deed what could be seen around them. In that deed, then, once they resolved to defend us and to suffer more than to preserve themselves by surrendering, they fled from the shame of a discreditable report and endured the ultimate suffering with their bodies. Therefore, because of the briefest opportunity, they were acquitted by chance while they were at the height of their glory more than of their fear.

43.     "These here men fittingly were of such sorts for their city. The rest of you ought to pray for greater security, but also to deem yourselves worthy and to have the resolve not to be less daring against your enemies. You should not examine the profit of such a spirit in speech alone, on which any might speak to you at great length (though you know it yourselves not any the worse) and might tell you how many goods are possible when you defend yourselves against your enemies. But rather, day by day, you should contemplate the power of the city in deed and become lovers of it. You should also reflect, when it might seem to you to be great, that since they were daring and understood what was required to be done, and were alive to shame in their deeds, men acquired these things. Whenever they might have failed in an attempt at anything, they did not therefore deem it at all worthy to deprive their city also of virtue, but conferred on it a most beautiful collective offering. For although in common they gave the city their bodies, in private they received a praise that never grows old and the most distinguished tomb. It is not the one wherein they are laid, but the one wherein their glory is left behind them to be everlastingly remembered at every occasion and opportunity both in speech and in deed. For illustrious men have the whole earth as a tomb. Not only does the inscription upon the columns in their own household signify it, but even in other households an unwritten memorial of the mind dwells for each of them that is more permanent than the deed. Therefore, emulating these men now and

judging happiness to consist in freedom, and freedom in courage, you must not ignore the dangers of war. For it would not be more just for the evil-doers to be unsparing of their lives, for whom there is no hope of good. But rather it would be more just for those who are in danger of the opposite change during their life, and to whom it would make the very greatest difference if they should blunder. For the evil accompanied by cowardice is more grievous, at least to the prudent man, than the unperceived death that comes upon him at once during his vigor and his hope for the common good.

44.     "For this very reason, I shall also not lament more than console the parents of these here, as many of you as are now present. For you know that the dead have been brought up subject to manifold misfortunes. Thus, it is good luck for them who have obtained by lot the most fitting end, just as these here now have, although you are still in pain. In addition, life has been so measured for them that they were happy and died amidst the same happiness. I know, of course, that it is difficult to persuade you of this good luck, when you will very often be reminded of them by the good luck of others, in which you might someday have exulted. However, pain should not be felt when one is deprived of goods with which one has no experience, but when one has goods taken away with which one has become habituated. Your pain ought also to be endurable, through the hope of other children, for those of you who are still in the prime of life to make offspring. For to some of you in private, the children who are subsequently born will be a reason to forget those who exist no more. To the city, it will also be expedient in two ways: it will not be deserted and it will remain secure. Because of this, it is not possible for anyone to deliberate about these things equitably and justly unless also he would equally have his children thrown into danger.

"On the other hand, as many of you as are beyond their prime, you must consider that the longer period of your life, during which you had good fortune, is a gain and that what remains of this life will be short. You must lighten your burden with the good fame of these, your lost ones. For the love of honor alone is ageless; and in the uselessness of old age material gain, as some have said, does not give very much delight, but honor does.

"Again, for those of you present, who are children or brothers of these here, I see that the struggle will be great to emulate them because every one is accustomed to praise the man who no longer exists. Even with an excess of virtue, you still could not even scarcely become equal to them and would be judged a little inferior. For the living have envy against their rivals, but the one who is no longer an impediment is honored without antagonism and with good will.

"If I must remember something about womanly virtue, for those of you who will now be in widowhood, I will signify it all with a brief piece of advice. Your reputation will be great, lest you be worse than the nature which you possess, who would be as little as possible famous among males either for virtue or vice.

"Such things have been said by me in speech, according to the law, as I held were fitting. Some of them, who are here entombed, have already been adorned with honors in deed. For the others, the city will bring up their children at the public expense, from this time up to their manhood, and set aside for these and their posterity a profitable reward for their struggles. For where the greatest prizes for virtue are laid down, there also the most virtuous men are citizens. Now, after you have lamented for your respective relative, depart."

Such was the funeral that took place this winter. After Pericles went through it, the first year of this war ended.

# THE MELIAN DIALOGUE

84.      The Athenians went on a military expedition against the island of Melos, with thirty ships of their own, six of the Chians, two of the Lesbians, sixteen hundred of their own *hoplites*, three hundred archers, twenty mounted archers, and at most five thousand and five hundred *hoplites* of the allies and the islanders. The Melians were colonists of the Lacedaemonians and were not willing to submit to the Athenians, like the rest of the islanders. At first, they remained at rest and were on neither side; later, since the Athenians compelled them by ravaging their land, they were openly in a state of war with them. The Athenian generals—Cleomedes, son of Lycomedes, and Tisias, son of Tisimachus—encamped with this preparation and, before they did injustice to any part of the land, first sent ambassadors to make speeches with them. These ambassadors, the Melians did not introduce to their multitude, but ordered them to speak with the magistrates and the few about why they had come. The ambassadors of the Athenians then spoke as follows:

85.     *Ath.* "Since our speeches are not addressed to your multitude so that, no doubt, the many may remain deceived by not hearing at once, in one continuous oration, influential and irrefutable arguments from us (for we understand that you have this in mind by introducing us to the few), you who are seated here might act still very carefully. For on each particular point and not in one continuous speech, but immediately interrupting where what is said does not seem suitable to you, answer us. First, however, tell us if it pleases you that we speak this way." The commissioners of the Melians answered.

86.     *Mel.* "The comeliness of instructing each other at rest is not to be faulted. But your preparations for war, which are already present and not future, appear to be at variance with it. For we see that you have come to be judges by yourselves of what will be said. The end of it will, in all likelihood, bring us either war, if we should prevail in the justice of our cause and not submit because of it, or slavery, if we are persuaded by you."

87.     *Ath.* "If now you have come together with us to calculate suspicions of the future, or if you have any other purpose except to deliberate for the salvation of your city from the present circumstances and from what you see, we should stop. But if you have come together with us for this purpose, we should speak."

88.     *Mel.* "It is likely [*Eikos*, also less literally "fairness." Throughout the Melian Dialogue, Thucydides has the Melians appeal to "fairness" (*eikos* or *ta eikota*) as opposed to the Athenians' appeal to "utility" (*xresimon*).] and pardonable in this circumstance to turn to many things both in speaking and opining. Nevertheless, since this meeting exists for our very preservation, let the speech continue, if it is so resolved, in the way which you propose."

89.     *Ath.* "We, then, shall not on our part present long, untrustworthy speeches in noble words to the effect either that we rule justly for putting down the Mede or that we now come out against you for being done injustice. Nor do we deem it worthy for you to think of persuading us by saying either that you did not go on military expeditions with us because you are a colony of the Lacedaemonians or that you have done us no injustice. Let us be of a mind to act in accord with what is truly possible for each of us. Let it also be understood by those who know that, in the speech of the human thing, justice is decided from the equality of necessity. As for what is possible, the superiors act and the weaker sorts submit."

90.     *Mel.* "Indeed, we surely believe that it is useful (for it is necessity, since you have established the premises of the discussion thus, that we speak of the expedient as opposed to the just) for you not to dissolve the common good. But for one who is always in danger the fair is also the just; and so, one should profit from what is only somewhat within the bounds of strict justice if he is persuasive. Moreover, this is not less a matter of fairness and justice for you inasmuch as you would be made an example to others, when you fall, by suffering the greatest vengeance."

91.     *Ath.* "We, on our part, are not dispirited about the end of our empire, even if it should cease. For it is not those who rule over others, just as the Lacedaemonians do, who are terrible to the conquered (although the contest for us here is not against the Lacedaemonians), but it is the

subjects who are terrible if they should somehow set upon their rulers and conquer them. So on this point let us face the danger by ourselves. That we are present here for the profit of our empire, and that we shall also speak now for the salvation of your city, we shall clarify these things because we wish to rule over you unlaboriously and to preserve you usefully for the both of us."

92      *Mel.* "How could utility befall us to be enslaved by you at the same time as you rule us?"

93.      *Ath.* "Because it would be useful for you to submit before suffering the most terrible things, and we would gain by not destroying you."

94.      *Mel.* "But would you not accept, as long as we stay at rest, that we be friends instead of enemies, but allies with neither side?"

95.      *Ath.* "No, for your mortal hatred is not so harmful to us as your friendship. To those who are ruled by us, your friendship is a clear example of our weakness; but your hatred, of our power."

96.      *Mel.* "Do your subjects so examine the likelihood that as many as are your colonists, and some others who have been taken in hand by you after revolting, are both reduced to the same condition of subjection as those who are not related to you?"

97.      *Ath.* "[Why not?] For they do not consider us to be lacking a justification in either case: some we prevail over by force; others do not attack us because of fear. Therefore, in addition to ruling over more subjects, you would also provide safety for us through your subjection, especially if you, who are islanders and weaker than some others, could not prevail over us, who have the command of the sea."

98.      *Mel.* "Do you not believe that there is safety in our neutrality? For here again, since you have stopped us from speaking of justice and persuade us to submit to your expedient interest, we must also teach what is useful for us and endeavor to persuade you of it in case the same thing also chances to befall you. For how can you not make enemies of as many as are now allied with no one, when they look at this and consider that at some time or other you will proceed against them also? By this course, what else are you doing but aggrandizing your present enemies and bringing those against you unwillingly, who were not about to become your enemies?"

99.      *Ath.* "No. We do not believe that the mainlanders anywhere, who will make a long delay from guarding against us because of their liberty, are more terrible to us than the islanders anywhere who are not ruled by us, like you, and who by the necessity of our rule are now exasperated with us. For they would most turn to irrationality and put both themselves and us into a foreseeable state of danger."

100.      *Mel.* "Surely, then, if your present slaves in fact cause you such danger, lest they put a stop to the empire and are set free, for us who at least are still free it is great evil and cowardice not to have recourse to everything before we become slaves."

101.      *Ath.* "No, not at all, if you would deliberate moderately. For you are not involved in a contest over manly goodness, on equal terms, lest you incur shame. You are rather involved in a deliberation for your salvation lest you oppose those who are much stronger. [*Kreisson*, also "better" or "far superior"] than yourselves."

102.      *Mel.* "But we know that the opportunities of war, because of chance, are sometimes more equal than might be expected despite the difference in number on each side. In our case, to yield is immediate hopelessness; but by doing something, there is still also hope that it will turn out well."

103.      *Ath.* "Hope is a comfort in danger when it is used by those with abundant means; and although it may injure, it does not ruin them. But in the case of those who hazard, by a throw of the dice, their whole existence on it (for it is by nature expensive), one understands it at once when it causes failure. But to the extent that one will guard against it in the future, once it is recognized, he is not deficient. Do not, then, since you are weak and balancing on one single turn of the scale, be desirous to suffer this nor to resemble the many. When they might still have been saved in the present by human means, after visible hopes have left them in their distress, they

betake themselves to invisible things: prophecy, oracles, and all such things as inflict outrage together with hopes."

104.     *Mel.* "Indeed, even we, as you know well, believe that it is difficult for us to contend against your power and chance unless it will be on equal terms. Nevertheless, we trust that from the gods we shall not have the worse in matters of chance because we are standing up with divine right on our side against unjust opponents. Our deficiency in power will be made up by our alliance with the Lacedaemonians, who are under a necessity of aiding us, if for no other reason than at least on account of our kinship with them and shame."

105.     *Ath.* "Now then, as for the favor of the gods, we think that we too shall not be left behind. For we do not seek a justification nor do anything beyond the beliefs of human beings in regard to the gods or beyond their desires in regard to themselves. For of the gods we believe as a matter of opinion, and of human beings we see clearly, that by a necessity of nature they always rule wherever they can conquer. We neither enacted this law nor were the first to use it after it was laid down. But since we received it already in existence and shall leave it after us in existence forever, we only make use of it. We also know that both you and others, after rising to the same power as us, would do the same. Therefore, with respect to the gods, we do not fear the likelihood of having the worse. As for your opinion of the Lacedaemonians, regarding which you trust that from a sense of shame they will surely assist you, although we bless your innocence, we do not envy your folly. For with respect to themselves and the laws of their country, the Lacedaemonians make the most extensive use of virtue. But with respect to others, though one might be able to say much about how they conduct themselves, to sum it up most concisely, it should be evident that of those whom we know, they most clearly believe the pleasant to be the noble and the expedient to be the just. And further, such thinking does not accord with your present unreasonable hopes of safety."

106.     *Mel.* "On this very ground, we now especially trust in their sense of expediency. They would not wish to betray us, the Melians who are their colonists, and become untrustworthy to those of the Greeks who favor them, but profit the Greeks who are enemies to them."

107.     *Ath.* "Then, you do not think that the expedient here is connected with security, whereas justice and nobility are here practiced with danger, which the Lacedaemonians for most purposes are the least daring to face."

108.     *Mel.* "But we suppose that they would take in hand even greater dangers for our sake than for others, and that they would believe our case to be a more secure risk than in the case of others, inasmuch as we lie near the Peloponnesus for the execution of their deeds and are more trustworthy than others because of the kinship of our minds."

109.     *Ath.* "Security, in fact, for those who will take part in a struggle, does not appear to be the mere goodwill of those who are invited to help, but it depends on whether or not one might have far superior power in the deeds. And the Lacedaemonians observe this rule even more than the rest. At any rate, because of mistrust in their own resources, only with many allies do they attack their neighbors. Thus, it is not likely at all that they will cross over to an island while we are masters of the sea."

110.     *Mel.* "They might have others to send. Moreover, the Cretan sea is wide; because of this, the capture of someone who crosses it is more perplexing for those who command it than preservation is for those who wish to elude observation. If the Lacedaemonians should fail in this, they could also turn against your country and the remainder of your allies, as many as Brasidas did not reach. You will, then, have to labor not more for what does not belong to you than for your personal alliance and even your country."

111.     *Ath.* "On these points, you may become somewhat experienced, and not remain ignorant, that from no single siege did the Athenians ever yet retreat through fear of others.

"As we are reflecting, although you said that you would deliberate for the safety of your country, you have in all this long speech said nothing that human beings might trust and believe in order to be saved. Your strongest points are future hopes, and your present resources are too scanty, compared with those at present arrayed against you, for you to prevail. Thus, you present great irrationality in your planning unless, by changing your mind again with respect to us, you might understand something more moderate than this. For surely, you will not turn your mind toward that shame that destroys human beings when they are in shameful and foreseeable danger. In the case of the many, while they are still foreseeing what dangers they are brought into, the thing called shame draws them in by the power of its seductive name. Once the many are mastered by that word in their deeds, they fall voluntarily into irretrievable disasters and incur a more shameful shame because it is the result of folly rather than of chance. Against this, then, if you would deliberate well, you must guard. You must also not believe that it is unfitting to submit to the greatest city after it invites you on measured terms to become tributary allies in possession of your own country. Since you have been given a choice between the alternatives of war and safety, do not choose the worse because of the love of victory. When someone does not yield to his equals, but conducts himself nobly with his superiors and is measured to his inferiors, he would be most correct. At all events, examine this and change your mind with respect to us. Reflect often that you are deliberating for your fatherland; and this deliberation will take place, whether fortunately or unfortunately, for only one fatherland and in one deliberation."

112.     The Athenians withdrew from the speeches. The Melians, once they were by themselves, had nearly the same opinions as they had in the dialogue and gave the following answer: "We do not have an opinion other than the very one that we had at first, Athenians, nor shall we in a short space of time take away the liberty from a city that has now been inhabited for seven hundred years. Entrusting it to chance from the gods, which up to this time has saved it, and to vengeance from human beings and from the Lacedaemonians, we shall endeavor to save ourselves. We propose to you that we be your friends, and the enemies of neither side, and that you should retire from our country after we make such a treaty as seems to be suitable to both sides."

113.     The Melians answered in such a way. The Athenians, who already put an end to the speeches, said: "Very well, then. You are indeed the only men, who on the basis of these deliberations, as you seem to us, judge the future to be more certain than what is seen in the present and who view the invisible as already occurring because you wish it. Since you have staked your all on and trusted most in the Lacedaemonians, chance, and hopes, you will also fail most."

114.     The Athenian ambassadors returned to their army. Their generals, when the Melians did not listen at all to them, immediately turned their attention to war. They divided the work between the several cities and built a wall around the Melians. Later, the Athenians, after they left behind a part of their own and the allies' troops to keep guard both by land and sea, returned with the larger part of the forces. Those who were left behind remained and besieged the place. . . . [Later], the Melians seized, in an assault by night, the part of the Athenian walls opposite to the marketplace and killed some of their men. As soon as they carried in corn and as many useful things as they were able, they returned and remained at rest. Accordingly, the Athenians made better preparation for their guard in future. And so, the summer ended.

116.     The following winter, the Melians again took some part of the Athenian walls, in another direction, because the garrison present was not large. Another army later came from Athens after these attacks occurred, with Philocrates, son of Demeas, commanding it. Once the Melians were strongly besieged and there had also been some treachery from their own men, they surrendered to the Athenians on the condition that they hold deliberations about them. The Athenians put to death as many of the Melian adults as they took and made slaves of the children and women. As for the country, they sent out five hundred colonists and inhabited it themselves.

# Selections from *The Politics*

## *Aristotle (384–322 B.C.)*

*Aristotle, the most famous student of Plato, conducted empirical and theoretical researches in virtually every subject—biology and psychology, metaphysics and physics, logic and rhetoric, to name a few. The* Politics, *which Aristotle considered to be closely connected with his* Ethics, *is the first treatise of political science. His political works encompass a very broad range of ideas and issues related to political life. Even in these brief selections, we encounter such important questions as the meaning of political life, as distinguished from other forms of life in common, and the best way of life for good men.*

*Consider the arguments Aristotle uses to support his controversial views on the authority of politics over the rest of human life, the situations in which slavery is justified, the criticisms of democracy and oligarchy, and the requirements for the happiest life in common for the best human beings. Is it reasonable to believe that human beings are, by nature, political animals? Why is human nature such an important problem for political thought? What does Aristotle mean by "justice" and why is it so significant for an inquiry into politics?*

## BOOK I

### CHAPTER 1

Since we see that every city is some sort of partnership, and that every partnership is constituted for the sake of some good (for everyone does everything for the sake of what is held to be good), it is clear that all partnerships aim at some good, and that the partnership that is most authoritative of all and embraces all the others does so particularly, and aims at the most authoritative good of all. This is what is called the city or the political partnership.

Those who suppose that the same person is expert in political [rule], kingly [rule], managing the household and being a master [of slaves] do not argue rightly. For they consider that each of these differs in the multitude or fewness [of those ruled] and not in kind—for example, [the ruler] of a few is a master, of more a household manager, and of still more an expert in political or kingly [rule]—the assumption being that there is no difference between a large household and a small city; and as for the experts in political and kingly [rule], they consider an expert in kingly [rule] one who has charge himself, and in political [rule] one who, on the basis of the precepts of this sort of science, rules and is ruled in turn. But these things are not true. This will be clear to those investigating in accordance with our normal sort of inquiry. For just as it is necessary elsewhere to divide a compound into its uncompounded elements (for these are the smallest parts of the whole), so too by investigating what the city is composed of we shall gain a better view concerning these [kinds of rulers] as well, both as to how they differ from one another and as to whether there is some expertise characteristic of an art that can be acquired in connection with each of those mentioned.

### CHAPTER 2

Now in these matters as elsewhere it is by looking at how things develop naturally from the beginning that one may best study them. First, then, there must of necessity be a conjunction of persons who cannot exist without one another: on the one hand, male and female, for the sake of reproduction (which occurs not from intentional choice but—as is also the case with the other animals and plants—from a natural striving to leave behind another that is like oneself); on the other, the naturally ruling and ruled, on account of preservation. For that which can foresee with the mind is the naturally ruling and naturally mastering element, while that which can do these things with the body is the naturally ruled and slave; hence the same thing is advantageous for the master and slave. Now the female is distinguished by nature from the slave. For nature makes nothing in an economizing spirit, as smiths make the Delphic knife, but one thing with a view to one thing, and each instrument would perform most finely if it served one task rather than many. The barbarians, though, have the same arrangement for female and slave. The reason for this is that they have no naturally ruling element; with them, the partnership [of man and woman] is that of female slave and male slave. This is why the poets say "it is fitting for Greeks to rule barbarians"—the assumption being that barbarian and slave are by nature the same thing.

From these two partnerships, then, the household first arose, and Hesiod's verse is rightly spoken: "first a house, and woman, and ox for ploughing"—for poor persons have an ox instead of a servant. The household is the partnership constituted by nature for [the needs of] daily life; Charondas calls its members "peers of the mess," Epimenides of Crete "peers of the manger." The first partnership arising from [the union of] several households and for the sake of nondaily needs is the village. By nature the village seems to be above all an extension of the household. Its members some call "milk-peers"; they are "the children and the children's children." This is why cities were at first under kings, and nations are even now. For those who joined together were already under kings: every household was under the eldest as king, and so also were the extensions [of the household constituting the village] as a result of kinship. This is what Homer meant when he says that "each acts as law to his children and wives"; for [men] were scattered and used to dwell in this manner in ancient times. And it is for this reason that all assert that the gods are under a king—because they themselves are under kings now, or were in ancient times. For human beings assimilate not only the looks of the gods to themselves, but their ways of life as well.

The partnership arising from [the union of] several villages that is complete is the city. It reaches a level of full self-sufficiency, so to speak; and while coming into being for the sake of living, it exists for the sake of living well. Every city, therefore, exists by nature, if such also are the first partnerships. For the city is their end, and nature is an end: what each thing is—for example, a human being, a horse, or a household—when its coming into being is complete is, we assert, the nature of that thing. Again, that for the sake of which [a thing exists], or the end, is what is best; and self-sufficiency is an end and what is best.

From these things it is evident, then, that the city belongs among the things that exist by nature, and that man is by nature a political animal. He who is without a city through nature rather than chance is either a mean sort or superior to man; he is "without clan, without law, without hearth," like the person reproved by Homer; for the one who is such by nature has by this fact a desire for war, as if he were an isolated piece in a game of chess. That man is much more a political animal than any kind of bee or any herd animal is clear. For, as we assert, nature does nothing in vain; and man alone among the animals has speech. The voice indeed indicates the painful or pleasant, and hence is present in other animals as well; for their nature has come this far, that they have a perception of the painful and pleasant and indicate these things to each other. But speech serves to reveal the advantageous and the harmful, and hence also the just and the unjust. For it is peculiar to man as compared to the other animals that he alone has a perception of good and bad and just and unjust and other things [of this sort]; and partnership in these things is what makes a household a city.

The city is thus prior by nature to the household and to each of us. For the whole must of necessity be prior to the part; for if the whole [body] is destroyed there will not be a foot or a hand, unless in the sense that the term is similar (as when one speaks of a hand made of stone), but the thing itself will be defective. Everything is defined by its task and its power, and if it is no longer the same in these respects it should not be spoken of in the same way, but only as something similarly termed. That the city is both by nature and prior to each individual, then, is clear. For if the individual when separated [from it] is not self-sufficient, he will be in a condition similar to that of the other parts in relation to the whole. One who is incapable of participating or who is in need of nothing through being self-sufficient is no part of a city, and so is either a beast or a god.

Accordingly, there is in everyone by nature an impulse toward this sort of partnership. And yet the one who first constituted [a city] is responsible for the greatest of goods. For just as man is the best of the animals when completed, when separated from law and adjudication he is the worst of all. For injustice is harshest when it is furnished with arms; and man is born naturally possessing arms for [the use of] prudence and virtue which are nevertheless very susceptible to being used for their opposites. This is why, without virtue, he is the most unholy and the most savage [of the animals], and the worst with regard to sex and food. [The virtue of] justice is a thing belonging to the city. For adjudication is an arrangement of the political partnership, and adjudication is judgment as to what is just.

## CHAPTER 3

Since it is evident out of what parts the city is constituted, it is necessary first to speak of household management; for every city is composed of households. The parts of household management correspond to the parts out of which the household itself is constituted. Now the complete household is made up of slaves and free persons. Since everything is to be sought for first in its smallest elements, and the first and smallest parts of the household are master, slave, husband, wife, father, and children, three things must be investigated to determine what each is and what sort of thing it ought to be. These are expertise in mastery, in marital [rule] (there is no term for the union of man and woman), and thirdly in parental [rule] (this too has not been assigned a term of its own). So much, then, for the three we spoke of. There is a certain part of it, however, which some hold to be [identical with] household management, and others its greatest part; how the matter really stands has to be studied. I am speaking of what is called business expertise.

Let us speak first about master and slave, so that we may see at the same time what relates to necessary needs and whether we cannot acquire something in the way of knowledge about these things that is better than current conceptions. For some hold that mastery is a kind of science, and that managing the household, mastery, and expertise in political and kingly [rule] are the same, as we said at the beginning. Others hold that exercising mastery is against nature; for [as they believe] it is by law that one person is slave and another free, there being no difference by nature, and hence it is not just, since it rests on force.

## CHAPTER 4

Now possessions are a part of the household, and expertise in acquiring possessions a part of household management (for without the necessary things it is impossible either to live or to live well); and just as the specialized arts must of necessity have their proper instruments if their work is to be performed, so too must the expert household manager. Now of instruments some are inanimate and others animate—the pilot's rudder, for example, is an inanimate one, but his lookout an animate one; for the subordinate is a kind of instrument for the arts. A possession too, then, is an instrument for life, and one's possessions are the multitude of such instruments; and the slave is a possession of the animate sort. Every subordinate, moreover, is an instrument that wields many instruments, for if each of the instruments were able to perform its work on command or by anticipation, as they assert those of Daedalus did, or the tripods of Hephaestus (which the poet says "of their own accord came to the gods' gathering"), so that shuttles would weave themselves and picks play the lyre, master craftsmen would no longer have a need for subordinates, or masters for slaves. Now the instruments mentioned are productive instruments, but a possession is an instrument of action. For from the shuttle comes something apart from the use of it, while from clothing or a bed the use alone. Further, since production and action differ in kind and both require instruments, these must of necessity reflect the same difference. Life is action, not production; the slave is therefore a subordinate in matters concerning action.

A possession is spoken of in the same way as a part. A part is not only part of something else, but belongs wholly to something else; similarly with a possession. Accordingly, while the master is only master of the slave and does not belong to him, the slave is not only slave to the master but belongs wholly to him.

What the nature of the slave is and what his capacity, then, is clear from these things. For one who does not belong to himself by nature but is another's, though a human being, is by nature a slave; a human being is another's who, though a human being, is a possession; and a possession is an instrument of action and separable [from its owner].

## CHAPTER 5

Whether anyone is of this sort by nature or not, and whether it is better and just for anyone to be a slave or not, but rather all slavery is against nature, must be investigated next. It is not difficult either to discern [the answer] by reasoning or to learn it from what actually happens. Ruling and being ruled belong not only among things necessary but also among things advantageous. And immediately from birth certain things diverge, some toward being ruled, others toward ruling. There are many kinds both of ruling and ruled [things], and the better rule is always that over ruled [things] that are better, for example over a human being rather than a beast; for the work performed by the better is better; and wherever something rules and something is ruled there is a certain work belonging to these together. For whatever is constituted out of a number of things—whether continuous or discrete—and becomes a single common thing always displays a ruling and a ruled element; this is something that animate things derive from all of nature, for even in things that do not share in life there is a sort of rule, for example in a harmony. But these matters perhaps belong to a more external sort of investigation. But an animal is the first thing constituted out of soul and body, of which the one is the ruling element by nature, the other the ruled. It is in things whose condition is according to nature that one ought particularly to investigate what is by nature, not in things that are defective. Thus the human being to be studied is one whose state is best both in body and in soul—in him this is clear; for in the case of the depraved, or those in a depraved condition, the body is often held to rule the soul on account of their being in a condition that is bad and unnatural.

It is then in an animal, as we were saying, that one can first discern both the sort of rule characteristic of a master and political rule. For the soul rules the body with the rule characteristic of a master, while intellect rules appetite with political and kingly rule; and this makes it evident that it is according to nature and advantageous for the body to be ruled by the soul, and the passionate part [of the soul] by intellect and the part having reason, while it is harmful to both if the relation is equal or reversed. The same holds with respect to man and the other animals: tame animals have a better nature than wild ones, and it is better for all of them to be ruled by man, since in this way their preservation is ensured. Further, the relation of male to female is by nature a relation of superior to inferior and ruler to ruled. The same must of necessity hold in the case of human beings generally.

Accordingly, those who are as different [from other men] as the soul from the body or man from beast—and they are in this state if their work is the use of the body, and if this is the best that can come from them—are slaves by nature. For them it is better to be ruled in accordance with this sort of rule, if such is the case for the other things mentioned. For he is a slave by nature who is capable of belonging to another—which is also why he belongs to another—and who participates in reason only to the extent of perceiving it, but does not have it. (The other animals, not perceiving reason, obey their passions.) Moreover, the need for them differs only slightly: bodily assistance in the necessary things is forthcoming from both, from slaves and from tame animals alike.

Nature indeed wishes to make the bodies of free persons and slaves different as well [as their souls]—those of the latter strong with a view to necessary needs, those of the former straight and useless for such tasks, but useful with a view to a political way of life (which is itself divided between the needs of war and those of peace); yet the opposite often results, some having the bodies of free persons while others have the souls. It is evident, at any rate, that if they were to be born as different only in body as the images of the gods, everyone would assert that those not so favored merit being their slaves. But if this is true in the case of the body, it is much more justifiable to make this distinction in the case of the soul; yet it is not as easy to see the beauty of the soul as it is that of the body. That some persons are free and others slaves by nature, therefore, and that for these slavery is both advantageous and just, is evident.

## CHAPTER 6

That those who assert the opposite are in a certain manner correct, however, is not difficult to see. Slavery and the slave are spoken of in a double sense. There is also a sort of slave or enslaved person according to law, the law being a certain agreement by which things conquered in war are said to belong to the conquerors. This [claim of] justice is challenged by many of those conversant with the laws—as they would challenge an orator—on a motion of illegality, on the grounds that it is a terrible thing if what yields to force is to be enslaved and ruled by what is able to apply force and is superior in power. And there are some of the wise as well who hold this opinion, though some hold the other. The cause of this dispute—and what makes the arguments converge—is that virtue, once it obtains equipment, is in a certain manner particularly able to apply force, and the dominant element is always preeminent in something that is good, so that it is held that there is no force without virtue, and that the dispute concerns only the justice of the matter; for on this account some hold that justice consists in benevolence, while the others hold that this very thing, the rule of the superior, is just. At any rate, if these arguments are set on one side, the other arguments—which assume that what is better in virtue ought not to rule or be master—have neither strength nor persuasiveness. Those who regard the slavery that results from war as just adhere wholly, as they suppose, to a sort of justice (for law is just in a certain sense); yet at the same time they deny [implicitly that it is in fact always just]. For the beginnings of wars are not always just, and no one would assert that someone not meriting enslavement ought ever to be a slave. Otherwise, the result will be that those held to be the best born will become slaves and the offspring of slaves if they happen to be captured and sold. Accordingly, they do not want to speak of these as slaves, but rather of barbarians. When they say this, however, they are in search of nothing other than the slave by nature of which we spoke at the beginning; for they must necessarily assert that there are some persons who are everywhere slaves, and others who are so nowhere. It is the same way with good birth as well; for they consider themselves well born not only among their own but everywhere, but barbarians only at home—the assumption being that there is something well born and free simply, and something not simply [but relatively], as Theodectes' Helen says:

> As offshoot of divine roots on either side
> Who would dare call me serving-maid?

When they speak in this way, it is by nothing other than virtue or vice that they define what is slave and what is free, who well born and who ill born. For they claim that from the good should come something good, just as a human being comes from a human being and a beast from beasts. But while nature wishes to do this, it is often unable to. That there is some reason in the dispute, therefore, and that it is not [simply] the case that the ones are slaves by nature and the others free, is clear; and also that such a distinction does exist for some, where it is advantageous as well as just for the one to be enslaved and the other to be master; and that the one ought to be ruled and other to rule, and to rule by the sort of rule that is natural for them, which is mastery, while bad rule is disadvantageous for both. For the same thing is advantageous for the part and the whole and for body and soul, and the slave is a sort of part of the master—a part of his body, as it were, animate yet separate. There is thus a certain advantage—and even affection of slave and master for one another—for those [slaves] who merit being such by nature; but for those who do not merit it in this way but [who are slaves] according to law and by force, the opposite is the case.

## CHAPTER 7

It is evident from these things as well that mastery and political [rule] are not the same thing and that all the sorts of rule are not the same as one another, as some assert. For the one sort is over those free by nature, the other over slaves; and household management is monarchy (for every household is run by one alone), while political rule is over free and equal persons. Now the master is so called not according to a science [he possesses] but through being a certain sort, and similarly with the slave and the free person. Yet there could be a science characteristic both of mastery and of slavery. The science characteristic of slavery would be the sort of thing provided through the education offered by the fellow in Syracuse—for someone there used to receive pay for teaching slave boys their regular serving chores; and there might be additional learning in such matters, for example in cookery and other service of this type. For certain works are more honored or more necessary than others, and as the proverb has it, "slave before slave, master before master." All things of this sort, then, are sciences characteristic of slavery; but the science characteristic of mastery is expertise in using slaves, since the master is what he is not in the acquiring of slaves but in the use of them. This science has nothing great or dignified about it: the master must know how to command the things that the slave must know how to do. Hence for those to whom it is open not to be bothered with such things, an overseer assumes this prerogative, while they themselves engage in politics or philosophy. Expertise in acquiring [slaves] is different from both of these—that is, the just sort of acquiring, which is like a certain kind of expertise in war or hunting.

## CHAPTER 8

(1) But let us examine generally, in accordance with our normal sort of approach, possessions as such and expertise in business, since the slave too turned out to be a part of one's possessions. In the first place, then, one might raise the question whether expertise in business is the same as expertise in household management, a part of it, or subordinate to it; and if subordinate, whether it is so in the way expertise in making shuttles is to expertise in weaving, or in the way expertise in casting bronze is to expertise in sculpture. For these are not subordinate in the same way, but the one provides instruments, the other the matter. (2) (By the matter I mean the substance out of

which some work is performed—for example, wool for the weaver or bronze for the sculptor.) Now it is clear that expertise in household management is not the same as expertise in business, for it belongs to the latter to supply and the former to use. For what is the expertise that uses the things in the house if not expertise in household management? But whether expertise in business is a part of it or different in kind is a matter of dispute. (3) For if it belongs to the expert businessman to discern how to get goods and possessions, and if possessions and wealth encompass many parts, [one must consider] in the first place whether expertise in farming is part of business expertise or different in kind, and [whether this is the case for] the concern with sustenance generally and the possessions connected with it. (4) There are indeed many kinds of sustenance, and therefore many ways of life both of animals and of human beings. For it is impossible to live without sustenance, so that the differences in sustenance have made the ways of life of animals differ. (5) For of beasts some live in herds and others scattered—whichever is advantageous for their sustenance, on account of some of them being carnivorous, some herbivorous, and some omnivorous; so that it is with a view to their convenience and their predilections in these matters that nature has determined their ways of life. And because the same thing is not pleasant to each [species of animal] according to nature but different things to different [species], among the carnivorous and the herbivorous themselves their ways of life differ from one another. (6) The same is the case for human beings as well; for there are great differences in their ways of life. The idlest are nomads: they derive sustenance from tame animals without exertion and amid leisure, though as it is necessary for their herds to move about on account of their pastures, they are compelled to follow along with them, as if they were farming a living farm. (7) Others live from hunting, and different sorts from different sorts of hunting. Some, for example, live from piracy; others from fishing, if they dwell near lakes, marshes, rivers, or a sea that is suitable; others from birds or wild beasts. But the type of human being that is most numerous lives from the land and from cultivated crops.

(8) The ways of life are, then, about this many, or at least those which involve self-generated work and do not supply sustenance through exchange and commerce: the way of life of the nomad, the farmer, the pirate, the fisher, and the hunter. There are also some who live pleasantly by combining several of these in order to compensate for the shortcomings of one way of life, where it happens to be deficient with regard to being self-sufficient. For example, some combine the nomad's with the pirate's, some the farmer's with the hunter's, and similarly with others as well—they pass their time in the manner that need [together with pleasure] compels them to. (9) Now possessions of this sort are evidently given by nature itself to all [animals], both immediately from birth and when they have reached completion. (10) For at birth from the very beginning some animals provide at the same time as much sustenance as is adequate until the offspring can supply itself—for example, those that give birth to larvae or eggs; while those that give birth to live offspring have sustenance for these in themselves for a certain period—the natural substance called milk. (11) It is clear in a similar way, therefore, that for grown things as well one must suppose both that plants exist for the sake of animals and that the other animals exist for the sake of human beings—the tame animals, both for use and sustenance, and most if not all of the wild animals, for sustenance and other assistance, in order that clothing and other instruments may be got from them. (12) If, then, nature makes nothing that is incomplete or purposeless, nature must necessarily have made all of these for the sake of human beings.

Hence expertise in war will also be in some sense a natural form of acquisitive expertise; for one part of it is expertise in hunting, which should be used with a view both to beasts and to those human beings who are naturally suited to be ruled but unwilling—this sort of war being by nature just. (13) One kind of acquisitive expertise, then, is by nature a part of expertise in household management, and must either be available or be supplied by the latter so as to be available—[expertise in acquiring] those goods a store of which is both necessary for life and useful for partnership in a city or a household. (14) At any rate, it would seem to be these things that make up genuine wealth. For self-sufficiency in possessions of this sort with a view to a good life is not limitless, as Solon asserts it to be in his poem: "of wealth no boundary lies revealed to men." (15) There is such a boundary, just as in the other arts; for there is no art that has an instrument that is without limit either in number or in size, and wealth is the multitude of instruments belonging to expert household managers and political [rulers]. That there is a natural expertise in acquisition for household managers and political [rulers], then, and the cause of this, is clear.

## CHAPTER 9

(1) But there is another type of acquisitive expertise that they particularly call—and justifiably so—expertise in business, on account of which there is held to be no limit to wealth and possessions. This is considered by many to be one and the same as the sort mentioned because of the resemblance between them; and while it is not the same as the one spoken of, it is not far from it either. The one is by nature, while the other is not by nature but arises rather through a certain experience and art.

(2) Concerning this, let us take the following as our beginning. Every possession has a double use. Both of these uses belong to it as such, but not in the same way, the one being proper and the other not proper to the thing. In the case of footwear, for example, one can wear it or one can exchange it. Both of these are uses of footwear; (3) for the one exchanging footwear with someone who needs it in return for money or sustenance uses footwear as footwear, but not in respect of its proper use; for it did not come to be for the sake of exchange. The same is the case concerning other possessions as well. (4) For there is an expertise in exchange for all things; it arises in the first place from something that is according to nature—the fact that human beings have either more or fewer things than what is adequate. Thus it is also clear that expertise in commerce does not belong by nature to expertise in business; for it was necessary to make an exchange in order to obtain what was adequate for them. (5) In the first partnership, then—that is, the household— it is evident that exchange has no function, but only when the partnership has already become more numerous. For those [in the household] were partners in their own things, while persons separated [into different households] were partners in many things of others as well, and it was necessary to make transfers of these things according to their needs, as many barbarian nations still do, through exchange. (6) For they exchange useful things for one another and nothing besides—giving, for example, wine and accepting grain, and similarly for other such things. This sort of expertise in exchange is not contrary to nature, nor is it any kind of expertise in business, for it existed in order to support natural self-sufficiency. (7) However, the latter arose from it reasonably enough. For as the assistance of foreigners became greater in importing what they were in need of and exporting what was in surplus, the use of money was necessarily devised. (8) For the things necessary by nature are not in each case easily portable; hence with a view to exchanges they made a compact with one another to give and accept something which was itself one of the useful things and could be used flexibly to suit the needs of life, such as iron and silver and whatever else might be of this sort. At first this was something [with its value] determined simply by size and weight, but eventually they impressed a mark on it in order to be relieved of having to measure it, the mark being put on as an indication of the amount. (9) Once a supply of money came into being as a result of such necessary exchange, then, the other kind of expertise in business arose—that is, commerce. At first this probably existed in a simple fashion, while later through experience it became more a matter of art—[the art of discerning] what and how to exchange in order to make the greatest profit. (10) It is on this account that expertise in business is held to be particularly connected with money, and to have as its task the ability to discern what will provide a given amount [of it]; for it is held to be productive of wealth and goods. Indeed, they often define wealth as a given amount of money, since this is what expertise in business or commerce is connected with. (11) At other times, however, money seems to be something nonsensical and [to exist] altogether [by] law, and in no way by nature, because when changed by

its users it is worth nothing and is not useful with a view to any of the necessary things; and it will often happen that one who is wealthy in money will go in want of necessary sustenance. Yet it would be absurd if wealth were something one could have in abundance and die of starvation—like the Midas of the fable, when everything set before him turned into gold on account of the greediness of his prayer. (12) Hence they seek another [definition] of wealth and expertise in business, and correctly so. For the expertise in business and the wealth that is according to nature is something different: this is expertise in household management, while the other is commercial expertise, which is productive of wealth not in every way but through trafficking in goods, and is held to be connected with money, since money is the medium and goal of exchange. (13) And the wealth deriving from this sort of business expertise is indeed without limit. For just as expertise in medicine has no limit with respect to being healthy, or any of the other arts with respect to its end (for this is what they particularly wish to accomplish), while there is a limit with respect to what exists for the sake of the end (since the end is a limit in the case of all of them), so with this sort of expertise in business there is no limit with respect to the end, and the end is wealth of this sort and possession of goods. (14) But of expertise in household management as distinguished from expertise in business there is a limit; for that is not the work of expertise in household management. Thus in one way it appears necessary that there be a limit to all wealth; yet if we look at what actually occurs we see that the opposite happens— all who engage in business increase their money without limit. (15) The cause of this is the nearness to one another of these [forms of expertise in business]. For they converge in the matter of use, the same thing being used in the case of either sort of expertise in business. For possessions serve the same use, though not in the same respect, but in the one case the end is increase, in the other something else. So some hold that this is the work of expertise in household management, and they proceed on the supposition that they should either preserve or increase without limit their property in money. (16) The cause of this state is that they are serious about living, but not about living well; and since that desire of theirs is without limit, they also desire what is productive of unlimited things. Even those who also aim at living well seek what conduces to bodily gratifications, and since this too appears to be available in and through possessions, their pursuits are wholly connected with business, and this is why the other kind of business expertise has arisen. (17) For as gratification consists in excess, they seek the sort that is productive of the excess characteristic of gratification; and if they are unable to supply it through expertise in business, they attempt this in some other fashion, using each sort of capacity in a way not according to nature. For it belongs to courage to produce not goods but confidence; nor does this belong to military or medical expertise, but it belongs to the former to produce victory, to the latter, health. (18) But all of these they make forms of expertise in business, as if this were the end and everything else had to march toward it.

Concerning the unnecessary sort of expertise in business, then, both as regards what it is and why we are in need of it, enough has been said; and also concerning the necessary sort—that it is different from the other, being expertise in household management according to nature (the sort connected with sustenance), and is not without limit like the other, but has a defining principle.

## CHAPTER 10

(1) It is also clear what the answer is to the question raised at the beginning whether business expertise belongs to the expert household manager or political [ruler] or not, but should rather be available to him. For just as political expertise does not create human beings but makes use of them after receiving them from nature, so also should nature provide land or sea or something else for sustenance, while it befits the household manager to have what comes from those things in the state it should be in. (2) For it does not belong to expertise in weaving to make wool, but to make use of it, and to know what sort is usable and suitable or poor and unsuitable. Otherwise one might raise the question why expertise in business should be a part of household

management but not medical expertise, since those in the household ought to be healthy, just as they must live or do any other necessary thing. (3) But just as seeing about health does indeed belong to the household manager and the ruler in a sense, but in another sense not but rather to the doctor, so in the case of goods it belongs to the household manager in a sense, but in another sense not but rather to the subordinate expertise. This should be available above all, as was said before, by nature. For it is a work of nature to provide sustenance to the newly born, everything deriving sustenance from what remains of that from which it is born. (4) Expertise in business relative to crops and animals is thus natural for all. But since it is twofold, as we said, part of it being commerce and part expertise in household management, the latter necessary and praised, while expertise in exchange is justly blamed since it is not according to nature but involves taking from others, usury is most reasonably hated because one's possessions derive from money itself and not from that for which it was supplied. (5) For it came into being for the sake of exchange, but interest actually creates more of it. And it is from this that it gets its name: offspring are similar to those who give birth to them, and interest is money born of money. So of the sorts of business this is the most contrary to nature.

## CHAPTER 11

(1) Since we have discussed adequately what relates to knowledge, what relates to practice must be treated. All things of this sort have room for a free sort of study, but experience in them is a necessity. The useful parts of expertise in business are: to be experienced regarding livestock—what sorts are most profitable in which places and under what conditions (for example, what sort of horses or cattle or sheep ought to be kept, and similarly with the other animals, (2) for one needs to be experienced as regards those that are most profitable both compared with one another and in particular places, since different kinds thrive in different areas); next, regarding farming, both of grain and fruit; and finally, regarding beekeeping and the raising of other animals, whether fish or fowl, from which it is possible to derive benefit. (3) Of expertise in business in its most proper sense, then, these are the parts and primary elements. Of expertise in exchange the greatest part is trade, of which there are three parts: provisioning the ship, transport, and marketing (these differ from each other by the fact that some are safer while others provide greater remuneration); the second is money-lending; and the third is wage labor, (4) of which one sort involves the vulgar arts, while the other [is performed by] those who lack any art but are useful only for their bodies. There is a third kind of expertise in business between this and the first, since it has some part both of the sort that is according to nature and of expertise in exchange: [this deals with] things from the earth and unfruitful but useful things that grow from the earth, [and includes activities] such as lumbering and every sort of mining (5) (this now encompasses many different types, as there are many kinds of things mined from the earth).

A general account has now been given of each of these things; a detailed and exact discussion would be useful in undertaking the works themselves, but to spend much time on such things is crude. (6) The most artful of these works are those which involve chance the least; the most vulgar, those in which the body is most damaged; the most slavish, those in which the body is most used; the most ignoble, those which are least in need of virtue.

(7) Since some have written on these matters—as Chares of Paros and Apollodoros of Lemnos on farming both of grain and fruit, for example, and others on other things—they may be studied there by anyone concerned with them; but, in addition, what has been said in various places concerning the ways some have succeeded in business should be collected. (8) For all these things are useful for those who honor expertise in business. There is, for example, the [way] of Thales of Miletus. This is a business scheme which is attributed to him on account of his wisdom, yet it happens to be general in application. (9) For they say that when some on account of his poverty reproached him with the uselessness of philosophy, Thales, observing through his knowledge of astronomy that there would be a good harvest of olives, was able during the winter

to raise a small sum of money to place in deposit on all the olive presses in both Miletus and Chios, which he could hire at a low rate because no one was competing with him; then, when the season came, and many of them were suddenly in demand at the same time, he hired them out on what terms he pleased and collected a great deal in the way of funds, thus showing how easy it is for philosophers to become wealthy if they so wish, but it is not this they are serious about. (10) Thales, then, is said to have made a display of his wisdom in this manner, though, as we said, this piece of business expertise is universal, if someone is able to establish a monopoly for himself. Thus even some cities raise revenue in this way when they are short of funds; they establish a monopoly on things being sold. (11) In Sicily, a man used some money deposited with him to buy all the iron from the iron foundries, and when traders came from their trading places he alone had it to sell; and though he did not greatly increase the price, he made a hundred talents' profit out of an original fifty. (12) When Dionysius heard of this, he ordered him to take his funds and leave Syracuse, on the grounds that he had discovered a way of raising revenue that was harmful to Dionysius' own affairs. Yet the insight was the same as that of Thales, for both artfully arranged a monopoly for themselves. (13) It is useful for political [rulers] also to be familiar with these things. For many cities need business and revenues of this sort, just as households do, yet more so. Thus there are some even among those engaged in politics who are concerned only with these matters.

## CHAPTER 12

(1) Since there are three parts of expertise in household management—expertise in mastery, which was spoken of earlier, expertise in paternal [rule], and expertise in marital [rule]—[the latter two must now be taken up. These differ fundamentally from the former, since one ought] to rule a wife and children as free persons, though it is not the same mode of rule in each case, the wife being ruled in political, the children in kingly fashion. For the male, unless constituted in some respect contrary to nature, is by nature more expert at leading than the female, and the elder and complete than the younger and incomplete. (2) In most political offices, it is true, there is an alternation of ruler and ruled, since they tend by their nature to be on an equal footing and to differ in nothing; all the same, when one rules and the other is ruled, [the ruler] seeks to establish differences in external appearance, forms of address, and prerogatives, as in the story Amasis told about his footpan. The male always stands thus in relation to the female. (3) But rule over the children is kingly. For the one who generates is ruler on the basis of both affection and age, which is the very mark of kingly rule. Homer thus spoke rightly of Zeus when he addressed as "father of men and gods" the king of them all. For by nature the king should be different, but he should be of the same stock; and this is the case of the elder in relation to the younger and the one who generates to the child.

## CHAPTER 13

(1) It is evident, then, that household management gives more serious attention to human beings than to inanimate possessions, to the virtue of these than that of possessions (which we call wealth), and to the virtue of free persons rather than that of slaves. (2) First, then, one might raise a question concerning slaves: whether there is a certain virtue belonging to a slave besides the virtues of an instrument and a servant and more honorable than these, such as moderation and courage and justice and the other dispositions of this sort, or whether there is none besides the bodily services. (3) Questions arise either way, for if there is [such a virtue], how will they differ from free persons? But if there is not, though they are human beings and participate in reason, it is odd. Nearly the same question arises concerning a woman and a child, whether there are virtues belonging to these as well—whether the woman should be moderate and courageous and just, and whether a child is [capable of being] licentious and moderate or not. (4) And in

general, then, this must be investigated concerning the ruled by nature and the ruler, whether virtue is the same or different. For if both should share in gentlemanliness, why should the one rule and the other be ruled once and for all? For it is not possible for them to differ by greater and less, since being ruled and ruling differ in kind, not by greater and less; (5) but that one should [have such virtue] and the other not would be surprising. For unless the ruler is moderate and just, how will he rule finely? And unless the ruled is, how will he be ruled finely? For if he is licentious and cowardly he will perform none of his duties. It is evident, then, that both must of necessity share in virtue, but that there are differences in their virtue, as there are in [that of] those who are by nature ruled. (6) Consideration of the soul guides us straightway [to this conclusion]. For in this there is by nature a ruling and a ruled element, and we assert there is a different virtue of each—that is, of the element having reason and of the irrational element. It is clear, then, that the same thing holds in the other cases as well. Thus by nature most things are ruling and ruled. (7) For the free person rules the slave, the male the female, and the man the child in different ways. The parts of the soul are present in all, but they are present in a different way. The slave is wholly lacking the deliberative element; the female has it but it lacks authority; the child has it but it is incomplete. (8) It is to be supposed that the same necessarily holds concerning the virtues of character: all must share in them, but not in the same way, but to each in relation to his own work. Hence the ruler must have complete virtue of character (for a work belongs in an absolute sense to the master craftsman, and reason is a master craftsman); while each of the others must have as much as falls to him. (9) It is thus evident that there is a virtue of character that belongs to all these mentioned, and that the moderation of a woman and a man is not the same, nor their courage or justice, as Socrates supposed, but that there is a ruling and a serving courage, and similarly with the other virtues. (10) This is further clear if we investigate the matter in more detail. For those who say in a general way that virtue is a good condition of the soul or acting correctly or something of this sort deceive themselves. Those who enumerate the virtues, like Gorgias, do much better than those who define it in this way. (11) One should thus consider that matters stand with everyone as the poet said of woman: "to a woman silence is an ornament," though this is not the case for a man. Since the child is incomplete, it is clear that its virtue too is not its own as relating to itself, but as relating to its end and the person leading it. (12) The same is true of that of the slave in relation to a master. We laid it down that the slave is useful with respect to the necessary things, so that he clearly needs only a small amount of virtue—as much as will prevent him from falling short in his work through licentiousness or cowardice. One might raise the question whether, if what has just been said is true, artisans too will need virtue, since they often fall short in their work through licentiousness. (13) Or is the case very different? For the slave is a partner in [the master's] life, while the other is more remote, and shares in virtue only so far as he also shares in slavery. For the vulgar artisan is under a special sort of slavery, and while the slave belongs among those [persons or things that are] by nature, no shoemaker does, nor any of the other artisans. (14) It is evident, therefore, that the master should be responsible for [instilling] this sort of virtue in the slave; he is not merely someone possessing an expertise in mastery which instructs the slave in his work. Those who deny reason to slaves and assert that commands only should be used with them do not argue rightly: admonition is to be used with slaves more than with children. (15) But concerning these matters let our discussion stand thus. Concerning husband and wife and children and father and the sort of virtue that is connected with each of these, and what is and what is not fine in their relations with one another and how one should pursue what is well and avoid the bad, these things must necessarily be addressed in the [discourses] connected with the regimes. For since the household as a whole is a part of the city, and these things of the household, and one should look at the virtue of the part in relation to the virtue of the whole, both children and women must necessarily be educated looking to the regime, at least if it makes any difference with a view to the city's being excellent that both its children and its women are excellent. (16) But it necessarily makes a difference: women are a part amounting to a half of the free persons, and from the children come those who are partners in the regime. So since there has been discussion of these matters, and we must speak elsewhere of those remaining, let us leave off the present discourses as having reached an end and make another beginning to the argument. Let us investigate in the first instance the views that have been put forward about the best regime.

# BOOK II

## CHAPTER 7

There are certain other regimes as well, some of private individuals, others of philosophers and political [rulers]; but all of them are closer than either of those [just discussed, i. e., Plato's *Republic* and *Laws*] to established regimes under which [men] are now governed. For no one else has shown originality regarding community of women and children or regarding common messes for women; they begin rather from the necessary things. For some of them hold that a fine arrangement concerning property is the greatest thing; it is about this, they assert, that all factional conflicts arise. The first to introduce this was Phaleas of Chalcedon, who asserts that the possessions of the citizens should be equal. He supposed this would not be difficult to do in [cities] just being settled; in those already settled he supposed it would be troublesome, but that a leveling could be quickly brought about by having the wealthy give dowries but not receive them, and the poor receive but not give them. Plato, when writing the *Laws*, supposed [increase in properties] should be allowed up to a certain point, no citizen being permitted to possess [a property] more than five times the size of the smallest one, as was said earlier. But those who legislate in this fashion should not overlook—what they overlook now—that an arrangement concerning the extent of property should properly include an arrangement concerning the number of children as well. If the number of children outstrips the size of the property, the law will surely be abrogated, and, abrogation aside, it is a bad thing to have many of the wealthy become poor, for such persons are apt to become subversives. Thus the leveling of property does indeed have a certain power to affect the political partnership. This was plainly recognized by some of former times, as in the legislation of Solon, and others have a law which forbids the acquisition of land in whatever amount one wishes. Similarly, some laws forbid the sale of property, for example among the Locrians, where there is a law against sale unless one can show he has suffered manifest misfortune; and some attempt to preserve original allotments [of land in colonies]. It was the abrogation of this [sort of law] at Leucas that led to their regime becoming overly popular; for the result was that offices were no longer filled from the designated assessments. Yet it is possible to have equality of property, but for [the amount of property] to be either too great (so that luxury results) or too little (so that they live in penury). It is clear, then, that it is not enough for the legislator to make property equal; he must also aim at a mean.

Yet even if one were to arrange a moderate level of property for all, it would not help. For one ought to level desires sooner than property; but this is impossible for those not adequately educated by the laws. Phaleas would perhaps object that this is what he himself is saying; for he supposes that cities must have equality in these two things, possessions and education. But one ought to say what the education is to be: having it one and the same is no help, for it is possible for it to be one and the same, and yet of such a sort that they intentionally choose to aggrandize themselves with respect to goods or honor or both. Further, factional conflict occurs not only because of inequality of possessions, but also because of inequality of honors, though in an opposite way in each case; for the many [engage in factional conflict] because possessions are unequal, but the refined do so if honors are equal—hence the verse "in single honor whether vile or worthy." Nor do human beings commit injustice only because of the necessary things—for which Phaleas considers equality of property a remedy, so that no one will steal through being cold or hungry; they also do it for enjoyment and the satisfaction of desire. For if they have a desire beyond the necessary things, they will commit injustice in order to cure it—and not only for this reason, for they might desire merely the enjoyment that comes with pleasures unaccompanied by pains.

What remedy is there, then, for these three things? For the one, a minimum of property and work; for the other, moderation. As for the third, if certain persons should want enjoyment through themselves alone, they should not seek a remedy except in connection with philosophy; for the other [pleasures] require human beings. The greatest injustices are committed out of excess, then, not because of the necessary things—no one becomes a tyrant in order to get in out of the cold (hence the honors too are great if one kills a tyrant rather than a thief). So it is only with a view to minor injustices that the mode of Phaleas' regime is of assistance.

Further, most of what Phaleas wants to institute is designed to enable them to engage in politics finely among themselves; but they should do so also with a view to their neighbors and all foreigners. Therefore it is necessary that the regime be organized with a view to military strength, and he has said nothing about this. And similarly concerning possessions: they should be adequate not only for political uses but also for foreign dangers. Hence the extent of them should neither be so much that those near at hand and superior will desire them and those having them will be unable to ward off the attackers, nor so little that they will be unable to sustain a war even against those who are equal and similar. Although he has not discussed this, then, one should not overlook the extent of possessions that is advantageous. Perhaps the best defining principle is that [there should be just so much that] those who are superior will not gain if they go to war because of the excess, but [will go to war only under such circumstances] as they would even if their property were not so great. For example, when Autophradates was about to besiege Atarneus, Euboulus bid him examine how much time would be required to take the place and calculate what the expense for this time would be, as he was willing to abandon Atarneus at once for less than this; and by saying this he caused Autophradates to have second thoughts and give up the siege.

For the property of the citizens to be equal, then, is indeed an advantage with a view to avoiding factional conflict between them, but it is by no means a great one. For the refined may well become disaffected, on the grounds that they do not merit [mere] equality, and for this reason they are frequently seen to attack [the people] and engage in factional conflict. Further, the wickedness of human beings is insatiable: at first the two obol allowance was adequate, but now that this is something traditional, they always ask for more, and go on doing so without limit. For the nature of desire is without limit, and it is with a view to satisfying this that the many live. To rule such persons, then, [requires] not so much leveling property as providing that those who are respectable by nature will be the sort who have no wish to aggrandize themselves, while the mean will not be able to, which will be the case if they are kept inferior but are done no injustice.

But not even what he has said about equality of property is right. For he equalizes only the possession of land; but there may also be wealth in slaves, livestock, or money, and there is a great supply of it in so-called furnishings. Either, then, equality is to be sought in all these things, or some moderate arrangement, or all are to be left alone. It is also evident from this legislation that he is instituting a small city; at any rate, all the artisans will be public slaves and will not contribute to the full complement of the city. But if there should be public slaves at all, it is those who work at common tasks who should be in this condition, as at Epidamnus, or as Diophantus once tried to institute at Athens. Concerning the regime of Phaleas, then, whether he happens to have argued rightly in some respect or not may be discerned from what has been said.

## CHAPTER 8

Hippodamus, the son of Euryphon, of Miletus, who invented the division of cities and laid out Peiraeus—and who was extraordinary in other aspects of his life through ambition, so that he seemed to some to live in a rather overdone manner, with long hair and expensive ornaments, and furthermore with cheap and warm clothing which he wore not only in winter but also in summer weather, and who wished to be learned with regard to nature as a whole—was the first of those not engaged in politics to undertake to give an account of the best regime. He wanted to institute a city of ten thousand men, divided into three parts, and to make one part artisans, one farmers, and the third the military part and that possessing arms. He also divided the territory into three parts, one sacred, one public and one private: the sacred to provide what custom requires to be tendered to the gods, the public for the warriors to live off of, and the private that belonging to the farmers. He supposed that there are three kinds of laws as well, since the things concerning which cases arise are three in number—arrogant behavior, injury, and death. He also wished to legislate a single authoritative court, to which all cases that are held not to have been rightly judged should be appealed; this he wanted to institute out of a certain number of elected elders. He supposed that decisions in the courts should not be rendered by a ballot, but that each should deposit a tablet on which, if he condemned simply, he should write the verdict, or if he acquitted simply, leave it blank, but if neither, he should make distinctions. For he supposed current legislation is not fine in this regard, as it compels [men] to perjure themselves if they judge one way or the other. He also wanted to enact a law concerning those who discover something useful to the city, so that they might obtain honor, and one providing that the children of those who die in war should receive sustenance from public funds (he supposed this had never been legislated by others, although such a law exists now both in Athens and in other cities). The rulers were all to be elected by the people, the people being the three parts of the city; those elected were to take care of common matters, matters affecting aliens, and matters affecting orphans.

These are most of the elements of Hippodamus' arrangement and those most deserving mention. The first question one might raise concerns the division of the multitude of the citizens. The artisans and the farmers and those possessing arms all participate in the regime, although the farmers have no arms and the artisans neither land nor arms—to that they become virtually slaves of those possessing arms. It is impossible, then, for them to share in all the prerogatives, since the generals and regime guardians and practically all the authoritative offices will necessarily be selected from among those possessing arms; yet if they do not share in the regime, how will they feel any affection toward the regime? Those possessing arms would then have to be superior to both of the other parts; but this would not be easy unless there were many of them. Yet if that is to be the case, why should the others share in the regime and have authority with respect to the selection of rulers? Furthermore, what use are the farmers to the city? It is necessary that there be artisans, for every city needs artisans, and they can subsist, as they do in other cities, from their arts. It would have been reasonable to make the farmers a part of the city if they provided sustenance to those possessing arms; as it is, however, they have private [land] and are to farm this privately. As for the common land, from which the warriors are to have their sustenance, if they are to farm it themselves there would be no difference between the fighting and the farming element, contrary to the wish of the legislator; but if there are to be others different from both those farming privately and from the fighters, this will be an additional fourth part of the city which shares in nothing and is hostile to the regime. On the other hand, if one makes the same persons farm both the private and the public land, will not the amount of crops from each one's farming be insufficient for two households? Or why is it they do not simply take sustenance for themselves from the land and their own allotments and also provide it to the fighters? In all of these things there is much confusion.

Nor is the law concerning judging a fine one—to require the one judging to make distinctions when the indictment in a case is simple, thus making the juror an arbitrator. This can be done in an arbitration, even by many persons, since they may confer together over the judgment; but it is not possible in courts where most legislators have made provision for the opposite of this—that the jurors do not confer together. But further, how will the judgment be other than confused, when the juror finds something owed, but not as much as claimed by the plaintiff? He claims twenty minas, but a juror judges ten minas (or the one more and the other less), another judges five, another four—it is clear they will split in this way; but others will condemn for all, and others for nothing. How then will they calculate the votes? Moreover, no one compels the one who simply acquits or condemns to perjure himself, at least if the indictment is simple (and justly so). For the one acquitting does not judge that he owes nothing, but that he does not owe the twenty minas, though the one indeed perjures himself who condemns without believing he owes the twenty minas.

Concerning the matter of those who discover something advantageous for the city, to legislate that they receive some honor is not safe, though it sounds appealing: it would involve harassments and, it might well happen, changes of regime. But this leads into another problem and a different investigation. For some raise the question whether it is harmful or advantageous for cities to change traditional laws, if some other one should be better. If indeed it is not advantageous, it would not be easy to agree readily with what has been said; but it is not impossible that some might propose the dissolution of the laws or the regime as something in the common good. Since we have made mention of this, it will be best to expand a bit further on it. For it involves, as we said, a question, and change might seem to be better. This has been advantageous, at any rate, in the other sciences—medicine, for example, has changed from its traditional ways, and gymnastic, and the arts and capacities generally, so that as political expertise too is to be regarded as one of these, it is clear that the same must necessarily hold concerning this as well. One might assert that evidence is provided by the facts themselves; the laws of ancient times were overly simple and barbaric. For the Greeks used to carry weapons and purchase their wives, and whatever other ancient ordinances still remain are altogether foolish. At Cyme, for example, there is a law concerning cases of homicide, to the effect that the accused shall be guilty of murder if the plaintiff can provide a certain number of witnesses from among his own relatives. In general, all seek not the traditional but the good. The first [human beings], whether they were earthborn or preserved from a cataclysm, are likely to have been similar to average or even simpleminded persons [today], as indeed is said of the earthborn; so it would be odd to abide by the opinions they hold. In addition to this, it is not best to leave written [laws] unchanged. For just as in the case of the other arts, so with respect to political arrangements it is impossible for everything to be written down precisely; for it is necessary to write them in universal fashion, while actions concern particulars. From these things it is evident, then, that some laws must be changed at some times; yet to those investigating it in another manner this would seem to require much caution. For when the improvement is small, and since it is a bad thing to habituate people to the reckless dissolution of laws, it is evident that some errors both of the legislators and of the rulers should be let go; for [the city] will not be benefited as much from changing them as it will be harmed through being habituated to disobey the rulers. And the argument from the example of the arts is false. Change in an art is not like change in law; for law has no strength with respect to obedience apart from habit, and this is not created except over a period of time. Hence the easy alteration of existing laws in favor of new and different ones weakens the power of law itself. Further, if they are indeed to be changeable, are all to be, and in every regime? And by anyone, or by whom? For these things make a great difference. Let us therefore set aside this investigation for the present; it belongs to other occasions.

# BOOK III

## CHAPTER 7

These things having been discussed, the next thing is to investigate regimes—how many in number and which sorts there are, and first of all the correct ones; for the deviations will be evident once these have been discussed. Since "regime" and "governing body" signify the same thing, since the governing body is the authoritative element in cities, and since it is necessary that the authoritative element be either one or a few or the many, when the one or the few or the many rule with a view to the common advantage, these regimes are necessarily correct, while those with a view to the private advantage of the one or the few or the multitude are deviations. For either it must be denied that persons sharing [in the regime] are citizens, or they must participate in its advantages. Now of monarchies, that [form] which looks toward the common advantage we are accustomed to call kingship; [rule] of the few (but of more than one person) we are accustomed to call aristocracy—either because the best persons are ruling, or because they are ruling with a view to what is best for the city and for those who participate in it; and when the multitude governs with a view to the common advantage, it is called by the term common to all regimes, polity. This happens reasonably. It is possible for one or a few to be outstanding in virtue, but where more are concerned it is difficult for them to be proficient with a view to virtue as a whole, but [some level of proficiency is possible] particularly regarding military virtue, as this arises in a multitude; hence in this regime the warrior element is the most authoritative, and it is those possessing [heavy] arms who share in it. Deviations from those mentioned are tyranny from kingship, oligarchy from aristocracy, democracy from polity. Tyranny is monarchy with a view to the advantage of the monarch, oligarchy [rule] with a view to the advantage of the well off, democracy [rule] with a view to the advantage of those who are poor; none of them is with a view to the common gain.

## CHAPTER 8

It is necessary to speak at somewhat greater length of what each of these regimes is. For certain questions are involved, and it belongs to one philosophizing in connection with each sort of inquiry and not merely looking toward action not to overlook or omit anything, but to make clear the truth concerning each thing. Tyranny, as we said, is monarchic rule of a master over the political partnership; oligarchy is when those with property have authority in the regime; and democracy is the opposite, when those have authority who do not possess a [significant] amount of property but are poor. The first question has to do with the definition. If a well-off majority has authority, and similarly in the other case, if it somewhere happened that the poor were a minority with respect to the well off but were superior and had authority in the regime, although when a small number has authority it is called oligarchy, this definition of the regimes would not be held to be a fine one. But even if one were to combine fewness with being well off and number with being poor and described the regimes accordingly (oligarchy being that in which those who are well off and few in number have the offices, and democracy that in which those who are poor and many in number have them), another question is involved. What shall we say of the regimes that were just mentioned—those in which the majority is well off and the poor are few and each has authority in the regime—if there is no other regime beside those we spoke of? The argument seems to make clear, therefore, that it is accidental that few or many have authority in oligarchies on the one hand and democracies on the other, and that this is because the well off are everywhere few and the poor many. Hence it also turns out that the causes of the differences are not what was mentioned. What makes democracy and oligarchy differ is poverty and wealth: wherever some rule on account of wealth, whether a minority or a majority, this is necessarily an oligarchy, and wherever those who are poor, a democracy. But it turns out, as we said, that the former are few and the latter many; for few are well off, but all share in freedom—which are the causes of both [groups] disputing over the regime.

## CHAPTER 9

It is necessary first to grasp what they speak of as the defining principles of oligarchy and democracy and what justice is [from] both oligarchic and democratic [points of view]. For all fasten on a certain sort of justice, but proceed only to a certain point, and do not speak of the whole of justice in its authoritative sense. For example, justice is held to be equality, and it is, but for equals and not for all; and inequality is held to be just and is indeed, but for unequals and not for all; but they disregard this element of persons and judge badly. The cause of this is that the judgment concerns themselves, and most people are bad judges concerning their own things. And so since justice is for certain persons, and is divided in the same manner with respect to objects and for persons, as was said previously in the [discourses on] ethics, they agree as to the equality, but dispute about it for persons. They do this particularly because of what was just spoken of, that they judge badly with respect to what concerns themselves, but also because both, by speaking to a point of a kind of justice, consider themselves to be speaking of justice simply. For the ones, if they are unequal in a certain thing, such as goods, suppose they are unequal generally, while the others suppose that if they are equal in a certain thing, such as freedom, they are equal generally.

But of the most authoritative [consideration] they say nothing. For if it were for the sake of possessions that they participated and joined together, they would share in the city just to the extent that they shared in possessions, so that the argument of the oligarches might be held a strong one; for [they would say] it is not just for one who has contributed one mina to share equally in a hundred minas with the one giving all the rest, whether [he derives] from those who were there originally or the later arrivals. But if [the city exists] not only for the sake of living but rather primarily for the sake of living well (for otherwise there could be a city of slaves or of animals—as things are, there is not, since they do not share in happiness or in living in accordance with intentional choice) and if it does not exist for the sake of an alliance to prevent their suffering injustice from anyone, nor for purposes of exchange and of use of one another—for otherwise the Tyrrhenians and Carthaginians, and all who have agreements with one another, would be as citizens of one city—at any rate, there are compacts between them concerning imports, agreements to abstain from injustice, and treaties of alliance. But no offices common to all have been established to deal with these things, but different ones in each [city]; nor do those [in one city] take thought that the others should be of a certain quality, or that none of those coming under the compacts should be unjust or depraved in any way, but only that they should not act unjustly toward one another. Whoever takes thought for good management, however, gives careful attention to political virtue and vice.

It is thus evident that virtue must be a care for every city, or at least every one to which the term applies truly and not merely in a manner of speaking. For otherwise the partnership becomes an alliance which differs from others—from [alliances of] remote allies—only by location. And law becomes a compact and, as the sophist Lycophron says, a guarantor among one another of the just things, but not the sort of thing to make the citizens good and just. But that the matter stands thus is evident. For even if one were to bring the locations together into one, so that the city of the Megarians were fastened to that of the Corinthians by walls, it would still not be a single city. Nor would it be if they practiced intermarriage with one another, although this is one of the aspects of the partnership that is peculiar to cities. Nor, similarly, if certain persons dwelled in separate places, yet were not so distant as to have nothing in common, but had laws not to commit injustice toward one another in their transactions—for example, if one were a carpenter, one a farmer, one a shoemaker, one something else of this sort, and the multitude of them were ten thousand, yet they had nothing in common except things of this sort, exchange and alliance; not even in this way would there be a city. What, then, is the reason for this? It is surely not on account of a lack of proximity of the partnership. For even if they joined together while participating in this way, but each nevertheless treated his own household as a city and each other as if there were a defensive alliance merely for assistance against those committing injustice, it would not by this fact be held a city by those studying the matter precisely—if, that is, they participated in a similar way when joined together as they had when separated. It is evident, therefore, that the city is not a partnership in a location and for the sake of not committing injustice against each other and of transacting business. These things must necessarily be present if there is to be a city, but not even when all of them are present is it yet a city, but [the city is] the partnership in living well both of households and families for the sake of a complete and self-sufficient life. This will not be possible, however, unless they inhabit one and the same location and make use of intermarriage. It was on this account that marriage connections arose in cities, as well as clans, festivals, and the pastimes of living together. This sort of thing is the work of affection; for affection is the intentional choice of living together. Living well, then, is the end of the city, and these things are for the sake of this end. A city is the partnership of families and villages in a complete and self-sufficient life. This, we assert, is living happily and finely. The political partnership must be regarded, therefore, as being for the sake of noble actions, not for the sake of living together. Hence those who contribute most to a partnership of this sort have a greater part in the city than those who are equal or greater in freedom and family but unequal in political virtue, or those who outdo them in wealth but are outdone in virtue.

That all who dispute about regimes speak of some part of justice, then, is evident from what has been said.

## CHAPTER 10

(1) There is a question as to what the authoritative element of the city should be. It is either the multitude, the wealthy, the respectable, the one who is best of all, or the tyrant; but all of these appear to involve difficulties. How could they not? If the poor by the fact of being the majority distribute among themselves the things of the wealthy, is this not unjust? "By Zeus, it was resolved in just fashion by the authoritative element!" (2) What, then, ought one to say is the extreme of injustice? Again, taking all [the citizens] into consideration, if the majority distributes among itself the things of a minority, it is evident that it will destroy the city. Yet it is certainly not virtue that destroys the element possessing it, nor is justice destructive of a city; so it is clear that this law cannot be just. (3) Further, [on such an assumption] any actions carried out by a tyrant are necessarily just: he is superior and uses force, like the multitude with respect to the wealthy.

But is it just, therefore, for the minority and the wealthy to rule? If they act in the same way and rob and plunder the possessions of the multitude, is this just? If so, the other is as well. (4) That all of these things are bad and unjust, then, is evident. But should the respectable rule and have authority over all [matters]? In this case, all the others are necessarily deprived of prerogatives, since they are not honored by [filling] political offices. For we say that offices are honors, and when the same persons always rule the others are necessarily deprived of [these honors or] prerogatives. (5) But is it better for the one who is most excellent of all to rule? But this is still more oligarchic, as more are deprived of prerogatives. One might perhaps assert, however, that it is bad for the authoritative element generally to be man instead of law, at any rate if he has the passions that result [from being human] in his soul. But if law may be oligarchic or democratic, what difference will it make with regard to the questions that have been raised? For what was said before will result all the same.

## CHAPTER 11

(1) Concerning the other matters there will be another discourse. That the multitude should be the authoritative element rather than those who are best but few, though, [is a position involving difficulties which] could be held to be [in need of being] resolved, and while questionable, it perhaps also involves some truth. (2) The many, of whom none is individually an excellent man, nevertheless can when joined together be better—not as individuals but all together—than those [who are best], just as dinners contributed [by many] can be better than those equipped from a single expenditure. For because they are many, each can have a part of virtue and prudence, and on their joining together, the multitude, with its many feet and hands and having many senses, becomes like a single human being, and so also with respect to character and mind. (3) Thus the many are also better judges of the works of music and of the

poets; some [appreciate] a certain part, and all of them all the parts. (4) But it is in this that the excellent men differ from each of the many individually, just as some assert beautiful persons differ from those who are not beautiful, and things painted by art from genuine things, by bringing together things scattered and separated into one; for taken separately, at any rate, this person's eye will be more beautiful than the painted one, as will another part of another person. (5) Whether this difference between the many and the few excellent can exist in the case of every people and every multitude is not clear.Or rather, [it might be objected,] "by Zeus, it is clear that in some cases it is impossible: the same argument would apply to beasts—for what difference is there between some [multitudes] and beasts, so to speak?" But nothing prevents what was said from being true of a certain kind of multitude.

(6) Through these things, accordingly, one might resolve both the question spoken of earlier [concerning who should rule] and one connected with it—over what [matters] free persons or the multitude of the citizens (these being whoever is neither wealthy nor has any claim at all deriving from virtue) should have authority. (7) For having them share in the greatest offices is not safe: [one might argue that] through injustice and imprudence they would act unjustly in some respects and err in others. On the other hand, to give them no part and for them not to share [in the offices] is a matter for alarm, for when there exist many who are deprived of prerogatives and poor, that city is necessarily filled with enemies. (8) What is left, then, is for them to share in deliberating and judging. Hence Solon and certain other legislators arrange to have them both choose officials and audit them, but do not allow them to rule alone. (9) For all of them when joined together have an adequate perception and, once mixed with those who are better, bring benefit to cities, just as impure sustenance mixed with the pure makes the whole more useful than the small amount of the latter, but each separately is incomplete with respect to judging.

(10) But this arrangement of the regime involves questions. In the first place, it might be held that it belongs to the same person to judge whether someone has healed in correct fashion and to heal and make healthy one who is suffering from a particular disease, this being the doctor; and similarly with respect to other kinds of experience and art. Just as a doctor must submit to audit by doctors, then, so must the others submit to audit by those similar to them. (11) But "doctor" [is a term that can be applied to] the [ordinary] craftsman, the master craftsman, and thirdly, the person who is educated with respect to the art; for there are some of this [latter] sort in the case of nearly all the arts, and we assign the task of judging to the educated no less than to those who know [the art]. (12) And it might be held that the case is the same with respect to the choice [of the officials]. Choosing correctly is indeed also the work of those who know—for example, choosing a geometer is the work of experts in geometry, and a pilot that of experts in piloting. If certain nonprofessionals share in some of these works and arts, however, they do not do so to a greater extent than those who know. (13) So according to this argument the multitude ought not to be given authority either over the choice of officials or over their auditing. (14) But perhaps not all of these things have been rightly argued, both because of the previous argument, provided the multitude is not overly slavish (for each individually will be a worse judge than those who know, but all when joined together will be either better or no worse), and because there are some [arts] concerning which the maker might not be the only or the best judge, but where those who do not possess the art also have some knowledge of its works. The maker of a house, for example, is not the only one to have some knowledge of it, but the one who uses it judges better than he does, and the one who uses it is the household manager; and a pilot judges rudders better than a carpenter, and the diner, not the cook, is the better judge of a banquet.

(15) This question, then, may perhaps be held to be adequately resolved in this fashion. But there is another connected with it. It is held to be absurd for mean persons to have authority over greater matters than the respectable; but auditing and the choice of officials are a very great thing, and in some regimes, as was said, these are given to the people, for the assembly has authority over everything of this sort. (16) Hence, persons from the lowest assessments and of whatever age share in the assembly and deliberate and adjudicate, while those from the greatest assessments

are the treasurers and generals and hold the greatest offices. Now one might resolve this question as well in a similar way. (17) For perhaps these things too are handled correctly: neither the juror nor the councilman nor the assemblyman acts as ruler, but the court, the council and the people, and each individual is [only] a part of these things just mentioned—I mean by "part" the councilman, the assemblyman, and the juror. (18) So the multitude justly has authority over greater things, for the people, the council, and the court are made up of many persons. Also, the assessment of all of them together is more than that of those who hold great offices, whether taken singly or as a [group of a] few.

(19) Let the discussion of these things stand thus, then. As regards the first question, it makes nothing more evident than that it is laws—correctly enacted—that should be authoritative and that the ruler, whether one person or more, should be authoritative with respect to those things about which the laws are completely unable to speak precisely on account of the difficulty of making clear general declarations about everything. (20) But as to what the quality of the laws should be if they are to be correctly enacted, it is not at all clear, and the question that was raised previously remains. Laws are necessarily poor or excellent and just or unjust in a manner similar to the regimes [to which they belong]: (21) if nothing else, it is evident that laws should be enacted with a view to the regime. But if this is the case, it is clear that those [enacted] in accordance with the correct regimes are necessarily just, and those [enacted] in accordance with the deviant ones, not just.

## CHAPTER 12

(1) Since in all the sciences and arts the end is some good, it is the greatest and primary good in that which is the most authoritative of all; this is the political capacity. The political good is justice, and this is the common advantage. Justice is held by all to be a certain equality, and up to a certain point they agree with the discourses based on philosophy in which ethics has been discussed; for they assert that justice is a certain thing for certain persons, and should be equal for equal persons. (2) But equality in what sort of things and inequality in what sort of things—this should not be overlooked. For this involves a question, and political philosophy. One might perhaps assert that offices should be unequally distributed in accordance with a preeminence in any good even among persons who do not differ in any other respect but happen to be similar, on the grounds that justice and what accords with merit is different for those who differ. (3) But if this is true, it will mean some aggrandizement in [claims to] political justice for those who are preeminent in complexion, height, or any other good. (4) Is this not plainly false? That it is false is evident in the case of the other sciences and capacities: where flute players are similar with respect to the art, aggrandizement in flutes is not granted to those who are better born. They will not play the flute better [on this account]; but it is to one who is preeminent in the work that preeminence in the instruments should be granted. If what has been said is in some way not clear, it will be still more evident if we take it further. (5) If someone were preeminent in flute playing, but very deficient in good birth or fine looks, even if each of those goods is greater than flute playing (I mean good birth and fine looks), and even if they are proportionately more preeminent with respect to flute playing than he is preeminent in flute playing, the outstanding flutes nevertheless ought to be given to him. For preeminence in wealth and good birth should contribute something to the work; but they contribute nothing. (6) Further, according to this argument every good would have to be commensurable with every other. For if being of a certain height [provided] more [in the way of a claim], then height generally would be in rivalry with both wealth and freedom. So if this person is more outstanding in height than that one in virtue, and is more preeminent generally in respect to height than virtue, everything would be commensurable. For if some amount of height is superior to some amount [of virtue], it is clear that some amount is equal. (7) Since this is impossible, it is clear that in political matters too it is reasonable for them not to dispute over offices on the basis of every inequality. If some are fast

and others slow, they should not have more or less on this account; it is in gymnastic contests that being outstanding in these things wins honor. (8) The dispute necessarily occurs in respect to those things that constitute a city. It is reasonable, therefore, that the well born, the free, and the wealthy lay claim to honor. For there must be both free persons and those paying an assessment, since a city cannot consist wholly of those who are poor, any more than of slaves; (9) yet if these things are needed, so also, it is clear, are [the virtue of] justice and military virtue. It is not possible for a city to be administered without these things. But whereas without the former elements there cannot be a city, without the latter one cannot be finely administered.

## CHAPTER 13

(1) Now with a view to the existence of a city, all or at least some of these things might be held to have a correct claim in the dispute; but with a view to a good life it is education and virtue above all that would have a just claim in the dispute, as was also said earlier. But since those who are equal in one thing alone should not have equality in everything, nor those who are unequal in a single thing inequality, all regimes of this sort are necessarily deviations. (2) It was also said previously that all dispute justly in a certain way, but not justly in an unqualified sense. The wealthy [have a claim] because they have the greater part of the territory, and the territory is something common; further, for the most part they are more trustworthy regarding agreements. The free and well born [have a claim] as being close to one another; for the better born are more particularly citizens than the ignoble, and good birth is honorable at home among everyone. (3) Further, [the well born have a claim] because it is likely that better persons come from those who are better, for good birth is virtue of a family. In a similar way, then, we shall assert that virtue has a just claim in the dispute, for we assert that [the virtue of] justice is a virtue characteristic of partnerships, and that all the other [virtues] necessarily follow on it. (4) Finally, the majority [has a just claim] in relation to a minority, for they are superior and wealthier and better when the majority is taken together in relation to the minority.

If, therefore, all should exist in a single city—I mean, both the good and the wealthy and well born, as well as a political multitude apart from them—will there be a dispute as to which should rule, or will there not? (5) Now the judgment as to who should rule is not disputed under each of the regimes that have been mentioned, for they differ from one another by their authoritative elements: for one the authoritative element is the wealthy, for another the excellent men, and in the same manner for each of the others. Still, we are investigating how the matter is to be determined when these things are present simultaneously. (6) Now if those possessing virtue were very few in number, in what way should one decide it? Or should the fact that they are few be investigated with a view to the work involved—whether they are capable of administering the city, or whether there is a multitude of them large enough to form a city? But there is a question affecting all of those who dispute over political honors. (7) Those who claim to merit rule on account of wealth could be held to have no argument of justice at all, and similarly with those claiming to merit rule on the basis of family; for it is clear that if there is one person wealthier than all of them, this one person should rule all of them in accordance with the same [claims of] justice, and similarly, that one who is outstanding in good birth should rule those who dispute on the basis of freedom. (8) And this same thing will perhaps result with respect to aristocracies in the case of virtue; for if one man should be better than the others in the governing body, even though they are excellent, this one should have authority in accordance with the same [claims of] justice, and if it is because they are superior to the few that the multitude should have authority, if one or more persons—though fewer than the many—should be superior to the rest, these should have authority rather than the multitude.

(9) All of these things seem to make it evident, then, that none of the defining principles on the basis of which they claim they merit rule, and all the others merit being ruled by them, is correct. (10) For, indeed, multitudes have an argument of some justice to make against those

claiming to merit authority over the governing body on the basis of virtue, and similarly also against those claiming it on the basis of wealth: nothing prevents the multitude from being at some point better than the few and wealthier—not as individuals but taken together. (11) Hence also it is possible to confront in this manner a question which certain persons pursue and put forward. For some raise the question whether the legislator who wants to enact the most correct laws should legislate with a view to the advantage of the better persons or that of the majority, when what was spoken of turns out to be the case. (12) But correctness must be taken to mean "in an equal spirit": what is [enacted] in an equal spirit is correct with a view both to the advantage of the city as a whole and to the common [advantage] of the citizens. A citizen in the common sense is one who shares in ruling and being ruled; but he differs in accordance with each regime. In the case of the best regime, he is one who is capable of and intentionally chooses being ruled and ruling with a view to the life in accordance with virtue.

(13) If there is one person so outstanding by his excess of virtue—or a number of persons, though not enough to provide a full complement for the city—that the virtue of all the others and their political capacity is not commensurable with their own (if there are a number) or his alone (if there is one), such persons can no longer be regarded as a part of the city. For they will be done injustice if it is claimed they merit equal things in spite of being so unequal in virtue and political capacity; for such a person would likely be like a god among human beings. (14) From this it is clear that legislation must necessarily have to do with those who are equal both in stock and capacity, and that for the other sort of person there is no law—they themselves are law. It would be ridiculous, then, if one attempted to legislate for them. They would perhaps say what Antisthenes says the lions say when the hares are making their harangue and claiming that everyone merits equality. (15) Hence democratically run cities enact ostracism for this sort of reason. For these are surely held to pursue equality above all others, and so they used to ostracize and banish for fixed periods from the city those who were held to be preeminent in power on account of wealth or abundance of friends or some other kind of political strength. (16) The tale is told that the Argonauts left Heracles behind for this sort of reason: the Argo was unwilling to have him on board because he so exceeded the other sailors. Hence also those who criticize tyranny and the advice Periander gave to Thrasyboulus must not be supposed to be simply correct in their censure. (17) It is reported that Periander said nothing by way of advice to the messenger who had been sent to him, but merely lopped off the preeminent ears of corn and so leveled the field. When the messenger, who was in ignorance of the reason behind what had happened, reported the incident, Thrasyboulus understood that he was to eliminate the preeminent men. (18) This is something that is advantageous not only to tyrants, nor are tyrants the only ones who do it, but the matter stands similarly with respect both to oligarchies and to democracies; for ostracism has the same power in a certain way as pulling down and exiling the preeminent. (19) And the same thing is done in the case of cities and nations alike by those with [military] power under their authority—for example, the Athenians in the case of the Samians, Chians, and Lesbians, for no sooner was their [imperial] rule firm than they humbled these [cities,] contrary to the compacts [they had with them]. And the king of the Persians frequently pruned back the Medes and Babylonians and others who harbored high thoughts on account of once exercising [imperial] rule themselves.

(20) The issue is one that concerns all regimes generally, including correct ones. For the deviant ones do this looking to the private [advantage of the rulers], yet even in the case of those that look to the common good the matter stands in the same way. (21) This is clear as well in the case of the other arts and sciences. For a painter would not allow himself to paint an animal with a foot that exceeded proportion, not even if it were outstandingly beautiful, nor would a shipbuilder permit himself to build a stern or any of the other parts of a ship that exceeded proportion, nor indeed would a chorus master allow someone with a voice louder and more beautiful than the entire chorus to be a member of it. (22) So on this account there is nothing that prevents monarchs from being in consonance with their cities when they do this, provided their

own rule is beneficial to their cities. Thus in connection with the [generally] agreed forms of preeminence the argument concerning ostracism involves a certain political justice. (23) Now it is better if the legislator constitutes the regime from the beginning in such a way that it does not need this sort of healing; but the "second voyage," if the contingency should arise, is to try to correct [the regime] with some corrective of this sort. But this is not what used to happen in the case of the cities [that used it]: they did not look to the advantage of their own regime but used ostracisms for purposes of factional conflict.

(24) In the deviant regimes it is evident that ostracism is advantageous [for the rulers] privately and is just; and perhaps that it is not simply just is also evident. In the case of the best regime, however, there is considerable question as to what ought to be done if there happens to be someone who is outstanding not on the basis of preeminence in the other goods such as strength, wealth, or abundance of friends, but on the basis of virtue. (25) For surely no one would assert that such a person should be expelled and banished. But neither would they assert that there should be rule over such a person: this is almost as if they should claim to merit ruling over Zeus by splitting the offices. What remains—and it seems the natural course—is for everyone to obey such a person gladly, so that persons of this sort will be permanent kings in their cities.

# BOOK VII

## CHAPTER 1

Concerning the best regime, one who is going to undertake the investigation appropriate to it must necessarily discuss first what the most choiceworthy way of life is. As long as this is unclear, the best regime must necessarily be unclear as well; for it is appropriate for those who govern themselves best on the basis of what is available to them to act in the best manner, provided nothing occurs contrary to reasonable expectation. Hence there should first be agreement on which is the most choiceworthy way of life for all, so to speak, and after this, whether the same or a different way of life is choiceworthy [for men] in common and separately [as individuals]. Considering as adequate, then, much of what is said in the external discourses concerning the best way of life, we must use that here as well.

For in truth no one would dispute that, there being a distinction among three groups [of good things], those that are external, those of the body, and those of the soul, all these things ought to be available to the blessed. No one would assert that a person is blessed who has no part of courage, moderation, [the virtue of] justice, or prudence, but is afraid of the flies buzzing around him, abstains from none of the extremes when he desires to eat or drink, destroys his dearest friends for a trifle, and similarly regarding the things connected with the mind, is as senseless and as thoroughly deceived [by a false perception of things] as a child or a madman. Yet while all would admit what has been said, they differ in regard to how much [of each type of good is desirable] and their [relative degree of] preeminence. For [men] consider any amount of virtue to be adequate, but wealth, goods, power, reputation, and all such things they seek to excess without limit. We shall say to them that it is easy to convince oneself concerning these matters through the facts as well [as through argument], when one sees that men do not acquire and safeguard the virtues by means of external things, but the latter by means of the former, and that living happily—whether human beings find it in enjoyment or in virtue or in both—is available to those who have to excess the adornments of character and mind but behave moderately in respect to the external acquisition of good things, rather than those who possess more of the latter than what is useful but are deficient in the former. Yet this can also be readily seen by those investigating on the basis of argument.

External things, like any instrument, have a limit: everything useful belongs among those things an excess of which must necessarily be either harmful or not beneficial to those who have them. In the case of each of the good things connected with the soul, however, the more it is in excess, the more useful it must necessarily be—if indeed one should attribute to these things not only nobility but utility as well. In general, it is clear, we shall assert, that the best state of each thing in relation to other things corresponds with respect to its preeminence to the distance between the things of which we assert that these are states. So if the soul is more honorable than both possessions and the body both simply and for us, the best state of each must necessarily stand in the same relation as these things [among themselves]. Further, it is for the sake of the soul that these things are naturally choiceworthy and that all sensible persons should choose them, and not the soul for the sake of them.

That the same amount of happiness falls to each person as of virtue and prudence and action in accordance with these, therefore, may stand as agreed by us. We may use the god as testimony to this: he is happy and blessed, yet not through any of the external good things but rather through himself and by being of a certain quality in his nature. And it is on this account that good fortune necessarily differs from happiness. Of the good things that are external to the soul the cause is chance and fortune; but no one is just or sound by fortune or through fortune.

Next, and requiring the same arguments, is [the assertion] that the best city is happy and acts nobly. It is impossible to act nobly without acting [to achieve] noble things; but there is no noble deed either of a man or of a city that is separate from virtue and prudence. The courage, justice, and prudence of a city have the same power and form as those things human beings share in individually who are called just, prudent, and sound.

These things, so far as they go, may stand as a preface to our discourse. For it is not possible either not to touch on them or to exhaust all of the arguments pertaining to them (these things are a task for [an inquiry belonging to] another sort of leisure). For the present let us presuppose this much, that the best way of life both separately for each individual and in common for cities is that accompanied by virtue—virtue that is equipped to such an extent as to [allow them to] share in the actions that accord with virtue. With regard to those who dispute [such an argument], we must pass over them for the purposes of the present inquiry, but shall make a thorough investigation later, if anyone happens not to be persuaded by what has been said.

## CHAPTER 4

Since this has been said by way of preface about these things, and since the other sorts of regimes were studied earlier, the beginning point of what remains is to speak in the first instance of the sorts of presuppositions there should be concerning the city that is to be constituted on the basis of what one would pray for. For it is impossible for the best regime to arise without equipment to match. Hence there are many things that we should presuppose for ourselves in advance, like persons offering prayer; yet none of these things should be impossible. I mean, for example, concerning the number of citizens and the amount of territory. For just as in the case of the other craftsmen—the weaver, for example, or the shipbuilder—material should be available that is suitable to work on (for to the extent that this has been better prepared, what is brought into being by the art is necessarily finer), so too in the case of the political expert and the legislator the proper material should be available in a suitable condition. To the equipment characteristic of the city belongs in the first instance, both the multitude of human beings—how many should be available and of what quality by nature—and the territory in the same way—how much there should be and of what quality. Now most persons suppose that it is appropriate for the happy city to be great. To the extent that this is true, they are ignorant of what sort of city is great and what sort small. They judge one to be great on the basis of the magnitude of the number of inhabitants, but one should look not to their number but to their capacity. For there exists a certain task of a city too, so that the city most capable of bringing this to completion is the one that must be supposed the greatest—just as one might assert that Hippocrates is greater not as a human being but as a doctor than someone excelling him in bodily size. Yet even if one should judge by looking to number, this must not be done on the basis of any chance multitude (for perhaps of necessity there is present in cities a large number of slaves as well as aliens and foreigners), but only those who are a part of the city—of those proper parts out of which a city is constituted. It is the preeminence of these things in a multitude that is an indication of a great city. One that can send out a large number of the vulgar but few heavy-armed troops cannot possibly be great. To be a great city and a populous one is not the same thing.

This too, at any rate, is evident from the facts: that it is difficult—perhaps impossible—for a city that is too populous to be well managed. Of those that are held to be finely governed, at any rate, we see none that is lax in regard to [restricting the] number [of citizens]. This is clear also through the proof afforded by arguments. For law is a certain sort of arrangement, and good management must of necessity involve good arrangement. But an overly excessive number is incapable of sharing in arrangement. This is, indeed, a task requiring divine power, which is what holds together the whole itself. [At the same time, too small a number is also inadequate for a good or beautiful arrangement,] since the beautiful, at any rate, comes to exist customarily in [things having a certain] number and size. Hence that city too must necessarily be the finest where, together with size, the defining principle mentioned is present. But there is a certain measure of size in a city as well, just as in all other things—animals, plants, instruments: none of these things will have its own capacity if it is either overly small or excessive with respect to size, but it will sometimes be wholly robbed of its nature, and at other times [be] in a poor condition. A ship that is a foot long, for example, will not be a ship at all, nor one of twelve hundred feet, and as it approaches a certain size it will make for a bad voyage, in the one case because of smallness, in the other because of excess. Similarly with the city as well, the one that is made up of too few persons is not self-sufficient, though the city is a self-sufficient thing, while the one that is made up of too many persons is with respect to the necessary things self-sufficient like a nation, but is not a city; for it is not easy for a regime to be present. Who will be general of an overly excessive number, or who will be herald, unless he has the voice of Stentor?

Hence the first city must necessarily be that made up of a multitude so large as to be the first multitude that is self-sufficient with a view to living well in the context of the political partnership. It is possible for one that exceeds this on the basis of number to be a greater city, but this is not possible, as we said, indefinitely. As to what the defining principle of the excess is, it is easy to see from the facts. The actions of the city belong on the one hand to the rulers, on the other to the ruled. The task of a ruler is command and judgment. With a view to judgment concerning the just things and with a view to distributing offices on the basis of merit, the citizens must necessarily be familiar with one another's qualities; where this does not happen to be the case, what is connected with the offices and with judging must necessarily be carried on poorly. For in connection with both it is not just to improvise—the very thing that manifestly happens in an overly populous city. Further, [in such cities] it is easy for aliens and foreigners to assume a part in the regime: it is not difficult for them to escape notice on account of the excess of number. It is clear, therefore, that the best defining principle for a city is this: the greatest excess of number with a view to self-sufficiency of life that is readily surveyable. Concerning the size of a city, then, let the discussion stand in this manner.

## CHAPTER 5

Something very similar holds as well in the case of what concerns the territory. As far as its being of a certain quality is concerned, it is clear that everyone would praise the territory that is the most self-sufficient. That which bears every sort of thing is of necessity such, for self-sufficiency is having everything available and being in need of nothing. In number and size [the territory should be] large enough so that the inhabitants are able to live at leisure in liberal fashion and at the same time with moderation. . . .

It is not difficult to speak of the kind of territory (regarding certain matters one should also be persuaded by those who are experienced in generalship)—that it ought to be difficult for enemies to enter, but readily exited by [the citizens] themselves, and further, just as we asserted that the multitude of human beings should be readily surveyable, that the territory too ought to be: being readily surveyable, the territory is readily defended. If the position of the city is to be fixed according to what one would pray for, it is appropriate for it to lie rightly in relation both to the sea and the land. One defining principle is that mentioned—the city should have access to all localities with a view to defensive sallies. The remaining one is that it should be accessible with a view to the conveyance of crops, and further of materials for lumber, and any other product of this sort the territory might happen to possess.

## CHAPTER 6

Concerning access to the sea, there is much dispute as to whether it is beneficial or harmful for well-managed cities. To have persons raised under other laws present as foreigners, it is asserted, is disadvantageous with respect to good management, as is overpopulation; for, [it is asserted,] as a result of their use of the sea for exporting and importing, a multitude of traders comes into existence, and this is contrary to their being finely governed. Now it is not unclear that, if these things do not result, it is better both with a view to safety and with a view to having a ready supply of necessary things for the city and the territory to have a share of the sea. With a view to bearing up under enemies more easily, they should be capable of a ready defense in both elements—both on land and at sea—if they are to preserve themselves. And with a view to injuring the attackers, if this is not possible in both elements, to do so in one element will still be easier for those who share in both. It is also necessary [for cities] both to import the things that happen not to be available at home and to export what exists in surplus. But the city should be involved in trade for itself, not for others: those who set themselves up as a market for all do so for the sake of revenue; a city that should not share in this sort of aggrandizement should not possess a trading center of this sort. Since we see at present many territories and cities having ports and harbors that are naturally well positioned in relation to the city, so that they neither form part of the same town nor are overly far away, but are dominated by walls and other fortifications of this sort, it is evident that if any good thing results from such access, this will be available to the city, while anything harmful can be guarded against easily by means of laws that stipulate and define which sorts of persons should and which should not have dealings with one another.

Concerning naval power, it is not unclear that it is best to have a certain amount of it. They should be formidable and capable of putting up a defense by sea as well as by land not only for themselves but also for certain of their neighbors. Concerning the amount and size of this force, one must look to the way of life of the city. If it is going to lead a way of life that involves leadership and is political, it must necessarily have this sort of power available as well to match its actions. Cities will not necessarily have the overpopulation that occurs in connection with the seafaring mass: these should be no part of the city. The marine element is free and belongs to the infantry; this is in authority and dominates the crew. And if there is available a multitude of subjects who farm the territory, there will necessarily be an abundance of sailors too. We see this too in certain [cities] at present, as for example the city of the Heracleots, which sends out many warships in spite of being more modest in size than other cities.

Concerning territory, harbors, cities, and the sea, and concerning naval power, then, let our discussion stand in this manner.

## CHAPTER 10

That the city should be divided among separate types [of persons], and that the fighting and farming elements should be different, seems not to be something that is familiar to those philosophizing about the regime only at present or in recent times. Things stand in this manner in Egypt even today, and also in Crete. Sesostris having legislated in this fashion for Egypt, so it is asserted, and Minos for Crete. The arrangement of common messes also seems to be ancient . . . One should therefore consider that practically everything has been discovered on many occasions—or rather an infinity of occasions—in the course of time. For it is likely that the necessary [discoveries] are taught by need, while those relating to elegance and superfluity may be reasonably expected to begin increasing once these are already present; and one should suppose that the things connected with regimes stand in the same manner. That all [such] things are ancient is indicated by those connected with Egypt. For [the Egyptians] are held to be the most ancient [of peoples], yet they have obtained laws and a political arrangement. Hence one should use what has been adequately discovered while attempting to seek out what has been passed over. . . .

We must now speak first about the distribution [of land] and, with regard to the farmers, who and of what sort they ought to be, since we assert both that possessions should not be common, as some have said, but rather should become common in use after the fashion of friends, and that none of the citizens should be in want of sustenance. Regarding common messes, all hold that it is useful for them to be present in well-instituted cities; the reason for our holding the same opinion will be spoken of later. All the citizens should participate in these, but it is not easy for the poor to contribute the required amount from their private [funds] and administer the rest of their household. Further, expenditures relating to the gods should be common to the entire city.

It is necessary, therefore, to divide the territory into two parts, one being common and the other for private individuals, and to divide each of these in two again. One part of the common territory should be for public service relating to the gods, the other for the expense of the common messes. Of the territory that belongs to private individuals, one part should be toward the frontiers, the other toward the city, so that, with two allotments assigned to each individual, all share in both locations. This provides equality and justice, as well as greater concord with a view to wars with their neighbors. For wherever things do not stand in this manner, some make light of an enmity toward those on the border, while others are concerned with it overly much and contrary to what is noble. Hence among some [peoples] there is a law that those who are neighbors of a bordering [people] may not share jointly in deliberation concerning wars against them, the assumption being that they are not capable of deliberating finely on account of their private [interest].

It is necessary to divide the territory in this manner, then, for the reasons just spoken of. As for the farmers, it is necessary above all—if one should [speak] on the basis of what one would pray for—that they be slaves who are neither all of the same stock nor of spirited ones, as in that way they would be useful with a view to the work and safe as regards engaging in subversion; or, second, they should be barbarian subjects resembling in their nature those just mentioned. Of these, the ones in private hands should belong privately to those possessing the properties, while those on the common land should be common. In what manner slaves should be treated, and why it is better to hold out freedom as a reward for all slaves, we will speak of later.

## CHAPTER 13

We must now speak of the regime itself, and of which and what sort of things the city that is going to be blessed and finely governed should be constituted from. There are two things that [living] well consists in for all: one of these is in correct positing of the aim and end of actions; the other, discovering the actions that bear on the end. These things can be consonant with one another or dissonant, for sometimes the aim is finely posited but in acting they miss achieving it, and sometimes they achieve everything with a view to the end, but the end they posited was bad. And sometimes they miss both. In connection with medicine, for example, [doctors] sometimes neither judge rightly what the quality of a healthy body should be nor achieve what is productive in relation to the object they set for themselves. But in all arts and sciences both of these should be kept in hand, the end and the actions directed to the end.

Now that everyone strives for living well and for happiness is evident. It is open to some to achieve these things, but to others not, on account of some sort of fortune or nature; for living nobly requires a certain equipment too—less of it for those in a better state, more for those in a worse one. Some, on the other hand, seek happiness incorrectly from the outset although it is open to them to achieve it. Since our object is to see the best regime, and this is one in accordance with which a city would be best governed, and it would be best governed in accordance with one that would make it possible for the city to be happy most of all, it is clear that one should not overlook what happiness is.

We assert—and we have defined it thus in the [discourses on] ethics, if there is anything of benefit in those discourses—that happiness is the actualization and complete practice of virtue, and this not on the basis of a presupposition but unqualifiedly. By "on the basis of a presupposition" I mean necessary things, by "unqualifiedly," nobly. In the case of just actions, for example, just retributions and punishments derive from virtue, but they are necessary, and have the element of nobility only in a necessary way (for it would be more choiceworthy if no man or city required anything of the sort); but actions directed to honors and to what makes one well off are very noble in an unqualified sense. For the one is the choice of an evil, but actions of this [latter] sort are the opposite; they are providers and generators of good things. An excellent man would deal in noble fashion with poverty, disease, and other sorts of bad fortune, but blessedness is in their opposites. Indeed, it was defined thus in the ethical discourses—that the excellent person is one of a sort for whom on account of his virtue the things that are good unqualifiedly are good; and it is clear that his uses of these [good things] must necessarily also be excellent and noble in an unqualified sense. Hence human beings consider the causes of happiness to be those good things that are external—as if the lyre rather than the art were to be held the cause of brilliant and beautiful lyre playing.

Necessarily, therefore, some of the things mentioned must be present, while others must be supplied by the legislator. Hence we pray for the city to be constituted on the basis of what one would pray for in those matters over which fortune has authority (we regard it as having authority [over the external things we regard as being desirable for the best city to have present]); but the city's being excellent is no longer the work of fortune, but of knowledge and intentional choice. But a city is excellent, at any rate, by its citizens'—those sharing in the regime—being excellent; and in our case all the citizens share in the regime. This, then, must be investigated— how a man becomes excellent. Now even if it is possible for all to be excellent but not each of the citizens individually, the latter is more choiceworthy; for all [being excellent] follows from [all] individually [being excellent].

Now [men] become good and excellent through three things. These three are nature, habit, and reason. For one must first develop naturally as a human being and not some one of the other animals, and so also be of a certain quality in body and soul. But there is no benefit in certain [qualities] developing naturally, since habits make them alter: certain [qualities] are through their nature ambiguous, through habits [tending] in the direction of worse or better. The other animals live by nature above all, but in some slight respects by habit as well, while man lives also by reason (for he alone has reason); so these things should be consonant with the other. For [men] act in many ways contrary to their habituation and their nature through reason, if they are persuaded that some other condition is better. Now as to the sort of nature those should have who are going to be readily taken in hand by the legislator, we discussed this earlier. What remains at this point is the work of education. For [men] learn some things by being habituated, others by listening.

## CHAPTER 14

Since every political partnership is constituted of rulers and ruled, this must then be investigated—if the rulers and the ruled should be different or the same throughout life; for it is clear that education too will have to follow in accordance with this distinction. Now if the ones were as different from the others as we believe gods and heroes differ from human beings—much exceeding them in the first place in body, and then in soul, so that the preeminence of the rulers is indisputable and evident to the ruled—it is clear that it would always be better for the same persons to rule and the same to be ruled once and for all. But since this is not easy to assume, there being none so different from the ruled as Scylax says the kings in India are, it is evident that for many reasons it is necessary for all in similar fashion to participate in ruling and being ruled in turn. For equality is the same thing [as justice] for persons who are similar, and it is difficult for a regime to last if its constitution is contrary to justice. For the ruled [citizens] will have with them all those [serfs] in the countryside who want to subvert it, and it is impossible that those in the governing body will be numerous enough to be superior to all of these. Nevertheless, that the rulers should differ from the ruled is indisputable. How this will be the case and how they will share [in ruling and being ruled], then, should be investigated by the legislator.

This was spoken of earlier. Nature has provided the distinction by making that which is the same by type have a younger and an older element, of which it is proper for the former to be ruled and the latter to rule. No one chafes at being ruled on the basis of age or considers himself superior, particularly when he is going to recover his contribution when he attains the age to come. In one sense, therefore, it must be asserted that the same persons rule and are ruled, but in another sense different persons. So education too must necessarily be the same in a sense, and in another sense different. For, so it is asserted, one who is going to rule finely should first have been ruled. Now rule, as was said in our first discourses, is on the one hand for the sake of the ruler, and on the other for the sake of the ruled. Of these [sorts of rule] we assert the former to be characteristic of a master, and the latter to belong to free persons. Now certain commands differ not by the works [involved] but by the [end] for the sake of which [they are carried out]. Hence it is noble for the free among the young to serve in many of the tasks that are held to be characteristic of servants; for, with a view to what is noble and what not noble, actions do not differ so much in themselves as in their end and that for the sake of which [they are performed].

Since we assert that the virtue of citizen and ruler is the same as that of the good man, and the same person must be ruled first and ruler later, the legislator would have to make it his affair to determine how men can become good and through what pursuits, and what the end of the best life is.

The soul is divided into two parts, of which the one has reason itself, while the other does not have it in itself, but is capable of obeying reason. To these belong, we assert, the virtues in accordance with which a man is spoken of as in some sense good. As to which of these the end is more to be found in, what must be said is not unclear to those who distinguish in the way we assert should be done. The worse is always for the sake of the better—this is evident in a similar way both in what accords with art and in what accords with nature; and the element having reason is better. This is divided in two in the manner we are accustomed to distinguish: there is reason of the active sort on the one hand and reason of the studying sort on the other. It is clear, therefore, that this part [of the soul] must also be divided in the same fashion. And we shall say that actions stand in a comparable relationship: those belonging to that [part] which is better by nature are more choiceworthy for those who are capable of achieving either all of them or [those belonging to] the two [lower parts]. For what is most choiceworthy for each individual is the highest it is possible for him to achieve.

Life as a whole is divided, too, into occupation and leisure and war and peace, and of matters involving action some are directed toward necessary and useful things, others toward noble things. Concerning these things there must of necessity be the same choice as in the case of the parts of the soul and their actions: war must be for the sake of peace, occupation for the sake of leisure, necessary and useful things for the sake of noble things. The political [ruler] must legislate, therefore, looking to all [these] things in the case both of the parts of the soul and of their actions, but particularly to the things that are better and [have more the character of] ends. And [he must do so] in the same manner in connection with the ways of life and the divisions among activities; for one should be capable of being occupied and going to war, but should rather remain at peace and be at leisure, and one should act [to achieve] necessary and useful things, but noble things more so. So it is with a view to these aims that they must be educated when still children as well as during the other ages that require education.

Those of the Greeks who are at present held to be the best governed and the legislators who established these regimes evidently did not organize the things pertaining to the regime with a view to the best end, or the laws and education with a view to all the virtues, but inclined in crude fashion toward those which are held to be useful and of a more aggrandizing sort. Certain persons writing later in a spirit similar to this have expressed the same opinion: in praising the regime of the Lacedaemonians they admire the aim of the legislator, because he legislated everything with a view to domination and war—[views] which are readily refutable on the basis of reason, and have now been refuted by the facts. For just as most human beings envy mastery over many persons because it provides much equipment in the things of fortune, so Thibron and each of the others who write about their regime evidently admire the Spartans' legislator because they ruled over many persons as a result of having exercised themselves with a view to dangers. And yet since now at least ruling [an empire] is no longer available to the Spartans, it clearly follows that they are not happy, and that their legislator was not a good one. But this is ridiculous—that they should have lost [the chance for] living nobly even while abiding by his laws, and in the absence of any impediment to putting the laws into practice. Nor do they have a correct conception concerning the sort of rule that the legislator should be seen to honor: rule over free persons is nobler and accompanied to a greater extent by virtue than ruling in the spirit of a master. Further, it is not on this account that one should consider the city happy and praise the legislator, that he trained it to dominate for the purpose of ruling those nearby; these things involve great harm. For it is clear that any citizen who is capable of doing so must attempt to pursue the capability to rule his own city—the very thing the Spartans accuse their king Pausanias of, even though he held so great a prerogative. There is, indeed, nothing in such arguments and laws that is either political, beneficial, or true. The same things are best [for men] both privately and in common, and the legislator should implant these in the souls of human beings. Training in matters related to war should be practiced not for the sake of reducing to slavery those who do not merit it, but in the first place in order that they themselves will not become slaves to others; next, so that they may seek leadership for the sake of benefiting the ruled, but not for the sake of mastery over everyone; and third, to be master over those who merit being slaves. That the legislator should give serious attention instead to arranging that legislation, and particularly that connected with matters related to war, is for the sake of being at leisure and of peace, is testified to by events as well as arguments. Most cities of this sort preserve themselves when at war, but once having acquired [imperial] rule they come to ruin; they lose their edge, like iron, when they remain at peace. The reason is that the legislator has not educated them to be capable of being at leisure.

## CHAPTER 15

Since the end is evidently the same for human beings both in common and privately, and there must necessarily be the same defining principle for the best man and the best regime, it is evident that the virtues directed to leisure should be present; for, as has been said repeatedly, peace is the end of war, and leisure of occupation. The virtues useful with a view to leisure and pastime are both those of which the work is in leisure and those of which it is in occupation. For many of the necessary things should be present for it to be open to them to be at leisure. Hence it is appropriate that the city have moderation, courage, and endurance, for as the proverb has it, "there is no leisure for slaves," and those who are incapable of facing danger in a courageous spirit are slaves of whomever comes along to attack them. Now courage and endurance are required with a view to occupation; philosophy, with a view to leisure; moderation and [the virtue of] justice, at both times, and particularly when they remain at peace and are at leisure. For war compels [men] to be just and behave with moderation, while the enjoyment of good fortune and being at leisure in peacetime tend to make them arrogant. There is, then, a need for much [of the virtue of] justice and much moderation on the part of those who are held to act in the best way and who have all the gratifications that are regarded as blessings, like those—if there are such—whom the poets assert are "in the islands of the blessed." For these will be most particularly in need of philosophy and moderation and [the virtue of] justice to the extent that they are at leisure in the midst of an abundance of good things of this sort.

Why a city that is going to exist happily and be excellent should share in these virtues, then, is evident. For if it is disgraceful not to be capable of using good things, it is still more so to be incapable of using them in leisure, but to be seen to be good [men] while occupied and at war but servile when remaining at peace and being at leisure. Hence one should not train in virtue as the city of the Lacedaemonians does. For it is not in this way that they differ from others, by not considering the greatest of good things to be the same things others do, but by considering that these things are got through some sort of virtue. But since [they consider] these good things and the gratification deriving from them to be greater than that deriving from the virtues, [the sort of virtue in which they are trained is only that useful and necessary for the acquisition of good things. That the sort of virtue is rather to be cultivated that governs the use of these good things, that this is preeminently the sort of virtue that is cultivated in leisure, and that it is to be cultivated] on its own account, is evident from these things. How and through what things it will exist is what must be studied now. . . .

# Selections from *An Essay Concerning the True Original, Extent, and End of Civil Government*

## John Locke (1632–1704)

*Educated extensively in many fields, including theology, medicine, physics, and economics, at Oxford University, John Locke was under the patronage of the Earl of Shaftesbury and served as a political advisor to the earl during the third quarter of the seventeenth century. In addition to his two treatises on government that sounded the death knell of the divine right of kings and formulated the groundwork for the liberal understanding of political life, Locke wrote what were to become politically influential works on religious toleration, economics, and education.*

*Consider Locke's view of the fundamental nature of human beings and contrast it with that of Aristotle. Is it more true to view ourselves as naturally solitary, free, and equal than to think of ourselves as essentially meant to live in an ordered lawful society, as Aristotle argues? Why is the source and meaning of property so important to Locke's political theory? What is political life like when a state understands itself primarily as the protector of the property of its citizens? Would Aristotle agree with Locke's view of the purpose of politics? What is the character of citizenship among men who believe they have a right to revolt against their government?*

### CHAPTER I

3.      Political power, . . . I take to be a right of making laws with penalties of death, and consequently all less penalties for the regulating and preserving of property, and of employing the force of the community, in the execution of such laws, and in the defence of the commonwealth from foreign injury; and all this only for the public good.

### CHAPTER II: OF THE STATE OF NATURE

4.      To understand political power right, and derive it from its original, we must consider what state all men are naturally in, and that is a state of perfect freedom to order their actions and dispose of their possessions and persons, as they think fit, within the bounds of the law of nature; without asking leave, or depending upon the will of any other man.

A state also of equality, wherein all the power and jurisdiction is reciprocal, no one having more than another; there being nothing more evident, than that creatures of the same species and rank, promiscuously born to all the same advantages of nature, and the use of the same faculties, should also be equal one amongst another without subordination or subjection; unless the lord and master of them all should, by any manifest declaration of his will, set one above another, and confer on him, by an evident and clear appointment, an undoubted right to dominion and sovereignty. . . .

6.    But though this be a state of liberty, yet it is not a state of licence: though man in that state have an uncontrollable liberty to dispose of his person or possessions, yet he has not liberty to destroy himself, or so much as any creature in his possession, but where some nobler use than its bare preservation calls for it. The state of nature has a law of nature to govern it, which obliges every one: and reason, which is that law, teaches all mankind, who will but consult it, that being all equal and independent, no one ought to harm another in his life, health, liberty, or possessions, for men being all the workmanship of one omnipotent and infinitely wise Maker; all the servants of one sovereign master, sent into the world by his order, and about his business; they are his property, whose workmanship they are, made to last during his, not one another's pleasure, and being furnished with like faculties, sharing all in one community of nature, there cannot be supposed any such subordination among us, that may authorize us to destroy another, as if we were made for one another's uses, as the inferior ranks of creatures are for ours. Every one, as he is bound to preserve himself, and not to quit his station willfully, so by the like reason, when his own preservation comes not in competition, ought he, as much as he can, to preserve the rest of mankind, and may not, unless it be to do justice to an offender, take away or impair the life, or what tends to the preservation of life; the liberty, health, limb, or goods of another.

7.    And that all men may be restrained from invading others rights, and from doing hurt to one another, and the law of nature be observed, which willeth the peace and preservation of all mankind, the execution of the law of nature is, in that state, put into every man's hands, whereby every one has a right to punish the transgressors of that law to such a degree as may hinder its violation, for the law of nature would, as all other laws that concern men in this world, be in vain, if there were nobody that in the state of nature had a power to execute that law, and thereby preserve the innocent and restrain offenders. And if any one in the state of nature may punish another for any evil he has done, every one may do so, for in that state of perfect equality, where naturally there is no superiority or jurisdiction of one over another, what any may do in prosecution of that law, every one must needs have a right to do.

8.    And thus, in the state of nature, "one man comes by a power over another;" but yet no absolute or arbitrary power, to use a criminal, when he has got him in his hand, according to the passionate heats, or boundless extravagancy of his own will; but only to retribute to him, so far as calm reason and conscience dictate, what is proportionate to his transgression; which is so much as may serve for reparation and restraint, for these two are the only reasons why one man may lawfully do harm to another, which is that we call punishment. In transgressing the law of nature, the offender declares himself to live by another rule than that of reason and common equity, which is that measure God has set to the actions of men, for their mutual security; and so he becomes dangerous to mankind, the tye, which is to secure them from injury and violence, being slighted and broken by him. Which being a trespass against the whole species, and the peace and safety of it, provided for by the law of nature; every man upon this score, by the right he hath to preserve mankind in general, may restrain, or, where it is necessary, destroy things noxious to them, and so may bring such evil on any one who hath transgressed that law, as may make him repent the doing of it and thereby deter him, and by his example others, from doing the like mischief. And in this case, and upon this ground, "every man hath a right to punish the offender, and be executioner of the law of nature." . . .

10.    Besides the crime which consists in violating the law, and varying from the right rule of reason, whereby a man so far becomes degenerate, and declares himself to quit the principles of human nature, and to be a noxious creature, there is commonly injury done to some person or

other, and some other man receives damage by his transgression, in which case he who hath received any damage, has, besides the right of punishment common to him with other men, a particular right to seek reparation from him that has done it, and any other person, who finds it just, may also join with him that is injured, and assist him in recovering from the offender so much as may make satisfaction for the harm he has suffered.

11.     From these two distinct rights, the one of punishing the crime for restraint, and preventing the like offence, which right of punishing is in every body; the other of taking reparation, which belongs only to the injured party; comes it to pass that the magistrate, who by being magistrate hath the common right of punishing put into his hands, can often, where the public good demands not the execution of the law, remit the punishment of criminal offences by his own authority, but yet cannot remit the satisfaction due to any private man for the damage he has received. That, he who has suffered the damage has a right to demand in his own name, and he alone can remit, the damnified person has this power of appropriating to himself the goods or service of the offender, by right of self-preservation, as every man has a power to punish the crime, to prevent its being committed again, "by the right he has of preserving all mankind;" and doing all reasonable things he can in order to that end, and thus it is, that every man, in the state of nature, has a power to kill a murderer, both to deter others from doing the like injury, which no reparation can compensate, by the example of the punishment that attends it from every body; and also to secure men from the attempts of a criminal, who having renounced reason, the common rule and measure God hath given to mankind, hath, by the unjust violence and slaughter he hath committed upon one, declared war against all mankind; and therefore may be destroyed as a lion or a tiger, one of those wild savage beasts, with whom men can have no society nor security: and upon this is grounded that great law of nature, "Whoso sheddeth man's blood, by man shall his blood be shed." And Cain was so fully convinced, that every one had a right to destroy such a criminal, that after the murder of his brother, he cries out, "Every one that findeth me, shall slay me;" so plain was it writ in the hearts of mankind.

12.     By the same reason may a man in the state of nature punish the lesser breaches of that law. It will perhaps be demanded, with death? I answer, each transgression may be punished to that degree, and with so much severity, as will suffice to make it an ill bargain to the offender, give him cause to repent, and terrify others from doing the like. Every offence, that can be committed in the state of nature, may in the state of nature be also punished equally, and as far forth as it may in a commonwealth, . . .

14.     It is often asked as a mighty objection, "Where are, or ever were there any men in such a state of nature?" To which it may suffice as an answer at present that, since all princes and rulers of independent governments, all through the world are in a state of nature, it is plain the world never was, nor ever will be, without numbers of men in that state. . . .

15.     . . . But I moreover affirm, that all men are naturally in that state, and remain so, till by their own consents they make themselves members of some politic society; and I doubt not in the sequel of this discourse to make it very clear.

## CHAPTER V:  OF PROPERTY

26.     God, who hath given the world to men in common, hath also given them reason to make use of it to the best advantage of life, and convenience. The earth and all that is therein is given to men for the support and comfort of their being. And though all the fruits it naturally produces, and beasts it feeds, belong to mankind in common, as they are produced by the spontaneous hand of nature; and nobody has originally a private dominion, exclusive of the rest of mankind, in any of them, as they are thus in their natural state; yet being given for the use of men, there must of necessity be a means to appropriate them some way or other, before they can be of any use, or at all beneficial to any particular man. The fruit, or venison, which nourishes the wild Indian, who knows no enclosure, and is still a tenant in common, must be his, and so his, i.e. a

part of him, that another can no longer have any right to it, before it can do him any good for the support of his life.

27.     Though the earth, and all inferior creatures be common to all men, yet every man has a property in his own person, this nobody has any right to but himself. The labour of his body, and the work of his hands, we may say, are properly his. Whatsoever then he removes out of the state that nature hath provided, and left it in, he hath mixed his labour with, and joined to it something that is his own, and thereby makes it his property. It being by him removed from the common state nature hath placed it in, it hath by this labour something annexed to it, that excludes the common right of other men. For this labour being the unquestionable property of the labourer, no man but he can have a right to what that is once joined to, at least where there is enough and as good, left in common for others.

28.     He that is nourished by the acorns he picked up under an oak, or the apples he gathered from the trees in the wood, has certainly appropriated them to himself. Nobody can deny but the nourishment is his. I ask then, when did they begin to be his? when he digested? or when he eat? or when he boiled? or when he brought them home? or when he picked them up? And it is plain, if the first gathering made them not his, nothing else could. That labour put a distinction between them and common, that added something to them more than nature, the common mother of all, had done; and so they became his private right. And will anyone say he had no right to those acorns or apples he thus appropriated, because he had not the consent of all mankind to make them his? was it a robbery thus to assume to himself what belonged to all in common? If such a consent as that was necessary, man had starved, notwithstanding the plenty God had given him. We see in commons, which remain so by compact, that it is the taking any part of what is common, and removing it out of the state nature leaves it in, which begins the property; without which the common is of no use. . . .

31.     It will perhaps be objected to this, that "if gathering the acorns, or other fruits of the earth, & makes a right to them, then any one may engross as much as he will." To which I answer, Not so. The same law of nature, that does by this means give us property, does also bound that property too. "God has given us all things richly," I Tim. vi. 17, is the voice of reason confirmed by inspiration. But how far has he given it us? To enjoy. As much as any one can make use of to any advantage of life before it spoils, so much he may by his labour fix a property in, whatever is beyond this, is more than his share, and belongs to others. Nothing was made by God for man to spoil or destroy. And thus, considering the plenty of natural provisions there was a long time in the world, and the few spenders; and to how small a part of that provision the industry of one man could extend itself, and engross it to the prejudice of others; especially keeping within the bounds, set by reason, of what might serve for his use; there could be then little room for quarrels or contentions about property so established.

32.     But the chief matter of property being now not the fruits of the earth and the beasts that subsist on it, but the earth itself; as that which takes in, and carries with it all the rest; I think it is plain, that property in that too is acquired as the former. As much land as a man tills, plants, improves, cultivates, and can use the product of, so much is his property. He by his labour does, as it were, enclose it from the common. Nor will it invalidate his right, to say everybody else has an equal title to it, and therefore he cannot appropriate, he cannot enclose, without the consent of all his fellow commoners, all mankind. God, when he gave the world in common to all mankind, commanded man also to labour, and the penury of his condition required it of him. God and his reason commanded him to subdue the earth, i.e., improve it for the benefit of life, and therein lay out something upon it that was his own, his labour. He that, in obedience to this command of God, subdued, tilled, and sowed any part of it, thereby annexed to it something that was his property, which another had no title to, nor could without injury take from him.

33.     Nor was this appropriation of any parcel of land, by improving it, any prejudice to any other man, since there was still enough, and as good left; and more than the yet unprovided

could use. So that, in effect, there was never the less left for others because of his enclosure for himself: for he that leaves as much as another can make use of, does as good as take nothing at all. Nobody could think himself injured by the drinking of another man, though he took a good draught, who had a whole river of the same water left him to quench his thirst; and the case of land and water, where there is enough for both, is perfectly the same.

34.     God gave the world to men in common; but since he gave it them for their benefit, and the greatest conveniences of life they were capable to draw from it, it cannot be supposed he meant it should always remain common and uncultivated. He gave it to the use of the industrious and rational, (and labour was to be his title to it) not to the fancy or covetousness of the quarrelsome and contentious. He that had as good left for his improvement, as was already taken up, needed not complain, ought not to meddle with what was already improved by another's labour: if he did, it is plain he desired the benefit of another's pains, which he had no right to, and not the ground which God has given him in common with others to labour on, and whereof there was as good left, as that already possessed, and more than he knew what to do with, or his industry could reach to. . . .

37.     This is certain, that in the beginning, before the desire of having more than man needed had altered the intrinsic value of things, which depends only on their usefulness to the life of man; or had agreed, that a little piece of yellow metal, which would keep without wasting or decay, should be worth a great piece of flesh, or a whole heap of corn; though men had a right to appropriate, by their labour, each one to himself as much of the things of nature as he could use: yet this could not be much, nor to the prejudice of others, where the same plenty was still left to those who would use the same industry. To which let me add, that he who appropriates land to himself by his labour, does not lessen, but increase the common stock of mankind: for the provisions serving to the support of human life, produced by one acre of enclosed and cultivated land, are (to speak much within compass) ten times more than those which are yielded by an acre of land of an equal richness lying waste in common. And therefore he that encloses land, and has a greater plenty of the conveniencies of life from ten acres, than he could have from an hundred left to nature, may truly be said to give ninety acres to mankind: for his labour now supplies him with provisions out of ten acres, which were by the product of an hundred lying in common. I have here rated the improved land very low, in making its product but as ten to one, when it is much nearer an hundred to one: for I ask, whether in the wild woods and uncultivated waste of America, left to nature, without any improvement, tillage, or husbandry, a thousand acres yield the needy and wretched inhabitants as many conveniencies of life, as ten acres equally fertile land do in Devonshire, where they are well cultivated. . . .

40.     Nor is it so strange, as perhaps before consideration it may appear, that the property of labour should be able to over-balance the community of land: for it is labour indeed that put the difference of value on every thing; and let any one consider what the difference is between an acre of land planted with tobacco or sugar, sown with wheat or barley, and an acre of the same land lying in common, without any husbandry upon it, and he will find, that the improvement of labour makes the far greater part of the value. I think it will be but a very modest computation to say, that of the products of the earth useful to the life of man, nine tenths are the effects of labour: nay, if we will rightly estimate things as they come to our use, and cast up the several expences about them, what in them is purely owing to nature, and what to labour, we shall find, that in most of them ninety-nine hundredths are wholly to be put on the account of labour.

41.     There cannot be a clearer demonstration of any thing, than several nations of the Americans are of this, who are rich in land, and poor in all the comforts of life; whom nature having furnished as liberally as any other people, with the materials of plenty, i.e., a fruitful soil, apt to produce in abundance what might serve for food, raiment, and delight; yet for want of improving it by labour have not one-hundredth part of the conveniencies we enjoy: and a king of

a large and fruitful territory there feeds, lodges, and is clad worse than a day-labourer in England. . . .

46.    The greatest part of things really useful to the life of man, and such as the necessity of subsisting made the first commoners of the world look after, as it doth the Americans now, are generally things of short duration; such as, if they are not consumed by use, will decay and perish of themselves: gold, silver, and diamonds, are things that fancy or agreement hath put the value on, more than real use, and the necessary support of life. Now of those good things which nature hath provided in common, every one had a right, (as hath been said) to as much as he could use, and property in all that he could effect with his labour; all that his industry could extend to, to alter from the state nature had put it in, was his. He that gathered a hundred bushels of acorns or apples, had thereby a property in them, they were his goods as soon as gathered. He was only to look, that he used them before they spoiled, else he took more than his share, and robbed others. And indeed it was a foolish thing, as well as dishonest, to hoard up more than he could make use of. If he gave away a part to any body else, so that it perished not uselessly in his possession, these he also made use of. And if he also bartered away plums, that would have rotted in a week, for nuts that would last good for his eating a whole year, he did no injury; he wasted not the common stock; destroyed no part of the portion of the goods that belonged to others, so long as nothing perished uselessly in his hands. Again, if he would give his nuts for a piece of metal, pleased with its colour; or exchange his sheep for shells, or wool for a sparkling pebble or a diamond, and keep those by him all his life, he invaded not the right of others, he might heap as much of these durable things as he pleased; the exceeding of the bounds of his just property not lying in the largeness of his possession, but the perishing of anything uselessly in it.

47.    And thus came in the use of money, some lasting thing that men might keep without spoiling, and that by mutual consent men would take in exchange for the truly useful, but perishable supports of life.

48.    And as different degrees of industry were apt to give men possessions in different proportions, so this invention of money gave them the opportunity to continue and enlarge them: for supposing an island, separate from all possible commerce with the rest of the world, wherein there were but an hundred families, but there were sheep, horses, and cows, with other useful animals, wholesome fruits, and land enough for corn for a hundred thousand times as many, but nothing in the island, either because of its commonness, or perishableness, fit to supply the place of money; what reason could any one have there to enlarge his possessions beyond the use of his family and a plentiful supply to its consumption, either in what their own industry produced, or they could barter for like perishable, useful commodities with others? Where there is not something, both lasting and scarce, and so valuable to be hoarded up, there men will not be apt to enlarge their possessions of land, were it ever so rich, ever so free for them to take: for I ask, what would a man value ten thousand, or an hundred thousand acres of excellent land, ready cultivated and well stocked too with cattle, in the middle of the inland parts of America, where he had no hopes of commerce with other parts of the world, to draw money to him by the sale of the product? It would not be worth the enclosing, and we should see him give up again to the wild common of nature, whatever was more than would supply the conveniencies of life to be had there for him and his family.

49.    Thus in the beginning all the world was America, and more so than that is now; for no such thing as money was any where known. Find out something that hath the use and value of money amongst his neighbours, you shall see the same man will begin presently to enlarge his possessions.

50.    But since gold and silver, being little useful to the life of man in proportion to food, raiment, and carriage, has its value only from the consent of men, whereof labour yet makes, in great part, the measure; it is plain, that men have agreed to a disproportionate and unequal possession of the earth, they having, by a tacit and voluntary consent, found out a way how a

man may fairly possess more land than he himself can use the product of, by receiving in exchange for the overplus, gold and silver, which may be hoarded up without injury to any one; these metals not spoiling or decaying in the hands of the possessor. This partage of things in an inequality of private possessions, men have made practicable out of the bounds of society, and without compact; only by putting a value on gold and silver, and tacitly agreeing in the use of money: for in governments, the laws regulate the right of property, and the possession of land is determined by positive constitutions.

51.     And thus, I think, it is very easy to conceive "how labour could at first begin a title of property" in the common things of nature, and how the spending it upon our uses bounded it. So that there could then be no reason of quarrelling about title, nor any doubt about the largeness of possession it gave. Right and conveniency went together; for as a man had a right to all he could employ his labour upon, so he had no temptation to labour for more than he could make use of. This left no room for controversy about the title, nor for encroachment on the right of others; what portion a man carved to himself, was easily seen: and it was useless, as well as dishonest, to carve himself too much, or take more than he needed.

## CHAPTER VII: OF POLITICAL OR CIVIL SOCIETY

87.     Man being born, as has been proved, with a title to perfect freedom, and uncontrolled enjoyment of all the rights and privileges of the law of nature, equally with any other man, or number of men in the world, hath by nature a power, not only to preserve his property, that is, his life, liberty, and estate, against the injuries and attempts of other men; but to judge of and punish the breaches of that law in others, as he is persuaded the offence deserves, even with death itself, in crimes where the heinousness of the fact, in his opinion, requires it. But because no political society can be, nor subsist, without having in itself the power to preserve the property, and, in order thereunto, punish the offences of all those of that society; there and there only is political society, where every one of the members hath quitted his natural power, resigned it up into the hands of the community in all cases that excludes him not from appealing for protection to the law established by it. And thus all private judgment of every particular member being excluded, the community comes to be umpire by settled standing rules, indifferent, and the same to all parties; and by men having authority from the community, for the execution of those rules, decides all the differences that may happen between any members of that society concerning any matter of right; and punishes those offences which any member hath committed against the society, with such penalties as the law has established, whereby it is easy to discern, who are, and who are not, in political society together. Those who are united into one body, and have a common established law and judicature to appeal to, with authority to decide controversies between them, and punish offenders, are in civil society one with another: but those who have no such common appeal, I mean on earth, are still in the state of nature, each being, where there is no other, judge for himself, and executioner: which is, as I have before showed, the perfect state of nature.

88.     And thus the commonwealth comes by a power to set down what punishment shall belong to the several transgressions which they think worthy of it committed amongst the members of that society, (which is the power of making laws) as well as it has the power to punish any injury done unto any of its members, by any one that is not of it, (which is the power of war and peace,) and all this for the preservation of the property of all the members of that society, as far as is possible. But though every man who has entered into civil society, and is become a member of any commonwealth, has thereby quitted his power to punish offences against the law of nature, in prosecution of his own private judgment; yet with the judgment of offences, which he has given up to the legislative in all cases, where he can appeal to the magistrate, he has given a right to the commonwealth to employ his force, for the execution of the judgments of the commonwealth, whenever he shall be called to it; which indeed are his own

judgments, they being made by himself, or his representative. And herein we have the original of the legislative and executive power of civil society which is to judge by standing laws, how far offences are to be punished, when committed within the commonwealth; and also to determine, by occasional judgments founded on the present circumstances of the fact, how far injuries from without are to be vindicated; and in both these to employ all the force of all the members, when there shall be need.

89.　　Whenever therefore any number of men are so united into one society, as to quit every one his executive power of the law of nature, and to resign it to the public, there and there only is a political, or civil society. And this is done, wherever any number of men, in the state of nature, enter into society to make one people, one body politic, under one supreme government; or else when any one joins himself to, and incorporates with any government already made: for hereby he authorizes the society, or, which is all one, the legislative thereof, to make laws for him, as the public good of the society shall require; to the execution whereof, his own assistance (as to his own degrees) is due. And this puts men out of a state of nature into that of a commonwealth, by setting up a judge on earth, with authority to determine all the controversies, and redress the injuries that may happen to any member of the commonwealth: which judge is the legislative, or magistrate appointed by it. And wherever there are any number of men, however associated, that have no such decisive power to appeal to, there they are still in the state of nature. . . .

## CHAPTER VIII: OF THE BEGINNING OF POLITICAL SOCIETIES

95.　　Men being, as has been said, by nature, all free, equal, and independent, no one can be put out of this estate, and subjected to the political power of another, without his own consent. The only way, whereby any one divests himself of his natural liberty, and puts on the bonds of civil society, is by agreeing with other men to join and unite into a community, for their comfortable, safe, and peaceable living one amongst another, in a secure enjoyment of their properties, and a greater security against any, that are not of it. This any number of men may do, because it injures not the freedom of the rest; they are left as they were in the liberty of the state of nature. When any number of men have so consented to make one community or government, they are thereby presently incorporated, and make one body politic, wherein the majority have a right to act and conclude the rest.

96.　　For when any number of men have, by the consent of every individual, made a community, they have thereby made that community one body, with a power to act as one body, which is only by the will and determination of the majority: for that which acts any community, being only the consent of the individuals of it, and it being necessary to that which is one body to move one way; it is necessary the body should move that way whither the greater force carries it, which is the consent of the majority: or else it is impossible it should act or continue one body, one community, which the consent of every individual that united into it, agreed that it should; and so every one is bound by that consent to be concluded by the majority. And therefore we see, that in assemblies, impowered to act by positive laws, where no number is set by that positive law which impowers them, the act of the majority passes for the act of the whole, and of course determines; as having by the law of nature and reason, the power of the whole.

97.　　And thus every man, by consenting with others to make one body politic under one government, puts himself under an obligation, to every one of that society, to submit to the determination of the majority, and to be concluded by it; or else this original compact, whereby he with others incorporates into one society, would signify nothing, and be no compact, if he be left free, and under no other ties than he was in before in the state of nature. For what appearance would there be of any compact? what new engagement if he were no farther tied by any decrees of the society, than he himself thought fit, and did actually consent to? This would be still as great a liberty as he himself had before his compact, or any one else in the state of nature hath, who may submit himself, and consent to any acts of it if he thinks fit. . . .

## CHAPTER IX:  OF THE ENDS OF POLITICAL SOCIETY AND GOVERNMENT

123.    If man in the state of nature be so free, as has been said; if he be absolute lord of his own person and possessions, equal to the greatest, and subject to nobody, why will he part with his freedom? why will he give up his empire, and subject himself to the dominion and control of any other power? To which it is obvious to answer, that though in the state of nature he hath such a right, yet the enjoyment of it is very uncertain, and constantly exposed to the invasion of others; for all being kings as much as he, every man his equal, and the greater part no strict observers of equity and justice, the enjoyment of the property he has in this state is very unsafe, very unsecure. This makes him willing to quit a condition, which, however free, is full of fears and continual dangers: and it is not without reason, that he seeks out, and is willing to join in society with others, who are already united, or have a mind to unite, for the mutual preservation of their lives, liberties, and estates, which I call by the general name, property.

124.    The great and chief end, therefore, of men's uniting into commonwealths, and putting themselves under government, is the preservation of their property. To which in the state of nature there are many things wanting.

First, There wants an established, settled, known law, received and allowed by common consent to be the standard of right and wrong, and the common measure to decide all controversies between them: for though the law of nature be plain and intelligible to all rational creatures, yet men being biassed by their interest, as well as ignorant for want of studying it, are not apt to allow of it as a law binding to them in the application of it to their particular cases.

125.    Secondly, In the state of nature there wants a known and indifferent judge, with authority to determine all differences according to the established law: for every one in that state being both judge and executioner of the law of nature, men being partial to themselves, passion and revenge is very apt to carry them too far, and with too much heat, in their own cases; as well as negligence, and unconcernedness, to make them too remiss in other men's.

126.    Thirdly, In the state of nature, there often wants power to back and support the sentence when right, and to give it due execution. They who by any injustice offend, will seldom fail, where they are able, by force to make good their injustice; such resistance many times makes the punishment dangerous, and frequently destructive, to those who attempt it.

127.    Thus mankind, notwithstanding all the privileges of the state of nature, being but in an ill condition, while they remain in it, are quickly driven into society. Hence it comes to pass that we seldom find any number of men live any time together in this state. The inconveniencies that they are therein exposed to, by the irregular and uncertain exercise of the power every man has of punishing the transgressions of others, make them take sanctuary under the established laws of government, and therein seek the preservation of their property. It is this makes them so willingly give up every one his single power of punishing, to be exercised by such alone, as shall be appointed to it amongst them; and by such rules as the community, or those authorized by them to that purpose, shall agree on. And in this we have the original right of both the legislative and executive power, as well as of the governments and societies themselves. . . .

## CHAPTER X:  OF THE FORMS OF A COMMONWEALTH

132.    The majority having, as has been showed, upon men's first uniting into society, the whole power of the community naturally in them, may employ all that power in making laws for the community from time to time, and executing those laws by officers of their own appointing; and then the form of the government is a perfect democracy: or else may put the power of making

laws into the hands of a few select men, and their heirs or successors; and then it is an oligarchy: or else into the hands of one man, and then it is a monarchy: if to him and his heirs, it is an hereditary monarchy: if to him only for life, but upon his death the power only of nominating a successor to return to them; an elective monarchy. And so accordingly of these the community may make compounded and mixed forms of government, as they think good. And if the legislative power be at first given by the majority to one or more persons only for their lives, or any limited time, and then the supreme power to revert to them again; when it is so reverted, the community may dispose of it again anew into what hands they please, and so constitute a new form of government: for the form of government depending upon the placing the supreme power, which is the legislative (it being impossible to conceive that an inferior power should prescribe to a superior, or any but the supreme make laws) according as the power of making laws is placed, such is the form of the commonwealth.

133.     By commonwealth, I must be understood all along to mean, not a democracy, or any form of government; but any independent community, which the Latines signified by the word civitas; to which the word which best answers in our language, is commonwealth, and most properly expresses such a society of men, which community or city in English does not: for there may be subordinate communities in government; and city amongst us has quite a different notion from commonwealth: and therefore, to avoid ambiguity, I crave leave to use the word commonwealth in that sense, in which I find it used by King James the First: and I take it to be its genuine signification; which if any body dislike, I consent with him to change it for a better.

## *CHAPTER XI: OF THE EXTENT OF THE LEGISLATIVE POWER*

134.     The great end of men's entering into society being the enjoyment of their properties in peace and safety, and the great instrument and means of that being the laws established in that society; the first and fundamental positive law of all commonwealths is the establishing of the legislative power; as the first and fundamental natural law, which is to govern even the legislative itself, is the preservation of the society, and (as far as will consist with the public good) of every person in it. This legislative is not only the supreme power of the commonwealth, but sacred and unalterable in the hands where the community have once place it; nor can any edict of any body else, in what form soever conceived, or by what power soever backed, have the force and obligation of a law, which has not its sanction from that legislative which the public has chosen and appointed; for without this the law could not have that, which is absolutely necessary to its being a law, the consent of the society; over whom nobody can have a power to make laws, but by their own consent, and by authority received from them. And therefore all the obedience, which by the most solemn ties any one can be obliged to pay, ultimately terminates in this supreme power, and is directed by those laws which it enacts; nor can any oaths to any foreign power whatsoever, or any domestic subordinate power, discharge any member of the society from his obedience to the legislative, acting pursuant to their trust; nor oblige him to any obedience contrary to the laws so enacted, or farther than they do allow; it being ridiculous to imagine one can be tied ultimately to obey any power in the society, which is not supreme.

135.     Though the legislative, whether placed in one or more, whether it be always in being, or only by intervals, though it be the supreme power in every commonwealth; yet,

First, It is not, nor can possibly be absolutely arbitrary over the lives and fortunes of the people: for it being but the joint power of every member of the society given up to that person, or assembly, which is legislator; it can be no more than those persons had in a state of nature before they entered into society, and gave up to the community: for nobody can transfer to another more power than he has in himself; and nobody has an absolute arbitrary power over himself, or over any other, to destroy his own life, or take away the life or property of another. A man, as has been proved, cannot subject himself to the arbitrary power of another; and having in the state of nature no arbitrary power over the life, liberty, or possession of another, but only so much as the law of nature gave him for the preservation of himself and the rest of mankind; this is all he doth, or can give up to the commonwealth, and by it to the legislative power, so that the legislative can have no more than this. Their power, in the utmost bounds of it, is limited to the public good of the society. It is a power, that hath no other end but preservation, and therefore can never have a right to destroy, enslave, or designedly to impoverish the subjects. The obligations of the law of nature cease not in society, but only in many cases are drawn closer, and have by human laws known penalties annexed to them, to enforce their observation. Thus the law of nature stands as an eternal rule to all men, legislators as well as others. The rules that they make for other men's actions, must, as well as their own and other men's actions, be conformable to the laws of nature, i.e. to the will of God, of which that is a declaration; and the "fundamental law of nature being the preservation of mankind," no human sanction can be good or valid against it.

136.    Secondly, The legislative or supreme authority cannot assume to itself a power to rule, by extemporary, arbitrary decrees; but is bound to dispense justice, and to decide the rights of the subject, by promulgated, standing laws, and known authorized judges. For the law of nature being unwritten, and so no-where to be found, but in the minds of men; they who through passion, or interest, shall miscite, or misapply it, cannot so easily be convinced of their mistake, where there is no established judge: and so it serves not, as it ought, to determine the rights, and fence the properties of those that live under it; especially where every one is judge, interpreter, and executioner of it too, and that in his own case: and he that has right on his side, having ordinarily but his own single strength, hath not force enough to defend himself from injuries, or to punish delinquents. To avoid these inconveniencies, which disorder men's properties in the state of nature, men unite into societies, that they may have the united strength of the whole society to secure and defend their properties, and may have standing rules to bound it, by which every one may know what is his. To this end it is that men give up all their natural power to the society which they enter into, and the community put the legislative power into such hands as they think fit: with this trust, that they shall be governed by declared laws, or else their peace, quiet, and property will still be at the same uncertainty, as it was in the state of nature.

137.    Absolute arbitrary power, or governing without settled standing laws, can neither of them consist with the ends of society and government, which men would not quit the freedom of the state of nature for, and tie themselves up under, were it not to preserve their lives, liberties, and fortunes, and by stated rules of right and property to secure their peace and quiet. It cannot be supposed that they should intend, had they a power so to do, to give to any one, or more, an absolute arbitrary power over their persons and estates, and put a force into the magistrate's hand to execute his unlimited will arbitrarily upon them. This were to put themselves into a worse condition than the state of nature, wherein they had a liberty to defend their right against the injuries of others, and were upon equal terms of force to maintain it, whether invaded by a single man, or many in combination. Whereas by supposing they have given up themselves to the absolute arbitrary power and will of a legislator, they have disarmed themselves, and armed him, to make a prey of them when he pleases; he being in a much worse condition, who is exposed to the arbitrary power of one man, who has the command of 100,000, than he that is exposed to the arbitrary power of 100,000 single men; nobody being secure, that his will, who has such a command, is better than that of other men, though his force be 100,000 times stronger. And therefore, whatever form the commonwealth is under, the ruling power ought to govern by declared and received laws, and not by extemporary dictates and undetermined resolutions: for then mankind will be in a far worse condition than in the state of nature, if they shall have armed one or a few men with the joint power of a multitude, to force them to obey at pleasure the exorbitant and unlimited degrees of their sudden thoughts, or unrestrained, and till that moment unknown wills, without having any measures set down

which may guide and justify their actions; for all the power the government has, being only for the good of the society, as it ought not to be arbitrary and at pleasure, so it ought to be exercised by established and promulgated laws; that both the people may know their duty, and be safe and secure within the limits of the law; and the rulers too kept within their bounds, and not be tempted, by the power they have in their hands, to employ it to such purposes, and by such measures, as they would not have known, and own not willingly.

138.     Thirdly, The supreme power cannot take from any man part of his property without his own consent, for the preservation of property being the end of government, and that for which men enter into society, it necessarily supposes and requires, that the people should have property, without which they must be supposed to lose that, by entering into society, which was the end for which they entered into it; too gross an absurdity for any man to own. Men therefore in society having property, they have such right to the goods, which by the law of the community are their's, that no body hath a right to take their substance or any part of it from them, without their own consent; without this they have no property at all; for I have truly no property in that, which another can by right take from me, when he pleases, against my consent. Hence it is a mistake to think, that the supreme or legislative power of any commonwealth can do what it will, and dispose of the estates of the subject arbitrarily, or take any part of them at pleasure. This is not much to be feared in governments where the legislative consists, wholly or in part, in assemblies which are variable, whose members, upon the dissolution of the assembly, are subjects under the common laws of their country, equally with the rest. But in governments, where the legislative is in one lasting assembly always in being, or in one man, as in absolute monarchies, there is danger still, that they will think themselves to have a distinct interest from the rest of the community; and so will be apt to increase their own riches and power, by taking what they think fit from the people: for a man's property is not at all secure, though there be good and equitable laws to set the bounds of it between him and his fellow-subjects, if he who commands those subjects, have power to take from any private man, what part he pleases of his property, and use and dispose of it as he thinks good.

139.     But government, into whatsoever hands it is put, being, as I have before showed, intrusted with this condition, and for this end, that men might have and secure their properties; the prince, or senate, however it may have power to make laws, for the regulating of property between the subjects one amongst another, yet can never have a power to take to themselves the whole, or any part of the subject's property, without their own consent: for this would be in effect to leave them no property at all. And to let us see, that even absolute power where it is necessary, is not arbitrary by being absolute, but is still limited by that reason, and confined to those ends, which required it in some cases to be absolute, we need look no farther than the common practice of martial discipline: for the preservation of the army, and in it of the whole commonwealth, requires an absolute obedience to the command of every superior officer, and it is justly death to disobey or dispute the most dangerous or unreasonable of them; but yet we see, that neither the sergeant, that could command a soldier to march up to the mouth of a cannon, or stand in a breach, where he is almost sure to perish, can command that soldier to give him one penny of his money; nor the general, that can condemn him to death for deserting his post, or for not obeying the most desperate orders, can yet, with all his absolute power of life and death, dispose of one farthing of that soldier's estate, or seize one jot of his goods; whom yet he can command any thing, and hang for the least disobedience: because such a blind obedience is necessary to that end, for which the commander has his power, viz. the preservation of the rest; but the disposing of his goods has nothing to do with it.

140.     It is true, governments cannot be supported without great charge, and it is fit every one who enjoys his share of the protection, should pay out of his estate his proportion for the maintenance of it. But still it must be with his own consent, i.e. the consent of the majority, giving it either by themselves, or their representatives chosen by them: for if any one shall

claim a power to lay and levy taxes on the people, by his own authority, and without such consent of the people, he thereby invades the fundamental law of property, and subverts the end of government: for what property have I in that, which another may by right take when he pleases, to himself?

141.　Fourthly, The legislative cannot transfer the power of making laws to any other hands: for it being but a delegated power from the people, they who have it cannot pass it over to others. The people alone can appoint the form of the commonwealth, which is by constituting the legislative, and appointing in whose hands that shall be. And when the people have said, we will submit to rules, and be governed by laws made by such men, and in such forms, nobody else can say other men shall make laws for them; nor can the people be bound by any laws, but such as are enacted by those whom they have chosen, and authorized to make laws for them. The power of the legislative being derived from the people by a positive voluntary grant and institution, can be no other than what that positive grant conveyed, which being only to make laws, and not to make legislators, the legislative can have no power to transfer their authority of making laws and place it in other hands.

142.　These are the bounds which the trust, that is put in them by the society and the law of God and nature, have set to the legislative power of every commonwealth, in all forms of government.

First, They are to govern by promulgated established laws, not to be varied in particular cases, but to have one rule for rich and poor, for the favourite at court, and the countryman at plough.

Secondly, These laws also ought to be designed for no other end ultimately, but the good of the people.

Thirdly, They must not raise taxes on the property of the people, without the consent of the people, given by themselves or their deputies. And this properly concerns only such governments where the legislative is always in being, or at least where the people have not reserved any part of the legislative to deputies, to be from time to time chosen by themselves.

Fourthly, The legislative neither must nor can transfer the power of making laws to any body else, or place it any where, but where the people have.

## CHAPTER XIX: OF THE DISSOLUTION OF GOVERNMENT

211.　He that will with any clearness speak of the dissolution of government, ought in the first place to distinguish between the dissolution of the society and the dissolution of the government. That which makes the community, and brings men out of the loose state of nature into one politic society, is the agreement which everyone has with the rest to incorporate, and act as one body, and so be one distinct commonwealth. The usual, and almost only way whereby this union is dissolved, is the inroad of foreign force making a conquest upon them; for in that case, (not being able to maintain and support themselves, as one entire and independent body) the union belonging to that body which consisted therein, must necessarily cease, and so everyone return to the state he was in before, with a liberty to shift for himself, and provide for his own safety, as he thinks fit, in some other society. Whenever the society is dissolved, it is certain the government of that society cannot remain. Thus conquerors' swords often cut up governments by the roots, and mangle societies to pieces, separating the subdued or scattered multitude from the protection of, and dependence on, that society which ought to have preserved them from violence. The world is too well instructed in, and too forward to allow of, this way of dissolving of governments, to need any more to be said of it; and there wants not much argument to prove, that where the society is dissolved, the government cannot remain; that being as impossible, as for the frame of a house to subsist when the materials of it are scattered and dissipated by a whirlwind, or jumbled into a confused heap by an earthquake.

212.    Besides this overturning from without, governments are dissolved from within.

First, When the legislative is altered. Civil society being a state of peace, amongst those who are of it, from whom the state of war is excluded by the umpirage, which they have provided in their legislative, for the ending all differences that may arise amongst any of them; it is in their legislative, that the members of a commonwealth are united, and combined together into one coherent living body. This is the soul that gives form, life, and unity to the commonwealth: from hence the several members have their mutual influence, sympathy, and connexion; and, therefore, when the legislative is broken, or dissolved, dissolution and death follows: for, the essence and union of the society consisting in having one will, the legislative, when once established by the majority, has the declaring, and as it were keeping of that will. The constitution of the legislative is the first and fundamental act of society, whereby provision is made for the continuation of their union under the direction of persons, and bonds of laws, made by persons authorized thereunto, by the consent and appointment of the people; without which no one man, or number of men, amongst them, can have authority of making laws that shall be binding to the rest. When any one, or more, shall take upon them to make laws, whom the people have not appointed so to do, they make laws without authority, which the people are not therefore bound to obey; by which means they come again to be out of subjection, and may constitute to themselves a new legislative, as they think best, being in full liberty to resist the force of those, who without authority would impose anything upon them. Every one is at the disposure of his own will, when those who had, by the delegation of the society the declaring of the public will, are excluded from it, and others usurp the place, who have no such authority or delegation . . . .

219.    There is one way more whereby such a government may be dissolved, and that is, when he who has the supreme executive power neglects and abandons that charge, so that the laws already made can no longer be put in execution. This is demonstratively to reduce all to anarchy, and so effectually to dissolve the government: for laws not being made for themselves, but to be, by their execution, the bonds of the society, to keep every part of the body politic in its due place and function; when that totally ceases, the government visibly ceases, and the people become a confused multitude, without order or connexion. Where there is no longer the administration of justice, for the securing of men's rights, nor any remaining power within the community to direct the force, or provide for the necessities of the public; there certainly is no government left. Where the laws cannot be executed, it is all one as if there were no laws; and a government without laws is, I suppose, a mystery in politics, inconceivable to human capacity, and inconsistent with human society.

220.    In these and the like cases, when the government is dissolved, the people are at liberty to provide for themselves, by erecting a new legislative, differing from the other, by the change of persons, or form, or both, as they shall find it most for their safety and good: for the society can never, by the fault of another, lose the native and original right it has to preserve itself; which can only be done by a settled legislative, and a fair and impartial execution of the laws made by it. But the state of mankind is not so miserable that they are not capable of using this remedy, till it be too late to look for any. To tell people they may provide for themselves, by erecting a new legislative, when by oppression, artifice, or being delivered over to a foreign power, their old one is gone, is only to tell them, they may expect relief when it is too late, and the evil is past cure. This is in effect no more than to bid them first be slaves, and then to take care of their liberty; and when their chains are on, tell them, they may act like freemen. This, if barely so, is rather mockery than relief; and men can never be secure from tyranny, if there be no means to escape it till they are perfectly under it: and therefore it is that they have not only a right to get out of it, but to prevent it.

221.    There is, therefore, secondly, another way whereby governments are dissolved, and that is, when the legislative, or the prince, either of them, act contrary to their trust.

First, the legislative acts against the trust reposed in them, when they endeavour to invade the property of the subject, and to make themselves, or any part of the community, masters, or arbitrary disposers of the lives, liberties, or fortunes of the people.

222.    The reason why men enter into society, is the preservation of their property; and the end why they choose and authorize a legislative, is, that there may be laws made, and rules set, as guards and fences to the properties of all the members of the society: to limit the power, and moderate the dominion, of every part and member of the society: for since it can never be supposed to be the will of the society, that the legislative should have a power to destroy that which every one designs to secure by entering into society, and for which the people submitted themselves to legislators of their own making; whenever the legislators endeavour to take away and destroy the property of the people, or to reduce them to slavery under arbitrary power, they put themselves into a state of war with the people, who are thereupon absolved from any farther obedience, and are left to the common refuge, which God hath provided for all men, against force and violence. Whensoever therefore the legislative shall transgress this fundamental rule of society; and either by ambition, fear, folly or corruption, endeavour to grasp themselves, or put into the hands of any other, an absolute power over the lives, liberties, and estates of the people; by this breach of trust they forfeit the power the people had put into their hands for quite contrary ends, and it devolves to the people, who have a right to resume their original liberty, and, by the establishment of a new legislative, (such as they shall think fit) provide for their own safety and security, which is the end for which they are in society. What I have said here, concerning the legislative in general, holds true also concerning the supreme executor, who having a double trust put in him, both to have a part in the legislative, and the supreme execution of the law, acts against both, when he goes about to set up his own arbitrary will as the law of the society . . . one cannot but see, that he, who has once attempted any such thing as this, cannot any longer be trusted.

223.    To this perhaps it will be said, that the people being ignorant, and always discontented, to lay the foundation of government in the unsteady opinion and uncertain humour of the people, is to expose it to certain ruin; and no government will be able long to subsist, if the people may set up a new legislative, whenever they take offence at the old one. To this I answer, quite the contrary. People are not so easily got out of their old forms as some are apt to suggest. They are hardly to be prevailed with to amend the acknowledged faults in the frame they have been accustomed to. And if there be any original defects, or adventitious ones introduced by time, or corruption: it is not an easy thing to get them changed, even when all the world sees there is an opportunity for it. This slowness and aversion in the people to quit their old constitutions, has in the many revolutions which have been seen in this kingdom, in this and former ages, still kept us to, or, after some interval of fruitless attempts, still brought us back again to, our old legislative of king, lords, and commons: and whatever provocations have made the crown be taken from some of our princes' heads, they never carried the people so far as to place it in another line.

224.    But it will be said, this hypothesis lays a ferment for frequent rebellion. To which I answer,

First, no more than any other hypothesis: for when the people are made miserable, and find themselves exposed to the ill-usage of arbitrary power, cry up their governors as much as you will, for sons of Jupiter; let them be sacred or divine, descended, or authorized from heaven; give them out for whom or what you please, the same will happen. The people generally ill-treated, and contrary to right, will be ready upon any occasion to ease themselves of a burden that sits heavy upon them. They will wish, and seek for the opportunity, which in the change, weakness, and accidents of human affairs, seldom delays long to offer itself. He must have lived but a little while in the world, who has not seen examples of this in his time; and he must have read very little, who cannot produce examples of it in all sorts of governments in the world.

225. Secondly, I answer, such revolutions happen not upon every little mismanagement in public affairs. Great mistakes in the ruling part, many wrong and inconvenient laws, and all the slips of human frailty, will be borne by the people without mutiny or murmur. But if a long train of abuses, prevarications and artifices, all tending the same way, make the design visible to the people, and they cannot but feel what they lie under, and see whither they are going; it is not to be wondered that they should then rouse themselves, and endeavour to put the rule into such hands which may secure to them the ends for which government was at first erected; and without which, ancient names, and specious forms, are so far from being better, that they are much worse, than the state of nature, or pure anarchy . . .

240. Here, it is like, the common question will be made: "Who shall be judge, whether the prince or legislative act contrary to their trust?" This, perhaps, ill-affected and factious men may spread amongst the people, when the prince only makes use of his due prerogative. To this I reply, "The people shall be judge;" for who shall be judge whether his trustee or deputy acts well, and according to the trust reposed in him, but he who deputes him, and must by having deputed him, have still a power to discard him, when he fails in his trust? If this be reasonable in particular cases of private men, why should it be otherwise in that of the greatest moment, where the welfare of millions is concerned, and also where the evil, if not prevented, is greater, and the redress very difficult, dear, and dangerous?

241. But farther, this question, ("Who shall be judge?") cannot mean that there is no judge at all: for where there is no judicature on earth, to decide controversies amongst men, God in heaven is judge. He alone, it is true, is judge of the right. But every man is judge for himself, as in all other cases, so in this, whether another hath put himself into a state of war with him, and whether he should appeal to the supreme judge, as Jephthah did. . . .

243. To conclude, The power that every individual gave the society, when he entered into it, can never revert to the individuals again, as long as the society lasts, but will always remain in the community; because without this there can be no community, no commonwealth, which is contrary to the original agreement: so also when the society hath placed the legislative in any assembly of men, to continue in them and their successors, with direction and authority for providing such successors, the legislative can never revert to the people whilst that government lasts; because, having provided a legislative with power to continue for ever, they have given up their political power to the legislative, and cannot resume it. But if they have set limits to the duration of their legislative, and made this supreme power in any person, or assembly, only temporary; or else, when by the miscarriages of those in authority, it is forfeited; upon the forfeiture, or at the determination of the time set, it reverts to the society, and the people have a right to act as supreme, and continue the legislative in themselves; or erect a new form, or under the old form place it in new hands, as they think good.

# The Declaration of Independence

## Thomas Jefferson (1743–1826)

*Battles raged between patriot militias and British and loyalist troops throughout the American colonies in 1775 and 1776. On June 11, 1776, the Continental Congress appointed a committee to compose a document declaring the colonies' independence from Britain. Thomas Jefferson was chosen to write the first draft. In a letter to Henry Lee in 1825, he described the composition of the document: "Neither aiming at originality of principle or sentiment, nor yet copied from any particular and previous writing, it was intended to be an expression of the American mind, and to give to that expression the proper tone and spirit called for by the occasion. All its authority rests then on the harmonizing sentiments of the day, whether expressed in conversation, in letters, printed essays, or in the elementary books of public right, as Aristotle, Cicero, Locke, Sidney, etc." The Declaration is reproduced here as it reads in the parchment original.*

*Consider the difference between a manifesto for a massive political movement and a work of political theory. In substance and in form, how does the Declaration resemble, and how does it differ from, Aristotle's treatise or Locke's essay? To what degree does the Declaration of Independence still represent what the United States of America stands for? How would Jefferson have to alter the text, if at all, to have it pass today's Congress?*

## THE UNANIMOUS DECLARATION OF THE THIRTEEN UNITED STATES OF AMERICA

When in the Course of human events, it becomes necessary for one people to dissolve the political bands, which have connected them with another, and to assume among the powers of the earth, the separate and equal station to which the Laws of Nature and of Nature's God entitle them, a decent respect to the opinions of mankind requires that they should declare the causes which impel them to the separation.—We hold these truths to be self-evident, that all men are created equal, that they are endowed by their Creator with certain unalienable Rights, that among these are Life, Liberty and the pursuit of Happiness.—That to secure these rights, Governments are instituted among Men, deriving their just powers from the consent of the governed,—That whenever any Form of Government becomes destructive of these ends, it is the right of the People to alter or to abolish it, and to institute new Government, laying its foundation on such principles and organizing its powers in such form, as to them shall seem most likely to effect their Safety and Happiness. Prudence, indeed, will dictate that Governments long established should not be changed for light and transient causes; and accordingly all experience hath shewn, that mankind are more disposed to suffer, while evils are sufferable, than to right themselves by abolishing the forms to which they are accustomed. But when a long train of abuses and usurpations, pursuing invariably the same Object evinces a design to reduce them under absolute Despotism, it is their right, it is their duty, to throw off such Government, and to provide new Guards for their future security.—Such has been the patient sufferance of these Colonies; and such is now the necessity which constrains them to alter their former System of Government. The history of the present King of Great Britain is a history of repeated injuries and usurpations, all having in direct object the establishment of an absolute Tyranny over these States. To prove this, let Facts be submitted to a candid world.—He has refused his Assent to Laws, the most wholesome and necessary for the public good.—He has forbidden his Governors to pass Laws of immediate and pressing importance, unless suspended in their operation till his Assent should be obtained; and when so suspended, he has utterly neglected to attend to them.—He has refused to pass other Laws for the accommodation of large districts of people, unless those people would relinquish the right of Representation in the Legislature, a right inestimable to them and formidable to tyrants only.—He has called together legislative bodies at places unusual, uncomfortable, and distant from the depository of their public Records, for the sole purpose of fatiguing them into compliance with his measures.—He has dissolved Representative Houses repeatedly, for opposing with manly firmness his invasions on the rights of the people.—He has refused for a long time, after such dissolutions, to cause others to be elected; whereby the Legislative powers, incapable of Annihilation, have returned to the People at large for their exercise; the State remaining in the meantime exposed to all the dangers of invasion from without, and convulsions within.—He has endeavoured to prevent the population of these States; for that purpose obstructing the Laws for Naturalization of Foreigners; refusing to pass others to encourage their migrations hither, and raising the conditions of new Appropriations of Lands.—He has obstructed the Administration of Justice, by refusing his Assent to Laws for establishing Judiciary powers.—He has made Judges dependent on his Will alone, for the tenure of their offices, and the amount and payment of their salaries.—He has erected a multitude of New Offices, and sent higher swarms of Officers to harass our people, and eat out their substance.—He has kept among us, in times of peace, Standing Armies without the Consent of our legislatures.—He has affected to render the Military independent of and superior to the Civil power.—He has combined with others to subject us to a jurisdiction foreign to our constitution, and unacknowledged by our laws; giving his Assent to their Acts of pretended Legislation.—For quartering large bodies of armed troops among us:—For protecting them, by a mock Trial, from punishment for any Murders which they should commit on the Inhabitants of these States:—For cutting off our Trade with all parts of the world:—For imposing Taxes on us without our Consent:—For depriving us in many cases, of the benefits of Trial by Jury:—For transporting us beyond Seas to be tried for pretended offenses:—For abolishing the free System of English Laws in a neighboring Province, establishing therein an Arbitrary government, and enlarging its Boundaries so as to render it at once an example and fit instrument for introducing the same absolute rule into these Colonies:—For taking away our Charters, abolishing our most valuable Laws, and altering fundamentally the Forms of our Governments:—for suspending our own Legislatures, and declaring themselves invested with power to legislate for us in all cases whatsoever,—He has abdicated Government here, by declaring us out of his Protection and waging War against us.—He has plundered our seas, ravaged our Coasts, burnt our towns, and destroyed the lives of our people.—He is at this time transporting large Armies of foreign Mercenaries to compleat the works of death, desolation and tyranny, already begun with circumstances of Cruelty & perfidy, scarcely paralleled in the most barbarous ages, and totally unworthy the Head of a civilized nation.—He has constrained our fellow Citizens taken Captive on the high Seas to bear Arms against their Country, to become the executioners of their friends and Brethren, or to fall themselves by their hands.—He has excited domestic insurrections amongst us, and has endeavoured to bring on the inhabitants of our frontiers, the merciless Indian Savages, whose known rule of warfare, is an undistinguished destruction of all ages, sexes and conditions. In every stage of these Oppressions We have Petitioned for Redress in the most humble terms: Our repeated Petitions have been answered only by repeated injury. A Prince whose character is thus marked by every act which may define a Tyrant, is unfit to be the ruler of a free people. Nor have We been wanting in attentions to our British brethren. We have warned them from time to time of attempts by their legislature to extend an unwarrantable jurisdiction over us. We have reminded them of the circumstances of our emigration and settlement here. We have appealed to their native justice and magnanimity, and we have conjured them by the ties of our common kindred to disavow these usurpations, which would inevitably interrupt our connections and correspondence. They too have been deaf to the voice of justice and of consanguinity. We must, therefore, acquiesce in the necessity, which denounces our Separation, and hold them, as we hold the rest of mankind, Enemies in War, in Peace Friends.—

We, therefore, the Representatives of the united States of America, in General Congress, Assembled, appealing to the Supreme Judge of the world for the rectitude of our intentions do, in the Name, and by the Authority of the good People of these Colonies, solemnly publish and declare, That these United Colonies are, and of Right ought to be Free and Independent States; that they are Absolved from all Allegiance to the British Crown, and that all political connection between them and the State of Great Britain, is and ought to be totally dissolved; and that as Free and Independent States, they have full Power to levy War, conclude Peace, contract Alliances, establish Commerce, and to do all other Acts and Things which Independent States may of right do.—And for the support of this Declaration, with a firm reliance on the protection of divine Providence, we mutually pledge to each other our Lives, our Fortunes and our sacred Honor.

*The Declaration of Independence was altered by Jefferson after consultation with John Adams and Benjamin Franklin, and by the Continental Congress before approval. In the following excerpts, the words lined out in parentheses and replaced in italics were suggested by Adams and Franklin; the bracketed words were removed and the underscored words added by Congress.*

When in the course of human events it becomes necessary for (a) *one* people to (advance from that subordination in which they have hitherto remained,& to) *dissolve the political bands which have connected them with another, and to* assume among the powers of the earth the (equal & independent) *separate and equal* station to which the laws of nature and of nature's god entitle them, a decent respect to the opinions of mankind requires that they should declare the causes which impel them to (the change) *the separation.*

We hold these truths to be (sacred & undeniable) *self-evident;* that all men are created equal (& independent;) that (from that equal creation they derive in rights) *they are endowed by their creator with* (equal rights, some of which are) certain [inherent &] inalienable *rights; that* among (which) *these* are (the preservation of) life, liberty, & the pursuit of happiness; that to secure these (ends) *rights* governments are instituted among men, deriving their just powers from the consent of the governed; that whenever any form of government (shall) becomes destructive of these ends, it is the right of the people to alter or abolish it . . .

[King George III] has refused his assent to laws the most wholesome and necessary for the public good: . . .

he has dissolved Representative houses repeatedly [& continually], for opposing with manly firmness his invasions on the rights of the people: . . .

he has [suffered] obstructed the administration of justice [totally to cease in some of these (colonies) states] . . .

he has made [our] judges dependent on his will alone . . .

he has kept among us in times of peace standing armies [& ships of war] *without the consent of our legislatures:*

he has combined with others to subject us to a jurisdiction foreign to our constitutions and unacknowledged by our laws; giving his assent to their *acts of* pretended (acts of) legislation . . .

for cutting off our trade with all parts of the world; for imposing taxes on us without our consent; for depriving us <u>in many cases</u> of the benefits of trial by jury . . .

[He has waged cruel war against human nature itself, violating its most sacred rights of life and liberty in the persons of a distant people who never offended him, captivating and carrying them into slavery in another hemisphere, or to incur miserable death in their transportation hither. This piratical warfare, the opprobrium of INFIDEL powers, is the warfare of the CHRISTIAN king of Great Britain. Determined to keep open a market where MEN should be bought and sold, he has prostituted his negative for suppressing every legislative attempt to prohibit or to restrain this execrable commerce. And that this assemblage of horrors might want no fact of distinguished die, he is now exciting those very people to rise in arms among us, and to purchase that liberty of which he has deprived them, by murdering the people on whom he also obtruded them: thus paying off former crimes committed against the LIBERTIES of one people, with crimes which he urges them to commit against the LIVES of another.] . . .

We therefore the representatives of the United states of America in General Congress assembled <u>appealing to the supreme judge of the world for the rectitude of our intentions</u>, do, in the name & by authority of the good people of these [states, reject & renounce all allegiance & subjection to the kings of Great Britain . . . & finally we do assert & declare these colonies to be free & independent states,] <u>colonies, solemnly publish and declare, that these United colonies are, and of right ought to be, free & independent states; that they are absolved from all allegiance to the British crown</u> & that as free & independent states they (shall hereafter) have *full* power to levy war, conclude peace, contract alliances, establish commerce, & to do all other acts and things which independent states may of right do. And for the support of this declaration, <u>with firm reliance on the protection of divine providence,</u> we mutually pledge to each other our lives, our fortunes & our sacred honour.

# Selections from *The Federalist*

## James Madison (1751–1836)
## Alexander Hamilton (ca. 1757–1804)
## John Jay (1745–1829)

*The 85* Federalist *papers were published pseudonymously in 1787-1788 in the New York press, and were designed to encourage the ratification of the new Constitution by the people of New York. Madison participated in political activities during the Revolution and became such an influential member of the Philadelphia Convention that he is often called the Father of the Constitution. As a member of the first House of Representatives, he led in the framing of the Bill of Rights, and later served as Secretary of State under Jefferson and as President. Hamilton served on Washington's staff and as a regimental commander during the Revolution, and became the first Secretary of the Treasury under Washington. Though he was not present at the Constitutional Convention, Jay was a prominent lawyer active in foreign affairs during and after the Revolution. He helped to conclude the peace with England, and became the first Chief Justice of the Supreme Court.*

*Like the Declaration of Independence, this series of essays waxes rhetorical in its attempt to influence political actions, but, because Madison and Hamilton were present at the Constitutional Convention, it also has served to instruct the nation in the meaning of the document and the intentions of the men who framed it. The two* Federalist *numbers reproduced here address crucial problems the founders of the new American government faced: Number 10, the danger that a free society will break up into a few warring groups or will be taken over by a selfish, unwise majority; Number 51, the danger that "parchment barriers" cannot sufficiently guard against the government's consolidation into a large tyrannical power to oppress the people. Consider the means the Constitution employs to combat these dangers. Again, as in studying Plutarch, Aristotle, and Locke, we are brought back to the essential nature of man. How much is human nature to be trusted? Is it a force for good or evil, or perhaps both?*

## THE FEDERALIST NO. 10

To the People of the State of New York:

Among the numerous advantages promised by a well-constructed Union, none deserves to be more accurately developed than its tendency to break and control the violence of faction. The friend of popular governments never finds himself so much alarmed for their character and fate as when he contemplates their propensity to this dangerous vice. He will not fail, therefore, to set a due value on any plan which, without violating the principles to which he is attached, provides a proper cure for it. The instability, injustice, and confusion introduced into the public councils, have, in truth, been the mortal diseases under which popular governments have everywhere perished; as they continue to be the favorite and fruitful topics from which the adversaries to liberty derive their most specious declamations. The valuable improvements made by the American constitutions on the popular models both ancient and modern, cannot certainly be too much admired; but it would be an unwarrantable partiality to contend that they have as effectually obviated the danger on this side as was wished and expected. Complaints are everywhere heard from our most considerate and virtuous citizens, equally the friends of public and private faith, and of public and personal liberty, that our governments are too unstable, that the public good is disregarded in the conflicts of rival parties, and that measures are too often decided, not according to the rules of justice and the rights of the minor party, but by the superior force of an interested and overbearing majority. However anxiously we may wish that these complaints had no foundation, the evidence of known facts will not permit us to deny that they are in some degree true. It will be found, indeed, on a candid review of our situation, that some of the distresses under which we labor have been erroneously charged on the operation of our governments; but it will be found, at the same time, that other causes will not alone account for many of our heaviest misfortunes; and, particularly, for that prevailing and increasing distrust of public engagements, and alarm for private rights, which are echoed from one end of the continent to the other. These must be chiefly, if not wholly, effects of the unsteadiness and injustice with which a factious spirit has tainted our public administrations.

By a faction, I understand a number of citizens, whether amounting to a majority or minority of the whole, who are united and actuated by some common impulse of passion, or of interest, adverse to the rights of other citizens, or to the permanent and aggregate interests of the community.

There are two methods of curing the mischiefs of faction: the one, by removing its causes; the other, by controlling its effects.

There are again two methods of removing the causes of faction: the one, by destroying the liberty which is essential to its existence; the other, by giving to every citizen the same opinions, the same passions, and the same interests.

It could never be more truly said than of the first remedy, that it was worse than the disease. Liberty is to faction what air is to fire, an aliment without which it instantly expires. But it could not be less folly to abolish liberty, which is essential to political life because it nourishes faction, than it would be to wish the annihilation of air, which is essential to animal life, because it imparts to fire its destructive agency.

The second expedient is as impracticable as the first would be unwise. As long as the reason of man continues fallible, and he is at liberty to exercise it, different opinions will be formed. As long as the connection subsists between his reason and his self-love, his opinions and his passions will have a reciprocal influence on each other; and the former will be objects to which the latter will attach themselves. The diversity in the faculties of men, from which the rights of property originate, is not less an insuperable obstacle to a uniformity of interests. The protection of these faculties is the first object of government. From the protection of different and unequal faculties of acquiring property, the possession of different degrees and kinds of property immediately results; and from the influence of these on the sentiments and views of the respective proprietors, ensues a division of the society into different interests and parties.

The latent causes of faction are thus sown in the nature of man; and we see them everywhere brought into different degrees of activity, according to the different circumstances of civil society. A zeal for different opinions concerning religion, concerning government, and many other points, as well of speculation as of practice; an attachment to different leaders ambitiously contending for pre-eminence and power; or to persons of other descriptions whose fortunes have been inter-esting to the human passions, have, in turn, divided mankind into parties, inflamed them with mutual animosity, and rendered them much more disposed to vex and oppress each other than to co-operate for their common good. So strong is this propensity of mankind to fall into mutual animosities that, where no substantial occasion presents itself, the most frivolous and fanciful distinctions have been sufficient to kindle their unfriendly passions and excite their most violent conflicts. But the most common and durable source of factions has been the various and unequal distribution of property. Those who hold and those who are without property have ever formed distinct interests in society. Those who are creditors, and those who are debtors, fall under a like discrimination. A landed interest, a manufacturing interest, a mercantile interest, a moneyed interest, with many lesser interests, grow up of necessity in civilized nations, and divide them into different classes actuated by different sentiments and views. The regulation of these various and interfering interests forms the principal task of modern legislation, and involves the spirit of party and faction in the necessary and ordinary operations of the government.

No man is allowed to be a judge in his own cause, because his interest would certainly bias his judgment and, not improbably, corrupt his integrity. With equal, nay with greater reason, a body of men are unfit to be both judges and parties at the same time; yet what are many of the most important acts of legislation, but so many judicial determinations, not indeed concerning the rights of single persons, but concerning the rights of large bodies of citizens? And what are the different classes of legislators but advocates and parties to the causes which they determine? Is a law proposed concerning private debts? It is a question to which the creditors are parties on one side and the debtors on the other. Justice ought to hold the balance between them. Yet the parties are, and must be, themselves the judges; and the most numerous party, or, in other words, the most powerful faction, must be expected to prevail. Shall domestic manufactures be encouraged, and in what degree, by restrictions on foreign manufactures? are questions which would be differently decided by the landed and the manufacturing classes, and probably by neither with a sole regard to justice and the public good. The apportionment of taxes on the various descriptions of property is an act which seems to require the most exact impartiality; yet there is, perhaps, no legislative act in which greater opportunity and temptation are given to a predominant party to trample on the rules of justice. Every shilling with which they overburden the inferior number, is a shilling saved to their own pockets.

It is in vain to say that enlightened statesmen will be able to adjust these clashing interests, and render them all subservient to the public good. Enlightened statesmen will not always be at the helm. Nor in many cases can such an adjustment be made at all without taking into view indirect and remote considerations, which will rarely prevail over the immediate interest which one party may find in disregarding the rights of another or the good of the whole.

The inference to which we are brought is that the *causes* of faction cannot be removed, and that relief is only to be sought in the means of controlling its *effects*.

If a faction consists of less than a majority, relief is supplied by the republican principle, which enables the majority to defeat its sinister views by regular vote. It may clog the administration, it may convulse the society; but it will be unable to execute and mask its violence under the forms of the Constitution. When a majority is included in a faction, the form of popular government, on the other hand, enables it to sacrifice to its ruling passion or interest both the public good and the rights of other citizens. To secure the public good and private rights against the danger of such a faction, and at the same time to preserve the spirit and the form of popular government, is then the great object to which our inquiries are directed. Let me add that it is the great desideratum by which this form of government can be rescued from the opprobrium under which it has so long labored, and be recommended to the esteem and adoption of mankind.

By what means is this object attainable? Evidently by one of two only: Either the existence of the same passion or interest in a majority at the same time must be prevented, or the majority, having such coexistent passion or interest, must be rendered, by their number and local situation, unable to concert and carry into effect schemes of oppression. If the impulse and the opportunity be suffered to coincide, we well know that neither moral nor religious motives can be relied on as an adequate control. They are not found to be such on the injustice and violence of individuals, and lose their efficacy in proportion to the number combined together, that is, in proportion as their efficacy becomes needful.

From this view of the subject it may be concluded that a pure democracy, by which I mean a society consisting of a small number of citizens, who assemble and administer the government in person, can admit of no cure for the mischiefs of faction. A common passion or interest will, in almost every case, be felt by a majority of the whole; a communication and concert result from the form of government itself; and there is nothing to check the inducements to sacrifice the weaker party or an obnoxious individual. Hence it is that such democracies have ever been spectacles of turbulence and contention; have ever been found incompatible with personal security or the rights of property; and have in general been as short in their lives as they have been violent in their deaths. Theoretic politicians, who have patronized this species of government, have erroneously supposed that by reducing mankind to a perfect equality in their political rights, they would, at the same time, be perfectly equalized and assimilated in their possessions, their opinions, and their passions.

A republic, by which I mean a government in which the scheme of representation takes place, opens a different prospect, and promises the cure for which we are seeking. Let us examine the points in which it varies from pure democracy, and we shall comprehend both the nature of the cure and the efficacy which it must derive from the Union.

The two great points of difference between a democracy and a republic are: first, the delegation of the government, in the latter, to a small number of citizens elected by the rest; secondly, the greater number of citizens, and greater sphere of country, over which the latter may be extended.

The effect of the first difference is, on the one hand, to refine and enlarge the public views, by passing them through the medium of a chosen body of citizens, whose wisdom may best discern the true interest of their country, and whose patriotism and love of justice will be least likely to sacrifice it to temporary or partial considerations. Under such a regulation, it may well happen that the public voice, pronounced by the representatives of the people, will be more consonant to the public good than if pronounced by the people themselves, convened for the purpose. On the other hand, the effect may be inverted. Men of factious tempers, of local prejudices, or of sinister designs, may, by intrigue, by corruption, or by other means, first obtain the suffrages, and then betray the interests, of the people. The question resulting is, whether small or extensive republics are more favorable to the election of proper guardians of the public weal; and it is clearly decided in favor of the latter by two obvious considerations:

In the first place, it is to be remarked that, however small the republic may be, the representatives must be raised to a certain number, in order to guard against the cabals of a few; and that, however large it may be, they must be limited to a certain number, in order to guard against the confusion of a multitude. Hence, the number of representatives in the two cases not being in proportion to that of the two constituents, and being proportionally greater in the small republic, it follows that, if the proportion of fit characters be not less in the large than in the small republic, the former will present a greater option, and consequently a greater probability of a fit choice.

In the next place, as each representative will be chosen by a greater number of citizens in the large than in the small republic, it will be more difficult for unworthy candidates to practice with success the vicious arts by which elections are too often carried; and the suffrages of the people being more free, will be more likely to center in men who possess the most attractive merit and the most diffusive and established characters.

It must be confessed that in this, as in most other cases, there is a mean, on both sides of which inconveniences will be found to lie. By enlarging too much the number of electors, you render the representative too little acquainted with all their local circumstances and lesser interests; as by reducing it too much, you render him unduly attached to these, and too little fit to comprehend and pursue great and national objects. The Federal Constitution forms a happy combination in this respect; the great and aggregate interests being referred to the national, the local and particular to the State legislatures.

The other point of difference is, the greater number of citizens and extent of territory which may be brought within the compass of republican than of democratic government; and it is this circumstance principally which renders factious combinations less to be dreaded in the former than in the latter. The smaller the society, the fewer probably will be the distinct parties and interests composing it; the fewer the distinct parties and interests, the more frequently will a majority be found of the same party; and the smaller the number of individuals composing a majority, and the smaller the compass within which they are placed, the more easily will they concert and execute their plans of oppression. Extend the sphere, and you take in a greater variety of parties and interests; you make it less probable that a majority of the whole will have a common motive to invade the rights of other citizens; or, if such a common motive exists, it will be more difficult for all who feel it to discover their own strength and to act in unison with each other. Besides other impediments, it may be remarked that where there is a consciousness of unjust or dishonorable purposes, communication is always checked by distrust in proportion to the number whose concurrence is necessary.

Hence it clearly appears that the same advantage which a republic has over a democracy, in controlling the effects of faction, is enjoyed by a large over a small republic—is enjoyed by the Union over the States composing it. Does the advantage consist in the substitution of representatives whose enlightened views and virtuous sentiments render them superior to local prejudices and to schemes of injustice? It will not be denied that the representation of the Union will be most likely to possess these requisite endowments. Does it consist in the greater security afforded by a greater variety of parties against the event of any one party being able to outnumber and oppress the rest? In an equal degree does the increased variety of parties comprised within the Union increase this security? Does it, in fine, consist in the greater obstacles opposed to the concert and accomplishment of the secret wishes of an unjust and interested majority? Here, again, the extent of the union gives it the most palpable advantage.

The influence of factious leaders may kindle a flame within their particular States, but will be unable to spread a general conflagration through the other States. A religious sect may degenerate into a political faction in a part of the Confederacy; but the variety of sects dispersed over the entire face of it must secure the national councils against any danger from that source. A rage for paper money, for an abolition of debts, for an equal division of property, or for any other improper or wicked project, will be less apt to pervade the whole body of the Union than a particular member of it; in the same proportion as such a malady is more likely to taint a particular county or district than an entire State.

In the extent and proper structure of the Union, therefore, we behold a republican remedy for the diseases most incident to republican government. And according to the degree of pleasure and pride we feel in being republicans ought to be our zeal in cherishing the spirit and supporting the character of Federalists.

PUBLIUS.

## THE FEDERALIST NO. 51

To the People of the State of New York:

To what expedient, then, shall we finally resort, for maintaining in practice the necessary partition of power among the several departments, as laid down in the Constitution? The only answer that can be given is, that as all these exterior provisions are found to be inadequate, the defect must be supplied, by so contriving the interior structure of the government as that its several constituent parts may, by their mutual relations, be the means of keeping each other in their proper places. Without presuming to undertake a full development of this important idea, I will hazard a few general observations, which may perhaps place it in a clearer light and enable us to form a more correct judgment of the principles and structure of the government planned by the Convention.

In order to lay a due foundation for that separate and distinct exercise of the different powers of government, which to a certain extent is admitted on all hands to be essential to the preservation of liberty, it is evident that each department should have a will of its own, and consequently should be so constituted that the members of each should have as little agency as possible in the appointment of the members of the others. Were this principle rigorously adhered to, it would require that all the appointments for the supreme executive, legislative, and judiciary magistracies should be drawn from the same fountain of authority, the people, through channels having no communication whatever with one another. Perhaps such a plan of constructing the several departments would be less difficult in practice than it may in contemplation appear. Some difficulties, however, and some additional expense would attend the execution of it. Some deviations, therefore, from the principle must be admitted. In the constitution of the judiciary department in particular, it might be inexpedient to insist rigorously on the principle: First, because peculiar qualifications being essential in the members, the primary consideration ought to be to select that mode of choice which best secures these qualifications; secondly, because the permanent tenure by which the appointments are held in that department, must soon destroy all sense of dependence on the authority conferring them.

It is equally evident that the members of each department should be as little dependent as possible on those of the others for the emoluments annexed to their offices. Were the executive magistrate, or the judges, not independent of the legislature in this particular, their independence in every other would be merely nominal.

But the great security against a gradual concentration of the several powers in the same department consists in giving to those who administer each department the necessary constitutional means and personal motives to resist encroachments of the others. The provision for defense must in this, as in all other cases, be made commensurate to the danger of attack. Ambition must be made to counteract ambition. The interest of the man must be connected with the constitutional rights of the place. It may be a reflection on human nature that such devices should be necessary to control the abuses of government. But what is government itself, but the greatest of all reflections on human nature? If men were angels, no government would be necessary. If angels were to govern men, neither external nor internal controls on government would be necessary. In framing a government which is to be administered by men over men, the great difficulty lies in this: you must first enable the government to control the governed; and in the next place oblige it to control itself. A dependence on the people is, no doubt, the primary control on the government; but experience has taught mankind the necessity of auxiliary precautions.

This policy of supplying, by opposite and rival interests, the defect of better motives, might be traced through the whole system of human affairs, private as well as public. We see it particularly displayed in all the subordinate distributions of power, where the constant aim is to divide and arrange the several offices in such a manner as that each may be a check on the other—that the private interest of every individual may be a sentinel over the public rights. These inventions of prudence cannot be less requisite in the distribution of the supreme powers of the State.

But it is not possible to give to each department an equal power of self-defense. In republican government, the legislative authority necessarily predominates. The remedy for this inconveniency is to divide the legislature into different branches; and to render them, by different modes of election and different principles of action, as little connected with each other as the nature of their common functions and their common dependence on the society will admit. It may even be necessary to guard against dangerous encroachments by still further precautions. As the weight of the legislative authority requires that it should be thus divided, the weakness of the executive may require, on the other hand, that it should be fortified. An absolute negative on the legislature appears, at first view, to be the natural defense with which the executive magistrate should be armed. But perhaps it would be neither altogether safe nor alone sufficient. On ordinary occasions it might not be exerted with the requisite firmness, and on extraordinary occasions it might be perfidiously abused. May not this defect of an absolute negative be supplied by some qualified connection between this weaker department and the weaker branch of the stronger department, by which the latter may be led to support the constitutional rights of the former, without being too much detached from the rights of its own department?

If the principles on which these observations are founded be just, as I persuade myself they are, and they be applied as a criterion to the several State constitutions, and to the federal Constitution, it will be found that if the latter does not perfectly correspond with them, the former are infinitely less able to bear such a test.

There are, moreover, two considerations particularly applicable to the federal system of America, which place that system in a very interesting point of view.

*First.* In a single republic, all the power surrendered by the people is submitted to the administration of a single government; and the usurpations are guarded against by a division of the government into distinct and separate departments. In the compound republic of America, the power surrendered by the people is first divided between two distinct governments, and then the portion allotted to each subdivided among distinct and separate departments. Hence a double security arises to the rights of the people. The different governments will control each other, at the same time that each will be controlled by itself.

*Second.* It is of great importance in a republic not only to guard the society against the oppression of its rulers, but to guard one part of the society against the injustice of the other part. Different interests necessarily exist in different classes of citizens. If a majority be united by a common interest, the rights of the minority will be insecure. There are but two methods of providing against this evil: the one by creating a will in the community independent of the majority—that is, of the society itself; the other, by comprehending in the society so many separate descriptions of citizens as will render an unjust combination of a majority of the whole very improbable, if not impracticable. The first method prevails in all governments possessing an hereditary or self-appointed authority. This at best is but a precarious security; because a power independent of the society may as well espouse the unjust views of the major as the rightful interests of the minor party, and may possibly be turned against both parties. The second method will be exemplified in the federal republic of the United States. Whilst all authority in it will be derived from and dependent on the society, the society itself will be broken into so many parts, interests, and classes of citizens that the rights of individuals, or of the minority, will be in little danger from interested combinations of the majority. In a free government the security for civil rights must be the same as that for religious rights. It consists in the one case in the multiplicity of interests, and in the other in the multiplicity of sects. The degree of security in both cases will depend on the number of interests and sects; and this may be presumed to depend on the extent of country and number of people comprehended under the same government. This view of the subject must particularly recommend a proper federal system to all the sincere and considerate friends of republican government, since it shows that in exact proportion as the territory of the Union may be formed into more circumscribed confederacies, or States, oppressive combinations of a majority will be facilitated; the best security, under the republican forms, for the rights of every class of citizens will be diminished; and consequently the stability and independence of some member of the government, the only other security, must be proportionally increased. Justice is the end of government. It is the end of civil society. It ever has been and ever will be pursued until it be obtained, or until liberty be lost in the pursuit. In a society under the forms of which the stronger faction can readily unite and oppress the weaker, anarchy may as truly be said to reign as in a state of nature, where the weaker individual is not secured against the violence of the stronger; and as, in the latter state, even the stronger individuals are prompted, by the uncertainty of their condition, to submit to a government which may protect the weak as well as themselves; so, in the former state, will the more powerful factions or parties be gradually induced, by a like motive, to wish for a government which will protect all parties, the weaker as well as the more powerful. It can be little doubted that if the State of Rhode Island was separated from the confederacy and left to itself, the insecurity of rights under the popular form of government within such narrow limits would be displayed by such reiterated oppressions of factious majorities, that some power altogether independent of the people would soon be called for by the voice of the very factions whose misrule had proved the necessity of it. In the extended republic of the United States, and among the great variety of interests, parties, and sects which it embraces, a coalition of a majority of the whole society could seldom take place on any other principles than those of justice and the general good; whilst there being thus less danger to a minor from the will of a major party, there must be less pretext, also, to provide for the security of the former, by introducing into the government a will not dependent on the latter, or, in other words, a will independent of the society itself. It is no less certain than it is important, notwithstanding the contrary opinions which have been entertained, that the larger the society, provided it lie within a practical sphere, the more duly capable it will be of self-government. And happily for the *republican cause*, the practicable sphere may be carried to a very great extent, by a judicious modification and mixture of the *federal principle*.

PUBLIUS.

# Selections from the
# Lincoln-Douglas Debates of 1858

## *Abraham Lincoln (1809–1865)*
## *Stephen A. Douglas (1813–1861)*

*As you read and think about the thorny problem of slavery in America, consider whether, under the scheme of Federalist No. 10, any issue can be exempted from the arena of compromises that is American politics. What makes slavery an issue above the fray of factional conflict for Lincoln? What can we learn from Lincoln's policy about the relative roles of moral principle and political compromise in statesmanship? Is Douglas being a good student of issue—or is he perhaps distorting either Lincoln's or Madison's argument? Does the fact that a devastating civil war was precipitated by these issues reflect on the Federalist's method of "breaking and controlling the violence of faction"?*

### NICOLAY AND HAY, VOLUME III

**Speech delivered at Springfield, Illinois, at the Close of the Republican State Convention by which Mr. Lincoln had been named as their Candidate for United States Senator, June 16, 1858**

Mr. President and Gentlemen of the Convention:

If we could first know where we are, and whither we are tending, we could better judge what to do, and how to do it. We are now far into the fifth year since a policy was initiated with the avowed object and confident promise of putting an end to slavery agitation. Under the operation of that policy, that agitation has not only not ceased but has constantly augmented. In my opinion, it will not cease until a crisis shall have been reached and passed. "A house divided against itself cannot stand." I believe this government cannot endure permanently half slave and half free. I do not expect the Union to be dissolved—I do not expect the house to fall—but I do expect it will cease to be divided. It will become all one thing, or all the other. Either the opponents of slavery will arrest the further spread of it, and place it where the public mind shall rest in the belief that it is in the course of ultimate extinction; or its advocates will push it forward till it shall become alike lawful in all the States, old as well as new, North as well as South. . . .

### LAPSLEY, VOLUME III

**Speech of Senator Douglas, Chicago, July 9, 1858**

. . . Mr. Lincoln made a speech before that Republican Convention which unanimously nominated him for the Senate,—a speech evidently well prepared and carefully written,—in which he states the basis upon which he proposes to carry on the campaign during the summer.

In it he lays down two distinct propositions which I shall notice, and upon which I shall take a direct and bold issue with him.

His first and main proposition I will give in his own language, Scripture quotations and all [laughter]; I give his exact language: "'A house divided against itself cannot stand.' I believe this government cannot endure, permanently, half *slave* and half *free*. I do not expect the Union to be *dissolved*, I do not expect the house to *fall*; but I do expect it to cease to be divided. It will become *all* one thing, or *all* the other."

In other words, Mr. Lincoln asserts as a fundamental principle of this government, that there must be uniformity in the local laws and domestic institutions of each and all the States of the Union; and he therefore invites all the non-slaveholding States to band together, organize as one body, and make war upon slavery in Kentucky, upon slavery in Virginia, upon the Carolinas, upon slavery in all the slaveholding States in this Union, and to persevere in that war until it shall be exterminated. He then notifies the slaveholding States to stand together as a unit and make an aggressive war upon the free States of this Union with a view of establishing slavery in them all; of forcing it upon Illinois, of forcing it upon New York, upon New England, and upon every other free State, and that they shall keep up the warfare until it has been formally established in them all. In other words, Mr. Lincoln advocates boldly and clearly a war of sections, a war of the North against the South, of the free States against the slave States,—a war of extermination, to be continued relentlessly until the one or the other shall be subdued, and all the States shall either become free or become slave.

Now, my friends, I must say to you frankly that I take bold, unqualified issue with him upon that principle. I assert that it is neither desirable nor possible that there should be uniformity in the local institutions and domestic regulations of the different States of the Union. The framers of our government never contemplated uniformity in its internal concerns. The fathers of the Revolution and the sages who made the Constitution well understood that the laws and domestic institutions which would suit the granite hills of New Hampshire would be totally unfit for the rice plantations of South Carolina; they well understood that the laws which would suit the agricultural districts of Pennsylvania and New York would be totally unfit for the large mining regions of the Pacific, or the lumber regions of Maine. They well understood that the great varieties of soil, of production, and of interests in a republic as large as this, required different local and domestic regulations in each locality, adapted to the wants and interests of each separate State; and for that reason it was provided in the Federal Constitution that the thirteen original States should remain sovereign and supreme within their own limits in regard to all that was local and internal and domestic, while the Federal Government should have certain specified powers which were general and national, and could be exercised only by Federal authority.

The framers of the Constitution well understood that each locality, having separate and distinct interests, required separate and distinct laws, domestic institutions, and police regulations adapted to its own wants and its own condition; and they acted on the presumption, also, that these laws and institutions would be as diversified and as dissimilar as the States would be numerous, and that no two would be precisely alike, because the interests of no two would be precisely the same. Hence I assert that the great fundamental principle which underlies our complex system of State and Federal governments contemplated diversity and dissimilarity in the local institutions and domestic affairs of each and every State then in the Union, or thereafter to be admitted into the Confederacy. I therefore conceive that my friend Mr. Lincoln has totally misapprehended the great principles upon which our government rests. Uniformity in local and domestic affairs would be destructive of State rights, of State sovereignty, of personal liberty and personal freedom. Uniformity is the parent of despotism the world over, not only in politics, but in religion. Wherever the doctrine of uniformity is proclaimed, that all the States must be free or all slave, that all labor must be white or all black, that all the citizens of the different States must have the same privileges or be governed by the same regulations, you have destroyed the greatest safeguard which our institutions have thrown around the rights of the citizen.

How could this uniformity be accomplished, if it was desirable and possible? There is but one mode in which it could be obtained, and that must be by abolishing the State legislatures, blotting out State sovereignty, merging the rights and sovereignty of the States in one consolidated empire, and vesting Congress with the plenary power to make all the police regulations, domestic and local laws, uniform throughout the limits of the Republic. When you shall have done this, you will have uniformity. Then the States will all be slave or all be free; then negroes will vote everywhere or nowhere; then you will have a Maine liquor law in every State or none; then you will have uniformity in all things, local and domestic, by the authority of the Federal Government. But when you attain that uniformity, you will have converted these thirty-two sovereign, independent States into one consolidated empire, with the uniformity of despotism reigning triumphant throughout the length and breadth of the land. . . .

## NICOLAY AND HAY, VOLUME III

### Senator Douglas' Reply at Freeport, August 27, 1858

. . . The next question propounded to me by Mr. Lincoln is : Can the people of a Territory in any lawful way, against the wishes of any citizen of the United States, exclude slavery from their limits prior to the formation of a State constitution? I answer emphatically, as Mr. Lincoln has heard me answer a hundred times from every stump in Illinois, that in my opinion the people of a Territory can, by lawful means, exclude slavery from their limits prior to the formation of a State constitution. Mr. Lincoln knew that I had answered that question over and over again. He heard me argue the Nebraska bill on that principle all over the State in 1854, in 1855, and in 1856, and he has no excuse for pretending to be in doubt as to my position on that question. It matters not what way the Supreme Court may hereafter decide as to the abstract question whether slavery may or may not go into a Territory under the Constitution, the people have the lawful means to introduce it or exclude it as they please, for the reason that slavery cannot exist a day or an hour anywhere unless it is supported by the local police regulations. Those police regulations can only be established by the local legislature, and if the people are opposed to slavery they will elect representatives to that body who will by unfriendly legislation effectually prevent the introduction of it into their midst. If, on the contrary, they are for it, their legislation will favor its extension. Hence, no matter what the decision of the Supreme Court may be on that abstract question, still the right of the people to make a slave Territory or a free Territory is perfect and complete under the Nebraska bill. I hope Mr. Lincoln deems my answer satisfactory on that point. . . .

## VOLUME IV

### Senator Douglas' Speech at Jonesboro, September 15, 1858

. . . As my time flies, I can only glance at these points and not present them as fully as I would wish, because I desire to bring all the points in controversy between the two parties before you in order to have Mr. Lincoln's reply. He makes war on the decision of the Supreme Court, in the case known as the Dred Scott case. I wish to say to you, fellow-citizens, that I have no war to make on that decision, or any other ever rendered by the Supreme Court. I am content to take that decision as it stands delivered by the highest judicial tribunal on earth, a tribunal established by the Constitution of the United States for that purpose, and hence that decision becomes the law of the land, binding on you, on me, and on every other good citizen, whether we like it or not. Hence I do not choose to go into an argument to prove, before this audience, whether or not Chief Justice Taney understood the law better than Abraham Lincoln.

Mr. Lincoln objects to that decision, first and mainly because it deprives the negro of the rights of citizenship. I am as much opposed to his reason for that objection as I am to the objection itself. I hold that a negro is not and never ought to be a citizen of the United States. I hold that this government was made on the white basis, by white men for the benefit of white men and their posterity forever, and should be administered by white men, and none others. I do not believe that the Almighty made the negro capable of self-government. I am aware that all the Abolition lecturers that you find traveling about through the country, are in the habit of reading the Declaration of Independence to prove that all men were created equal and endowed by their Creator with certain inalienable rights, among which are life, liberty, and the pursuit of happiness. Mr. Lincoln is very much in the habit of following in the track of Lovejoy in this particular, by reading that part of the Declaration of Independence to prove that the negro was endowed by the Almighty with the inalienable right of equality with white men. Now, I say to you, my fellow-citizens, that in my opinion the signers of the Declaration had no reference to the negro whatever, when they declared all men to be created equal. They desired to express by that phrase white men, men of European birth and European descent, and had no reference either to the negro, the savage Indians, the Feejee, the Malay, or any other inferior and degraded race, when they spoke of the equality of men. One great evidence that such was their understanding, is to be found in the fact that at that time every one of the thirteen colonies was a slaveholding colony, every signer of the Declaration represented a slaveholding constituency, and we know that no one of them emancipated his slaves, much less offered citizenship to them, when they signed the Declaration; and yet, if they intended to declare that the negro was the equal of the white man, and entitled by divine right to an equality with him, they were bound, as honest men, that day and hour to have put their negroes on an equality with themselves. Instead of doing so, with uplifted eyes to heaven they implored the divine blessing upon them, during the seven years' bloody war they had to fight to maintain that Declaration, never dreaming that they were violating divine law by still holding the negroes in bondage and depriving them of equality.

My friends, I am in favor of preserving this government as our fathers made it. It does not follow by any means that because a negro is not your equal or mine, that hence he must necessarily be a slave. On the contrary, it does follow that we ought to extend to the negro every right, every privilege, every immunity which he is capable of enjoying, consistent with the good of society. When you ask me what these rights are, what their nature and extent is, I tell you that that is a question which each State of this Union must decide for itself. Illinois has already decided the question. We have decided that the negro must not be a slave within our limits; but we have also decided that the negro shall not be a citizen within our limits; that he shall not vote, hold office, or exercise any political rights. I maintain that Illinois, as a sovereign State, has a right thus to fix her policy with reference to the relation between the white man and the negro; but while we had that right to decide the question for ourselves, we must recognize the same right in Kentucky and in every other State to make the same decision, or a different one. Having decided our own policy with reference to the black race, we must leave Kentucky and Missouri and every other State perfectly free to make just such a decision as they see proper on that question.

Kentucky has decided that question for herself. She has said that within her limits a negro shall not exercise any political rights, and she has also said that a portion of the negroes under the laws of that State shall be slaves. She had as much right to adopt that as her policy as we had to adopt the contrary for our policy. New York has decided that in that State a negro may vote if he has two hundred and fifty dollars' worth of property, and if he owns that much he may vote upon an equality with the white man. I, for one, am utterly opposed to negro suffrage anywhere and under any circumstances; yet, inasmuch as the Supreme Court has decided in the celebrated Dred Scott case that a State has a right to confer the privilege of voting upon free negroes, I am not going to make war upon New York because she has adopted a policy repugnant to my feelings. But New York must mind her own business, and keep her negro suffrage to herself, and not attempt to force it upon us.

In the State of Maine they have decided that a negro may vote and hold office on an equality with a white man. I had occasion to say to the senators from Maine, in a discussion last session, that if they thought that the white people within the limits of their State were no better than negroes, I would not quarrel with them for it, but they must not say that my white constituents of Illinois were no better than negroes, or we would be sure to quarrel.

The Dred Scott decision covers the whole question, and declares that each State has the right to settle this question of suffrage for itself, and all questions as to the relations between the white man and the negro. Judge Taney expressly lays down the doctrine. I receive it as law, and I say that while those States are adopting regulations on that subject disgusting and abhorrent, according to my views, I will not make war on them if they will mind their own business and let us alone.

I now come back to the question, why cannot this Union exist forever divided into free and slave States, as our fathers made it? It can thus exist if each State will carry out the principles upon which our institutions were founded—to wit, the right of each State to do as it pleases, without meddling with its neighbors. Just act upon that great principle, and this Union will not only live forever, but it will extend and expand until it covers the whole continent, and makes this confederacy one grand, ocean-bound republic. We must bear in mind that we are yet a young nation, growing with a rapidity unequaled in the history of the world, that our national increase is great, and that the emigration from the Old World is increasing, requiring us to expand and acquire new territory from time to time, in order to give our people land to live upon.

If we live up to the principle of State rights and State sovereignty, each State regulating its own affairs and minding its own business, we can go on and extend indefinitely, just as fast and as far as we need the territory. The time may come, indeed has now come, when our interests would be advanced by the acquisition of the island of Cuba. When we get Cuba we must take it as we find it, leaving the people to decide the question of slavery for themselves, without interference on the part of the Federal Government, or of any State of this Union. So when it becomes necessary to acquire any portion of Mexico or Canada, or of this continent or the adjoining islands, we must take them as we find them, leaving the people free to do as they please—to have slavery or not, as they choose. I never have inquired, and never will inquire, whether a new State applying for admission has slavery or not for one of her institutions. If the constitution that is presented be the act and deed of the people, and embodies their will, and they have the requisite population, I will admit them with slavery or without it, just as that people shall determine. . . .

### Lincoln's Reply at Jonesboro, September 15, 1858

. . . The second interrogatory that I propounded to him was this:

> Question 2. Can the people of a United States Territory, in any lawful way, against the wish of any citizen of the United States, exclude slavery from its limits prior to the formation of a State constitution?

To this Judge Douglas answered that they can lawfully exclude slavery from the Territory prior to the formation of a constitution. He goes on to tell us how it can be done. As I understand him, he holds that it can be done by the territorial legislature refusing to make any enactments for the protection of slavery in the Territory, and especially by adopting unfriendly legislation to it. For the sake of clearness, I state it again: that they can exclude slavery from the Territory—first, by withholding what he assumes to be an indispensable assistance to it in the way of legislation; and, second, by unfriendly legislation. If I rightly understand him, I wish to ask your attention for a while to his position.

In the first place, the Supreme Court of the United States has decided that any congressional prohibition of slavery in the Territories is unconstitutional—they have reached this proposition as a conclusion from their former proposition, that the Constitution of the United States expressly recognizes property in slaves; and from that other constitutional provision, that no person shall be deprived of property without due process of law. Hence they reach the conclusion that as the Constitution of the United States expressly recognizes property in slaves, and prohibits any person from being deprived of property without due process of law, to pass an act of Congress by which a man who owned a slave on one side of a line would be deprived of him if he took him on the other side is depriving him of that property without due process of law. That I understand to be the decision of the Supreme Court. I understand also that Judge Douglas adheres most firmly to that decision; and the difficulty is, how is it possible for any power to exclude slavery from the Territory unless in violation of that decision? That is the difficulty. . . .

I hold that the proposition that slavery cannot enter a new country without police regulations is historically false. It is not true at all. I hold that the history of this country shows that the institution of slavery was originally planted upon this continent without these "police regulations" which the judge now thinks necessary for the actual establishment of it. Not only so, but is there not another fact—how came this Dred Scott decision to be made? It was made upon the case of a negro being taken and actually held in slavery in Minnesota Territory, claiming his freedom because the act of Congress prohibited his being so held there. Will the judge pretend that Dred Scott was not held there without police regulations? There is at least one matter of record as to his having been held in slavery in the Territory, not only without police regulations, but in the teeth of congressional legislation supposed to be valid at the time. This shows that there is vigor enough in slavery to plant itself in a new country even against unfriendly legislation. It takes not only law but the enforcement of law to keep it out. That is the history of this country upon the subject.

I wish to ask one other question. It being understood that the Constitution of the United States guarantees property in slaves in the Territories, if there is any infringement of the right of that property, would not the United States courts, organized for the government of the Territory, apply such remedy as might be necessary in that case? It is a maxim held by the courts, that there is no wrong without its remedy; and the courts have a remedy for whatever is acknowledged and treated as a wrong.

Again: I will ask you, my friends, if you were elected members of the legislature, what would be the first thing you would have to do before entering upon your duties? Swear to support the Constitution of the United States. Suppose you believe, as Judge Douglas does, that the Constitution of the United States guarantees to your neighbor the right to hold slaves in that Territory—that they are his property—how can you clear your oaths unless you give him such legislation as is necessary to enable him to enjoy that property? What do you understand by supporting the Constitution of a State, or of the United States? Is it not to give such constitutional helps to the rights established by that Constitution as may be practically needed? Can you, if you swear to support the Constitution, and believe that the Constitution establishes a right, clear your oath, without giving it support? Do you support the Constitution if, knowing or believing there is a right established under it which needs specific legislation, you withhold that legislation? Do you not violate and disregard your oath. I can conceive of nothing plainer in the world. There can be nothing in the words "support the Constitution," if you may run counter to it by refusing support to any right established under the Constitution. And what I say here will hold with still more force against the judge's doctrine of "unfriendly legislation." How could you, having sworn to support the Constitution, and believing that it guaranteed the right to hold slaves in the Territories, assist in legislation intended to defeat that right? That would be violating your own view of the Constitution. Not only so, but if you were to do so, how long would it take the courts to hold your votes unconstitutional and void? Not a moment.

Lastly I would ask—Is not Congress itself under obligation to give legislative support to any right that is established under the United States Constitution? I repeat the question—Is not Congress itself bound to give legislative support to any right that is established in the United

States Constitution? A member of Congress swears to support the Constitution of the United States, and if he sees a right established by that Constitution which needs specific legislative protection, can he clear his oath without giving that protection? Let me ask you why many of us who are opposed to slavery upon principle give our acquiescence to a fugitive-slave law? Why do we hold ourselves under obligations to pass such a law, and abide by it when it is passed? Because the Constitution makes provision that the owners of slaves shall have the right to reclaim them. It gives the right to reclaim slaves, and that right is, as Judge Douglas says, a barren right, unless there is legislation that will enforce it.

The mere declaration, "No person held to service or labor in one State under the laws thereof, escaping into another, shall in consequence of any law or regulation therein be discharged from such service or labor, but shall be delivered up on claim of the party to whom such service or labor may be due," is powerless without specific legislation to enforce it. Now, on what ground would a member of Congress who is opposed to slavery in the abstract vote for a fugitive-slave law, as I would deem it my duty to do? Because there is a constitutional right which needs legislation to enforce it. And although it is distasteful to me, I have sworn to support the Constitution, and having so sworn, I cannot conceive that I do support it if I withhold from that right any necessary legislation to make it practical. And if that is true in regard to a fugitive-slave law, is the right to have fugitive slaves reclaimed any better fixed in the Constitution than the right to hold slaves in the Territories? For this decision is a just exposition of the Constitution, as Judge Douglas thinks. Is the one right any better than the other? Is there any man who, while a member of Congress, would give support to the one any more than the other? If I wished to refuse to give legislative support to slave property in the Territories, if a member of Congress, I could not do it, holding the view that the Constitution establishes that right. If I did it at all, it would be because I deny that this decision properly construes the Constitution. But if I acknowledge, with Judge Douglas, that this decision properly construes the Constitution, I cannot conceive that I would be less than a perjured man if I should refuse in Congress to give such protection to that property as in its nature it needed. . . .

### Lincoln's Speech at Charleston, September 18, 1858

Ladies and Gentlemen: It will be very difficult for an audience so large as this to hear distinctly what a speaker says, and consequently it is important that as profound silence be preserved as possible.

While I was at the hotel to-day, an elderly gentleman called upon me to know whether I was really in favor of producing a perfect equality between the negroes and white people. While I had not proposed to myself on this occasion to say much on that subject, yet as the question was asked me I thought I would occupy perhaps five minutes in saying something in regard to it. I will say then that I am not, nor ever have been, in favor of bringing about in any way the social and political equality of the white and black races—that I am not, nor ever have been, in favor of making voters or jurors of negroes, nor of qualifying them to hold office, nor to intermarry with white people; and I will say in addition to this that there is a physical difference between the white and black races which I believe will forever forbid the two races living together on terms of social and political equality. And inasmuch as they cannot so live, while they do remain together there must be the position of superior and inferior, and I as much as any other man am in favor of having the superior position assigned to the white race. I say upon this occasion I do not perceive that because the white man is to have the superior position the negro should be denied everything. I do not understand that because I do not want a negro woman for a slave I must necessarily want her for a wife. My understanding is that I can just let her alone. I am now in my fiftieth year, and I certainly never have had a black woman for either a slave or a wife. So it seems to me quite possible for us to get along without making either slaves or wives of negroes. I will add to this that I have never seen, to my knowledge, a man, woman, or child who was in favor of producing a perfect equality, social and political, between negroes and white men. I recollect of but one distinguished instance that I ever heard of so frequently as to be entirely satisfied of its correctness, and that is the case of Judge Douglas's old friend Colonel Richard M. Johnson. I will also add to the remarks I have made (for I am not going to enter at large upon this subject), that I have never had the least apprehension that I or my friends would marry negroes if there was no law to keep them from it; but as Judge Douglas and his friends seem to be in great apprehension that they might, if there was no law to keep them from it, I give him the most solemn pledge that I will to the very last stand by the law of this State, which forbids the marrying of white people with negroes. I will add one further word, which is this: that I do not understand that there is any place where an alteration of the social and political relations of the negro and the white man can be made except in the State legislature—not in the Congress of the United States; and as I do not really apprehend the approach of any such thing myself, and as Judge Douglas seems to be in constant horror that some such danger is rapidly approaching, I propose, as the best means to prevent it, that the judge be kept at home and placed in the State legislature to fight the measure. I do not propose dwelling longer at this time on the subject. . . .

### Senator Douglas' Speech at Galesburg, October 7, 1858

. . . Now, let me ask you whether the country has any interest in sustaining this organization known as the Republican party. That party is unlike all other political organizations in this country. All other parties have been national in their character—have avowed their principles alike in the slave and free States, in Kentucky as well as Illinois, in Louisiana as well as in Massachusetts. Such was the case with the Old Whig party, and such was and is the case with the Democratic party. Whigs and Democrats could proclaim their principles boldly and fearlessly in the North and in the South, in the East and in the West, wherever the Constitution ruled and the American flag waved over American soil.

But now you have a sectional organization, a party which appeals to the Northern section of the Union against the Southern, a party which appeals to Northern passion, Northern pride, Northern ambition, and Northern prejudices, against Southern people, the Southern States, and Southern institutions. The leaders of that party hope that they will be able to unite the Northern States in one great sectional party, and inasmuch as the North is the stronger section, that they will thus be enabled to outvote, conquer, govern, and control the South. Hence you find that they now make speeches advocating principles and measures which cannot be defended in any slave-holding State of this Union. Is there a Republican residing in Galesburg who can travel into Kentucky, and carry his principles with him across the Ohio? What Republican from Massachusetts can visit the Old Dominion without leaving his principles behind him when he crosses Mason's and Dixon's line? Permit me to say to you in perfect good humor, but in all sincerity, that no political creed is sound which cannot be proclaimed fearlessly in every State of this Union where the Federal Constitution is the supreme law of the land. . . .

I ask you, my friends, why cannot Republicans avow their principles alike everywhere? I would despise myself if I thought that I was procuring your votes by concealing my opinions, and by avowing one set of principles in one part of the State, and a different set in another part.

If I do not truly and honorably represent your feelings and principles, then I ought not to be your senator; and I will never conceal my opinions, or modify or change them a hair's-breadth, in order to get votes. . . .

But Mr. Lincoln cannot be made to understand, and those who are determined to vote for him, no matter whether he is a pro-slavery man in the south and a negro-equality advocate in the north, cannot be made to understand, how it is that in a Territory the people can do as they please on the slavery question under the Dred Scott decision. Let us see whether I cannot explain it to the satisfaction of all impartial men. Chief Justice Taney has said, in his opinion in the Dred Scott case, that a negro slave, being property, stands on an equal footing with other property, and that the owner may carry them into United States territory the same as he does other property. Suppose any two of you neighbors shall conclude to go to Kansas, one carrying $100,000 worth of negro slaves and the other $100,000 worth of mixed merchandise, including quantities of liquors. You both agree that under that decision you may carry your property to Kansas, but when you get it there, the merchant who is possessed of the liquors is met by the Maine liquor law, which prohibits the sale or use of his property, and the owner of the slaves is met by equally unfriendly legislation, which makes his property worthless after he gets it there. What is the right to carry your property into the the Territory worth to either, when unfriendly legislation in the Territory renders it worthless after you get there? The slaveholder, when he gets his slaves there, finds that there is no local law to protect him in holding them, no slave code, no police regulations maintaining and supporting him in his right, and he discovers at once that the absence of such friendly legislation excludes his property from Territory just as irresistibly as if there was a positive constitutional prohibition excluding it. . . .

### Lincoln's Reply at Galesburg, October 7, 1858

. . . The judge has alluded to the Declaration of Independence, and insisted that negroes are not included in that Declaration; and that it is, a slander upon the framers of that instrument to suppose that negroes were meant therein; and he asks you: Is it possible to believe that Mr. Jefferson, who penned the immortal paper, could have supposed himself applying the language of that instrument to the negro race, and yet held a portion of that race in slavery? Would he not at once have freed them? I only have to remark upon this part of the judge's speech (and that, too, very briefly, for I shall not detain myself, or you, upon that point for any great length of time), that I believe the entire records of the world, from the date of the Declaration of Independence up to within three years ago, may be searched in vain for one single affirmation, from one single man, that the negro was not included in the Declaration of Independence; I think I may defy Judge Douglas to show that he ever said so, that Washington ever said so, that any president ever said so, that any member of Congress ever said so, or that any living man upon the whole earth ever said so, until the necessities of the present policy of the Democratic party, in regard to slavery, had to invent that affirmation. And I will remind Judge Douglas and this audience that while Mr. Jefferson was the owner of slaves, as undoubtedly he was, in speaking upon this very subject, he used the strong language that "he trembled for his country when he remembered that God was just"; and I will offer the highest premium in my power to Judge Douglas if he will show that he, in all his life, ever uttered a sentiment at all akin to that of Jefferson. . . .

The judge has also detained us awhile in regard to the distinction between his party and our party. His he assumes to be a national party—ours a sectional one. He does this in asking the question whether this country has any interest in the maintenance of the Republican party? He assumes that our party is altogether sectional—that the party to which he adheres is national; and the argument is that no party can be a rightful party—can be based upon rightful principles—unless it can announce its principles everywhere. I presume that Judge Douglas could not go into Russia and announce the doctrine of our national Democracy; he could not denounce the doctrine of kings and emperors and monarchies in Russia; and it may be true of this country, that in some places we may not be able to proclaim a doctrine as clearly true as the truth of Democracy, because there is a section so directly opposed to it that they will not tolerate us in doing so. Is it the true test of the soundness of a doctrine, that in some places people won't let you proclaim it? Is that the way to test the truth of any doctrine? Why, I understand that at one time the people of Chicago would not let Judge Douglas preach a certain favorite doctrine of his. I commend to his consideration the question, whether he takes that as a test of the unsoundness of what he wanted to preach. . . .

The judge tells us, in proceeding, that he is opposed to making any odious distinctions between free and slave States. I am altogether unaware that the Republicans are in favor of making any odious distinctions between the free and slave States. But there still is a difference, I think, between Judge Douglas and the Republicans in this. I suppose that the real difference between Judge Douglas and his friends and the Republicans, on the contrary, is that the judge is not in favor of making any difference between slavery and liberty—that he is in favor of eradicating, of pressing out of view, the questions of preference in this country for free or slave institutions; and consequently every sentiment he utters discards the idea that there is any wrong in slavery. Everything that emanates from him or his coadjutors in their course of policy carefully excludes the thought that there is anything wrong in slavery. All their arguments, if you will consider them, will be seen to exclude the thought that there is anything whatever wrong in slavery. If you will take the judge's speeches, and select the short and pointed sentences expressed by him,—as his declaration that he "don't care whether slavery is voted up or down,"—you will see at once that this is perfectly logical, if you do not admit that slavery is wrong. If you do admit that it is wrong, Judge Douglas cannot logically say he don't care whether a wrong is voted up or voted down. Judge Douglas declares that if any community wants slavery they have a right to have it. He can say that logically, if he says that there is no wrong in slavery; but if you admit that there is a wrong in it, he cannot logically say that anybody has a right to do wrong. He insists that, upon the score of equality, the owners of slaves and owners of property— of horses and every other sort of property—should be alike, and hold them alike in a new Territory. That is perfectly logical, if the two species of property are alike, and are equally founded in right. But if you admit that one of them is wrong, you cannot institute any equality between right and wrong. And from this difference of sentiment—the belief on the part of one that the institution is wrong, and a policy springing from that belief which looks to the arrest of the enlargement of that wrong; and this other sentiment, that it is no wrong, and a policy sprung from that sentiment which will tolerate no idea of preventing that wrong from growing larger, and looks to there never being an end of it through all the existence of things—arises the real difference between Judge Douglas and his friends on the one hand, and the Republicans on the other. Now, I confess myself as belonging to that class in the country who contemplate slavery as a moral, social, and political evil, having due regard for its actual existence amongst us, and the difficulties of getting rid of it in any satisfactory way, and to all the constitutional obligations which have been thrown about it; but who, nevertheless, desire a policy that looks to the prevention of it as a wrong, and looks hopefully to the time when as a wrong it may come to an end. . . .

### Lincoln's Rejoinder at Quincy, October 13, 1858

. . . I wish to return to Judge Douglas my profound thanks for his public annunciation here to-day to be put on record, that his system of policy in regard to the institution of slavery contemplates that it shall last forever. We are getting a little nearer the true issue of this controversy, and I am profoundly grateful for this one sentence. Judge Douglas asks you, "Why cannot the institution of slavery, or rather, why cannot the nation, part slave and part free, continue as our fathers made it forever?" In the first place, I insist that our fathers did not make this nation half slave and half free, or part slave and part free. I insist that they found the institution of slavery existing here. They did not make it so, but they left it so because they knew of no way to get rid of it at that time. When Judge Douglas undertakes to say that, as a matter of choice, the fathers of the government made this nation part slave and part free, he assumes what is historically a falsehood. More than that: when the fathers of the government cut off the source of slavery by the abolition of the slave-trade, and adopted a system of restricting it from the new Territories where it had not existed, I maintain that they placed it where they understood, and all sensible men understood, it was in the course of ultimate extinction; and when Judge Douglas asks me why it cannot continue as our fathers made it, I ask him why he and his friends could not let it remain as our fathers made it?

It is precisely all I ask of him in relation to the institution of slavery, that it shall be placed upon the basis that our fathers placed it upon. Mr. Brooks, of South Carolina, once said, and truly said, that when this government was established, no one expected the institution of slavery to last until this day; and that the men who formed this government were wiser and better than the men of these days; but the men of these days had experience which the fathers had not, and that experience had taught them the invention of the cotton-gin, and this had made the perpetuation of the institution of slavery a necessity in this country. Judge Douglas could not let it stand upon the basis where our fathers placed it, but removed it, and put it upon the cotton-gin basis. It is a question, therefore, for him and his friends to answer—why they could not let it remain where the fathers of the government originally placed it. . . .

## VOLUME V

### Senator Douglas' Speech at Alton, October 15, 1858

Ladies and Gentlemen: It is now nearly four months since the canvass between Mr. Lincoln and myself commenced. On the 16th of June the Republican convention assembled at Springfield, and nominated Mr. Lincoln as their candidate for the United States Senate, and he, on that occasion, delivered a speech in which he laid down what he understood to be the Republican creed, and the platform on which he proposed to stand during the contest. The principal points in that speech of Mr. Lincoln's were: First, that this government could not endure permanently divided into free and slave States, as our fathers made it; that they must all become free or all become slave; all become one thing or all become the other, otherwise this Union could not continue to exist. I give you his opinions almost in the identical language he used. His second proposition was a crusade against the Supreme Court of the United States, because of the Dred Scott decision; urging as an especial reason for his opposition to that decision that it deprived the negroes of the rights and benefits of that clause in the Constitution of the United States which guarantees to the citizens of each State all the rights, privileges, and immunities of the citizens of the several States. On the 10th of July I returned home, and delivered a speech to the people of Chicago, in which I announced it to be my purpose to appeal to the people of Illinois to sustain the course I had pursued in Congress. In that speech I joined issue with Mr. Lincoln on the points which he had presented. Thus there was an issue clear and distinct made up between us on these two propositions laid down in the speech of Mr. Lincoln at Springfield, and controverted by me in my reply to him at Chicago. On the next day, the 11th of July, Mr. Lincoln replied to me at Chicago, explaining at some length, and reaffirming the positions which he had taken in his Springfield speech. In that Chicago speech he even went further than he had before, and uttered sentiments in regard to the negro being on an equality with the white man. He adopted in support of this position the argument which Lovejoy, and Codding, and other Abolition lecturers had made familiar in the northern and central portions of the State, to wit: that the Declaration of Independence having declared all men free and equal by Divine law, negro equality was also an inalienable right, of which they could not be deprived. He insisted, in that speech, that the Declaration of Independence included the negro in the clause asserting that all men were created equal, and went so far as to say that if one man was allowed to take the position that it did not include the negro, others might take the position that it did not include other men. He said that all these distinctions between this man and that man, this race and the other race, must be discarded, and we must all stand by the Declaration of Independence, declaring that all men were created equal. . . .

In my speeches I confined myself closely to those three positions which he had taken, controverting his proposition that this Union could not exist as our fathers made it, divided into free and slave States, controverting his proposition of a crusade against the Supreme Court because of the Dred Scott decision, and controverting his proposition that the Declaration of

Independence included and meant the negroes as well as the white men, when it declared all men to be created equal. I supposed at that time that these propositions constituted a distinct issue between us, and that the opposite positions we had taken upon them we would be willing to be held to in every part of the State. I never intended to waver one hair's breadth from that issue either in the north or the south, or wherever I should address the people of Illinois. I hold that when the time arrives that I cannot proclaim my political creed in the same terms not only in the northern but the southern part of Illinois, not only in the Northern but the Southern States, and wherever the American flag waves over American soil, that then there must be something wrong in that creed—so long as we live under a common Constitution, so long as we live in a confederacy of sovereign and equal States, joined together as one for certain purposes, that any political creed is radically wrong which cannot be proclaimed in every State and every section of that Union, alike. I took up Mr. Lincoln's three propositions in my several speeches, analyzed them, and pointed out what I believe to be the radical errors contained in them. First, in regard to his doctrine that this government was in violation of the law of God, which says that a house divided against itself cannot stand; I repudiated it as a slander upon the immortal framers of our Constitution. I then said, I have often repeated, and now again assert, that in my opinion our government can endure forever, divided into free and slave States as our fathers made it—each State having the right to prohibit, abolish, or sustain slavery, just as it pleases. This government was made upon the great basis of the sovereignty of the States, the right of each State to regulate its own domestic institutions to suit itself, and that right was conferred with the understanding and expectation that inasmuch as each locality had separate interests, each locality must have different and distinct local and domestic institutions, corresponding to its wants and interests. Our fathers knew, when they made the government, that the laws and institutions which were well adapted to the green mountains of Vermont were unsuited to the rice plantations of South Carolina. They knew then, as well as we know now, that the laws and institutions which would be well adapted to the beautiful prairies of Illinois would not be suited to the mining regions of California. They knew that in a republic as broad as this, having such a variety of soil, climate, and interest, there must necessarily be a corresponding variety of local laws—the policy and institutions of each State adapted to its condition and wants. For this reason this Union was established on the right of each State to do as it pleased on the question of slavery, and every other question, and the various States were not allowed to complain of, much less interfere with, the policy of their neighbors. . . .

You see that if this Abolition doctrine of Mr. Lincoln had prevailed when the government was made, it would have established slavery as a permanent institution, in all the States, whether they wanted it or not; and the question for us to determine in Illinois now, as one of the free States, is whether or not we are willing, having become the majority section, to enforce a doctrine on the minority which we would have resisted with our heart's blood had it been attempted on us when we were in a minority. How has the South lost her power as the majority section in this Union, and how have the free States gained it, except under the operation of that principle which declares the right of the people of each State and each Territory to form and regulate their domestic institutions in their own way? It was under that principle that slavery was abolished in New Hampshire, Rhode Island, Connecticut, New York, New Jersey, and Pennsylvania; it was under that principle that one half of the slave-holding States became free; it was under that principle that the number of free States increased until, from being one out of twelve States, we have grown to be the majority of States of the whole Union, with the power to control the House of Representatives and Senate, and the power, consequently, to elect a President by Northern votes without the aid of a Southern State. Having obtained this power under the operation of that great principle, are you now prepared to abandon the principle, and declare that merely because we have the power you will wage a war against the Southern States and their institutions until you force them to abolish slavery everywhere . . . ?

My friends, there never was a time when it was as important for the Democratic party, for all national men, to rally and stand together as it is to-day. We find all sectional men giving up past differences and uniting on the one question of slavery, and when we find sectional men thus uniting, we should unite to resist them and their treasonable designs. Such was the case in 1850, when Clay left the quiet and peace of his home, and again entered upon public life to quell agitation and restore peace to a distracted Union. Then we Democrats, with Cass at our head, welcomed Henry Clay, whom the whole nation regarded as having been preserved by God for the times. He became our leader in that great fight, and we rallied around him the same as the Whigs rallied around Old Hickory in 1832 to put down nullification. Thus you see that while Whigs and Democrats fought fearlessly in old times about banks, the tariff, distribution, the specie circular, and the sub-treasury, all united as a band of brothers when the peace, harmony, or integrity of the Union was imperiled. It was so in 1850, when Abolitionism had even so far divided this country, North and South, as to endanger the peace of the Union. Whigs and Democrats united in establishing the compromise measures of that year, and restoring tranquillity and good feeling. These measures passed on the joint action of the two parties. They rested on the great principle that the people of each State and each Territory should be left perfectly free to form and regulate their domestic institutions to suit themselves. You Whigs and we Democrats justified them in that principle. In 1854, when it became necessary to organize the Territories of Kansas and Nebraska, I brought forward the bill on the same principle. In the Kansas-Nebraska bill you find it declared to be the true intent and meaning of the act not to legislate slavery into any State or Territory, nor to exclude it therefrom, but to leave the people thereof perfectly free to form and regulate their domestic institutions in their own way....

. . . I answer specifically, if you want a further answer, and say that while under the decision of the Supreme Court, as recorded in the opinion of Chief Justice Taney, slaves are property like all other property, and can be carried into any Territory of the United States the same as any other description of property, yet when you get them there they are subject to the local law of the Territory just like all other property. You will find in a recent speech delivered by that able and eloquent statesman, Hon. Jefferson Davis, at Bangor, Maine, that he took the same view of this subject that I did in my Freeport speech. He there said:

> If the inhabitants of any Territory should refuse to enact such laws and police regulations as would give security to their property or to his, it would be rendered more or less valueless in proportion to the difficulties of holding it without such protection. In the case of property in the labor of man, or what is usually called slave property, the insecurity would be so great that the owner could not ordinarily retain it. Therefore, though the right would remain, the remedy being withheld, it would follow that the owner would be practically debarred, by the circumstances of the case, from taking slave property into a Territory where the sense of the inhabitants was opposed to its introduction. So much for the often repeated fallacy of forcing slavery upon any community.

You will also find that the distinguished Speaker of the present House of Representatives, Hon. James L. Orr, construed the Kansas and Nebraska bill in this same way in 1856, and also that great intellect of the South, Alexander H. Stephens, put the same construction upon it in Congress that I did in my Freeport speech. The whole South is rallying to the support of the doctrine that if the people of that Territory want slavery they have a right to have it, and if they do not want it that no power on earth can force it upon them. I hold that there is no principle on earth more sacred to all the friends of freedom than that which says that no institution, no law, no constitution, should be forced on an unwilling people contrary to their wishes; and I assert that the Kansas and Nebraska bill contains that principle. It is the great principle contained in that bill. It is the principle on which James Buchanan was made President. Without that principle he never would have been made President of the United States. I will never violate or abandon that doctrine, if I have to stand alone. I have resisted the blandishments and threats of power on the one side, and seduction on the other, and have stood immovably for that principle, fighting for it when assailed by Northern mobs, or threatened by Southern hostility. I have defended it against the North and the South, and I will defend it against whoever assails it, and I will follow it wherever its logical conclusions lead me. I say to you that there is but one hope, one safety for this country, and that is to stand immovably by that principle which declares the right of each State and each Territory to decide these questions for themselves. This government was founded on that principle, and must be administered in the same sense in which it was founded.

But the Abolition party really think that under the Declaration of Independence the negro is equal to the white man, and that negro equality is an inalienable right conferred by the Almighty, and hence that all human laws in violation of it are null and void. . . .

We in Illinois have decided it for ourselves. We tried slavery, kept it up for twelve years, and finding that it was not profitable, we abolished it for that reason, and became a free State. We adopted in its stead the policy that a negro in this State shall not be a slave and shall not be a citizen. We have a right to adopt that policy. For my part, I think it is a wise and sound policy for us. You in Missouri must judge for yourselves whether it is a wise policy for you. . . .

. . . Why can we not thus have peace? Why should we thus allow a sectional party to agitate this country, to array the North against the South, and convert us into enemies instead of friends, merely that a few ambitious men may ride into power on a sectional hobby? How long is it since these ambitious Northern men wished for a sectional organization? Did any one of them dream of a sectional party as long as the North was the weaker section and the South the stronger? Then all were opposed to sectional parties. But the moment the North obtained the majority in the House and Senate by the admission of California, and could elect a President without the aid of Southern votes, that moment ambitious Northern men formed a scheme to excite the North against the South, and make the people be governed in their votes by geographical lines, thinking that the North, being the stronger section, would outvote the South, and consequently they, the leaders, would ride into office on a sectional hobby. I am told that my hour is out. It was very short.

### Lincoln's Reply at Alton, October 15, 1858

. . . You have heard him frequently allude to my controversy with him in regard to the Declaration of Independence. I confess that I have had a struggle with Judge Douglas on that matter, and I will try briefly to place myself right in regard to it on this occasion. I said—and it is between the extracts Judge Douglas has taken from this speech, and put in his published speeches:

> It may be argued that there are certain conditions that make necessities and impose them upon us, and to the extent that a necessity is imposed upon a man he must submit to it. I think that was the condition in which we found ourselves when we established this government. We had slaves among us; we could not get our Constitution unless we permitted them to remain in slavery; we could not secure the good we did secure if we grasped for more: and having by necessity submitted to that much, it does not destroy the principle that is the charter of our liberties. Let that charter remain as our standard.

Now I have upon all occasions declared as strongly as Judge Douglas against the disposition to interfere with the existing institution of slavery. You hear me read it from the same speech from which he takes garbled extracts for the purpose of proving upon me a disposition to interfere with the institution of slavery, and establish a perfect social and political equality between negroes and white people.

Allow me, while upon this subject, briefly to present one other extract from a speech of mine, made more than a year ago, at Springfield, in discussing this very same question, soon after Judge Douglas took his ground that negroes were not included in the Declaration of Independence:

I think the authors of that notable instrument intended to include all men, but they did not intend to declare all men equal in all respects. They did not mean to say that all men were equal in color, size, intellect, moral development, or social capacity. They defined with tolerable distinctness in what respects they did consider all men created equal—equal in certain inalienable rights, among which are life, liberty, and the pursuit of happiness. This they said, and this they meant. They did not mean to assert the obvious untruth, that all were then actually enjoying that equality, nor yet that they were about to confer it immediately upon them. In fact, they had no power to confer such a boon. They meant simply to declare the right, so that the enforcement of it might follow as fast as circumstances should permit.

They meant to set up a standard maxim for free society which should be familiar to all and revered by all—constantly looked to, constantly labored for, and even, though never perfectly attained, constantly approximated; and thereby constantly spreading and deepening its influence and augmenting the happiness and value of life to all people, of all colors, everywhere.

. . . At Galesburg the other day, I said, in answer to Judge Douglas, that three years ago there never had been a man, so far as I knew or believed, in the whole world, who had said that the Declaration of Independence did not include negroes in the term "all men." I reassert it to-day. I assert that Judge Douglas and all his friends may search the whole records of the country, and it will be a matter of great astonishment to me if they shall be able to find that one human being three years ago had ever uttered the astounding sentiment that the term "all men" in the Declaration did not include the negro. Do not let me be misunderstood. I know that more than three years ago there were men who, finding this assertion constantly in the way of their schemes to bring about the ascendancy and perpetuation of slavery, denied the truth of it. I know that Mr. Calhoun and all the politicians of his school denied the truth of the Declaration. I know that it ran along in the mouth of some Southern men for a period of years, ending at last in that shameful though rather forcible declaration of Pettit of Indiana, upon the floor of the United States Senate, that the Declaration of Independence was in that respect "a self-evident lie," rather than a self-evident truth. But I say, with a perfect knowledge of all this hawking at the Declaration without directly attacking it, that three years ago there never had lived a man who had ventured to assail it in the sneaking way of pretending to believe it and then asserting it did not include the negro. I believe the first man who ever said it was Chief Justice Taney in the Dred Scott case, and the next to him was our friend, Stephen A. Douglas. And now it has become the catchword of the entire party. I would like to call upon his friends everywhere, to consider how they have come in so short a time to view this matter in a way so entirely different from their former belief; to ask whether they are not being borne along by an irresistible current—whither, they know not. . . .

I have intimated that I thought the agitation would not cease until a crisis should have been reached and passed. I have stated in what way I thought it would be reached and passed. I have said that it might go one way or the other. We might, by arresting the further spread of it, and placing it where the fathers originally placed it, put it where the public mind should rest in the belief that it was in the course of ultimate extinction. Thus the agitation may cease. It may be pushed forward until it shall become alike lawful in all the States, old as well as new, North as well as South. I have said, and I repeat, my wish is that the further spread of it may be arrested, and that it may be placed where the public mind shall rest in the belief that it is in the course of ultimate extinction. I have expressed that as my wish. I entertain the opinion, upon evidence sufficient to my mind, that the fathers of this government placed that institution where the public mind did rest in the belief that it was in the course of ultimate extinction. Let me ask why they made provision that the source of slavery—the African slave-trade—should be cut off at the end of twenty years? Why did they make provision that in all the new territory we owned at that time, slavery should be forever inhibited? Why stop its spread in one direction and cut off its source in another, if they did not look to its being placed in the course of ultimate extinction?

Again, the institution of slavery is only mentioned in the Constitution of the United States two or three times, and in neither of these cases does the word "slavery" or "negro race" occur; but covert language is used each time, and for a purpose full of significance. What is the language in regard to the prohibition of the African slave-trade? It runs in about this way: "The migration or importation of such persons as any of the States now existing shall think proper to admit, shall not be prohibited by the Congress prior to the year 1808."

The next allusion in the Constitution to the question of slavery and the black race, is on the subject of the basis of representation, and there the language used is: "Representatives and direct taxes shall be apportioned among the several States which may be included within this Union, according to their respective numbers, which shall be determined by adding to the whole number of free persons, including those bound to service for a term of years, and excluding Indians not taxed, three fifths of all other persons."

It says "persons," not slaves, not negroes; but this "three fifths" can be applied to no other class among us than the negroes.

Lastly, in the provision for the reclamation of fugitive slaves, it is said: "No person held to service or labor in one State, under the laws thereof, escaping into another, shall in consequence of any law or regulation therein be discharged from such service or labor, but shall be delivered up, on claim of the party to whom such service or labor may be due." There, again, there is no mention of the word "negro," or of slavery. In all three of these places, being the only allusion to slavery in the instrument, covert language is used. Language is used not suggesting that slavery existed or that the black race were among us. And I understand the contemporaneous history of those times to be that covert language was used with a purpose, and that purpose was that in our Constitution, which it was hoped, and is still hoped, will endure forever,—when it should be read by intelligent and patriotic men, after the institution of slavery had passed from among us,—there should be nothing on the face of the great charter of liberty suggesting that such a thing as negro slavery had ever existed among us.

This is part of the evidence that the fathers of the government expected and intended the institution of slavery to come to an end. They expected and intended that it should be in the course of ultimate extinction. And when I say that I desire to see the further spread of it arrested, I only say I desire to see that done which the fathers have first done. When I say I desire to see it placed where the public mind will rest in the belief that it is in the course of ultimate extinction, I only say I desire to see it placed where they placed it. It is not true that our fathers, as Judge Douglas assumes, made this government part slave and part free. Understand the sense in which he puts it. He assumes that slavery is a rightful thing within itself—was introduced by the framers of the Constitution.

The exact truth is that they found the institution existing among us, and they left it as they found it. But in making the government they left this institution with many clear marks of disapprobation upon it. They found slavery among them, and they left it among them because of the difficulty—the absolute impossibility—of its immediate removal. And when Judge Douglas asks me why we cannot let it remain part slave and part free, as the fathers of the government made it, he asks a question based upon an assumption which is itself a falsehood; and I turn upon him and ask him the question, when the policy that the fathers of the government had adopted in relation to this element among us was the best policy in the world,—the only wise policy, the only policy that we can ever safely continue upon, that will ever give us peace, unless this dangerous element masters us all and becomes a national institution,—I turn upon him and ask him why he could not leave it alone. I turn and ask him why he was driven to the necessity of introducing a new policy in regard to it. He has himself said he introduced a new policy. He said so in his speech on the 22nd of March of the present year, 1858. I ask him why he could not let it remain where our fathers placed it. I ask, too, of Judge Douglas and his friends, why we shall not again place this institution upon the basis on which the fathers left it? I ask you, when he infers that I am in favor of setting the free and the slaves States at war, when the institution was placed in that attitude by those who made the Constitution, did they make any war? If we had no war out of it when thus placed, wherein is the ground of belief that we shall have war out of it if we return to that policy? Have we had any peace upon this matter springing from any other basis? I maintain that we have not. I have proposed nothing more than a return to the policy of the fathers.

I confess, when I propose a certain measure of policy, it is not enough for me that I do not intend anything evil in the result, but it is incumbent on me to show that it has not a tendency to that result. I have met Judge Douglas in that point of view. I have not only made the declaration that I do not mean to produce a conflict between the States, but I have tried to show by fair reasoning, and I think I have shown to the minds of fair men, that I propose nothing but what has a most peaceful tendency. The quotation that I happened to make in that Springfield speech, that "a house divided against itself cannot stand, " and which has proved so offensive to the judge, was part and parcel of the same thing. He tries to show that variety in the domestic institutions of the different States is necessary and indispensable. I do not dispute it. I have no controversy with Judge Douglas about that . . . . I understand, I hope, quite as well as Judge Douglas, or anybody else, that the variety in the soil and climate and face of the country, and consequent variety in the industrial pursuits and productions of a country, require systems of laws conforming to this variety in the natural features of the country. I understand quite as well as Judge Douglas, that if we here raise a barrel of flour more than we want, and the Louisianans raise a barrel of sugar more than they want, it is of mutual advantage to exchange. That produces commerce, brings us together, and makes us better friends. We like one another the more for it. And I understand as well as Judge Douglas, or anybody else, that these mutual accommodations are the cements which bind together the different parts of this Union; that instead of being a thing to "divide the house"—figuratively expressing the Union—they tend to sustain it; they are the props of the house tending always to hold it up.

But when I have admitted all this, I ask if there is any parallel between these things and this institution of slavery? I do not see that there is any parallel at all between them. Consider it. When have we had any difficulty or quarrel amongst ourselves about the cranberry laws of Indiana, or the oyster laws of Virginia, or the pine-lumber laws of Maine, or the fact that Louisiana produces sugar, and Illinois flour? When have we had any quarrels over these things? When have we had perfect peace in regard to this thing which I say is an element of discord in this Union? We have sometimes had peace, but when was it? It was when the institution of slavery remained quiet where it was. We have had difficulty and turmoil whenever it has made a struggle to spread itself where it was not. I ask, then, if experience does not speak in thunder-tones, telling us that the policy which has given peace to the country heretofore, being returned to, gives the greatest promise of peace again. You may say, and Judge Douglas has intimated the same thing, that all this difficulty in regard to the institution of slavery is the mere agitation of office-seekers and ambitious northern politicians. He thinks we want to get "his place," I suppose. I agree that there are office-seekers among us. The Bible says somewhere that we are desperately selfish. I think we would have discovered that fact without the Bible. I do not claim that I am any less so than the average of men, but I do claim that I am not more selfish than Judge Douglas.

But is it true that all the difficulty and agitation we have in regard to this institution of slavery springs from office-seeking—from the mere ambition of politicians?. . . But where is the philosophy or statesmanship which assumes that you can quiet that disturbing element in our society which has disturbed us for more than half a century, which has been the only serious danger that has threatened our institutions—I say, where is the philosophy or the statesmanship based on the assumption that we are to quit talking about it, and that the public mind is all at once to cease being agitated by it? Yet this is the policy here in the North that Douglas is advocating—that we are to care nothing about it! I ask you if it is not a false philosophy? Is it not a false statesmanship that undertakes to build up a system of policy upon the basis of caring nothing about the very thing that everybody does care the most about—a thing which all experience his shown we care a very great deal about?

The judge alludes very often in the course of his remarks to the exclusive right which the States have to decide the whole thing for themselves. I agree with him very readily that the different States have that right. He is but fighting a man of straw when he assumes that I am contending against the rights of the States to do as they please about it. Our controversy with him is in regard to the new Territories. We agree that when the States come in as States they have the right and the power to do as they please. We have no power as citizens of the free States, or in our federal capacity as members of the Federal Union through the General Government, to disturb slavery in the States where it exists. We profess constantly that we have no more inclination than belief in the power of the government to disturb it; yet we are driven constantly to defend ourselves from the assumption that we are warring upon the rights of the States. What I insist upon is, that the new Territories shall be kept free from it while in the territorial condition. Judge Douglas assumes that we have no interest in them—that we have no right whatever to interfere. I think we have some interest. I think that as white men we have. Do we wish for an outlet for our surplus population, if I may so express myself? Do we not feel an interest in getting to that outlet with such institutions as we would like to have prevail there? If you go to the Territory opposed to slavery, and another man comes upon the same ground with his slave, upon the assumption that the things are equal, it turns out that he has the equal right all his way, and you have no part of it your way. If he goes in and makes it a slave Territory, and by consequence a slave State, is it not time that those who desire to have it a free State were on equal ground? Let me suggest it in a different way. How many democrats are there about here ["A thousand"] who have left slave states and come into the free State of Illinois to get rid of the institution of slavery? [Another voice: "A thousand and one."] I reckon there are a thousand and one. I will ask you, if the policy you are now advocating had prevailed when this country was in a territorial condition, where would you have gone to get rid of it? Where would you have found your free State or Territory to go to? And when hereafter, for any cause, the people in this place shall desire to find new homes, if they wish to be rid of the institution, where will they find the place to go to?

Now, irrespective of the moral aspect of this question as to whether there is a right or wrong in enslaving a negro, I am still in favor of our new Territories being in such a condition that white men may find a home—may find some spot where they can better their condition—where they can settle upon new soil, and better their condition in life. I am in favor of this not merely (I must say it here as I have elsewhere) for our own people who are born amongst us, but as an outlet for free white people everywhere, the world over—in which Hans, and Baptiste, and Patrick, and all other men from all the world, may find new homes and better their condition in life.

I have stated upon former occasions, and I may as well state again, what I understand to be the real issue of this controversy between Judge Douglas and myself. On the point of my wanting to make war between the free and the slave States, there has been no issue between us. So, too, when he assumes that I am in favor of introducing a perfect social and political equality between the white and black races. These are false issues, upon which Judge Douglas has tried to force the controversy. There is no foundation in truth for the charge that I maintain either of these propositions. The real issue in this controversy—the one pressing upon every mind—is the sentiment on the part of one class that looks upon the institution of slavery as a wrong, and of another class that does not look upon it as a wrong. The sentiment that contemplates the institution of slavery in this country as a wrong is the sentiment of the Republican party. It is the sentiment around which all their actions, all their arguments, circle; from which all their propositions radiate. They look upon it as being a moral, social, and political wrong; and while they contemplate it as such, they nevertheless have due regard for its actual existence among us, and the difficulties of getting rid of it in any satisfactory way, and to all the constitutional obligations thrown about it. Yet having a due regard for these, they desire a policy in regard to it that looks to its not creating any more danger. They insist that it, as far as may be, be treated as a wrong, and one of the methods of treating it as a wrong is to make provision that it shall grow no larger. They also desire a policy that looks to a peaceful end of slavery some time, as being a wrong. These are the views they entertain in regard to it, as I understand them; and all their sentiments, all their arguments and propositions, are brought within this range. I have said, and I repeat it here, that if there be a man amongst us who does not think that the institution of slavery is wrong in any one of the aspects of which I have spoken, he is misplaced, and ought not to be with us. And if there be a man amongst us who is so impatient of it as a wrong as to disregard its actual presence among us and the difficulty of getting rid of it suddenly in a satisfactory way, and to disregard the constitutional obligations thrown about it, that man is misplaced if he is on our platform. We disclaim sympathy with him in practical action. He is not placed properly with us.

On this subject of treating it as a wrong, and limiting its spread, let me say a word. Has anything ever threatened the existence of this Union save and except this very institution of slavery? What is it that we hold most dear amongst us? Our own liberty and prosperity. What has ever threatened our liberty and prosperity save and except this institution of slavery? If this is true, how do you propose to improve the condition of things by enlarging slavery—by spreading it out and making it bigger? You may have a wen or cancer upon your person, and not be able to cut it out lest you bleed to death; but surely it is no way to cure it, to engraft it and spread it over your whole body. That is no proper way of treating what you regard as a wrong. You see this peaceful way of dealing with it as a wrong—restricting the spread of it, and not allowing it to go into new countries where it has not already existed. That is the peaceful way, the old-fashioned way, the way in which the fathers themselves set us the example.

On the other hand, I have said there is a sentiment which treats it as not being wrong. That is the Democratic sentiment of this day. I do not mean to say that every man who stands within that range positively asserts that it is right. That class will include all who positively assert that it is right, and all who, like Judge Douglas, treat it as indifferent, and do not say it is either right or wrong. These two classes of men fall within the general class of those who do not look upon it as a wrong. . . .

The Democratic policy in regard to that institution will not tolerate the merest breath, the slightest hint, of the least degree of wrong about it. Try it by some of Judge Douglas's arguments. He says he "don't care whether it is voted up or voted down" in the Territories. I do not care myself, in dealing with that expression, whether it is intended to be expressive of his individual sentiments on the subject, or only of the national policy he desires to have established. It is alike valuable for my purpose. Any man can say that who does not see anything wrong in slavery, but no man can logically say it who does see a wrong in it because no man can logically say he don't care whether a wrong is voted up or voted down. He may say he don't care whether an indifferent thing is voted up or down, but he must logically have a choice between a right thing and a wrong thing. He contends that whatever community wants slaves has a right to have them. So they have if it is not a wrong. But if it is a wrong, he cannot say people have a right to do wrong.

He says that, upon the score of equality, slaves should be allowed to go into a new Territory like other property. This is strictly logical if there is no difference between it and other property. If it and other property are equal, his argument is entirely logical. But if you insist that one is wrong and the other right there is no use to institute a comparison between right and wrong. You may turn over everything in the Democratic policy from beginning to end, whether in the shape it takes on the statute-book, in the shape it takes in the Dred Scott decision, in the shape it takes in conversation, or the shape it takes in short maxim-like arguments—it everywhere carefully excludes the idea that there is anything wrong in it.

That is the real issue. That is the issue that will continue in this country when these poor tongues of Judge Douglas and myself shall be silent. It is the eternal struggle between these two principles—right and wrong—throughout the world. They are the two principles that have stood face to face from the beginning of time; and will ever continue to struggle. The one is the common right of humanity, and the other the divine right of kings. It is the same principle in whatever shape it develops itself. It is the same spirit that says, "You toil and work and earn bread, and I'll eat it." No matter in what shape it comes, whether from the mouth of a king who seeks to bestride the people of his own nation and live by the fruit of their labor, or from one race of men as an apology for enslaving another race, it is the same tyrannical principle. . . .

# Selections From *An Inquiry Into the Nature and Causes of the Wealth of Nations*

## Adam Smith (1723–1790)

*Along with John Locke, Adam Smith stands as one of the chief designers of the liberal capitalist way of life. A Professor of Logic and of Moral Philosophy at the University of Glasgow from 1751 to the early 1760s, Smith published the* Theory of Moral Sentiments *in 1759 and* The Wealth of Nations *in 1776. Both works laud the economic virtues of rational "self-love" combined with individual freedom.*

*What fundamental assumptions does Smith share with John Locke? How does the famous "invisible hand" regulate the production and distribution of goods to the benefit of society as a whole? Consider the consequences of making self-interest the principle of social order. What are the political implications of this theory of the free market? Compare Smith's view of the most efficient economic order with Publius' view of the most free and most stable political order in* Federalist Nos. 10 and 51.

## BOOK I

### CHAPTER I:  OF DIVISION OF LABOUR

The greatest improvement in the productive powers of labour, and the greater part of the skill, dexterity, and judgment with which it is any where directed, or applied, seem to have been the effects of the division of labour.

The effects of the division of labour, in the general business of society, will be more easily understood by considering in what manner it operates in some particular manufactures. It is commonly supposed to be carried furthest in some very trifling ones; not perhaps that it really is carried further in them than in others of more importance:  but in those trifling manufactures which are destined to supply the small wants of but a small number of people, the whole number of workmen must necessarily be small; and those employed in every different branch of the work can often be collected into the same workhouse, and placed at once under the view of the spectator. In those great manufactures, on the contrary, which are destined to supply the great wants of the great body of the people, every different branch of the work employs so great a number of workmen, that it is impossible to collect them all into the same workhouse. We can seldom see more, at one time, than those employed in one single branch. Though in such manufactures, therefore, the work may really be divided into a much greater number of parts, than in those of a more trifling nature, the division is not near so obvious, and has accordingly been much less observed.

To take an example, therefore, from a very trifling manufacture; but one in which the division of labour has been very often taken notice of, the trade of the pin-maker; a workman not educated to this business (which the division of labour has rendered a distinct trade,) nor acquainted with the use of the machinery employed in it (to the invention of which the same division of labour has probably given occasion,) could scarce, perhaps, with his utmost industry, make one pin in a day, and certainly could not make twenty. But in the way in which the business is now carried on, not only the whole work is a peculiar trade, but it is divided into a number of branches, of which the greater part are likewise peculiar trades. One man draws out the wire, another straights it, a third cuts it, a fourth points it, a fifth grinds it at the top for receiving the head; to make the head requires two or three distinct operations; to put it on, is a peculiar business, to whiten the pins is another; it is even a trade by itself to put them into the paper; and the important business of making a pin is, in this manner, divided into about eighteen distinct operations, which, in some manufactories, are all performed by distinct hands, though in others the same man will sometimes perform two or three of them. I have seen a small manufactory of this kind where ten men only were employed, and where some of them consequently performed two or three distinct operations. But though they were very poor, and therefore but indifferently accommodated with the necessary machinery, they could, when they exerted themselves, make among them about twelve pounds of pins in a day. There are in a pound upwards of four thousand pins of a middling size. Those ten persons, therefore, could make among them upwards of forty-eight thousand pins in a day. Each person, therefore, making a tenth part of forty-eight thousand pins, might be considered as making four thousand eight hundred pins a day. But if they had all wrought separately and independently, and without any of them having been educated to this peculiar business, they certainly could not each of them have made twenty, perhaps not one pin in a day; that is, certainly, not the two hundred and fortieth, perhaps not the four thousand eight hundredth part of what they are at present capable of performing, in consequence of a proper division and combination of their different operations.

In every other art and manufacture, the effects of the division of labour are similar to what they are in this very trifling one; though in many of them, the labour can neither be so much subdivided, nor reduced to so great a simplicity of operation. The division of labour, however, so far as it can be introduced, occasions, in every art, a proportionable increase of the productive powers of labour. The separation of different trades and employments from one another, seems to have taken place, in consequence of this advantage. This separation too is generally carried furthest in those countries which enjoy the highest degree of industry and improvement; what is the work of one man in a rude state of society, being generally that of several in an improved one. In every improved society, the farmer is generally nothing but a farmer; the manufacturer, nothing but a manufacturer. The labour too which is necessary to produce any one complete manufacture, is almost always divided among a great number of hands. How many different trades are employed in each branch of the linen and woollen manufactures, from the growers of the flax and the wool, to the bleachers and smoothers of the linen, or to the dyers and dressers of the cloth! The nature of agriculture, indeed, does not admit of so many subdivisions of labour, nor of so complete a separation of one business from another, as manufactures. It is impossible to separate so entirely the business of the grazier from that of the corn-farmer, as the trade of the carpenter is commonly separated from that of the smith. The spinner is almost always a distinct person from the weaver; but the ploughman, the harrower, the sower of the seed, and the reaper of the corn, are often the same. The occasions for those different sorts of labour returning with the different seasons of the year, it is impossible that one man should be constantly employed in any one of them. This impossibility of making so complete and entire a separation of all the different branches of labour employed in agriculture, is perhaps the reason why the improvement of the productive powers of labour in this art, does not always keep pace with their improvement in manufactures. The most opulent nations, indeed, generally excel all their neighbours in agriculture as well as in manufactures; but they are commonly more distinguished by their superiority in the latter than in the former. Their lands are in general better cultivated, and having more labour and expence bestowed upon them, produce more in proportion to the extent and natural fertility of the ground. But this superiority of produce is seldom much more than in proportion to the superiority of labour and expence. In agriculture, the labour of the rich country is not always much more productive than that of the poor; or, at least, it is never so much more productive, as it commonly is in manufactures. The corn of the rich country, therefore, will not always, in the same degree of goodness, come cheaper to market than that of the poor. The corn of Poland, in the same degree of goodness, is as cheap as that of France, notwithstanding the superior opulence and improvement of the latter country. The corn of France is, in the corn provinces, fully as good, and in most years nearly about the same price with the corn of England, though, in opulence and improvement, France is perhaps inferior to England. The corn-lands of England, however, are better cultivated than those of France, and the corn-lands of France are said to be much better cultivated than those of Poland. But though the poor country, notwithstanding the inferiority of its cultivation, can in some measure, rival the rich in the cheapness and goodness of its corn, it can pretend to no such competition in its manufactures; at least if those manufactures suit the soil, climate, and situation of the rich country. The silks of France are better and cheaper than those of England, because the silk manufacture, at least under the present high duties upon the importation of raw silk, does not so well suit the climate of England as that of France. But the hard-ware and the coarse woollens of England are beyond all comparison superior to those of France, and much cheaper too in the same degree of goodness. In Poland there are said to be scarce any manufactures of any kind, a few of those coarser household manufactures excepted, without which no country can well subsist.

This great increase in the quantity of work, which, in consequence of the division of labour, the same number of people are capable of performing, is owing to three different circumstances; first, to the increase of dexterity in every particular workman; secondly, to the saving of the time which is commonly lost in passing from one species of work to another; and lastly, to the invention of a great number of machines which facilitate and abridge labour, and enable one man to do the work of many.

First, the improvement of the dexterity of the workman necessarily increases the quantity of the work he can perform; and the division of labour, by reducing every man's business to some one simple operation, and by making this operation the sole employment of his life, necessarily increases very much the dexterity of the workman. A common smith, who, though accustomed to handle the hammer, has never been used to make nails, if upon some particular occasion he is obliged to attempt it, will scarce, I am assured, be able to make above two or three hundred nails in a day, and those too very bad ones. A smith who has been accustomed to make nails, but whose sole or principal business has not been that of a nailer, can seldom with his utmost diligence make more than eight hundred or a thousand nails in a day. I have seen several boys under twenty years of age who had never exercised any other trade but that of making nails, and who, when they exerted themselves, could make, each of them, upwards of two thousand three hundred nails in a day. The making of a nail, however, is by no means one of the simplest operations. The same person blows the bellows, stirs or mends the fire as there is occasion, heats the iron, and forges every part of the nail: In forging the head too he is obliged to change his tools. The different operations into which the making of a pin, or of a metal button, is subdivided, are all of them much more simple, and the dexterity of the person, of whose life it has been the sole business to perform them, is usually much greater. The rapidity with which some of the operations of those manufactures are performed, exceeds what the human hand could, by those who had never seen them, be supposed capable of acquiring.

Secondly, the advantage which is gained by saving the time commonly lost in passing from one sort of work to another, is much greater than we should at first view be apt to imagine it. It is impossible to pass very quickly from one kind of work to another, that is carried on in a different place, and with quite different tools. A country weaver, who cultivates a small farm, must lose a good deal of time in passing from his loom to the field, and from the field to his loom. When the two trades can be carried on in the same workhouse, the loss of time is no doubt much less. It is even in this case, however, very considerable. A man commonly saunters a little in turning his hand from one sort of employment to another. When he first begins the new work he is seldom very keen and hearty; his mind, as they say, does not go to it, and for some time he rather trifles than applies to good purpose. The habit of sauntering and of indolent careless application, which is naturally, or rather necessarily, acquired by every country workman who is obliged to change his work and his tools every half hour, and to apply his hand in twenty different ways almost every day of his life; renders him almost always slothful and lazy, and incapable of any vigorous application even on the most pressing occasions. Independent, therefore, of his deficiency in point of dexterity, this cause alone must always reduce considerably the quantity of work which he is capable of performing.

Thirdly, and lastly, every body must be sensible how much labour is facilitated and abridged by the application of proper machinery. It is unnecessary to give any example. I shall only observe, therefore, that the invention of all those machines by which labour is so much facilitated and abridged, seems to have been originally owing to the division of labour. Men are much more likely to discover easier and readier methods of attaining any object, when the whole attention of their minds is directed  towards that single object, than when it is dissipated among a great variety of things. But in consequence of the division of labour, the whole of every man's attention comes naturally to be directed towards some one very simple object. It is naturally to be expected, therefore, that some one or other of those who are employed in each particular branch of labour should soon find out easier and readier methods of performing their own particular work, wherever the nature of it admits of such improvement. A great part of the machines made use of in those manufactures in which labour is most subdivided, were originally the inventions of common workmen, who, being each of them employed in some very simple operation, naturally turned their thoughts towards finding out easier and readier methods of performing it. Whoever has been much accustomed to visit such manufactures, must frequently have been  shewn very pretty machines, which were the inventions of such workmen, in order to facilitate and quicken their own particular part of the work. In the first fire-engines, a boy was constantly employed to open and shut alternately the communication between the boiler and the cylinder, according as the piston either ascended or descended. One of those boys, who loved to play with his companions, observed that, by tying a string from the handle of the valve which opened this communication to another part of the machine, the valve would open and shut without his assistance, and leave him at liberty to divert himself with his playfellows. One of the greatest improvements that has been made upon this machine, since it was first invented, was in this manner the discovery of a boy who wanted to save his own labour.

All the improvements in machinery, however, have by no means been the inventions of those who had occasion to use the machines. Many improvements have been made by the ingenuity of the makers of the machines, when to make them became the business of a peculiar trade; and some by that of those who are called philosophers or men of speculation, whose trade it is not to do any thing; but to observe every thing; and who, upon that account, are often capable of combining together the powers of the most distant and dissimilar objects. In the progress of society, philosophy or speculation becomes, like every other employment, the principal or sole trade and occupation of a particular class of citizens. Like every other employment too, it is subdivided into a great number of different branches, each of which affords occupation to a peculiar tribe or class of philosophers; and this subdivision of employment in philosophy, as well as in every other business, improves dexterity, and saves time. Each individual becomes more expert in his own peculiar branch, more work is done upon the whole, and the quantity of science is considerably increased by it.

It is the great multiplication of the production of all the different arts in consequence of the division of labour, which occasions, in a well-governed society, that universal opulence which extends itself to the lowest ranks of the people. Every workman has a great quantity of his own work to dispose of beyond what he himself has occasion for; and every other workman being exactly in the same situation, he is enabled to exchange a great quantity of his own goods for a great quantity, or, what comes to the same thing, for the price of a great quantity of theirs. He supplies them abundantly with what they have occasion for, and they accommodate him as amply with what he has occasion for, and a general plenty diffuses itself through all the different ranks of the society.

Observe the accommodation of the most common artificer or day-labourer in a civilized and thriving country, and you will perceive that the number of people of whose industry a part, though but a small part, has been employed in procuring him this accommodation, exceeds all computation. The woollen coat for example, which covers the day-labourer, as coarse and rough as it may appear, is the produce of the joint labour of a great multitude of workmen. The shepherd, the sorter of the wool, the wool-comber or carder, the dyer, the scribbler, the spinner, the weaver, the fuller, the dresser, with many others, must all join their different arts in order to complete even this homely production. How many merchants and carriers, besides, must have been employed in transporting the materials from some of those workmen to others who often live in a very distant part of the country! How much commerce and navigation in particular, how many ship-builders, sailors, sail-makers, rope-makers, must have been employed in order to bring together the different drugs made use of by the dyer, which often come from the remotest corners of the world? What a variety of labour too is necessary in order to produce the tools of the meanest of those workmen! To say nothing of such complicated machines as the ship of the sailor, the mill of the fuller, or even the loom of the weaver, let us consider only what a variety of labour is requisite in order to form that very simple machine, the shears with which the shepherd clips the wool. The miner, the builder of the furnace for smelting the ore, the feller of the timber, the burner of the charcoal to be made use of in the smelting house, the brick-maker, the bricklayer, the workmen who attend the furnace, the mill-wright, the forger, the smith, must all of them join their different arts in order to produce them. Were we to examine in the same manner, all the different parts of his dress and household furniture, the coarse linen shirt which he wears next his skin, the shoes which cover his feet, the bed which he lies on, and all the different parts which compose it, the kitchen grate at which he prepares his victuals, the coals which he makes use of for that purpose, dug from the bowels of the earth, and brought to him perhaps by a long sea and a long land carriage, all the other utensils of his kitchen, all the furniture of his table, the knives and forks, the earthen or pewter plates upon which he serves up and divides his victuals, the different hands employed in preparing his bread and his beer, the glass window which lets in the heat and the light, and keeps out the wind and the rain, with all the knowledge and art requisite for preparing that beautiful and happy invention, without which these northern parts of the world could scarce have afforded a very comfortable habitation, together with the tools of all the different workmen employed in producing those different conveniencies; if we examine, I say, all these things, and consider what a variety of labour is employed about each of them, we shall be sensible that without the assistance and cooperation of many thousands, the very meanest person in a civilized country could not be provided, even according to, what we very falsely imagine, the easy and simple manner in which he is commonly accommodated. Compared, indeed, with the more extravagant luxury of the great, his accommodation must no doubt appear extremely simple and easy; and yet it may be true, perhaps, that the accommodation of an European prince does not always so much exceed that of an industrious and frugal peasant, as the accommodation of the latter exceeds that of many an African king, the absolute master of the lives and liberties of ten thousand naked savages.

## CHAPTER II:   *OF THE PRINCIPLE WHICH GIVES OCCASION TO THE DIVISION OF LABOUR*

This division of labour, from which so many advantages are derived, is not originally the effect of any human wisdom, which foresees and intends that general opulence to which it gives occasion. It is the necessary, though very slow and gradual, consequence of a certain propensity in human nature which has in view no such extensive utility; the propensity to truck, barter, and exchange one thing for another.

Whether this propensity be one of those original principles in human nature, of which no further account can be given; or whether, as seems more probable, it be the necessary consequence of the faculties of reason and speech, it belongs not to our present subject to enquire. It is common to all men, and to be found in no other race of animals, which seem to know neither this nor any other species of contracts. Two greyhounds, in running down the same hare, have sometimes the appearance of acting in some sort of concert. Each turns her towards his companion, or endeavors to intercept her when his companion turns her towards himself. This, however, is not the effect of any contract, but of the accidental concurrence of their passions in the same object at that particular time. Nobody ever saw a dog make a fair and deliberate exchange of one bone for another with another dog. Nobody ever saw one animal by its gestures and natural cries signify to another, this is mine, that yours; I am willing to give this for that. When an animal wants to obtain something either of a man, or of another animal, it has no other means of persuasion, but to gain the favour of those whose service it requires. A puppy fawns upon its dam, and a spaniel endeavours by a thousand attractions to engage the attention of its master who is at dinner, when it wants to be fed by him. Man sometimes uses the same arts with his brethren, and when he has no other means of engaging them to act according to his inclinations, endeavours by every servile and fawning attention to obtain their good will. He has not time, however, to do this upon every occasion. In civilized society he stands at all times in need of the cooperation and assistance of great multitudes, while his whole life is scarce sufficient to gain the friendship of a few persons. In almost every other race of animals, each individual, when it is grown up to maturity, is entirely independent, and in its natural state has occasion for the assistance of no other living creature. But man has almost constant occasion for the help of his brethren, and it is in vain for him to expect it from their benevolence only. He will be more likely to prevail if he can interest their self-love in his favour, and shew them that it is for their own advantage to do for him what he requires of them. Whoever offers to another a bargain of any kind, proposes to do this:  Give me that which I want, and you shall have this which you want, is the meaning of every such offer; and it is in this manner that we obtain from one another the far greater part of those good offices which we stand in need of. It is not from the benevolence of the butcher, the brewer, or the baker, that we expect our dinner, but from their regard to their own interest. We address ourselves, not to their humanity but to their self-love, and never talk to them of our own necessities but of their advantages. Nobody but a beggar chooses to depend chiefly upon the benevolence of his fellow-citizens. Even a beggar does not depend upon it entirely. The charity of well-disposed people, indeed, supplies him with the whole fund of his subsistence. But though this principle ultimately provides him with all the necessaries of life which he has occasion for, it neither does nor can provide him with them as he has occasion for them. The greater part of his occasional wants are supplied in the same manner as those of other people, by treaty, by barter, and by purchase. With the money which one man gives him he purchases food. The old cloaths which another bestows upon him he exchanges for other old cloaths which suit him better, or for lodging, or for food, or for money, with which he can buy either food, cloaths, or lodging, as he has occasion.

As it is by treaty, by barter, and by purchase, that we obtain from one another the greater part of those mutual good offices which we stand in need of, so it is the same trucking disposition which originally gives occasion to the division of labour. In a tribe of hunters or shepherds a particular person makes bows and arrows, for example, with more readiness and dexterity than any other. He frequently exchanges them for cattle or for venison with his companions; and he finds at last that he can in this manner get more cattle and venison, than if he himself went to the field to catch them. From a regard to his own interest, therefore, the making of bows and arrows grows to be his chief business, and he becomes a sort of armourer. Another excels in making the frames and covers of their little huts or moveable houses. He is accustomed to be of use in this way to his neighbours, who reward him in the same manner with cattle and with venison, till at last he finds it his interest to dedicate himself entirely to this employment, and to become a sort of house-carpenter. In the same manner a third becomes a smith or a brazier; a fourth a tanner or dresser of hides or skins, the principal part of the cloathing of savages. And thus the certainty of being able to exchange all that surplus part of the produce of his own labour, which is over and above his own consumption, for such parts of the produce of other men's labour as he may have occasion for, encourages every man to apply himself to a particular occupation, and to cultivate and bring to perfection whatever talent or genius he may possess for that particular species of business.

The difference of natural talents in different men is, in reality, much less than we are aware of; and the very different genius which appears to distinguish men of different professions, when grown up to maturity, is not upon many occasions so much the cause, as the effect of the division of labour. The difference between the most dissimilar characters, between a philosopher and a common street porter, for example, seems to arise not so much from nature, as from habit, custom, and education. When they came into the world, and for the first six or eight years of their existence, they were, perhaps, very much alike, and neither their parents nor play fellows could perceive any remarkable difference. About that age, or soon after, they come to be employed in very different occupations. The difference of talents comes then to be taken notice of, and widens by degrees, till at last the vanity of the philosopher is willing to acknowledge scarce any resemblance. But without the disposition to truck, barter, and exchange, every man must have procured to himself every necessary and conveniency of life which he wanted. All must have had the same duties to perform, and the same work to do, and there could have been no such difference of employment as could alone give occasion to any great difference of talents.

As it is this disposition which forms that difference of talents, so remarkable among men of different professions, so it is this same disposition which renders that difference useful. Many tribes of animals acknowledged to be all of the same species, derive from nature a much more remarkable distinction of genius, than what, antecedent to custom and education, appears to take place among men. By nature a philosopher is not in genius and disposition half so different from a street-porter, as a mastiff is from a greyhound, or a greyhound from a spaniel, or this last from a shepherd's dog. Those different tribes of animals, however, though all of the same species, are of scarce any use to one another. The strength of the mastiff is not in the least supported either by the swiftness of the greyhound, or by the sagacity of the spaniel, or by the docility of the shepherd's dog. The effects of those different geniuses and talents, for want of the power or disposition to barter and exchange, cannot be brought into a common stock, and do not in the least contribute to the better accommodation and conveniency of the species. Each animal is still obliged to support and defend itself, separately and independently, and derives no sort of advantage from that variety of talents with which nature has distinguished its fellows. Among men, on the contrary, the most dissimilar geniuses are of use to one another; the different produces of their respective talents, by the general disposition to truck, barter, and exchange, being brought, as it were, into a common stock, where every man may purchase whatever part of the produce of other men's talents he has occasion for. . . .

### CHAPTER V:  *OF THE REAL AND NOMINAL PRICE OF COMMODITIES, OR OF THEIR PRICE IN LABOUR, AND THEIR PRICE IN MONEY*

Every man is rich or poor according to the degree in which he can afford to enjoy the necessaries, conveniences, and amusements of human life. But after the division of labour has once thoroughly taken place, it is but a very small part of these with which a man's own labour can supply him. The far greater part of them he must derive from the labour of other people, and he must be rich or poor according to the quantity of that labour, which he can command, or which he can afford to purchase. The value of any commodity, therefore, to the person who possesses it, and who means not to use or consume it himself, but to exchange it for other commodities, is equal to the quantity of labor which it enables him to purchase or command. Labour, therefore, is the real measure of the exchangeable value of all commodities.

The real price of every thing, what every thing really costs to the man who wants to acquire it, is the toil and trouble of acquiring it. What every thing is really worth to the man who has acquired it, and who wants to dispose of it or exchange it for something else, is the toil and trouble which it can save to himself, and which it can impose upon other people. What is bought with money or with goods is purchased by labour, as much as what we acquire by the toil of our own body. That money or those goods indeed save us this toil. They contain the value of a certain quantity of labour which we exchange for what is supposed at the time to contain the value of an equal quantity. Labour was the first price, the original purchase-money that was paid for all things. It was not by gold or by silver, but by labour, that all the wealth of the world was originally purchased; and its value, to those who possess it, and who want to exchange it for some new productions, is precisely equal to the quantity of labour which it can enable them to purchase or command.

Wealth, as Mr. Hobbes says, is power. But the person who either acquires, or succeeds to a great fortune, does not necessarily acquire or succeed to any political power, either civil or military. His fortune may, perhaps, afford him the means of acquiring both, but the mere possession of that fortune does not necessarily convey to him either. The power which that possession immediately and directly conveys to him, is the power of purchasing a certain command over all the labour, or over all the produce of labour which is then in the market. His fortune is greater or less, precisely in proportion to the extent of this power; or to the quantity either of other men's labour, or, what is the same thing, of the produce of other men's labour, which it enables him to purchase or command. The exchangeable value of every thing must always be precisely equal to the extent of power which it conveys to its owner.

But though labour be the real measure of the exchangeable value of all commodities, it is not that by which their value is commonly estimated. It is often difficult to ascertain the proportion between two different quantities of labour. The time spent in two different sorts of work will not always alone determine this proportion. The different degrees of hardship endured, and of ingenuity exercised, must likewise be taken into account. There may be more labour in an hour's hard work, than in two hours' easy business; or in an hour's application to a trade which it cost ten years labour to learn, than in a month's industry, at an ordinary and obvious employment. But it is not easy to find any accurate measure either of hardship or ingenuity. In exchanging indeed the different productions of different sorts of labour for one another, some allowance is commonly made for both. It is adjusted, however, not by any accurate measure, but by the higgling and bargaining of the market, according to that sort of rough equality which, though not exact, is sufficient for carrying on the business of common life.

Every commodity besides, is more frequently exchanged for, and thereby compared with, other commodities than with labour. It is more natural therefore, to estimate its exchangeable value by the quantity of some other commodity than by that of the labour which it can purchase. The greater part of people too understand better what is meant by a quantity of a particular commodity, than by a quantity of labour. The one is a plain palpable object; the other an abstract notion, which, though it can be made sufficiently intelligible, is not altogether so natural and obvious.

But when barter ceases, and money has become the common instrument of commerce, every particular commodity is more frequently exchanged for money than for any other commodity. The butcher seldom carries his beef or his mutton to the baker, or the brewer, in order to exchange them for bread or for beer; but he carries them to the market, where he exchanges them for money, and afterwards exchanges that money for bread and for beer. The quantity of money which he gets for them regulates too the quantity of bread and beer which he can afterwards purchase. It is more natural and obvious to him, therefore, to estimate their value by the quantity of money, the commodity for which he immediately exchanges them, than by that of bread and beer, the commodities for which he can exchange them only by the intervention of another commodity; and rather to say that his butcher's meat is worth threepence or fourpence a pound, than that it is worth three or four pounds of bread, or three or four quarts of small beer. Hence it come to pass, that the exchangeable value of every commodity is more frequently estimated by the quantity of money, than by the quantity either of labour or of any other commodity which can be had in exchange for it.

Gold and silver, however, like every other commodity, vary in their value, are sometimes cheaper and sometimes dearer, sometimes of easier and sometimes of more difficult purchase. The quantity of labour which any particular quantity of them can purchase or command, or the quantity of other goods which it will exchange for, depends always upon the fertility or barrenness of the mines which happen to be known about the time when such exchanges are made. The discovery of the abundant mines of America reduced, in the sixteenth century, the value of gold and silver in Europe to about a third of what it had been before. As it costs less labour to bring those metals from the mine to the market, so when they were brought thither they could purchase or command less labour; and this revolution in their value, though perhaps the greatest, is by no means the only one of which history gives some account. But as a measure of quantity, such as the natural foot, fathom, or handful, which is continually varying in its own quantity, can never be an accurate measure of the quantity of other things; so a commodity which is itself continually varying in its own value, can never be an accurate measure of the value of other commodities. Equal quantities of labour, at all times and places, may be said to be of equal value to the labourer. In his ordinary state of health, strength, and spirits, in the ordinary degree of his skill and dexterity, he must always lay down the same portion of his ease, his liberty and his happiness. The price which he pays must always be the same, whatever may be the quantity of goods which he receives in return for it. Of these, indeed, it may sometimes purchase a greater and sometimes a smaller quantity; but it is their value which varies, not that of the labour which purchases them. At all times and places that is dear which it is difficult to come at, or which it costs much labour to acquire; and that cheap which is to be had easily, or with very little labour. Labour alone, therefore, never varying in its own value, is alone the ultimate and real standard by which the value of all commodities can at all times and places be estimated and compared. It is their real price; money is their nominal price only.

But though equal quantities of labour are always of equal value to the labourer, yet to the person who employs him they appear sometimes to be of greater and sometimes of smaller value. He purchases them sometimes with a greater and sometimes with a smaller quantity of goods, and to him the price of labour seems to vary like that of all other things. It appears to him dear in the one case, and cheap in the other. In reality, however, it is the goods which are cheap in the one case, and dear in the other.

In this popular sense, therefore, labour like commodities, may be said to have a real and a nominal price. Its real price may be said to consist in the quantity of the necessaries and conveniences of life which are given for it; its nominal price, in the quantity of money. The labourer is rich or poor, is well or ill rewarded, in proportion to the real, not to the nominal price of his labour. . . .

### CHAPTER VII: OF THE NATURAL AND MARKET PRICE OF COMMODITIES

There is in every society or neighbourhood an ordinary or average rate both of wages and profit in every different employment of labour and stock. This rate is naturally regulated, as I shall show hereafter, partly by the general circumstances of the society, their riches or poverty, their advancing, stationary, or declining condition; and partly, by the particular nature of each employment.

There is likewise in every society or neighbourhood an ordinary or average rate of rent, which is regulated too, as I shall show hereafter, partly by the general circumstances of the society or neighbourhood in which the land is situated, and partly by the natural or improved fertility of the land.

These ordinary or average rates may be called the natural rates of wages, profit, and rent, at the time and place in which they commonly prevail.

When the price of any commodity is neither more nor less than what is sufficient to pay the rent of the land, the wages of the labour, and the profits of the stock employed in raising, preparing, and bringing it to market, according to their natural rates, the commodity is then sold for what may be called its natural price.

The commodity is then sold precisely for what it is worth, or for what it really costs the person who brings it to market; for though in common language what is called the prime cost of any commodity does not comprehend the profit of the person who is to sell it again, yet if he sells it at a price which does not allow him the ordinary rate of profit in his neighbourhood, he is evidently a loser by the trade; since by employing his stock in some other way he might have made that profit. His profit, besides, is his revenue, the proper fund of his subsistence. As, while he is preparing and bringing the goods to market, he advances to his workmen their wages, or their subsistence; so he advances to himself, in the same manner, his own subsistence, which is generally suitable to the profit which he may reasonably expect from the sale of his goods. Unless they yield him this profit, therefore, they do not repay him what they may very properly be said to have really cost him.

Though the price, therefore, which leaves him this profit, is not always the lowest at which a dealer may sometimes sell his goods, it is the lowest at which he is likely to sell them for any considerable time; at least where there is perfect liberty, or where he may change his trade as often as he pleases.

The actual price at which any commodity is commonly sold is called its market price. It may either be above, or below, or exactly the same with its natural price.

The market price of every particular commodity is regulated by the proportion between the quantity which is actually brought to market, and the demand of those who are willing to pay the natural price of the commodity, or the whole value of the rent, labour, and profit, which must be paid in order to bring it thither. Such people may be called the effectual demanders, and their demand the effectual demand; since it may be sufficient to effectuate the bringing of the commodity to market. It is different from the absolute demand. A very poor man may be said in some sense to have a demand for a coach and six; he might like to have it; but his demand is not an effectual demand, as the commodity can never be brought to market in order to satisfy it.

When the quantity of any commodity which is brought to market falls short of the effectual demand, all those who are willing to pay the whole value of the rent, wages, and profit, which must be paid in order to bring it thither, cannot be supplied with the quantity which they want. Rather than want it altogether, some of them will be willing to give more. A competition will immediately begin among them, and the market price will rise more or less above the natural price, according as either the greatness of the deficiency, or the wealth and wanton luxury of the competitors, happen to animate more or less the eagerness of the competition. Among competitors of equal wealth and luxury the same deficiency will generally occasion a more or less eager competition, according as the acquisition of the commodity happens to be of more or less importance to them. Hence the exorbitant price of the necessaries of life during the blockade of a town or in a famine.

When the quantity brought to market exceeds the effectual demand, it cannot be all sold to those who are willing to pay the whole value of the rent, wages and profit, which must be paid in order to bring it thither. Some part must be sold to those who are willing to pay less, and the low price which they give for it must reduce the price of the whole. The market price will sink more or less below the natural price, according as the greatness of the excess increases more or less the competition of the sellers, or according as it happens to be more or less important to them to get immediately rid of the commodity. The same excess in the importation of perishable, will occasion a much greater competition than in that of durable commodities; in the importation of oranges, for example, than in that of old iron.

When the quantity brought to market is just sufficient to supply the effectual demand and no more, the market price naturally comes to be either exactly, or as nearly as can be judged of, the same with the natural price. The whole quantity upon hand can be disposed of for this price, and cannot be disposed of for more. The competition of the different dealers obliges them all to accept of this price, but does not oblige them to accept of less.

The quantity of every commodity brought to market naturally suits itself to the effectual demand. It is the interest of all those who employ their land, labour, or stock, in bringing any commodity to market, that the quantity never should exceed the effectual demand; and it is the interest of all other people that it never should fall short of that demand.

If at any time it exceeds the effectual demand, some of the component parts of its price must be paid below their natural rate. If it is rent, the interest of the landlords will immediately prompt them to withdraw a part of their land; and if it is wages or profit, the interest of the labourers in the one case, and of their employers in the other, will prompt them to withdraw a part of their labour or stock from this employment. The quantity brought to market will soon be no more than sufficient to supply the effectual demand. All the different parts of its price will rise to their natural rate, and the whole price to its natural price.

If, on the contrary, the quantity brought to market should at any time, fall short of the effectual demand, some of the component parts of its price must rise above their natural rate. If it is rent, the interest of all other landlords will naturally prompt them to prepare more land for the raising of this commodity; if it is wages or profit, the interest of all other labourers, and dealers will soon prompt them to employ more labour and stock in preparing and bringing it to market. The quantity brought thither will soon be sufficient to supply the effectual demand. All the different parts of its price will soon sink to their natural rate, and the whole price to its natural price.

The natural price, therefore, is, as it were, the central price, to which the prices of all commodities are continually gravitating. Different accidents may sometimes keep them suspended a good deal above it, and sometimes force them down even somewhat below it. But whatever may be the obstacles which hinder them from settling in this center of repose and continuance, they are constantly tending towards it.

The whole quantity of industry annually employed in order to bring any commodity to market, naturally suits itself in this manner to the effectual demand. It naturally aims at bringing always that precise quantity thither which may be sufficient to supply, and no more than supply, that demand.

But in some employments the same quantity of industry will, in different years, produce very different quantities of commodities; while in others it will produce always the same, or very nearly the same. The same number of labourers in husbandry will, in different years, produce very different quantities of corn, wine, oil, hops, &c. But the same number of spinners and weavers will every year produce the same or very nearly the same quantity of linen and woolen cloth. It is only the average produce of the one species of industry which can be suited in any respect to the effectual demand; and as its actual produce is frequently much greater and frequently much less than its average produce, the quantity of the commodities brought to market will sometimes exceed a good deal, and sometimes fall short a good deal, of the effectual demand. Even though that demand, therefore, should continue always the same, their market price will be liable to great fluctuations, will sometimes fall a good deal below, and sometimes rise a good deal above, their natural price. In the other species of industry, the produce of equal quantities of labour being always the same, or very nearly the same, it can be more exactly suited to the effectual demand. While that demand continues the same, therefore, the market price of the commodities is likely to do so too, and to be either altogether, or as nearly as can be judged of, the same with the natural price. That the price of linen and woolen cloth is liable neither to such frequent nor to such great variations as the price of corn, every man's experience will inform him. The price of the one species of commodities varies only with the variations in the demand: that of the other varies not only with the variations in the demand, but with the much greater and more frequent variations in the quantity of what is brought to market in order to supply that demand.

The occasional and temporary fluctuations in the market price of any commodity fall chiefly upon those parts of its price which resolve themselves into wages and profit. That part which resolves itself into rent is less affected by them. A rent certain in money is not in the least affected by them either in its rate or in its value. A rent which consists either in a certain proportion or in a certain quantity of the rude produce, is no doubt affected in its yearly value by all the occasional and temporary fluctuations in the market price of that rude produce; but it is seldom affected by them in its yearly rate. In settling the terms of the lease, the landlord and farmer endeavour, according to their best judgment, to adjust that rate, not to the temporary and occasional, but to the average and ordinary price of the produce.

Such fluctuations affect both the value and the rate either of wages or of profit, according as the market happens to be either over-stocked or under-stocked with commodities or with labour; with work done, or with work to be done. A public mourning raises the price of black cloth (with which the market is almost always under-stocked upon such occasions), and augments the profits of the merchants who possess any considerable quantity of it. It has no effect upon the wages of the weavers. The market is under-stocked with commodities, not with labour; with work done, not with work to be done. It raises the wages of journeymen taylors. The market is here under-stocked with labour. There is an effectual demand for more labour, for more work to be done than can be had. It sinks the price of coloured silks and cloths, and thereby reduces the profits of the merchants who have any considerable quantity of them upon hand. It sinks too the wages of the workmen employed in preparing such commodities, for which all demand is stopped for six months, perhaps for a twelve month. The market is here over-stocked both with commodities and with labour.

But though the market price of every particular commodity is in this manner continually gravitating, if one may say so, towards the natural price, yet sometimes particular accidents, sometimes natural causes, and sometimes particular regulations of policy, may, in many commodities, keep up the market price for a long time together, a good deal above the natural price.

When by an increase in the effectual demand, the market price of some particular commodity happens to rise a good deal above the natural price, those who employ their stocks in supplying that market are generally careful to conceal this change. If it was commonly known, their great profit would tempt so many new rivals to employ their stocks in the same way, that, the effectual demand being fully supplied, the market price would soon be reduced to the natural price, and perhaps for some time even below it. If the market is at a great distance from the residence of those who supply it, they may sometimes be able to keep the secret for several years together, and may so long enjoy their extraordinary profits without any new rivals. Secrets of this kind, however, it must be acknowledged can seldom be long kept; and the extraordinary profit can last very little longer than they are kept.

Secrets in manufactures are capable of being longer kept than secrets in trade. A dyer who has found the means of producing a particular colour with materials which cost only half the price of those commonly made use of, may, with good management, enjoy the advantage of his discovery as long as he lives, and even leave it as a legacy to his posterity. His extraordinary gains arise from the high price which is paid for his private labour. They properly consist in the high wages of that labour. But as they are repeated upon every part of his stock, and as their whole amount bears, upon that account, a regular proportion to it, they are commonly considered as extraordinary profits of stock.

Such enhancements of the market price are evidently the effects of particular accidents, of which, however, the operation may sometimes last for many years together.

Some natural productions require such a singularity of soil and situation, that all the land in a great country, which is fit for producing them, may not be sufficient to supply the effectual demand. The whole quantity brought to market, therefore, may be disposed of to those who are willing to give more than what is sufficient to pay the rent of the land which produced them, together with the wages of the labour and the profits of the stock which were employed in preparing and bringing them to market, according to their natural rates. Such commodities may continue for whole centuries together to be sold at this high price; and that part of it which resolves itself into the rent of land is in this case the part which is generally paid above its natural rate. The rent of the land which affords such singular and esteemed productions, like the rent of some vineyards in France of a peculiar happy soil and situation, bears no regular proportion to the rent of other equally fertile and equally well-cultivated land in its neighbourhood. The wages of the labour and the profits of the stock employed in bringing such commodities to market, on the contrary, are seldom out of their natural proportion to those of the other employments of labour and stock in their neighbourhood.

Such enhancements of the market price are evidently the effect of natural causes which may hinder the effectual demand from ever being fully supplied, and which may continue, therefore, to operate forever.

A monopoly granted either to an individual or to a trading company has the same effect as a secret in trade or manufactures. The monopolists, by keeping the market constantly under-stocked, by never fully supplying the effectual demand, sell their commodities much above the natural price, and raise their emoluments whether they consist in wages or profit, greatly above their natural rate.

The price of monopoly is upon every occasion the highest which can be got. The natural price, or the price of free competition, on the contrary, is the lowest which can be taken, not upon every occasion indeed, but for any considerable time together. The one is upon every occasion the highest which can be squeezed out of the buyers, or which, it is supposed, they will consent to give: the other is the lowest which the sellers can commonly afford to take, and at the same time continue their business.

The exclusive privileges of corporations, statutes of apprenticeship, and all those laws which restrain, in particular employments, the competition to a smaller number than might otherwise go into them, have the same tendency, though in a less degree. They are a sort of enlarged monopolies, and may frequently, for ages together, and in whole classes of employments, keep up the market price of particular commodities above the natural price, and maintain both the wages of the labour and the profits of the stock employed about them somewhat above their natural rate.

Such enhancements of the market price may last as long as the regulations of policy which give occasion to them.

The market price of any particular commodity, though it may continue long above, can seldom continue long below, its natural price. Whatever part of it was paid below the natural rate, the persons whose interest it affected would immediately feel the loss, and would immediately withdraw either so much land, or so much labour, or so much stock, from being employed about it, that the quantity brought to market would soon be no more than sufficient to supply the effectual demand. Its market price, therefore, would soon rise to the natural price. This at least would be the case where there was perfect liberty. . . .

### CHAPTER VIII: OF WAGES OF LABOUR

The produce of labour constitutes the natural recompence or wages of labour.

In that original state of things, which precedes both the appropriation of land and the accumulation of stock, the whole produce of labour belongs to the labourer. He has neither landlord nor master to share with him.

Had this state continued, the wages of labour would have augmented with all those improvements in its productive powers, to which the division of labour gives occasion. All things would gradually have become cheaper. They would have been produced by a smaller quantity of labour; and as the commodities produced by equal quantities of labour would naturally in this state of things be exchanged for one another, they would have been purchased likewise with the produce of a smaller quantity.

But though all things would have become cheaper in reality, in appearance many things might have become dearer than before, or have been exchanged for a greater quantity of other goods. Let us suppose, for example, that in the greater part of employments the productive powers of labour had been improved to ten fold, or that a day's labour could produce ten times the quantity of work which it had done originally; but that in a particular employment they had improved only to double, or that a day's labour could produce only twice the quantity of work which it had done before. In exchanging the produce of a day's labour in the greater part of employments, for that of a day's labour in this particular one, ten times the original quantity of work in them would purchase only twice the original quantity in it. Any particular quantity in it, therefore, a pound weight for example, would appear to be five times dearer than before. In reality, however, it would be twice as cheap. Though it required five times the quantity of other goods to purchase it, it would require only half the quantity of labour either to purchase or to produce it. The acquisition, therefore, would be twice as easy as before.

But this original state of things, in which the labourer enjoyed the whole produce of his own labour, could not last beyond the first introduction of the appropriation of land and the accumulation of stock. It was at an end, therefore, long before the most considerable improvements were made in the productive powers of labour, and it would be to no purpose to trace further what might have been its effects upon the recompence or wages of labour.

As soon as land becomes private property, the landlord demands a share of almost all the produce which the labourer can either raise, or collect from it. His rent makes the first deduction from the produce of the labour which is employed upon land.

It seldom happens that the person who tills the ground has wherewithal to maintain himself till he reaps the harvest. His maintenance is generally advanced to him from the stock of a master, the farmer who employs him, and who would have no interest to employ him, unless he was to share in the produce of his labour, or unless his stock was to be replaced to him with a profit. This profit makes a second deduction from the produce of the labour which is employed upon land.

The produce of almost all other labour is liable to the like deduction of profit. In all arts and manufactures the greater part of the workmen stand in need of a master to advance them the materials of their work, and their wages and maintenance till it be completed. He shares in the produce of their labour, or in the value which it adds to the materials upon which it is bestowed; and in this share consist his profit.

It sometimes happens, indeed, that a single independent workman has stock sufficient both to purchase the materials of his work, and to maintain himself till it be completed. He is both master and workman, and enjoys the whole produce of his own labour, or the whole value which it adds to the materials upon which it is bestowed. It includes what are usually two distinct revenues, belonging to two distinct persons, the profits of stock, and the wages of labour.

Such cases, however, are not very frequent, and in every part of Europe, twenty workmen serve under a master for one that is independent; and the wages of labour are every-where understood to be, what they usually are, when the labourer is one person, and the owner of the stock which employs him another.

What are the common wages of labour, depends every-where upon the contract usually made between those two parties, whose interests are by no means the same. The workmen desire to get as much, the masters to give as little as possible. The former are disposed to combine in order to raise, the latter in order to lower, the wages of labour.

It is not, however, difficult to foresee which of the two parties must, upon all ordinary occasions, have the advantage in the dispute, and force the other into a compliance with their terms. The masters, being fewer in number, can combine much more easily; and the law, besides, authorises, or at least does not prohibit their combinations, while it prohibits those of the workmen. We have no acts of parliament against combining to lower the price of work; but many against combining to raise it. In all such disputes the masters can hold out much longer. A landlord, a farmer, a master manufacturer, or merchant, though they did not employ a single workman, could generally live a year or two upon the stocks which they have already acquired. Many workmen could not subsist a week, few could subsist a month, and scarce any a year without employment. In the long run the workman may be as necessary to his master as his master is to him; but the necessity is not so immediate.

We rarely hear, it has been said, of the combinations of masters, though frequently of those of workmen. But whoever imagines, upon this account, that masters rarely combine, is as ignorant of the world as of the subject. Masters are always and every-where in a sort of tacit, but constant and uniform, combination, not to raise the wages of labour above their actual rate. To violate this combination is every-where a most unpopular action, and a sort of reproach to a master among his neighbours and equals. We seldom, indeed, hear of this combination, because it is the usual, and one may say, the natural state of things which nobody ever hears of. Masters too sometimes enter into particular combinations to sink the wages of labour even below this rate. These are always conducted with the utmost silence and secrecy, till the moment of execution, and when the workmen yield, as they sometimes do, without resistance, though severely felt by them, they are never heard of by other people. Such combinations, however, are frequently resisted by a contrary defensive combination of the workmen; who sometimes too, without any provocation of this kind, combine of their own accord to raise the price of their labour. Their usual pretences are, sometimes the high price of provisions; sometimes the great profit which their masters make by their work. But whether their combinations be offensive or defensive, they are always abundantly heard of. In order to bring the point to a speedy decision, they have always recourse to the loudest clamour, and sometimes to the most shocking violence and outrage. They are desperate, and act with the folly and extravagance of desperate men, who must either starve, or frighten their masters into an immediate compliance with their demands. The masters upon these occasions are just as clamorous upon the other side, and never cease to call aloud for the assistance of the civil magistrate, and the rigorous execution of those laws which have been enacted with so much severity against the combinations of servants, labourers, and journeymen. The workmen, accordingly, very seldom derive any advantage from the violence of those tumultuous combinations, which, partly from the interposition of the civil magistrate, partly from the superior steadiness of the masters, partly from the necessity which the greater part of the workmen are under of submitting for the sake of present subsistence, generally end in nothing, but the punishment or ruin of the ringleaders.

But though in disputes with their workmen, masters must generally have the advantage, there is however a certain rate, below which it seems impossible to reduce, for any considerable time, the ordinary wages even of the lowest species of labour.

A man must always live by his work, and his wages must at least be sufficient to maintain him. They must even upon most occasions be somewhat more; otherwise it would be impossible for him to bring up a family, and the race of such workmen could not last beyond the first generation. Mr. Cantillon seems, upon this account, to suppose that the lowest species of common labourers must every-where earn at least double their own maintenance, in order that one with another they may be enabled to bring up two children; the labour of the wife, on account of her necessary attendance on the children, being supposed no more than sufficient to provide for herself. But one half the children born, it is computed, die before the age of manhood. The poorest labourers, therefore, according to this account, must, one with another, attempt to rear at least four children in order that two may have an equal chance of living to that age. But the necessary maintenance of four children, it is supposed, may be nearly equal to that of one man. The labour of an able-bodied slave, the same author adds, is computed to be worth double his maintenance; and that of the meanest labourer, he thinks, cannot be worth less than that of an able-bodied slave. Thus far at least seems certain, that, in order to bring up a family, the labour of the husband and wife together must, even in the lowest species of common labour, be able to earn something more than what is precisely necessary for their own maintenance; but in what proportion, whether in that above mentioned, or in any other, I shall not take upon me to determine.

There are certain circumstances, however, which sometimes give the labourers an advantage, and enable them to raise their wages considerably above this rate; evidently the lowest which is consistent with common humanity.

When in any country the demand for those who live by wages, labourers, journeymen, servants of every kind, is continually increasing; when every year furnishes employment for a greater number than had been employed the year before, the workmen have no occasion to combine in order to raise their wages. The scarcity of hands occasions a competition among masters, who bid against one another, in order to get workmen, and thus voluntarily break through the natural combination of masters not to raise wages.

The demand for those who live by wages, it is evident, cannot increase but in proportion to the increase of the funds which are destined to the payment of wages. These funds are of two kinds: first, the revenue which is over and above what is necessary for the maintenance; and, secondly, the stock which is over and above what is necessary for the employment of their masters.

When the landlord, annuitant, or monied man, has a greater revenue than what he judges sufficient to maintain his own family, he employs either the whole or a part of the surplus in maintaining one or more menial servants. Increase this surplus, and he will naturally increase the number of those servants.

When an independent workman, such as a weaver or shoemaker has got more stock than what is sufficient to purchase the materials of his own work, and to maintain himself till he can dispose of it, he naturally employs one or more journeymen with the surplus, in order to make a profit by their work. Increase this surplus, and he will naturally increase the number of his journeymen.

The demand for those who live by wages, therefore, necessarily increases with the increase of the revenue and stock of every country, and cannot possibly increase without it. The increase of revenue and stock is the increase of national wealth. The demand for those who live by wages, therefore, naturally increases with the increase of national wealth, and cannot possibly increase without it.

It is not the actual greatness of national wealth, but its continual increase, which occasions a rise in the wages of labour. It is not accordingly, in the richest countries, but in the most thriving, or in those which are growing rich the fastest, that the wages of labour are highest. England is certainly, in the present times, a much richer country than any part of North America. The wages of labour, however, are much higher in North America than in any part of England. In the province of New York, common labourers earn three shillings and sixpence currency, equal to two shillings sterling, a day; ship carpenters, ten shillings and sixpence currency, with a pint of rum worth sixpence sterling, equal in all to six shillings and sixpence sterling; house carpenters and bricklayers, eight shillings currency, equal to four shillings and sixpence sterling; journeymen taylors, five shillings currency, equal to about two shillings and ten-pence sterling. These prices are all above the London price; and wages are said to be as high in the other colonies as in New York. The price of provisions is every-where in North America much lower than in England. A dearth has never been known there. In the worst seasons, they have always had a sufficiency for themselves, though less for exportation. If the money price of labour, therefore, be higher than it is any-where in the mother country, its real price, the real command of the necessaries and conveniences of life which it conveys to the labourer, must be higher in a still greater proportion....

The real recompence of labour, the real quantity of the necessaries and conveniencies of life which it can procure to the labourer, has, during the course of the present century, increased perhaps in a still greater proportion than its money price. Not only grain has become somewhat cheaper, but many other things from which the industrious poor derive an agreeable and wholesome variety of food, have become a great deal cheaper.... The great improvements in the coarser manufactories of both linen and woolen cloth furnish the labourers with cheaper and better cloathing; and those in the manufactures of the coarser metals, with cheaper and better instruments of trade, as well as with many agreeable and convenient pieces of household furniture. Soap, salt, candles, leather, and fermented liquors, have indeed, become a good deal dearer; chiefly from the taxes which have been laid upon them. The quantity of these, however, which the labouring poor are under any necessity of consuming, is so very small, that the increase in their price does not compensate the diminution in that of so many other things. The common complaint that luxury extends itself even to the lowest ranks of the people, and that the labouring poor will not now be contented with the same food, cloathing and lodging, which satisfied them in former times, may convince us that it is not the money price of labour only, but its real recompence, which has augmented.

Is this improvement in the circumstances of the lower ranks of the people to be regarded as an advantage or as an inconveniency to the society? The answer seems at first sight abundantly plain. Servants, labourers, and workmen of different kinds, make up the far greater part of every great political society. But what improves the circumstances of the greater part can never be regarded as an inconveniency to the whole. No society can surely be flourishing and happy, of which the far greater part of the members are poor and miserable. It is but equity, besides, that they who feed, cloath and lodge the whole body of the people, should have such a share of the produce of their own labour as to be themselves tolerably well fed, cloathed, and lodged.

Poverty, though it no doubt discourages, does not always prevent marriage. It seems even to be favourable to generation. A half-starved Highland woman frequently bears more than twenty children, while a pampered fine lady is often incapable of bearing any, and is generally exhausted by two or three. Barrenness, so frequent among women of fashion, is very rare among those of inferior station. Luxury in the fair sex, while it inflames perhaps the passion for enjoyment, seems always to weaken, and frequently to destroy altogether, the powers of generation.

But poverty, though it does not prevent the generation, is extremely unfavourable to the rearing of children. The tender plant is produced, but in so cold a soil, and so severe a climate, soon withers and dies. It is not uncommon, I have been frequently told, in the Highlands of Scotland for a mother who has born twenty children not to have two alive.... In some places one half the children born die before they are four years of age; in many places before they are seven; and in almost all places before they are nine or ten. This great mortality, however, will every where be found chiefly among the children of the common people, who cannot afford to tend them with the same care as those of better station. Though their marriages are generally more fruitful than those of people of fashion, a smaller proportion of their children arrive at maturity.

In foundling hospitals, and among the children brought up by parish charities, the mortality is still greater than among those of the common people.

Every species of animals naturally multiplies in proportion to the means of their subsistence, and no species can ever multiply beyond it. But in civilized society it is only among the inferior ranks of people that the scantiness of subsistence can set limits to the further multiplication of the human species; and it can do so in no other way than by destroying a great part of the children which their fruitful marriages produce.

The liberal reward of labour, by enabling them to provide better for their children, and consequently to bring up a greater number, naturally tends to widen and extend those limits. It deserves to be remarked, too, that it necessarily does this as nearly as possible in the proportion which the demand for labour requires. If this demand is continually increasing, the reward of labour must necessarily encourage in such a manner the marriage and multiplication of labourers, as may enable them to supply that continually increasing demand by a continually increasing population. If the reward should at any time be less than what was requisite for this purpose, the deficiency of hands would soon raise it; and if it should at any time be more, their excessive multiplication would soon lower it to this necessary rate. The market would be so much under-stocked with labour in the one case, and so much over-stocked in the other, as would soon force back its price to that proper rate which the circumstances of the society required. It is in this manner that the demand for men, like that for any other commodity, necessarily regulates the production of men; quickens it when it goes on too slowly, and stops it when it advances too fast. It is this demand which regulates and determines the state of propagation in all the different countries of the world, in North America, in Europe, and in China; which renders it rapidly progressive in the first, slow and gradual in the second, and altogether stationary in the last. . . .

# BOOK IV

## CHAPTER II: *OF RESTRAINTS UPON THE IMPORTATION FROM FOREIGN COUNTRIES OF SUCH GOODS AS CAN BE PRODUCED AT HOME*

By restraining, either by high duties, or by absolute prohibitions, the importation of such goods from foreign countries as can be produced at home, the monopoly of the home market is more or less secured to the domestic industry employed in producing them. Thus the prohibition of importing either live cattle or salt provisions from foreign countries secures to the graziers of Great Britain the monopoly of the home market for butchers' meat. The high duties upon the importation of corn, which in times of moderate plenty amount to a prohibition, give a like advantage to the growers of that commodity. The prohibition of the importation of foreign woolens is equally favourable to the woolen manufactures. The silk manufacture, though altogether employed upon foreign materials, has lately obtained the same advantage. The linen manufacture has not yet obtained it, but is making great strides towards it. Many other sorts of manufactures have, in the same manner, obtained in Great Britain, either altogether, or very nearly a monopoly against their countrymen. The variety of goods of which the importation into Great Britain is prohibited, either absolutely, or under certain circumstances, greatly exceeds what can easily be suspected by those who are not well acquainted with the laws of the customs.

That this monopoly of the home market frequently gives great encouragement to that particular species of industry which enjoys it, and frequently turns towards that employment a greater share of both the labour and stock of the society than would otherwise have gone to it, cannot be doubted. But whether it tends either to increase the general industry of the society, or to give it the most advantageous direction, is not, perhaps, altogether so evident.

The general industry of the society never can exceed what the capital of the society can employ. As the number of workmen that can be kept in employment by any particular person must bear a certain proportion to his capital, so the number of those that can be continually employed by all the members of a great society, must bear a certain proportion to the whole capital of that society, and never can exceed that proportion. No regulation of commerce can increase the quantity of industry in any society beyond what its capital can maintain. It can only divert a part of it into a direction into which it might not otherwise have gone; and it is by no means certain that this artificial direction is likely to be more advantageous to the society than that into which it would have gone of its own accord.

Every individual is continually exerting himself to find out the most advantageous employment for whatever capital he can command. It is his own advantage indeed, and not that of the society, which he has in view. But the study of his own advantage naturally, or rather necessarily, leads him to prefer that employment which is most advantageous to the society.

First, every individual endeavours to employ his capital as near home as he can, and consequently as much as he can in the support of domestic industry; provided always that he can thereby obtain the ordinary, or not a great deal less than the ordinary profits of stock.

Thus, upon equal or nearly equal profits, every wholesale merchant naturally prefers the home-trade to the foreign trade of consumption, and the foreign trade of consumption to the carrying trade. In the home-trade his capital is never so long out of his sight as it frequently is in the foreign trade of consumption. He can know better the character and situation of the persons whom he trusts, and if he should happen to be deceived, he knows better the laws of the country from which he must seek redress. In the carrying trade, the capital of the merchant is, as it were, divided between two foreign countries, and no part of it is ever necessarily brought home, or placed under his own immediate view and command. The capital which an Amsterdam merchant employs in carrying corn from Konnigsberg to Lisbon, and fruit and wine from Lisbon to Konnigsberg, must generally be the one-half of it at Konnigsberg and the other half at Lisbon. No part of it need ever come to Amsterdam. The natural residence of such a merchant should either be at Konnigsberg or Lisbon, and it can only be some very particular circumstances which can make him prefer the residence of Amsterdam. The uneasiness, however, which he feels at being separated so far from his capital, generally determines him to bring part both of the Konnigsberg goods which he destines for the market of Lisbon, and of the Lisbon goods which he destines for that of Konnigsberg, to Amsterdam: and though this necessarily subjects him to a double charge of loading and unloading, as well as to the payment of some duties and customs, yet for the sake of having some part of his capital always under his own view and command, he willingly submits to this extraordinary charge; and it is in this manner that every country which has any considerable share of the carrying trade, becomes always the emporium, or general market, for the goods of all the different countries whose trade it carries on. The merchant, in order to save a second loading and unloading, endeavours always to sell in the home-market as much of the goods of all those different countries as he can, and thus, so far as he can, to convert his carrying trade into a foreign trade of consumption. A merchant, in the same manner, who is engaged in the foreign trade of consumption, when he collects goods for foreign markets, will always be glad, upon equal or nearly equal profits, to sell as great a part of them at home as he can. He saves himself the risk and trouble of exportation, when, so far as he can, he thus converts his foreign trade of consumption into a home-trade. Home is in this manner the centre, if I may say so, round which the capitals of the inhabitants of every country are continually circulating, and towards which they are always tending, though by particular causes they may sometimes be driven off and repelled from it towards more distant employments. But a capital employed in the home-trade, it has already been shown, necessarily puts into motion a greater quantity of domestic industry, and gives revenue and employment to a greater number of the inhabitants of the country, than an equal capital employed in the foreign trade of consumption: and one employed in the foreign trade of consumption has the same advantage over an equal capital employed in the carrying trade. Upon equal, or only nearly equal profits, therefore, every individual naturally inclines to employ his capital in the manner in which it is likely to afford the greatest support to domestic industry, and to give revenue and employment to the greatest number of people of his own country.

Secondly, every individual who employs his capital in the support of domestic industry, necessarily endeavours so to direct that industry, that its produce may be of the greatest possible value.

The produce of industry is what it adds to the subject or materials upon which it is employed. In proportion as the value of this produce is great or small, so will likewise be the profits of the employer. But it is only for the sake of profit that any man employs a capital in the support of industry; and he will always, therefore, endeavour to employ it in the support of that industry of which the produce is likely to be of the greatest value, or to exchange for the greatest quantity either of money or of other goods.

But the annual revenue of every society is always precisely equal to the exchangeable value of the whole annual produce of its industry, or rather is precisely the same thing with that exchangeable value. As every individual, therefore, endeavours as much as he can both to employ his capital in the support of domestic industry, and so to direct that industry that its produce may be of the greatest value; every individual necessarily labours to render the annual revenue of the society as great as he can. He generally, indeed, neither intends to promote the public interest, nor knows how much he is promoting it. By preferring the support of domestic to that of foreign industry, he intends only his own security; and by directing that industry in such a manner as its produce may be of the greatest value, he intends only his own gain, and he is in this as in many other cases, led by an invisible hand to promote an end which was no part of his intention. Nor is it always the worse for the society that it was no part of it. By pursuing his own interest he frequently promotes that of the society more effectually than when he really intends to promote it. I have never known much good done by those who affected to trade for the public good. It is an affectation indeed, not very common among merchants, and very few words need be employed in dissuading them from it.

What is the species of domestic industry which his capital can employ, and of which the produce is likely to be of the greatest value, every individual, it is evident, can, in his local situation, judge much better than any statesman or lawgiver can do for him. The statesman, who should attempt to direct private people in what manner they ought to employ their capitals, would not only load himself with a most unnecessary attention, but assume an authority which could safely be trusted, not only to no single person, but to no council or senate whatever, and which would no-where be so dangerous as in the hands of a man who had folly and presumption enough to fancy himself fit to exercise it.

To give the monopoly of the home market to the produce of domestic industry, in any particular art or manufacture, is in some measure to direct private people in what manner they ought to employ their capitals, and must, in almost all cases, be either a useless or a hurtful regulation. If the produce of domestic can be brought there as cheap as that of foreign industry, the regulation is evidently useless. If it cannot, it must generally be hurtful. It is the maxim of every prudent master of a family, never to attempt to make at home what it will cost him more to make than to buy. The tailor does not attempt to make his own shoes, but buys them of the shoemaker. The shoemaker does not attempt to make his own clothes, but employs a tailor. The farmer attempts to make neither the one nor the other, but employs those different artificers. All of them find it for their interest to employ their whole industry in a way in which they have some advantage over their neighbours, and to purchase with a part of its produce, or what is the same thing, with the price of a part of it, whatever else they have occasion for.

What is prudence in the conduct of every private family, can scarce be folly in that of a great kingdom. If a foreign country can supply us with a commodity cheaper than we ourselves can make it, better buy it of them with some part of the produce of our own industry, employed in a way in which we have some advantage. The general industry of the country, being always in proportion to the capital which employs it, will not thereby be diminished, no more than that of the above mentioned artificers; but only left to find out the way in which it can be employed with the greatest advantage. It is certainly not employed to the greatest advantage, when it is thus directed towards an object which it can buy cheaper than it can make. The value of its annual produce is certainly more or less diminished, when it is thus turned away from producing commodities evidently of more value than the commodity which it is directed to produce. According to the supposition, that commodity could be purchased from foreign countries cheaper than it can be made at home. It could, therefore, have been purchased with a part only of the commodities, or, what is the same thing, with a part only of the price of the commodities, which the industry employed by an equal capital would have produced at home, had it been left to follow its natural course. The industry of the country, therefore, is thus turned away from a more to a less advantageous employment, and the exchangeable value of its annual produce, instead of being increased, according to the intention of the lawgiver, must necessarily be diminished by every such regulation.

By means of such regulations, indeed, a particular manufacture may sometimes be acquired sooner than it could have been otherwise, and after a certain time may be made at home as cheap or cheaper than in the foreign country. But though the industry of the society may be thus carried with advantage into a particular channel sooner than it could have been otherwise, it will by no means follow that the sum total, either of its industry or of its revenue, can ever be augmented by any such regulation. The industry of the society can augment only in proportion as its capital augments, and its capital can augment only in proportion to what can be gradually saved out of its revenue. But the immediate effects of every such regulation is to diminish its revenue, and what diminishes its revenue is certainly not very likely to augment its capital faster than it would have augmented of its own accord, had both capital and industry been left to find out their natural employments.

Though for want of such regulations, the society should never acquire the proposed manufacture, it would not, upon that account, necessarily be the poorer in any one period of its duration. In every period of its duration its whole capital and industry might still have been employed, though upon different objects, in the manner that was most advantageous at the time. In every period its revenue might have been the greatest which its capital could afford, and both capital and revenue might have been augmented with the greatest possible rapidity.

The natural advantages which one country has over another in producing particular commodities are sometimes so great, that it is acknowledged by all the world to be in vain to struggle with them. By means of glasses, hotbeds, and hotwalls, very good grapes can be raised in Scotland, and very good wine too can be made of them at about thirty times the expence for which at least equally good can be brought from foreign countries. Would it be a reasonable law to prohibit the importation of all foreign wines, merely to encourage the making of claret and burgundy in Scotland? But if there would be a manifest absurdity in turning towards any employment, thirty times more of the capital and industry of the country than would be necessary to purchase from foreign countries an equal quantity of the commodities wanted, there must be an absurdity, though not altogether so glaring, yet exactly of the same kind, in turning towards any such employment a thirtieth, or even a three hundredth part or more of either. Whether the advantages which one country has over another, be natural or acquired, is in this respect of no consequence. As long as the one country has those advantages, and the other wants them, it will always be more advantageous for the latter, rather to buy of the former than to make. It is an acquired advantage only, which one artificer has over his neighbour, who exercises another trade; and yet they both find it more advantageous to buy of one another, than to make what does not belong to their particular trades.

Merchants and manufacturers are the people who derive the greatest advantages from this monopoly of the home market. The prohibition of the importation of foreign cattle, and of salt provisions, together with the high duties upon foreign corn, which in times of moderate plenty amount to a prohibition, are not near so advantageous to the graziers and farmers of Great

Britain, as other regulations of the same kind are to its merchants and manufacturers. Manufactures, those of the finer kind especially, are more easily transported from one country to another than corn or cattle. It is in the fetching and carrying manufactures, accordingly the foreign trade is chiefly employed. In manufactures, a very small advantage will enable foreigners to undersell our own workmen, even in the home-market. It will require a very great one to enable them to do so in the rude produce of the soil. If the free importation of foreign manufacture were permitted, several of the home manufactures would probably suffer, and some of them perhaps go to ruin altogether, and a considerable part of the stock and industry at present employed in them would be forced to find out some other employment. But the freest importation of the rude produce of the soil could have no such effect upon the agriculture of the country. . . .

To expect, indeed, that the freedom of trade should ever be entirely restored in Great Britain, is as absurd as to expect that an Oceana or Utopia should ever be established in it. Not only the prejudices of the public, but what is much more unconquerable, the private interests of many individuals, irresistibly oppose it. Were the officers of the army to oppose with the same zeal and unanimity any reduction in the number of forces, with which master manufacturers set themselves against every law that is likely to increase the number of their rivals in the home-market; were the former to animate their soldiers, in the same manner as the latter inflame their workmen, to attack with violence and outrage the proposers of any such regulation; to attempt to reduce the army would be as dangerous as it has now become to attempt to diminish in any respect the monopoly which our manufacturers have obtained against us. This monopoly has so much increased the number of some particular tribes of them, that, like an overgrown standing army, they have become formidable to the government, and upon many occasions intimidate the legislature. The member of parliament who supports every proposal for strengthening this monopoly, is sure to acquire not only the reputation of understanding trade, but great popularity and influence with an order of men whose numbers and wealth render them of great importance. If he opposes them, on the contrary, and still more if he has authority enough to be able to thwart them, neither the most acknowledged probity, nor the highest rank, nor the greatest public services can protect him from the most infamous abuse and detraction, from personal insults, nor sometimes from real danger, arising from the insolent outrage of furious and disappointed monopolists.

The undertaker of a great manufacture, who by the home-markets being suddenly laid open to the competition of foreigners, should be obliged to abandon his trade, would no doubt suffer very considerably. That part of his capital which had usually been employed in purchasing materials and in paying his workmen, might, without much difficulty, perhaps find another employment. But that part of it which was fixed in workhouses, and in the instruments of trade, could scarce be disposed of without considerable loss. The equitable regard, therefore, to his interest requires that changes of this kind should never be introduced suddenly, but slowly, gradually, and after a very long warning. The legislature, were it possible that its deliberations could be always directed, not by the clamorous importunity of partial interests, but by an extensive view of the general good, ought upon this very account, perhaps, to be particularly careful neither to establish any new monopolies of this kind, nor to extend further those which are already established. Every such regulation introduces some degree of real disorder into the constitution of the state, which it will be difficult afterwards to cure without occasioning another disorder.

How far it may be proper to impose taxes upon the importation of foreign goods, in order not to prevent their importation, but to raise a revenue for government, I shall consider hereafter when I come to treat of taxes. Taxes imposed with a view to prevent or even to diminish importation, are evidently as destructive of the revenue of the customs as of the freedom of trade. . . .

# BOOK V

## CHAPTER I, PART III

### Article II:   Of the Expense of the Institutions for the Education of Youth

. . . In the progress of the division of labour, the employment of the far greater part of those who live by labour, that is of the great body of the people, comes to be confined to a few very simple operations; frequently to one or two. But the understandings of the greater part of men are necessarily formed by their ordinary employments. The man whose whole life is spent in performing a few simple operations, of which the effects too are, perhaps, always the same, or very nearly the same, has no occasion to exert his understanding, or to exercise his invention in finding out expedients for removing difficulties which never occur. He naturally loses, therefore, the habit of such exertion, and generally becomes as stupid and ignorant as it is possible for a human creature to become. The torpor of his mind renders him not only incapable of relishing or bearing a part in any rational conversation, but of conceiving any generous, noble, or tender sentiment, and consequently of forming any just judgment concerning many even of the ordinary duties of private life. Of the great and extensive interests of his country he is altogether incapable of judging; and unless very particular pains have been taken to render him otherwise, he is equally incapable of defending his country in war. The uniformity of his stationary life naturally corrupts the courage of his mind, and makes him regard with abhorrence the irregular, uncertain, and adventurous life of a soldier. It corrupts even the activity of his body; and renders him incapable of exerting his strength with vigour and perseverance, in any other employment than that to which he has been bred. His dexterity at his own particular trade seems, in this manner, to be acquired at the expence of his intellectual, social, and martial virtues. But in every improved and civilized society this is the state into which the labouring poor, that is, the great body of the people, must necessarily fall, unless government takes some pains to prevent it.

It is otherwise in the barbarous societies, as they are commonly called, of hunters, of shepherds, and even of husbandmen in that rude state of husbandry which precedes the improvement of manufactures, and the extension of foreign commerce. In such societies the varied occupations of every man oblige every man to exert his capacity, and to invent expedients for removing difficulties which are continually occurring. Invention is kept alive, and the mind is not suffered to fall into that drowsy stupidity, which, in a civilized society, seems to benumb the understanding of almost all the inferior ranks of people. In those barbarous societies, as they are called, every man, it has already been observed, is a warrior. Every man too is in some measure a statesman, and can form a tolerable judgment concerning the interest of the society, and the conduct of those who govern it. How far their chiefs are good judges in peace, or good leaders in war, is obvious to the observation of almost every single man among them. In such a society, indeed, no man can well acquire that improved and refined understanding, which a few men sometimes possess in a more civilized state. Though in a rude society there is a good deal of variety in the occupations of every individual, there is not a great deal in those of the whole society. Every man does, or is capable of doing, almost every thing which any other man does, or is capable of doing. Every man has a considerable degree of knowledge, ingenuity, and invention; but scarce any man has a great degree. The degree, however, which is commonly possessed, is generally sufficient for conducting the whole simple business of the society.  In a civilized state, on the contrary, though there is little variety in the occupations of the greater part of individuals, there is an almost infinite variety in those of the whole society. These varied occupations present an almost infinite variety of objects to the contemplation of those few, who being attached to no particular occupation themselves, have leisure and inclination to examine the occupations of other people. The contemplation of so great a variety of objects necessarily exercises their minds in endless comparisons and combinations, and renders their understanding, in an extraordinary degree, both acute and comprehensive. Unless those few, however, happen to be placed in some very particular situations, their great abilities, though honourable to themselves, may contribute very little to the good government or happiness of their society. Notwithstanding the great abilities of those few, all the nobler parts of the human character may be, in a great measure, obliterated and extinguished in the great body of the people.

The education of the common people requires, perhaps, in a civilized and commercial society, the attention of the public more than that of people of some rank and fortune. People of some rank and fortune are generally eighteen or nineteen years of age before they enter upon the particular business, profession, or trade, by which they propose to distinguish themselves in the world. They have before that full time to acquire, or at least to fit themselves for afterwards acquiring, every accomplishment which can recommend them to the public esteem, or render them worthy of it. Their parents or guardians are generally sufficiently anxious that they should be so accomplished, and are, in most cases willing enough to lay out the expence which is necessary for the purpose. If they are not always properly educated, it is seldom from the want of expence laid out upon their education; but from the improper application of that expence. It is seldom from the want of masters; but from the negligence and incapacity of the masters who are to be had, and from the difficulty, or rather from the impossibility which there is, in the present state of things, of finding any better. The employments too in which people of some rank or fortune spend the greater part of their lives, are not, like those of the common people, simple and uniform. They are almost all of them extremely complicated, and such as exercise the head more than the hands. The understandings of those who are engaged in such employments can seldom grow torpid for want of exercise. The employments of people of some rank and fortune, besides, are seldom such as harrass them from morning to night. They generally have a good deal of leisure, during which they may perfect themselves in every branch either of useful or ornamental knowledge of which they may have laid the foundation, or for which they may have acquired some taste in the earlier part of life.

It is otherwise with the common people. They have little time to spare for education. Their parents can scarce afford to maintain them even in infancy. As soon as they are able to work, they must apply to some trade by which they can can earn their subsistence. That trade too is generally so simple and uniform as to give little exercise to the understanding; while, at the same time, their labour is both so constant and so severe, that it leaves them little leisure and less inclination to apply to, or even to think of anything else.

But though the common people cannot, in any civilized society, be so well instructed as people of some rank and fortune, the most essential parts of education, however, to read, write, and account, can be acquired at so early a period of life, that the greater part even of those who are to be bred to the lowest occupations, have time to acquire them before they can be employed in those occupations. For a very small expence the public can facilitate, can encourage, and can even impose upon almost the whole body of the people, the necessity of acquiring those most essential parts of education. . . .

# Selections from *Democracy in America,* Volumes I & II

## *Alexis de Tocqueville (1805–1859)*

*Young Alexis de Tocqueville came to America in 1831 with his friend, Gustave de Beaumont, to study a democratic nation in action and to report on the American prison system to the government of France. As a result of several months of travelling throughout the United States, Tocqueville wrote the first volume of his* Democracy in America *on the characteristics of the American political system, emphasizing the pervasive democratic tendencies of state and national institutions. About five years later, he published the second volume of this work, attempting, as he says in his preface, "to show how far both [our inclinations and our ideas] are affected by the equality of men's conditions." Characterizing himself as a friend of democracy, he believes he must point out to democratic nations and those who aspire to democracy the social and political dangers peculiar to the pursuit of equality.* Democracy in America, *despite its author's relatively brief acquaintance with the United States, is still widely regarded as one of the best books written on the American polity.*

*In contrast to the prevailing view of individualism today, Tocqueville shows us a perspective from which it appears dangerous and quite unattractive. What does he see as lacking in an individualistic society? What links this phenomenon with democratic political and social institutions? Despite its original intent, Tocqueville says individualistic democracy can lead to a new and pernicious form of tyranny. Why and how? Do you find his analysis and predictions convincing? What does he see as the particularly American responses to individualism? How do these institutions and attitudes discourage democratic despotism? Does America still practice these or comparable measures?*

## VOLUME I

### Chapter XV:  Unlimited Power of the Majority in the United States, and Its Consequences

The very essence of democratic government consists in the absolute sovereignty of the majority: for there is nothing in democratic states which is capable of resisting it. Most of the American constitutions have sought to increase this natural strength of the majority by artificial means.[1]

---

[1] We observed in examining the federal constitution that the efforts of the legislators of the Union had been diametrically opposed to the present tendency. The consequence has been that the federal government is more independent in its sphere than that of the states. But the federal government scarcely ever interferes in any but external affairs; and the governments of the states are in reality the authorities which direct society in America.

The legislature is, of all political institutions, the one which is most easily swayed by the wishes of the majority. The Americans determined that the members of the legislature should be elected by the people immediately, and for a very brief term, in order to subject them, not only to the general convictions, but even to the daily passions of their constituents. The members of both houses are taken from the same class in society, and are nominated in the same manner; so that the modifications of the legislative bodies are almost as rapid and quite as irresistible as those of a single assembly. It is to a legislature thus constituted, that almost all the authority of the government has been intrusted.

But while the law increased the strength of those authorities which of themselves were strong, it enfeebled more and more those which were naturally weak. It deprived the representatives of the executive of all stability and independence; and by subjecting them completely to the caprices of the legislature, it robbed them completely of the slender influence which the nature of a democratic government might have allowed them to retain. In several states the judicial power was also submitted to the elective discretion of the majority; and in all them its existence was made to depend on the pleasure of the legislative authority, since the representatives were empowered annually to regulate the stipend of the judges.

Custom, however, has done even more than law. A proceeding which will in the end set all the guarantees of representative government at naught, is becoming more and more general in the United States: it frequently happens that the electors, who choose a delegate, point out a certain line of conduct to him, and impose upon him a certain number of positive obligations which he is pledged to fulfill. With the exception of the tumult, this comes to the same thing as if the majority of the populace held its deliberations in the marketplace.

Several other circumstances concur in rendering the power of the majority in America, not only preponderant, but irresistible. The moral authority of the majority is partly based upon the notion, that there is more intelligence and more wisdom in a great number of men collected together than in a single individual, and that the quantity of legislators is more important than their quality. The theory of equality is in fact applied to the intellect of man; and human pride is thus assailed in its last retreat, by a doctrine which the minority hesitate to admit, and in which they very slowly concur. Like all other powers, and perhaps more than all other powers, the authority of the many requires the sanction of time; at first it enforces obedience by constraint; but its laws are not respected until they have long been maintained.

The right of governing society, which the majority supposes itself to derive from its superior intelligence, was introduced into the United States by the first settlers; and this idea, which would be sufficient of itself to create a free nation, has now been amalgamated with the manners of the people, and the minor incidents of social intercourse.

The French, under the old monarchy, held it for a maxim (which is still a fundamental principle of the English constitution), that the king could do no wrong; and if he did wrong, the blame was imputed to his advisers. This notion was highly favorable to habits of obedience; and it enabled the subject to complain of the law, without ceasing to love and honor the lawgiver. The Americans entertain the same opinion with respect to the majority.

The moral power of the majority is founded upon yet another principle, which is, that the interests of the many are to be preferred to those of the few. It will readily be perceived that the respect here professed for the rights of the majority must naturally increase or diminish according to the state of parties. When a nation is divided into several irreconcilable factions, the privilege of the majority is often overlooked, because it is intolerable to comply with its demands.

If there existed in America a class of citizens whom the legislating majority sought to deprive of exclusive privileges, which they had possessed for ages, and to bring down from an elevated station to the level of the ranks of the multitude, it is probable that the minority would be less ready to comply with its laws. But as the United States were colonized by men holding an equal rank among themselves, there is as yet no natural or permanent source of dissension between the interests of its different inhabitants.

There are certain communities in which the persons who constitute the minority can never hope to draw over the majority to their side, because they must then give up the very point which is at issue between them. Thus, an aristocracy can never become a majority while it retains its exclusive privileges, and it cannot cede its privileges without ceasing to be an aristocracy.

In the United States, political questions cannot be taken up in so general and absolute a manner; and all parties are willing to recognize the rights of the majority, because they all hope to turn those rights to their own advantage at some future time. The majority therefore in that country exercises a prodigious actual authority, and a moral influence which is scarcely less preponderant; no obstacles exist which can impede, or so much as retard its progress, or which can induce it to heed the complaints of those whom it crushes upon its path. This state of things is fatal in itself and dangerous for the future. . . .

**Tyranny of the Majority**

I hold it to be an impious and an execrable maxim that, politically speaking, a people has a right to do whatsoever it pleases; and yet I have asserted that all authority originates in the will of the majority. Am I, then, in contradiction with myself?

A general law—which bears the name of justice—has been made and sanctioned, not only by a majority of this or that people, but by a majority of mankind. The rights of every people are consequently confined within the limits of what is just. A nation may be considered in the light of a jury which is empowered to represent society at large, and to apply the great and general law of justice. Ought such a jury, which represents society, to have more power than the society in which the laws it applies originate?

When I refuse to obey an unjust law, I do not contest the right which the majority has of commanding, but I simply appeal from the sovereignty of the people to the sovereignty of mankind. It has been asserted that a people can never entirely outstep the boundaries of justice and of reason in those affairs which are more peculiarly its own; and that consequently full power may fearlessly be given to the majority by which it is represented. But this language is that of a slave.

A majority taken collectively may be regarded as a being whose opinions, and most frequently whose interests, are opposed to those of another being, which is styled a minority. If it be admitted that a man, possessing absolute power, may misuse that power by wronging his adversaries, why should a majority not be liable to the same reproach? Men are not apt to change their characters by agglomeration; nor does their patience in the presence of obstacles increase with the consciousness of their strength.[2] And for these reasons I can never willingly invest any number of my fellow-creatures with that unlimited authority which I should refuse to any one of them.

I do not think that it is possible to combine several principles in the same government, so as at the same time to maintain freedom, and really to oppose them to one another. The form of government which is usually termed *mixed* has always appeared to me to be a mere chimera. Accurately speaking, there is no such thing as a mixed government (with the meaning usually given to that word), because in all communities some one principle of action may be discovered, which preponderates over the others. England in the last century, which has been more especially cited as an example of this form of government, was in point of fact an essentially aristocratic state, although it comprised very powerful elements of democracy: for the laws and customs of the country were such, that the aristocracy could not but preponderate in the end, and subject the

---

[2] No one will assert that a people cannot forcibly wrong another people: but parties may be looked upon as lesser nations within a greater one, and they are aliens to each other: if therefore it be admitted that a nation can act tyrannically toward another nation, it cannot be denied that a party may do the same toward another party.

direction of public affairs to its own will. The error arose from too much attention being paid to the actual struggle which was going on between the nobles and the people, without considering the probable issue of the contest, which was in reality the important point. When a community really has a mixed government, that is to say, when it is equally divided between two adverse principles, it must either pass through a revolution, or fall into complete dissolution.

I am therefore of opinion that some one social power must always be made to predominate over the others; but I think that liberty is endangered when this power is checked by no obstacles which may retard its course, and force it to moderate its own vehemence.

Unlimited power is in itself a bad and dangerous thing; human beings are not competent to exercise it with discretion; and God alone can be omnipotent, because his wisdom and his justice are always equal to his power. But no power upon earth is so worthy of honor for itself, or of reverential obedience to the rights which it represents, that I would consent to admit its uncontrolled and all-predominant authority. When I see that the right and the means of absolute command are conferred on a people or upon a king, upon an aristocracy or a democracy, a monarchy or a republic, I recognize the germe of tyranny, and I journey onward to a land of more hopeful institutions.

In my opinion the main evil of the present democratic institutions of the United States does not arise, as is often asserted in Europe, from their weakness, but from their overpowering strength; and I am not so much alarmed at the excessive liberty which reigns in that country, as at the very inadequate securities which exist against tyranny.

When an individual or a party is wronged in the United States, to whom can he apply for redress? If to public opinion, public opinion constitutes the majority; if to the legislature, it represents the majority, and implicitly obeys its instructions; if to the executive power, it is appointed by the majority and is a passive tool in its hands; the public troops consist of the majority under arms; the jury is the majority invested with the right of hearing judicial cases; and in certain states even the judges are elected by the majority. However iniquitous or absurd the evil of which you complain may be, you must submit to it as well as you can.[3]

---

[3] A striking instance of the excesses which may be occasioned by the despotism of the majority occurred at Baltimore in the year 1812. At that time the war was very popular in Baltimore. A journal which had taken the other side of the question excited the indignation of the inhabitants by its opposition. The populace assembled, broke the printing-presses, and attacked the houses of the newspaper editors. The militia was called out, but no one obeyed the call; and the only means of saving the poor wretches who were threatened by the phrensy of the mob, was to throw them into prison as common malefactors. But even this precaution was ineffectual; the mob collected again during the night; the magistrates again made a vain attempt to call out the militia; the prison was forced, one of the newspaper editors were killed upon the spot, and the others were left for dead: the guilty parties were acquitted by the jury when they were brought to trial.

I said one day to an inhabitant of Pennsylvania: "Be so good as to explain to me how it happens, that in a state founded by quakers, and celebrated for its toleration, freed blacks are not allowed to exercise civil rights. They pay the taxes: is it not fair that they should have a vote.

"You insult us," replied my informant, "if you imagine that our legislators could have committed so gross an act of injustice and intolerance."

"What, then, the blacks possess the right of voting in this country?"

"Without the smallest doubt."

"How comes it, then, that at the polling-booth this morning I did not perceive a single negro in the whole meeting?"

"This is not the fault of the law; the negroes have an undisputed right of voting; but they voluntarily abstain from making their appearance."

"A very pretty piece of modesty on their parts," rejoined I.

"Why, the truth is, that they are not disinclined to vote, but they are afraid of being maltreated; in this country the law is sometimes unable to maintain its authority without the support of the majority. But in this case the majority entertains very strong prejudices against the blacks, and the magistrates are unable to protect them in the exercise of their legal privileges."

If, on the other hand, a legislative power could be so constituted as to represent the majority without necessarily being the slave of its passions; an executive, so as to retain a certain degree of uncontrolled authority; and a judiciary, so as to remain independent of the two other powers; a government would be formed which would still be democratic, without incurring any risk of tyrannical abuse.

I do not say that tyrannical abuses frequently occur in America at the present day; but I maintain that no sure barrier is established against them, and that the causes which mitigate the government are to be found in the circumstances and the manners of the country more than in its laws. . . .

### Power Exercised by the Majority in America Upon Opinion

It is in the examination of the display of public opinion in the United States, that we clearly perceive how far the power of the majority surpasses all the powers with which we are acquainted in Europe. Intellectual principles exercise an influence which is so invisible and often so inappreciable, that they baffle the toils of oppression. At the present time the most absolute monarchs in Europe are unable to prevent certain notions, which are opposed to their authority, from circulating in secret throughout their dominions, and even in their courts. Such is not the case in America; so long as the majority is still undecided, discussion is carried on; but as soon as its decision is irrevocably pronounced, a submissive silence is observed; and the friends, as well as the opponents of the measure, unite in assenting to its propriety. The reason of this is perfectly clear: no monarch is so absolute as to combine all the powers of society in his own hands, and to conquer all opposition, with the energy of a majority, which is invested with the right of making and of executing the laws.

The authority of a king is purely physical, and it controls the actions of the subject without subduing his private will; but the majority possesses a power which is physical and moral at the same time; it acts upon the will as well as upon the actions of men, and it represses not only all contest, but all controversy.

I know no country in which there is so little true independence of mind and freedom of discussion as in America. In any constitutional state in Europe every sort of religious and political theory may be advocated and propagated abroad; for there is no country in Europe so subdued by any single authority, as not to contain citizens who are ready to protect the man who raises his voice in the cause of truth, from the consequences of his hardihood. If he is unfortunate enough to live under an absolute government, the people is upon his side; if he inhabits a free country, he may find a shelter behind the authority of the throne, if he require one. The aristocratic part of society supports him in some countries, and the democracy in others. But in a nation where democratic institutions exist, organized like those of the United States, there is but one sole authority, one single element of strength and of success, with nothing beyond it.

In America, the majority raises very formidable barriers to the liberty of opinion: within these barriers an author may write whatever he pleases, but he will repent it if he ever step beyond them. Not that he is exposed to the terrors of an auto-da-fé, but he is tormented by the slights and persecutions of daily obloquy. His political career is closed for ever, since he has offended the only authority which is able to promote his success. Every sort of compensation, even that of celebrity, is refused to him. Before he published his opinions, he imagined that he held them in common with many others; but no sooner has he declared them openly, than he is loudly censured by his overbearing opponents, while those who think, without having the courage to speak, like him, abandon him in silence. He yields at length, oppressed by the daily efforts he has been making, and he subsides into silence as if he was tormented by remorse for having spoken the truth.

---

"What, then, the majority claims the right not only of making the laws, but of breaking the laws it has made?"

Fetters and headsmen were the course instruments which tyranny formerly employed; but the civilization of our age has refined the arts of despotism, which seemed however to have been sufficiently perfected before. The excesses of monarchical power had devised a variety of physical means of oppression; the democratic republics of the present day have rendered it as entirely an affair of the mind, as that will which it is intended to coerce. Under the absolute sway of an individual despot, the body was attacked in order to subdue the soul; and the soul escaped the blows which were directed against it, and rose superior to the attempt; but such is not the course adopted by tyranny in democratic republics; there the body is left free, and the soul is enslaved. The sovereign can no longer say, "You shall think as I do on pain of death;" but he says, "You are free to think differently from me, and to retain your life, your property, and all that you possess; but if such be your determination, you are henceforth an alien among your people. You may retain your civil rights, but they will be useless to you, for you will never be chosen by your fellow-citizens, if you solicit their suffrages; and they will affect to scorn you, if you solicit their esteem. You will remain among men, but you will be deprived of the rights of mankind. Your fellow-creatures will shun you like an impure being; and those who are most persuaded of your innocence will abandon you too, lest they should be shunned in their turn. Go in peace! I have given you your life, but it is an existence incomparably worse than death."

Absolute monarchies have thrown an odium upon despotism; let us beware lest democratic republics should restore oppression, and should render it less odious and less degrading in the eyes of the many, by making it still more onerous to the few.

Works have been published in the proudest nations of the Old World, expressly intended to censure the vices and deride the follies of the time; Labruyère inhabited the palace of Louis XIV, when he composed his chapter upon the Great, and Molière criticized the courtiers in the very pieces which were acted before the court. But the ruling power in the United States is not to be made game of; the smallest reproach irritates its sensibility, and the slightest joke which has any foundation in truth renders it indignant; from the style of its language to the more solid virtues of its character, everything must be made the subject of encomium. No writer, whatever be his eminence, can escape from this tribute of adulation to his fellow-citizens. The majority lives in the perpetual exercise of self-applause; and there are certain truths which the Americans can only learn from strangers or from experience.

If great writers have not at present existed in America, the reason is very simply given in these facts; there can be no literary genius without freedom of opinion, and freedom of opinion does not exist in America. The inquisition has never been able to prevent a vast number of anti-religious books from circulating in Spain. The empire of the majority succeeds much better in the United States, since it actually removes the wish of publishing them. Unbelievers are to be met with in America, but, to say the truth, there is no public organ of infidelity. Attempts have been made by some governments to protect the morality of nations by prohibiting licentious books. In the United States no one is punished for this sort of works, but no one is induced to write them; not because all the citizens are immaculate in their manners, but because the majority of the community is decent and orderly.

In these cases the advantages derived from the exercise of this power are unquestionable; and I am simply discussing the nature of the power itself. This irresistible authority is a constant fact, and its beneficent exercise is an accidental occurrence. . . .

### The Greatest Dangers of the American Republics Proceed from the Unlimited Power of the Majority

Governments usually fall a sacrifice to impotence or to tyranny. In the former case their power escapes from them: it is wrested from their grasp in the latter. Many observers who have noticed the anarchy of democratic states, have imagined that the government of those states was naturally weak and impotent. The truth is, that when once hostilities are begun between parties, the government loses its control over society. But I do not think that a democratic power is naturally without resources: say rather, that it is almost always by the abuse of its force, and the misemployment of its resources, that a democratic government fails. Anarchy is almost always produced by its tyranny or its mistakes, but not by its want of strength.

It is important not to confound stability with force, or the greatness of a thing with its duration. In democratic republics, the power which directs[4] society is not stable; for it often changes hands and assumes a new direction. But whichever way it turns, its force is almost irresistible. The governments of the American republics appear to me to be as much centralized as those of the absolute monarchies of Europe, and more energetic than they are. I do not, therefore, imagine that they will perish from weakness.[5]

If ever the free institutions of America are destroyed, that event may be attributed to the unlimited authority of the majority, which may at some future time urge the minorities to desperation, and oblige them to have recourse to physical force. Anarchy will then be the result, but it will have been brought about by despotism.

Mr. Hamilton expresses the same opinion in the Federalist, No. 51. "It is of great importance in a republic not only to guard the society against the oppression of its rulers, but to guard one part of the society against the injustice of the other part. Justice is the end of government. It is the end of civil society. It ever has been, and ever will be pursued until it be obtained, or until liberty be lost in the pursuit. In a society, under the forms of which the stronger faction can readily unite and oppress the weaker, anarchy may as truly be said to reign as in a state of nature, where the weaker individual is not secured against the violence of the stronger: and as in the latter state even the stronger individuals are prompted by the uncertainty of their condition to submit to a government which may protect the weak as well as themselves, so in the former state will the more powerful factions be gradually induced by a like motive to wish for a government which will protect all parties, the weaker as well as the more powerful. It can be little doubted, that if the state of Rhode Island was separated from the confederacy and left to itself, the insecurity of rights under the popular form of government within such narrow limits, would be displayed by such reiterated oppressions of the factious majorities, that some power altogether independent of the people would soon be called for by the voice of the very factions whose misrule had proved the necessity of it."

Jefferson has also thus expressed himself in a letter to Madison:[6] "The executive power in our government is not the only, perhaps not even the principal object of my solicitude. The tyranny of the legislature is really the danger most to be feared, and will continue to be so for many years to come. The tyranny of the executive power will come in its turn, but at a more distant period."

I am glad to cite the opinion of Jefferson upon this subject rather than that of another, because I consider him to be the most powerful advocate democracy has ever sent forth.

---

[4] This power may be centred in an assembly, in which case it will be strong without being stable; or it may be centred in an individual, in which case it will be less strong, but more stable.

[5] I presume that it is scarcely necessary to remind the reader here, as well as throughout the remainder of this chapter, that I am speaking not of the federal government, but of the several governments of each state which the majority controls at its pleasure.

[6] 15th March, 1789.

# VOLUME II

### BOOK II: *INFLUENCE OF DEMOCRACY ON THE FEELINGS OF THE AMERICANS*

**Chapter I:** **Why Democratic Nations Show a More Ardent and Enduring Love of Equality than of Liberty**

The first and most intense passion which is produced by equality of conditions is, I need hardly say, the love of that equality. My readers will therefore not be surprised that I speak of this feeling before all others.

Everybody has remarked, that in our time, and especially in France, this passion for equality is every day gaining ground in the human heart. It has been said a hundred times that our contemporaries are far more ardently and tenaciously attached to equality than to freedom; but, as I do not find that the causes of the fact have been sufficiently analyzed, I shall endeavour to point them out.

It is possible to imagine an extreme point at which freedom and equality would meet and be confounded together. Let us suppose that all the people take a part in the government, and that each one of them has an equal right to take a part in it. As none is different from his fellows, none can exercise a tyrannical power; men will be perfectly free, because they are all entirely equal; and they will all be perfectly equal, because they are all entirely free. To this ideal state democratic nations tend. Such is the completest form that equality can assume upon earth; but there are a thousand others which, without being equally perfect, are not less cherished by those nations.

The principle of equality may be established in civil society, without prevailing in the political world. Equal rights may exist of indulging in the same pleasures, of entering the same professions, of frequenting the same places; in a word, of living in the same manner and seeking wealth by the same means—although all men do not take an equal share in the government. A kind of equality may even be established in the political world, though there should be no political freedom there. A man may be the equal of all his countrymen save one, who is the master of all without distinction, and who selects equally from among them all the agents of his power. Several other combinations might be easily imagined, by which very great equality would be united to institutions more or less free, or even to institutions wholly without freedom.

Although men cannot become absolutely equal unless they be entirely free; and consequently equality, pushed to its furthest extent, may be confounded with freedom, yet there is good reason for distinguishing the one from the other. The taste which men have for liberty, and that which they feel for equality, are, in fact, two different things; and I am not afraid to add, that, amongst democratic nations, they are two unequal things.

Upon close inspection, it will be seen that there is in every age some peculiar and preponderating fact with which all others are connected; this fact almost always gives birth to some pregnant idea or some ruling passion, which attracts to itself, and bears away in its course, all the feelings and opinions of the time: it is like a great stream, towards which each of the neighboring rivulets seems to flow.

Freedom has appeared in the world at different times and under various forms; it has not been exclusively bound to any social condition, and it is not confined to democracies. Freedom cannot, therefore, form the distinguishing characteristic of democratic ages. The peculiar and preponderating fact which marks those ages as its own is the equality of condition; the ruling passion of men in those periods is the love of this equality. Ask not what singular charm the men of democratic ages find in being equal, or what special reasons they may have for clinging so tenaciously to equality rather than to the other advantages which society holds out to them: equality is the distinguishing characteristic of the age they live in; that, of itself, is enough to explain that they prefer it to all the rest.

But independently of this reason there are several others, which will at all times habitually lead men to prefer equality to freedom.

If a people could ever succeed in destroying, or even in diminishing, the equality which prevails in its own body, this could only be accomplished by long and laborious efforts. Their social condition must be modified, their laws abolished, their opinions superseded, their habits changed, their manners corrupted. But political liberty is more easily lost; to neglect to hold it fast, is to allow it to escape. Men therefore not only cling to equality because it is dear to them; they also adhere to it because they think it will last forever.

That political freedom may compromise in its excesses the tranquillity, the property, the lives of individuals, is obvious to the narrowest and most unthinking minds. On the contrary, none but attentive and clear-sighted men perceive the perils with which equality threatens us, and they commonly avoid pointing them out. They know that the calamities they apprehend are remote, and flatter themselves that they will only fall upon future generations, for which the present generation takes but little thought. The evils which freedom sometimes brings with it are immediate; they are apparent to all, and all are more or less affected by them. The evils which extreme equality may produce are slowly disclosed; they creep gradually into the social frame; they are only seen at intervals, and at the moment at which they become most violent, habit already causes them to be no longer felt.

The advantages which freedom brings are only shown by lapse of time; and it is always easy to mistake the cause in which they originate. The advantages of equality are immediate, and they may always be traced from their source.

Political liberty bestows exalted pleasures, from time to time, upon a certain number of citizens. Equality every day confers a number of small enjoyments on every man. The charms of equality are every instant felt, and are within the reach of all; the noblest hearts are not insensible to them, and the most vulgar souls exult in them. The passion which equality engenders must therefore be at once strong and general. Men cannot enjoy political liberty unpurchased by some sacrifices, and they never obtain it without great exertions. But the pleasures of equality are self-proffered: each of the petty incidents of life seems to occasion them, and in order to taste them nothing is required but to live.

Democratic nations are at all times fond of equality, but there are certain epochs at which the passion they entertain for it swells to the height of fury. This occurs at the moment when the old social system, long menaced, is overthrown after a severe intestine struggle, and the barriers of rank are at length thrown down. At such times, men pounce upon equality as their booty, and they cling to it as to some precious treasure which they fear to lose. The passion for equality penetrates on every side into men's hearts, expands there, and fills them entirely. Tell them not that by this blind surrender of themselves to an exclusive passion, they risk their dearest interests: they are deaf. Show them not freedom escaping from their grasp, whilst they are looking another way: they are blind, or rather, they can discern but one object to be desired in the universe.

What I have said is applicable to all democratic nations: what I am about to say concerns the French alone. Amongst most modern nations, and especially amongst all those of the continent of Europe, the taste and the idea of freedom only began to exist and to be developed at the time when social conditions were tending to equality, and as a consequence of that very equality. Absolute kings were the most efficient levellers of ranks amongst their subjects. Amongst these nations equality preceded freedom: equality was therefore a fact of some standing, when freedom was still a novelty: the one had already created customs, opinions, and laws belonging to it, when the other, alone and for the first time, came into actual existence. Thus the latter was still only an affair of opinion and of taste, whilst the former had already crept into the habits of the people, possessed itself of their manners, and given a particular turn to the smallest actions in their lives. Can it be wondered that the men of our own time prefer the one to the other?

I think that democratic communities have a natural taste for freedom: left to themselves, they will seek it, cherish it, and view any privation of it with regret. But for equality, their passion is ardent, insatiable, incessant, invincible: they call for equality in freedom; and if they cannot obtain that, they still call for equality in slavery. They will endure poverty, servitude, barbarism; but they will not endure aristocracy.

This is true at all times, and especially true in our own day. All men and all powers seeking to cope with this irresistible passion, will be overthrown and destroyed by it. In our age, freedom cannot be established without it, and despotism itself cannot reign without its support.

**Chapter II:    Of Individualism in Democratic Countries**

I have shown how it is that, in ages of equality, every man seeks for his opinions within himself: I am now about to show how it is that, in the same ages, all his feelings are turned towards himself alone. *Individualism* is a novel expression, to which a novel idea has given birth. Our fathers were only acquainted with *egoisme* (selfishness). Selfishness is a passionate and exaggerated love of self, which leads a man to connect everything with himself, and to prefer himself to everything in the world. Individualism is a mature and calm feeling, which disposes each member of the community to sever himself from the mass of his fellows, and to draw apart with his family and his friends; so that, after he has thus formed a little circle of his own, he willingly leaves society at large to itself. Selfishness originates in blind instinct: individualism proceeds from erroneous judgment more than from depraved feelings; it originates as much in deficiencies of mind as in perversity of heart.

Selfishness blights the germ of all virtue: individualism, at first, only saps the virtues of public life; but, in the long run, it attacks and destroys all others, and is at length absorbed in downright selfishness. Selfishness is a vice as old as the world, which does not belong to one form of society more than to another: individualism is of democratic origin, and it threatens to spread in the same ratio as the equality of conditions.

Amongst aristocratic nations, as families remain for centuries in the same condition, often on the same spot, all generations become as it were contemporaneous. A man almost always knows his forefathers, and respects them: he thinks he already sees his remote descendants, and he loves them. He willingly imposes duties on himself towards the former and the latter; and he will frequently sacrifice his personal gratifications to those who went before and to those who will come after him. Aristocratic institutions have, moreover, the effect of closely binding every man to several of his fellow-citizens. As the classes of an aristocratic people are strongly marked and permanent, each of them is regarded by its own members as a sort of lesser country, more tangible and more cherished than the country at large. As, in aristocratic communities, all the citizens occupy fixed positions, one above the other, the result is, that each of them always sees a man above himself whose patronage is necessary to him, and, below himself, another man whose co-operation he may claim. Men living in aristocratic ages are therefore almost always closely attached to something placed out of their own sphere, and they are often disposed to forget themselves. It is true that, in these ages, the notion of human fellowship is faint, and that men seldom think of sacrificing themselves for mankind; but they often sacrifice themselves for other men. In democratic ages, on the contrary, when the duties of each individual to the race are much more clear, devoted service to any one man becomes more rare; the bond of human affection is extended, but it is relaxed.

Amongst democratic nations, new families are constantly springing up, others are constantly falling away, and all that remain change their condition; the woof of time is every instant broken, and the track of generations effaced. Those who went before are soon forgotten; of those who will come after, no one has any idea: the interest of man is confined to those in close propinquity to himself. As each class approximates to other classes, and intermingles with them, its members become indifferent, and as strangers to one another. Aristocracy had made a chain of all the members of the community, from the peasant to the king: democracy breaks that chain, and severs every link of it.

As social conditions become more equal, the number of persons increases who, although they are neither rich enough nor powerful enough to exercise any great influence over their fellows, have nevertheless acquired or retained sufficient education and fortune to satisfy their own wants. They owe nothing to any man, they expect nothing from any man; they acquire the habit of always considering themselves as standing alone, and they are apt to imagine that their whole destiny is in their own hands.

Thus, not only does democracy make every man forget his ancestors, but it hides his descendants and separates his contemporaries from him; it throws him back forever upon himself alone, and threatens in the end to confine him entirely within the solitude of his own heart.

### Chapter IV:   That the Americans Combat the Effects of Individualism by Free Institutions

Despotism, which is of a very timorous nature, is never more secure of continuance than when it can keep men asunder; and all its influence is commonly exerted for that purpose. No vice of the human heart is so acceptable to it as selfishness: a despot easily forgives his subjects for not loving him, provided they do not love each other. He does not ask them to assist him in governing the state; it is enough that they do not aspire to govern it themselves. He stigmatizes as turbulent and unruly spirits those who would combine their exertions to promote the prosperity of the community; and, perverting the natural meaning of words, he applauds as good citizens those who have no sympathy for any but themselves.

Thus the vices which despotism produces are precisely those which equality fosters. These two things mutually and perniciously complete and assist each other. Equality places men side by side, unconnected by any common tie; despotism raises barriers to keep them asunder: the former predisposes them not to consider their fellow-creatures, the latter makes general indifference a sort of public virtue.

Despotism, then, which is at all times dangerous, is more particularly to be feared in democratic ages. It is easy to see that in those same ages men stand most in need of freedom. When the members of a community are forced to attend to public affairs, they are necessarily drawn from the circle of their own interests, and snatched at times from self-observation. As soon as a man begins to treat of public affairs in public, he begins to perceive that he is not so independent of his fellow-men as he had at first imagined, and that, in order to obtain their support, he must often lend them his co-operation.

When the public governs, there is no man who does not feel the value of public good-will, or who does not endeavor to court it by drawing to himself the esteem and affection of those amongst whom he is to live. Many of the passions which congeal and keep asunder human hearts, are then obliged to retire and hide below the surface. Pride must be dissembled; disdain dares not break out; selfishness fears its own self. Under a free government, as most public offices are elective, the men whose elevated minds or aspiring hopes are too closely circumscribed in private life constantly feel that they cannot do without the people who surround them. Men learn at such times to think of their fellow-men from ambitious motives; and they frequently find it, in a manner, their interest to forget themselves.

I may here be met by an objection derived from electioneering intrigues, the meanesses of candidates, and the calumnies of their opponents. These are occasions of enmity which occur the oftener, the more frequent elections become. Such evils are doubtless great, but they are transient; whereas the benefits which attend them remain. The desire of being elected may lead some men for a time to violent hostility; but this same desire leads all men in the long run mutually to support each other; and, if it happens that an election accidentally severs two friends, the electoral system brings a multitude of citizens permanently together, who would always have remained unknown to each other. Freedom engenders private animosities, but despotism gives birth to general indifference.

The Americans have combated by free institutions the tendency of equality to keep men asunder, and they have subdued it. The legislators of America did not suppose that a general representation of the whole nation would suffice to ward off a disorder at once so natural to the frame of democratic society, and so fatal: they also thought that it would be well to infuse political life into each portion of the territory, in order to multiply to an infinite extent opportunities of acting in concert for all the members of the community, and to make them constantly feel their mutual dependence on each other. The plan was a wise one. The general affairs of a country only engage the attention of leading politicians, who assemble from time to time in the same places; and, as they often lose sight of each other afterwards, no lasting ties are established between them. But if the object be to have the local affairs of a district conducted by the men who reside there, the same persons are always in contact, and they are, in a manner, forced to be acquainted, and to adapt themselves to one another.

It is difficult to draw a man out of his own circle to interest him in the destiny of the state, because he does not clearly understand what influence the destiny of the state can have upon his own lot. But if it be proposed to make a road cross the end of his estate, he will see at a glance that there is a connection between this small public affair and his greatest private affairs; and he will discover, without its being shown to him, the close tie which unites private to general interest. Thus, far more may be done by intrusting to the citizens the administration of minor affairs than by surrendering to them the control of important ones, towards interesting them in the public welfare, and convincing them that they constantly stand in need one of an other in order to provide for it. A brilliant achievement may win for you the favor of a people at one stroke; but to earn the love and respect of the population which surrounds you, a long succession of little services rendered and of obscure good deeds,—a constant habit of kindness, and an established reputation for disinterestedness, —will be required. Local freedom, then, which leads a great number of citizens to value the affection of their neighbors and of their kindred, perpetually brings men together, and forces them to help one another, in spite of the propensities which sever them.

In the United States, the more opulent citizens take great care not to stand aloof from the people; on the contrary, they constantly keep on easy terms with the lower classes: they listen to them, they speak to them every day. They know that the rich in democracies always stand in need of the poor; and that, in democratic ages, you attach a poor man to you more by your manner than by benefits conferred. The magnitude of such benefits, which sets off the difference of conditions, causes a secret irritation to those who reap advantage from them; but the charm of simplicity of manners is almost irresistible: affability carries men away, and even want of polish is not always displeasing. This truth does not take root at once in the minds of the rich. They generally resist it as long as the democratic revolution lasts, and they do not acknowledge it immediately after that revolution is accomplished. They are very ready to do good to the people, but they still choose to keep them at arm's length; they think that is sufficient, but they are mistaken. They might spend fortunes thus without warming the hearts of the population around them;—that population does not ask them for the sacrifice of their money, but of their pride.

It would seem as if every imagination in the United States were upon the stretch to invent means of increasing the wealth and satisfying the wants of the public. The best-informed inhabitants of each district constantly use their information to discover new truths which may augment the general prosperity; and, if they have made any such discoveries, they eagerly surrender them to the mass of the people.

When the vices and weaknesses frequently exhibited by those who govern in America are closely examined, the prosperity of the people occasions, but improperly occasions, surprise. Elected magistrates do not make the American democracy flourish; it flourishes because the magistrates are elective.

It would be unjust to suppose that the patriotism and the zeal which every American displays for the welfare of his fellow-citizens are wholly insincere. Although private interest directs the greater part of human actions in the United States, as well as elsewhere, it does not regulate them all. I must say that I have often seen Americans make great and real sacrifices to the public welfare; and I have remarked a hundred instances in which they hardly ever failed to lend faithful support to each other. The free institutions which the inhabitants of the United States possess, and the political rights of which they make so much use, remind every citizen, and in a thousand ways, that he lives in society. They every instant impress upon his mind the notion that it is the duty, as well as the interest, of men to make themselves useful to their fellow-creatures; and as he sees no particular ground of animosity to them, since he is never either their master or their slave, his heart readily leans to the side of kindness. Men attend to the interests of the public, first by necessity, afterwards by choice: what was intentional becomes an instinct; and by dint of working for the good of one's fellow-citizens, the habit and the taste for serving them is at length acquired.

Many people in France consider equality of condition as one evil, and political freedom as a second. When they are obliged to yield to the former, they strive at least to escape from the latter. But I contend, that in order to combat the evils which equality may produce, there is only one effectual remedy—namely, political freedom.

### Chapter V:     Of the Use Which the Americans Make of Public Associations in Civil Life

I do not propose to speak of those political associations by the aid of which men endeavor to defend themselves against the despotic action of a majority, or against the aggressions of regal power. That subject I have already treated. If each citizen did not learn, in proportion as he individually becomes more feeble, and consequently more incapable of preserving his freedom single-handed, to combine with his fellow-citizens for the purpose of defending it, it is clear that tyranny would unavoidably increase together with equality.

Those associations only which are formed in civil life, without reference to political objects, are here adverted to. The political associations which exist in the United States are only a single feature in the midst of the immense assemblage of associations in that country. Americans of all ages, all conditions, and all dispositions, constantly form associations. They have not only commercial and manufacturing companies, in which all take part, but associations of a thousand other kinds, —religious, moral, serious, futile, general or restricted, enormous or diminutive. The Americans make associations to give entertainments, to found seminaries, to build inns, to construct churches, to diffuse books, to send missionaries to the antipodes; they found in this manner hospitals, prisons, and schools. If it be proposed to inculcate some truth, or to foster some feeling, by the encouragement of a great example, they form a society. Wherever, at the head of some new undertaking, you see the government in France, or a man of rank in England, in the United States you will be sure to find an association.

I met with several kinds of associations in America of which I confess I had no previous notion; and I have often admired the extreme skill with which the inhabitants of the United States succeed in proposing a common object to the exertions of a great many men, and in inducing them voluntarily to pursue it.

I have since travelled over England, whence the Americans have taken some of their laws and many of their customs; and it seemed to me that the principle of association was by no means so constantly or adroitly used in that country. The English often perform great things singly, whereas the Americans form associations for the smallest undertakings. It is evident that the former people consider association as a powerful means of action, but the latter seem to regard it as the only means they have of acting.

Thus, the most democratic country on the face of the earth is that in which men have, in our time, carried to the highest perfection the art of pursuing in common the object of their common desires, and have applied this new science to the greatest number of purposes. Is this the result of accident? or is there in reality any necessary connection between the principle of association and that of equality?

Aristocratic communities always contain, amongst a multitude of persons who by themselves are powerless, a small number of powerful and wealthy citizens, each of whom can achieve great undertakings single-handed. In aristocratic societies, men do not need to combine in order to act, because they are strongly held together. Every wealthy and powerful citizen constitutes the head of a permanent and compulsory association, composed of all those who are dependent upon him, or whom he makes subservient to the execution of his designs.

Amongst democratic nations, on the contrary, all the citizens are independent and feeble; they can do hardly anything by themselves, and none of them can oblige his fellow-men to lend him their assistance. They all, therefore, become powerless, if they do not learn voluntarily to help each other. If men living in democratic countries had no right and no inclination to associate for political purposes, their independence would be in great jeopardy; but they might long preserve their wealth and their cultivation: whereas, if they never acquired the habit of forming associations in ordinary life, civilization itself would be endangered. A people amongst whom individuals should lose the power of achieving great things single-handed, without acquiring the means of producing them by united exertions, would soon relapse into barbarism.

Unhappily, the same social condition which renders associations so necessary to democratic nations, renders their formation more difficult amongst those nations than amongst all other. When several members of an aristocracy agree to combine, they easily succeed in doing so: as each of them brings great strength to the partnership, the number of its members may be very limited; and when the members of an association are limited in number, they may easily become mutually acquainted, understand each other, and establish fixed regulations. The same opportunities do not occur amongst democratic nations, where the associated members must always be very numerous for their association to have any power.

I am aware that many of my countrymen are not in the least embarrassed by this difficulty. They contend, that, the more enfeebled and incompetent the citizens become, the more able and active the Government ought to be rendered, in order that society at large may execute what individuals can no longer accomplish. They believe this answers the whole difficulty, but I think they are mistaken.

A government might perform the part of some of the largest American companies; and several States, members of the Union, have already attempted it; but what political power could ever carry on the vast multitude of lesser undertakings which the American citizens perform every day, with the assistance of the principle of association? It is easy to foresee that the time is drawing near when man will be less and less able to produce, of himself alone, the commonest necessaries of life. The task of the governing power will therefore perpetually increase, and its very efforts will extend it every day. The more it stands in the place of associations, the more will individuals, losing the notion of combining together, require its assistance: these are causes and effects which unceasingly create each other. Will the administration of the country ultimately assume the management of all the manufactures which no single citizen is able to carry on? And if a time at length arrives when, in consequence of the extreme subdivision of landed property, the soil is split into an infinite number of parcels, so that it can only be cultivated by companies of husbandmen, will it be necessary that the head of the government should leave the helm of state to follow the plough? The morals and the intelligence of a democratic people would be as much endangered as its business and manufactures, if the government ever wholly usurped the place of private companies.

Feelings and opinions are recruited, the heart is enlarged, and the human mind is developed, only by the reciprocal influence of men upon each other. I have shown that these influences are almost null in democratic countries; they must therefore be artificially created, and this can only be accomplished by associations.

When the members of an aristocratic community adopt a new opinion, or conceive a new sentiment, they give it a station, as it were, beside themselves, upon the lofty platform where they stand; and opinions or sentiments so conspicuous to the eyes of the multitude are easily introduced into the minds or hearts of all around. In democratic countries, the governing power alone is naturally in a condition to act in this manner; but it is easy to see that its action is always inadequate, and often dangerous. A government can no more be competent to keep alive and to renew the circulation of opinions and feelings amongst a great people, than to manage all the speculations of productive industry. No sooner does a government attempt to go beyond its political sphere, and to enter upon this new track, than it exercises, even unintentionally, an insupportable tyranny; for a government can only dictate strict rules, the opinions which it favors are rigidly enforced, and it is never easy to discriminate between its advice and its commands. Worse still will be the case, if the government really believes itself interested in preventing all circulation of ideas; it will then stand motionless and oppressed by the heaviness of voluntary torpor. Governments, therefore, should not be the only active powers: associations ought, in democratic nations, to stand in lieu of those powerful private individuals whom the equality of conditions has swept away.

As soon as several of the inhabitants of the United States have taken up an opinion or a feeling which they wish to promote in the world, they look out for mutual assistance; and as soon as they have found each other out, they combine. From that moment they are no longer isolated men, but a power seen from afar, whose actions serve for an example, and whose language is listened to. The first time I heard in the United States that a hundred thousand men had bound themselves publicly to abstain from spirituous liquors, it appeared to me more like a joke than a serious engagement; and I did not at once perceive why these temperate citizens could not content themselves with drinking water by their own firesides. I at last understood that these hundred thousand Americans, alarmed by the progress of drunkenness around them, had made up their minds to patronize temperance. They acted just in the same way as a man of high rank who should dress very plainly, in order to inspire the humbler orders with a contempt of luxury. It is probable that, if these hundred thousand men had lived in France, each of them would singly have memorialized the government to watch the public houses all over the kingdom.

Nothing, in my opinion, is more deserving of our attention than the intellectual and moral associations of America. The political and industrial associations of that country strike us forcibly; but the others elude our observation, or, if we discover them, we understand them imperfectly, because we have hardly ever seen anything of the kind. It must, however, be acknowledged, that they are as necessary to the American people as the former, and perhaps more so. In democratic countries, the science of association is the mother of science; the progress of all the rest depends upon the progress it has made.

Amongst the laws which rule human societies, there is one which seems to be more precise and clear than all others. If men are to remain civilized, or to become so, the art of associating together must grow and improve in the same ratio in which the equality of conditions is increased.

### Chapter VI: Of the Relation Between Public Associations and Newspapers

When men are no longer united amongst themselves by firm and lasting ties, it is impossible to obtain the co-operation of any great number of them, unless you can persuade every man whose help you require that his private interest obliges him voluntarily to unite his exertions to the exertions of all the others. This can be habitually and conveniently effected only by means of a newspaper: nothing but a newspaper can drop the same thought into a thousand minds at the same moment. A newspaper is an adviser who does not require to be sought, but who comes of his own accord, and talks to you briefly every day of the common weal, without distracting you from your private affairs.

Newspapers therefore become more necessary in proportion as men become more equal, and individualism more to be feared. To suppose that they only serve to protect freedom would be to diminish their importance: they maintain civilization. I shall not deny that, in democratic countries, newspapers frequently lead the citizens to launch together into very ill-digested schemes; but if there were no newspapers, there would be no common activity. The evil which they produce is therefore much less than that which they cure.

The effect of a newspaper is not only to suggest the same purpose to a great number of persons, but to furnish means for executing in common the designs which they may have singly conceived. The principal citizens who inhabit an aristocratic country discern each other from afar; and if they wish to unite their forces, they move towards each other, drawing a multitude of men after them. It frequently happens, on the contrary, in democratic countries, that a great number of men who wish or who want to combine cannot accomplish it, because, as they are very insignificant and lost amidst the crowd, they cannot see, and know not where to find, one another. A newspaper then takes up the notion or the feeling which had occurred simultaneously, but singly, to each of them. All are then immediately guided towards this beacon; and these wandering minds, which had long sought each other in darkness, at length meet and unite. The newspaper brought them together, and the newspaper is still necessary to keep them united.

In order that an association amongst a democratic people should have any power, it must be a numerous body. The persons of whom it is composed are therefore scattered over a wide extent, and each of them is detained in the place of his domicile by the narrowness of his income, or by the small unremitting exertions by which he earns it. Means must then be found to converse every day without seeing each other, and to take steps in common without having met. Thus hardly any democratic association can do without newspapers.

There is, consequently, a necessary connection between public associations and newspapers: newspapers make associations, and associations make newspapers; and if it has been correctly advanced, that associations will increase in number as the conditions of men become more equal, it is not less certain that the number of newspapers increases in proportion to that of associations. Thus it is, in America, that we find at the same time the greatest number of associations and of newspapers.

This connection between the number of newspapers and that of associations leads us to the discovery of a further connection between the state of the periodical press and the form of the administration in a country and shows that the number of newspapers must diminish or increase amongst a democratic people, in proportion as its administration is more or less centralized. For, amongst democratic nations, the exercise of local powers cannot be intrusted to the principal members of the community, as in aristocracies. Those powers must either be abolished, or placed in the hands of very large numbers of men, who then in fact constitute an association permanently established by law, for the purpose of administering the affairs of a certain extent of territory; and they require a journal, to bring to them every day, in the midst of their own minor concerns, some intelligence of the state of their public weal. The more numerous local powers are, the greater is the number of men in whom they are vested by law; and as this want is hourly felt, the more profusely do newspapers abound.

The extraordinary subdivision of administrative power has much more to do with the enormous number of American newspapers, than the great political freedom of the country and the absolute liberty of the press. If all the inhabitants of the Union had the suffrage, but a suffrage which should extend only to the choice of their legislators in Congress,—they would require but few newspapers, because they would have to act together only on very important, but very rare, occasions. But within the great national association, of the nation, lesser associations have been established by law in every country, every city, and indeed in every village, for the purposes of local administration. The laws of the country thus compel every American to co-operate every day of his life with some of his fellow-citizens for a common purpose, and each one of them requires a newspaper to inform him what all the others are doing.

I am of opinion that a democratic people,[7] without any national representative assemblies, but with a great number of small local powers, would have in the end more newspapers than another people governed by a centralized administration and an elective legislature. What best explains to me the enormous circulation of the daily press in the United States is, that, amongst the Americans, I find the utmost national freedom combined with local freedom of every kind.

There is a prevailing opinion in France and England, that the circulation of newspapers would be indefinitely increased by removing the taxes which have been laid upon the press. This is a very exaggerated estimate of the effects of such a reform. Newspapers increase in numbers, not according to their cheapness, but according to the more or less frequent want which a great number of men may feel for intercommunication and combination.

In like manner, I should attribute the increasing influence of the daily press to causes more general than those by which it is commonly explained. A newspaper can only subsist on the condition of publishing sentiments or principles common to a large number of men. A newspaper, therefore, always represents an association which is composed of its habitual readers. This association may be more or less defined, more or less restricted, more or less numerous; but the fact that the newspaper keeps alive, is a proof that at least the germ of such an association exists in the minds of its readers.

This leads me to a last reflection, with which I shall conclude this chapter. The more equal the conditions of men become, and the less strong men individually are, the more easily do they give way to the current of the multitude, and the more difficult is it for them to adhere by themselves to an opinion which the multitude discard. A newspaper represents an association; it may be said to address each of its readers in the name of all the others, and to exert its influence over them in proportion to their individual weakness. The power of the newspaper press must therefore increase as the social conditions of men become more equal.

### Chapter VII:    Relation of Civil to Political Associations

There is only one country on the face of the earth where the citizens enjoy unlimited freedom of association for political purposes. This same country is the only one in the world where the continual exercise of the right of association has been introduced into civil life, and where all the advantages which civilization can confer are procured by means of it.

In all the countries where political associations are prohibited, civil associations are rare. It is hardly probable that this is the result of accident; but the inference should rather be, that there is a natural, and perhaps a necessary, connection between these two kinds of associations.

Certain men happen to have a common interest in some concern; either a commercial undertaking is to be managed, or some speculation in manufactures to be tried: they meet, they combine, and thus, by degrees, they become familiar with the principle of association. The greater the multiplicity of small affairs, the more do men, even without knowing it, acquire facility in prosecuting great undertakings in common.

Civil associations, therefore, facilitate political association; but, on the other hand, political association singularly strengthens and improves associations for civil purposes. In civil life, every man may, strictly speaking, fancy that he can provide for his own wants; in politics, he can fancy no such thing. When a people, then, have any knowledge of public life, the notion of association, and the wish to coalesce, present themselves every day to the minds of the whole community: whatever natural repugnance may restrain men from acting in concert, they will always be ready to combine for the sake of a party. Thus political life makes the love and practice of association

---

[7] I say a *democratic people*: the administration of an aristocratic people may be the reverse of centralized, and yet the want of newspapers be little felt, because local powers are then vested in the hands of a very small number of men, who either act apart, or who know each other, and can easily meet and come to an understanding.

more general; it imparts a desire of union, and teaches the means of combination to numbers of men who otherwise would have always lived apart.

Politics not only give birth to numerous associations, but to associations of great extent. In civil life, it seldom happens that any one interest draws a very large number of men to act in concert; much skill is required to bring such an interest into existence: but in politics, opportunities present themselves every day. Now it is solely in great associations that the general value of the principle of association is displayed. Citizens who are individually powerless do not very clearly anticipate the strength which they may acquire by uniting together; it must be shown to them in order to be understood. Hence it is often easier to collect a multitude for a public purpose than a few persons; a thousand citizens do not see what interest they have in combining together; ten thousand will be perfectly aware of it. In politics, men combine for great undertakings; and the use they make of the principle of association in important affairs practically teaches them that it is their interest to help each other in those of less moment. A political association draws a number of individuals at the same time out of their own circle; however they may be naturally kept asunder by age, mind, and fortune, it places them nearer together, and brings them into contact. Once met, they can always meet again.

Men can embark in few civil partnerships without risking a portion of their possessions; this is the case with all manufacturing and trading companies. When men are as yet but little versed in the art of association, and are unacquainted with its principal rules, they are afraid, when first they combine in this manner, of buying their experience dear. They therefore prefer depriving themselves of a powerful instrument of success, to running the risks which attend the use of it. They are, however, less reluctant to join political associations, which appear to them to be without danger, because they adventure no money in them. But they cannot belong to these associations for any length of time, without finding out how order is maintained amongst a large number of men, and by what contrivance they are made to advance, harmoniously and methodically, to the same object. Thus they learn to surrender their own will to that of all the rest, and to make their own exertions subordinate to the common impulse,—things which it is not less necessary to know in civil than in political associations. Political associations may therefore be considered as large free schools, where all the members of the community go to learn the general theory of association.

But even if political association did not directly contribute to the progress of civil association, to destroy the former would be to impair the latter. When citizens can only meet in public for certain purposes, they regard such meetings as a strange proceeding of rare occurrence, and they rarely think at all about it. When they are allowed to meet freely for all purposes, they ultimately look upon public association as the universal, or in a manner the sole, means which men can employ to accomplish the different purposes they may have in view. Every new want instantly revives the notion. The art of association then becomes, as I have said before, the mother of action, studied and applied by all.

When some kinds of associations are prohibited and others allowed, it is difficult to distinguish the former from the latter beforehand. In this state of doubt, men abstain from them altogether, and a sort of public opinion passes current, which tends to cause any association whatsoever to be regarded as a bold, and almost an illicit enterprise.[8]

---

[8]This is more especially true when the executive government has a discretionary power of allowing or prohibiting associations. When certain associations are simply prohibited by law, and the courts of justice have to punish infringements of that law, the evil is far less considerable. Then, every citizen knows beforehand pretty nearly what he has to expect. He judges himself before he is judged by the law, and, abstaining from prohibited associations, he embarks in those which are legally sanctioned. It is by these restrictions that all free nations have always admitted that the right of association might be limited. But if the legislature should invest a man with a power of ascertaining beforehand which associations are dangerous and which are useful, and should authorize him to destroy all associations in the bud or to allow them to be

It is therefore chimerical to suppose that the spirit of association, when it is repressed on some one point, will nevertheless display the same vigor on all others; and that, if men be allowed to prosecute certain undertakings in common, that is quite enough for them eagerly to set about them. When the members of a community are allowed and accustomed to combine for all purposes, they will combine as readily for the lesser as for the more important ones; but if they are only allowed to combine for small affairs, they will be neither inclined nor able to effect it. It is in vain that you will leave them entirely free to prosecute their business on joint-stock account: they will hardly care to avail themselves of the rights you have granted to them; and, after having exhausted your strength in vain efforts to put down prohibited associations, you will be surprised that you cannot persuade men to form the associations you encourage.

I do not say that there can be no civil associations in a country where political association is prohibited; for men can never live in society without embarking in some common undertakings: but I maintain that, in such a country, civil associations will always be few in number, feebly planned, unskillfully managed, that they will never form any vast designs, or that they will fail in the execution of them.

This naturally leads me to think that freedom of association in political matters is not so dangerous to public tranquillity as is supposed; and that possibly, after having agitated society for some time, it may strengthen the state in the end. In democratic countries, political associations are, so to speak, the only powerful persons who aspire to rule the state. Accordingly, the governments of our time look upon associations of this kind just as sovereigns in the Middle Ages regarded the great vassals of the crown: they entertain a sort of instinctive abhorrence of them, and combat them on all occasions. They bear, on the contrary, a natural good-will to civil associations, because they readily discover that, instead of directing the minds of the community to public affairs, these institutions serve to divert them from such reflections; and that, by engaging them more and more in the pursuit of objects which cannot be attained without public tranquillity, they deter them from revolutions. But these governments do not attend to the fact, that political associations tend amazingly to multiply and facilitate those of a civil character, and that, in avoiding a dangerous evil, they deprive themselves of an efficacious remedy.

When you see the Americans freely and constantly forming associations for the purpose of promoting some political principle, of raising one man to the head of affairs, or of wresting power from another, you have some difficulty in understanding that men so independent do not constantly fall into the abuse of freedom. If, on the other hand, you survey the infinite number of trading companies which are in operation in the United States, and perceive that the Americans are on every side unceasingly engaged in the execution of important and difficult plans, which the slightest revolution would throw into confusion, you will readily comprehend why people so well employed are by no means tempted to perturb the state, nor to destroy that public tranquillity by which they all profit.

Is it enough to observe these things separately, or should we not discover the hidden tie which connects them? In their political associations, the Americans of all conditions, minds, and ages, daily acquire a general taste for association, and grow accustomed to the use of it. There they meet together in large numbers,—they converse, they listen to each other, and they are mutually stimulated to all sorts of undertakings. They afterwards transfer to civil life the notions they have thus acquired, and make them subservient to a thousand purposes. Thus it is by the enjoyment of a dangerous freedom that the Americans learn the art of rendering the dangers of freedom less formidable.

---

formed, as nobody would be able to foresee in what cases associations might be established, and in what cases they would be put down, the spirit of association would be entirely paralyzed. The former of these laws would only assail certain associations; the latter would apply to society itself, and inflict an injury upon it. I can conceive that a regular government may have recourse to the former, but I do not concede that any government has the right of enacting the latter.

If a certain moment in the existence of a nation be selected, it is easy to prove that political associations perturb the state, and paralyze productive industry; but take the whole life of a people, and it may perhaps be easy to demonstrate that freedom of association in political matters is favorable to the prosperity, and even to the tranquillity, of the community.

I said in the former part of this work: "The unrestrained liberty of political association cannot be entirely assimilated to the liberty of the press. The one is at the same time less necessary and more dangerous than the other. A nation may confine it within certain limits, without ceasing to be mistress of itself; and it may sometimes be obliged to do so, in order to maintain its own authority." And, further on, I added: "It cannot be denied that the unrestrained liberty of association for political purposes is the last degree of liberty which a people is fit for. If it does not throw them into anarchy, it perpetually brings them, as it were, to the verge of it." Thus, I do not think that a nation is always at liberty to invest its citizens with an absolute right of association for political purposes; and I doubt whether, in any country or in any age, it be wise to set no limits to freedom of association.

A certain nation, it is said, could not maintain tranquillity in the community, cause the laws to be respected, or establish a lasting government, if the right of association were not confined within narrow limits. These blessings are doubtless invaluable; and I can imagine that, to acquire or to preserve them, a nation may impose upon itself severe temporary restrictions: but still it is well that the nation should know at what price these blessings are purchased. I can understand that it may be advisable to cut off a man's arm in order to save his life; but it would be ridiculous to assert that he will be as dexterous as he was before he lost it.

### Chapter VIII: How the Americans Combat Individualism by the Principle of Interest Rightly Understood

When the world was managed by a few rich and powerful individuals, these persons loved to entertain a lofty idea of the duties of man. They were fond of professing that it is praiseworthy to forget one's self, and that good should be done without hope of reward, as it is by the Deity himself. Such were the standard opinions of that time in morals.

I doubt whether men were more virtuous in aristocratic ages than in others; but they were incessantly talking of the beauties of virtue, and its utility was only studied in secret. But since the imagination takes less lofty flights and every man's thoughts are centred in himself, moralists are alarmed by this idea of self-sacrifice, and they no longer venture to present it to the human mind. They therefore content themselves with inquiring, whether the personal advantage of each member of the community does not consist in working for the good of all; and when they have hit upon some point on which private interest and public interest meet and amalgamate, they are eager to bring it into notice. Observations of this kind are gradually multiplied: what was only a single remark becomes a general principle; and it is held as a truth, that man serves himself in serving his fellow-creatures, and that his private interest is to do good.

I have already shown, in several parts of this work, by what means the inhabitants of the United States almost always manage to combine their own advantage with that of their fellow-citizens: my present purpose is to point out the general rule which enables them to do so. In the United States, hardly anybody talks of the beauty of virtue; but they maintain that virtue is useful, and prove it every day. The American moralists do not profess that men ought to sacrifice themselves for their fellow-creatures *because* it is noble to make such sacrifices; but they boldly aver that such sacrifices are as necessary to him who imposes them upon himself, as to him for whose sake they are made.

They have found out that, in their country and their age, man is brought home to himself by an irresistible force; and, losing all hope of stopping that force, they turn all their thoughts to the direction of it. They therefore do not deny that every man may follow his own interest; but they endeavor to prove that it is the interest of every man to be virtuous. I shall not here enter into the reasons they allege, which would divert me from my subject: suffice it to say, that they have convinced their fellow-countrymen.

Montaigne said long ago, "Were I not to follow the straight road for its straightness, I should follow it for having found by experience that, in the end, it is commonly the happiest and most useful track." The doctrine of interest rightly understood is not then new, but amongst the Americans of our time it finds universal acceptance: it has become popular there; you may trace it at the bottom of all their actions, you will remark it in all they say. It is as often asserted by the poor man as by the rich. In Europe, the principle of interest is much grosser than it is in America, but it is also less common, and especially it is less avowed; amongst us, men still constantly feign great abnegation which they no longer feel.

The Americans, on the contrary, are fond of explaining almost all the actions of their lives by the principle of interest rightly understood; they show with complacency how an enlightened regard for themselves constantly prompts them to assist each other, and inclines them willingly to sacrifice a portion of their time and property to the welfare of the state. In this respect, I think they frequently fail to do themselves justice; for, in the United States, as well as elsewhere, people are sometimes seen to give way to those disinterested and spontaneous impulses which are natural to man: but the Americans seldom allow that they yield to emotions of this kind; they are more anxious to do honor to their philosophy than to themselves.

I might here pause, without attempting to pass a judgment on what I have described. The extreme difficulty of the subject would be my excuse, but I shall not avail myself of it; and I had rather that my readers, clearly perceiving my object, should refuse to follow me, than that I should leave them in suspense.

The principle of interest rightly understood is not a lofty one, but it is clear and sure. It does not aim at mighty objects, but it attains without excessive exertion all those at which it aims. As it lies within the reach of all capacities, every one can without difficulty apprehend and retain it. By its admirable conformity to human weaknesses, it easily obtains great dominion; nor is that dominion precarious, since the principle checks one personal interest by another, and uses, to direct the passions, the very same instrument which excites them.

The principle of interest rightly understood produces no great acts of self-sacrifice, but it suggests daily small acts of self-denial. By itself, it cannot suffice to make a man virtuous; but it disciplines a number of citizens in habits of regularity, temperance, moderation, foresight, self-command; and, if it does not lead men straight to virtue by the will, it gradually draws them in that direction by their habits. If the principle of interest rightly understood were to sway the whole moral world, extraordinary virtues would doubtless be more rare; but I think that gross depravity would then also be less common. The principle of interest rightly understood perhaps prevents men from rising far above the level of mankind; but a great number of other men, who were falling far below it, are caught and restrained by it. Observe some few individuals, they are lowered by it; survey mankind, it is raised.

I am not afraid to say, that the principle of interest rightly understood appears to me the best suited of all philosophical theories to the wants of the men of our time, and that I regard it as their chief remaining security against themselves. Towards it, therefore, the minds of the moralists of our age should turn; even should they judge it to be incomplete, it must nevertheless be adopted as necessary.

I do not think, upon the whole, that there is more selfishness amongst us than in America; the only difference is, that there it is enlightened, here it is not. Every American will sacrifice a portion of his private interests to preserve the rest; we would fain preserve the whole, and oftentimes the whole is lost. Everybody I see about me seems bent on teaching his contemporaries, by precept and example, that what is useful is never wrong. Will nobody undertake to make them understand how what is right may be useful?

No power upon earth can prevent the increasing equality of conditions from inclining the human mind to seek out what is useful, or from leading every member of the community to be wrapped up in himself. It must therefore be expected that personal interest will become more than ever the principal, if not the sole, spring of men's actions; but it remains to be seen how each man will understand his personal interest. If the members of a community, as they become more equal, become more ignorant and coarse, it is difficult to foresee to what pitch of stupid excesses their selfishness may lead them; and no one can foretell into what disgrace and wretchedness they would plunge themselves, lest they should have to sacrifice something of their own well-being to the prosperity of their fellow-creatures.

I do not think that the system of interest, as it is professed in America, is, in all its parts, self-evident; but it contains a great number of truths so evident, that men, if they are but educated, cannot fail to see them. Educate, then, at any rate; for the age of implicit self-sacrifice and instinctive virtues is already flitting far away from us, and the time is fast approaching when freedom, public peace, and social order itself will not be able to exist without education.

### Chapter IX: That the Americans Apply the Principle of Interest Rightly Understood to Religious Matters

If the principle of interest rightly understood had nothing but the present world in view, it would be very insufficient, for there are many sacrifices which can only find their recompense in another; and whatever ingenuity may be put forth to demonstrate the utility of virtue, it will never be an easy task to make that man live aright who has no thought of dying.

It is therefore necessary to ascertain whether the principle of interest rightly understood can be easily reconciled with religious belief. The philosophers who inculcate this system of morals tell men that, to be happy in this life, they must watch their passions, and steadily control their excess; that lasting happiness can be secured only by renouncing a thousand transient gratifications; and that a man must perpetually triumph over himself in order to secure his own advantage. The founders of almost all religions have held the same language. The track they point out to man is the same, only the goal is more remote; instead of placing in this world the reward of the sacrifices they impose, they transport it to another.

Nevertheless, I cannot believe that all those who practise virtue from religious motives are actuated only by the hope of a recompense. I have known zealous Christians who constantly forgot themselves, to work with greater ardor for the happiness of their fellow-men; and I have heard them declare that all they did was only to earn the blessings of a future state. I cannot but think that they deceive themselves: I respect them too much to believe them.

Christianity, indeed, teaches that a man must prefer his neighbor to himself, in order to gain eternal life; but Christianity also teaches that men ought to benefit their fellow-creatures for the love of God. A sublime expression! Man searches by his intellect into the Divine conception, and sees that order is the purpose of God; he freely gives his own efforts to aid in prosecuting this great design, and, whilst he sacrifices his personal interests to this consummate order of all created things, expects no other recompense than the pleasure of contemplating it.

I do not believe that interest is the sole motive of religious men: but I believe that interest is the principal means which religions themselves employ to govern men, and I do not question that in this way they strike the multitude and become popular. I do not see clearly why the principle of interest rightly understood should undermine the religious opinions of men; it seems to me more easy to show why it should strengthen them. Let it be supposed that, in order to attain happiness in this world, a man combats his instincts on all occasions, and deliberately calculates every action of his life; that, instead of yielding blindly to the impetuosity of first desires, he has learned the art of resisting them, and that he has accustomed himself to sacrifice without an effort the pleasure of a moment to the lasting interest of his whole life. If such a man believes in the religion which he professes, it will cost him but little to submit to the restrictions it may impose. Reason herself counsels him to obey, and habit has prepared him to endure these limitations. If he should have conceived any doubts as to the object of his hopes, still he will not easily allow himself to be stopped by them; and he will decide that it is wise to risk some of the advantages of this world, in order to preserve his rights to the great inheritance promised him in another. "To be mistaken in believing that the Christian religion is true," says Pascal, "is no great loss to any one; but how dreadful to be mistaken in believing it to be false!"

The Americans do not affect a brutal indifference to a future state; they affect no puerile pride in despising perils which they hope to escape from. They therefore profess their religion without shame and without weakness; but there generally is, even in their zeal, something so indescribably tranquil, methodical, and deliberate, that it would seem as if the head, far more than the heart, brought them to the foot of the altar.

The Americans not only follow their religion from interest, but they often place in this world the interest which makes them follow it. In the Middle Ages, the clergy spoke of nothing but a future state; they hardly cared to prove that a sincere Christian may be a happy man here below. But the American preachers are constantly referring to the earth; and it is only with great difficulty that they can divert their attention from it. To touch their congregations, they always show them how favorable religious opinions are to freedom and public tranquillity; and it is often difficult to ascertain from their discourses whether the principal object of religion is to procure eternal felicity in the other world, or prosperity in this.

### BOOK III: INFLUENCE OF DEMOCRACY ON MANNERS PROPERLY SO CALLED

#### Chapter VIII: Influence of Democracy on Kindred

I have just examined the changes which the equality of conditions produces in the mutual relations of the several members of the community among democratic nations, and among the Americans in particular. I would now go deeper, and inquire into the closer ties of kindred: my object here is not to seek for new truths, but to show in what manner facts already known are connected with my subject.

It has been universally remarked, that in our time the several members of a family stand upon an entirely new footing toward each other; that the distance which formerly separated a father from his sons has been lessened; and that paternal authority, if not destroyed, is at least impaired.

Something analogous to this, but even more striking, may be observed in the United States. In America, the family, in the Roman and aristocratic signification of the word, does not exist. All that remains of it are a few vestiges in the first years of childhood, when the father exercises, without opposition, that absolute domestic authority, which the feebleness of his children renders necessary, and which their interest, as well as his own incontestable superiority, warrants. But as soon as the young American approaches manhood, the ties of filial obedience are relaxed day by day: master of his thoughts, he is soon master of his conduct. In America there is, strictly speaking, no adolescence: at the close of boyhood the man appears, and begins to trace out his own path.

It would be an error to suppose that this is preceded by a domestic struggle, in which the son has obtained by a sort of moral violence the liberty that his father refused him. The same habits, the same principles which impel the one to assert his independence, predispose the other to consider the use of that independence as an incontestable right. The former does not exhibit any of those rancorous or irregular passions which disturb men long after they have shaken off an established authority; the latter feels none of that bitter and angry regret which is apt to survive a by-gone power. The father foresees the limits of his authority long beforehand, and when the time arrives he surrenders it without a struggle: the son looks forward to the exact period at which he will be his own master; and he enters upon his freedom without precipitation and without effort, as a possession which is his own, and which no one seeks to wrest from him.[9]

It may perhaps not be without utility to show how these changes which take place in family relations, are closely connected with the social and political revolution which is approaching its consummation under our own observation.

There are certain great social principles, which a people either introduces everywhere, or tolerates nowhere. In countries which are aristocratically constituted with all the gradations of rank, the government never makes a direct appeal to the mass of the governed: as men are united together, it is enough to lead the foremost—the rest will follow. This is equally applicable to the family, as to all aristocracies which have a head.

Among aristocratic nations, social institutions recognize, in truth, no one in the family but the father; children are received by society at his hands; society governs him, he governs them. Thus the parent has not only a natural right, but he acquires a political right, to command them: he is the author and the support of his family; but he is also its constituted ruler.

In democracies, where the government picks out every individual singly from the mass, to make him subservient to the general laws of the community, no such intermediate person is required: a father is there, in the eye of the law, only a member of the community, older and richer than his sons.

When most of the conditions of life are extremely unequal, and the inequality of these conditions is permanent, the notion of a superior grows upon the imaginations of men: if the law invested him with no privileges, custom and public opinion would concede them. When, on the contrary, men differ but little from each other, and do not always remain in dissimilar conditions of life, the general notion of a superior becomes weaker and less distinct: it is vain for legislation to strive to place him who obeys very much beneath him who commands; the manners of the time bring the two men nearer to one another, and draw them daily toward the same level.

Although the legislation of an aristocratic people should grant no peculiar privileges to the heads of families, I shall not be the less convinced that their power is more respected and more extensive than in a democracy; for I know that, whatsoever the laws may be, superiors always appear higher and inferiors lower in aristocracies than among democratic nations.

When men live more for the remembrance of what has been than for the care of what is, and when they are more given to attend to what their ancestors thought than to think themselves, the father is the natural and necessary tie between the past and the present—the link by which the ends of these two chains are connected. In aristocracies, then, the father is not only the civil head of the family, but the oracle of its traditions, the expounder of its customs, the arbiter of its manners. He is listened to with deference, he is addressed with respect, and the love which is felt for him is always tempered with fear.

---

[9] The Americans however have not yet thought fit to strip the parent, as has been done in France, of one of the chief elements of parental authority, by depriving him of the power of disposing of his property at his death. In the United States there are no restrictions on the powers of a testator.

In this respect, as in almost all others, it is easy to perceive, that if the political legislation of the Americans is much more democratic than that of the French, the civil legislation of the latter is infinitely more democratic than that of the former. This may easily be accounted for. The civil legislation of France was the work of a man who saw that it was his interest to satisfy the democratic passions of his contemporaries in all that was not directly and immediately hostile to his own power. He was willing to allow some popular principles to regulate the distribution of property and the government of families, provided they were not to be introduced into the administration of public affairs. While the torrent of democracy overwhelmed the civil laws of the country, he hoped to find an easy shelter behind its political institutions. This policy was at once both adroit and selfish; but a compromise of this kind could not last; for in the end political institutions never fail to become the image and expression of civil society; and in this sense it may be said that nothing is more political in a nation than its civil legislation.

When the condition of society becomes democratic, and men adopt as their general principle that it is good and lawful to judge of all things for oneself, using former points of belief not as a rule of faith but simply as a means of information, the power which the opinions of a father exercise over those of his sons diminishes as well as his legal power.

Perhaps the subdivision of estates which democracy brings with it contributes more than anything else to change the relations existing between a father and his children. When the property of the father of a family is scanty, his son and himself constantly live in the same place, and share the same occupations: habit and necessity bring them together, and force them to hold constant communication: the inevitable consequence is a sort of familiar intimacy, which renders authority less absolute, and which can ill be reconciled with the external forms of respect.

Now in democratic countries the class of those who are possessed of small fortunes is precisely that which gives strength to the notions, and a particular direction to the manners, of the community. That class makes its opinions preponderate as universally as its will, and even those who are most inclined to resist its commands are carried away in the end by its example. I have known eager opponents of democracy who allowed their children to address them with perfect colloquial equality.

Thus, at the same time that the power of aristocracy is declining, the austere, the conventional, and the legal part of parental authority vanishes, and a species of equality prevails around the domestic hearth. I know not, upon the whole, whether society loses by the change, but I am inclined to believe that man individually is a gainer by it. I think that, in proportion as manners and laws become more democratic, the relation of father and son becomes more intimate and more affectionate; rules and authority are less talked of; confidence and tenderness are oftentimes increased, and it would seem that the natural bond is drawn closer in proportion as the social bond is loosened.

In a democratic family the father exercises no other power than that with which men love to invest the affection and the experience of age: his orders would perhaps be disobeyed, but his advice is for the most part authoritative. Though he be not hedged in with ceremonial respect, his sons at least accost him with confidence; no settled form of speech is appropriated to the mode of addressing him, but they speak to him constantly and are ready to consult him day by day: the master and the constituted ruler have vanished—the father remains.

Nothing more is needed, in order to judge of the difference between the two states of society in this respect, than to peruse the family correspondence of aristocratic ages. The style is always correct, ceremonious, stiff, and so cold that the natural warmth of the heart can hardly be felt in the language. The language on the contrary addressed by a son to this father in democratic countries is always marked by mingled freedom, familiarity and affection, which at once show that new relations have sprung up in the bosom of the family.

A similar revolution takes place in the mutual relations of children. In aristocratic families, as well as in aristocratic society, every place is marked out beforehand. Not only does the father occupy a separate rank, in which he enjoys extensive privileges, but even the children are not equal among themselves. The age and sex of each irrevocably determine his rank, and secure to him certain privileges: most of these distinctions are abolished or diminished by democracy.

In aristocratic families the eldest son, inheriting the greater part of the property and almost all the rights of the family, becomes the chief, and to a certain extent the master, of his brothers. Greatness and power are for him—for them, mediocrity and dependance. Nevertheless it would be wrong to suppose that, among aristocratic nations, the privileges of the eldest son are advantageous to himself alone, or that they excite nothing but envy and hatred in those around him. The eldest son commonly endeavors to procure wealth and power for his brothers, because the general splendor of the house is reflected back on him who represents it; the younger sons seek to back the elder brother in all his undertakings, because the greatness and power of the head of the family better enable him to provide for all its branches. The different members of an aristocratic family are therefore very closely bound together; their interests are connected, their minds agree, but their hearts are seldom in harmony.

Democracy also binds brothers to each other, but by very different means. Under democratic laws all the children are perfectly equal, and consequently independent: nothing brings them forcibly together, but nothing keeps them apart; and as they have the same origin, as they are trained under the same roof, as they are treated with the same care, and as no peculiar privilege distinguishes or divides them, the affectionate and youthful intimacy of early years easily springs up between them. Scarcely any opportunities occur to break the tie thus formed at the outset of life; for their brotherhood brings them daily together, without embarrassing them. It is not then by interest, but by common associations and by the free sympathy of opinion and of taste, that democracy unites brothers to each other. It divides their inheritance, but it allows their hearts and minds to mingle together.

Such is the charm of these democratic manners, that even the partisans of aristocracy are caught by it; and after having experienced it for some time, they are by no means tempted to revert to the respectful and frigid observances of aristocratic families. They would be glad to retain the domestic habits of democracy, if they might throw off its social conditions and its laws; but these elements are indissolubly united, and it is impossible to enjoy the former without enduring the latter.

The remarks I have made on filial love and fraternal affection are applicable to all the passions which emanate spontaneously from human nature itself.

If a certain mode of thought or feeling is the result of some peculiar condition of life, when that condition is altered nothing whatever remains of the thought or feeling. Thus a law may bind two members of the community very closely to one another; but that law being abolished, they stand asunder. Nothing was more strict than the tie which united the vassal to the lord under the feudal system: at the present day the two men know not each other; the fear, the gratitude, and the affection which formerly connected them have vanished, and not a vestige of the tie remains.

Such, however, is not the case with those feelings which are natural to mankind. Whenever a law attempts to tutor these feelings in any particular manner, it seldom fails to weaken them; by attempting to add to their intensity, it robs them of some of their elements, for they are never stronger than when left to themselves.

Democracy, which destroys or obscures almost all the old conventional rules of society, and which prevents men from readily assenting to new ones, entirely effaces most of the feelings to which these conventional rules have given rise; but it only modifies some others, and frequently imparts to them a degree of energy and sweetness unknown before.

Perhaps it is not impossible to condense into a single proposition the whole meaning of this chapter, and of several others that preceded it. Democracy loosens social ties, but it draws the ties of nature more tight; it brings kindred more closely together, while it places the various members of the community more widely apart.

### Chapter IX:     Education of Young Women in the United States

No free communities ever existed without morals; and, as I observed in the former part of this work, morals are the work of woman. Consequently, whatever affects the condition of women, their habits and their opinions, has great political importance in my eyes.

Among almost all Protestant nations young women are far more the mistresses of their own actions than they are in Catholic countries. This independence is still greater in Protestant countries like England, which have retained or acquired the right of self-government; the spirit of freedom is then infused into the domestic circle by political habits and by religious opinions. In the United States the doctrines of Protestantism are combined with great political freedom and a most democratic state of society; and nowhere are young women surrendered so early or so completely to their own guidance.

Long before an American girl arrives at the age of marriage, her emancipation from maternal control begins: she has scarcely ceased to be a child, when she already thinks for herself, speaks with freedom, and acts on her own impulse. The great scene of the world is constantly open to her view; far from seeking concealment, it is every day disclosed to her more completely, and she is taught to survey it with a firm and calm gaze. Thus the vices and dangers of society are early revealed to her; as she sees them clearly, she views them without illusions, and braves them without fear; for she is full of reliance on her own strength, and her reliance seems to be shared by all who are about her.

An American girl scarcely ever displays that virginal bloom in the midst of young desires, or that innocent and ingenuous grace which usually attend the European woman in the transition from girlhood to youth. It is rarely that an American woman at any age displays childish timidity or ignorance. Like the young women of Europe, she seeks to please, but she knows precisely the cost of pleasing. If she does not abandon herself to evil, at least she knows that it exists; and she is remarkable rather for purity of manners than for chastity of mind.

I have been frequently surprised, and almost frightened, at the singular address and happy boldness with which young women in America contrive to manage their thoughts and their language, amid all the difficulties of stimulating conversation; a philosopher would have stumbled at every step along the narrow path which they trod without accidents and without effort. It is easy indeed to perceive that, even amid the independence of early youth, an American woman is always mistress of herself: she indulges in all permitted pleasures, without yielding herself up to any of them; and her reason never allows the reigns of self-guidance to drop, though it often seems to hold them loosely.

In France, where remnants of every age are still so strangely mingled in the opinions and tastes of the people, women commonly receive a reserved, retired, and almost conventional education, as they did in aristocratic times; and then they are suddenly abandoned, without a guide and without assistance, in the midst of all the irregularities inseparable from democratic society.

The Americans are more consistent. They have found out that in a democracy the independence of individuals cannot fail to be very great, youth premature, tastes ill-restrained, customs fleeting, public opinion often unsettled and powerless, paternal authority weak, and marital authority contested. Under these circumstances, believing that they had little chance of repressing in woman the most vehement passions of the human heart, they held that the surer way was to teach her the art of combating those passions for herself. As they could not prevent her virtue from being exposed to frequent danger, they determined that she should know how best to defend it; and more reliance was placed on the free vigor of her will, than on safeguards which have been shaken or overthrown. Instead then of inculcating mistrust of herself, they constantly seek to enhance her confidence in her own strength of character. As it is neither possible nor desirable to keep a young woman in perpetual and complete ignorance, they hasten to give her a precocious knowledge on all subjects. Far from hiding the corruptions of the world from her, they prefer that she should see them at once and train herself to shun them; and they hold it of more importance to protect her conduct, than to be over-scrupulous of her innocence.

Although the Americans are a very religious people, they do not rely on religion alone to defend the virtue of woman; they seek to arm her reason also. In this they have followed the same method as in several other respects: they first make the most vigorous efforts to bring individual independence to exercise a proper control over itself, and they do not call in the aid of religion until they have reached the utmost limits of human strength.

I am aware that an education of this kind is not without danger; I am sensible that it tends to invigorate the judgement at the expense of the imagination, and to make cold and virtuous women instead of affectionate wives and agreeable companions to man. Society may be more tranquil and better regulated, but domestic life has often fewer charms. These however are secondary evils, which may be braved for the sake of higher interests. At the stage at which we are now arrived the time for choosing is no longer within our control; a democratic education is indispensable, to protect women from the dangers with which democratic institutions and manners surround them.

### Chapter X:     The Young Woman in the Character of a Wife

In America the independence of women is irrecoverably lost in the bonds of matrimony: if an unmarried woman is less constrained there than elsewhere, a wife is subjected to stricter obligations. The former makes her father's house an abode of freedom and of pleasure; the latter lives in the home of her husband as if it were a cloister. Yet these two different conditions of life are perhaps not so contrary as may be supposed, and it is natural that the American women should pass through the one to arrive at the other.

Religious peoples and trading nations entertain peculiarly serious notions of marriage: the former consider the regularity of woman's life as the best pledge and most certain sign of the purity of her morals; the latter regard it as the highest security for the order and prosperity of the household. The Americans are at the same time a puritanical people and a commercial nation: their religious opinions, as well as their trading habits, consequently lead them to require much abnegation on the part of women, and a constant sacrifice of her pleasures to her duties which is seldom demanded of her in Europe. Thus in the United States the inexorable opinion of the public carefully circumscribes woman within the narrow circle of domestic interests and duties, and forbids her to step beyond it.

Upon her entrance into the world a young American woman finds these notions firmly established; she sees the rules which are derived from them; she is not slow to perceive that she cannot depart for an instant from the established usages of her contemporaries, without putting in jeopardy her peace of mind, her honor, nay even her social existence; and she finds the energy required for such an act of submission in the firmness of her understanding and in the virile habits which her education has given her. It may be said that she has learned by the use of her independence, to surrender it without a struggle and without a murmur when the time comes for making the sacrifice.

But no American woman falls into the toils of matrimony as into a snare held out to her simplicity and ignorance. She has been taught beforehand what is expected of her, and voluntarily and freely does she enter upon this engagement. She supports her new condition with courage, because she chose it. As in America paternal discipline is very relaxed and the conjugal tie very strict, a young woman does not contract the latter without considerable circumspection and apprehension. Precocious marriages are rare. Thus American women do not marry until their understandings are exercised and ripened; whereas in other countries most women generally only begin to exercise and to ripen their understandings after marriage.

I by no means suppose, however, that the great change which takes place in all the habits of women in the United States, as soon as they are married, ought solely to be attributed to the constraint of public opinion; it is frequently imposed upon themselves by the sole effort of their own will. When the time for choosing a husband is arrived, that cold and stern reasoning power which has been educated and invigorated by the free observation of the world, teaches an American woman that a spirit of levity and independence in the bonds of marriage is a constant subject of annoyance, not of pleasure; it tells her that the amusements of the girl cannot become the recreations of the wife, and that the sources of a married woman's happiness are in the home of her husband. As she clearly discerns beforehand the only road which can lead to domestic happiness, she enters upon it at once, and follows it to the end without seeking to turn back.

The same strength of purpose which the young wives of America display, in bending themselves at once and without repining to the austere duties of their new condition, is no less manifest in all the great trials of their lives. In no country in the world are private fortunes more precarious than in the United States. It is not uncommon for the same man, in the course of his life, to rise and sink again through all the grades which lead from opulence to poverty. American women support these vicissitudes with calm and unquenchable energy: it would seem that their desires contract, as easily as they expand, with their fortunes.[10]

---

[10] I find in my travelling-journal a passage which may serve to convey a more complete notion of the trials to which the women of America, who consent to follow their husbands into the wilds, are often subjected. This description has nothing to recommend it to the reader but its strict accuracy.

. . . "From time to time we come to fresh clearings; all these places are alike: I shall describe the one at which we have halted to-night, for it will serve to remind me of all the others.

"The bell which the pioneers hang round the necks of their cattle, in order to find them again in the woods, announced our approach to a clearing, when we were yet a long way off; and we soon afterward heard the stroke of the hatchet, hewing down the trees of the forest. As we came nearer, traces of destruction marked the presence of civilized man: the road was strewn with shattered boughs; trunks of trees, half consumed by fire, or cleft by the wedge, were still standing in the track we were following. We continued to proceed till we reached a wood in which all the trees seemed to have been suddenly struck dead; in the height of summer their boughs were as leafless as in winter; and upon closer examination, we found that a deep circle had been cut round the bark, which, by stopping the circulation of the sap, soon kills the tree. We were informed that this is commonly the first thing a pioneer does; as he cannot, in the first year, cut down all the trees which cover his new parcel of land, he sows Indian corn under their branches, and puts the trees to death in order to prevent them from injuring his crop. Beyond this field, at present imperfectly traced out, we suddenly came upon the cabin of its owner, situated in the center of a plot of ground more carefully cultivated than the rest, but where man was still waging unequal warfare with the forest; there the trees were cut down, but their roots were not removed, and the trunks still encumbered the ground which they so recently shaded. Around these dry blocks, wheat, suckers of trees, and plants of every kind grow and intertwine in all the luxuriance of wild untutored nature. Amid this vigorous and various vegetation stands the house of the pioneer, or, as they call it, the log-house. Like the ground about it, this rustic dwelling bore marks of recent and hasty labour; its length seemed not to exceed thirty feet, its height fifteen; the walls as well as the roof were formed of rough trunks of trees, between which a little moss and clay had been inserted to keep out the cold and rain.

"As night was coming on, we determined to ask the master of the log-house for a lodging. At the sound of our footsteps, the children who were playing among the scattered branches sprang up and ran toward the house, as if they were frightened at the sight of man; while two large dogs, almost wild, with ears erect and outstretched nose, came growling out of their hut, to cover the retreat of their young masters. The pioneer himself made his appearance at the door of his dwelling; he looked at us with a rapid and inquisitive glance, made a sign to the dogs to go into the house, and set them the example, without betraying either curiosity or apprehension at our arrival.

"We entered the log-house: the inside is quite unlike that of the cottages of the peasantry of Europe: it contains more that is superfluous, less that is necessary. A single window with a muslin blind; on a hearth of trodden clay an immense fire, which lights the whole structure; above the hearth a good rifle, a deer's skin, and plumes of eagles' feathers; on the right hand of the chimney a map of the United States, raised and shaken by the wind through the crannies in the wall; near the map, upon a shelf formed of a roughly hewn plank, a few volumes of books—a bible, the six first books of Milton, and two of Shakespeare's plays; along the wall, trunks instead of closets; in the center of the room a rude table, with legs of green wood, and with the bark still upon them, looking as if they grew out of the ground on which they stood; but on this table a teapot of British ware, silver spoons, cracked teacups, and some newspapers.

"The master of this dwelling has the strong angular features and lank limbs peculiar to the native of New England. It is evident that this man was not born in the solitude in which we have met with him: his physical constitution suffices to show that his earlier years were spent in the midst of civilized society, and that he belongs to that restless, calculating and adventurous race of men, who do with the utmost coolness things only to be accounted for by the ardor of the passions, and who endure the life of savages for a time, in order to conquer and civilize the back-woods.

"When the pioneer perceived that we were crossing his threshold, he came to meet us and shake hands, as is their custom; but his face was quite unmoved; he opened the conversation by inquiring what was going on in the world; and when his curiosity was satisfied, he held his peace, as if he were tired by the noise and importunity of mankind. When we questioned him in our turn, he gave us all the information we required; he then attended sedulously, but without eagerness, to our personal wants. While he was engaged in

The greater part of the adventurers who migrate every year to people the western wilds, belong, as I observed in the former part of this work, to the old Anglo-American race of the Northern States. Many of these men, who rush so boldly onward in pursuit of wealth, were already in the enjoyment of a competency in their own part of the country. They take their wives along with them, and make them share the countless perils and privations which always attend the commencement of these expeditions. I have often met, even on the verge of the wilderness, with young women, who after having been brought up amid all the comforts of the large towns of New England, had passed, almost without any intermediate stage, from the wealthy abode of their parents to a comfortless hovel in a forest. Fever, solitude, and a tedious life had not broken the springs of their courage. Their features were impaired and faded, but their looks were firm: they appeared to be at once sad and resolute. I do not doubt that these young American women had amassed, in the education of their early years, that inward strength which they displayed under these circumstances. The early culture of the girl may still therefore be traced, in the United States, under the aspect of marriage: her part is changed, her habits are different, but her character is the same.

### Chapter XII: How the Americans Understand the Equality of the Sexes

I have shown how democracy destroys or modifies the different inequalities which originate in society: but is this all? or does it not ultimately affect that great inequality of man and woman which has seemed, up to the present day, to be eternally based in human nature? I believe that the social changes which bring nearer to the same level the father and son, the master and servant, and superiors and inferiors generally speaking, will raise woman and make her more and more the equal of man. But here, more than ever, I feel the necessity of making myself clearly understood; for there is no subject on which the coarse and lawless fancies of our age have taken a freer range.

There are people in Europe who, confounding together the different characteristics of the sexes, would make of man and woman beings not only equal but alike. They would give to both the same functions, impose on both the same duties, and grant to both the same rights: they would mix them in all things—their occupations, their pleasures, their business. It may readily be conceived, that by thus attempting to make one sex equal to the other, both are degraded; and from so preposterous a medley of the works of nature, nothing could ever result but weak men and disorderly women.

It is not thus that the Americans understand that species of democratic equality which may be established between the sexes. They admit, that as nature has appointed such wide differences

---

providing thus kindly for us, how came it that in spite of ourselves we felt our gratitude die upon our lips? it is, that our host, while he performs the duties of hospitality, seems to be obeying an irksome necessity of his condition: he treats it as a duty imposed upon him by his situation, not as a pleasure.

"By the side of the hearth sits a woman with a baby on her lap: she nods to us, without disturbing herself. Like the pioneer, this woman is in the prime of life; her appearance would seem superior to her condition, and her apparel even betrays a lingering taste for dress; but her delicate limbs appear shrunken, her features are drawn in, her eye is mild and melancholy; her whole physiognomy bears marks of a degree of religious resignation, a deep quiet of all passions, and some sort of natural and tranquil firmness, ready to meet all the ills of life, without fearing and without braving them.

"Her children cluster about her, full of health, turbulence and energy: they are true children of the wilderness; their mother watches them from time to time with mingled melancholy and joy: to look at their strength and her languor, one might imagine that the life she has given them had exhausted her own, and still she regrets not what they have cost her.

"The house inhabited by these emigrants has no internal partition or loft. In the one chamber of which it consists the whole family is gathered for the night. The dwelling is itself a little world—an ark of civilization amid an ocean of foliage: a hundred steps beyond it the primeval forest spreads its shades, and solitude resumes its sway."

between the physical and moral constitutions of man and woman, her manifest design was to give a distinct employment to their various faculties; and they hold that improvement does not consist in making beings so dissimilar do pretty nearly the same things, but in getting each of them to fulfill their respective tasks in the best possible manner. The Americans have applied to the sexes the great principle of political economy which governs the manufacturers of our age, by carefully dividing the duties of man from those of woman, in order that the great work of society may be the better carried on.

In no country has such constant care been taken as in America to trace two clearly distinct lines of action for the two sexes, and to make them keep pace one with the other, but in two pathways which are always different. American women never manage the outward concerns of the family, or conduct a business, or take a part in political life; nor are they, on the other hand, ever compelled to perform the rough labor of the fields, or to make any of those laborious exertions which demand the exertion of physical strength. No families are so poor as to form an exception to this rule. If on the one hand an American woman cannot escape from the quiet circle of domestic employments, on the other hand she is never forced to go beyond it. Hence it is that the women of America, who often exhibit a masculine strength of understanding and a manly energy, generally preserve great delicacy of personal appearance and always retain the manners of women, although they sometimes show that they have the hearts and minds of men.

Nor have the Americans ever supposed that one consequence of democratic principles is the subversion of marital power, or the confusion of the natural authorities in families. They hold that every association must have a head in order to accomplish its object, and that the natural head of the conjugal association is man. They do not therefore deny him the right of directing his partner; and they maintain, that in the smaller association of husband and wife, as well as in the great social community, the object of democracy is to regulate and legalize the powers which are necessary, not to subvert all power.

This opinion is not peculiar to one sex, and contested by the other: I never observed that the women of America consider conjugal authority as a fortunate usurpation of their rights, nor that they thought themselves degraded by submitting to it. It appeared to me, on the contrary, that they attach a sort of pride to the voluntary surrender of their own will, and make it their boast to bend themselves to the yoke, not to shake it off. Such at least is the feeling expressed by the most virtuous of their sex; the others are silent; and in the United States it is not the practice for a guilty wife to clamor for the rights of woman, while she is trampling on her holiest duties.

It has often been remarked that in Europe a certain degree of contempt lurks even in the flattery which men lavish upon women: although a European frequently affects to be the slave of woman, it may be seen that he never sincerely thinks her his equal. In the United States men seldom compliment women, but they daily show how much they esteem them. They constantly display an entire confidence in the understanding of a wife, and a profound respect for her freedom; they have decided that her mind is just as fitted as that of a man to discover the plain truth, and her heart as firm to embrace it; and they have never sought to place her virtue, any more than his, under the shelter of prejudice, ignorance, and fear.

It would seem that in Europe, where man so easily submits to the despotic sway of women, they are nevertheless curtailed of some of the greatest qualities of the human species, and considered as seductive but imperfect beings; and (what may well provoke astonishment) women ultimately look upon themselves in the same light, and almost consider it as a privilege that they are entitled to show themselves futile, feeble, and timid. The women of America claim no such privileges.

Again, it may be said, that in our morals we have reserved strange immunities to man; so that there is, as it were, one virtue for his use, and another for the guidance of his partner; and that, according to the opinion of the public, the very same act may be punished alternately as a crime or only as a fault. The Americans know not this iniquitous division of duties and rights; among them the seducer is as much dishonored as his victim.

It is true that the Americans rarely lavish upon women those eager attentions which are commonly paid them in Europe; but their conduct to women always implies that they suppose them to be virtuous and refined; and such is the respect entertained for the moral freedom of the sex, that in the presence of a woman the most guarded language is used, lest her ear should be offended by an expression. In America a young unmarried woman may, alone and without fear, undertake a long journey.

The legislators of the United States, who have mitigated almost all the penalties of criminal law, still make rape a capital offence, and no crime, is visited with more inexorable severity by public opinion. This may be accounted for; as the Americans can conceive nothing more precious than a woman's honor, and nothing which ought so much to be respected as her independence, they hold that no punishment is too severe for the man who deprives her of them against her will. In France, where the same offence is visited with far milder penalties, it is frequently difficult to get a verdict from a jury against the prisoner. Is this a consequence of contempt of decency or contempt of woman? I cannot but believe that it is a contempt of one and of the other.

Thus the Americans do not think that man and woman have either the duty or the right to perform the same offices, but they show an equal regard for both their respective parts; and though their lot is different, they consider both of them as beings of equal value. They do not give to the courage of woman the same form or the same direction as to that of man; but they never doubt her courage: and if they hold that man and his partner ought not always to exercise their intellect and understanding in the same manner, they at least believe the understanding of the one to be as sound as that of the other, and her intellect to be as clear. Thus, then, while they have allowed the social inferiority of woman to subsist, they have done all they could to raise her morally and intellectually to the level of man; and in this respect they appear to me to have excellently understood the true principle of democratic improvement.

As for myself, I do not hesitate to avow, that, although the women of the United States are confined within the narrow circle of domestic life, and their situation is in some respects one of extreme dependance, I have nowhere seen women occupying a loftier position; and if I were asked, now that I am drawing to the close of this work, in which I have spoken of so many important things done by the Americans, to what the singular prosperity and growing strength of that people ought mainly to be attributed, I should reply—to the superiority of their women.

### BOOK IV: INFLUENCE OF DEMOCRATIC IDEAS AND FEELINGS ON POLITICAL SOCIETY

**Chapter I:    Equality Naturally Gives Men a Taste for Free Institutions**

The principle of equality, which makes men independent of each other, gives them a habit and a taste for following, in their private actions, no other guide but their own will. This complete independence, which they constantly enjoy towards their equals and in the intercourse of private life, tends to make them look upon all authority with a jealous eye, and speedily suggests to them the notion and the love of political freedom. Men living at such times have a natural bias to free institutions. Take any one of them at a venture, and search if you can his most deep-seated instincts; you will find that of all governments he will soonest conceive and most highly value that government, whose head he has himself elected, and whose administration he may control.

Of all the political effects produced by the equality of conditions, this love of independence is the first to strike the observing, and to alarm the timid; nor can it be said that their alarm is wholly misplaced, for anarchy has a more formidable aspect in democratic countries than elsewhere. As the citizens have no direct influence on each other, as soon as the supreme power of the nation fails, which kept them all in their several stations, it would seem that disorder must instantly reach its utmost pitch, and that, every man drawing aside in a different direction, the fabric of society must at once crumble away.

-I am persuaded, however, that anarchy is not the principal evil which democratic ages have to fear, but the least. For the principle of equality begets two tendencies: the one leads men straight to independence, and may suddenly drive them into anarchy; the other conducts them by a longer, more secret, but more certain road, to servitude. Nations readily discern the former tendency, and are prepared to resist it; they are led away by the latter, without perceiving its drift; hence it is peculiarly important to point it out.

For myself, I am so far from urging it as a reproach to the principle of equality that it renders men intractable, that this very circumstance principally calls forth my approbation. I admire to see how it deposits in the mind and heart of man the dim conception and instinctive love of political independence, thus preparing the remedy for the evil which it produces: it is on this very account that I am attached [to it].

### Chapter II: The the Opinions of Democratic Nations About Government are Naturally Favorable to the Concentration of Power

The notion of secondary powers, placed between the sovereign and his subjects, occurred naturally to the imagination of aristocratic nations, because those communities contained individuals or families raised above the common level, and apparently destined to command by their birth, their education, and their wealth. This same notion is naturally wanting in the minds of men in democratic ages, for converse reasons; it can only be introduced artificially, it can only be kept there with difficulty; whereas they conceive, as it were without thinking upon the subject, the notion of a single and central power which governs the whole community by its direct influence. Moreover, in politics as well as in philosophy and in religion, the intellect of democratic nations is peculiarly open to simple and general notions. Complicated systems are repugnant to it, and its favorite conception is that of a great nation composed of citizens all formed upon one pattern, and governed by a single power.

The very next notion to that of a single and central power, which presents itself to the minds of men in the ages of equality, is the notion of uniformity of legislation. As every man sees that he differs but little from those about him, he cannot understand why a rule which is applicable to one man should not be equally applicable to all others. Hence the slightest privileges are repugnant to his reason; the faintest dissimilarities in the political institutions of the same people offend him, and uniformity of legislation appears to him to be the first condition of good government.

I find, on the contrary, that this notion of a uniform rule, equally binding on all the members of the community, was almost unknown to the human mind in aristocratic ages; it was either never broached, or it was rejected.

These contrary tendencies of opinion ultimately turn on both sides to such blind instincts and such ungovernable habits, that they still direct the actions of men, in spite of particular exceptions. Notwithstanding the immense variety of conditions in the Middle Ages, a certain number of persons existed at that period in precisely similar circumstances; but this did not prevent the laws then in force from assigning to each of them distinct duties and different rights. On the contrary, at the present time, all the powers of government are exerted to impose the same customs and the same laws on populations which have as yet but few points of resemblance.

As the conditions of men become equal amongst a people, individuals seem of less, and society of greater importance; or rather, every citizen, being assimilated to all the rest, is lost in the crowd, and nothing stands conspicuous but the great and imposing image of the people at large. This naturally gives the men of democratic periods a lofty opinion of the privileges of society, and a very humble notion of the rights of individuals; they are ready to admit that the interests of the former are everything, and those of the latter nothing. They are willing to acknowledge that the power which represents the community has far more information and wisdom than any of the members of that community; and that it is the duty, as well as the right, of that power, to guide as well as govern each private citizen.

If we closely scrutinize our contemporaries, and penetrate to the root of their political opinions, we shall detect some of the notions which I have just pointed out, and we shall perhaps be surprised to find so much accordance between men who are so often at variance.

The Americans hold, that in every state the supreme power ought to emanate from the people; but when once that power is constituted, they can conceive, as it were, no limits to it, and they are ready to admit that it has the right to do whatever it pleases. They have not the slightest notion of peculiar privileges granted to cities, families, or persons: their minds appear never to have foreseen that it might be possible not to apply with strict uniformity the same laws to every part, and to all the inhabitants.

These same opinions are more and more diffused in Europe; they even insinuate themselves amongst those nations which most vehemently reject the principle of the sovereignty of the people. Such nations assign a different origin to the supreme power, but they ascribe to that power the same characteristics. Amongst them all, the idea of intermediate powers is weakened and obliterated: the idea of rights inherent in certain individuals is rapidly disappearing from the minds of men; the idea of the omnipotence and sole authority of society at large rises to fill its place. These ideas take root and spread in proportion as social conditions become more equal, and men more alike; they are engendered by equality, and in turn they hasten the progress of equality.

In France, where the revolution of which I am speaking has gone further than in any other European country, these opinions have got complete hold of the public mind. If we listen attentively to the language of the various parties in France, we shall find that there is not one which has not adopted them. Most of these parties censure the conduct of the government, but they all hold that the government ought perpetually to act and interfere in everything that is done. Even those which are most at variance are nevertheless agreed upon this head. The unity, the ubiquity, the omnipotence of the supreme power, and the uniformity of its rules, constitute the principal characteristics of all the political systems which have been put forward in our age. They recur even in the wildest visions of political regeneration: the human mind pursues them in its dreams.

If these notions spontaneously arise in the minds of private individuals, they suggest themselves still more forcibly to the minds of princes. Whilst the ancient fabric of European society is altered and dissolved, sovereigns acquire new conceptions of their opportunities and their duties; they learn for the first time that the central power which they represent may and ought to administer by its own agency, and on a uniform plan, all the concerns of the whole community. This opinion, which, I will venture to say, was never conceived before our time by the monarchs of Europe, now sinks deeply into the minds of kings, and abides there amidst all the agitation of more unsettled thoughts.

Our contemporaries are therefore much less divided than is commonly supposed; they are constantly disputing as to the hands in which supremacy is to be vested, but they readily agree upon the duties and the rights of that supremacy. The notion they all form of government is that of a sole, simple, providential, and creative power.

All secondary opinions in politics are unsettled; this one remains fixed, invariable, and consistent. It is adopted by statesmen and political philosophers; it is eagerly laid hold of by the multitude; those who govern and those who are governed agree to pursue it with equal ardour; it is the foremost notion of their minds, it seems connatural with their feelings. It originates therefore in no caprice of the human intellect, but it is a necessary condition of the present state of mankind.

**Chapter III:    That the Sentiments of Democratic Nations Accord With Their Opinions in Leading Them to Concentrate Political Power**

If it be true that, in ages of equality, men readily adopt the notion of a great central power, it cannot be doubted, on the other hand, that their habits and sentiments predispose them to recognize such a power, and to give it their support. This may be demonstrated in a few words, as the greater part of the reasons to which the fact may be attributed have been previously stated.

As the men who inhabit democratic countries have no superiors, no inferiors, and no habitual or necessary partners in their undertakings, they readily fall back upon themselves and consider themselves as beings apart. I had occasion to point this out at considerable length in treating of individualism. Hence such men can never, without an effort, tear themselves from their private affairs to engage in public business; their natural bias leads them to abandon the latter to the sole visible and permanent representative of the interests of the community, that is to say, to the state. Not only are they naturally wanting in a taste for public business, but they have frequently no time to attend to it. Private life in democratic periods is so busy, so excited, so full of wishes and of work, that hardly any energy or leisure remains to each individual for public life. I am the last man to contend that these propensities are unconquerable, since my chief object in writing this book has been to combat them. I only maintain that at the present day a secret power is fostering them in the human heart, and that if they are not checked they will wholly overgrow it.

I have also had occasion to show how the increasing love of well-being, and the fluctuating character of property cause democratic nations to dread all violent disturbance. The love of public tranquillity is frequently the only passion which these nations retain, and it becomes more active and powerful amongst them in proportion as all other passions droop and die. This naturally disposes the members of the community constantly to give or to surrender additional rights to the central power, which alone seems to be interested in defending them by the same means that it uses to defend itself.

As in periods of equality, no man is compelled to lend his assistance to his fellow-men, and none has any right to expect much support from them, every one is at once independent and powerless. These two conditions, which must never be either separately considered or confounded together, inspire the citizen of a democratic country with very contrary propensities. His independence fills him with self-reliance and pride amongst his equals; his debility makes him feel from time to time the want of some outward assistance, which he cannot expect from any of them, because they are all impotent and unsympathizing. In this predicament he naturally turns his eyes to that imposing power which alone rises above the level of universal depression. Of that power his wants and especially his desires continually remind him; until he ultimately views it as the sole and necessary support of his own weakness.[11]

---

[11]In a democratic communities nothing but the central power has any stability in its position or any permanence in its undertakings. All the members of society are in ceaseless stir and transformation. Now it is in the nature of all governments to seek constantly to enlarge their sphere of action; hence it is almost impossible that such a government should not ultimately succeed, because it acts with a fixed principle and a constant will, upon men, whose position, whose notions, and whose desires are in continual vacillation.

It frequently happens that the members of the community promote the influence of the central power without intending it. Democratic ages are periods of experiment, innovation, and adventure. At such times there are always a multitude of men engaged in difficult or novel undertakings, which they follow alone, without caring for their fellow-men. Such persons may be ready to admit, as a general principle, that the public authority ought not to interfere in private concerns; but, by an exception to that rule, each of them craves its assistance in the particular concern on which he is engaged, and seeks to draw upon the influence of the government for his own benefit, though he would restrict it on all other occasions. If a large number of men apply this particular exception to a great variety of different purposes, the sphere of the central power extends insensible in all directions, although each of them wishes it to be circumscribed.

This may more completely explain what frequently takes place in democratic countries, where the very men who are so impatient of superiors patiently submit to a master, exhibiting at once their pride and their servility.

The hatred which men bear to privilege increases in proportion as privileges become fewer and less considerable, so that democratic passions would seem to burn most fiercely at the very time when they have least fuel. I have already given the reason of this phenomenon. When all conditions are unequal, no inequality is so great as to offend the eye; whereas the slightest dissimilarity is odious in the midst of general uniformity: the more complete is this uniformity, the more insupportable does the sight of such a difference become. Hence it is natural that the love of equality should constantly increase together with equality itself, and that it should grow by what it feeds upon.

This never-dying ever-kindling hatred, which sets a democratic people against the smallest privileges, is peculiarly favourable to the gradual concentration of all political rights in the hands of the representative of the state alone. The sovereign, being necessarily and incontestably above all the citizens, excites not their envy, and each of them thinks that he strips his equals of the prerogative which he concedes to the crown. The man of a democratic age is extremely reluctant to obey his neighbour who is his equal; he refuses to acknowledge in such a person ability superior to his own; he mistrusts his justice, and is jealous of his power; he fears and he condemns him; and he loves continually to remind him of the common dependence in which both of them stand to the same master.

Every central power which follows its natural tendencies courts and encourages the principle of equality; for equality singularly facilitates, extends, and secures the influence of a central power.

In like manner it may be said that every central government worships uniformity: uniformity relieves it from inquiry into an infinite number of small details which must be attended to if rules have to be adapted to different men, instead of indiscriminately subjecting all men to the same rule: thus the government likes what the citizens like, and naturally hates what they hate. These common sentiments, which, in democratic nations, constantly unite the sovereign and every member of the community in one and the same conviction, establish a secret and lasting sympathy between them. The faults of the government are pardoned for the sake of its tastes; public confidence is only reluctantly withdrawn in the midst even of its excesses and its errors, and it is restored at the first call. Democratic nations often hate those in whose hands the central power is vested; but they always love that power itself.

Thus, by two separate paths, I have reached the same conclusion. I have shown that the principle of equality suggests to men the notion of a sole, uniform, and strong government: I have now shown that the principle of equality imparts to them a taste for it. To governments of this kind the nations of our age are therefore tending. They are drawn thither by the natural inclination of mind and heart; and in order to reach that result, it is enough that they do not check themselves in their course.

I am of opinion, that, in the democratic ages which are opening upon us, individual independence and local liberties will ever be the product of artificial contrivance; that centralization will be the natural form of government.

Thus a democratic government increases its power simply by the fact of its permanence. Time is on its side; every incident befriends it; the passions of individuals unconsciously promote it; and it may be asserted, that the older a democratic community is, the more centralized will its government become.

**Chapter IV:** **Of Certain Peculiar and Accidental Causes Which Either Lead a People to Complete Centralization of Government, or Which Divert Them From It**

If all democratic nations are instinctively led to the centralization of government, they tend to this result in an unequal manner. This depends on the particular circumstances which may promote or prevent the natural consequences of that state of society,—circumstances which are exceedingly numerous; but I shall only advert to a few of them.

Amongst men who have lived free long before they became equal, the tendencies derived from free institutions combat, to a certain extent, the propensities superinduced by the principle of equality; and although the central power may increase its privileges amongst such a people, the private members of such a community will never entirely forfeit their independence. But when the equality of conditions grows up amongst a people which has never known, or has long ceased to know, what freedom is (and such is the case upon the continent of Europe), as the former habits of the nation are suddenly combined, by some sort of natural attraction, with the new habits and principles engendered by the state of society, all powers seem spontaneously to rush to the centre. These powers accumulate there with astonishing rapidity, and the state instantly attains the utmost limits of its strength, whilst private persons allow themselves to sink as suddenly to the lowest degree of weakness.

The English who emigrated three hundred years ago to found a democratic commonwealth on the shores of the New World, had all learned to take a part in public affairs in their mother country; they were conversant with trial by jury; they were accustomed to liberty of speech and of the press,—to personal freedom, to the notion of rights and the practice of asserting them. They carried with them to America these free institutions and manly customs, and these institutions preserved them against the encroachments of the state. Thus amongst the Americans it is freedom which is old,—equality is of comparatively modern date. The reverse is occurring in Europe, where equality, introduced by absolute power and under the rule of kings, was already infused into the habits of nations long before freedom had entered into their conceptions.

I have said that amongst democratic nations the notion of government naturally presents itself to the mind under the form of a sole and central power, and that the notion of intermediate powers is not familiar to them. This is peculiarly applicable to the democratic nations which have witnessed the triumph of the principle of equality by means of a violent revolution. As the classes which managed local affairs have been suddenly swept away by the storm, and as the confused mass which remains has as yet neither the organization nor the habits which fit it to assume the administration of these same affairs, the State alone seems capable of taking upon itself all the details of government, and centralization becomes, as it were, the unavoidable state of the country.

Napoleon deserves neither praise nor censure for having centred in his own hands almost all the administrative power of France; for, after the abrupt disappearance of the nobility and the higher rank of the middle classes, these powers devolved on him of course: it would have been almost as difficult for him to reject as to assume them. But no necessity of this kind has ever been felt by the Americans, who, having passed through no revolution, and having governed themselves from the first, never had to call upon the state to act for a time as their guardian. Thus the progress of centralization amongst a democratic people depends not only on the progress of equality, but on the manner in which this equality has been established.

At the commencement of a great democratic revolution, when hostilities have but just broken out between the different classes of society, the people endeavour to centralize the public administration in the hands of the government, in order to wrest the management of local affairs from the aristocracy. Towards the close of such a revolution, on the contrary, it is usually the conquered aristocracy that endeavours to make over the management of all affairs to the state, because such an aristocracy dreads the tyranny of a people which has become their equal, and not unfrequently their master. Thus it is not always the same class of the community which strives to increase the prerogative of the government; but as long as the democratic revolution lasts, there is always one class in the nation, powerful in numbers or in wealth, which is induced, by peculiar passions or interests, to centralize the public administration, independently of that hatred of being governed by one's neighbour, which is a general and permanent feeling amongst democratic nations.

It may be remarked, that at the present day the lower orders in England are striving with all their might to destroy local independence, and to transfer the administration from all the points of the circumference to the centre; whereas the higher classes are endeavouring to retain this administration within its ancient boundaries. I venture to predict that a time will come when the very reverse will happen.

These observations explain why the supreme power is always stronger, and private individuals weaker, amongst a democratic people which has passed through a long and arduous struggle to reach a state of equality, than amongst a democratic community in which the citizens have been equal from the first. The example of the Americans completely demonstrates the fact. The inhabitants of the United States were never divided by any privileges; they have never known the mutual relation of master and inferior, and as they neither dread nor hate each other, they have never known the necessity of calling in the supreme power to manage their affairs. The lot of the Americans is singular: they have derived from the aristocracy of England the notion of private rights and the taste for local freedom; and they have been able to retain both the one and the other, because they have had no aristocracy to combat.

If education enables men at all times to defend their independence, this is most especially true in democratic times. When all men are alike, it is easy to found a sole and all-powerful government, by the aid of mere instinct. But men require much intelligence, knowledge, and art to organize and to maintain secondary powers under similar circumstances, and to create amidst the independence and individual weakness of the citizens such free associations as may be able to struggle against tyranny without destroying public order.

Hence the concentration of power and the subjection of individuals will increase amongst democratic nations, not only in the same proportion as their equality, but in the same proportion as their ignorance. It is true, that in ages of imperfect civilization the government is frequently as wanting in the knowledge required to impose a despotism upon the people as the people are wanting in the knowledge required to shake it off; but the effect is not the same on both sides. However rude a democratic people may be, the central power which rules them is never completely devoid of cultivation, because it readily draws to its own uses what little cultivation is to be found in the country, and, if necessary, may seek assistance elsewhere. Hence, amongst a nation which is ignorant as well as democratic, an amazing difference cannot fail speedily to arise between the intellectual capacity of the ruler and that of each of his subjects. This completes the easy concentration of all power in his hands: the administrative function of the state is perpetually extended, because the state alone is competent to administer the affairs of the country.

Aristocratic nations, however unenlightened they may be, never afford the same spectacle, because in them instruction is nearly equally diffused between the monarch and the leading members of the community.

The Pasha, who now rules in Egypt, found the population of that country composed of men exceedingly ignorant and equal, and he has borrowed the science and ability of Europe to govern that people. As the personal attainments of the sovereign are thus combined with the ignorance and democratic weakness of his subjects, the utmost centralization has been established without impediment, and the Pasha has made the country his manufactory, and the inhabitants his workmen.

I think that extreme centralization of government ultimately enervates society, and thus after a length of time weakens the government itself; but I do not deny that a centralized social power may be able to execute great undertakings with facility in a given time and on a particular point. This is more especially true of war, in which success depends much more on the means of transferring all the resources of a nation to one single point, than on the extent of those resources.

Hence it is chiefly in war that nations desire and frequently require to increase the powers of the central government. All men of military genius are fond of centralization, which increases their strength; and all men of centralizing genius are fond of war, which compels nations to combine all their powers in the hands of the government. Thus the democratic tendency which leads men unceasingly to multiply the privileges of the state, and to circumscribe the rights of private persons, is much more rapid and constant amongst those democratic nations which are exposed by their position to great and frequent wars, than amongst all others.

I have shown how the dread of disturbance and the love of well-being insensibly lead democratic nations to increase the functions of central government, as the only power which appears to be intrinsically sufficiently strong, enlightened, and secure, to protect them from anarchy. I would now add, that all the particular circumstances which tend to make the state of a democratic community agitated and precarious, enhance this general propensity, and lead private persons more and more to sacrifice their rights to their tranquillity.

A people is therefore never so disposed to increase the functions of central government as at the close of a long and bloody revolution, which, after having wrested property from the hands of its former possessors, has shaken all belief, and filled the nation with fierce hatreds, conflicting interests, and contending factions. The love of public tranquillity becomes at such times an indiscriminate passion, and the members of the community are apt to conceive a most inordinate devotion to order.

I have already examined several of the incidents which may concur to promote the centralization of power, but the principal cause still remains to be noticed. The foremost of the incidental causes which may draw the management of all affairs into the hands of the ruler in democratic countries, is the origin of that ruler himself, and his own propensities. Men who live in the ages of equality are naturally fond of central power, and are willing to extend its privileges; but if it happens that this same power faithfully represents their own interests, and exactly copies their own inclinations, the confidence they place in it knows no bounds, and they think that whatever they bestow upon it is bestowed upon themselves.

The attraction of administrative powers to the centre will always be less easy and less rapid under the reign of kings who are still in some way connected with the old aristocratic order, than under new princes, the children of their own achievements, whose birth, prejudices, propensities, and habits appear to bind them indissolubly to the cause of equality. I do not mean that princes of aristocratic origin who live in democratic ages do not attempt to centralize; I believe they apply themselves as diligently as any others to that object. For them, the sole advantages of equality lie in that direction; but their opportunities are less great, because the community, instead of volunteering compliance with their desires, frequently obey them with reluctance. In democratic communities, the rule is, that centralization must increase in proportion as the sovereign is less aristocratic.

When an ancient race of kings stands at the head of an aristocracy, as the natural prejudices of the sovereign perfectly accord with the natural prejudices of the nobility, the vices inherent in aristocratic communities have a free course, and meet with no corrective. The reverse is the case when the scion of a feudal stock is placed at the head of a democratic people. The sovereign is constantly led, by his education, his habits, and his associations, to adopt sentiments suggested by the inequality of conditions, and the people tend as constantly, by their social condition, to those manners which are engendered by equality. At such times it often happens that the citizens seek to control the central power far less as a tyrannical than as an aristocratical power, and that they persist in the firm defence of their independence, not only because they would remain free, but especially because they are determined to remain equal.

A revolution which overthrows an ancient regal family in order to place new men at the head of a democratic people may temporarily weaken the central power; but however anarchical such a revolution may appear at first, we need not hesitate to predict that its final and certain consequence will be to extend and to secure the prerogatives of that power.

The foremost or indeed the sole condition which is required in order to succeed in centralizing the supreme power in a democratic community, is to love equality, or to get men to believe you love it. Thus the science of despotism, which was once so complex, is simplified, and reduced as it were to a single principle.

### Chapter VI: What Sort of Despotism Democratic Nations Have to Fear

I had remarked during my stay in the United States, that a democratic state of society, similar to that of the Americans, might offer singular facilities for the establishment of despotism; and I perceived, upon my return to Europe, how much use had already been made, by most of our rulers, of the notions, the sentiments, and the wants created by this same social condition, for the purpose of extending the circle of their power. This led me to think that the nations of Christendom would perhaps eventually undergo some sort of oppression like that which hung over several of the nations of the ancient world.

A more accurate examination of the subject, and five years of further meditation, have not diminished my fears, but have changed the object of them.

No sovereign ever lived in former ages so absolute or so powerful as to undertake to administer by his own agency, and without the assistance of intermediate powers, all the parts of a great empire: none ever attempted to subject all his subjects indiscriminately to strict uniformity of regulation, and personally to tutor and direct every member of the community. The notion of such an undertaking never occurred to the human mind; and if any man had conceived it, the want of information, the imperfection of the administrative system, and, above all, the natural obstacles caused by the inequality of conditions, would speedily have checked the execution of so vast a design.

When the Roman emperors were at the height of their power, the different nations of the empire still preserved manners and customs of great diversity; although they were subject to the same monarch, most of the provinces were separately administered; they abounded in powerful and active municipalities; and although the whole government of the empire was centred in the hands of the Emperor alone, and he always remained, in case of need, the supreme arbiter in all matters, yet the details of social life and private occupations lay for the most part beyond his control. The Emperors possessed, it is true, an immense and unchecked power, which allowed them to gratify all their whimsical tastes, and to employ for that purpose the whole strength of the state. They frequently abused that power arbitrarily to deprive their subjects of property or of life: their tyranny was extremely onerous to the few, but it did not reach the many; it was fixed to some few main objects, and neglected the rest; it was violent, but its range was limited.

It would seem that, if despotism were to be established amongst the democratic nations of our days, it might assume a different character; it would be more extensive and more mild, it would degrade men without tormenting them. I do not question, that in an age of instruction and equality like our own, sovereigns might more easily succeed in collecting all political power into their own hands, and might interfere more habitually and decidedly with the circle of private interests, than any sovereign of antiquity could ever do. But this same principle of equality which facilitates despotism, tempers its rigor. We have seen how the manners of society become more humane and gentle, in proportion as men become more equal and alike. When no member of the community has much power or much wealth, tyranny is, as it were, without opportunities and a field of action. As all fortunes are scanty, the passions of men are naturally circumscribed, their imagination limited, their pleasures simple. This universal moderation moderates the sovereign himself, and checks within certain limits the inordinate stretch of his desires.

Independently of these reasons drawn from the nature of the state of society itself, I might add many others arising from causes beyond my subject; but I shall keep within the limits I have laid down.

Democratic governments may become violent, and even cruel, at certain periods of extreme effervescence or of great danger; but these crises will be rare and brief. When I consider the petty passions of our contemporaries, the mildness of their manners, the extent of their education, the purity of their religion, the gentleness of their morality, their regular and industrious habits, and the restraint which they almost all observe in their vices no less than in their virtues, I have no fear that they will meet with tyrants in their rulers, but rather with guardians.

I think, then, that the species of oppression by which democratic nations are menaced is unlike anything which ever before existed in the world: our contemporaries will find no prototype of it in their memories. I seek in vain for an expression which will accurately convey the whole of the idea I have formed of it, the old words despotism and tyranny are inappropriate: the thing itself is new, and since I cannot name I must attempt to define it.

I seek to trace the novel features under which despotism may appear in the world. The first thing that strikes the observation is an innumerable multitude of men, all equal and alike, incessantly endeavouring to procure the petty and paltry pleasures with which they glut their lives. Each of them, living apart, is as a stranger to the fate of all the rest,—his children and his private friends constitute to him the whole of mankind; as for the rest of his fellow-citizens, he is close to them, but he sees them not; he touches them, but he feels them not; he exists but in himself and for himself alone; and if his kindred still remain to him, he may be said at any rate to have lost his country.

Above this race of men stands an immense and tutelary power, which takes upon itself alone to secure their gratifications, and to watch over their fate. That power is absolute, minute, regular, provident, and mild. It would be like the authority of a parent, if, like that authority, its object was to prepare men for manhood; but it seeks, on the contrary, to keep them in perpetual childhood: it is well content that the people should rejoice, provided they think of nothing but rejoicing. For their happiness such a government willingly labors, but it chooses to be the sole agent and the only arbiter of that happiness; it provides for their security, foresees and supplies their necessities, facilitates their pleasures, manages their principal concerns, directs their industry, regulates the descent of property, and subdivides their inheritances: what remains, but to spare them all the care of thinking and all the trouble of living?

Thus, it every day renders the exercise of the free agency of man less useful and less frequent; it circumscribes the will within a narrower range, and gradually robs a man of all the uses of himself. The principle of equality has prepared men for these things; it has predisposed men to endure them, and oftentimes to look on them as benefits.

After having thus successively taken each member of the community in its powerful grasp, and fashioned him at will, the supreme power then extends its arm over the whole community. It covers the surface of society with a network of small complicated rules, minute and uniform, through which the most original minds and the most energetic characters cannot penetrate, to rise above the crowd. The will of man is not shattered, but softened, bent, and guided; men are seldom forced by it to act, but they are constantly restrained from acting: such a power does not destroy, but it prevents existence; it does not tyrannize, but it compresses, enervates, extinguishes, and stupefies a people, till each nation is reduced to be nothing better than a flock of timid and industrious animals, of which the government is the shepherd.

I have always thought that servitude of the regular, quiet, and gentle kind which I have just described, might be combined more easily than is commonly believed with some of the outward forms of freedom, and that it might even establish itself under the wing of the sovereignty of the people.

Our contemporaries are constantly excited by two conflicting passions; they want to be led, and they wish to remain free: as they cannot destroy either the one or the other of these contrary propensities, they strive to satisfy them both at once. They devise a sole, tutelary, and all-powerful form of government, but elected by the people. They combine the principle of centralization and that of popular sovereignty; this gives them a respite: they console themselves for being in tutelage by the reflection that they have chosen their own guardians. Every man allows himself to be put in leading-strings, because he sees that it is not a person or a class of persons, but the people at large, that hold the end of his chain.

By this system, the people shake off their state of dependence just long enough to select their master, and then relapse into it again. A great many persons at the present day are quite contented with this sort of compromise between administrative despotism and the sovereignty of the people; and they think they have done enough for the protection of individual freedom when they have surrendered it to the power of the nation at large. This does not satisfy me: the nature of him I am to obey signifies less to me than the fact of extorted obedience.

I do not, however, deny that a constitution of this kind appears to me to be infinitely preferable to one which, after having concentrated all the powers of government, should vest them in the hands of an irresponsible person or body of persons. Of all the forms which democratic despotism could assume, the latter would assuredly be the worst.

When the sovereign is elective, or narrowly watched by a legislature which is really elective and independent, the oppression which he exercises over individuals is sometimes greater, but it is always less degrading; because every man, when he is oppressed and disarmed, may still imagine that, whilst he yields obedience, it is to himself he yields it, and that it is to one of his own inclinations that all the rest give way. In like manner, I can understand that, when the sovereign represents the nation, and is dependent upon the people, the rights and the power of which every citizen is deprived not only serve the head of the state, but the state itself; and that private persons derive some return from the sacrifice of their independence which they have made to the public. To create a representation of the people in every centralized country is, therefore, to diminish the evil which extreme centralization may produce, but not to get rid of it.

I admit that, by this means, room is left for the intervention of individuals in the more important affairs; but it is not the less suppressed in the smaller and more private ones. It must not be forgotten that it is especially dangerous to enslave men in the minor details of life. For my own part, I should be inclined to think freedom less necessary in great things than in little ones, if it were possible to be secure of the one without possessing the other.

Subjection in minor affairs breaks out every day, and is felt by the whole community indiscriminately. It does not drive men to resistance, but it crosses them at every turn, till they are led to surrender the exercise of their will. Thus their spirit is gradually broken and their character enervated; whereas that obedience which is exacted on a few important but rare occasions, only exhibits servitude at certain intervals, and throws the burden of it upon a small number of men. It is in vain to summon a people, who have been rendered so dependent on the central power, to choose from time to time the representatives of that power; this rare and brief exercise of their free choice, however important it may be, will not prevent them from gradually losing the faculties of thinking, feeling, and acting for themselves, and thus gradually falling below the level of humanity.[12]

I add, that they will soon become incapable of exercising the great and only privilege which remains to them. The democratic nations which have introduced freedom into their political

---

[12] It cannot be absolutely or generally affirmed that the greatest danger of the present age is license or tyranny, anarchy or despotism. Both are equally to be feared; and the one may as easily proceed as the other from the self-same cause, namely, that *general apathy*, which is the consequence of what I have termed individualism: it is because this apathy exists, that the executive government, having mustered a few troops, is able to commit acts of oppression one day, and the next day, a party which has mustered some thirty men in its ranks can also commit acts of oppression. Neither one nor the other can found anything to last; and the causes which enable them to succeed easily prevent them from succeeding long: they rise because nothing opposes them, and they sink because nothing supports them. The proper object, therefore, of our most strenuous resistance, is far less either anarchy or despotism, than that apathy which may almost indifferently beget either the one or the other.

constitution, at the very time when they were augmenting the despotism of their administrative constitution, have been led into strange paradoxes. To manage those minor affairs in which good sense is all that is wanted,—the people are held to be unequal to the task; but when the government of the country is at stake, the people are invested with immense powers; they are alternately made the playthings of their ruler, and his masters—more than kings, and less than men. After having exhausted all the different modes of election, without finding one to suit their purpose, they are still amazed, and still bent on seeking further; as if the evil they remark did not originate in the constitution of the country, far more than in that of the electoral body.

It is, indeed, difficult to conceive how men who have entirely given up the habit of self-government should succeed in making a proper choice of those by whom they are to be governed; and no one will ever believe that a liberal, wise, and energetic government can spring from the suffrages of a subservient people.

A constitution which should be republican in its head, and ultra-monarchical in all its other parts, has ever appeared to me to be a short-lived monster. The vices of rulers and the inaptitude of the people would speedily bring about its ruin; and the nation, weary of its representatives and of itself, would create freer institutions, or soon return to stretch itself at the feet of a single master.

### Chapter VII:   Continuation of the Preceding Chapters

I believe that it is easier to establish an absolute and despotic government amongst a people in which the conditions of society are equal, than amongst any other; and I think, that if such a government were once established amongst such a people, it would not only oppress men, but would eventually strip each of them of several of the highest qualities of humanity. Despotism, therefore, appears to me peculiarly to be dreaded in democratic times. I should have loved freedom, I believe, at all times, but in the time in which we live I am ready to worship it.

On the other hand, I am persuaded that all who shall attempt, in the ages upon which we are entering, to base freedom upon aristocratic privilege, will fail; that all who shall attempt to draw and to retain authority within a single class, will fail. At the present day, no ruler is skilful or strong enough to found a despotism by re-establishing permanent distinctions of rank amongst his subjects: no legislator is wise or powerful enough to preserve free institutions, if he does not take equality for his first principle and his watchword. All those of our contemporaries who would establish or secure the independence and the dignity of their fellow-men, must show themselves the friends of equality; and the only worthy means of showing themselves as such, is to be so: upon this depends the success of their holy enterprise. Thus, the question is not how to reconstruct aristocratic society, but how to make liberty proceed out of that democratic state of society in which God has placed us.

These two truths appear to me simple, clear, and fertile in consequences; and they naturally lead me to consider what kind of free government can be established amongst a people in which social conditions are equal.

It results, from the very constitution of democratic nations and from their necessities, that the power of government amongst them must be more uniform, more centralized, more extensive, more searching, and more efficient than in other countries. Society at large is naturally stronger and more active, the individual more subordinate and weak; the former does more, the latter less; and this is inevitably the case.

It is not, therefore, to be expected that the range of private independence will ever be as extensive in democratic as in aristocratic countries;—nor is this to be desired; for, amongst aristocratic nations, the mass is often sacrificed to the individual, and the prosperity of the greater number to the greatness of the few. It is both necessary and desirable that the government of a democratic people should be active and powerful: and our object should not be to render it weak or indolent, but solely to prevent it from abusing its aptitude and its strength.

The circumstance which most contributed to secure the independence of private persons in aristocratic ages was, that the supreme power did not affect to take upon itself alone the government and administration of the community; those functions were necessarily partially left to the members of the aristocracy: so that, as the supreme power was always divided, it never weighed with its whole weight and in the same manner on each individual.

Not only did the government not perform everything by its immediate agency; but, as most of the agents who discharged its duties derived their power, not from the state, but from the circumstance of their birth, they were not perpetually under its control. The government could not make or unmake them in an instant, at pleasure, or bend them in strict uniformity to its slightest caprice; this was an additional guarantee of private independence.

I readily admit that recourse cannot be had to the same means at the present time; but I discover certain democratic expedients which may be substituted for them. Instead of vesting in the government alone all the administrative powers of which corporations and nobles have been deprived, a portion of them may be entrusted to secondary public bodies temporarily composed of private citizens: thus the liberty of private persons will be more secure, and their equality will not be diminished.

The Americans, who care less for words than the French, still designate by the name of County the largest of their administrative districts; but the duties of the count or lord-lieutenant are in part performed by a provincial assembly.

At a period of equality like our own, it would be unjust and unreasonable to institute hereditary officers; but there is nothing to prevent us from substituting elective public officers to a certain extent. Election is a democratic expedient, which insures the independence of the public officer in relation to the government as much as hereditary rank can insure it amongst aristocratic nations, and even more so.

Aristocratic countries abound in wealthy and influential persons who are competent to provide for themselves, and who cannot be easily or secretly oppressed: such persons restrain a government within general habits of moderation and reserve. I am well aware that democratic countries contain no such persons naturally; but something analogous to them may be created by artificial means. I firmly believe that an aristocracy cannot again be founded in the world; but I think that private citizens, by combining together, may constitute bodies of great wealth, influence, and strength, corresponding to the persons of an aristocracy. By this means, many of the greatest political advantages of aristocracy would be obtained, without its injustice or its dangers. An association for political, commercial, or manufacturing purposes, or even for those of science and literature, is a powerful and enlightened member of the community, which cannot be disposed of at pleasure, or oppressed without remonstrance; and which, by defending its own rights against the encroachments of the government, saves the common liberties of the country.

In periods of aristocracy every man is always bound so closely to many of his fellow-citizens that he cannot be assailed without their coming to his assistance. In ages of equality every man naturally stands alone; he has no hereditary friends whose co-operation he may demand; no class upon whose sympathy he may rely: he is easily got rid of, and he is trampled on with impunity. At the present time, an oppressed member of the community has therefore only one method of self-defence,—he may appeal to the whole nation; and if the whole nation is deaf to his complaint, he may appeal to mankind: the only means he has of making this appeal is by the press. Thus, the liberty of the press is infinitely more valuable amongst democratic nations than amongst all others; it is the only cure for the evils which equality may produce. Equality sets men apart and weakens them; but the press places a powerful weapon within every man's reach, which the weakest and loneliest of them all may use. Equality deprives a man of the support of his connections; but the press enables him to summon all his fellow-countrymen and all his fellow-men to his assistance. Printing has accelerated the progress of equality, and it is also one of its best correctives.

I think that men living in aristocracies may, strictly speaking, do without the liberty of the press: but such is not the case with those who live in democratic countries. To protect their personal independence I trust not to great political assemblies, to parliamentary privilege, or to the assertion of popular sovereignty. All these things may, to a certain extent, be reconciled with personal servitude. But that servitude cannot be complete if the press is free: the press is the chiefest democratic instrument of freedom.

Something analogous may be said of the judicial power. It is a part of the essence of judicial power to attend to private interests, and to fix itself with predilection on minute objects submitted to its observation: another essential quality of judicial power is never to volunteer its assistance to the oppressed, but always to be at the disposal of the humblest of those who solicit it; their complaint, however feeble they may themselves be, will force itself upon the ear of justice and claim redress, for this is inherent in the very constitution of the courts of justice.

A power of this kind is therefore peculiarly adapted to the wants of freedom, at a time when the eye and finger of the government are constantly intruding into the minutest details of human actions, and when private persons are at once too weak to protect themselves, and too much isolated for them to reckon upon the assistance of their fellows. The strength of the courts of law has ever been the greatest security which can be offered to personal independence; but this is more especially the case in democratic ages: private rights and interests are in constant danger, if the judicial power does not grow more extensive and more strong to keep pace with the growing equality of conditions.

Equality awakens in men several propensities extremely dangerous to freedom, to which the attention of the legislator ought constantly to be directed. I shall only remind the reader of the most important amongst them.

Men living in democratic ages do not readily comprehend the utility of forms: they feel an instinctive contempt for them, I have elsewhere shown for what reasons. Forms excite their contempt, and often their hatred; as they commonly aspire to none but easy and present gratifications, they rush onwards to the object of their desires, and the slightest delay exasperates them. This same temper, carried with them into political life, renders them hostile to forms, which perpetually retard or arrest them in some of their projects.

Yet this objection, which the men of democracies make to forms, is the very thing which renders forms so useful to freedom; for their chief merit is to serve as a barrier between the strong and the weak, the ruler and the people, to retard the one, and give the other time to look about him. Forms become more necessary in proportion as the government becomes more active and more powerful, whilst private persons are becoming more indolent and more feeble. Thus democratic nations naturally stand more in need of forms than other nations, and they naturally respect them less. This deserves most serious attention.

Nothing is more pitiful than the arrogant disdain of most of our contemporaries for questions of form; for the smallest questions of form have acquired in our time an importance which they never had before: many of the greatest interests of mankind depend upon them. I think, that, if the statesmen of aristocratic ages could sometimes contemn forms with impunity, and frequently rise above them, the statesmen to whom the government of nations is now confided ought to treat the very least among them with respect, and not neglect them without imperious necessity. In aristocracies the observance of forms was superstitious; amongst us they ought to be kept with a deliberate and enlightened deference.

Another tendency, which is extremely natural to democratic nations and extremely dangerous, is that which leads them to despise and undervalue the rights of private persons. The attachment which men feel to a right, and the respect which they display for it, is generally proportioned to its importance, or to the length of time during which they have enjoyed it. The rights of private persons amongst democratic nations are commonly of small importance, of recent growth, and extremely precarious; the consequence is, that they are often sacrificed without regret, and almost always violated without remorse.

But it happens that, at the same period and amongst the same nations in which men conceive a natural contempt for the rights of private persons, the rights of society at large are naturally extended and consolidated: in other words, men become less attached to private rights just when it is most necessary to retain and defend what little remains of them. It is therefore most especially in the present democratic times, that the true friends of the liberty and the greatness of man ought constantly to be on the alert, to prevent the power of government from lightly sacrificing the private rights of individuals to the general execution of its designs. At such times, no citizen is so obscure that it is not very dangerous to allow him to be oppressed; no private rights are so unimportant that they can be surrendered with impunity to the caprices of a government. The reason is plain:—if the private right of an individual is violated at a time when the human mind is fully impressed with the importance and the sanctity of such rights, the injury done is confined to the individual whose right is infringed; but to violate such a right at the present day is deeply to corrupt the manners of the nation, and to put the whole community in jeopardy, because the very notion of this kind of right constantly tends amongst us to be impaired and lost.

There are certain habits, certain notions, and certain vices which are peculiar to a state of revolution, and which a protracted revolution cannot fail to create and to propagate, whatever be, in other respects, its character, its purpose, and the scene on which it takes place. When any nation has, within a short space of time, repeatedly varied its rulers, its opinions, and its laws, the men of whom it is composed eventually contract a taste for change, and grow accustomed to see all changes effected by sudden violence. Thus they naturally conceive a contempt for forms which daily prove ineffectual; and they do not support, without impatience, the dominion of rules which they have so often seen infringed.

As the ordinary notions of equity and morality no longer suffice to explain and justify all the innovations daily begotten by a revolution, the principle of public utility is called in, the doctrine of political necessity is conjured up, and men accustom themselves to sacrifice private interests without scruple, and to trample on the rights of individuals in order more speedily to accomplish any public purpose.

These habits and notions, which I shall call revolutionary, because all revolutions produce them, occur in aristocracies just as much as amongst democratic nations; but amongst the former they are often less powerful and always less lasting, because there they meet with habits, notions, defects, and impediments, which counteract them: they consequently disappear as soon as the revolution is terminated, and the nation reverts to its former political courses. This is not always the case in democratic countries, in which it is ever to be feared that revolutionary tendencies, becoming more gentle and more regular, without entirely disappearing from society, will be gradually transformed into habits of subjection to the administrative authority of the government. I know of no countries in which revolutions are more dangerous than in democratic countries; because, independently of the accidental and transient evils which must always attend them, they may always create some evils which are permanent and unending.

I believe that there are such things as justifiable resistance and legitimate rebellion: I do not therefore assert, as an absolute proposition, that the men of democratic ages ought never to make revolutions; but I think that they have especial reason to hesitate before they embark in them, and that it is far better to endure many grievances in their present condition, than to have recourse to so perilous a remedy.

I shall conclude by one general idea, which comprises not only all the particular ideas which have been expressed in the present chapter, but also most of those which it is the object of this book to treat of. In the ages of aristocracy which preceded our own, there were private persons of great power, and a social authority of extreme weakness. The outline of society itself was not easily discernible, and constantly confounded with the different powers by which the community was ruled. The principal efforts of the men of those times were required to strengthen, aggrandize, and secure the supreme power; and, on the other hand, to circumscribe individual independence within narrower limits, and to subject private interests to the interests of the public. Other perils and other cares await the men of our age. Amongst the greater part of modern nations, the government, whatever may be its origin, its constitution, or its name, has become almost omnipotent, and private persons are falling, more and more, into the lowest stage of weakness and dependence.

In olden society, everything was different; unity and uniformity were nowhere to be met with. In modern society, everything threatens to become so much alike, that the peculiar characteristics of each individual will soon be entirely lost in the general aspect of the world. Our forefathers were ever prone to make an improper use of the notion that private rights ought to be respected; and we are naturally prone, on the other hand, to exaggerate the idea that the interest of a private individual ought always to bend to the interest of the many.

The political world is metamorphosed: new remedies must henceforth be sought for new disorders. To lay down extensive but distinct and settled limits to the action of the government; to confer certain rights on private persons, and to secure to them the undisputed enjoyment of those rights; to enable individual man to maintain whatever independence, strength, and original power he still possesses; to raise him by the side of society at large, and uphold him in that position,—these appear to me the main objects of legislators in the ages upon which we are now entering.

It would seem as if the rulers of our time sought only to use men in order to make things great; I wish that they would try a little more to make great men; that they would set less value on the work, and more upon the workman; that they would never forget that a nation cannot long remain strong when every man belonging to it is individually weak; and that no form or combination of social polity has yet been devised to make an energetic people out of a community of pusillanimous and enfeebled citizens.

I trace amongst our contemporaries two contrary notions which are equally injurious. One set of men can perceive nothing in the principle of equality but the anarchical tendencies which it engenders: they dread their own free agency, they fear themselves. Other thinkers, less numerous but more enlightened, take a different view: beside that track which starts from the principle of equality to terminate in anarchy, they have at last discovered the road which seems to lead men to inevitable servitude. They shape their souls beforehand to this necessary condition; and, despairing of remaining free, they already do obeisance in their hearts to the master who is soon to appear. The former abandon freedom because they think it dangerous; the latter, because they hold it to be impossible.

If I had entertained the latter conviction, I should not have written this book, but I should have confined myself to deploring in secret the destiny of mankind. I have sought to point out the dangers to which the principle of equality exposes the independence of man, because I firmly believe that these dangers are the most formidable, as well as the least foreseen, of all those which futurity holds in store; but I do not think that they are insurmountable.

The men who live in the democratic ages upon which we are entering have naturally a taste for independence; they are naturally impatient of regulation, and they are wearied by the permanence even of the condition they themselves prefer. They are fond of power; but they are prone to despise and hate those who wield it, and they easily elude its grasp by their own mobility and insignificance.

These propensities will always manifest themselves, because they originate in the groundwork of society, which will undergo no change: for a long time they will prevent the establishment of any despotism, and they will furnish fresh weapons to each succeeding generation which shall struggle in favor of the liberty of mankind. Let us, then, look forward to the future with that salutary fear which makes men keep watch and ward for freedom, not with that faint and idle terror which depresses and enervates the heart.

### Chapter VIII: General Survey of the Subject

Before closing forever the subject that I have now discussed, I would fain take a parting survey of all the different characteristics of modern society, and appreciate at last the general influence to be exercised by the principle of equality upon the fate of mankind; but I am stopped by the difficulty of the task, and, in presence of so great a theme, my sight is troubled, and my reason fails.

The society of the modern world, which I have sought to delineate, and which I seek to judge, has but just come into existence. Time has not yet shaped it into perfect form; the great revolution by which it has been created is not yet over; and, amidst the occurrences of our time, it is almost impossible to discern what will pass away with the revolution itself, and what will survive its close. The world which is rising into existence is still half encumbered by the remains of the world which is waning into decay; and, amidst the vast perplexity of human affairs, none can say how much of ancient institutions and former manners will remain, or how much will completely disappear.

Although the revolution which is taking place in the social condition, the laws, the opinions, and the feelings of men is still very far from being terminated, yet its results already admit of no comparison with anything that the world has ever before witnessed. I go back from age to age up to the remotest antiquity, but I find no parallel to what is occurring before my eyes: as the past has ceased to throw its light upon the future, the mind of man wanders in obscurity.

Nevertheless, in the midst of a prospect so wide, so novel and so confused, some of the more prominent characteristics may already be discerned and pointed out. The good things and the evils of life are more equally distributed in the world: great wealth tends to disappear, the number of small fortunes to increase; desires and gratifications are multiplied, but extraordinary prosperity and irremediable penury are alike unknown. The sentiment of ambition is universal, but the scope of ambition is seldom vast. Each individual stands apart in solitary weakness; but society at large is active, provident, and powerful: the performances of private persons are insignificant, those of the state immense.

There is little energy of character, but manners are mild, and laws humane. If there be few instances of exalted heroism or of virtues of the highest, brightest, and purest temper, men's habits are regular, violence is rare, and cruelty almost unknown. Human existence becomes longer, and property more secure: life is not adorned with brilliant trophies, but it is extremely easy and tranquil. Few pleasures are either very refined or very coarse; and highly polished manners are as uncommon as great brutality of tastes. Neither men of great learning, nor extremely ignorant communities, are to be met with; genius becomes more rare, information more diffused. The human mind is impelled by the small efforts of all mankind combined together, not by the strenuous activity of a few men. There is less perfection, but more abundance, in all the productions of the arts. The ties of race, of rank, and of country are relaxed; the great bond of humanity is strengthened.

If I endeavour to find out the most general and the most prominent of all these different characteristics, I perceive that what is taking place in men's fortunes manifests itself under a thousand other forms. Almost all extremes are softened or blunted: all that was most prominent is superseded by some middle term, at once less lofty and less low, less brilliant and less obscure, than what before existed in the world.

When I survey this countless multitude of beings, shaped in each other's likeness, amidst whom nothing rises and nothing falls, the sight of such universal uniformity saddens and chills me, and I am tempted to regret that state of society which has ceased to be. When the world was full of men of great importance and extreme insignificance, of great wealth and extreme poverty, of great learning and extreme ignorance, I turned aside from the latter to fix my observation on the former alone, who gratified my sympathies. But I admit that this gratification arose from my own weakness: it is because I am unable to see at once all that is around me, that I am allowed thus to select and separate the objects of my predilection from among so many others. Such is not the case with that Almighty and Eternal Being, whose gaze necessarily includes the whole of created things and who surveys distinctly, though at once, mankind and man.

We may naturally believe that it is not the singular prosperity of the few, but the greater well-being of all, which is most pleasing in the sight of the Creator and Preserver of men. What appears to me to be man's decline is, to His eye, advancement; what afflicts me is acceptable to Him. A state of equality is perhaps less elevated, but it is more just: and its justice constitutes its greatness and its beauty. I would strive, then, to raise myself to this point of the Divine contemplation, and thence to view and to judge the concerns of men.

No man, upon the earth, can as yet affirm, absolutely and generally, that the new state of the world is better than its former one; but it is already easy to perceive that this state is different. Some vices and some virtues were so inherent in the constitution of an aristocratic nation, and are so opposite to the character of a modern people, that they can never be infused into it; some good tendencies and some bad propensities which were unknown to the former, are natural to the latter; some ideas suggest themselves spontaneously to the imagination of the one, which are utterly repugnant to the mind of the other. They are like two distinct orders of human beings, each of which has its own merits and defects, its own advantages and its own evils. Care must therefore be taken not to judge the state of society which is now coming into existence, by notions derived from a state of society which no longer exists; for, as these states of society are exceedingly different in their structure, they cannot be submitted to a just or fair comparison. It would be scarcely more reasonable to require of our own contemporaries the peculiar virtues which originated in the social condition of their forefathers, since that social condition is itself fallen, and has drawn into one promiscuous ruin the good and evil which belonged to it.

But as yet these things are imperfectly understood. I find that a great number of my contemporaries undertake to make a selection from amongst the institutions, the opinions, and the ideas which originated in the aristocratic constitution of society as it was: a portion of these elements they would willingly relinquish, but they would keep the remainder and transplant them into their new world. I apprehend that such men are wasting their time and their strength in virtuous but unprofitable efforts. The object is, not to retain the peculiar advantages which the inequality of conditions bestows upon mankind, but to secure the new benefits which equality may supply. We have not to seek to make ourselves like our progenitors, but to strive to work out that species of greatness and happiness which is our own.

For myself, who now looks back from this extreme limit of my task, and discovers from afar, but at once, the various objects which have attracted my more attentive investigation upon my way, I am full of apprehensions and of hopes. I perceive mighty dangers which it is possible to ward off,—mighty evils which may be avoided or alleviated; and I cling with a firmer hold to the belief, that, for democratic nations to be virtuous and prosperous, they require but to will it.

I am aware that many of my contemporaries maintain that nations are never their own masters here below, and that they necessarily obey some insurmountable and unintelligent power, arising from anterior events, from their race, or from the soil and climate of their country. Such principles are false and cowardly; such principles can never produce aught but feeble men and pusillanimous nations. Providence has not created mankind entirely independent or entirely free. It is true, that around every man a fatal circle is traced, beyond which he cannot pass; but within the wide verge of that circle he is powerful and free: as it is with man, so with communities. The nations of our time cannot prevent the conditions of men from becoming equal; but it depends upon themselves whether the principle of equality is to lead them to servitude or freedom, to knowledge or barbarism, to prosperity or to wretchedness.

# "'When Virtue Loses all Her Loveliness'—Some Reflections on Capitalism and 'The Free Society'"

*Irving Kristol (1920–        )*

*Author of many essays on the capitalist system and its relationships to democratic politics and to the good life for human beings, Kristol is considered one of the theorists of the contemporary "neo-conservative" movement. Kristol defines a neo-conservative as "a liberal who has been mugged by reality." In this piece, Kristol raises questions about the justice and goodness of capitalist society from the perspective of one who appreciates its capacity to produce prosperity for most and to support political freedom.*

*Consider whether capitalism really promised a just society in addition to affluence and freedom. Why would the founders of this system believe that there would be a link among these three aims? Why has the free market failed to produce a social order that all the people can view as just? What alternative understandings of politics and justice does Kristol suggest for the restoration of the spiritual satisfaction of Americans amid material enrichment? What does Kristol mean by "virtue" and do you agree with him about its importance?*

When we lack the will to see things as they really are, there is nothing so mystifying as the obvious. This is the case, I think, with the new upsurge of radicalism that is now shaking much of Western society to its foundations. We have constructed the most ingenious sociological and psychological theories—as well as a few disingenuously naive ones—to explain this phenomenon. But there is in truth no mystery here. Our youthful rebels are anything but inarticulate; and though they utter a great deal of nonsense, the import of what they are saying is clear enough. What they are saying is that they dislike—to put it mildly—the liberal, individualist, capitalist civilization that stands ready to receive them as citizens. They are rejecting this offer of citizenship and are declaring their desire to see some other kind of civilization replace it.

That most of them do not always put the matter as explicitly or as candidly as this is beside the point. Some of them do, of course; we try to dismiss them as "the lunatic fringe." But the mass of dissident young are not, after all, sufficiently educated to understand the implications of everything they say. Besides, it is so much easier for the less bold among them to insist that what they find outrageous are the defects and shortcomings of the present system. Such shortcomings undeniably exist and are easy polemical marks. And, at the other end, it is so much easier for the adult generations to accept such polemic as representing the sum and substance of their dissatisfaction. It is consoling to think that the turmoil among them is provoked by the extent to which our society falls short of realizing its ideals. But the plain truth is that it is these ideals themselves that are being rejected. Our young radicals are far less dismayed at America's failure to become what it ought to be than they are contemptuous of what it thinks it ought to be. For them, as for Oscar Wilde, it is not the average American who is disgusting; it is the ideal American.

This is why one can make so little impression on them with arguments about how much progress has been made in the past decades, or is being made today, toward racial equality, or abolishing poverty, or fighting pollution, or whatever it is that we conventionally take as a sign of "progress." The obstinacy with which they remain deaf to such "liberal" arguments is not all perverse or irrational, as some would like to think. It arises, rather, out of a perfectly sincere, if often inchoate, animus against the American system itself. This animus stands for a commitment—*to* what, remains to be seen, but *against* what is already only too evident.

### CAPITALS THREE PROMISES

Dissatisfaction with the liberal-capitalist ideal, as distinct from indignation at failures to realize this ideal, are coterminous with the history of capitalism itself. Indeed, the cultural history of the capitalist epoch is not much more than a record of the varying ways such dissatisfaction could be expressed—in poetry, in the novel, in the drama, in painting, and today even in the movies. Nor, again, is there any great mystery why, from the first stirrings of the romantic movement, poets and philosophers have never had much regard for the capitalist civilization in which they lived and worked. But to understand this fully, one must be able to step outside the "progressive" ideology which makes us assume that liberal capitalism is the "natural" state of man toward which humanity has always aspired. There is nothing more natural about capitalist civilization than about many others that have had, or will have, their day. Capitalism represents a sum of human choices about the good life and the good society. These choices inevitably have their associated costs, and after two hundred years the conviction seems to be spreading that the costs have got out of line.

What did capitalism promise? First of all, it promised continued improvement in the material conditions of all its citizens, a promise without precedent in human history. Secondly, it promised an equally unprecedented measure of individual freedom for all of these same citizens. And lastly, it held out the promise that, amidst this prosperity and liberty, the individual could satisfy his instinct for self-perfection—for leading a virtuous life that satisfied the demands of his spirit (or, as one used to say, his soul)—and that the free exercise of such individual virtue would aggregate into a just society.

Now, it is important to realize that, though these aims were in one sense more ambitious than any previously set forth by a political ideology, in another sense they were far more modest. Whereas, as Joseph Cropsey has pointed out, Adam Smith defined "prudence" democratically as "the care of the health, of the fortune, of the rank of the individual," Aristotle had defined that term aristocratically, to mean "the quality of mind concerned with things just and noble and good for man." By this standard, all pre-capitalist systems had been, to one degree or another, Aristotelian: they were interested in creating a high and memorable civilization even if this were shared only by a tiny minority. In contrast, capitalism lowered its sights, but offered its shares in bourgeois civilization to the entire citizenry. Tocqueville, as usual, astutely caught this difference between the aristocratic civilizations of the past and the new liberal capitalism he saw emerging in the United States:

> In aristocratic societies the class that gives the tone to opinion and has the guidance of affairs, being permanently and hereditarily placed above the multitude, naturally conceives a lofty idea of itself and man. It loves to invent for him noble pleasures, to carve out splendid objects for his

ambition. Aristocracies often commit very tyrannical and inhuman actions, but they rarely entertain groveling thoughts. . . .

In democracies, in contrast there is little energy of character but customs are mild and laws humane. If there are few instances of exalted heroism or of virtues of the highest, brightest, and purest temper, men's habits are regular, violence is rare, and cruelty almost unknown. . . . Genius becomes rare, information more diffused. . . . There is less perfection, but more abundance, in all the productions of the arts.

It is because "high culture" inevitably has an aristocratic bias—it would not be "high" if it did not—that, from the beginnings of the capitalist era, it has always felt contempt for the bourgeois mode of existence. That mode of existence purposively depreciated the very issues that were its *raison d'être*. It did so by making them, as no society had ever dared or desired to do, matters of personal taste, according to the prescription of Adam Smith in his *Theory of Moral Sentiments*:

Though you despise that picture, or that poem, or even that system of philosophy, which I admire, there is little danger of our quarreling upon that account. Neither of us can reasonably be much interested about them. They ought all of them to be matters of great indifference to us both; so that, though our opinions may be opposite, our affections shall be very nearly the same.

In short, an amiable philistinism was inherent in bourgeois society, and this was bound to place its artists and intellectuals in an antagonistic posture toward it. This antagonism was irrepressible—the bourgeois world could not suppress it without violating its own liberal creed; the artists could not refrain from expressing their hostility without denying their most authentic selves. But the conflict could, and was, contained so long as capitalist civilization delivered on its three basic promises. It was only when the third promise, of a virtuous life and a just society, was subverted by the dynamics of capitalism itself, as it strove to fulfill the other two—affluence and liberty—that the bourgeois order came, in the minds of the young especially, to possess a questionable legitimacy.

## FROM BOURGEOIS SOCIETY TO A "FREE SOCIETY"

I can think of no better way of indicating the distance that capitalism has travelled from its original ideological origins than by contrasting the most intelligent defender of capitalism today with his predecessors. I refer to Friederich von Hayek, who has as fine and as powerful a mind as is to be found anywhere, and whose *Constitution of Liberty* is one of the most thoughtful works of the last decades. In that book, he offers the following argument against viewing capitalism as a system that incarnates any idea of justice:

Most people will object not to the bare fact of inequality but to the fact that the differences in reward do not correspond to any recognizable differences in the merit of those who receive them. The answer commonly given to this is that a free society on the whole achieves this kind of justice. This, however, is an indefensible contention if by justice is meant proportionality of reward to moral merit. Any attempt to found the case for freedom on this argument is very damaging to it, since it concedes that material rewards ought to be made to correspond to recognizable merit and then opposes the conclusion that most people will draw from this by an assertion which is untrue. The proper answer is that in a free society it is neither desirable nor practicable that material rewards should be made generally to correspond to what men recognize as merit and that it is an essential characteristic of a free society that an individual's position should not necessarily depend on the views that his fellows hold about the merit he has acquired. . . . A society in which the posi-tion of the individual was made to correspond to human ideas of moral merit would therefore be the exact opposite of a free society. It would be a society in which people were rewarded for duty performed instead of for success. . . . But if nobody's knowledge is sufficient to guide all human action, there is also no human being who is competent to reward all efforts according to merit.

This argument is admirable both for its utter candor and for its firm opposition to all those modern authoritarian ideologies, whether rationalist or irrationalist, which give a self-selected elite the right to shape men's lives and fix their destinies according to its preconceived notions of good and evil, merit and demerit. But it is interesting to note what Hayek is doing: he is opposing a *free* society to a *just* society—because, he says, while we know what freedom is, we have no generally accepted knowledge of what justice is. Elsewhere he writes:

> Since they [i.e., differentials in wealth and income] are not the effect of anyone's design or intentions, it is meaningless to describe the manner in which the market distributed the good things of this world among particular people as just or unjust. . . . No test or criteria have been found or can be found by which such rules of "social justice" can be assessed. . . . They would have to be determined by the arbitrary will of the holders of power.

Now, it may be that this is the best possible defense that can be made of a free society. But if this is the case, one can fairly say that "capitalism" is (or was) one thing, and a "free society" another. For capitalism, during the first hundred years or so of its existence, did lay claim to being a just social order, in the meaning later given to that concept by Paul Elmer More: ". . .Such a distribution of power and privilege, and of property as the symbol and instrument of these, as at once will satisfy the distinctions of reason among the superior, and will not outrage the feelings of the inferior." As a matter of fact, capitalism at its apogee saw itself as the most just social order the world has ever witnessed, because it replaced all arbitrary (e.g., inherited) distributions of power, privilege, and property with a distribution that was directly and intimately linked to personal merit—this latter term being inclusive of both personal abilities and personal virtues.

Writing shortly before the Civil War, George Fitzhugh, the most gifted of Southern apologists for slavery, attacked the capitalist North in these terms:

> In a free society none but the selfish virtues are in repute, because none other help a man in the race of competition. In such a society virtue loses all her loveliness, because of her selfish aims. Good men and bad men have the same end in view—self-promotion and self-elevation. . . .

At the time, this accusation was a half-truth. The North was not yet "a free society" in Hayek's sense or Fitzhugh's. It was still in good measure a bourgeois society in which the capitalist mode of existence involved moral self-discipline and had a visible aura of spiritual grace. It was a society in which "success" was indeed seen as having what Hayek has said it ought never to have: a firm connection with "duty performed." It was a society in which Theodore Parker could write of a leading merchant: "He had no uncommon culture of the understanding or the imagination, and of the higher reason still less. But in respect of the *greater faculties*—in respect of conscience, affection, the religious element—he was well born, well bred." In short, it was a society still permeated by the Puritan ethic, the Protestant ethic, the capitalist ethic—call it what you will. It was a society in which it was agreed that there was a strong correlation between certain personal virtues—frugality, industry, sobriety, reliability, piety—and the way in which power, privilege, and property were distributed. And this correlation was taken to be the sign of a just society, not merely of a free one. Samuel Smiles or Horatio Alger would have regarded Professor Hayek's writings as slanderous of his fellow Christians, blasphemous of God, and ultimately subversive of the social order. I am not sure about the first two of these accusations, but I am fairly certain of the validity of the last.

This is not the place to recount the history and eventual degradation of the capitalist ethic in America. Suffice it to say that, with every passing decade, Fitzhugh's charge, that "virtue loses all her loveliness, because of her selfish aims," became more valid. From having been a *capitalist, republican community*, with shared values and a quite unambiguous claim to the title of a just order, the United States became a *free, democratic society* where the will to success and privilege was severed from its moral moorings.

## THREE CURRENT APOLOGIA

But can men live in a free society if they have no reason to believe it is also a just society? I do not think so. My reading of history is that, in the same way as men cannot for long tolerate a sense of spiritual meaninglessness in their individual lives, so they cannot for long accept a society in which power, privilege, and property are not distributed according to some morally meaningful criteria. Nor is equality itself any more acceptable than inequality—neither is more "natural" than the other—if equality is merely a brute fact rather than a consequence of an ideology or social philosophy. This explains what otherwise seems paradoxical: that small inequalities in capitalist countries can become the source of intense controversy while relatively larger inequalities in socialist or communist countries are blandly overlooked. Thus, those same young radicals who are infuriated by trivial inequalities in the American economic system are quite blind to grosser inequalities in the Cuban system. This is usually taken as evidence of hypocrisy or self-deception. I would say it shows, rather, that people's notions of equality or inequality have extraordinarily little to do with arithmetic and almost everything to do with political philosophy.

I believe that what holds for equality also holds for liberty. People feel free when they subscribe to a prevailing social philosophy; they feel unfree when the prevailing social philosophy is unpersuasive; and the existence of constitutions or laws or judiciaries have precious little to do with these basic feelings. The average working man in nineteenth-century America had far fewer "rights" than his counterpart today; but he was far more likely to boast about his being a free man.

So I conclude, despite Professor Hayek's ingenious analysis, that men cannot accept the historical accidents of the marketplace—seen merely as accidents—as the basis for an enduring and legitimate entitlement to power, privilege, and property. And, in actual fact, Professor Hayek's rationale for modern capitalism is never used outside a small academic enclave; I even suspect it cannot be believed except by those whose minds have been shaped by overlong exposure to scholasticism. Instead, the arguments offered to justify the social structure of capitalism now fall into three main categories:

1) *The Protestant Ethic*–This, however, is now reserved for the lower socioeconomic levels. It is still believed, and it is still reasonable to believe, that worldly success among the working class, lower-middle class, and even middle class has a definite connection with personal virtues such as diligence, rectitude, sobriety, honest ambition, etc., etc. And, so far as I can see, the connection is not only credible but demonstrable. It does seem that the traditional bourgeois virtues are efficacious among these classes—at least, it is rare to find successful men emerging from these classes who do not to a significant degree exemplify them. But no one seriously claims that these traditional virtues will open the corridors of corporate power to anyone, or that the men who now occupy the executive suites are—or even aspire to be—models of bourgeois virtue.

2) *The Darwinian Ethic*—This is to be found mainly among small businessmen who are fond of thinking that their "making it" is to be explained as "the survival of the fittest." They are frequently quite right, of course, in believing the metaphor appropriate to their condition and to the ways in which they achieved it. But it is preposterous to think that the mass of men will ever accept as legitimate a social order formed in accordance with the laws of the jungle. Men may be animals, but they are political animals—and, what comes to not such a different thing, moral animals too. The fact that for several decades after the Civil War, the Darwinian ethic, as popularized by Herbert Spencer, could be taken seriously by so many social theorists represents one of the most bizarre and sordid episodes in American intellectual history. It could not last; and did not.

3) *The Technocratic Ethic*—This is the most prevalent justification of corporate capitalism today, and finds expression in an insistence on "performance." Those who occupy the seats of

corporate power, and enjoy the prerogatives and privileges thereof, are said to acquire legitimacy by their superior ability to achieve superior "performance"—in economic growth, managerial efficiency, technological innovation. In a sense, what is claimed is that these men are accomplishing social tasks, and fulfilling social responsibilities, in an especially efficacious way.

There are, however, two fatal flaws in this argument. First, if one defines "performance" in a strictly limited and measurable sense, then one is applying a test that any ruling class is bound, on fairly frequent occasions, to fail. Life has its ups and downs; so do history and economics, and men who can only claim legitimacy *via* performance are going to have to spend an awful lot of time and energy explaining why things are not going as well as they ought to. Such repeated, defensive apologias, in the end, will be hollow and unconvincing. Indeed, the very concept of "legitimacy," in its historical usages, is supposed to take account of and make allowances for all those rough passages a society will have to navigate. If the landed gentry of Britain during those centuries of its dominance, or the business class in the United States during the first century and a half of our national history, had insisted that it be judged by performance alone, it would have flunked out of history. So would every other ruling class that ever existed.

Secondly, if one tries to avoid this dilemma by giving the term "performance" a broader and larger meaning, then one inevitably finds oneself passing beyond the boundaries of bourgeois propriety. It is one thing to say with Samuel Johnson that men honestly engaged in business are doing the least mischief than men are capable of; it is quite another thing to assert that they are doing the greatest good—this is only too patently untrue. For the achievement of the greatest good, more than successful performance in business is necessary. Witness how vulnerable our corporate managers are to accusations that they are befouling our environment. What these accusations really add up to is the statement that the business system in the United States does not create a beautiful, refined, gracious, and tranquil civilization. To which our corporate leaders are replying: "Oh, we can perform that mission too—just give us time." But there is no good reason to think they can accomplish this noncapitalist mission; nor is there any reason to believe that they have any proper entitlement even to try.

### *"PARTICIPATION" OR LEADERSHIP?*

It is, I think, because of the decline of the bourgeois ethic, and the consequent drainage of legitimacy out of the business system, that the issue of "participation" has emerged with such urgency during these past years. It is a common error to take this word at its face value—to assume that, in our organized and bureaucratized society, the average person is more isolated, alienated, or powerless than ever before, and that the proper remedy is to open new avenues of "participation." We are then perplexed when, the avenues having been open, we find so little traffic passing through. We give college students the right to representation on all sorts of committees—and then discover they never bother to come to meetings. We create new popularly-elected "community" organizations in the ghettos—and then discover that ghetto residents won't come out to vote. We decentralize New York City's school system—only to discover that the populace is singularly uninterested in local school board elections.

I doubt very much that the average American is actually more isolated or powerless today than in the past. The few serious studies that have been made on this subject indicate that we have highly romanticized notions of the past—of the degree to which ordinary people were ever involved in community activities—and highly apocalyptic notions of the present. If one takes membership in civic-minded organizations as a criterion, people are unquestionably more "involved" today than ever before in our history. Maybe that's not such a good criterion; but it is a revealing aspect of this whole problem that those who make large statements on this matter rarely give us any workable or testable criteria at all.

But I would not deny that more people, even if more specifically "involved" than ever before, also feel more "alienated" in a general way. And this, I would suggest, is because the institutions of our society have lost their vital connection with the values which are supposed to govern the private lives of our citizenry. They no longer exemplify these values; they no longer magnify them; they no longer reassuringly sustain them. When it is said that the institutions of our society have become appallingly "impersonal," I take this to mean that they have lost any shape that is congruent with the private moral codes which presumably govern individual life. (That presumption, of course, may be factually weak; but it is nonetheless efficacious so long as people hold it.) The "outside" of our social life has ceased being harmonious with the "inside"—the mode of distribution of power, privilege, and property, and hence the very principle of authority, no longer "makes sense" to the bewildered citizen. And when institutions cease to "make sense" in this way, all the familiar criteria of success or failure become utterly irrelevant.

As I see it, then, the demand for "participation" is best appreciated as a demand for authority—for leadership that holds the promise of reconciling the inner and outer worlds of the citizen. So far from its being a hopeful reawakening of the democratic spirit, it signifies a hunger for authority that leads toward some kind of plebiscitary democracy at best, and is in any case not easy to reconcile with liberal democracy as we traditionally have known it. I find it instructive that such old-fashioned populists as Hubert Humphrey and Edmund Muskie, whose notions of "participation" are both liberal and traditional, fail to catch the imagination of our dissidents in the way that Robert Kennedy did. The late Senator Kennedy was very much a leader—one can imagine Humphrey or Muskie participating in an old-fashioned town meeting, one can only envision Kennedy dominating a town rally. One can also envision those who "participated" in such a rally feeling that they had achieved a kind of "representation" previously denied them.

## A CASE OF REGRESSION

For a system of liberal, representative government to work, free elections are not enough. The results of the political process and of the exercise of individual freedom—the distribution of power, privilege, and property—must also be seen as in some profound sense expressive of the values that govern the lives of individuals. An idea of self-government, if it is to be viable, must encompass both the private and the public sectors. If it does not—if the principles that organize public life seem to have little relation to those that shape private lives—you have "alienation," and *anomie*, and a melting away of established principles of authority.

Milton Friedman, arguing in favor of Hayek's extreme libertarian position, has written that the free man "recognizes no national purpose except as it is the consensus of the purposes for which the citizens severally strive." If he is using the term "consensus" seriously, then he must be assuming that there is a strong homogeneity of values among the citizenry, and that these values give a certain corresponding shape to the various institutions of society, political and economic. Were that the case, then it is indeed true that a "national purpose" arises automatically and organically out of the social order itself. Something like this did happen when liberal capitalism was in its prime, vigorous and self-confident. But is that our condition today? I think not—just as I think Mr. Friedman doesn't really mean "consensus" but rather the mere aggregation of selfish aims. In such a blind and accidental arithmetic, the sum floats free from the addenda, and its legitimacy is infinitely questionable.

The inner spiritual chaos of the times, so powerfully created by the dynamics of capitalism itself, is such as to make nihilism an easy temptation. A "free society" in Hayek's sense gives birth in massive numbers to "free spirits"—emptied of moral substance but still driven by primordial moral aspirations. Such people are capable of the most irrational actions. Indeed, it is my impression that, under the strain of modern life, whole classes of our population—and the educated classes most of all—are entering what can only be called, in the strictly clinical sense, a phase of infantile regression. With every passing year, public discourse becomes sillier and more petulant, while human emotions become, apparently, more ungovernable. Some of our most intelligent university professors are now loudly saying things that, had they been uttered by one of their students twenty years ago, would have called forth gentle and urbane reproof.

## THE REFORMING SPIRIT AND THE CONSERVATIVE IDEAL

And yet, if the situation of liberal capitalism today seems so precarious, it is likely nevertheless to survive for a long while, if only because the modern era has failed to come up with any plausible alternatives. Socialism, communism, and fascism have all turned out to be either utopian illusions or sordid frauds. So we shall have time—though not an endless amount of it, for we have already wasted a great deal. We are today in a situation not very different from that described by Herbert Croly in *The Promise of American Life* (1912):

> The substance of our national Promise has consisted . . . of an improving popular economic condition, guaranteed by democratic political institutions, and resulting in moral and social amelioration. These manifold benefits were to be obtained merely by liberating the enlightened self-enterprise of the American people. . . . The fulfillment of the American Promise was considered inevitable because it was based upon a combination of self-interest and the natural goodness of human nature. On the other hand, if the fulfillment of our national Promise can no longer be considered inevitable, if it must be considered as equivalent to a conscious national purpose instead of an inexorable national destiny, the implication necessarily is that the trust reposed in individual self-interest has been in some measure betrayed. No pre-established harmony can then exist between the free and abundant satisfaction of private needs and the accomplishment of a morally and socially desirable result.

Croly is not much read these days. He was a liberal reformer with essentially conservative goals. So was Matthew Arnold, fifty years earlier—and he isn't much read these days, either. Neither of them can pass into the conventional anthologies of liberal or conservative thought. I think this is a sad commentary on the ideological barrenness of the liberal and conservative creeds. I also think it is a great pity. For if our private and public worlds are ever again, in our lifetimes, to have a congenial relationship—if virtue is to regain her lost loveliness—then some such combination of the reforming spirit with the conservative ideal seems to me to be what is most desperately wanted.

I use the word "conservative" advisedly. Though the discontents of our civilization express themselves in the rhetoric of "liberation" and "equality," one can detect beneath the surface an acute yearning for order and stability—but a legitimate order, of course, and a legitimized stability. In this connection, I find the increasing skepticism as to the benefits of economic growth and technological innovation most suggestive. Such skepticism has been characteristic of conservative critics of liberal capitalism since the beginning of the nineteenth century. One finds it in Coleridge, Carlyle, and Newman—in all those who found it impossible to acquiesce in a "progressive" notion of human history or social evolution. Our dissidents today may think they are exceedingly progressive; but no one who puts greater emphasis on "the quality of life" than on "mere" material enrichment can properly be placed in that category. For the idea of progress in the modern era has always signified that the quality of life would inevitably be improved by material enrichment. To doubt this is to doubt the political metaphysics of modernity and to start the long trek back to pre-modern political philosophy—Plato, Aristotle, Thomas Aquinas, Hooker, Calvin, etc. It seems to me that this trip is quite necessary. Perhaps there we shall discover some of those elements that are most desperately needed by the spiritually impoverished civilization that we have constructed on what once seemed to be sturdy bourgeois foundations.

# Selections from the *German Ideology*, Part I

## Karl Marx (1818–1883)
## Frederick Engels (1820–1895)

*Just two years before the promulgation of the* Communist Manifesto, *Marx and Engels collaborated on this work, their "critique of the latest German philosophy . . . and of German Socialism." Here they set forth their most comprehensive statement of what they call the "materialist conception of history" that grounds the Marxian vision of the proletarian revolution and the coming of communist society. Though they submitted the work for publication in 1846, they "abandoned the manuscript to the gnawing criticism of the mice," and it was not published until 1932.*

*In this selection, Marx and Engels present an outline of their analysis of the history of mankind, including a rare forecast of the end of history, life in a fully developed communist society. How does this view of the nature of man (or the lack thereof) differ from those of Plutarch's Lycurgus, Aristotle, Locke, or Smith? What is the significance of history for Marx and Engels? What would it mean for history to come to an end? Do they view the beginnings of human society differently from Aristotle? From Locke and Smith? Consider their criticism of the division of labor in light of Smith's praise of this economic practice.*

. . . We must begin by stating the first premise of all human existence and, therefore, of all history, the premise, namely, that men must be in a position to live in order to be able to "make history." But life involves before everything else eating and drinking, housing, clothing and various other things. The first historical act is thus the production of the means to satisfy these needs, the production of material life itself. And indeed this is an historical act, a fundamental condition of all history, which today, as thousands of years ago, must daily and hourly be fulfilled merely in order to sustain human life. . . .

The second point is that the satisfaction of the first need, the action of satisfying and the instrument of satisfaction which has been acquired, leads to new needs; and this creation of new needs is the first historical act. . . .

The third circumstance which, from the very outset, enters into historical development, is that men, who daily re-create their own life, begin to make other men, to propagate their kind: the relation between man and woman, parents and children, the *family*. The family, which to begin with is the only social relation, becomes later, when increased needs create new social relations and the increased population new needs, a subordinate one . . .

These three aspects of social activity are not of course to be taken as three different stages, but just as three aspects or, to make it clear to the Germans, three "moments" which have existed simultaneously since the dawn of history and the first men, and which still assert themselves in history today.

The production of life, both of one's own in labour and of fresh life in procreation, now appears as a twofold relation: on the one hand as a natural, on the other as a social relation—social in the sense that it denotes the co-operation of several individuals, no matter under what conditions, in what manner and to what end. It follows from this that a certain mode of production, or industrial stage, is always combined with a certain mode of co-operation, or social stage, and this mode of co-operation is itself a "productive force." Further, the aggregate of productive forces accessible to men determines the condition of society, hence, the "history of humanity" must always be studied and treated in relation to the history of industry and exchange. . . . Thus it is quite obvious from the start that there exists a materialist connection of men with one another, which is determined by their needs and their mode of production, and which is as old as men themselves. This connection is ever taking on new forms, and thus presents a "history" irrespective of the existence of any political or religious nonsense which would especially hold men together.

Only now, after having considered four moments, four aspects of primary historical relations, do we find that man also possesses "consciousness." But even from the outset this is not "pure" consciousness. The "mind" is from the outset afflicted with the curse of being "burdened" with matter, which here makes its appearance in the form of agitated layers of air, sounds, in short, of language. Language is as old as consciousness, language *is* practical, real consciousness that exists for other men as well, and only therefore does it also exist for me; language, like consciousness, only arises from the need, the necessity, of intercourse with other men. Where there exists a relationship, it exists for me: the animal does not "*relate*" itself to anything, it does not "*relate*" itself at all. For the animal its relation to other does not exist as a relation. Consciousness is, therefore, from the very beginning a social product, and remains so as long as men exist at all. Consciousness is at first, of course, merely consciousness concerning the *immediate* sensuous environment and consciousness of the limited connection with other persons and things outside the individual who is growing self-conscious. At the same time it is consciousness of nature, which first confronts men as a completely alien, all-powerful and unassailable force, with which men's relations are purely animal and by which they are overawed like beasts; it is thus a purely animal consciousness of nature (natural religion) precisely because nature is as yet hardly altered by history—on the other hand, it is man's consciousness of the necessity of associating with the individuals around him, the beginning of the consciousness that he is living in society at all. This beginning is as animal as social life itself at this stage. It is mere herd-consciousness, and at this point man is distinguished from sheep only by the fact that with him consciousness takes the place of instinct or that his instinct is a conscious one. This sheep-like or tribal consciousness receives its further development and extension through increased productivity, the increase of needs, and, what is fundamental to both of these, the increase of population. With these there develops the division of labour, which was originally nothing but the division of labour in the sexual act, then the division of labour which develops spontaneously or "naturally" by virtue of natural predisposition (e.g., physical strength), needs, accidents, etc., etc. Division of labour only becomes truly such from the moment when a division of material and mental labour appears. From this moment onwards consciousness *can* really flatter itself that it is something other than consciousness of existing practice, that it *really* represents something without representing something real; from now on consciousness is in a position to emancipate itself from the world and to proceed to the formation of "pure" theory, theology, philosophy, morality, etc. But even if this theory, theology, philosophy, morality, etc., come into contradiction with the existing relations, this can only occur because existing social relations have come into contradiction with existing productive forces . . .

The division of labour in which all these contradictions are implicit, and which in its turn is based on the natural division of labour in the family and the separation of society into individual families opposed to one another, simultaneously implies the *distribution*, and indeed the *unequal* distribution, both quantitative and qualitative, of labour and its products, hence property, the nucleus, the first form of which lies in the family, where wife and children are the slaves of the husband. This latent slavery in the family, though still very crude, is the first form of property, but even at this stage it corresponds perfectly to the definition of modern economists, who call it the power of disposing of the labour-power of others. Division of labour and private property are, after all, identical expressions: in the one the same thing is affirmed with reference to activity as is affirmed in the other with reference to the product of the activity.

Further, the division of labour also implies the contradiction between the interest of the separate individual or the individual family and the common interest of all individuals who have intercourse with one another. And indeed, this common interest does not exist merely in the imagination, as the "general interest," but first of all in reality, as the mutual interdependence of the individuals among whom the labour is divided.

Out of this very contradiction between the particular and the common interests, the common interest assumes an independent form as the *state*, which is divorced from the real individual and collective interests, and at the same time as an illusory community, always based, however, on the real ties existing in every family conglomeration and tribal conglomeration—such as flesh and blood, language, division of labour on a larger scale, and other interests—and especially, as we shall show later, on the classes, already implied by the division of labour, which in every such mass of men separate out, and one of which dominates all the others. It follows from this that all struggles within the state, the struggle between democracy, aristocracy, and monarchy, the struggle for the franchise, etc., etc., are merely the illusory forms—altogether the general interest is the illusory form of common interests—in which the real struggles of the different classes are fought out among one another . . . Further, it follows that every class which is aiming at domination, even when its domination, as is the case with the proletariat, leads to the abolition of the old form of society in its entirety and of domination in general, must first conquer political power in order to represent its interest in turn as the general interest, which in the first moment it is forced to do.

Just because individuals seek *only* their particular interest, which for them does not coincide with their common interest, the latter is asserted as an interest "alien" ["*fremd*"] to them, and "independent" of them, as in its turn a particular and distinctive "general" interest; or they themselves must remain within this discord, as in democracy. On the other hand, too, the *practical* struggle of these particular interests, which *actually* constantly run counter to the common and illusory common interests necessitates *practical* intervention and restraint by the illusory "general" interest in the form of the state.

And finally, the division of labour offers us the first example of the fact that, as long as man remains in naturally evolved society, that is, as long as a cleavage exists between the particular and the common interest, as long, therefore, as activity is not voluntarily, but naturally, divided, man's own need becomes an alien power opposed to him, which enslaves him instead of being controlled by him. For as soon as the division of labour comes into being, each man has a particular, exclusive sphere of activity, which is forced upon him and from which he cannot escape. He is a hunter, a fisherman, a shepherd, or a critical critic, and he must remain so if he does not want to lose his means of livelihood; whereas in communist society, where nobody has one exclusive sphere of activity but each can become accomplished in any branch he wishes, society regulates the general production and thus makes it possible for me to do one thing today and another tomorrow, to hunt in the morning, fish in the afternoon, rear cattle in the evening, criticise after dinner, just as I have a mind, without ever becoming hunter, fisherman, shepherd or critic.

This fixation of social activity, this consolidation of what we ourselves produce into a material power above us, growing out of our control, thwarting our expectations, bringing to naught our calculations, is one of the chief factors in historical development up till now. The social power, i.e., the multiplied productive force, which arises through the co-operation of different individuals as it is caused by the division of labour, appears to these individuals, since their co-operation is not voluntary but has come about naturally, not as their own united power, but as an alien force existing outside them, of the origin and goal of which they are ignorant, which they thus are no longer able to control, which on the contrary passes through a peculiar series of phases and stages independent of the will and the action of man, nay even being the prime governor of these. . . .

. . . This "estrangement" *[Entfremdung]* (to use a term which will be comprehensible to the philosophers) can, of course, only be abolished given two *practical* premises. In order to become an "unendurable" power, i.e., a power against which men make a revolution, it must necessarily have rendered the great mass of humanity "propertyless," and moreover in contradiction to an existing world of wealth and culture; both these premises presuppose a great increase in productive power, a high degree of its development. And, on the other hand, this development of productive forces (which at the same time implies the actual empirical existence of men in their *world-historical*, instead of local, being) is an absolutely necessary practical premise, because without it privation, *want* is merely made general, and with *want* the struggle for necessities would begin again, and all the old filthy business would necessarily be restored; and furthermore, because only with this universal development of productive forces is a *universal* intercourse between men established, which on the one side produces in *all* nations simultaneously the phenomenon of the "propertyless" mass (universal competition), making each nation dependent on the revolutions of the others, and finally puts *world-historical*, empirically universal individuals in place of local ones. Without this, 1) communism could only exist as a local phenomenon; 2) the forces of intercourse themselves could not have developed as *universal*, hence unendurable powers: they would have remained home-bred "conditions" surrounded by superstition; and 3) each extension of intercourse would abolish local communism. Empirically, communism is only possible as the act of the dominant peoples "all at once" and simultaneously, which presupposes the universal development of productive forces and the world intercourse bound up with them.

Moreover, the mass of workers who are *nothing but workers*—labour-power on a mass scale cut off from capital or from even a limited satisfaction [of their needs] and, hence, as a result of competition their utterly precarious position, the no longer merely temporary loss of work as a secure source of life—presupposes the *world market*. The proletariat can thus only exist *world-historically*, just as communism, its activity, can only have a "world-historical" existence. World-historical existence of individuals, i.e., existence of individuals which is directly linked up with world history.

Communism is for us not a *state of affairs* which is to be established, an *ideal* to which reality [will] have to adjust itself. We call communism the *real* movement which abolishes the present state of things. . . .

. . . In history up to the present it is certainly likewise an empirical fact that separate individuals have, with the broadening of their activity into world-historical activity, become more and more enslaved under a power alien to them ( a pressure which they have conceived of as a dirty trick on the part of the so-called world spirit, etc.), a power which has become more and more enormous and, in the last instance, turns out to be the *world market*. But it is just as empirically established that, by the overthrow of the existing state of society by the communist revolution (of which more below) and the abolition of private property which is identical with it, this power, which so baffles the German theoreticians, will be dissolved; and that then the liberation of each single individual will be accomplished in the measure in which history becomes wholly transformed into world history. From the above it is clear that the real intellectual wealth of the individual depends entirely on the wealth of his real connections. Only this will liberate the separate individuals from the various national and local barriers, bring them into practical connection with the production (including intellectual production) of the whole world and make it possible for them to acquire the capacity to enjoy this all-sided production of the whole earth (the creations of man). *All-round* dependence, this primary natural form of the *world-historical* co-operation of individuals, will be transformed by this communist revolution into the control and conscious mastery of these powers, which, born of the action of men on one another, have till now overawed and ruled men as powers completely alien to them. . . .

# Selections from *State and Revolution*

## V.I. Lenin (1870–1924)

*As is indicated by Lenin's postscript to* State and Revolution, *it was written on the eve of the Russian Revolution. Its author became the founder and first leader of the new Soviet order. Lenin was no newcomer to the revolutionary movement in Russia; he had been an active revolutionary since the late nineteenth century and took a large part in the failed uprising of 1905 as a leader of the newly formed Bolshevik (majority) wing of the Russian Social Democratic Party.* State and Revolution *lays out his understanding of the political actions necessitated by a Marxian revolution, especially in Russia, but generally in any country.*

*Consider whether Lenin is successful in translating Marxian theories of history and politics into a workable program of revolutionary practice. Why does he demand a small group of educated and committed leaders at the head of the masses? What actions must the leaders perform after the seizure of power?*

*Compare Lenin with Lycurgus and with Jefferson and the Federalists as founders of new regimes. What were their primary aims? Why did they believe they could succeed? Did they succeed?*

### POSTSCRIPT TO THE FIRST EDITION

This pamphlet was written in August and September, 1917 . . . However, the second part of the pamphlet (devoted to the "Experience of the Russian Revolutions of 1905 and 1917") will probably have to be put off for a long time. It is more pleasant and useful to go through the "experience of the revolution" than to write about it.

### CHAPTER I:     CLASS SOCIETY AND THE STATE

#### 1.   The State as the Product of the Irreconcilability of Class Antagonisms

What is now happening to Marx's doctrine has, in the course of history, often happened to the doctrines of other revolutionary thinkers and leaders of oppressed classes struggling for emancipation. During the lifetime of great revolutionaries, the oppressing classes have visited relentless persecution on them and received their teaching with the most savage hostility, the most furious hatred, the most ruthless campaign of lies and slanders. After their death, attempts are made to turn them into harmless icons, canonize them, and surround their *names* with a certain halo for the "consolation" of the oppressed classes and with the object of duping them, while at the same time emasculating and vulgarizing the *real essence* of their revolutionary theory and blunting their revolutionary edge. At the present time, the bourgeoisie and the opportunists within the labour movement are co-operating in this work of adulterating Marxism. They omit, obliterate, and distort the revolutionary side of its teaching, its revolutionary soul. They push to the foreground and extol what is, or seems, acceptable to the bourgeoisie. . . .

In such circumstances, the distortion of Marxism being so widespread, it is our first task to *resuscitate* the real teachings of Marx on the state. For this purpose it will be necessary to quote at length from the works of Marx and Engels themselves. . . .

Let us begin with the most popular of Engels' works, *The Origin of the Family, Private Property, and the State*. . . .

Summarizing his historical analysis Engels says:

> The state is therefore by no means a power imposed on society from the outside; just as little is it "the reality of the moral idea," "the image and reality of reason," as Hegel asserted. Rather, it is a product of society at a certain stage of development; it is the admission that this society has become entangled in an insoluble contradiction with itself, that it is cleft into irreconcilable antagonisms which it is powerless to dispel. But in order that these antagonisms, classes with conflicting economic interests, may not consume themselves and society in sterile struggle, a power apparently standing above society becomes necessary, whose purpose is to moderate the conflict and keep it within the bounds of "order"; and this power arising out of society, but placing itself above it, and increasingly separating itself from it, is the state.

Here we have, expressed in all its clearness, the basic idea of Marxism on the question of the historical role and meaning of the state. The state is the product and the manifestation of the *irreconcilability* of class antagonisms. The state arises when, where, and to the extent that the class antagonisms *cannot* be objectively reconciled. And, conversely, the existence of the state proves that the class antagonisms *are* irreconcilable.

It is precisely on this most important and fundamental point that distortions of Marxism arise along two main lines.

On the one hand, the bourgeois, and particularly the petty bourgeois, ideologists, compelled under the pressure of indisputable historical facts to admit that the state only exists where there are class antagonisms and the class struggle, "correct" Marx in such a way as to make it appear that the state is an organ for *reconciling* the classes. According to Marx, the state could neither arise nor maintain itself if a reconciliation of classes were possible. But with the petty-bourgeois and philistine professors and publicists, the state—and this frequently on the strength of benevolent references to Marx!—becomes a conciliator of the classes. According to Marx, the state is an organ of class *domination*, an organ of *oppression* of one class by another; its aim is the creation of "order" which legalizes and perpetuates this oppression by moderating the collisions between the classes. . . .

If the state is the product of the irreconcilable character of class antagonisms, if it is a force standing *above* society and "increasingly separating itself from it," then it is clear that the liberation of the oppressed class is impossible not only without a violent revolution, *but also without the destruction* of the apparatus of state power, which was created by the ruling class and in which this "separation" is embodied. . . .

## 2. Special Bodies of Armed Men, Prisons, Etc.

Engels develops the conception of that "power" which is termed the state—a power arising from society, but placing itself above it and becoming more and more separated from it. What does this power mainly consist of? It consists of special bodies of armed men who have at their disposal prisons, etc.

We are justified in speaking of special bodies of armed men, because the public power peculiar to every state is not "absolutely identical" with the armed population, with its "self-acting armed organization."

Like all the great revolutionary thinkers, Engels tries to draw the attention of the class-conscious workers to that very fact which to prevailing philistinism appears least of all worthy of attention, most common and sanctified by solid, indeed, one might say, petrified prejudices. A standing army and police are the chief instruments of state power. But can this be otherwise? . . .

Here the question regarding the privileged position of the officials as organs of state power is clearly stated. The main point is indicated as follows: what is it that places them *above* society? . . .

### 3. The State as an Instrument for the Exploitation of the Oppressed Class

As the state arose out of the need to hold class antagonisms in check; but as it, at the same time, arose in the midst of the conflict of these classes, it is, as a rule, the state of the most powerful, economically dominant class, which by virtue thereof becomes also the dominant class politically, and thus acquires new means of holding down and exploiting the oppressed class. . . .

Not only the ancient and feudal states were organs of exploitation of the slaves and serfs, but

the modern representative state is the instrument of the exploitation of wage-labour by capital. By way of exception, however, there are periods when the warring classes so nearly attain equilibrium that the state power, ostensibly appearing as a mediator, assumes for the moment a certain independence in relation to both. . . .

In a democratic republic, Engels continues, "wealth wields its power indirectly, but all the more effectively," first, by means of "direct corruption of the officials" (America); second, by means of "the alliance of the government with the stock exchange" (France and America).

At the present time, imperialism and the domination of the banks have "developed" to an unusually fine art both these methods of defending and asserting the omnipotence of wealth in democratic republics of all descriptions. . . .

We must also note that Engels quite definitely regards universal suffrage as a means of bourgeois domination. Universal suffrage, he says, obviously summing up the long experience of German Social-Democracy, is "an index of the maturity of the working class; it cannot, and never will, be anything else but that in the modern state."

A general summary of his views is given by Engels in the most popular of his works in the following words:

The state, therefore, has not existed from all eternity. There have been societies which managed without it, which had no conception of the state and state power. At a certain stage of economic development, which was necessarily bound up with the cleavage of society into classes, the state became a necessity owing to this cleavage. We are now rapidly approaching a stage in the development of production at which the existence of these classes has not only ceased to be a necessity, but is becoming a positive hindrance to production. They will disappear as inevitably as they arose at an earlier stage. Along with them, the state will inevitably disappear. The society that organizes production anew on the basis of a free and equal association of the producers will put the whole state machine where it will then belong: in the museum of antiquities, side by side with the spinning wheel and the bronze axe. . . .

### 4. The "Withering Away" of the State and Violent Revolution

Engels' words regarding the "withering away" of the state enjoy such popularity, they are so often quoted, and they show so clearly the essence of the usual adulteration by means of which Marxism is made to look like opportunism, that we must dwell on them in detail. Let us quote the whole passage from which they are taken.

The proletariat seizes state power, and then transforms the means of production into state property. But in doing this, it puts an end to itself as the proletariat, it puts an end to all class differences and class antagonisms, it puts an end also to the state as the state. Former society, moving in class antagonisms, had need of the state, that is, an organization of the exploiting class at each period for the maintenance of its external conditions of production; therefore, in particular, for the forcible holding down of the exploited class in the conditions of oppression (slavery, bondage or serfdom, wage-labour) determined by the existing mode of production. The state was the official representative of society as a whole, its embodiment in a visible corporate body; but it was this only in so far as it was the state of that class which itself, in its epoch, represented society as a whole: in ancient times, the state of the slave-owning citizens; in the Middle Ages, of the feudal nobility; in our epoch, of the bourgeoisie. When ultimately it becomes really representative of society as a whole, it makes itself superfluous. As soon as there is no longer any class of society to be held in subjection; as soon as, along with class domination and the struggle for individual existence based on the former anarchy of production, the collisions and excesses arising from these have also been abolished, there is nothing more to be repressed, and a special repressive force, a state, is no longer necessary. The first act in which the state really comes forward as the representative of society as a whole—the seizure of the means of production in the name of society—is at the same time its last independent act as a state. The interference of a state power in social relations becomes superfluous in one sphere after another, and then becomes dormant of itself. Government over persons is replaced by the administration of things and the direction of the processes of production. The state is not "abolished," *it withers away.* It is from this standpoint that we must appraise the phrase "people's free state"—both its justification at times for agitational purposes, and its ultimate scientific inadequacy—and also the demand of the so-called Anarchists that the state should be abolished overnight. (*Anti-Dühring*)

. . . Engels at the very outset of his argument says that, in assuming state power, the proletariat by that very act "puts an end to the state as the state.". . . Engels speaks here of the destruction of the bourgeois state by the proletarian revolution, while the words about its withering away refer to the remains of *proletarian* statehood *after* the socialist revolution. The bourgeois state does not "wither away," according to Engels, but is "put an end to" by the proletariat in the course of the revolution. What withers away after the revolution is the proletarian state or semi-state.

Secondly, the state is a "special repressive force." This splendid and extremely profound definition of Engels' is given by him here with complete lucidity. It follows from this that the "special repressive force" of the bourgeoisie for the suppression of the proletariat, of the millions of workers by a handful of the rich, must be replaced by a "special repressive force" of the proletariat for the suppression of the bourgeoisie (the dictatorship of the proletariat). It is just this that constitutes the destruction of "the state as the state." It is just this that constitutes the "act" of "the seizure of the means of production in the name of society." And it is obvious that such a substitution of one (proletarian) "special repressive force" for another (bourgeois) "special repressive force" can in no way take place in the form of a "withering away."

Thirdly, as to the "withering away" or, more expressively and colourfully, as to the state "becoming dormant," Engels refers quite clearly and definitely to the period *after* "the seizure of the means of production (by the state) in the name of society," that is, *after* the Socialist revolution. We all know that the political form of the "state" at that time is complete democracy. But it never enters the head of any of the opportunists who shamelessly distort Marx that when Engels speaks here of the state "withering away," or "becoming dormant," he speaks of *democracy.* At first sight this seems very strange. But it is "unintelligible" only to one who has not reflected on the fact that democracy is *also* a state and that, consequently, democracy will *also* disappear when the state disappears. The bourgeois state can only be "put an end to" by a revolution. The state in general, *i.e.,* most complete democracy, can only "wither away."

Fourthly, having formulated his famous proposition that "the state withers away," Engels at once explains concretely that this proposition is directed equally against the opportunists and the Anarchists. . . .

Fifthly, in the same work of Engels, from which every one remembers his argument on the "withering away" of the state, there is also a disquisition on the significance of a violent revolution. The historical analysis of its role becomes, with Engels, a veritable panegyric on violent revolution. This, of course, "no one remembers"; to talk or even to think of the importance of this idea is not considered good form by contemporary Socialist parties, and in the daily propaganda and agitation among the masses it plays no part whatever. Yet it is indissolubly bound up with the "withering away" of the state in one harmonious whole.

Here is Engels' argument:

> . . . That force, however, plays another role (other than that of a diabolical power) in history, a revolutionary role; that, in the words of Marx, it is the midwife of every old society which is pregnant with the new; that it is the instrument with whose aid social movement forces its way through and shatters the dead, fossilized political forms—of this there is not a word in Herr Dühring. It is only with sighs and groans that he admits the possibility that force will perhaps be necessary for the overthrow of the economic system of exploitation—unfortunately! because all use of force, forsooth, demoralizes the person who uses it. And this in spite of the immense moral and spiritual impetus which has resulted from every victorious revolution! . . .

How can this panegyric on violent revolution . . . be combined with the theory of the "withering away" of the state to form one doctrine? . . .

We have already said above and shall show more fully later that the teaching of Marx and Engels regarding the inevitability of a violent revolution refers to the bourgeois state. It *cannot* be replaced by the proletarian state (the dictatorship of the proletariat) through "withering away," but, as a general rule, only through a violent revolution. . . . The necessity of systematically fostering among the masses *this* and just this point of view about violent revolution lies at the root of the *whole* of Marx's and Engels' teaching. . . .

The replacement of the bourgeois by the proletarian state is impossible without a violent revolution. The abolition of the proletarian state, *i.e.*, of all states, is only possible through "withering away."

## CHAPTER II:    THE EXPERIENCES OF 1848-1851

### 1.   On the Eve of Revolution

It is instructive to compare with this general statement of the idea of the state disappearing after classes have disappeared, the statement contained in the *Communist Manifesto*, written by Marx and Engels . . .

> In depicting the most general phases of the development of the proletariat, we traced the more or less veiled civil war, raging within existing society, up to the point where that war breaks out into open revolution, and where the violent overthrow of the bourgeoisie lays the foundation for the sway of the proletariat. . . .

> The proletariat will use its political supremacy to wrest by degrees all capital from the bourgeoisie, to centralize all instruments of production in the hands of the state, *i.e.*, of the proletariat organized as the ruling class; and to increase the total of productive forces as rapidly as possible.

Here we have a formulation of one of the most remarkable and most important ideas of Marxism on the subject of the state, namely, the idea of the "dictatorship of the proletariat" . . . *"the state, i.e., the proletariat organized as the ruling class."* . . .

The doctrine of the class struggle, as applied by Marx to the question of the state and of the Socialist revolution, leads inevitably to the recognition of the *political rule* of the proletariat, of its dictatorship, *i.e.*, of a power shared with none and relying directly upon the armed force of the masses. The overthrow of the bourgeoisie is realizable only by the transformation of the proletariat into the *ruling class*, able to crush the inevitable and desperate resistance of the bourgeoisie, and to organize, for the new economic order, *all* the toiling and exploited masses.

The proletariat needs state power, the centralized organization of force, the organization of violence, both for the purpose of crushing the resistance of the exploiters and for the purpose of *guiding* the great mass of the population—the peasantry, the petty-bourgeoisie, the semi-proletarians—in the work of organizing Socialist economy.

By educating a workers' party, Marxism educates the vanguard of the proletariat, capable of assuming power and of *leading the whole people* to Socialism, of directing and organizing the new order, of being the teacher, guide and leader of all the toiling and exploited in the task of building up their social life without the bourgeoisie and against the bourgeoisie. . . .

But, if the proletariat needs the state, as a *special* form of organization of violence *against* the capitalist class, the following question arises almost automatically: is it thinkable that such an organization can be created without a preliminary break-up and destruction of the state machinery created for *its own* use by the bourgeoisie? The *Communist Manifesto* leads straight to this conclusion. . . .

## 2. Results of the Revolution

The problem of the state is put concretely: how did the bourgeois state, the state machinery necessary for the rule of the bourgeoisie, come into being? What were its changes, what its evolution in the course of the bourgeois revolutions and in the face of the independent actions of the oppressed classes? What are the tasks of the proletariat relative to this state machinery?

The centralized state power peculiar to bourgeois society came into being in the period of the fall of absolutism. Two institutions are especially characteristic of this state machinery: bureaucracy and the standing army. . . .

The development, perfecting and strengthening of the bureaucratic and military apparatus has been going on through all the bourgeois revolutions of which Europe has seen so many since the fall of feudalism. It is particularly the petty-bourgeoisie that is attracted to the side of the big bourgeoisie and to its allegiance, largely by means of this apparatus, which provides the upper strata of the peasantry, small artisans and tradesmen with a number of comparatively comfortable, quiet and respectable berths raising their holders *above* the people. . . .

But the longer the process of "re-apportioning" the bureaucratic apparatus among the various bourgeois and petty-bourgeois parties (among the Cadets, S.-R.'s and Mensheviks, if we take the case of Russia) goes on, the more clearly the oppressed classes, with the proletariat at their head, realize that they are irreconcilably hostile to the *whole* of bourgeois society. Hence the necessity for all bourgeois parties, even for the most democratic and "revolutionary-democratic" among them, to increase their repressive measures against the revolutionary proletariat, to strengthen the apparatus of repression, *i.e.*, the same state machinery. Such a course of events compels the revolution "*to concentrate all its forces of destruction*" against the state power, and to regard the problem as one, not of perfecting the machinery of the state, but of *breaking up and annihilating it.* . . .

At the present time, world history is undoubtedly leading, on an incomparably larger scale than in 1852, to the "concentration of all the forces" of the proletarian revolution for the purpose of "destroying" the state machinery. . . .

### 3.  The Formulation of the Question by Marx in 1852

In 1907 Mehring published . . . extracts from a letter by Marx to Weydemeyer dated March 5, 1852. In this letter, among other things, is the following noteworthy observation:

> As far as I am concerned, the honour does not belong to me for having discovered the existence either of classes in modern society or of the struggle between the classes. Bourgeois historians a long time before me expounded the historical development of this class struggle, and bourgeois economists, the economic anatomy of classes. What was new on my part, was to prove the following: (1) that the existence of classes is connected only with certain historical struggles which arise out of the development of production [*historische Entwicklungskampfe der Produktion*]; (2) that class struggle necessarily leads to the dictatorship of the proletariat; (3) that this dictatorship is itself only a transition to the abolition of all classes and to a classless society.

. . . The theory of the class struggle was *not* created by Marx, but by the bourgeoisie *before* Marx and is, generally speaking, *acceptable* to the bourgeoisie. He who recognizes *only* the class struggle is not yet a Marxist; he may be found not to have gone beyond the boundaries of bourgeois reasoning and politics. To limit Marxism to the teaching of the class struggle means to curtail Marxism—to distort it, to reduce it to something which is acceptable to the bourgeoisie. A Marxist is one who *extends* the acceptance of class struggle to the acceptance of the *dictatorship of the proletariat.* . . .

The state during this period inevitably must be a state that is democratic *in a new way* (for the proletariat and the poor in general) and dictatorial *in a new way* (against the bourgeoisie).

Further, the substance of the teachings of Marx about the state is assimilated only by one who understands that the dictatorship of a *single* class is necessary not only for any class society generally, not only for the *proletariat* which has overthrown the bourgeoisie, but for the entire *historic period* which separates capitalism from "classless society," from Communism. The forms of bourgeois states are exceedingly variegated, but their essence is the same: in one way or another, all these states are in the last analysis inevitably a *dictatorship of the bourgeoisie*. The transition from capitalism to Communism will certainly bring a great variety and abundance of political forms, but the essence will inevitably be only one: *the dictatorship of the proletariat*.

## CHAPTER III:    *EXPERIENCE OF THE PARIS COMMUNE OF 1871: MARX'S ANALYSIS*

### 2.  What is to Replace the Shattered State Machinery?

. . . To replace this machinery by "the proletariat organized as the ruling class," by "establishing democracy"—such was the answer of the *Communist Manifesto*.

Without resorting to Utopias, Marx waited for the *experience* of a mass movement to produce the answer to the problem as to the exact forms which this organization of the proletariat as the ruling class will assume and as to the exact manner in which this organization will be combined with the most complete, most consistent "establishment of democracy."

The experiment of the Commune, meagre as it was, was subjected by Marx to the most careful analysis in his *The Civil War in France.* . . .

> The Commune was formed of municipal councillors, chosen by universal suffrage in various wards of the town, responsible and revocable at short terms. The majority of its members were naturally working men, or acknowledged representatives of the working class. . . . Instead of continuing to be the agent of the Central Government, the police was at once stripped of its political attributes, and turned into the responsible and at all times revocable agent of the Commune. So were the officials of all other branches of the administration. From the members of the Commune downwards, the public service had to be done at *workmen's wages.* . . .

Thus the Commune would appear to have replaced the shattered state machinery "only" by fuller democracy: abolition of the standing army; all officials to be fully elective and subject to recall. But, as a matter of fact this "only" signifies a gigantic replacement of one type of institution by others of a fundamentally different order. Here we observe a case of "transformation of quantity into quality."...

In this connection the Commune's measure emphasized by Marx, particularly worthy of note, is: the abolition of all representation allowances, and of all money privileges in the case of officials, the reduction of the remuneration of *all* servants of the state to "workingmen's wages." Here is shown, more clearly than anywhere else, the *break* from a bourgeois democracy to a proletarian democracy, from the democracy of the oppressors to the democracy of the oppressed classes, from the state as a "special force for suppression" of a given class to the suppression of the oppressors by the *whole force* of the majority of the people—the workers and the peasants....

The reduction of the remuneration of the highest state officials seems "simply" a demand of naive, primitive democracy . . . the transition from capitalism to Socialism is *impossible* without "return," in a measure, to "primitive" democracy (how can one otherwise pass on to the discharge of all the state functions by the majority of the population and by every individual of the population?). . . . Capitalist culture has *created* large-scale production, factories, railways, the postal service, telephones, etc., and *on this basis* the great majority of functions of the old "state power" have become so simplified and can be reduced to such simple operations of registration, filing and checking that they will be quite within the reach of every literate person, and it will be possible to perform them for "workingmen's wages," which circumstance can (and must) strip those functions of every shadow of privilege, of every appearance of "official grandeur."...

### 3.  The Destruction of Parliamentarism

The Commune—says Marx—was to be a working, not a parliamentary body, executive and legislative at the same time....

To decide once every few years which member of the ruling class is to repress and oppress the people through parliament—this is the real essence of bourgeois parliamentarism, not only in parliamentary-constitutional monarchies, but also in the most democratic republics....

The venal and rotten parliamentarism of bourgeois society is replaced in the Commune by institutions in which freedom of opinion and discussion does not degenerate into deception, for the parliamentarians must themselves work, must themselves execute their own laws, must themselves verify their results in actual life, must themselves be directly responsible to their electorate. Representative institutions remain, but parliamentarism as a special system, as a division of labour between the legislative and the executive functions, as a privileged position for the deputies, *no longer exists.* Without representative institutions we cannot imagine democracy, not even proletarian democracy; but we can and *must* think of democracy without parliamentarism....

We are not Utopians, we do not indulge in "dreams" of how best to do away *immediately* with all administration, with all subordination; these Anarchist dreams, based upon a lack of understanding of the task of proletarian dictatorship, are basically foreign to Marxism, and, as a matter of fact, they serve but to put off the Socialist revolution until human nature is different. No, we want the Socialist revolution with human nature as it is now, with human nature that cannot do without subordination, control, and "managers."

But if there be subordination, it must be to the armed vanguard of all the exploited and the labouring—to the proletariat. The specific "commanding" methods of the state officials can and must begin to be replaced—immediately, within twenty-four hours—by the simple functions of "managers" and bookkeepers, functions which are now already within the capacity of the average city dweller and can well be performed for "workingmen's wages."...

Such a beginning, on the basis of large-scale production, of itself leads to the gradual "withering away" of all bureaucracy, to the gradual creation of a new order . . . an order which has nothing to do with wage slavery, an order in which the more and more simplified functions of control and accounting will be performed by each in turn, will then become a habit, and will finally die out as *special* functions of a special stratum of the population. . . .

To organize the *whole* national economy like the postal system, in such a way that the technicians, managers, bookkeepers as well as *all* officials, should receive no higher wages than "workingmen's wages," all under the control and leadership of the armed proletariat—this is our immediate aim. This is the kind of state and economic basis we need. This is what will produce the destruction of parliamentarism, while retaining representative institutions. This is what will free the labouring classes from the prostitution of these institutions by the bourgeoisie. . . .

## CHAPTER IV:    SUPPLEMENTARY EXPLANATIONS BY ENGELS

> If anything is certain, it is that our party and the working class can only come to power under the form of the democratic republic. This is, indeed, the specific form for the dictatorship of the proletariat, as has already been shown by the great French Revolution. . . .

Engels repeats here in a particularly emphatic form the fundamental idea which runs like a red thread throughout all Marx's work, namely, that the democratic republic is the nearest approach to the dictatorship of the proletariat. For such a republic—without in the least setting aside the domination of capital, and, therefore, the oppression of the masses and the class struggle—inevitably leads to such an extension, development, unfolding and sharpening of that struggle that, as soon as the possibility arises for satisfying the fundamental interests of the oppressed masses, this possibility is realized inevitably and solely in the dictatorship of the proletariat, in the guidance of these masses by the proletariat. . . .

From the point of view of the proletariat and the proletarian revolution, Engels, like Marx, insists on democratic centralism, on one indivisible republic. The federal republic he considers either as an exception and a hindrance to development, or as a transitional form from a monarchy to a centralized republic, as a "step forward" under certain special conditions. . . .

When Engels says that in a democratic republic, "no less" than in a monarchy, the state remains a "machine for the oppression of one class by another," this by no means signifies that the *form* of oppression is a matter of indifference to the proletariat, as some Anarchists "teach." A wider, freer and more open *form* of the class struggle and of class oppression enormously assists the proletariat in its struggle for the abolition of all classes.

. . . Why only a new generation will be able completely to throw out all the state rubbish—this question is bound up with the question of overcoming democracy, to which we now turn.

### 6.  Engels on the Overcoming of Democracy

In the current arguments about the state, the mistake is constantly made against which Engels cautions here, and which we have indicated above, namely, it is constantly forgotten that the destruction of the state means also the destruction of democracy; that the withering away of the state also means the withering away of democracy.

At first sight such a statement seems exceedingly strange and incomprehensible; indeed, some one may even begin to fear lest we be expecting the advent of such an order of society in which the principle of the subordination of the minority to the majority will not be respected—for is not a democracy just the recognition of this principle?

No, democracy is *not* identical with the subordination of the minority to the majority. Democracy is a *state* recognizing the subordination of the minority to the majority, *i.e.*, an organization for the systematic use of *violence* by one class against the other, by one part of the population against another.

We set ourselves the ultimate aim of destroying the state, *i.e.*, every organized and systematic violence, every use of violence against man in general. We do not expect the advent of an order of society in which the principle of subordination of minority to majority will not be observed. But, striving for Socialism, we are convinced that it will develop into Communism; that, side by side with this, there will vanish all need for force, for the *subjection* of one man to another, and of one part of the population to another, since people will *grow accustomed* to observing the elementary conditions of social existence *without force and without subjection.*

In order to emphasize this element of habit, Engels speaks of a *new generation*, "reared under new and free social conditions,"which "will be able to throw on the scrap heap all this state rubbish"—every kind of state, including even the democratic-republican state. . . .

## CHAPTER V: *THE ECONOMIC BASIS OF THE WITHERING AWAY OF THE STATE*

### 1. Formulation of the Question by Marx

On the basis of what *data* can the future development of future Communism be considered?

On the basis of the fact that it *has its origin* in capitalism, that it develops historically from capitalism, that it is the result of the action of a social force to which capitalism *has given birth*. There is no shadow of an attempt on Marx's part to conjure up a Utopia, to make idle guesses about that which cannot be known. Marx treats the question of Communism in the same way as a naturalist would treat the question of the development of, say, a new biological species, if he knew that such and such was its origin, and such and such the direction in which it changed. . . .

Historically, there must undoubtedly be a special stage or epoch of *transition* from capitalism to Communism. . . .

### 2. Transition From Capitalism to Communism

> Between capitalist and Communist society—Marx continues—lies the period of the revolutionary transformation of the former into the latter. To this also corresponds a political transition period, in which the state can be no other than *the revolutionary dictatorship of the proletariat.*

This conclusion Marx bases on an analysis of the role played by the proletariat in modern capitalist society, on the data concerning the development of this society, and on the irreconcilability of the opposing interests of the proletariat and the bourgeoisie.

Earlier the question was put thus: to attain its emancipation, the proletariat must overthrow the bourgeoisie, conquer political power and establish its own revolutionary dictatorship.

Now the question is put somewhat differently: the transition from capitalist society, developing towards Communism, towards a Communist society, is impossible without a "political transition period," and the state in this period can only be the revolutionary dictatorship of the proletariat.

What, then, is the relation of this dictatorship to democracy?

. . . On the basis of all that has been said above, one can define more exactly how democracy changes in the transition from capitalism to Communism.

In capitalist society, under the conditions most favourable to its development, we have more or less complete democracy in the democratic republic. But this democracy is always bound by the narrow framework of capitalist exploitation, and consequently always remains, in reality, a democracy for the minority, only for the possessing classes, only for the rich. Freedom in capitalist society always remains just about the same as it was in the ancient Greek republics: freedom for the slave-owners. The modern wage-slaves, owing to the conditions of capitalist exploitation, are so much crushed by want and poverty that "democracy is nothing to them,""politics is nothing to them"; that, in the ordinary peaceful course of events, the majority of the population is debarred from participating in social and political life. . . .

But from this capitalist democracy—inevitably narrow, subtly rejecting the poor, and therefore hypocritical and false to the core—progress does not march onward, simply, smoothly and directly, to "greater and greater democracy," as the liberal professors and petty-bourgeois opportunists would have us believe. No, progress marches onward, *i.e.*, towards Communism, through the dictatorship of the proletariat; it cannot do otherwise, for there is no one else and no other way to *break the resistance* of the capitalist exploiters. . . .

And the dictatorship of the proletariat, i.e., the organization of the vanguard of the oppressed as the ruling class for the purpose of suppressing the oppressors, cannot result merely in an expansion of democracy. *Simultaneously* with an immense expansion of democracy, which *for the first time*, becomes democracy for the poor, democracy for the people, and not democracy for the moneybags, the dictatorship of the proletariat imposes a series of restrictions on the freedom of the oppressors, the exploiters, the capitalists. We must suppress them in order to free humanity from wage slavery. Their resistance must be crushed by force; and it is clear that where there is suppression, where there is violence, there is no freedom and no democracy.

Engels expressed this splendidly . . . when he said . . . that "the proletariat uses the state not in the interests of freedom but in order to hold down its adversaries, and as soon as it becomes possible to speak of freedom the state as such ceases to exist."

Democracy for the vast majority of the people, and suppression by force, i.e., exclusion from democracy, of the exploiters and oppressors of the people—this is the modification of democracy during the *transition* from capitalism to Communism.

Only in Communist society, when the resistance of the capitalists has been completely broken, when the capitalists have disappeared, when there are no classes (*i.e.*, there is no difference between the members of society in their relation to the social means of production), *only then* "the state ceases to exist," and "*it becomes possible to speak of freedom.*" Only then a really full democracy, a democracy without any exceptions, will be possible and will be realized. And only then will democracy itself begin to *wither away* due to the simple fact that, freed from capitalist slavery, from the untold horrors, savagery, absurdities and infamies of capitalist exploitation, people will gradually *become accustomed* to the observance of the elementary rules of social life that have been known for centuries and repeated for thousands of years in all school books; they will become accustomed to observing them without force, without compulsion, without subordination, without the *special apparatus* for compulsion which is called the state.

The expression "the state *withers away*," is very well chosen, for it indicates both the gradual and the elemental nature of the process. Only habit can, and undoubtedly will, have such an effect; for we see around us millions of times how readily people get accustomed to observe the necessary rules of life in common, if there is no exploitation, if there is nothing that causes indignation, that calls forth protest and revolt and has to be *suppressed*.

Thus, in capitalist society, we have a democracy that is curtailed, poor, false; a democracy only for the rich, for the minority. The dictatorship of the proletariat, the period of transition to Communism, will, for the first time, produce democracy for the people, for the majority, side by side with the necessary suppression of the minority—the exploiters. Communism alone is capable of giving a really complete democracy, and the more complete it is the more quickly will it become unnecessary and wither away of itself.

In other words: under capitalism we have a state in the proper sense of the word, that is, special machinery for the suppression of one class by another, and of the majority by the minority at that. Naturally, for the successful discharge of such a task as the systematic suppression by the exploiting minority of the exploited majority, the greatest ferocity and savagery of suppression are required, seas of blood are required, through which mankind is marching in slavery, serfdom, and wage-labour. . . .

Finally, only Communism renders the state absolutely unnecessary, for there is *no one* to be suppressed—"no one" in the sense of a *class*, in the sense of a systematic struggle with a definite section of the population. We are not Utopians, and we do not in the least deny the possibility and inevitability of excesses on the part of *individual persons*, nor the need to suppress *such* excesses. But, in the first place, no special machinery, no special apparatus of repression is needed for this; this will be done by the armed people itself, as simply and as readily as any crowd of civilized people, even in modern society, parts a pair of combatants or does not allow a woman to be outraged. And, secondly, we know that the fundamental social cause of excesses which consist in violating the rules of social life is the exploitation of the masses, their want and their poverty. With the removal of this chief cause, excesses will inevitably begin to *"wither away."* We do not know how quickly and in what succession, but we know that they will wither away. With their withering away, the state will also *wither away.*

Without going into Utopias, Marx defined more fully what can now be defined regarding this future, namely, the difference between the lower and higher phases (degrees, stages) of Communist society.

### 3. First Phase of Communist Society

> What we are dealing with here [analysing the programme of the party] is not a Communist society which has *developed* on its own foundations, but, on the contrary, one which is just *emerging* from capitalist society, and which therefore in all respects—economic, moral and intellectual—still bears the birthmarks of the old society from whose womb it sprung.

And it is this Communist society—a society which has just come into the world out of the womb of capitalism, and which, in all respects, bears the stamp of the old society—that Marx terms the "first,"or lower, phase of Communist society. . . .

The first phase of Communism, therefore, still cannot produce justice and equality; differences, and unjust differences, in wealth will still exist, but the *exploitation* of man by man will have become impossible, because it will be impossible to seize as private property the *means of production*, the factories, machines, land, and so on. . . .

Marx not only takes into account with the greatest accuracy the inevitable inequality of men; he also takes into account the fact that the mere conversion of the means of production into the common property of the whole of society ("Socialism" in the generally accepted sense of the word) *does not remove* the defects of distribution and the inequality of "bourgeois right" which *continue to rule* as long as the products are divided "according to work performed."

> But these defects—Marx continues—are unavoidable in the first phase of Communist society, when, after long travail, it first emerges from capitalist society. Justice can never rise superior to the economic conditions of society and the cultural development conditioned by them.

And so, in the first phase of Communist society (generally called Socialism) "bourgeois right" is *not* abolished in its entirety. . . .

"He who does not work, shall not eat"—this Socialist principle is *already* realized; "for an equal quantity of labour, an equal quantity of products"—this Socialist principle is also *already* realized. However, this is not yet Communism, and this does not abolish "bourgeois right," which gives to unequal individuals, in return for an unequal (in reality unequal) amount of work, an equal quantity of products.

This is a "defect," says Marx, but it is unavoidable during the first phase of Communism; for, if we are not to fall into Utopianism, we cannot imagine that, having overthrown capitalism, people will at once learn to work for society *without any standards of right*; indeed, the abolition of capitalism *does not immediately lay* the economic foundations for *such* a change. . . .

### 4.   Higher Phase of Communist Society

Marx continues:

> In a higher phase of Communist society, when the enslaving subordination of individuals in the division of labour has disappeared, and with it also the antagonism between mental and physical labour; when labour has become not only a means of living, but itself the first necessity of life; when, along with the all-round development of individuals, the productive forces too have grown, and all the springs of social wealth are flowing more freely—it is only at that stage that it will be possible to pass completely beyond the narrow horizon of bourgeois rights, and for society to inscribe on its banners: from each according to his ability: to each according to his needs!

The economic basis for the complete withering away of the state is that high stage of development of Communism when the antagonism between mental and physical labour disappears, that is to say, when one of the principal sources of modern *social* inequality disappears—a source, moreover, which it is impossible to remove immediately by the mere conversion of the means of production into public property, by the mere expropriation of the capitalists.

This expropriation will make a gigantic development of the productive forces *possible*. And seeing how incredibly, even now, capitalism *retards* this development, how much progress could be made even on the basis of modern technique at the level it has reached, we have a right to say, with the fullest confidence, that the expropriation of the capitalists will inevitably result in a gigantic development of the productive forces of human society. But how rapidly this development will go forward, how soon it will reach the point of breaking away from the division of labour, of removing the antagonism between mental and physical labour, of transforming work into the "first necessity of life"—this we do not and *cannot* know.

Consequently, we have a right to speak solely of the inevitable withering away of the state, emphasizing the protracted nature of this process and its dependence upon the rapidity of development of the *higher phase* of Communism; leaving quite open the question of lengths of time, or the concrete forms of withering away, since material for the solution of such questions is *not available.*

The state will be able to wither away completely when society has realized the rule: "From each according to his ability; to each according to his needs," *i.e.,* when people have become accustomed to observe the fundamental rules of social life, and their labour is so productive, that they voluntarily work *according to their ability*. "The narrow horizon of bourgeois rights," which compels one to calculate, with the hard-heartedness of a Shylock, whether he has not worked half an hour more than another, whether he is not getting less pay than another—this narrow horizon will then be left behind. There will then be no need for any exact calculation by society of the quantity of products to be distributed to each of its members; each will take freely "according to his needs."

From the bourgeois point of view, it is easy to declare such a social order "a pure Utopia," and to sneer at the Socialists for promising each the right to receive from society, without any control of the labour of the individual citizen, any quantity of truffles, automobiles, pianos, etc. Even now, most bourgeois "savants" deliver themselves of such sneers, thereby displaying at once their ignorance and their self-seeking defence of capitalism.

Ignorance—for it has never entered the head of any Socialist to "promise" that the highest phase of Communism will arrive; while the great Socialists, in *foreseeing* its arrival, presupposed both a productivity of labour unlike the present and a person not like the present man in the street, capable of spoiling, without reflection, . . . the stores of social wealth, and of demanding the impossible.

Until the "higher" phase of Communism arrives, the Socialists demand the *strictest* control, *by society and by the state*, of the quantity of labour and the quantity of consumption; only this control must *start* with the expropriation of the capitalists, with the control of the workers over the capitalists, and must be carried out, not by a state of bureaucrats, but by a state of *armed workers....*

Consequently, for a certain time not only bourgeois rights, but even the bourgeois state remains under Communism, without the bourgeoisie!

This may look like a paradox, or simply a dialectical puzzle for which Marxism is often blamed by people who would not make the least effort to study its extraordinarily profound content.

But, as a matter of fact, the old surviving in the new confronts us in life at every step, in nature as well as in society. Marx did not smuggle a scrap of "bourgeois" rights into Communism of his own accord; he indicated what is economically and politically inevitable in a society issuing *from the womb* of capitalism.

Democracy is of great importance for the working class in its struggle for freedom against the capitalists. But democracy is by no means a limit one may not overstep; it is only one of the stages in the course of development from feudalism to capitalism, and from capitalism to Communism.

Democracy means equality. The great significance of the struggle of the proletariat for equality, and the significance of equality as a slogan, are apparent, if we correctly interpret it as meaning the abolition of *classes.* But democracy means only *formal* equality. Immediately after the attainment of equality for all members of society *in respect of* the ownership of the means of production, that is, of equality of labour and equality of wages, there will inevitably arise before humanity the question of going further from formal equality to real equality, *i.e.,* to realizing the rule, "From each according to his ability; to each according to his needs." By what stages, by means of what practical measures humanity will proceed to this higher aim—this we do not and cannot know....

Democracy is a form of the state—one of its varieties. Consequently, like every state, it consists in organized, systematic application of force against human beings. This on the one hand. On the other hand, however, it signifies the formal recognition of the equality of all citizens, the equal right of all to determine the structure and administration of the state. This, in turn, is connected with the fact that, at a certain stage in the development of democracy, it first rallies the proletariat as a revolutionary class against capitalism, and gives it an opportunity to crush, to smash to bits, to wipe off the face of the earth the bourgeois state machinery—even its republican variety: the standing army, the police, and bureaucracy; then it substitutes for all this a *more* democratic, but still a state machinery in the shape of armed masses of workers, which becomes transformed into universal participation of the people in the militia.

Here "quantity turns into quality": *such* a degree of democracy is bound up with the abandonment of the framework of bourgeois society, and the beginning of its Socialist reconstruction. If *every one* really takes part in the administration of the state, capitalism cannot retain its hold. In its turn, capitalism, as it develops, itself creates *prerequisites* for "every one" *to be able* really to take part in the administration of the state. Among such prerequisites are: universal literacy, already realized in most of the advanced capitalist countries, then the "training and disciplining" of millions of workers by the huge, complex, and socialized apparatus of the post-office, the railways, the big factories, large-scale commerce, banking, etc., etc.

With such *economic* prerequisites it is perfectly possible, immediately, within twenty-four hours after the overthrow of the capitalists and bureaucrats, to replace them, in the control of production and distribution, in the business of *control* of labour and products, by the armed workers, by the whole people in arms. The question of control and accounting must not be confused with the question of the scientifically educated staff of engineers, agronomists and so on. These gentlemen work today, obeying the capitalists; they will work even better tomorrow, obeying the armed workers.

Accounting and control—these are the *chief* things necessary for the organizing and correct functioning of the *first phase* of Communist society. *All* citizens are here transformed into hired employees of the state, which is made up of the armed workers. *All* citizens become employees and workers of *one* national state "syndicate."All that is required is that they should work equally, should regularly do their share of work, and should receive equal pay. The accounting and control necessary for this have been *simplified* by capitalism to the utmost, till they have become the extraordinarily simple operations of watching, recording and issuing receipts, within the reach of anybody who can read and write and knows the first four rules of arithmetic.

When the *majority* of the people begin everywhere to keep such accounts and maintain such control over the capitalists (now converted into employees) and over the intellectual gentry, who still retain capitalist habits, this control will really become universal, general, national; and there will be no way of getting away from it, there will be "nowhere to go."

The whole of society will have become one office and one factory, with equal work and equal pay.

But this "factory" discipline, which the proletariat will extend to the whole of society after the defeat of the capitalists and the overthrow of the exploiters, is by no means our ideal, or our final aim. It is but a *foothold* necessary for the radical cleansing of society of all the hideousness and foulness of capitalist exploitation, *in order to advance further.*

From the moment when all members of society, or even only the overwhelming majority, have learned how to govern the state *themselves,* have taken this business into their own hands, have "established" control over the insignificant minority of capitalists, over the gentry with capitalist leanings, and the workers thoroughly demoralized by capitalism—from this moment the need for any government begins to disappear. The more complete the democracy, the nearer the moment when it begins to be unnecessary. The more democratic the "state" consisting of armed workers, which is "no longer a state in the proper sense of the word,"the more rapidly does *every* state begin to wither away.

For when *all* have learned to manage, and independently are actually managing by themselves social production, keeping accounts, controlling the idlers, the gentlefolk, the swindlers and similar "guardians of capitalist traditions," then the escape from this national accounting and control will inevitably become so increasingly difficult, such a rare exception, and will probably be accompanied by such swift and severe punishment (for the armed workers are men of practical life, not sentimental intellectuals, and they will scarcely allow any one to trifle with them), that very soon the *necessity* of observing the simple, fundamental rules of every-day social life in common will have become a *habit.*

The door will then be wide open for the transition from the first phase of Communist society to its higher phase, and along with it to the complete withering away of the state.

# "What Socialism Means:
# A Call to the Unconverted"

## Sidney Webb (1859–1947)

*This lecture was delivered before the Fabian Society of London in 1886, whose name is a reference to the Roman general Fabius Maximus, who defeated Hannibal by a policy of harassment, rather than risk a pitched battle. Among the earliest members of this socialist organization, Webb was quite influential in the first half of the twentieth century in the socialist movement and the Labour Party in England. Webb served many years on the London County Council and then as a Member of Parliament, and he helped in the development of the London School of Economics. Together with his wife, Beatrice Potter, he wrote the manifesto of the Labour Party for the elections of 1918-1924 as well as many books on various economic and political issues. After a trip to the Soviet Union in the 1930s, they wrote* Soviet Communism: A New Civilization?, *in which they showed a new tendency to embrace a socialist revolution, but this lecture outlines the more gradualist or evolutionary approach Webb espoused during most of his political life.*

*To what class does Webb address his remarks? Compare his rhetoric and the intent of his speech to that of* State and Revolution. *Why might Webb use so many terms drawn from religious discourse? What does he offer as the stark alternative to a conscious evolution toward a socialist society? Compare the view of socialism Webb sketches with the Marxian "end of history" described in the* German Ideology.

Nothing is more universal than the widespread illusion as to what Socialism really means, and as to how Socialists intend to obtain its adoption. It seems almost impossible to bring people to understand that the abstract word "Socialism," denotes like "radicalism," not an elaborate plan of Society, but a principle of social action. Socialists easily recognise that the adoption of the principle can only be extended by bringing about a slowly dawning conviction in the minds of men; it is certain that no merely forcible "revolution" organised by a minority, can ever avail, either in England or elsewhere. We seek therefore to influence only convictions, so as thereby to bring about the great bugbear of our opponents, the "Social Revolution"—a revolution in the opinions men form of the proper Society in which to live, and in the kind of action to which those opinions lead them.

There are many who desire to help in social reconstruction, but who are not quite decided to act; many who sympathise, but who are timid; many, indeed, who are Socialists, but are not conscious of their Socialism. It is to these especially that we must address ourselves asking them always to remember that Socialism is more than any Socialist, and its principle more than any detailed system or scheme of reform. The Fabian Society has no such plan or scheme; its members are led by their Socialist principles to work for social reform in a certain definite direction, but the future evolution of Society no man can exactly forecast, and to human evolution no final goal can be set. The moment will never come when we can say, "Now Socialism is established; let us keep things as they are." Constant evolution is the lesson of history: of endings, as of beginnings, we know nothing.

Socialism inevitably suffers if identified with any particular scheme, or even with the best vision we can yet form of Collectivism itself. In this, as in many other cases, the public are so much concerned with details, that they miss the principle: they "cannot see the forest for the trees." But it is no more fair to identify Socialism with any modern prophet's forecast of it, than it would be to identify Christianity with the "New Jerusalem" of the Swedenborgians. Nevertheless, such misconceptions will inevitably persist, and those who may embrace Socialism, must be warned that they are not likely to receive "honour among men" in consequence; they are certain to be misconstrued, misrepresented, and reviled, and to be regarded as advocates of dynamite outrages or childish absurdities, even by those who are gradually learning their very doctrines.

Socialism is emphatically a new thing, a thing of the present century—and one of the unforeseen results of the great industrial revolution of the past 150 years. During this period man's power over the rest of nature has suddenly and largely increased: new means of accumulating wealth and also new means of utilising land and capital have come into being.

Many do not realise what a change has resulted from this industrial revolution. At the beginning of the last century, the whole value of the land and capital of this country is estimated to have amounted to less than 500 millions sterling; now it is supposed to be over 9,000 millions; an increase eighteenfold. Two hundred years ago, rent and interest cannot have amounted to 30 million sterling annually—now they absorb over 450 millions. Socialism arose as soon as rent and interest became important factors; it began with our own century: in its birthplace in England it was, however, beaten back for a time by the hasty misunderstandings of Malthus, followed by the "acute outbreak of individualism unchecked by the old restraints, and invested with almost a religious sanction by a certain soulless school of writers," from which even Professor Foxwell asserts England to have suffered for the last century.

This hasty misinterpretation of economic science was set right by John Stuart Mill, (who describes in his "Autobiography" (p. 231) his own conversion from more extreme Democracy to a complete Socialism), and at the present moment Socialism, which had never ceased on the Continent, permeates the whole world of thought and politics here as elsewhere. Even the tide of "Orthodox Political Economy" is now running strongly in its favour, and we have Cambridge professors publicly claiming to be Socialists, and turning out Socialists by scores as their pupils.

What is the cause of this new criticism of the existing order? It has arisen because the great increase in wealth has been allowed to flow mainly to individuals, so that the enormous increase per head of the wealth production has failed to exterminate or even to alleviate poverty. In this London, the wealthiest city of the world, there is also the greatest mass of poverty and misery. It has miles upon miles of palaces, serried ranks of costly carriages in Hyde Park, such signs of abundant wealth as no other land can show. Its mere rental value is nearly forty millions sterling annually. Yet in this city homeless little children beg for bread, strong men die of starvation and want every night, and there is an array of over 300,000 persons, as many as would make the whole city of Brussels or Birmingham, in frequent receipt of workhouse relief. We should dwell a little on this. So dazed are we by the perfection of the organisation, that we are only too unconscious of the misery around us. Think of this army of 300,000 strong men, brave women and little children, absolutely destitute in this city where we are so comfortable; an army of 300,000 unable to get bread, or to obtain shelter from the cutting blast, and obliged during any one year to resort to the cold mercy of official charity. One in every five of the population dies in the workhouse or hospital. This is not a picture of London alone: things are much the same throughout the Kingdom. We have a total of over 3,000,000 in the pauper class; one in ten of the population, or one in eight of the wage earning classes.

These men, our brothers, were not born paupers; they, too, had once hope, and some youthful aspirations, which the hard world has gradually quenched in the pitiless struggle from which we favoured ones have reaped so much of the benefit; the iron has entered into their souls during that dreadful losing fight down the hill of poverty, until our brother once erect and toiling for our benefit, is borne down before us to a pauper's grave.

Not only do we exact life-long labour from the poor, for which, as we have seen, so many receive in return just sufficient to keep them alive: we take their lives also. In the worst parts of London the death rate is four times that of neighbouring "respectable" districts, and any doctor who has practised among the poor knows that their most fatal disease is poverty.

"At present the average age at death among the nobility, gentry and professional classes in England and Wales was 55 years: but among the artisan classes of Lambeth it only amounted to 29; and while the infantile death-rate among the well-to-do classes was such that only 8 children died in the first year of life out of 100 born, as many as 30 per cent, succumbed at that age among the children of the poor in some districts of our large cities. The only real cause of this enormous difference in the position of the rich and poor with respect to their chances of existence lay in the fact that at the bottom of society wages were so low that food and other requisites of health were obtained with too great difficulty" (Dr. C. R. Drysdale, "Report of Industrial Remuneration Conference" 1886, p. 130).

Our Society, it appears according to this non-Socialist, robs the wage workers of Lambeth of 26 years of life each; they die before their time, like worn-out draught horses, and their innocent children like flies. They die in their own slums of diseases, which we, in our wealth, know how to prevent; one or two will die to-night in London alone of actual starvation.

This is not all. Year by year our comforts and our pleasures increase, and year by year those iron-monsters, the never ceasing machines, grow in number and complexity. Do we realise that year by year the accidents to the workers also increase, the number of fatal accidents doubling every 20 years? Last year we raised more coal than 20 years ago, smelted more iron, made more journeys, and all at less money cost: but we also killed many thousand of the workers, unhonoured martyrs of our civilization. How many we merely maimed is not to be ascertained. The cheap fuel with which we warmed ourselves last winter was not coal but lives of men.

This is what we have come to after 150 years of the greatest wealth-production the world has known; not only a greater aggregate production, but also an increased production per head of population. There is a small rich class endowed with every comfort the mind can describe; a middle-class, well-off, educated, leisured, powerful, and all roads open to it. These two, taken together and including all above the manual labour class *make up less than one fifth of the population.* On the other hand, is the great mass of the people (of whom one-eighth are actually in the pauper class), earning on an average perhaps 25/- per family per week. These are with necessarily rare exceptions, condemned to a life of unremitting toil; without leisure or higher education, no opportunity for real improvement, and also no hope of better things.

"To me, at least, it would be enough to condemn modern society as hardly an advance on slavery or serfdom, if the permanent condition of industry were to be that which we behold, that 90 per cent of the actual producers of wealth have no home that they can call their own beyond the end of the week; have no bit of soil, or so much as a room that belongs to them; have nothing of any kind except as much old furniture as will go in a cart; have the precarious chance of weekly wages which barely suffice to keep them in health; are housed for the most part in places that no man thinks fit for his horse; are separated by so narrow a margin from destitution, that a month of bad trade, sickness or unexpected loss, brings them face to face with hunger and pauperism. . . . *This is the normal state of the average workman in town or country*" (Mr. Frederic Harrison, p. 429 "Report of Industrial Remuneration Conference," 1886).

What is the remedy of Socialism! We search—and have not to search long—for the causes of this misery. Nature itself has not, it is true, been exceedingly kind to us and we Socialists, as strongly as the Economists, demand that no useless mouths grow up to consume the too scanty store we can produce. We too, insist that there is no place at nature's table for any one who cannot or does not produce his quota, and we too, assert that there is—especially just now—grave danger that the number of such mouths may increase. We claim, indeed, that only in a Socialist community can any general limitation of population really be brought about. But we also call for a proper administration of that which is produced, so that if we must go upon short rations, these may at any rate be fairly shared.

Political Economists show us the causes of the existing poverty, and explain clearly enough the nature and extent of the deductions that go for rent, interest and the monopoly wages of exceptional ability. Official statisticians themselves enumerate these—in England at present—at two thirds of the annual produce of the workers.

There is no mystery about these things, though it may suit those who benefit by them to pretend that there is. The operations of unrestrained competition, with private ownership of land and industrial capital, is fully explained by Karl Marx, but even better by such writers as Mill, Cairnes and Walker. Economic rent and interest, they say, consists in reality of a toll levied upon production by the monopolist, and in exchange the monopolist, as such, gives nothing but permission to use the land and already accumulated capital.

"That useful function, therefore, which some profound writers fancy they discover in abundant expenditure of the idle rich, turns out to be a sheer illusion. Political economy furnishes no such palliation of unmitigated selfishness. Not that I would breathe a word against the sacredness of contracts. But I think it is important, on moral no less than on economic grounds, to insist upon this, that no public benefit of any kind arises from the existence of an idle rich class. The wealth accumulated by their ancestors and others on their behalf, where it is employed as capital, no doubt helps to sustain industry; but what they consume in luxury and idleness is not capital, and helps to sustain nothing but their own unprofitable lives. By all means they must have their rents and interest, as it is written in the bond; but let them take their proper place as drones in the hive, gorging at a feast to which they have contributed nothing" ("Some Leading Principles of Political Economy" p. 32, by the late John Elliott Cairnes, M.A., Emeritus Professor of Political Economy at University College, London; 1874).

Yet it is clearly inevitable that, so long as land and capital are in individual ownership, rent and interest must continue to exist, creating what Mill called "the great social evil of a non-labouring class." For them the great mass of the workers are deprived of at least half the product of labour.

This is the Socialist case. It is founded on no new system of political economy, upon no new statistics. It is mainly the emphatic assertion of two leading principles. We recognise first, as the central truth of modern society, the interdependence of all. No man now works alone; by division of labour and mutual exchange all are sharing in each one's toil. Each worker, by the marvelously complex exchange-system shares in the fruits of the labour of those in the most remote parts of the earth, and is in unconscious partnership with every other worker. No individual can now claim as his own the product to which he is in reality giving only certain final touches.

We claim, in the second place, to apply the doctrines of economic science to the art of Government in insisting on the ethical right of the joint workers, *and the workers alone*, to the whole produce of their labour, without any deduction for rent and interest, or any other form of mere monopolist's toll. We contend for the full recognition of the admitted fact that the whole produce of labour is created by labour alone—whether labour of hand or labour of brain—and that any form of society which enables idle owners of certain social products to exact for personal consumption a toll from helpless fellow citizens, although perhaps useful in the earlier stage of social evolution, is now bad; guilty as Mill and Cairnes themselves have in effect said, of causing unnecessary deaths and misery to the poorer classes.

This is essentially the Socialistic platform. We do not expect to realise this ideal all at once. Society is evolving fast under our eyes, and it is in this direction that it is changing. We have but the option of helping or resisting the change.

It is obvious that the scope of unrestrained private ownership will be once more altered. The limits, which have already gradually excluded slaves, public offices, highway tolls, post offices, "sound dues," and other monopolist freaks, must now be drawn so as to leave in the hands, or at least under the full control, of the community, that without which no man can live—the great means of wealth production, land and industrial capital.

Individual Socialists, whilst agreeing in this necessity, entertain different views as to the form of the social organisation to which we are now tending. There are three main schools of Socialist thought.

1. *Collectivists* lay stress on the necessity for equality of opportunity lest some be otherwise compelled to lead lives unnecessarily cramped and fettered. They wish with this end to extend public administration and public control of the means of production, the tendency to which has marked off modern society from the extreme individualism of the earlier part of the century.

2. *Anarchists* lay more stress upon the moral objections to any government coercion, and contend for private administration in a state of free co-operation with no other than moral regulation. Consumption is to be eventually according to real social needs, and to be regulated by voluntary restriction. Most Anarchists admit, however, that a period of Collectivism will precede the attainment of their ideal, during which humanity will gradually learn to become fit for it.

3. *Positivists*, so far as they have thought out their economic system, come clearly under this definition of Socialism. They would leave administration ostensibly in private hands but under increased government regulations; equal personal consumption, and by workers only, being realised chiefly by an advance in personal morality, and by the influence on public opinion of a philosophic priesthood. It is fair to add that most Positivists repudiate the name of Socialists. On the other hand the extreme Radical party in England is now practically Socialist of this type, often without being conscious of the fact.

But all forms of Socialism agree in the two general principles stated above. All agree in repudiating any claim by particular workers to the competitive exchange value of their particular products, which could be set up only by ignoring the unconscious co-operation by their fellows all over the world or by reverting to the wild individualism which is a characteristic of barbarism. And all agree with the Economist, in repudiating any moral claim in the monopolist as such, to the toll which he can levy.

It may be said that these are mere ideals which we hope to realise one day—not perhaps in our own lives, but living again in lives to come. What has Socialism hitherto done for the workers? What is its remedy for the present distress? The Socialist is, in the meantime, the most practical of politicians, the truest opportunist. While repudiating as unscientific, the idea that any mere palliative of existing evils can effect a cure of them, he is constantly urging the adoption of every practical measure of immediate relief. It is in his principles rather than in his practical politics that the Socialist differs from the mere "social reformer." But principles are the only lasting springs of action.

Socialism, therefore, does not mean any particular plan or scheme of social re-organisation, nor the vain dream of equality of wealth. It means no contempt for machinery, no dislike of education or culture, no enmity to brain work or invention. It is, in fact, because we want more of these things that we are Socialists.

It is easy to bring objections against Socialism. There are always a thousand reasons against every social change. Yet the change comes, and the objectors silently learn wisdom. We need hardly trouble to reason with the man who says merely that he means to keep what he has got. Dawning conscience and increased social intelligence will bring the sons of such men over to our ranks. But may not the clever artisan or the skilled brain worker who now earns huge wages because of the scarcity of his talent, be justly allowed to consume the whole wages of his labour? There need be nothing to prevent him from doing this, in a society organised on a Socialist basis, but he should remember that countless other workers are helping him, and that his brain or skill is not his alone; it is the result of past ages; a social and not an individual product; while his training and education are essentially the fruit of social capital expended upon him.

Loss of liberty and independence, what of these? This is perhaps felt by most of those who enjoy a fair share under existing arrangements to be the weightiest objection to any increase in the present tendency to collectivism. On questions of personal liberty, Mill may be allowed some weight, and Mill emphatically declared that "the restraints of Communism would be freedom in comparison with the present condition of the majority of the human race." [*Principles of Political Economy*] As to the present liberty and independence of the comfortable classes, on what are they based? The king's house at Dahomey stands solid on its mighty corner piles in the African sand, but their solidity is secured—so the natives will tell you—by the blood of the slave girls, crushed in the holes in which the piles were driven. The smiling landlord or mill-owner leans back in his saloon-carriage, rejoicing in the freedom to travel given by his long holiday, but he heeds not the extra hours of toil which his very liberty thus adds to the task of his serfs all over the world. There is economic servitude for the ordinary worker as unrelenting in its impersonal grip as the harshest trammels of the slave-owner.

Yes, Socialism means a loss of such liberty. Freedom which can only be enjoyed by the oppression of the rest is but the license of the tyrant, and

> "True freedom is to share
> All the bonds our brothers wear."

Any loss of personal liberty which the few may suffer, (in any case, the liberty only to control the labour of others) will be far outweighed by the greater safety, independence and leisure of the many. Socialism necessarily implies by its fairer distribution of social pressure, an aggregate gain in personal freedom.

But, whatever the seeming objections, those who recognise the economic causes of social evolution, are constrained, of necessity, to join forces with the Socialist movement.

It is not a comfortable gospel that we preach to the middle and upper classes—no glad tidings of great joy—but it is one of which you will not be able to escape the unpleasant conviction. Perhaps those are happier who do not know, who have never thought of the source of their income: coming to them like manna from heaven. But you who do know whence comes your rent and interest, will see discomforting visions. As you feed the fire, you will see the miner, bent double underground, in his toil, giving up his life that you may be warmed. As you look upon your daughters growing up around you in your sheltered and cultured home, you will see behind them the daughters of other mothers, slaving seamstresses, working sixteen hours for "eleven pence ha'penny"; nay, selling themselves into a life of infamy, for want of that bread which you, by your position of social vantage, are forcing them to give up to you.

Then there will be no escape. Those of you who do know, those of you who are no longer in blissful ignorance; those of you who realise this economic toll levied on the scanty earnings of the poor—will be compelled to come over to us for very shame, and work with all your might to stop the sooner this fearful drain upon the insufficient average pittance, which is all that we can as yet extract from the rest of nature.

You have but one alternative. By steadily turning away your eyes, and caring only for your own comforts, by luxurious and selfish living, by making to yourself a false idol of art, or religion, or literature you may perhaps be able in time to stifle your conscience, and drown the despairing cries of the misery which you are taking your part in creating. But then do not be surprised if the long suffering masses, roused at last from their ignorant patience, and deserted by those who ought to have been their leaders, shake in their despair the whole social structure about your ears, crying of your class, of its good as of its evil, "cut it down, why cumbereth it the ground?" It is to prevent matters coming to such indiscriminate ruin that we are, and you should be, Socialists.

# Selections From
## *The Ethics of Redistribution*

## *Bertrand de Jouvenel (1903–       )*

*Bertrand de Jouvenel is the author of many books and articles on economics and politics, chief among them* Sovereignty, Power, *and* The Pure Theory of Politics. *As a journalist between the wars, he interviewed such influential political men as Huey Long and Adolph Hitler. Jouvenel is the founder of* Futuribles, *a journal devoted to conjecture about the future. This selection is taken from a series of lectures he gave at Cambridge University in 1949.*

*Consider Jouvenel's case for a non-materialistic basis for sharing one's wealth. Is something like a monastic life the only sound foundation for the "brotherly love" sought in communal life? Are socialism's promises of equality of reward, justice, and material advancement contradictory in principle? Why does Jouvenel reject redistribution as the ethical solution to the "scandal of poverty"? What important link does Jouvenel see between the capitalist and the socialist economic arguments? Compare these ethical arguments against redistribution with those of Aristotle in his criticism of Phaleas of Chalcedon.*

### LECTURE I:   THE SOCIALIST IDEAL

I propose to discuss a predominant preoccupation of our day:  the redistribution of incomes.

#### The Process of Redistribution

In the course of a lifetime, current ideas as to what may be done in a society by political decision have altered radically. It is now generally regarded as within the proper province of the State, and indeed as one of its major functions, to shift wealth from its richer to its poorer members. . . .

#### Our Subject: The Ethical Aspect

A spirited controversy is now raging on what is termed "the disincentive effect of excessive redistribution." It is known from experience that in most cases, though by no means in all, men are spurred by material rewards proportional or even more than proportional to their effort, as for example in "time and a half." Making each increase of effort less rewarding than those which preceded it, whilst at the same time lowering, by the provision of benefits, the basic effort necessary to sustain existence, can be held to affect the pace of production and economic progress. Thus the policy of redistribution is subject to heavy fire. The attack, however, is made on grounds of expediency. Current criticism of redistribution is not based on its being undesirable but on its being, beyond a certain point, imprudent. Nor do champions of redistribution deny that there are limits to what can be achieved, if it is proposed, as they wish, to maintain economic progress. This whole conflict, of which so much is made today is a borderline quarrel, involving no fundamentals.

I propose to skirt this field of combat, and shall assume here that redistribution, however far it may be carried, exerts no disincentive influence, and leaves the volume and growth of production entirely unaffected. This assumption is made in order to centre attention upon other aspects of redistribution. To some the assumption may seem to do away with the need for discussion. If it were not going to affect production, they will say, redistribution would have to proceed to its extreme of total equality of incomes. This would be good and desirable. But would it? Why would it? And how far would it? This is my starting-point.

Dealing with redistribution purely on ethical grounds, our first concern must be to distinguish sharply between the social ideal of income equalization and others with which it is sentimentally, but not logically, associated. It is a common but ill-founded belief that ideals of social reform are somehow lineal descendants of one another. It is not so: redistributionism is not descended from socialism; nor can any but a purely verbal link be discovered between it and agrarian egalitarianism. It will greatly clarify the problem if we stress the contrasts between these ideals.

### Land Redistribution in Perspective

What was demanded in the name of social justice over thousands of years was land redistribution. This may be said to belong to a past phase of history when agriculture was by far the major economic activity. Yet the agrarian demand comes right down to our own times: did not the First World War bring in its train an ample redistribution of land over all of Eastern Europe? . . .

### Land Redistribution Not Equivalent to Redistribution of Income

There is a clear contrast between redistribution of land and redistribution of incomes. Agrarianism does not advocate the equalization of the produce, but of natural resources out of which the several units will autonomously provide themselves with the produce. This is justice, in the sense that inequality of rewards between units equally provided with natural resources will reflect inequality of toil. In other words, the role played by inequality of "capital" in bringing about unequal rewards is nullified. What is equalized is the supply of "capital". . . .

### Socialism as the City of Brotherly Love

Agrarianism can be summed up under the heading of *fair rewards*. Socialism aims even higher than the establishment of "mere" justice. It seeks to establish a new order of brotherly love. The basic socialist feeling is not that things are out of proportion and thus unjust, that reward is not proportional to effort, but an emotional revolt against the antagonisms within society, against the ugliness of men's behaviour to each other.

It is of course logically possible to minimize antagonism by minimizing the occasions on which men's paths cross. Thus, the agrarian solution lies in the economic sovereignty of each several owner on his well delimited field, which is equal in size to that of his neighbour. But this is not possible in modern societies, where interests are intertwined as in a Gordian knot. To cut the knot means reversion to a ruder state. But there is another solution: it is a new spirit of joyful acceptance of this interdependence; it is that men, called to serve one another ever increasingly by economic progress and division of labour, should do so "in newness of spirit," not as the "old" man did who grudgingly measured his service against his reward, but as a "new" man who finds his delight in the welfare of his brethren. . . .

[S]ocialism has singled out private property as the basic "situation" creating antagonisms: it creates firstly the essential antagonism between those with property and those without, and secondly the struggle among the propertied.

### How to Do Away With Antagonism: Socialist Goal, and Socialist Means

The socialist solution then is the destruction of private property as such. This is to erase the contrast between men's positions and thereby do away with tension. The proletariat, made conscious of its solidarity in its struggle to do away with property, will, when victorious, absorb into itself the now proletarianized remainder. Social antagonisms would thereby be extinguished and the force of repression formerly called for by the existence of antagonisms in order to preserve civil peace in an atmosphere of war, that is, the power of the State, will become unnecessary. This power must then of itself wither away.

This promise that the State will wither away is fundamental to socialist doctrine, because the disappearance of antagonisms is the fundamental aim of socialism; but it has somewhat suffered from being bandied about in political controversy. Some shrewd critics of socialism have very properly taken the withering away of the State as the criterion of socialist success, thereby causing annoyance to their opponents. In the dust of combat the fact that the State is expected to wither away as an instrument of repression and of police power has been somewhat lost sight of, and in fairness it does not seem that enlarged functions of the State, by themselves, prove a failure of socialism but only the preservation and *a fortiori* the enlargement of police powers. It is, however, only too evident that police powers are at their greatest where the destruction of private property has been most completely achieved: a plain fact which refutes socialist belief.

It is clear for all to see that the destruction of private property has not done away with antagonisms or given rise to a spirit of solidarity permitting men to dispense with police powers; and it is further apparent that what spirit of solidarity there is seems to have as its necessary ingredient the distrust and hatred of another society, or of another section of society. The warlike intentions of foreign powers seem to be a basic postulate of the collectivist State, and may even be attributed by one collectivist State to another, or, if the process of socialization has not been completed, to the aggressive disposition of the capitalist classes, backed by foreign capitalists. Thus the solidarity obtained is not, as intended, a solidarity of love, but, at least in part, a solidarity in strife. Clearly this is not consonant with the basic intention of socialism: "the fruit of righteousness is sown in peace of them that make peace."

Yet the socialist ideal is not to be summarily dismissed. We do aspire to something more than a society of good neighbours who do not displace landmarks, who return stray sheep to their owner, and refrain from coveting their neighbour's ass. And indeed a community based not upon economic independence but upon a fraternal partaking of the common produce and inspired by the deep-seated feeling that its members are of one family, should not be called utopian.

### The Inner Contradiction of Socialism

Such a community works. It has worked for centuries and we can see it at work under our very eyes, in every monastic community. But it is to be noticed that these are cities of brotherly love *because* they were originally cities built up by love of the Father. It is further to be noticed that material goods are shared without question *because* they are spurned. The members of the community are not anxious to increase their individual well-being at the expense of one another, but then they are not very anxious to increase it *at all*. Their appetites are not addressed to scarce material commodities, and thus competitive; they are addressed to God, who is infinite. In short, they are members of one another not because they form a social body but because they are part of a mystical body.

Socialism seeks to restore this unity without the faith that causes it. It seeks to restore sharing as amongst brothers without contempt for worldly goods, without recognition of their worthlessness. It does not accept the view that consumption is a trivial thing, to be kept down to the minimum. On the contrary it adheres to the fundamental belief of modern society that there must be ever more worldly goods to be enjoyed, the spoils of a conquest of nature which is held to be man's noblest venture. The socialist ideal is grafted on to the progressive society and adheres to this society's veneration of commodities, its encouragement of fleshly appetites and pride in technical imperialism.

The moral seduction of socialism lies in the fact that it repudiates the methodical exploitation of the personal interest motive, of the fleshly appetites, of egoism, which held pride of place in the economic society it has undertaken to supersede; yet that, in so far as it has endorsed this society's pursuit of ever-increasing consumption, it has become a heterogeneous system, torn by an inner contradiction.

If "more goods" are the goal to which society's efforts are to be addressed, why should "more goods" be a disreputable objective for the individual? Socialism suffers from ambiguity in its judgment of values: if the good of society lies in greater riches, why not the good of the individual? If society should press towards that good, why not the individual? If this appetite for riches is wrong in the individual, why not in society? Here, then, is at least a *prima facie* incoherence, indeed a blatant heterogeneity.

Further, so long as the general purpose of society is the conquest of nature and the enjoyment of its spoils, is it not logical that this purpose should determine the characteristics of that society? Is not society shaped by its predominant desire, by the end towards which it tends? Is it not possible that many unpleasant traits of society are functionally related to its basic purpose? And is not their unpleasantness inherent in the purpose, so that any different society one seeks to build up with the same purpose must display the same characteristics, possibly under a different guise?

The productivist society may be likened to the military society. That which is meant for war must in its structure show characteristics appropriate to war. An army, or a military society, embodies many traits which are indefensible, by the standards of a "good society." But military hierarchy and discipline cannot be done away with as long as victory remains the purpose—though of course they can be amended. In the same manner, there may be a relation between the structure of productivist society and its purpose. And there is much to be said for the view that socialism's higher aspirations were doomed when it accepted the general purpose of modern society—as Rousseau indeed foresaw.

The socialist belief, that is to say the noble ethical aim of a society rid of its antagonisms and transformed into a city of brotherly love, has gone into decline. The measures which were once believed to lead towards that goal are still pressed for and in no small degree achieved. But they are increasingly advocated as ends, or as means to something other than the "good society" previously pictured, the vision of which now floats free from its anchor to what was formerly believed to be its means of achievement. Socialism, properly so called, is disintegrating, in that the component parts of a formerly compact edifice of beliefs seem to be operating almost autonomously, and for something differing from the original socialist ideal. This would please Sorel or Pareto, as an illustration of their theories of myths.

### Redistribution and the Scandal of Poverty

What has now come to the fore, as against the ideal of fair rewards, and brotherly love, is the ideal of more equal consumption. It may be regarded as compounded of two convictions: *one*, that it is good and necessary to remove want and that the surplus of some should be sacrificed to the urgent needs of others; and *two*, that inequality of means between the several members of a society is bad in itself and should be more or less radically removed.

The two ideas are not logically related. The first rests squarely upon the Christian idea of brotherhood. Man is his brother's keeper, must act as the Good Samaritan, has a moral obligation to help the unfortunate, an obligation which rests most heavily, though not exclusively, upon the most fortunate. There is, on the other hand, no *prima facie* evidence for the current contention that justice demands near equality of material conditions. Justice means proportion. The individualist is entitled to hold that justice demands individual rewards proportionate to individual endeavours; and the socialist is entitled to hold that it demands individual rewards proportionate to the services received by the community. It seems therefore reasonable to deny simultaneously that our present society is just, and that justice is to be achieved by the equalization of incomes.

It is however a loose modern habit to call "just" whatever is thought emotionally desirable. Attention was legitimately called in the nineteenth century to the sorry condition of the labouring classes. It was felt to be wrong that their human needs were so ill-satisfied. The idea of proportion then came to be applied to the relation between needs and resources. Just as it seemed improper that some should have less than what was adjudged necessary, so it also seemed improper that others should have so much more.

The first feeling was almost the only one at work in the early stage of redistributionism. The second has gained almost the upper hand in the latter stage.

Socialists, at the inception of the move towards redistribution, took rather a disdainful attitude; the initial measures were in their eyes mere bribes offered to the working classes in an attempt to divert them from the higher aims of socialism.

Here however powerful feelings were aroused. While it is difficult for men to imagine the suppression of private property, that is, of something that all desire, it is natural to them to compare their condition with that of others; the poorer can easily imagine the uses to which they would put some of the riches of others, and the richer, if once awakened to the condition of the poorer, are bound to feel some remorse on account of their luxuries.

At all times the revelation of poverty has come as a shock to the chosen few: it has impelled them to regard their personal extravagance with a sense of guilt, has driven them to distribute their riches and to mingle with the poor. In every case one knows of in the past, this has been associated with a religious experience: the mind may have been turned to God by the discovery of the poor, or to the poor by the discovery of God: in any case the two were linked, and a revulsion away from riches as evil was always implied.

However, in our century the feeling that has assailed not merely a few spirits but practically all the members of the leading classes has been of a different kind. Upon a society inordinately proud of its ever increasing riches it dawned that "in the midst of plenty," as the saying went, misery was still rife; and this called for action to raise the standard of the poor. While the discovery of poverty, coupled with an assumption of the impossibility of removing it, had formerly brought about a revulsion against riches, this time a deep-rooted appreciation of worldly goods, coupled with a sense of power, caused an onslaught on poverty itself. Riches had been a scandal in the face of poverty; now poverty was a scandal in the face of riches. . . . To the pace-making middle classes, profoundly committed to the religion of progress, the existence of poverty was not only emotionally but intellectually disturbing: in the same manner as is the existence of evil to the simpler sort of deist. The increasing goodness of civilization, the increasing power of man, were to be finally demonstrated by the eradication of poverty.

Thus charity and pride went hand in hand. In stressing the role played by pride it is not intended to belittle the part given to charity. Assuredly there are moments in history when the human heart is suddenly mellowed and some phenomenon of this kind occurs. Thus redistribution was sped on its way by a feeling, or pattern of feelings. . . .

## The Notions of Relief and of Lifting Working-Class Standards Merged

We must, however, note that redistribution appears as a novelty only in contrast to the practices immediately preceding it and in the choice of its agent, the State. It is inherent in the very notion of society that those in direct want must be taken care of. The principle is applied in every family and in every small community, and in fact went out of practice only a few generations ago as a result of the disruption of smaller communities by the Industrial Revolution. This caused the isolation of the individual, and the new "master" he acquired did not regard himself as bound to him by the same ties as the former lord. It is characteristic that the feasts of consumption of the landed class were feasts *for all*, whereas the consumption of the rich in the new era is purely selfish. It is moreover almost needless to point out that the church, when it enjoyed enormous gifts from the powerful and the rich, was a great redistributive agency. Between the old customs and the age of the welfare state stretch the "hard times," when the individual was left helpless in his need.

This cannot be ascribed to lack of feeling in generations which were fired with sympathy for slaves, for oppressed nationalities, and with indignation at the news of the "Bulgarian atrocities." One is tempted to conclude that men's powers of sympathy vary in their direction over periods of time, and are somewhat limited at any one moment. However, concern for the least favoured was certainly not absent, as Malthus, Sismondi and many others testify.

The twentieth century offers no more forceful statement of maldistribution than that of John Stuart Mill. But it was assumed that the standard of life of "the people" would be raised by the cheapening of goods, of which the cheapening of salt and spices offered a promising instance. Moreover the relative position of the labourer would be improved by the cheapening of capital. Faith in the benefits of a competitive economy for "the common man" was not ill-grounded, as the American example testifies. But perhaps there was some confusion between two different notions: *one*, that the situation of the "median" worker is best improved by the play of productive forces; and *two*, that there is no call to take care of an unfortunate "rearguard." Such is the "stickiness" of social thinking that as long as emphasis was laid on the raising of the median by the processes of the market, there was reluctance to intervene on behalf of the unfortunate (compare the attitude of the American Federation of Labor in the first years of the Great Depression), while as soon as attention was focussed upon this rearguard, it came to be held that the median condition was also to be raised by political measures.

While relief is an unquestionable social obligation which the destruction of neighbourliness, of responsible aristocracies and of Church wealth has laid on the State for want of any other agency, it is open to discussion whether policies of redistribution are the best means of dealing with the problem of raising *median* working incomes, whether they can be effective, and whether they do not come into conflict with other legitimate social objectives.

The distinction drawn here is admittedly a difficult one. The two things are confused in practice, and it is not always clear to which end the enormous social machinery set up in our generation is actually working; this creation of ours presents a structure not easily amenable to our intellectual categories. When, through the working of the social services, a man in actual want is provided with the means of subsistence, whether it be a minimum income in days of unemployment, or basic medical care for which he could not have paid, this is a primary manifestation of solidarity. And it does not come under redistribution as we understand it here.

What does come under redistribution is everything which relieves the individual of an expenditure that he could and presumably would have undertaken out of his own purse, and which, freeing a proportion of his income, is therefore equivalent to a raising of this income. A family which would have bought the same amount of food at non-subsidized prices and gets it so much cheaper, an individual who would have sought the same medical services and gets them free, see their incomes raised. And this is what we want to discuss.

As we know, this does not apply only to poorer people: in some countries, especially in England, all incomes are raised in this manner while most incomes are drawn upon to finance the raising. The impact upon incomes of this enormous diversion and redistribution is a very complicated subject with which we are not ready to deal. It is far from being a simple redistribution from the richer to the the poorer. And yet it is to a large degree sustained by the belief that this is what the whole process comes to. This basic motivating thought is what we want to deal with.

### Indecent Low-Living and Indecent High-Living

We propose to deal with redistribution in its pure form: that is, taking from the higher incomes to add to the lower incomes. Such a policy is sustained by a pattern of feeling from which we shall try to extract some implied judgments of value. The urge to redistribute is closely attended by a sense of scandal: it is scandalous that so many should be in dire need, it is also scandalous that so many more should have an inadequate mode of life, which seems to us, in the original sense of the word, indecent. Thus the urge to redistribute is associated more or less with an idea of a *floor* beneath which no one should be left.

In thinking of the higher incomes, we are also conscious of an indecency: the upper modes of life seem to us wasteful of riches which could cover far more legitimate needs. That is, if you will, condemnation by comparison. But there is moreover a certain "way of the rich" which seems to us to call for absolute condemnation. We should in any event have scant sympathy with expenditure in night-clubs, casinos, on horse-racing and so on.

These two judgments of value are generally fused in the very general feeling which may be termed the "caviar into bread" motive. Not only do we disapprove of the feast of caviar when others lack bread but we disapprove of it absolutely. . . .

### The Floor and the Ceiling. Intellectual Harmony and Financial Harmony

We now need a terminology which we shall keep within modest bounds. We call *floor* the minimum income regarded as necessary and *ceiling* the maximum income regarded as desirable. We call floor and ceiling "intellectually harmonious" in so far as they are the floor and ceiling acceptable to the same mind or minds. Further, we shall call a floor and ceiling "financially harmonious" in so far as there is sufficient surplus to be taken from "above the ceiling" incomes to make up the deficiency in "beneath the floor" incomes. . . .

Redistributionism is a spontaneous feeling. And in its more naive forms it carries with it an implied conviction that the floor and ceiling which are intellectually harmonious will also prove to be financially harmonious. This, like so many spontaneous assumptions of the human mind, is an error. Questioning members of the western intelligentsia, unfamiliar with income statistics, on the suitable floor and ceiling of incomes is absorbingly interesting. . . .

[O]ur calculations bring out the neglected fact that the present degree of redistribution would already be impracticable were it, as one believes, essentially a redistribution from the rich to the poor; it proves possible because it is quite as much a horizontal shift as an oblique drift.

The outcome of this exploration comes as something of a surprise. It jolts a widely held belief that our societies are extremely rich and that their wealth is merely maldistributed: a belief unwisely disseminated by the well-meaning abundance-mongers of the 'thirties. What we do find is that such surpluses as we might be willing ruthlessly to take away—always assuming that this would have no effect upon production—are by a long way inadequate to raise our nether incomes to a desirable level. The pursuit of our purpose involves the debasement of even the lower-middle-class standard of life.

Redistributionism was at the outset given its impetus by two absolute disapprovals; the unrightness of underconsumption was matched by the unrightness of overconsumption. What luck if, in order to achieve a worthy purpose, you have to sacrifice nothing of value, if indeed your means to the suppression of an evil are also desirable of themselves! Thus the problem appeared to the intellectual, sitting in judgment upon society. There were bad patterns of life, those of the poor, which he wished to do away with; and he expected that this could be accomplished merely by the suppression of other bad patterns of life, those of the rich. The intellectual (not the artist) is naturally out of sympathy with the extrovert way of life of the rich. There was thus no social loss, in his eyes, implied in redistribution policies. But if the income ceiling is to be brought as low as we have suggested, then there is a great change. It is now worthy patterns of life which are to be destroyed, standards which the intellectual has been accustomed to and which he holds necessary to the performance of those social functions he most appreciates.

And so, while it still seems right to give, the rightness of taking away is far less obvious. It is easy to say: "Rothschild must forgo his yacht." It is quite another thing to say: "I am afraid Bergson must lose the modest competence which made it possible for him to do his work." Nor is it only a question of unearned income: the executive, the public servant, the engineer, the intellectual, the artist are to be cramped. Is this desirable? Is this right? . . .

## A Discussion of Satisfactions

Redistribution started with a feeling that some have too little and some too much. When attempts are made to express this feeling more precisely, two formulae are spontaneously offered. The first we may call objective, the second subjective. The objective formula is based upon an idea of a decent way of life beneath which no one should fall and above which other ways of life are desirable and acceptable within a certain range. The subjective formula is not based upon a notion of what is objectively good for men but can be roughly stated as follows: "The richer would feel their loss less than the poorer would appreciate their gain"; or even more roughly: "A certain loss of income would mean less to the richer than the consequent gain would mean to the poorer."

Here a comparison of satisfactions is made. Can such a comparison be rendered effective? Can we with any precision come to weigh losses of satisfaction to some and gains of satisfaction to others? . . .

It is not to be proven that the sum of individual satisfactions of people benefited is greater than the sum of dissatisfactions of people despoiled. In fact there is every reason to believe that if what is taken from a number of people were distributed among an equal number of people, the latter would gain less total satisfaction than the former were losing. But the fact is that the takings are distributed among a far greater number of people. And there will be more people pleased than displeased, more positive signs than negative: and as the intensity of the values is not to be measured, all one can do is state that there are more positive signs than negative and take the result as a gain; which is what in fact is currently done.

It is, however, generally granted that the intensity of dissatisfactions should not be pushed too far, and the process of reducing upper incomes is therefore to be effected over a period of time.

It has been suggested that the assumed impossibility of measuring dissatisfactions against satisfactions might be overcome by empirical means. If indeed we took Lansing's view of democracy as a regime of well-regulated strife where force is made to prevail without violence, we might say that the dissatisfaction caused by loss of income is measured by the political resistance opposed to measures of redistribution, and that success or failure of this resistance denotes the excess of dissatisfaction over satisfaction or the contrary. Thus the outcome of the political struggle over incomes would always maximize welfare.

However, it would be so only if all protagonists were concerned with nothing but their personal satisfaction, and were indifferent to any moral imperative. Then indeed, the vigour of their several demands would be expressive of the intensity of their satisfactions. Fortunately the struggle occurs nowhere in such a climate of clear and conscious selfishness.

## Discrimination Against Minorities

The inexpediency of radical levelling in the short run is easily granted. The psychologist warns of the violent, socially disruptive discontent of those suddenly toppled down from their customary modes of life. The economist warns that the conversion to popular use of those productive resources which specifically served the well-to-do will not, in the short run, yield in popular goods and services anything like the value previously yielded in luxury goods and services.

Conceding objections to short run levelling does not weaken the case for long-run levelling. Indeed it strengthens it. For the greater willingness one shows to postpone radical equalization in order to accommodate acquired tastes, the more one implies that differences in subjective wants are a matter of habit, a historic phenomenon. While it would seem excessive to equalize incomes between the men of today, known to us and whom we know to have different needs, it seems plausible to do so in the case of men whose personalities we can imagine to differ less from one another—for the very good reason that they have as yet no personalities. Thereby we can project forward as reasonable what might in reality strike us as absurd.

It is a common behaviour of the mind, naturally enamoured of simplicity, to build its schemes far away from the annoying complexities of a familiar reality, in the future or in a mythical past, where things have no shapes of their own. After this first operation resulting in a rational scheme, that scheme can be used as a rational model against which the disorderly architecture of today can be measured, and thereby condemned.

Let us however notice a certain consequence of equalization, valid in whatever future we care to place the completion of reform. Let us grant that any differences in tastes due to social habits have been erased. Men will not however be uniform in character; some differences in tastes must exist among individuals. Economic demand will not any more be weighted by differences in individual incomes that will have been abolished: it will be weighted solely by numbers. It is clear that those goods and services in demand by greater collections of individuals will be provided to those individuals more cheaply than other goods and services wanted by smaller collections of individuals will be provided to these latter. The satisfaction of minority wants will be more expensive than the satisfaction of majority wants. Members of a minority will be discriminated against.

There is nothing novel in this phenomenon. It is a regular feature of any economic society. People of uncommon tastes are at a disadvantage for the satisfaction of their wants. But they can and do endeavour to raise their incomes in order to pay for their distinctive wants. And this by the way is a most potent incentive; its efficiency is illustrated by the more than average effort, the higher incomes and the leading positions achieved by racial and religious minorities; what is true of these well-defined minorities is just as true of individuals presenting original traits. Sociologists will readily grant that, in a society where free competition obtains, the more active and the more successful are also those with the more uncommon personalities.

If, however, it is not open to those whose tastes differ from the common run to remedy their economic disadvantage by an increase in their incomes, then, in the name of equality, they will be enduring discrimination.

Four consequences deserve notice. Firstly, personal hardship for individuals of original tastes; secondly, the loss to society of the special effort these people would make in order to satisfy their special needs; thirdly, the loss to society of the variety in ways of life resulting from successful efforts to satisfy special wants; fourthly, the loss to society of those activities which are supported by minority demands.

With respect to the latter point, it is a commonplace that things which are now provided inexpensively to the many, say spices or the newspaper, were originally luxuries which could be offered only because some few were willing and able to buy them at high prices. It is difficult to say what the economic development of the West would have been, had first things been put first, as reformers urge; that is, if the productive effort had been aimed at providing more of the things needed by all, to the exclusion of a greater variety of things desired by minorities. But the onus of proving that economic progress would have been as impressive surely rests with the reformers. History shows us that each successive enlargement of the opportunities to consume was linked with unequal distribution of means to consume.

### The Effect of Redistribution Upon Society

No one has attempted to draw the picture of the society which would result from radical redistribution, as called for by the logic of reasoning on the maximization of satisfactions. Even if one were to compromise on such a floor-and-ceiling society . . . it would still be one which would exclude the present modes of life of our leaders in every field: whether they are business men, public servants, artists, intellectuals or trade-unionists.

We have forbidden ourselves to contemplate any decrease in the activity of anyone, any lowering of production as a whole. But the reallocation of incomes would bring about a great shift in activities. The demand for some goods and services would be increased. The demand for others would drop or disappear. It is not beyond the skill of those economists who have specialized in consumer behaviour to calculate roughly how far the demand of certain items would rise and how far the demand of certain others would drop. . . .

I for one would see without chagrin the disappearance of many activities which serve the richer, but no one surely would gladly accept the disappearance of all the activities which find their market in the classes enjoying more than 500 pounds of net income. The production of all first quality goods would cease. The skill they demand would be lost and the taste they shape would be coarsened. The production of artistic and intellectual goods would be affected first and foremost. Who would buy paintings? Who even could buy books other than pulp?

Can we reconcile ourselves to the loss suffered by civilization if creative intellectual and artistic activities fail to find a market? We must if we follow the logic of the felicific calculus. If the two thousand guineas heretofore spent by two thousand buyers of an original piece of historical or philosophical research, are henceforth spent by forty-two thousand buyers of shilling books, aggregate satisfaction is very probably enhanced. There is therefore a gain to society, according to this mode of thought which represents society as a collection of independent consumers. Felicific calculus, counting in units of satisfactions afforded to individuals, cannot enter into its accounts the loss involved in the suppression of the piece of research. A fact which, by the way, brings to light the radically individualistic assumptions of a viewpoint usually labelled socialistic.

In fact, and although this entails an intellectual inconsistency, the most eager champions of income redistribution are highly sensitive to the cultural losses involved. And they press upon us a strong restorative. It is true that individuals will not be able to build up private libraries; but there will be bigger and better and ever more numerous public libraries. It is true that the producer of the book will not be sustained by individual buyers; but the author will be given a public grant, and so forth. All advocates of extreme redistribution couple it with most generous measures of state support for the whole superstructure of cultural activities. This calls for two comments. We shall deal first with the measures of compensation, and then with their significance.

### The More Redistribution, The More Power to the State

Already, when stressing the loss of investment capital which would result from a redistribution of incomes, we found that the necessary counterpart of lopping off the tops of higher incomes was the diversion by the State from these incomes of as much, or almost as much, as they used to pour into investment; the assumption which followed logically was that the State would take care of investment: a great function, a great responsibility, and a great power.

Now we find that by making it impossible for individuals to support cultural activities out of their shrunken incomes, we have devolved upon the State another great function, another great power.

It then follows that the State finances, and therefore chooses, investments; and that it finances cultural activities, and must thenceforth, choose which it supports. There being no private buyers left for books or paintings or other creative work, the State must support literature and the arts either as buyer or as provider of *beneficia* to the producers, or in both capacities.

This is a rather disquieting thought. How quickly this State mastery follows upon measures of redistribution we can judge by the enormous progress towards such mastery which has already followed from limited redistribution.

## Values and Satisfactions

But the fact that redistributionists are eager to repair by State expenditure the degradation of higher activities which would result from redistribution left to itself is very significant. They want to prevent a loss of values. Does this make sense? . . .

Surely, when we achieve the distribution of incomes which, it is claimed, maximizes the sum of satisfactions, we must let this distribution of incomes exert its influence upon the allocation of resources and productive activities, for it is only through this adjustment that the distribution of incomes is made meaningful. And when resources are so allocated, we must not interfere with their disposition, since by doing so we shall, as a matter of course, decrease the sum of satisfactions. It is then an inconsistency, and a very blatant one, to intervene with state support for such cultural activities as do not find a market. Those who spontaneously correct their schemes of redistribution by schemes for such support are in fact denying that the ideal allocation of resources and activities is that which maximizes the sum of satisfactions.

But it is clear that by this denial the whole process of reasoning by which redistribution is justified falls to the ground. If we say that, although people would be better satisfied to spend a certain sum on needs they are more conscious of, we deprive them of this satisfaction in order to support a painter, we obviously lose the right to argue that James's income must go to the mass of the people because satisfaction will thereby be increased. For all we know, James may be supporting the painter. We cannot accept the criterion of maximizing satisfactions when we are destroying private incomes, and then reject it when we are planning state expenditure.

The recognition that maximizing satisfactions may destroy values which we are all willing to restore at the cost of moving away from the position of maximal satisfaction destroys the criterion of maximizing satisfactions.

## Are Subjective Satisfactions an Exclusive Standard?

Indeed, the foregoing discussion reaches beyond a mere refutation of the formal argument for income redistribution. Economists as such are interested in the play of consumer's preferences through the market, and in showing how this play guides the allocation of productive resources so that it comes to correspond with the consumer's preferences. The perfection of the correspondence is general equilibrium. It is perfection of a kind: and it is quite legitimate to speak of such allocation of resources as the best, it being understood that it is the best from the angle of subjective wants, weighted by the actual distribution of incomes. . . . Calling it the best without qualification implies a value judgment which equates the good with the desired, on Hobbesian lines. Now it is quite legitimate for the economist to deal only with the desired and not with the good. But it is not legitimate to treat the optimum in relation to desires as an optimum in any other sense. And that the allocation of resources in relation to desires should fail to be optimal by other standards should not come as a surprise to us.

That a society which we may assume to have maximized the sum of subjective satisfactions should, when we survey it as a whole, strike us as falling far short of a "good society," could have been foreseen by anyone with a Christian background or a classical education.

To the many, however, who were apt to think so much in terms of satisfactions that the "badness" of society seemed to them due to the uneven distribution of satisfactions, it must come as a most useful lesson that the outcome of this viewpoint leads them into an unacceptable state of affairs. The error must then lie in the original assumption that incomes are to be regarded solely as means to consumer-enjoyment. In so far as they are so regarded, the form of society which maximizes the sum of consumer-enjoyments should be best: and yet it is unacceptable. It follows that incomes are not to be so regarded.

### Redistributionism the End Result of Utilitarian Individualism

There is no doubt that incomes are currently regarded as means to consumer-enjoyment, and society as an association for the promotion of consumption. This is made clear by the character of the controversy now proceeding on the theme of redistribution. The arguments set against one another are cut from the same cloth. It is fair, some say, to equalize consumer-satisfactions. It is prudent, the others retort, to allow greater rewards to spur production and thereby provide greater means of consumption.

There is an Armenian proverb: "The world is a pot and man a spoon in it." In this image our two sides might choose slogans: an expanding pot with unequal spoons, or a static and possibly declining pot with equal spoons. But perhaps the world is not a pot and surely man is not a spoon. Here we have completely slipped away from any conception of the "good life" and the "good society." It is quite inadmissible to consider the "good life" as a buyer's spree or the "good society" as a suitable queueing up of buyers. And the redistributionist ideal represents a disastrous fall from socialism.

Socialism, before its disastrous decay into a new version of enlightened despotism, was an ethical social doctrine. And as such a doctrine must, to merit the double epithet, it looked to a "good society", which it saw as one wherein men would have better relations with one another, and feel more kindly towards their fellows. This spirit seems to have evaporated from modern reformist tendencies. Redistributionism takes its cue wholly from the society it seeks to reform. An increased consuming power is the promise held out, and fulfilled, by capitalist mercantile society: so is it the promise of the modern reformer. And in fact the choice of right or left is to be finally regarded as not an ethical choice at all, but a bet. Taking, say, the period 1956-65, do we bet that redistributionism with its probable negative effect on economic progress will provide a majority with a higher standard of living than capitalism with its inequality? Or do we put our money—it seems the proper term—on the other horse?

There is no question of ethics here. The end-product of society is anyhow taken to be personal consumption: this is, under socialistic colours, the extremity of individualism. Finally my probable consumption under one or the other system is to be my criterion. Nothing quite so trivial has ever been made into a social ideal. But it is wrong to accuse our reformers of having invented it: they found it.

What is to be held against them is not that they are utopian, it is that they completely fail to be so; it is not their excessive imagination, but their complete lack of it; not that they wish to transform society beyond the realm of possibility, but that they have renounced any essential transformation; not that their means are unrealistic, but that their ends are flat-footed. In fact the mode of thought which tends to predominate in advanced circles is nothing but the tail-end of nineteenth century utilitarianism.

# Selections from *Mein Kampf*

## *Adolf Hitler (1889–1945)*

*As the leader of the National Socialist Workers Party (the Nazis), Hitler was jailed in Bavaria in 1923 for his part in the failed Beer Hall Putsch. With the collaboration of others, he wrote this long diatribe against critics within and without the party, describing his "struggle" against the decadence of democracy and his plans for world domination by the "Aryan" race with himself at its head. The author says in his preface, "I know men are won over less by the written than by the spoken word, that every great movement on this earth owes its growth to great orators and not to great writers. Nevertheless, for a doctrine to be disseminated uniformly and coherently, its basic elements must be set down for all time." The book was published in 1925 and eventually received wide circulation through pressure by the Nazi Party, but, although it accurately reflected Hitler's goals and purposes, it was largely ignored by the German people and the world.*

*Hitler appears to give arguments for his charges against the Jewish people, the liberal form of government, and the socialist movement. What are they? What is the difference between political argument and rhetorical assertion? Does Hitler make a sound case for the radical inequality of men? Is social life rightly understood in terms of survival of the fittest? What does Hitler mean by "Germanic democracy"? Compare it with Aristotle's and Publius' definitions of democracy.*

### NATION AND RACE

Any crossing of two beings not at exactly the same level produces a medium between the level of the two parents. This means: the offspring will probably stand higher than the racially lower parent, but not as high as the higher one. Consequently, it will later succumb in the struggle against the higher level. Such mating is contrary to the will of Nature for a higher breeding of all life. The precondition for this does not lie in associating superior and inferior, but in the total victory of the former. The stronger must dominate and not blend with the weaker, thus sacrificing his own greatness. Only the born weakling can view this as cruel, but he after all is only a weak and limited man; for if this law did not prevail, any conceivable higher development of organic living beings would be unthinkable.

The consequence of this racial purity, universally valid in Nature, is not only the sharp outward delimitation of the various races, but their uniform character in themselves. The fox is always a fox, the goose a goose, the tiger a tiger, etc., and the difference can lie at most in the varying measure of force, strength, intelligence, dexterity, endurance, etc., of the individual specimens. But you will never find a fox who in his inner attitude might, for example, show humanitarian tendencies toward geese, as similarly there is no cat with a friendly inclination toward mice.

Therefore, here, too, the struggle among themselves arises less from inner aversion than from hunger and love. In both cases, Nature looks on calmly, with satisfaction, in fact. In the struggle for daily bread all those who are weak and sickly or less determined succumb, while the struggle of the males for the female grants the right or opportunity to propagate only to the healthiest. And struggle is always a means for improving a species' health and power of resistance and, therefore, a cause of its higher development.

If the process were different, all further and higher development would cease and the opposite would occur. For, since the inferior always predominates numerically over the best, if both had the same possibility of preserving life and propagating, the inferior would multiply so much more rapidly that in the end the best would inevitably be driven into the background, unless a correction of this state of affairs were undertaken. Nature does just this by subjecting the weaker part to such severe living conditions that by them alone the number is limited, and by not permitting the remainder to increase promiscuously, but making a new and ruthless choice according to strength and health.

No more than Nature desires the mating of weaker with stronger individuals, even less does she desire the blending of a higher with a lower race, since, if she did, her whole work of higher breeding, over perhaps hundreds of thousands of years, might be ruined with one blow.

Historical experience offers countless proofs of this. It shows with terrifying clarity that in every mingling of Aryan blood with that of lower peoples the result was the end of the cultured people. North America, whose population consists in by far the largest part of Germanic elements who mixed but little with the lower colored peoples, shows a different humanity and culture from Central and South America, where the predominantly Latin immigrants often mixed with the aborigines on a large scale. By this one example, we can clearly and distinctly recognize the effect of racial mixture. The Germanic inhabitant of the American continent, who has remained racially pure and unmixed, rose to be master of the continent; he will remain the master as long as he does not fall a victim to defilement of the blood.

The result of all racial crossing is therefore in brief always the following:

(a)  Lowering of the level of the higher race;
(b)  Physical and intellectual regression and hence the beginning of a slowly but surely progressing sickness.

To bring about such a development is, then, nothing else but to sin against the will of the eternal creator.

And as a sin this act is rewarded.

When man attempts to rebel against the iron logic of Nature, he comes into struggle with the principles to which he himself owes his existence as a man. And this attack must lead to his own doom. . . .

Everything we admire on this earth today—science and art, technology and inventions—is only the creative product of a few peoples and originally perhaps of *one* race. On them depends the existence of this whole culture. If they perish, the beauty of this earth will sink into the grave with them.

However much the soil, for example, can influence men, the result of the influence will always be different depending on the races in question. The low fertility of a living space may spur the one race to the highest achievements; in others it will only be the cause of bitterest poverty and final undernourishment with all its consequences. The inner nature of peoples is always determining for the manner in which outward influences will be effective. What leads the one to starvation trains the other to hard work.

All great cultures of the past perished only because the originally creative race died out from blood poisoning.

The ultimate cause of such a decline was their forgetting that all culture depends on men and not conversely; hence that to preserve a certain culture the man who creates it must be preserved.

This preservation is bound up with the rigid law of necessity and the right to victory of the best and stronger in this world.

Those who want to live, let them fight, and those who do not want to fight in this world of eternal struggle do not deserve to live.

Even if this were hard—that is how it is! Assuredly, however, by far the harder fate is that which strikes the man who thinks he can overcome Nature, but in the last analysis only mocks her. Distress, misfortune, and disease are her answer.

The man who misjudges and disregards the racial laws actually forfeits the happiness that seems destined to be his. He thwarts the triumphal march of the best race and hence also the precondition for all human progress, and remains, in consequence, burdened with all the sensibility of man, in the animal realm of helpless misery.

It is idle to argue which race or races were the original representative of human culture and hence the real founders of all that we sum up under the word humanity. It is simpler to raise this question with regard to the present, and here an easy, clear answer results. All the human culture, all the results of art, science, and technology that we see before us today, are almost exclusively the creative product of the Aryan. This very fact admits of the not unfounded inference that he alone was the founder of all higher humanity, therefore representing the prototype of all that we understand by the word man. He is the Prometheus of mankind from whose bright forehead the divine spark of genius has sprung at all times, forever kindling anew that fire of knowledge which illumined the night of silent mysteries and thus caused man to climb the path to mastery over the other beings of this earth. Exclude him—and perhaps after a few thousand years darkness will again descend on the earth, human culture will pass, and the world turn to a desert.

If we were to divide mankind into three groups, the founders of culture, the bearers of culture, the destroyers of culture, only the Aryan could be considered as the representative of the first group. From him originate the foundations and walls of all human creation, and only the outward form and color are determined by the changing traits of character of the various peoples. He provides the mightiest building stones and plans for all human progress and only the execution corresponds to the nature of the varying men and races. In a few decades, for example, the entire east of Asia will possess a culture whose ultimate foundation will be Hellenic spirit and Germanic technology, just as much as in Europe. Only the *outward* form—in part at least—will bear the features of Asiatic character. It is not true, as some people think, that Japan adds European technology to its culture; no, European science and technology are trimmed with Japanese characteristics. The foundation of actual life is no longer the special Japanese culture, although it determines the color of life—because outwardly, in consequence of its inner difference, it is more conspicuous to the European—but the gigantic scientific-technical achievements of Europe and America; that is, of Aryan peoples. Only on the basis of these achievements can the Orient follow general human progress. They furnish the basis of the struggle for daily bread, create weapons and implements for it, and only the outward form is gradually adapted to Japanese character.

If beginning today all further Aryan influence on Japan should stop, assuming that Europe and America should perish, Japan's present rise in science and technology might continue for a short time; but even in a few years the well would dry up, the Japanese special character would gain, but the present culture would freeze and sink back into the slumber from which it was awakened seven decades ago by the wave of Aryan culture. Therefore, just as the present Japanese development owes its life to Aryan origin, long ago in the gray past foreign influence and foreign spirit awakened the Japanese culture of that time. The best proof of this is furnished by the fact of its subsequent sclerosis and total petrifaction. This can occur in a people only when the original creative racial nucleus has been lost, or if the external influence which furnished the impetus and the material for the first development in the cultural field was later lacking. But if it is established that a people receives the most essential basic materials of its culture from foreign races, that it assimilates and adapts them, and that then, if further external influence is lacking, it rigidifies again and again, such a race may be designated as *"culture-bearing,"* but never as *"culture-creating."* An examination of the various peoples from this standpoint points to the fact that practically none of them were originally *culture-founding* but almost always *culture-bearing.*

Approximately the following picture of their development always results:

Aryan races—often absurdly small numerically—subject foreign peoples, and then, stimulated by the special living conditions of the new territory (fertility, climatic conditions, etc.) and assisted by the multitude of lower-type beings standing at their disposal as helpers, develop the intellectual and organizational capacities dormant within them. Often in a few millenniums or even centuries they create cultures which originally bear all the inner characteristics of their nature, adapted to the above-indicated special qualities of the soil and subjected beings. In the end, however, the conquerors transgress against the principle of blood purity, to which they had first adhered; they begin to mix with the subjugated inhabitants and thus end their own existence; for the fall of man in paradise has always been followed by his expulsion.

After a thousand years and more, the last visible trace of the former master people is often seen in the lighter skin color which its blood left behind in the subjugated race, and in a petrified culture which it had originally created. For, once the actual and spiritual conqueror lost himself in the blood of the subjected people, the fuel for the torch of human progress was lost! Just as, through the blood of the former masters, the color preserved a feeble gleam in their memory, likewise the night of cultural life is gently illumined by the remaining creations of the former light-bringers. They shine through all the returned barbarism and too often inspire the thoughtless observer of the moment with the opinion that he beholds the picture of the present people before him, whereas he is only gazing into the mirror of the past.

It is then possible that such a people will a second time, or even more often in the course of its history, come into contact with the race of those who once brought it culture, and the memory of former encounters will not necessarily be present. Unconsciously the remnant of the former master blood will turn toward the new arrival, and what was first possible only by compulsion can now succeed through the people's own will. A new cultural wave makes its entrance and continues until those who have brought it are again submerged in the blood of foreign peoples. . . .

The progress of humanity is like climbing an endless ladder; it is impossible to climb higher without first taking the lower steps. Thus, the Aryan had to take the road to which reality directed him and not the one that would appeal to the imagination of a modern pacifist. The road of reality is hard and difficult, but in the end it leads where our friend would like to bring humanity by dreaming, but unfortunately removes more than bringing it closer.

Hence it is no accident that the first cultures rose in places where the Aryan, in his encounters with lower peoples, subjugated them and bent them to his will. They then became the first technical instrument in the service of a developing culture.

Thus, the road which the Aryan had to take was clearly marked out. As a conquerer he subjected the lower beings and regulated their practical activity under his command, according to his will and for his aims. But in directing them to a useful, though arduous activity, he not only spared the life of those he subjected; perhaps he gave them a fate that was better than their previous so-called freedom. As long as he ruthlessly upheld the master attitude, not only did he really remain master, but also the preserver and increaser of culture. For culture was based exclusively on his abilities and hence on his actual survival. As soon as the subjected people began to raise themselves up and probably approached the conqueror in language, the sharp dividing wall between master and servant fell. The Aryan gave up the purity of his blood and, therefore, lost his sojourn in the paradise which he had made for himself. He became submerged in the racial mixture, and gradually, more and more, lost his cultural capacity, until at last, not only mentally but also physically, he began to resemble the subjected aborigines more than his own ancestors. For a time he could live on the existing cultural benefits, but then petrifaction set in and he fell a prey to oblivion.

Thus cultures and empires collapsed to make place for new formations.

Blood mixture and the resultant drop in the racial level is the sole cause of the dying out of old cultures; for men do not perish as a result of lost wars, but by the loss of that force of resistance which is contained only in pure blood.

All who are not of good race in this world are chaff.

And all occurrences in world history are only the expression of the races' instinct of self-preservation, in the good or bad sense. . . .

The mightiest counterpart to the Aryan is represented by the Jew. In hardly any people in the world is the instinct of self-preservation developed more strongly than in the so-called chosen. Of this, the mere fact of the survival of this race may be considered the best proof. Where is the people which in the last two thousand years has been exposed to so slight changes of inner disposition, character, etc., as the Jewish people? What people, finally, has gone through greater upheavals than this one—and nevertheless issued from the mightiest catastrophes of mankind unchanged? What an infinitely tough will to live and preserve the species speaks from these facts!

The mental qualities of the Jew have been schooled in the course of many centuries. Today he passes as smart, and this in a certain sense he has been at all times. But his intelligence is not the result of his own development, but of visual instruction through foreigners. For the human mind cannot climb to the top without steps; for every step upward he needs the foundation of the past, and this in the comprehensive sense in which it can be revealed only in general culture. All thinking is based only in small part on man's own knowledge, and mostly on the experience of the time that has preceded. The general cultural level provides the individual man, without his noticing it as a rule, with such a profusion of preliminary knowledge that, thus armed, he can more easily take further steps of his own. The boy of today, for example, grows up among a truly vast number of technical acquisitions of the last centuries, so that he takes for granted and no longer pays attention to much that a hundred years ago was a riddle to even the greatest minds, although for following and understanding our progress in the field in question it is of decisive importance to him. If a very genius from the twenties of the past century should suddenly leave his grave today, it would be harder for him even intellectually to find his way in the present era than for an average boy of fifteen today. For he would lack all the infinite preliminary education which our present contemporary unconsciously, so to speak, assimilates while growing up amidst the manifestations of our present general civilization.

Since the Jew—for reasons which will at once become apparent—was never in possession of a culture of his own, the foundations of his intellectual work were always provided by others. His intellect at all times developed through the cultural world surrounding him.

The reverse process never took place.

For if the Jewish people's instinct of self-preservation is not smaller but larger than that of other peoples, if his intellectual faculties can easily arouse the impression that they are equal to the intellectual gifts of other races, he lacks completely the most essential requirement for a cultured people, the idealistic attitude.

In the Jewish people the will to self-sacrifice does not go beyond the individual's naked instinct of self-preservation. Their apparently great sense of solidarity is based on the very primitive herd instinct that is seen in many other living creatures in this world. It is a noteworthy fact that the herd instinct leads to mutual support only as long as a common danger makes this seem useful or inevitable. The same pack of wolves which has just fallen on its prey together disintegrates when hunger abates into its individual beasts. The same is true of horses which try to defend themselves against an assailant in a body, but scatter again as soon as the danger is past.

It is similar with the Jew. His sense of sacrifice is only apparent. It exists only as long as the existence of the individual makes it absolutely necessary. However, as soon as the common enemy is conquered, the danger threatening all averted and the booty hidden, the apparent harmony of the Jews among themselves ceases, again making way for their old causal tendencies. The Jew is only united when a common danger forces him to be or a common booty entices him; if these two grounds are lacking, the qualities of the crassest egoism come into their own, and in the twinkling of an eye the united people turns into a horde of rats, fighting bloodily among themselves.

If the Jews were alone in this world, they would stifle in filth and offal; they would try to get ahead of one another in hate-filled struggle and exterminate one another, in so far as the absolute absence of all sense of self-sacrifice, expressing itself in their cowardice, did not turn battle into comedy here too.

So it is absolutely wrong to infer any ideal sense of sacrifice in the Jews from the fact that they stand together in struggle, or, better expressed, in the plundering of their fellow men.

Here again the Jew is led by nothing but the naked egoism of the individual.

That is why the Jewish state—which should be the living organism for preserving and increasing a race—is completely unlimited as to territory. For a state formation to have a definite spatial setting always presupposes an idealistic attitude on the part of the state-race, and especially a correct interpretation of the concept of work. In the exact measure in which this attitude is lacking, any attempt at forming, even of preserving, a spatially delimited state fails. And thus the basis on which alone culture can arise is lacking.

Hence the Jewish people, despite all apparent intellectual qualities, is without any true culture, and especially without any culture of its own. For what sham culture the Jew today possesses is the property of other peoples, and for the most part it is ruined in his hands.

In judging the Jewish people's attitude on the question of human culture, the most essential characteristic we must always bear in mind is that there has never been a Jewish art and accordingly there is none today either; that above all the two queens of all the arts, architecture and music, owe nothing original to the Jews. What they do accomplish in the field of art is either patchwork or intellectual theft. Thus, the Jew lacks those qualities which distinguish the races that are creative and hence culturally blessed.

To what an extent the Jew takes over foreign culture, imitating or rather ruining it, can be seen from the fact that he is mostly found in the art which seems to require least original invention, the art of acting. But even here, in reality, he is only a juggler, or rather an ape; for even here he lacks the last touch that is required for real greatness; even here he is not the creative genius, but a superficial imitator, and all the twists and tricks that he uses are powerless to conceal the inner lifelessness of his creative gift. Here the Jewish press most lovingly helps him along by raising such a roar of hosannahs about even the most mediocre bungler, just so long as he is a Jew, that the rest of the world actually ends up by thinking that they have an artist before them, while in truth it is only a pitiful comedian.

No, the Jew possesses no culture-creating force of any sort, since the idealism, without which there is no true higher development of man, is not present in him and never was present. Hence his intellect will never have a constructive effect, but will be destructive, and in very rare cases perhaps will at most be stimulating, but then as the prototype of the force which always wants evil and nevertheless creates good. Not through him does any progress of mankind occur, but in spite of him.

Since the Jew never possessed a state with definite territorial limits and therefore never called a culture his own, the conception arose that this was a people which should be reckoned among the ranks of the *nomads*. This is a fallacy as great as it is dangerous. The nomad does possess a definitely limited living space, only he does not cultivate it like a sedentary peasant, but lives from the yield of his herds with which he wanders about in his territory. The outward reason for this is to be found in the small fertility of a soil which simply does not permit of settlement. The deeper cause, however, lies in the disparity between the technical culture of an age or people and the natural poverty of a living space. There are territories in which even the Aryan is enabled only by his technology, developed in the course of more than a thousand years, to live in regular settlements, to master broad stretches of soil and obtain from it the requirements of life. If he did not possess this technology, either he would have to avoid these territories or likewise have to struggle along as a nomad in perpetual wandering, provided that his thousand-year-old education and habit of settled residence did not make this seem simply unbearable to him. We must bear in mind that in the time when the American continent was being opened up, numerous Aryans fought for their livelihood as trappers, hunters, etc., and often in larger troops with wife and children, always on the move, so that their existence was completely like that of the nomads. But as soon as their increasing number and better implements permitted them to clear the wild soil and make a stand against the natives, more and more settlements sprang up in the land.

Probably the Aryan was also first a nomad, settling in the course of time, but for that very reason he was never a Jew! No, the Jew is no nomad; for the nomad had also a definite attitude toward the concept of work which could serve as a basis for his later development in so far as the necessary intellectual premises were present. In him the basic idealistic view is present, even if in infinite dilution, hence in his whole being he may seem strange to the Aryan peoples, but not unattractive. In the Jew, however, this attitude is not at all present; for that reason he was never a nomad, but only and always a *parasite* in the body of other peoples. That he sometimes left his previous living space has nothing to with his own purpose, but results from the fact that from time to time he was thrown out by the host nations he had misused. His spreading is a typical phenomenon for all parasites; he always seeks a new feeding ground for his race.

This, however, has nothing to do with nomadism, for the reason that a Jew never thinks of leaving a territory that he has occupied, but remains where he is, and he sits so fast that even by force it is very hard to drive him out. His extension to ever-new countries occurs only in the moment in which certain conditions for his existence are there present, without which—unlike the nomad—he would not change his residence. He is and remains the typical parasite, a sponger who like a noxious bacillus keeps spreading as soon as a favorable medium invites him. And the effect of his existence is also like that of spongers: wherever he appears, the host people dies out after a shorter or longer period.

Thus, the Jew of all times has lived in the states of other peoples, and there formed his own state, which, to be sure, habitually sailed under the disguise of religious community as long as outward circumstances made a complete revelation of his nature seem inadvisable. But as soon as he felt strong enough to do without the protective cloak, he always dropped the veil and suddenly became what so many of the others previously did not want to believe and see: the Jew. . . .

## GENERAL POLITICAL CONSIDERATIONS BASED ON MY VIENNA PERIOD

. . . I had always hated parliament, but not as an institution in itself. On the contrary, as a freedom-loving man I could not even conceive of any other possibility of government, for the idea of any sort of dictatorship would, in view of my attitude toward the House of Habsburg, have seemed to me a crime against freedom and all reason.

What contributed no little to this was that as a young man, in consequence of my extensive newspaper reading, I had, without myself realizing it, been inoculated with a certain admiration for the British Parliament, of which I was not easily able to rid myself. The dignity with which the Lower House there fulfilled its tasks (as was so touchingly described in our press) impressed me immensely. Could a people have any more exalted form of self-government?

But for this very reason I was an enemy of the Austrian parliament. I considered its whole mode of conduct unworthy of the great example. To this the following was now added:

The fate of the Germans in the Austrian state was dependent on their position in the Reichsrat. Up to the introduction of universal and secret suffrage, the Germans had had a majority, though an insignificant one, in parliament. Even this condition was precarious, for the Social Democrats, with their unreliable attitude in national questions, always turned against German interests in critical matters affecting the Germans—in order not to alienate the members of the various foreign nationalities. Even in those days the Social Democracy could not be regarded as a German party. And with the introduction of universal suffrage the German superiority ceased even in a purely numerical sense. There was no longer any obstacle in the path of the further de-Germanization of the state.

For this reason my instinct of national self-preservation caused me even in those days to have little love for a representative body in which the Germans were always misrepresented rather than represented. Yet these were deficiencies which, like so many others, were attributable, not to the thing in itself, but to the Austrian state. I still believed that if a German majority were restored in the representative bodies, there would no longer be any reason for a principled opposition to them, that is, as long as the old state continued to exist at all.

These were my inner sentiments when for the first time I set foot in these halls as hallowed as they were disputed. For me, to be sure, they were hallowed only by the lofty beauty of the magnificent building. A Hellenic miracle on German soil!

How soon was I to grow indignant when I saw the lamentable comedy that unfolded beneath my eyes!

Present were a few hundred of these popular representatives who had to take a position on a question of most vital economic importance.

The very first day was enough to stimulate me to thought for weeks on end.

The intellectual content of what these men said was on a really depressing level, in so far as you could understand their babbling at all; for several of the gentlemen did not speak German, but their native slavic languages or rather dialects. I now had occasion to hear with my own ears what previously I had known only from reading the newspapers. A wild gesticulating mass screaming all at once in every different key, presided over by a good-natured old uncle who was striving in the sweat of his brow to revive the dignity of the House by violently ringing his bell and alternating gentle reproof with grave admonitions.

I couldn't help laughing.

A few weeks later I was in the House again. The picture was changed beyond recognition. The hall was absolutely empty. Down below everybody was asleep. A few deputies were in their places, yawning at one another; one was speaking. A vice-president of the House was present, looking into the hall with obvious boredom.

The first misgivings arose in me. From now on, whenever time offered me the slightest opportunity, I went back and, with silence and attention, viewed whatever picture presented itself, listened to the speeches in so far as they were intelligible, studied the more or less intelligent faces of the elect of the peoples of this woe-begone state—and little by little formed my own ideas.

A year of this tranquil observation sufficed totally to change or eliminate my former view of the nature of this institution. My innermost position was no longer against the misshapen form which this idea assumed in Austria; no, by now I could no longer accept the parliament as such. Up till then I had seen the misfortune of the Austrian parliament in the absence of a German majority, now I saw that its ruination lay in the whole nature and essence of the institution as such.

A whole series of questions rose up in me.

I began to make myself familiar with the democratic principle of majority rule as the foundation of this whole institution, but devoted no less attention to the intellectual and moral values of these gentlemen, supposedly the elect of the nations, who were expected to serve this purpose.

Thus I came to know the institution and its representatives at once.

In the course of a few years, my knowledge and insight shaped a plastic model of that most dignified phenomenon of modern times: the parliamentarian. He began to impress himself upon me in a form which has never since been subjected to any essential change.

Here again the visual instruction of practical reality had prevented me from being stifled by a theory which at first sight seemed seductive to so many, but which none the less must be counted among the symptoms of human degeneration.

The Western democracy of today is the forerunner of Marxism which without it would not be thinkable. It provides this world plague with the culture in which its germs can spread. In its most extreme form, parliamentarianism created a monstrosity of excrement and fire, in which, however, sad to say, the fire seems to me at the moment to be burned out.

I must be more than thankful to Fate for laying this question before me while I was in Vienna, for I fear that in Germany at that time I would have found the answer too easily. For if I had first encountered this absurd institution known as parliament in Berlin, I might have fallen into the opposite fallacy, and not without seemingly good cause have sided with those who saw the salvation of the people and the Reich exclusively in furthering the power of the imperial idea, and who nevertheless were alien and blind at once to the times and the people involved.

In Austria this was impossible.

Here it was not so easy to go from one mistake to the other. If parliament was worthless, the Habsburgs were even more worthless—in no event, less so. To reject parliamentarianism was not enough, for the question still remained open: what then? The rejection and abolition of the Reichsrat would have left the House of Habsburg the sole governing force, a thought which, especially for me, was utterly intolerable.

The difficulty of this special case led me to a more thorough contemplation of the problem as such than would otherwise have been likely at such tender years.

What gave me most food for thought was the obvious absence of any responsibility in a single person.

The parliament arrives at some decision whose consequences may be ever so ruinous—nobody bears any responsibility for this, no one can be taken to account. For can it be called an acceptance of responsibility if, after an unparalleled catastrophe, the guilty government resigns? Or if the coalition changes, or even if parliament is itself dissolved?

Can a fluctuating majority of people ever be made responsible in any case?

Isn't the very idea of responsibility bound up with the individual?

But can an individual directing a government be made practically responsible for actions whose preparation and execution must be set exclusively to the account of the will and inclination of a multitude of men?

Or will not the task of a leading statesman be seen, not in the birth of a creative idea or plan as such, but rather in the art of making the brilliance of his projects intelligible to a herd of sheep and blockheads, and subsequently begging for their kind approval?

Is it the criterion of the statesman that he should possess the art of persuasion in as high degree as that of political intelligence in formulating great policies or decisions? Is the incapacity of a leader shown by the fact that he does not succeed in winning for a certain idea the majority of a mob thrown together by more or less savory accidents?

Indeed, has this mob ever understood an idea before success proclaimed its greatness?

Isn't every deed of genius in this world a visible protest of genius against the inertia of the mass?

And what should the statesman do, who does not succeed in gaining the favor of this mob for his plans by flattery?

Should he buy it?

Or, in view of the stupidity of his fellow citizens, should he renounce the execution of the tasks which he has recognized to be vital necessities? Should he resign or should he remain at his post?

In such a case, doesn't a man of true character find himself in a hopeless conflict between knowledge and decency, or rather honest conviction?

Where is the dividing line between his duty toward the general public and his duty toward his personal honor?

Mustn't every true leader refuse to be thus degraded to the level of a political gangster?

And, conversely, mustn't every gangster feel that he is cut out for politics, since it is never he, but some intangible mob, which has to bear the ultimate responsibility?

Mustn't our principle of parliamentary majorities lead to the demolition of any idea of leadership?

Does anyone believe that the progress of this world springs from the mind of majorities and not from the brains of individuals?

Or does anyone expect that the future will be able to dispense with this premise of human culture?

Does it not, on the contrary, today seem more indispensable than ever?

By rejecting the authority of the individual and replacing it by the numbers of some momentary mob, the parliamentary principle of majority rule sins against the basic aristocratic principle of Nature, though it must be said that this view is not necessarily embodied in the present-day decadence of our upper ten thousand.

The devastation caused by this institution of modern parliamentary rule is hard for the reader of Jewish newspapers to imagine, unless he has learned to think and examine independently. It is, first and foremost, the cause of the incredible inundation of all political life with the most inferior, and I mean the most inferior, characters of our time. Just as the true leader will withdraw from all political activity which does not consist primarily in creative achievement and work, but in bargaining and haggling for the favor of the majority, in the same measure this activity will suit the small mind and consequently attract it.

The more dwarfish one of these present-day leather-merchants is in spirit and ability, the more clearly his own insight makes him aware of the lamentable figure he actually cuts—that much more will he sing the praises of a system which does not demand of him the power and genius of a giant, but is satisfied with the craftiness of a village mayor, preferring in fact this kind of wisdom to that of a Pericles. And this kind doesn't have to torment himself with responsibility for his actions. He is entirely removed from such worry, for he well knows that, regardless what the result of his "statesmanlike" bungling may be, his end has long been written in the stars: one day he will have to cede his place to another equally great mind, for it is one of the characteristics of this decadent system that the number of great statesmen increases in proportion as the stature of the individual decreases. With increasing dependence on parliamentary majorities it will inevitably continue to shrink, since on the one hand great minds will refuse to be the stooges of idiotic incompetents and big-mouths, and on the other, conversely, the representatives of the majority, hence of stupidity, hate nothing more passionately than a superior mind.

For such an assembly of wise men of Gotham, it is always a consolation to know that they are headed by a leader whose intelligence is at the level of those present: this will give each one the pleasure of shining from time to time—and, above all, if Tom can be master, what is to prevent Dick and Harry from having their turn too?

This invention of democracy is most intimately related to a quality which in recent times has grown to be a real disgrace, to wit, the cowardice of a great part of our so-called leadership. What luck to be able to hide behind the skirts of a so-called majority in all decisions of any real importance!

Take a look at one of these political bandits. How anxiously he begs the approval of the majority for every measure, to assure himself of the necessary accomplices, so he can unload the responsibility at any time. And this is one of the main reasons why this type of political activity is always repulsive and hateful to any man who is decent at heart and hence courageous, while it attracts all low characters—and anyone who is unwilling to take personal responsibility for his acts, but seeks a shield, is a cowardly scoundrel. When the leaders of a nation consist of such vile creatures, the results will soon be deplorable. Such a nation will be unable to muster the courage for any determined act; it will prefer to accept any dishonor, even the most shameful, rather than rise to a decision; for there is no one who is prepared of his own accord to pledge his person and his head for the execution of a dauntless resolve.

For there is one thing which we must never forget: in this, too, the majority can never replace the man. It is not only a representative of stupidity, but of cowardice as well. And no more than a hundred empty heads make one wise man will an heroic decision arise from a hundred cowards.

The less the responsibility of the individual leader, the more numerous will be those who, despite their most insignificant stature, feel called upon to put their immortal forces in the service of the nation. Indeed, they will be unable to await their turn; they stand in a long line, and with pain and regret count the number of those waiting ahead of them, calculating almost the precise hour at which, in all probability, their turn will come. Consequently, they long for any change in the office hovering before their eyes, and are thankful for any scandal which thins out the ranks ahead of them. And if some man is unwilling to move from the post he holds, this in their eyes is practically a breach of a holy pact of solidarity. They grow vindictive, and they do not rest until the impudent fellow is at last overthrown, thus turning his warm place back to the public. And, rest assured, he won't recover the position so easily. For as soon as one of these creatures is forced to give up a position, he will try at once to wedge his way into the waiting-line unless the hue and cry raised by the others prevents him. . . . The haggling and bargaining for the individual portfolios represented Western democracy of the first water. And the results corresponded to the principles applied. Particularly the change of individual personalities occurred in shorter and shorter terms, ultimately becoming a veritable chase. In the same measure, the stature of the statesmen steadily diminished until finally no one remained but that type of parliamentary gangster whose statesmanship could only be measured and recognized by their ability in pasting together the coalitions of the moment; in other words, concluding those pettiest of political bargains which alone demonstrate the fitness of these representatives of the people for practical work. . . .

But what attracted me no less was to compare the ability and knowledge of these representatives of the people and the tasks which awaited them. In this case, whether I liked it or not, I was impelled to examine more closely the intellectual horizon of these elect of the nations themselves, and in so doing, I could not avoid giving the necessary attention to the processes which lead to the discovery of these ornaments of our public life.

The way in which the real ability of these gentlemen was applied and placed in the service of the fatherland—in other words, the technical process of their activity—was also worthy of thorough study and investigation.

The more determined I was to penetrate these inner conditions, to study the personalities and material foundations with dauntless and penetrating objectivity, the more deplorable became my total picture of parliamentary life. Indeed, this is an advisable procedure in dealing with an institution which, in the person of its representatives, feels obliged to bring up objectivity in every second sentence as the only proper basis for every investigation and opinion. Investigate these gentlemen themselves and the laws of their sordid existence, and you will be amazed at the result.

There is no principle which, objectively considered, is as false as that of parliamentarianism.

Here we may totally disregard the manner in which our fine representatives of the people are chosen, how they arrive at their office and their new dignity. That only the tiniest fraction of them rise in fulfillment of a general desire, let alone a need, will at once be apparent to anyone who realizes that the political understanding of the broad masses is far from being highly enough developed to arrive at definite general political views of their own accord and seek out the suitable personalities.

The thing we designate by the word public opinion rests only in the smallest part on experience or knowledge which the individual has acquired by himself, but rather on an idea which is inspired by so-called enlightenment, often of a highly persistent and obtrusive type.

Just as a man's denominational orientation is the result of upbringing, and only the religious need as such slumbers in his soul, the political opinion of the masses represents nothing but the final result of an incredibly tenacious and thorough manipulation of their mind and soul.

By far the greatest share in their political education, which in this case is most aptly designated by the word propaganda, falls to the account of the press. It is foremost in performing this work of enlightenment and thus represents a sort of school for grown-ups. This instruction however, is not in the hands of the state, but in the claws of forces which are in part very inferior. In Vienna as a very young man I had the best opportunity to become acquainted with the owners and spiritual manufacturers of this machine for educating the masses. At first I could not help but be amazed at how short a time it took this great evil power within the state to create a certain opinion even where it meant totally falsifying profound desires and views which surely existed among the public. In a few days a ridiculous episode had become a significant state action, while, conversely, at the same time, vital problems fell a prey to public oblivion, or rather were simply filched from the memory and consciousness of the masses. . . .

These scum manufacture more than three quarters of the so-called public opinion, from whose foam the parliamentarian Aphrodite arises. To give an accurate description of this process and depict it in all its falsehood and improbability, one would have to write volumes. But even if we disregard all this and examine only the given product along with its activity, this seems to me enough to make the objective lunacy of this institution dawn on even the naivest mind.

This human error, as senseless as it is dangerous, will most readily be understood as soon as we compare democratic parliamentarianism with a truly Germanic democracy.

The distinguishing feature of the former is that a body of, let us say five hundred men, or in recent times even women, is chosen and entrusted with making the ultimate decision in any and all matters. And so for practical purposes they alone are the government; for even if they do choose a cabinet which undertakes the external direction of the affairs of state, this is a mere sham. In reality this so-called government cannot take a step without first obtaining the approval of the general assembly. Consequently, it cannot be made responsible for anything, since the ultimate decision never lies with it, but with the majority of parliament. In every case it does nothing but carry out the momentary will of the majority. Its political ability can only be judged according to the skills with which it understands how either to adapt itself to the will of the majority or to pull the majority over to its side. Thereby it sinks from the heights of real government to the level of a beggar confronting the momentary majority. Indeed, its most urgent task becomes nothing more than either to secure the favor of the existing majority, as the need arises, or to form a majority with more friendly inclinations. If this succeeds, it may govern a little while longer; if it doesn't succeed, it can resign. The soundness of its purposes as such is beside the point.

For practical purposes, this excludes all responsibility.

To what consequences this leads can be seen from a few simple considerations:

The internal composition of the five hundred chosen representatives of the people, with regard to profession or even individual abilities, gives a picture as incoherent as it is usually deplorable. For no one can believe that these men elected by the nation are elect of spirit or even of intelligence! It is to be hoped that no one will suppose that the ballots of an electorate which is anything else than brilliant will give rise to statesmen by the hundreds. Altogether we cannot be too sharp in condemning the absurd notion that geniuses can be born from general elections. In the first place, a nation only produces a real statesman once in a blue moon and not a hundred or more at once; and in the second place, the revulsion of the masses for every outstanding genius is positively instinctive. Sooner will a camel pass through a needle's eye than a great man be discovered by an election.

In world history the man who really rises above the norm of the broad average usually announces himself personally.

As it is, however, five hundred men, whose stature is to say the least modest, vote on the most important affairs of the nation, appoint governments which in every single case and in every special question have to get the approval of the exalted assembly, so that policy is really made by five hundred.

And that is just what it usually looks like.

But even leaving the genius of these representatives of the people aside, bear in mind how varied are the problems awaiting attention, in what widely removed fields solutions and decisions must be made, and you will realize how inadequate a governing institution must be which transfers the ultimate right of decision to a mass assembly of people, only a tiny fraction of which possess knowledge and experience of the matter to be treated. The most important economic measures are thus submitted to a forum, only a tenth of whose members have any economic education to show. This is nothing more nor less than placing the ultimate decision in a matter in the hands of men totally lacking in every prerequisite for the task.

The same is true of every other question. The decision is always made by a majority of ignoramuses and incompetents, since the composition of this institution remains unchanged while the problems under treatment extend to nearly every province of public life and would thereby presuppose a constant turn-over in the deputies who are to judge and decide on them, since it is impossible to let the same persons decide matters of transportation as, let us say, a question of high foreign policy. Otherwise these men would all have to be universal geniuses such as we actually seldom encounter once in centuries. Unfortunately we are here confronted, for the most part, not with thinkers but with dilettantes as limited as they are conceited and inflated, intellectual *demi-monde* of the worst sort. And this is the source of the often incomprehensible frivolity with which these gentry speak and decide on things which would require careful meditation even in the greatest minds. Measures of the gravest significance for the future of a whole state, yes, of a nation, are passed as though a game of *schafkopf* or *tarock*, which would certainly be better suited to their abilities, lay on the table before them and not the fate of a race. . . .

And thereby every practical responsibility vanishes. For responsibility can lie only in the obligation of an individual and not in a parliamentary bull session. . . .

Juxtaposed to this is the truly Germanic democracy characterized by the free election of a leader and his obligation fully to assume all responsibility for his actions and omissions. In it there is no majority vote on individual questions, but only the decision of an individual who must answer with his fortune and his life for his choice.

If it be objected that under such conditions scarcely anyone would be prepared to dedicate his person to so risky a task, there is but one possible answer:

Thank the Lord, Germanic democracy means just this: that any old climber or moral slacker cannot rise by devious paths to govern his national comrades, but that, by the very greatness of the responsibility to be assumed, incompetents and weaklings are frightened off.

But if, nevertheless, one of these scoundrels should attempt to sneak in, we can find him more easily, and mercilessly challenge him: Out, cowardly scoundrel! Remove your foot, you are besmirching the steps; the front steps of the Pantheon of history are not for sneak-thieves, but for heroes!

## PERSONALITY AND THE CONCEPTION OF THE FOLKISH STATE

The folkish National Socialist state sees its chief task in *educating and preserving the bearer of the state*. It is not sufficient to encourage the racial elements as such, to educate them and finally instruct them in the needs of practical life; the state must also adjust its own organization to this task.

It would be lunacy to try to estimate the value of man according to his race, thus declaring war on the Marxist idea that men are equal, unless we are determined to draw the ultimate consequences. And the ultimate consequence of recognizing the importance of blood—that is, of the racial foundation in general—is the transference of this estimation to the individual person. In general, I must evaluate peoples differently on the basis of the race they belong to, and the same applies to the individual men within a national community. The realization that peoples are not equal transfers itself to the individual man within a national community, in the sense that men's minds cannot be equal, since here too, the blood components, though equal in their broad outlines, are, in particular cases, subject to thousands of the finest differentiations.

The first consequence of this realization might at the same time be called the cruder one: an attempt to promote in the most exemplary way those elements within the national community that have been recognized as especially valuable from the racial viewpoint and to provide for their special increase.

This task is cruder because it can be recognized and solved almost mechanically. It is more difficult to recognize among the whole people the minds that are most valuable in the intellectual and ideal sense, and to gain for them that influence which not only is the due of these superior minds, but which above all is beneficial to the nation. This sifting according to capacity and ability cannot be undertaken mechanically; it is a task which the struggle of daily life unceasingly performs.

*A philosophy of life which endeavors to reject the democratic mass idea and give this earth to the best people—that is, the highest humanity—must logically obey the same aristocratic principle within this people and make sure that the leadership and the highest influence in this people fall to the best minds. Thus, it builds, not upon the idea of the majority, but upon the idea of personality.*

Anyone who believes today that a folkish National Socialist state must distinguish itself from other states only in a purely mechanical sense, by a superior construction of its economic life— that is, by a better balance between rich and poor, or giving broad sections of the population more right to influence the economic process, or by fairer wages by elimination of excessive wage differentials—has not gone beyond the most superficial aspect of the matter and has not the faintest idea of what we call a philosophy. All the things we have just mentioned offer not the slightest guaranty of continued existence, far less of any claim to greatness. A people which did not go beyond these really superficial reforms would not obtain the least guaranty of victory in the general struggle of nations. A movement which finds the content of its mission only in such a general leveling, assuredly just as it may be, will truly bring about no great and profound, hence real, reform of existing conditions, since its entire activity does not, in the last analysis, go beyond externals, and does not give the people that inner armament which enables it, with almost inevitable certainty I might say, to overcome in the end those weaknesses from which we suffer today.

To understand this more easily, it may be expedient to cast one more glance at the real origins and causes of human cultural development.

The first step which outwardly and visibly removed man from the animal was that of invention. Invention itself is originally based on the finding of stratagems and ruses, the use of which facilitates the life struggle with other beings, and is sometimes the actual prerequisite for its favorable course. These most primitive inventions do not yet cause the personality to appear with sufficient distinctness, because, of course, they enter the consciousness of the future, or rather the present, human observer, only as a mass phenomenon. Certain dodges and crafty measures which man, for example, can observe in the animal catch his eye only as a summary fact, and he is no longer in a position to establish or investigate their origin, but must simply content himself with designating such phenomena as instinctive.

But in our case this last word means nothing at all. For anyone who believes in a higher development of living creatures must admit that every expression of their life urge and life struggle must have had a beginning; that *one* subject must have started it, and that subsequently such a phenomenon repeated itself more and more frequently and spread more and more, until at last it virtually entered the subconscious of all members of a given species, thus manifesting itself as an instinct.

This will be understood and believed more readily in the case of man. His first intelligent measures in the struggle with other beasts assuredly originate in the actions of individual, particularly able subjects. Here, too, the personality was once unquestionably the cause of decisions and acts which later were taken over by all humanity and regarded as perfectly self-evident. Just as any obvious military principle, which today has become, as it were, the basis of all strategy, originally owed its appearance to one absolutely distinct mind, and only in the course of many, perhaps even thousands of years, achieved universal validity and was taken entirely for granted.

Man complements this first invention by a second: he learns to place other objects and also living creatures in the service of his own struggle for self-preservation; and thus begins man's real inventive activity which today is generally visible. These material inventions, starting with the use of stone as a weapon and leading to the domestication of beasts, giving man artificial fire, and so on up to the manifold and amazing inventions of our day, show the individual creator the more clearly, the closer the various inventions lie to the present day, or the more significant and incisive they are. At all events, we know that all the material inventions we see about us are the result of the creative power and ability of the individual personality. And all these inventions in the last analysis help to raise man more and more above the level of the animal world and finally to remove him from it. Thus, fundamentally, they serve the continuous process of higher human development. But the very same thing which once, in the form of the simplest ruse, facilitated the struggle for existence of the man hunting in the primeval forest, again contributes, in the shape of the most brilliant scientific knowledge of the present era, to alleviate mankinds' struggle for existence and to forge its weapons for the struggles of the future. All human thought and invention, in their ultimate effects, primarily serve man's struggle for existence on this planet, even when the so-called practical use of an invention or a discovery or a profound scientific insight into the essence of things is not visible at the moment. All these things together, by contributing to raise man above the living creatures surrounding him, strengthen him and secure his position, so that in every respect he develops into the dominant being on this earth.

Thus, all inventions are the result of an individual's work. All these individuals, whether intentionally or unintentionally, are more or less great benefactors of all men. Their work subsequently gives millions, nay, billions of human creatures, instruments with which to facilitate and carry out their life struggle.

If in the origin of our present material culture we always find individuals in the form of inventors, complementing one another and one building upon another, we find the same in the practice and execution of the things devised and discovered by the inventors. For all productive processes in turn must in their origin be considered equivalent to inventions, hence dependent on the individual. Even purely theoretical intellectual work, which in particular cases is not measurable, yet is the premise for all further material inventions, appears as the exclusive product of the individual person. It is not the mass that invents and not the majority that organizes or thinks, but in all things only and always the individual man, the person.

A human community appears well organized only if it facilitates the labors of these creative forces in the most helpful way and applies them in a manner beneficial to all. The most valuable thing about the invention itself, whether it lie in the material field or in the world of ideas, is primarily the inventor as a personality. Therefore, to employ him in a way benefiting the totality is the first and highest task in the organization of a national community. Indeed, the organization itself must be a realization of this principle. Thus, also, it is redeemed from the curse of mechanism and becomes a living thing. *It must itself be an embodiment of the endeavor to place thinking individuals above the masses, thus subordinating the latter to the former.*

Consequently, the organization must not only not prevent the emergence of thinking individuals from the mass; on the contrary it must in the highest degree make this possible and easy by the nature of its own being. In this it must proceed from the principle that the salvation of mankind has never lain in the masses, but in its creative minds, which must therefore really be regarded as benefactors of the human race. To assure them of the most decisive influence and facilitate their work is in the interest of the totality. Assuredly this interest is not satisfied, and is not served by the domination of the unintelligent or incompetent, in any case uninspired masses, but solely by the leadership of those to whom Nature has given special gifts for this purpose.

The selection of these minds, as said before, is primarily accomplished by the hard struggle for existence. Many break and perish, thus showing that they are not destined for the ultimate and in the end only a few appear to be chosen. In the fields of thought, artistic creation, even, in fact, of economic life, this selective process is still going on today, though, especially in the latter field, it faces a grave obstacle. The administration of the state and likewise the power embodied in the organized military might of the nation are also dominated by these ideas. Here, too, the idea of personality is everywhere dominant—its authority downward and its responsibility toward the higher personality above. Only political life has today completely turned away from this most natural principle. While all human culture is solely the result of the individual's creative activity, everywhere, and particularly in the highest *leadership* of the national community, the *principle of the value of the majority* appears decisive, and from that high place begins to gradually poison all life; that is, in reality to dissolve it. The destructive effect of the Jew's activity in other national bodies is basically attributable only to his eternal efforts to undermine the position of the personality in the host-peoples and to replace it by the mass. Thus, the organizing principle of Aryan humanity is replaced by the destructive principle of the Jew. He becomes a ferment of decomposition among peoples and races, and in the broader sense a dissolver of human culture.

Marxism presents itself as the perfection of the Jew's attempt to exclude the pre-eminence of personality in all fields of human life and replace it by the numbers of the mass. To this, in the political sphere, corresponds the parliamentary form of government, which, from the smallest germ cells of the municipality up to the supreme leadership of the Reich, we see in such disastrous operation, and in the economic sphere, the system of a trade-union movement which does not serve the real interests of the workers, but exclusively the destructive purposes of the international world Jew. In precisely the measure in which the economy is withdrawn from the influence of the personality principle and instead exposed to the influences and effects of the masses, it must lose its efficacy in serving all and benefiting all, and gradually succumb to a sure retrogression. All the shop organizations which, instead of taking into account the interests of their employees, strive to gain influence on production, serve the same purpose. They injure collective achievement, and thus in reality injure individual achievement. For the satisfaction of the members of a national body does not in the long run occur exclusively through mere theoretical phrases, but by the goods of daily life that fall to the individual and the ultimate resultant conviction that a national community in the sum of its achievement guards the interests of individuals.

It is of no importance whether Marxism, on the basis of its mass theory, seems capable of taking over and carrying on the economy existing at the moment. Criticism with regard to the soundness or unsoundness of this principle is not settled by the proof of its capacity to *administer* the existing order for the future, but exclusively by the proof that it can itself *create* a higher culture. Marxism might a thousand times take over the existing economy and make it continue to work under its leadership, but even success in this activity would prove nothing in the face of the fact that it would not be in a position, by applying its principle *itself*, to create the same thing which today it takes over in a finished state.

Of this Marxism has furnished practical proof. Not only that it has nowhere been able to found and create a culture by itself; actually it has not been able to continue the existing ones in accordance with its principles, but after a brief time has been forced to return to the ideas embodied in the personality principle, in the form of *concessions*;—even in its own organization it cannot dispense with these principles.

*The folkish philosophy is basically distinguished from the Marxist philosophy by the fact that it not only recognizes the value of race, but with it the importance of the personality, which it therefore makes one of the pillars of its entire edifice.* These are the factors which sustain its view of life.

If the National Socialist movement did not understand the fundamental importance of this basic realization, but instead were merely to perform superficial patchwork on the present-day state, or even adopt the mass standpoint as its own—then it would really constitute nothing but a party in competition with the Marxists; in that case, it would not possess the right to call itself a philosophy of life. If the social program of the movement consisted only in pushing aside the personality and replacing it by the masses, National Socialism itself would be corroded by the poison of Marxism, as is the case with our bourgeois parties.

The folkish state must care for the welfare of its citizens by recognizing in all and everything the importance of the value of personality, thus in all fields preparing the way for that highest measure of productive performance which grants to the individual the highest measure of participation.

And accordingly, the folkish state must free all leadership and especially the highest—that is, the political leadership—entirely from the parliamentary principle of majority rule—in other words, mass rule—and instead absolutely guarantee the right of the personality.

From this the following realization results:

*The best state constitution and state form is that which, with the most unquestioned certainty, raises the best minds in the national community to leading position and leading influence.*

But as, in economic life, the able men cannot be appointed from above, but must struggle through for themselves, and just as here the endless schooling, ranging from the smallest business to the largest enterprise, occurs spontaneously, with life alone giving the examinations, obviously political minds cannot be discovered. Extraordinary geniuses permit of no consideration for normal mankind.

From the smallest community cell to the highest leadership of the entire Reich, the state must have the personality principle anchored in its organization.

There must be no majority decisions, but only responsible persons, and the word council must be restored to its original meaning. Surely every man will have advisers by his side, but *the decisions will be made by one man.*

The principle which made the Prussian army in its time into the most wonderful instrument of the German people must some day, in a transferred sense, become the principle of the construction of our whole state conception: *authority of every leader downward and responsibility upward.*

Even then it will not be possible to dispense with those corporations which today we designate as parliaments. But their councillors will then actually give counsel; responsibility, however, can and may be borne only by *one* man, and therefore only he alone may possess the authority and right to command.

Parliaments as such are necessary, because in them, above all, personalities to which special responsible tasks can later be entrusted have an opportunity gradually to rise up.

This gives the following picture:

The folkish state, from the township up to the Reich leadership, has no representative body which decides anything by the majority, but only *advisory bodies* which stand at the side of the elected leader, receiving their share of work from him, and in turn if necessary assuming unlimited responsibility in certain fields, just as on a larger scale the leader or chairman of the various corporations himself possesses.

As a matter of principle, the folkish state does not tolerate asking advice or opinions in special matters—say, of an economic nature—of men who, on the basis of their education and activity, can understand nothing of the subject. It, therefore, divides its representative bodies from the start into *political and professional chambers.*

In order to guarantee a profitable cooperation between the two, a special *senate* of the elite always stands over them.

In no chamber and in no senate does a vote ever take place. They are working institutions and not voting machines. The individual member has an advisory, but never a determining, voice. The latter is the exclusive privilege of the responsible chairman.

This principle—absolute responsibility unconditionally combined with absolute authority—will gradually breed an elite of leaders such as today, in this era of irresponsible parliamentarianism, is utterly inconceivable.

Thus, the political form of the nation will be brought into agreement with that law to which it owes its greatness in the cultural and economic field.

As regards the possibility of putting these ideas into practice, I beg you not to forget that the parliamentary principle of democratic majority rule has by no means always dominated mankind, but on the contrary is to be found only in brief periods of history, which are always epochs of the decay of peoples and states.

But it should not be believed that such a transformation can be accomplished by purely theoretical measures from above, since logically it may not even stop at the state constitution, but must permeate all other legislation, and indeed all civil life. Such a fundamental change can and will only take place through a movement which is itself constructed in the spirit of these ideas and hence bears the future state within itself.

Hence the National Socialist movement should today adapt itself entirely to these ideas and carry them to practical fruition within its own organization, so that some day it may not only show the state these same guiding principles, but can also place the completed body of its own state at its disposal.

# Selections from *The City of God,* Book XIX

## St. Augustine (354–430)

*Augustine was born in North Africa to a Christian mother and educated extensively in Latin grammar, poetry, and rhetoric. Seduced by the pleasures of Carthage as a young man, he followed a winding path through Ciceronian philosophy, Manichaeism, and skepticism to a final reconversion to Christianity in 386, under the influence of Ambrose, the Bishop of Milan, and some Christian Neoplatonists. He eventually became a priest, and then Bishop of Hippo in North Africa. In* The City of God *(written in 413-427), Augustine tries to come to terms with the place of political life, which he views as not natural to innocent man, in the life of a fallen man striving for salvation.*

*Consider the stance Augustine takes toward political society. He puts many of the questions of politics taken up in previous readings in the perspective of something higher than politics. To what extent can a good Christian be a good citizen, according to Augustine? Is he correct that most of political life involves the pursuit of ungodly ends and that one should not be attracted to it for its own sake? Should we wait and hope for our happiness in another life or try to procure it here and now by collective and individual ingenuity?*

## BOOK NINETEENTH

### CHAPTER I
*That Varro has made out that two hundred and eighty-eight different sects of philosophy might be formed by the various opinions regarding the supreme good.*

As I see that I have still to discuss the fit destinies of the two cities, the earthly and the heavenly, I must first explain, so far as the limits of this work allow me, the reasonings by which men have attempted to make for themselves a happiness in this unhappy life, in order that it may be evident, not only from divine authority, but also from such reasons as can be adduced to unbelievers, how the empty dreams of the philosophers differ from the hope which God gives to us, and from the substantial fulfillment of it which He will give us as our blessedness. Philosophers have expressed a great variety of diverse opinions regarding the ends of goods and of evils, and this question they have eagerly canvassed, that they might, if possible, discover what makes a man happy. For the end of our good is that for the sake of which other things are to be desired, while it is to be desired for its own sake; and the end of evil is that on account of which other things are to be shunned, while it is avoided on its own account. Thus, by the *end of good*, we at present mean, not that by which good is destroyed, so that it no longer exists, but that by which it is finished, so that it becomes complete; and by the *end of evil* we mean, not that which abolishes it, but that which completes its development. These two ends, therefore, are the supreme good and the supreme evil; and, as I have said, those who have in this vain life professed the study of wisdom have been at great pains to discover these ends, and to obtain the supreme good and avoid the supreme evil in this life. And although they erred in a variety of ways, yet natural insight has prevented them from wandering from the truth . . .

### CHAPTER IV
*What the Christians believe regarding the supreme good and evil, in opposition to the philosophers, who have maintained that the supreme good is in themselves.*

If, then, we be asked what the city of God has to say upon these points, and, in the first place, what its opinion regarding the supreme good and evil is, it will reply that life eternal is the supreme good, death eternal the supreme evil, and that to obtain the one and escape the other we must live rightly. And thus it is written, "The just lives by faith," for we do not as yet see our good, and must therefore live by faith; neither have we in ourselves power to live rightly, but can do so only if He who has given us faith to believe in His help do help us when we believe and pray. As for those who have supposed that the sovereign good and evil are to be found in this life, and have placed it either in the soul or the body, or in both, or, to speak more explicitly, either in pleasure or in virtue, or in both; in repose or in virtue, or in both; in pleasure and repose, or in virtue, or in all combined; in the primary objects of nature, or in virtue, or in both—all these have, with a marvelous shallowness, sought to find their blessedness in this life and in themselves. Contempt has been poured upon such ideas by the Truth, saying by the prophet, "The Lord knoweth the thoughts of men" (or, as the Apostle Paul cites the passage, "The Lord knoweth the thoughts of the *wise*") "that they are vain."

For what flood of eloquence can suffice to detail the miseries of this life? Cicero, in the *Consolation* on the death of his daughter, has spent all his ability in lamentation; but how inadequate was even his ability here? For when, where, how, in this life can these primary objects of nature be possessed so that they may not be assailed by unforeseen accident? Is the body of the wise man exempt from any pain which may dispel pleasure, from any disquietude which may banish repose? The amputation or decay of the members of the body puts an end to its integrity, deformity blights its beauty, weakness its health, lassitude its vigour, sleepiness or sluggishness its activity—and which of these is it that may not assail the flesh of the wise man? Comely and fitting attitudes and movements of the body are numbered among the prime natural blessings; but what if some sickness makes the members tremble? What if a man suffers from curvature of the spine to such an extent that his hands reach the ground, and he goes upon all fours like a quadruped? Does not this destroy all beauty and grace in the body, whether at rest or in motion? What shall I say of the fundamental blessings of the soul, sense and intellect, of which the one is given for the perception, and the other for the comprehension of truth? But what kind of sense is it that remains when a man becomes deaf and blind? Where are reason and intellect when disease makes a man delirious? We can scarcely, or not at all, refrain from tears, when we think of or see the actions and words of such frantic persons, and consider how different from and even opposed to their own sober judgment and ordinary conduct their present demeanor is. And what shall I say of those who suffer from demoniacal possession? Where is their own intelligence hidden and buried while the malignant spirit is using their body and soul according to his own will? And who is quite sure that no such thing can happen to the wise man in this life? Then, as to the perception of truth, what can we hope for even in this way while in the body, as we read in the true book of Wisdom, "The corruptible body weigheth down the soul, and the earthly tabernacle presseth down the mind that museth upon many things?" And eagerness, or desire of action, if this is the right meaning to put upon the Greek *horme* is also reckoned among the primary advantages of nature; and yet is it not this which produces those pitiable movements of the insane, and those actions which we shudder to see, when sense is deceived and reason deranged?

In fine, virtue itself, which is not among the primary objects of nature, but succeeds to them as the result of learning, though it holds the highest place among human good things, what is its occupation save to wage perpetual war with vices—not those that are outside of us, but within; not other mens', but our own—a war which is waged especially by that virtue which the Greeks call and we temperance, and which bridles carnal lusts, and prevents them from winning the constant of the spirit to wicked deeds? For we must not fancy that there is no vice in us, when, as the apostle says, "The flesh lusteth against the spirit"; for to this vice there is a contrary virtue, when, as the same writer says, "The spirit lusteth against the flesh." "For these two," he says, "are contrary one to the other, so that you cannot do the things which you would." But what is it we wish to do when we seek to attain the supreme good, unless that the flesh should cease to lust against the spirit, and that there be no vice in us against which the spirit may lust? And as we cannot attain to this in the present life, however ardently we desire it, let us by God's help accomplish at least this, to preserve the soul from succumbing and yielding to the flesh that lusts against it, and to refuse our consent to the perpetration of sin. Far be it from us, then, to fancy that while we are still engaged in this intestine  war, we have already found the happiness which we seek to reach by victory. And who is there so wise that he has no conflict at all to maintain against his vices?

What shall I say of that virtue which is called prudence? Is not all its vigilance spent in the discernment of good from evil things, so that no mistake may be admitted about what we should desire and what avoid? And thus it is itself a proof that we are in the midst of evils, or that evils are in us; for it teaches us that it is an evil to consent to sin, and a good to refuse this consent. And yet this evil, to which prudence teaches and temperance enables us not to consent, is removed from this life neither by prudence nor by temperance. And justice, whose office it is to render to every man his due, whereby there is in man himself a certain just order of nature, so that the soul is subjected to God, and the flesh to the soul, and consequently both soul and flesh to God—does not this virtue demonstrate that it is as yet rather laboring towards its end than resting in its finished work? For the soul is so much the less subjected to God as it is less occupied with the thought of God; and the flesh is so much the less subjected to the spirit as it lusts more vehemently against the spirit. So long, therefore, as we are beset by this weakness, this plague, this disease, how shall we dare to say that we are safe? and if not safe, then how can we be already enjoying our final beatitude? Then that virtue which goes by the name of fortitude is the plainest proof of the ills of life, for it is these ills which it is compelled to bear patiently. And this holds good, no matter though the ripest wisdom co-exists with it. And I am at a loss to understand how the Stoic philosophers can presume to say that these are no ills, though at the same time they allow the wise man to commit suicide and pass out of this life if they become so grievous that he cannot or ought not to endure them. But such is the stupid pride of these men who fancy that the supreme good can be found in this life, and that they can become happy by their own resources, that their wise man, or at least the man whom they fancifully depict as such, is always happy, even though he become blind, deaf, dumb, mutilated, racked with pains, or suffer any conceivable calamity such as may compel him to make away with himself; and they are not ashamed to call the life that is beset with these evils happy. O happy life, which seeks the aid of death to end it! If it is happy, let the wise man remain in it; but if these ills drive him out of it, in what sense is it happy? Or how can they say that these are not evils which conquer the virtue of fortitude, and force it not only to yield, but so to rave that it in one breath calls life happy and recommends it to be given up? For who is so blind as not to see that if it were happy it would not be fled from? And if they say we should flee from it on account of the infirmities that beset it, why then do they not lower their pride and acknowledge that it is miserable? Was it, I would ask, fortitude or weakness which prompted Cato to kill himself? For he would not have done so had he not been too weak to endure Caesar's victory. Where, then, is his fortitude? It has yielded, it has succumbed, it has been so thoroughly overcome as to abandon, forsake, flee this happy life. Or was it no longer happy? Then it was miserable. How, then, were these not evils which made life miserable, and a thing to be escaped from?

And therefore those who admit that these are evils, as the Peripatetics do, and the Old Academy, the sect which Varro advocates, express a more intelligible doctrine; but theirs also is a surprising mistake, for they contend that this is a happy life which is beset by these evils, even though they be so great that he who endures them should commit suicide to escape them. "Pains and anguish of body," says Varro, "are evils, and so much the worse in proportion to their severity; and to escape them you must quit this life." What life, I pray? This life, he says, which is oppressed by such evils. Then it is happy in the midst of these very evils on account of which you say we must quit it? Or do you call it happy because you are at liberty to escape these evils by death? What, then, if by some secret judgment of God you were held fast and not permitted to die, nor suffered to live without these evils? In that case, at least, you would say that such a life was miserable. It is soon relinquished, no doubt, but this does not make it not miserable; for were it eternal, you yourself would pronounce it miserable. Its brevity, therefore, does not clear it of misery; neither ought it to be called happiness because it is a brief misery. Certainly there is a mighty force in these evils which compel a man—according to them, even a wise man—to cease to be a man that he may escape them, though they say, and say truly, that it is as it were the first and strongest demand of nature that a man cherish himself, and naturally therefore avoid death, and should so stand his own friend as to wish and vehemently aim at continuing to exist as a living creature, and subsisting in this union of soul and body. There is a mighty force in these evils to overcome this natural instinct by which death is by every means and with all a man's efforts avoided, and to overcome it so completely that what was avoided is desired, sought after, and if it cannot in any other way be obtained, is inflicted by the man on himself. There is a mighty force in these evils which make fortitude a homicide—if, indeed, that is to be called fortitude which is so thoroughly overcome by these evils, that it not only cannot preserve by patience the man whom it undertook to govern and defend, but is itself obliged to kill him. The wise man, I admit, ought to bear death with patience, but when it is inflicted by another. If, then, as these men maintain, he is obliged to inflict it on himself, certainly it must be owned that the ills which compel him to this are not only evils, but intolerable evils. The life, then, which is either subject to accidents, or environed with evils so considerable and grievous, could never have been called happy, if the men who give it this name had condescended to yield to the truth, and to be conquered by valid arguments, when they inquired after the happy life, as they yield to unhappiness, and are overcome by overwhelming evils, when they put themselves to death, and if they had not fancied that the supreme good was to be found in this mortal life; for the very virtues of this life, which are certainly its best and most useful possessions, are all the more telling proofs of its miseries in proportion as they are helpful against the violence of its dangers, toils, and woes. For if these are true virtues—and such cannot exist save in those who have true piety— they do not profess to be able to deliver the men who possess them from all miseries; for true virtues tell no such lies, but they profess that by the hope of the future world this life, which is miserably involved in the many and great evils of this world, is happy as it is also safe. For if not yet safe, how could it be happy? And therefore the Apostle Paul, speaking not of men without prudence, temperance, fortitude, and justice, but of those whose lives were regulated by true piety, and whose virtues were therefore true, says "For we are saved by hope: now hope which is seen is not hope; for what a man seeth, why doth he yet hope for? But if we hope for that we see not, then do we with patience wait for it." As, therefore, we are saved, so we are made happy by hope. And as we do not as yet possess a present, but look for a future salvation, so is it with our happiness, and this "with patience"; for we are encompassed with evils, which we ought patiently to endure, until we come to the ineffable enjoyment of unmixed good; for there shall be no longer anything to endure. Salvation, such as it shall be in the world to come, shall itself be our final happiness. And this happiness these philosophers refuse to believe in, because they do not see it, and attempt to fabricate for themselves a happiness in this life, based upon a virtue which is as deceitful as it is proud.

## CHAPTER V
*Of the social life, which, though most desirable, is frequently disturbed by many distresses.*

We give a much more unlimited approval to their idea that the life of the wise man must be social. For how could the city of God (concerning which we are already writing no less than the nineteenth book of this work) either take a beginning or be developed, or attain its proper destiny, if the life of the saints were not a social life? But who can enumerate all the great grievances with which human society abounds in the misery of this mortal state? Who can weigh them? Hear how one of their comic writers makes one of his characters express the common feelings of all men in this matter: "I am married; this is one misery. Children are born to me; they are additional cares." What shall I say of the miseries of love which Terence also recounts—"slights, suspicions, quarrels, war to-day, peace to-morrow?" Is not human life full of such things? Do they not often occur even in honorable friendships? On all hands we experience these slights, suspicions, quarrels, war, all of which are undoubted evils; while, on the other hand, peace is a doubtful good, because we do not know the heart of our friend, and though we did know it to-day, we should be as ignorant of what it might be to-morrow. Who ought to be, or who are more friendly than those who live in the same family? And yet who can rely even upon this friendship, seeing that secret treachery has often broken it up, and produced enmity as bitter as the amity was sweet, or seemed sweet by the most perfect dissimulation? It is on this account that the words of Cicero so move the heart of every one, and provoke a sigh: "There are no snares more dangerous than those which lurk under the guise of duty or the name of relationship. For the man who is your declared foe you can easily baffle by precaution; but this hidden, intestine, and domestic danger not merely exists, but overwhelms you before you can foresee and examine it." It is also to this that allusion is made by the divine saying, "A man's foes are those of his own household"—words which one cannot hear without pain; for though a man have sufficient fortitude to endure it with equanimity, and sufficient sagacity to baffle the malice of a pretended friend, yet if he himself is a good man, he cannot but be greatly pained at the discovery of the perfidy of wicked men, whether they have always been wicked and merely feigned goodness, or have fallen from a better to a malicious disposition. If, then, home, the natural refuge from the ills of life, is itself not safe, what shall we say of the city, which, as it is larger, is so much the more filled with lawsuits civil and criminal, and is never free from the fear, if sometimes from the actual outbreak, of disturbing and bloody insurrections and civil wars?

## CHAPTER VI
*Of the error of human judgments when the truth is hidden.*

What shall I say of these judgments which men pronounce on men, and which are necessary in communities, whatever outward peace they enjoy? Melancholy and lamentable judgments they are, since the judges are men who cannot discern the consciences of those at their bar, and are therefore frequently compelled to put innocent witnesses to the torture to ascertain the truth regarding the crimes of other men. What shall I say of torture applied to the accused himself? He is tortured to discover whether he is guilty, so that, though innocent, he suffers most undoubted punishment for crime that is still doubtful, not because it is proved that he committed it, but because it is not ascertained that he did not commit it. Thus the ignorance of the judge frequently involves an innocent person in suffering. And what is still more unendurable—a thing, indeed, to be bewailed, and, if that were possible, watered with fountains of tears—is this, that when the judge puts the accused to the question, that he may not unwittingly put an innocent man to death, the result of this lamentable ignorance is that this very person, whom he tortured that he might not condemn him if innocent, is condemned to death both tortured and innocent. For if he has chosen, in obedience to the philosophical instructions to the wise man, to quit this life rather than endure any longer such tortures, he declares that he has committed the crime which in fact he has not committed. And when he has been condemned and put to death, the judge is still in ignorance whether he has put to death an innocent or a guilty person, though he put the accused to the torture for the very purpose of saving himself from condemning the innocent; and consequently he has both tortured an innocent man to discover his innocence, and has put him to death without discovering it. If such darkness shrouds social life, will a wise judge take his seat on the bench or no? Beyond question he will. For human society, which he thinks it a wickedness to abandon, constrains him and compels him to this duty. And he thinks it no wickedness that innocent witnesses are tortured regarding the crimes of which other men are accused; or that the accused are put to the torture, so that they are often overcome with anguish, and, though innocent, make false confessions regarding themselves, and are punished; or that, though they be not condemned to die, they often die during, or in consequence of, the torture; or that sometimes the accusers, who perhaps have been prompted by a desire to benefit society by bringing criminals to justice, are themselves condemned through the ignorance of the judge, because they are unable to prove the truth of their accusations though they are true, and because the witnesses lie, and the accused endures the torture without being moved to confession. These numerous and important evils he does not consider sins; for the wise judge does these things, not with any intention of doing harm, but because his ignorance compels him, and because human society claims him as a judge. But though we therefore acquit the judge of malice, we must none the less condemn human life as miserable. And if he is compelled to torture and punish the innocent because his office and his ignorance constrain him, is he a happy as well as a guiltless man? Surely it were proof of more profound considerateness and finer feeling were he to recognise the misery of these necessities, and shrink from his own implication in that misery; and had he any piety about him, he would cry to God, "From my necessities deliver Thou me."

### CHAPTER VII
*Of the diversity of languages, by which the intercourse of men is prevented; and of the misery of wars, even of those called just.*

After the state or city comes the world, the third circle of human society—the first being the house, and the second the city. And the world, as it is larger, so it is fuller of dangers, as the greater sea is more dangerous. And here, in the first place, man is separated from man by the difference of languages. For if two men, each ignorant of the other's language, meet, and are not compelled to pass, but, on the contrary, to remain in company, dumb animals, though of different species, would more easily hold intercourse than they, human beings though they be. For their common nature is no help to friendliness when they are prevented by diversity of language from conveying their sentiments to one another; so that a man would more readily hold intercourse with his dog than with a foreigner. But the imperial city has endeavoured to impose on subject nations not only her yoke, but her language, as a bond of peace, so that interpreters, far from being scarce, are numberless. This is true; but how many great wars, how much slaughter and bloodshed, have provided this unity! And though these are past the end of these miseries has not yet come. For though there have never been wanting, nor are yet wanting, hostile nations beyond the empire, against whom wars have been and are waged, yet, supposing there were no such nations, the very extent of the empire itself has produced wars of a more obnoxious description— social and civil wars—and with these the whole race has been agitated, either by the actual conflict or the fear of a renewed outbreak. If I attempted to give an adequate description of these manifold disasters, these stern and lasting necessities, though I am quite unequal to the task, what limit could I set? But, say they, the wise man will wage just wars. As if he would not all the rather lament the necessity of just wars, if he remembers that he is a man; for if they were not just he would not wage them, and would therefore be delivered from all wars. For it is the wrong-doing of the opposing party which compels the wise man to wage just wars; and this wrong-doing, even though it gave rise to no war, would still be matter of grief to man because it is man's wrong-doing. Let every one, then, who thinks with pain on all these great evils, so horrible, so ruthless, acknowledge that this is misery. And if any one either endures or thinks of them without mental pain, this is a more miserable plight still, for he thinks himself happy because he has lost human feeling.

### CHAPTER VIII
*That the friendship of good men cannot be securely rested in, so long as the dangers of this life force us to be anxious.*

In our present wretched condition we frequently mistake a friend for an enemy, and an enemy for a friend. And if we escape this pitiable blindness, is not the unfeigned confidence and mutual love of true and good friends our one solace in human society, filled as it is with misunderstandings and calamities? And yet the more friends we have, and the more widely they are scattered, the more numerous are our fears that some portion of the vast masses of the disasters of life may light upon them. For we are not only anxious lest they suffer from famine, war, disease, captivity, or the inconceivable horrors of slavery, but we are also affected with the much more painful dread that their friendship may be changed into perfidy, malice, and injustice. And when these contingencies actually occur—as they do the more frequently the more friends we have, and the more widely they are scattered—and when they come to our knowledge, who but the man who has experienced it can tell with what pangs the heart is torn? We would, in fact, prefer to hear that they were dead, although we could not without anguish hear of even this. For if their life has solaced us with the charms of friendship, can it be that their death should affect us with no sadness? He who will have none of this sadness must, if possible, have no friendly intercourse. Let him interdict or extinguish friendly affection; let him burst with ruthless insensibility the bonds of every human relationship; or let him contrive so to use them that no sweetness shall distil into his spirit. But if this is utterly impossible, how shall we contrive to feel no bitterness in the death of those whose life has been sweet to us? Hence arises that grief which affects the tender heart like a wound or a bruise, and which is healed by the application of kindly consolation. For though the cure is affected all the more easily and rapidly the better condition the soul is in, we must not on this account suppose that there is nothing at all to heal. Although, then, our present life is afflicted, sometimes in a milder, sometimes in a more painful degree, by the death of those very dear to us, and especially of useful public men, yet we would prefer to hear that such men were dead rather than to hear or perceive that they had fallen from the faith, or from virtue—in other words, that they were spiritually dead. Of this vast material for misery the earth is full, and therefore it is written, "Is not human life upon earth a trial?" And with the same reference the Lord says, "Woe to the world because of offences!" and again, "Because iniquity abounded, the love of many shall wax cold." And hence we enjoy some gratification when our good friends die; for though their death leaves us in sorrow, we have the consolatory assurance that they are beyond the ills by which in this life even the best of men are broken down or corrupted, or are in danger of both results.

### CHAPTER IX
*Of the friendship of the holy angels, which men cannot be sure of in this life, owing to the deceit of the demons who hold in bondage the worshippers of a plurality of gods.*

The philosophers who wished us to have the gods for our friends rank the friendship of the holy angels in the fourth circle of society, advancing now from the three circles of society on earth to the universe, and embracing heaven itself. And in this friendship we have indeed no fear that the angels will grieve us by their death or deterioration. But as we cannot mingle with them as familiarly as with men (which itself is one of the grievances of this life), and as Satan, as we read, sometimes transforms himself into an angel of light, to tempt those whom it is necessary to discipline, or just to deceive, there is great need of God's mercy to preserve us from making friends of demons in disguise, while we fancy we have good angels for our friends; for the astuteness and deceitfulness of these wicked spirits is equalled by their hurtfulness. And is this not a great misery of human life, that we are involved in such ignorance as, but for God's mercy, makes us a prey to these demons? And it is very certain that the Philosophers of the godless city, who have maintained that the gods were their friends, had fallen a prey to the malignant demons who rule that city, and whose eternal punishment is to be shared by it. For the nature of these beings is sufficiently evinced by the sacred or rather sacrilegious observances which form their worship, and by the filthy games in which their crimes are celebrated, and which they themselves originated and exacted from their worshippers as a fit propitiation.

### CHAPTER X
*The reward prepared for the saints after they have endured the trial of this life.*

But not even the saints and faithful worshippers of the one true and most high God are safe from the manifold temptations and deceits of the demons. For in this abode of weakness, and in these wicked days, this state of anxiety has also its use, stimulating us to seek with keener longing for that security where peace is complete and unassailable. There we shall enjoy the gifts of nature, that is to say, all that God the Creator of all natures has bestowed upon ours—gifts not only good, but eternal—not only of the spirit, healed now by wisdom, but also of the body renewed by the resurrection. There the virtues shall no longer be struggling against any vice or evil, but shall enjoy the reward of victory, the eternal peace which no adversary shall disturb. This is the final blessedness, this the ultimate consummation, the unending end. Here, indeed, we are said to be blessed when we have such peace as can be enjoyed in a good life; but such blessedness is mere misery compared to that final felicity. When we mortals possess such peace as this mortal life can afford, virtue, if we are living rightly, makes a right use of the advantages of this peaceful condition; and when we have it not, virtue makes a good use even of the evils a man suffers. But this is true virtue, when it refers all the advantages it makes a good use of, and all that it does in making good use of good and evil things, and itself also, to that end in which we shall enjoy the best and greatest peace possible.

### CHAPTER XI
*Of the happiness of the eternal peace, which constitutes the end or true perfection of the saints.*

And thus we may say of peace, as we have said of eternal life, that it is the end of our good; and the rather because the Psalmist says of the city of God, the subject of this laborious work, "Praise the Lord, O Jerusalem; praise thy God, O Zion: for He hath strengthened the bars of thy gates; He hath blessed thy children within thee; who hath made thy borders peace." For when the bars of her gates shall be strengthened, none shall go in or come out from her; consequently we ought to understand the peace of her borders as that final peace we are wishing to declare. For even the mystical name of the city itself, that is, *Jerusalem*, means, as I have already said, "Vision of Peace." But as the word peace is employed in connection with things in this world in which certainly life eternal has no place, we have preferred to call the end or supreme good of this city life eternal rather than peace. Of this end the apostle says, "But now, being freed from sin, and become servants to God, ye have your fruit unto holiness, and the end life eternal." But, on the other hand, as those who are not familiar with Scripture may suppose that the life of the wicked is eternal life, either because of the immortality of the soul, which some of the philosophers even have recognised, or because of the endless punishment of the wicked, which forms a part of our faith, and which seems impossible unless the wicked live for ever, it may therefore be advisable, in order that every one may readily understand what we mean, to say that the end or supreme good of this city is either peace in eternal life, or eternal life in peace. For peace is a good so great, that even in this earthly and mortal life there is no word we hear with such pleasure, nothing we desire with such zest, or find to be more thoroughly gratifying. So that if we dwell for a little longer on this subject, we shall not, in my opinion, be wearisome to our readers, who will attend both for the sake of understanding what is the end of this city of which we speak, and for the sake of the sweetness of peace which is dear to all. . . .

### CHAPTER XIV
*Of the order and law which obtain in heaven and earth, whereby it comes to pass that human society is served by those who rule it.*

The whole use, then, of things temporal has a reference to this result of earthly peace in the earthly community, while in the city of God it is connected with eternal peace. And therefore, if we were irrational animals, we should desire nothing beyond the proper arrangement of the parts of the body and the satisfaction of the appetites—nothing, therefore, but bodily comfort and abundance of pleasures, that the peace of the body might contribute to the peace of the soul. For if bodily peace be awanting, a bar is put to the peace even of the irrational soul, since it cannot obtain the gratification of its appetites. And these two together help out the mutual peace of soul and body, the peace of harmonious life and health. For as animals, by shunning pain, show that they love bodily peace, and, by pursuing pleasure to gratify their appetites, show that they love peace of soul, so their shrinking from death is a sufficient indication of their intense love of that peace which binds soul and body in close alliance. But, as man has a rational soul, he subordinates all this which he has in common with the beasts to the peace of his rational soul, that his intellect may have free play and may regulate his actions, and that he may thus enjoy the well-ordered harmony of knowledge and action which constitutes, as we have said, the peace of the rational soul. And for this purpose he must desire to be neither molested by pain, nor disturbed by desire, nor extinguished by death, that he may arrive at some useful knowledge by which he may regulate his life and manners. But, owing to the liability of the human mind to fall into mistakes, this very pursuit of knowledge may be a snare to him unless he has a divine Master, whom he may obey without misgiving, and who may at the same time give him such help as to preserve his own freedom. And because, so long as he is in this mortal body, he is a stranger to God, he walks by faith, not by sight; and he therefore refers all peace, bodily or spiritual or both, to that peace which mortal man has with the immortal God, so that he exhibits the well-ordered obedience of faith to eternal law. But as this divine Master inculcates two precepts—the love of God and the love of our neighbour—and as in these precepts a man finds three things he has to love—God, himself, and his neighbour—and that he who loves God loves himself thereby, it follows that he must endeavour to get his neighbour to love God, since he is ordered to love his neighbour as himself. He ought to make this endeavour in behalf of his wife, his children, his household, all within his reach, even as he would wish his neighbour to do the same for him if he needed it; and consequently he will be at peace, or in well-ordered concord, with all men, as far as in him lies. And this is the order of this concord, that a man, in the first place, injure no one, and, in the second, do good to every one he can reach. Primarily, therefore, his own household are his care, for the law of nature and of society gives him readier access to them and greater opportunity of serving them. And hence the apostle says, "Now, if any provide not for his own, and specially for those of his own house, he hath denied the faith, and is worse than an infidel." This is the origin of domestic peace, or the well-ordered concord of those in the family who rule and those who obey. For they who care for the rest rule—the husband the wife, the parents the children, the masters the servants; and they who are cared for obey—the women their husbands, the children their parents, the servants their masters. But in the family of the just man who lives by faith and is as yet a pilgrim journeying on to the celestial city, even those who rule serve those whom they seem to command; for they rule not from a love of power, but from a sense of the duty they owe to others—not because they are proud of authority, but because they love mercy.

## CHAPTER XV
*Of the liberty proper to man's nature, and the servitude introduced by sin,—a servitude in which the man whose will is wicked is the slave of his own lust, though he is free so far as regards other men.*

This is prescribed by the order of nature: it is thus that God has created man. For "let them," He says, "have dominion over the fish of the sea, and over the fowl of the air, and over every creeping thing which creepeth on the earth." He did not intend that His rational creature, who was made in His image, should have dominion over anything but the irrational creation—not man over man, but man over the beasts. And hence the righteous men in primitive times were made shepherds of cattle rather than kings of men, God intending thus to teach us what the relative position of the creatures is, and what the desert of sin; for it is with justice, we believe, that the condition of slavery is the result of sin. And this is why we do not find the word "slave" in any part of Scripture until righteous Noah branded the sin of his son with this name. It is a name, therefore, introduced by sin and not by nature. The origin of the Latin word for slave is supposed to be found in the circumstance that those who by the law of war were liable to be killed were sometimes preserved by their victors, and were hence called servants. And these circumstances could never have arisen save through sin. For even when we wage a just war, our adversaries must be sinning; and every victory, even though gained by wicked men, is a result of the first judgment of God, who humbles the vanquished either for the sake of removing or of punishing their sins. Witness that man of God, Daniel, who, when he was in captivity, confessed to God his own sins and the sins of his people, and declares with pious grief that these were the cause of the captivity. The prime cause, then, of slavery is sin, which brings man under the dominion of his fellow—that which does not happen save by the judgment of God, with whom is no unrighteousness, and who knows how to award fit punishments to every variety of offence. But our Master in heaven says, "Every one who doeth sin is the servant of sin." And thus there are many wicked masters who have religious men as their slaves, and who are yet themselves in bondage; "for of whom a man is overcome, of the same is he brought in bondage." And beyond question it is a happier thing to be the slave of a man than of a lust; for even this very lust of ruling, to mention no others, lays waste men's hearts with the most ruthless dominion. Moreover, when men are subjected to one another in a peaceful order, the lowly position does as much good to the servant as the proud position does harm to the master. But by nature, as God first created us, no one is the slave either of man or of sin. This servitude is, however, penal, and is appointed by that law which enjoins the preservation of the natural order and forbids its disturbance; for if nothing had been done in violation of that law, there would have been nothing to restrain by penal servitude. And therefore the apostle admonishes slaves to be subject to their masters, and to serve them heartily and with good-will, so that, if they cannot be freed by their masters, they may themselves make their slavery in some sort free, by serving not in crafty fear, but in faithful love, until all unrighteousness pass away, and all principality and every human power be brought to nothing, and God be all in all.

## CHAPTER XVI
*Of equitable rule.*

And therefore, although our righteous fathers had slaves, and administered their domestic affairs so as to distinguish between the condition of slaves and the heirship of sons in regard to the blessings of this life, yet in regard to the worship of God, in whom we hope for eternal blessings, they took an equally loving oversight of all the members of their household. And this is so much in accordance with the natural order, that the head of the household was called *paterfamilias*; and this name has been so generally accepted, that even those whose rule is unrighteous are glad to apply it to themselves. But those who are true fathers of their households desire and endeavour that all the members of their household, equally with their own children, should worship and win God, and should come to that heavenly home in which the duty of ruling men is no longer necessary, because the duty of caring for their everlasting happiness has also ceased; but, until they reach that home, masters ought to feel their position of authority a greater burden than servants their service. And if any member of the family interrupts the domestic peace by disobedience, he is corrected either by word or blow, or some kind of just and legitimate punishment, such as society permits, that he may himself be the better for it, and be readjusted to the family harmony from which he had dislocated himself. For as it is not benevolent to give a man help at the expense of some greater benefit he might receive, so it is not innocent to spare a man at the risk of his falling into graver sin. To be innocent, we must not only do harm to no man, but also restrain him from sin or punish his sin, so that either the man himself who is punished may profit by his experience, or others be warned by his example. Since, then, the house ought to be the beginning or element of the city, and every beginning bears reference to some end of its own kind, and every element to the integrity of the whole of which it is an element, it follows plainly enough that domestic peace has a relation to civic peace—in other words, that the well-ordered concord of domestic obedience and domestic rule has a relation to the well-ordered concord of civic obedience and civic rule. And therefore it follows, further, that the father of the family ought to frame his domestic rule in accordance with the law of the city, so that the household may be in harmony with the civic order.

### CHAPTER XVII
*What produces peace, and what discord, between the heavenly and earthly cities.*

But the families which do not live by faith seek their peace in the earthly advantages of this life; while the families which live by faith look for those eternal blessings which are promised, and use as pilgrims such advantages of time and of earth as do not fascinate and divert them from God, but rather aid them to endure with greater ease, and to keep down the number of those burdens of the corruptible body which weigh upon the soul. Thus the things necessary for this mortal life are used by both kinds of men and families alike, but each has its own peculiar and widely different aim in using them. The earthly city, which does not live by faith, seeks an earthly peace, and the end it proposes, in the well-ordered concord of civic obedience and rule, is the combination of men's wills to attain the things which are helpful to this life. The heavenly city, or rather the part of it which sojourns on earth and lives by faith, makes use of this peace only because it must, until this mortal condition which necessitates it shall pass away. Consequently, so long as it lives like a captive and a stranger in the earthly city, though it has already received the promise of redemption, and the gift of the Spirit as the earnest of it, it makes no scruple to obey the laws of the earthly city, whereby the things necessary for the maintenance of this mortal life are administered; and thus, as this life is common to both cities, so there is a harmony between them in regard to what belongs to it. But, as the earthly city has had some philosophers whose doctrine is condemned by the divine teaching, and who, being deceived either by their own conjectures or by demons, supposed that many gods must be invited to take an interest in human affairs, and assigned to each a separate function and a separate department—to one the body, to another the soul; and in the body itself, to one the head, to another the neck, and each of the other members to one of the gods; and in like manner, in the soul, to one god the natural capacity was assigned, to another education, to another anger, to another lust; and so the various affairs of life were assigned—cattle to one, corn to another, wine to another, oil to another, the woods to another, money to another, navigation to another, wars and victories to another, marriages to another, births and fecundity to another, and other things to other gods: and as the celestial city, on the other hand, knew that one god only was to be worshipped, and that to Him alone was due that service which the Greeks call *latria*, and which can be given only to a god, it has come to pass that the two cities could not have common laws of religion, and that the heavenly city has been compelled in this matter to dissent, and to become obnoxious to those who think differently, and to stand the brunt of their anger and hatred and persecutions, except in so far as the minds of their enemies have been alarmed by the multitude of the Christians and quelled by the manifest protection of God accorded to them. This heavenly city, then, while it sojourns on earth, calls citizens out of all nations, and gathers together a society of pilgrims of all languages, not scrupling about diversities in the manners, laws, and institutions whereby earthly peace is secured and maintained but recognising that, however various these are, they all tend to one and the same end of earthly peace. It therefore is so far from rescinding and abolishing these diversities, that it even preserves and adapts them, so long only as no hindrance to the worship of the one supreme and true God is thus introduced. Even the heavenly city, therefore, while in its state of pilgrimage, avails itself of the peace of earth, and, so far as it can without injuring faith and godliness, desires and maintains a common agreement among men regarding the acquisition of the necessaries of life, and makes this earthly peace bear upon the peace of heaven; for this alone can be truly called and esteemed the peace of the reasonable creatures, consisting as it does in the perfectly ordered and harmonious enjoyment of God and of one another in God. When we shall have reached that peace, this mortal life shall give place to one that is eternal, and our body shall be no more this animal body which by its corruption weighs down the soul, but a spiritual body feeling no want, and in all its members subjected to the will. In its pilgrim state the heavenly city possesses this peace by faith; and by this faith it lives righteously when it refers to the attainment of that peace every good action towards God and man; for the life of the city is a social life.

### CHAPTER XVIII
*How different the uncertainty of the New Academy is from the certainty of the Christian faith.*

As regards the uncertainty about everything which Varro alleges to be the differentiating characteristic of the New Academy, the city of God thoroughly detests such doubt as madness. Regarding matters which it apprehends by the mind and reason it has most absolute certainty, although its knowledge is limited because of the corruptible body pressing down the mind, for, as the apostle says, "We know in part." It believes also the evidence of the senses which the mind uses by aid of the body; for (if one who trusts his senses is sometimes deceived), he is more wretchedly deceived who fancies he should never trust them. It believes also the Holy Scriptures, old and new, which we call canonical, and which are the source of the faith by which the just lives, and by which we walk without doubting whilst we are absent from the Lord. So long as this faith remains inviolate and firm, we may without blame entertain doubts regarding some things which we have neither perceived by sense nor by reason, and which have not been revealed to us by the canonical Scriptures, nor come to our knowledge through witnesses whom it is absurd to disbelieve.

### CHAPTER XIX
*Of the dress and habits of the Christian people.*

It is a matter of no moment in the city of God whether he who adopts the faith that brings men to God adopts it in one dress and manner of life or another, so long only as he lives in conformity with the commandments of God. And hence, when philosophers themselves become Christians, they are compelled, indeed, to abandon their erroneous doctrines, but not their dress and mode of living, which are no obstacle to religion. So that we make no account of that distinction of sects which Varro adduced in connection with the Cynic school, provided always nothing indecent or self-indulgent is retained. As to these three modes of life, the contemplative, the active, and the composite, although, so long as a man's faith is preserved, he may choose any of them without detriment to his eternal interests, yet he must never overlook the claims of truth and duty. No man has a right to lead such a life of contemplation as to forget in his own ease the service due to his neighbour; nor has any man a right to be so immersed in active life as to neglect the contemplation of God. The charm of leisure must not be indolent vacancy of mind, but the investigation or discovery of truth, that thus every man may make solid attainments without grudging that others do the same. And, in active life, it is not the honors or power of this life we should covet, since all things under the sun are vanity, but we should aim at using our position and influence, if these have been honorably attained, for the welfare of those who are under us, in the way we have already explained. It is to this the apostle refers when he says, "He that desireth the episcopate desireth a good work." He wished to show that the episcopate is the title of a work, not of an honor. It is a Greek word, and signifies that he who governs superintends or takes care of those whom he governs: for *epi* means *over*, and *skopain, to see*; therefore *episkopain* means "to oversee." So that he who loves to govern rather than to do good is no bishop. Accordingly no one is prohibited from the search after truth, for in this leisure may most laudably be spent; but it is unseemly to covet the high position requisite for governing the people, even though that position be held and that government be administered in a seemly manner. And therefore holy leisure is longed for by the love of truth; but it is the necessity of love to undertake requisite business. If no one imposes this burden upon us, we are free to sift and contemplate truth; but if it be laid upon us, we are necessitated for love's sake to undertake it. And yet not even in this case are we obliged wholly to relinquish the sweets of contemplation; for were these to be withdrawn, the burden might prove more than we could bear.

### CHAPTER XX
*That the saints are in this life blessed in hope.*

Since, then, the supreme good of the city of God is perfect and eternal peace, not such as mortals pass into and out of by birth and death, but the peace of freedom from all evil, in which the immortals ever abide, who can deny that that future life is most blessed, or that, in comparison with it, this life which now we live is most wretched, be it filled with all blessings of body and soul and external things? And yet, if any man uses this life with a reference to that other which he ardently loves and confidently hopes for, he may well be called even now blessed, though not in reality so much as in hope. But the actual possession of the happiness of this life, without the hope of what is beyond, is but a false happiness and profound misery. For the true blessings of the soul are not now enjoyed; for that is no true wisdom which does not direct all its prudent observations, manly actions, virtuous self-restraint, and just arrangements, to that end in which God shall be all and all in a secure eternity and perfect peace.

### CHAPTER XXI
*Whether there ever was a Roman republic answering to the definitions of Scipio in Cicero's dialogue.*

This, then, is the place where I should fulfil the promise I gave in the second book of this work, and explain, as briefly and clearly as possible, that if we are to accept the definitions laid down by Scipio in Cicero's *De Republica*, there never was a Roman republic; for he briefly defines a republic as the weal of the people. And if this definition be true, there never was a Roman republic, for the people's weal was never attained among the Romans. For the people, according to his definition, is an assemblage associated by a common acknowledgement of right and by a community of interests. And what he means by a common acknowledgement of right he explains at large, showing that a republic cannot be administered without justice. Where, therefore, there is no true justice there can be no right. For that which is done by right is justly done, and what is unjustly done cannot be done by right. For the unjust inventions of men are neither to be considered nor spoken of as rights; for even they themselves say that right is that which flows from the fountain of justice, and deny the definition which is commonly given by those who misconceive the matter, that right is that which is useful to the stronger party. Thus, where there is not true justice there can be no assemblage of men associated by a common acknowledgement of right, and therefore there can be no people, as defined by Scipio or Cicero; and if no people, then no weal of the people, but only of some promiscuous multitude unworthy of the name of people. Consequently if the republic is the weal of the people, and there is no people if it be not associated by a common acknowledgment of right, and if there is no right where there is no justice, then most certainly it follows that there is no republic where there is no justice. Further, justice is that virtue which gives every one his due. Where, then, is the justice of man, when he deserts the true God and yields himself to impure demons? Is this to give every one his due? Or is he who keeps back a piece of ground from the purchaser and gives it to a man who has no right to it, unjust, while he who keeps back himself from the God who made him, and serves wicked spirits, is just?

This same book, *De Republica,* advocates the cause of justice against injustice with great force and keenness. The pleading for injustice against justice was first heard, and it was asserted that without injustice a republic could neither increase nor even subsist, for it was laid down as an absolutely unassailable position that it is unjust for some men to rule and some to serve; and yet the imperial city to which the republic belongs cannot rule her provinces without having recourse to this injustice. It was replied in behalf of justice, that this ruling of the provinces is just, because servitude may be advantageous to the provincials, and is so when rightly administered—that is to say, when lawless men are prevented from doing harm. And further, as they became worse and worse so long as they were free, they will improve by subjection. To confirm this reasoning there is added an eminent example drawn from nature: for "why," it is asked, "does God rule man, the soul the body, the reason the passions and other vicious parts of the soul?" This example leaves no doubt that, to some, servitude is useful; and, indeed, to serve God is useful to all. And it is when the soul serves God that it exercises a right control over the body; and in the soul itself the reason must be subject to God if it is to govern as it ought the passions and other vices. Hence, when a man does not serve God, what justice can we ascribe to him, since in this case his soul cannot exercise a just control over the body, nor his reason over his vices? And if there is no justice in such an individual, certainly there can be none in a community composed of such persons. Here, therefore, there is not that common acknowledgement of right which makes an assemblage of men a people whose affairs we call a republic. And why need I speak of the advantageousness, the common participation in which, according to the definition, makes a people? For although, if you choose to regard the matter attentively, you will see that there is nothing advantageous to those who live godlessly, as every one lives who does not serve God but demons, whose wickedness you may measure by their desire to receive the worship of men though they are most impure spirits, yet what I have said of the common acknowledgement of right is enough to demonstrate that, according to the above definition, there can be no people, and therefore no republic, where there is no justice. For if they assert that in their republic the Romans did not serve unclean spirits, but good and holy gods, must we therefore again reply to this evasion, though already we have said enough, and more than enough, to expose it? He must be an uncommonly stupid, or a shamelessly contentious person, who has read through the foregoing books to this point, and can yet question whether the Romans served wicked and impure demons. But, not to speak of their character, it is written in the law of the true God, "He that sacrificeth unto any god save unto the Lord only, he shall be utterly destroyed." He, therefore, who uttered so menacing a commandment decreed that no worship should be given either to good or bad gods. . . .

And therefore, where there is not this righteousness whereby the one supreme God rules the obedient city according to His grace, so that it sacrifices to none but Him, and whereby, in all the citizens of this obedient city, the soul consequently rules the body and reason the vices in the rightful order, so that, as the individual just man, so also the community and people of the just, live by faith, which works by love, that love whereby man loves God as He ought to be loved, and his neighbour as himself—there, I say, there is not an assemblage associated by a common acknowledgement of right, and by a community of interests. But if there is not this, there is not a people, if our definition be true, and therefore there is no republic; for where there is no people there can be no republic.

## CHAPTER XXIV
*The definition which must be given of a people and a republic, in order to vindicate the assumption of these titles by the Romans and by other kingdoms.*

But if we discard this definition of a people, and, assuming another, say that a people is an assemblage of reasonable beings bound together by a common agreement as to the objects of their love, then, in order to discover the character of any people, we have only to observe what they love. Yet whatever it loves, if only it is an assemblage of reasonable beings and not of beasts, and is bound together by an agreement as to the objects of love, it is reasonably called a people; and it will be a superior people in proportion as it is bound together by higher interests, inferior in proportion as it is bound together by lower. According to this definition of ours, the Roman people is a people, and its weal is without doubt a commonwealth or republic. But what its tastes were in its early and subsequent days, and how it declined into sanguinary seditions and then to social and civil wars, and so burst asunder or rotted off the bond of concord in which the health of a people consists, history shows, and in the preceding books I have related at large. And yet I would not on this account say either that it was not a people, or that its administration was not a republic, so long as there remains an assemblage of reasonable beings bound together by a common agreement as to the objects of love. But what I say of this people and of this republic I must be understood to think and say of the Athenians or any Greek state, of the Egyptians, of the early Assyrian Babylon, and of every other nation, great or small, which had a public government. For, in general, the city of the ungodly, which did not obey the command of God that it should offer no sacrifice save to Him alone, and which, therefore, could not give to the soul its proper command over the body, nor to the reason its just authority over the vices, is void of true justice.

## CHAPTER XXV
*That where there is no true religion there are no true virtues.*

For though the soul may seem to rule the body admirably, and the reason the vices, if the soul and reason do not themselves obey God, as God has commanded them to serve Him, they have no proper authority over the body and the vices. For what kind of mistress of the body and the vices can that mind be which is ignorant of the true God, and which, instead of being subject to His authority, is prostituted to the corrupting influences of the most vicious demons? It is for this reason that the virtues which it seems to itself to possess, and by which it restrains the body and the vices that it may obtain and keep what it desires, are rather vices than virtues so long as there is no reference to God in the matter. For although some suppose that virtues which have a reference only to themselves, and are desired only on their own account, are yet true and genuine virtues, the fact is that even then they are inflated with pride, and are therefore to be reckoned vices rather than virtues. For as that which gives life to the flesh is not derived from flesh, but is above it, so that which gives blessed life to man is not derived from man, but is something above him; and what I say of man is true of every celestial power and virtue whatsoever.

### CHAPTER XXVI
*Of the peace which is enjoyed by the people that are alienated from God, and the use made of it by the people of God in the time of its pilgrimage.*

Wherefore, as the life of the flesh is the soul, so the blessed life of man is God, of whom the sacred writings of the Hebrews say, "Blessed is the people whose God is the Lord." Miserable, therefore, is the people which is alienated from God. Yet even this people has a peace of its own which is not to be lightly esteemed, though, indeed, it shall not in the end enjoy it, because it makes no good use of it before the end. But it is our interest that it enjoy this peace meanwhile in this life; for as long as the two cities are commingled, we also enjoy the peace of Babylon. For from Babylon the people of God is so freed that it meanwhile sojourns in its company. And therefore the apostle also admonished the Church to pray for kings and those in authority, assigning as the reason, "that we may live a quiet and tranquil life in all godliness and love." And the prophet Jeremiah, when predicting the captivity that was to befall the ancient people of God, and giving them the divine command to go obediently to Babylonia, and thus serve their God, counselled them also to pray for Babylonia, saying, "In the peace thereof shall ye have peace"— the temporal peace which the good and the wicked together enjoy.

### CHAPTER XXVII
*That the peace of those who serve God cannot in this mortal life be apprehended in its perfection.*

But the peace which is peculiar to ourselves we enjoy now with God by faith, and shall hereafter enjoy eternally with Him by sight. But the peace which we enjoy in this life, whether common to all or peculiar to ourselves, is rather the solace of our misery than the positive enjoyment of felicity. Our very righteousness, too, though true in so far as it has respect to the true good, is yet in this life of such a kind that it consists rather in the remission of sins than in the perfecting of virtues. Witness the prayer of the whole city of God in its pilgrim state, for it cries to God by the mouth of all its members, "Forgive us our debts as we forgive our debtors." And this prayer is efficacious not for those whose faith is "without works and dead," but for those whose faith "worketh by love." For as reason, though subjected to God, is yet "pressed down by the corruptible body," so long as it is in this mortal condition, it has not perfect authority over vice, and therefore this prayer is needed by the righteous. For though it exercises authority, the vices do not submit without a struggle. For however well one maintains the conflict, and however thoroughly he has subdued these enemies, there steals in some evil thing, which, if it do not find ready expression in act, slips out by the lips, or insinuates itself into the thought; and therefore his peace is not full so long as he is at war with his vices. For it is a doubtful conflict he wages with those that resist, and his victory over those that are defeated is not secure, but full of anxiety and effort. Amidst these temptations, therefore, of all which it has been summarily said in the divine oracles, "Is not human life upon earth a temptation?" who but a proud man can presume that he so lives that he has no need to say to God, "Forgive us our debts"? And such a man is not great, but swollen and puffed up with vanity, and is justly resisted by Him who abundantly gives grace to the humble. Whence it is said, "God resisteth the proud, but giveth grace to the humble." In this, then, consists the righteousness of a man, that he submit himself to God, his body to his soul, and his vices, even when they rebel, to his reason, which either defeats or at least resists them; and also that he beg from God grace to do his duty, and the pardon of his sins, and that he render to God thanks for all the blessings he receives. But, in that final peace to which all our righteousness has reference, and for the sake of which it is maintained, as our nature shall enjoy a sound immortality and incorruption, and shall have no more vices, and as we shall experience no resistance either from ourselves or from others, it will not be necessary that reason should rule vices which no longer exist, but God shall rule the man, and the soul shall rule the body, with a sweetness and facility suitable to the felicity of a life which is done with bondage. And this condition shall there be eternal, and we shall be assured of its eternity; and thus the peace of this blessedness and the blessedness of this peace shall be the supreme good.

### CHAPTER XXVIII
*The end of the wicked.*

But, on the other hand, they who do not belong to this city of God shall inherit eternal misery, which is also called the second death, because the soul shall then be separated from God its life, and therefore cannot be said to live, and the body shall be subjected to eternal pains. And consequently this second death shall be the more severe, because no death shall terminate it. But war being contrary to peace, as misery to happiness, and life to death, it is not without reason asked what kind of war can be found in the end of the wicked answering to the peace which is declared to be the end of the righteous? The person who puts this question has only to observe what it is in war that is hurtful and destructive, and he shall see that it is nothing else than the mutual opposition and conflict of things. And can he conceive a more grievous and bitter war than that in which the will is so opposed to passion, and passion to the will, that their hostility can never be terminated by the victory of either, and in which the violence of pain so conflicts with the nature of the body, that neither yields to the other? For in this life, when this conflict has arisen, either pain conquers and death expels the feeling of it, or nature conquers and health expels the pain. But in the world to come the pain continues that it may torment, and the nature endures that it may be sensible of it; and neither ceases to exist, lest punishment also should cease. Now, as it is through the last judgment that men pass to these ends, the good to the supreme good, the evil to the supreme evil, I will treat of this judgment in the following book.

Devotion to the charisma of the prophet, or the leader in war, or to the great demagogue in the *ecclesia* or in parliament, means that the leader is personally recognized as the innerly "called" leader of men. Men do not obey him by virtue of tradition or statute, but because they believe in him. If he is more than a narrow and vain upstart of the moment, the leader lives for his cause and "strives for his work." The devotion of his disciples, his followers, his personal party friends is oriented to his person and to its qualities.

Charismatic leadership has emerged in all places and in all historical epochs. Most importantly in the past, it has emerged in the two figures of the magician and the prophet on the one hand, and in the elected war lord, the gang leader and *condotierre* on the other hand. *Political* leadership in the form of the free "demagogue" who grew from the soil of the city state is of greater concern to us; like the city state, the demagogue is peculiar to the Occident and especially to Mediterranean culture. Furthermore, political leadership in the form of the parliamentary "party leader" has grown on the soil of the constitutional state, which is also indigenous only to the Occident.

These politicians by virtue of a "calling," in the most genuine sense of the word, are of course nowhere the only decisive figures in the cross-currents of the political struggle for power. The sort of auxiliary means that are at their disposal is also highly decisive. How do the politically dominant powers manage to maintain their domination? The question pertains to any kind of domination, hence also to political domination in all its forms, traditional as well as legal and charismatic.

Organized domination, which calls for continuous administration, requires that human conduct be conditioned to obedience towards those masters who claim to be the bearers of legitimate power. On the other hand, by virtue of this obedience, organized domination requires the control of those material goods which in a given case are necessary for the use of physical violence. Thus, organized domination requires control of the personal executive staff and the material implements of administration.

The administrative staff, which externally represents the organization of political domination, is, of course, like any other organization, bound by obedience to the power-holder and not alone by the concept of legitimacy, of which we have just spoken. There are two other means, both of which appeal to personal interests: material reward and social honor. The fiefs of vassals, the prebends of patrimonial officials, the salaries of modern civil servants, the honor of knights, the privileges of estates, and the honor of the civil servant comprise their respective wages. The fear of losing them is the final and decisive basis for solidarity between the executive staff and the power-holder. There is honor and booty for the followers in war; for the demagogue's following, there are "spoils"—that is, exploitation of the dominated through the monopolization of office— and there are politically determined profits and premiums of vanity. All of these rewards are also derived from the domination exercised by a charismatic leader.

\* \* \*

. . . Now then, what inner enjoyments can this career offer and what personal conditions are presupposed for one who enters this avenue?

Well, first of all, the career of politics grants a feeling of power. The knowledge of influencing men, of participating in power over them, and above all, the feeling of holding in one's hands a nerve fiber of historically important events can elevate the professional politician above everyday routine even when he is placed in formally modest positions. But now the question for him is: Through what qualities can I hope to do justice to this power (however narrowly circumscribed it may be in the individual case)? How can he hope to do justice to the responsibility that power imposes upon him? With this we enter the field of ethical questions, for that is where the problem belongs: What kind of a man must one be if he is to be allowed to put his hand on the wheel of history?

One can say that three pre-eminent qualities are decisive for the politician: passion, a feeling of responsibility, and a sense of proportion.

This means passion in the sense of *matter-of-factness*, of passionate devotion to a "cause," to the god or demon who is its overlord. It is not passion in the sense of that inner bearing which my late friend, Georg Simmel, used to designate as "sterile excitation," and which was peculiar especially to a certain type of Russian intellectual (by no means all of them!). It is an excitation that plays so great a part with our intellectuals in this carnival we decorate with the proud name of "revolution." It is a "romanticism of the intellectually interesting," running into emptiness devoid of all feeling of objective responsibility.

To be sure, mere passion, however genuinely felt, is not enough. It does not make a politician, unless passion as devotion to a "cause" also makes responsibility to this cause the guiding star of action. And for this, a sense of proportion is needed. This is the decisive psychological quality of the politician: his ability to let realities work upon him with inner concentration and calmness. Hence his *distance* to things and men. "Lack of distance" *per se* is one of the deadly sins of every politician. It is one of those qualities the breeding of which will condemn the progeny of our intellectuals to political incapacity. For the problem is simply how can warm passion and a cool sense of proportion be forged together in one and the same soul? Politics is made with the head, not with other parts of the body or soul. And yet devotion to politics, if it is not to be frivolous intellectual play but rather genuinely human conduct, can be born and nourished from passion alone. However, that firm taming of the soul, which distinguishes the passionate politician and differentiates him from the "sterilely excited" and mere political dilettante, is possible only through habituation to detachment in every sense of the word. The "strength" of a political "personality" means, in the first place, the possession of these qualities of passion, responsibility, and proportion.

Therefore, daily and hourly, the politician inwardly has to overcome a quite trivial and all-too-human enemy: a quite vulgar vanity, the deadly enemy of all matter-of-fact devotion to a cause, and of all distance, in this case, of distance towards one's self.

Vanity is a very widespread quality and perhaps nobody is entirely free from it. In academic and scholarly circles, vanity is a sort of occupational disease, but precisely with the scholar, vanity—however disagreeably it may express itself—is relatively harmless; in the sense that as a rule it does not disturb scientific enterprise. With the politician the case is quite different. He works with the striving for power as an unavoidable means. Therefore, "power instinct," as is usually said, belongs indeed to his normal qualities. The sin against the lofty spirit of his vocation, however, begins where this striving for power ceases to be *objective* and becomes purely personal self-intoxication instead of exclusively entering the service of "the cause." For ultimately there are only two kinds of deadly sins in the field of politics: lack of objectivity and—often but not always identical with it—irresponsibility. Vanity, the need personally to stand in the foreground as clearly as possible, strongly tempts the politician to commit one or both of these sins. This is more truly the case as the demagogue is compelled to count upon "effect." He therefore is constantly in danger of becoming an actor as well as taking lightly the responsibility for the outcome of his actions and of being concerned merely with the "impression" he makes. His lack of objectivity tempts him to strive for the glamorous semblance of power rather than for actual power. His irresponsibility, however, suggests that he enjoy power merely for power's sake without a substantive purpose. Although, or rather just because, power is the unavoidable means, and striving for power is one of the driving forces of all politics, there is no more harmful distortion of political force than the parvenu-like braggart with power, and the vain self-reflection in the feeling of power, and in general every worship of power *per se*. The mere "power politician" may get strong effects, but actually his work leads nowhere and is senseless. (Among us, too, an ardently promoted cult seeks to glorify him.) In this, the critics of "power politics" are absolutely right. From the sudden inner collapse of typical representatives of this mentality, we can see what inner weakness and impotence hides behind this boastful but entirely empty gesture. It is a product of a shoddy and superficially blase attitude towards the meaning of human conduct; and it has no relation whatsoever to the knowledge of tragedy with which all action, but especially political action, is truly interwoven.

The final result of political action often, no, even regularly, stands in completely inadequate and often even paradoxical relation to its original meaning. This is fundamental to all history, a point not to be proved in detail here. But because of this fact, the serving of a cause must not be absent if action is to have inner strength. Exactly what the cause, in the service of which the politician strives for power and uses power, looks like is a matter of faith. The politician may serve national, humanitarian, social, ethical, cultural, worldly, or religious ends. The politician may be sustained by a strong belief in "progress"—no matter in which sense—or he may coolly reject this kind of belief. He may claim to stand in the service of an "idea" or, rejecting this in principle, he may want to serve external ends of everyday life. However, some kind of faith must always exist. Otherwise, it is absolutely true that the curse of the creature's worthlessness overshadows even the externally strongest political successes.

With the statement above we are already engaged in discussing the last problem that concerns us tonight: the *ethos* of politics as a "cause." What calling can politics fulfill quite independently of its goals within the total ethical economy of human conduct—which is, so to speak, the ethical locus where politics is at home? Here, to be sure, ultimate *Weltanschauungen* clash, world views among which in the end one has to make a choice. Let us resolutely tackle this problem, which recently has been opened again, in my view in a very wrong way.

But first, let us free ourselves from a quite trivial falsification: namely, that ethics may first appear in a morally highly compromised role. Let us consider examples. Rarely will you find that a man whose love turns from one woman to another feels no need to legitimate this before himself by saying: she was not worthy of my love, or, she has disappointed me, or whatever other like "reasons" exist. This is an attitude that, with a profound lack of chivalry, adds a fancied "legitimacy" to the plain fact that he no longer loves her and that the woman has to bear it. By virtue of this "legitimation," the man claims a right for himself and besides causing the misfortune seeks to put her in the wrong. The successful amatory competitor proceeds exactly in the same way: namely, the opponent must be less worthy, otherwise he would not have lost out. It is no different, of course, if after a victorious war the victor in undignified self-righteousness claims, "I have won because I was right." Or, if somebody under the frightfulness of war collapses psychologically, and instead of simply saying it was just too much, he feels the need of legitimizing his war weariness to himself by substituting the feeling, "I could not bear it because I had to fight for a morally bad cause." And likewise with the defeated in war. Instead of searching like old women for the "guilty one" after the war—in a situation in which the structure of society produced the war—everyone with a manly and controlled attitude would tell the enemy, "We lost the war. You have won it. That is now all over. Now let us discuss what conclusions must be drawn according to the *objective* interests that came into play and what is the main thing in view of the responsibility towards the *future* which above all burdens the victor." Anything else is undignified and will become a boomerang. A nation forgives if its interests have been damaged, but no nation forgives if its honor has been offended, especially by bigoted self-righteousness. Every new document that comes to light after decades revives the undignified lamentations, the hatred and scorn, instead of allowing the war at its end to be buried, at least morally. This is possible only through objectivity and chivalry and above all only through dignity. But never is it possible through an "ethic," which in truth signifies a lack of dignity on both sides. Instead of being concerned about what the politician is interested in, the future and the responsibility towards the future, this ethic is concerned about politically sterile questions of past guilt, which are not to be settled politically. To act in this way is politically guilty, if such guilt exists at all. And it overlooks the unavoidable falsification of the whole problem, through very material interests: namely, the victor's interest in the greatest possible moral and material gain; the hopes of the defeated to trade in advantages through confessions of guilt. If anything is "vulgar," then, this is, and it is the result of this fashion of exploiting "ethics" as a means of "being in the right."

Now then, what relations do ethics and politics actually have? Have the two nothing whatever to do with one another, as has occasionally been said? Or, is the reverse true: that the ethic of political conduct is identical with that of any other conduct? Occasionally an exclusive choice has been believed to exist between the two propositions—either the one or the other proposition must be correct. But is it true that any ethic of the world could establish commandments of identical content for erotic, business, familial, and official relations; for the relations to one's wife, to the greengrocer, the son, the competitor, the friend, the defendant? Should it really matter so little for the ethical demands on politics that politics operates with very special means, namely, power backed up by *violence*? Do we not see that the Bolshevik and the Spartacist ideologists bring about exactly the same results as any militaristic dictator just because they use this political means? In what but the persons of the power-holders and their dilettantism does the rule of the workers' and soldiers' councils differ from the rule of any power-holder of the old regime? In what way does the polemic of most representatives of the presumably new ethic differ from that of the opponents which they criticized, or the ethic of any other demagogues? In their noble intention, people will say. Good! But it is the means about which we speak here, and the adversaries, in complete subjective sincerity, claim, in the very same way, that their ultimate intentions are of lofty character. "All they that take the sword shall perish with the sword" and fighting is everywhere fighting. Hence, the ethic of the Sermon on the Mount.

By the Sermon on the Mount, we mean the absolute ethic of the gospel, which is a more serious matter than those who are fond of quoting these commandments today believe. This ethic is no joking matter. The same holds for this ethic as has been said of causality in science: it is not a cab, which one can have stopped at one's pleasure; it is all or nothing. This is precisely the meaning of the gospel, if trivialities are not to result. Hence, for instance, it was said of the wealthy young man, "He went away sorrowful: for he had great possessions." The evangelist commandment, however, is unconditional and unambiguous: give what thou hast—absolutely everything. The politician will say that this is a socially senseless imposition as long as it is not carried out everywhere. Thus the politician upholds taxation, confiscatory taxation, outright confiscation; in a word, compulsion and regulation for all. The ethical commandment, however, is not at all concerned about that, and this unconcern is its essence. Or, take the example, "turn the other cheek": This command is unconditional and does not question the source of the other's authority to strike. Except for a saint it is an ethic of indignity. This is it: one must be saintly in everything; at least in intention, one must live like Jesus, the apostles, St. Francis, and their like. *Then* this ethic makes sense and expresses a kind of dignity; otherwise it does not. For if it is said, in line with the acosmic ethic of love, "Resist not him that is evil with force," for the politician the reverse proposition holds, "thou *shalt* resist evil by force," or else you are responsible for the evil winning out. He who wishes to follow the ethic of the gospel should abstain from strikes, for strikes mean compulsion; he may join the company unions. Above all things, he should not talk of "revolution." After all, the ethic of the gospel does not wish to teach that civil war is the only legitimate war. The pacifist who follows the gospel will refuse to bear arms or will throw them down; in Germany this was the recommended ethical duty to end the war and therewith all wars. The politician would say the only sure means to discredit the war for all foreseeable time would have been a *status quo* peace. Then the nations would have questioned, what was this war for? And then the war would have been argued *ad absurdum*, which is now impossible. For the victors, at least for part of them, the war will have been politically profitable. And the responsibility for this rests on behavior that made all resistance impossible for us. Now, as a result of the ethics of absolutism, when the period of exhaustion will have passed, *the peace will be discredited, not the war.*

Finally, let us consider the duty of truthfulness. For the absolute ethic it holds unconditionally. Hence the conclusion was reached to publish all documents, especially those placing blame on one's own country. On the basis of these one-sided publications the confessions of guilt followed—and they were one-sided, unconditional, and without regard to consequences. The politician will find that as a result truth will not be furthered but certainly obscured through abuse and unleashing of passion; only an all-round methodical investigation by non-partisans could bear fruit; any other procedure may have consequences for a nation that cannot be remedied for decades. But the absolute ethic just does not *ask* for "consequences." That is the decisive point.

We must be clear about the fact that all ethically oriented conduct may be guided by one of two fundamentally different and irreconcilably opposed maxims: conduct can be oriented to an "ethic of ultimate ends" or to an "ethic of responsibility." This is not to say that an ethic of ultimate ends is identical with irresponsibility, or that an ethic of responsibility is identical with unprincipled opportunism. Naturally nobody says that. However, there is an abysmal contrast between conduct that follows the maxim of an ethic of ultimate ends—that is, in religious terms, "The Christian does rightly and leaves the results with the Lord"—and conduct that follows the maxim of an ethic of responsibility, in which case one has to give an account of the foreseeable results of one's action.

You may demonstrate to a convinced syndicalist, believing in an ethic of ultimate ends, that his action will result in increasing the opportunities of reaction, in increasing the oppression of his class, and obstructing its ascent—and you will not make the slightest impression upon him. If an action of good intent leads to bad results, then, in the actor's eyes, not he but the world, or the stupidity of other men, or God's will who made them thus, is responsible for the evil. However a man who believes in an ethic of responsibility takes account of precisely the average deficiencies of people; as Fichte has correctly said, he does not even have the right to presuppose their goodness and perfection. He does not feel in a position to burden others with the results of his own actions so far as he was able to foresee them; he will say: these results are ascribed to my action. The believer in an ethic of ultimate ends feels "responsible" only for seeing to it that the flame of pure intentions is not quelched: for example, the flame of protesting against the injustice of the social order. To rekindle the flame ever anew is the purpose of his quite irrational deeds, judged in view of their possible success. They are acts that can and shall have only exemplary value.

But even herewith the problem is not yet exhausted. No ethics in the world can dodge the fact that in numerous instances the attainment of "good" ends is bound to the fact that one must be willing to pay the price of using morally dubious means or at least dangerous ones—and facing the possibility or even the probability of evil ramifications. From no ethics in the world can it be concluded when and to what extent the ethically good purpose "justifies" the ethically dangerous means and ramifications.

The decisive means for politics is violence. You may see the extent of the tension between means and ends, when viewed ethically, from the following: as is generally known, even during the war the revolutionary socialists (Zimmerwald faction) professed a principle that one might strikingly formulate: "If we face the choice either of some more years of war and then revolution, or peace now and no revolution, we choose—some more years of war!" Upon the further question: "What can this revolution bring about?" every scientifically trained socialist would have had the answer: One cannot speak of a transition to an economy that in our sense could be called socialist; a bourgeois economy will re-emerge, merely stripped of the feudal elements and the dynastic vestiges. For this very modest result, they are willing to face "some more years of war." One may well say that even with a very robust socialist conviction one might reject a purpose that demands such means. With Bolshevism and Spartacism, and, in general, with any kind of revolutionary socialism, it is precisely the same thing. It is of course utterly ridiculous if the power politicians of the old regime are morally denounced for their use of the same means, however justified the rejection of their *aims* may be.

The ethic of ultimate ends apparently must go to pieces on the problem of the justification of means by ends. As a matter of fact, logically it has only the possibility of rejecting all action that employs morally dangerous means—in theory! In the world of realities, as a rule, we encounter the ever-renewed experience that the adherent of an ethic of ultimate ends suddenly turns into a chiliastic prophet. Those, for example, who have just preached "love against violence" now call for the use of force for the *last* violent deed, which would then lead to a state of affairs in which *all* violence is annihilated. In the same manner, our officers told the soldiers before every offensive: "This will be the last one; this one will bring victory and therewith peace." The proponent of an ethic of absolute ends cannot stand up under the ethical irrationality of the world. He is a cosmic-ethical "rationalist." Those of you who know Dostoievski will remember the scene of the "Grand Inquisitor" where the problem is poignantly unfolded. If one makes any concessions at all to the principle that the end justifies the means, it is not possible to bring an ethic of ultimate ends and an ethic of responsibility under one roof or to decree ethically which end should justify which means.

My colleague, Mr. F. W. Förster, whom personally I highly esteem for his undoubted sincerity, but whom I reject unreservedly as a politician, believes it is possible to get around this difficulty by the simple thesis: "from good comes only good; but from evil only evil follows." In that case this whole complex of questions would not exist. But it is rather astonishing that such a thesis could come to light two thousand five hundred years after the Upanishads. Not only the whole course of world history, but every frank examination of everyday experience points to the very opposite. The development of religions all over the world is determined by the fact that the opposite is true. The age-old problem of theodicy consists of the very question of how it is that a power which is said to be at once omnipotent and kind could have created such an irrational world of undeserved suffering, unpunished injustice, and hopeless stupidity. Either this power is not omnipotent or not kind, or, entirely different principles of compensation and reward govern our life—principles we may interpret metaphysically, or even principles that forever escape our comprehension.

This problem—the experience of the irrationality of the world—has been the driving force of all religious evolution. The Indian doctrine of karma, Persian dualism, the doctrine of original sin, predestination and the *deus absconditus*, all these have grown out of this experience. Also the early Christians knew full well the world is governed by demons and that he who lets himself in for politics, that is, for power and force as means, contracts with diabolical powers and for his action it is not true that good can follow only from good and evil only from evil, but that often the opposite is true. Anyone who fails to see this is, indeed, a political infant.

We are placed into various life-spheres, each of which is governed by different laws. Religious ethics have settled with this fact in different ways. Hellenic polytheism made sacrifices to Aphrodite and Hera alike, to Dionysus and to Apollo, and knew these gods were frequently in conflict with one another. The Hindu order of life made each of the different occupations an object of a specific ethical code, a Dharma, and forever segregated one from the other as castes, thereby placing them into a fixed hierarchy of rank. For the man born into it, there was no escape from it, lest he be twice-born in another life. The occupations were thus placed at varying distances from the highest religious goods of salvation. In this way, the caste order allowed for the possibility of fashioning the Dharma of each single caste, from those of the ascetics and Brahmins to those of the rogues and harlots, in accordance with the immanent and autonomous laws of their respective occupations. War and politics were also included. You will find war integrated into the totality of life-spheres in the *Bhagavad-Gita*, in the conversation between Krishna and Arduna. "Do what must be done," i.e. do that work which, according to the Dharma of the warrior caste and its rules, is obligatory and which, according to the purpose of the war, is objectively necessary. Hinduism believes that such conduct does not damage religious salvation but, rather, promotes it. When he faced the hero's death, the Indian warrior was always sure of Indra's heaven, just as was the Teuton warrior of Valhalla. The Indian hero would have despised Nirvana just as much as the Teuton would have sneered at the Christian paradise with its angels' choirs. This specialization of ethics allowed for the Indian ethic's quite unbroken treatment of politics by following politics' own laws and even radically enhancing this royal art.

A really radical "Machiavellianism," in the popular sense of this word, is classically represented in Indian literature, in the *Kautaliya Arthasastra* (long before Christ, allegedly dating from Chandragupta's time). In contrast with this document Machiavelli's *Principe* is harmless. As is known in Catholic ethics—to which otherwise Professor Förster stands close—the *consilia evangelica* are a special ethic for those endowed with the charisma of a holy life. There stands the monk who must not shed blood or strive for gain, and beside him stand the pious knight and the burgher, who are allowed to do so, the one to shed blood, the other to pursue gain. The gradation of ethics and its organic integration into the doctrine of salvation is less consistent than in India. According to the presuppositions of Christian faith, this could and had to be the case. The wickedness of the world stemming from original sin allowed with relative ease the integration of violence into ethics as a disciplinary means against sin and against the heretics who endangered the soul. However, the demands of the Sermon on the Mount, an acosmic ethic of ultimate ends, implied a natural law of absolute imperatives based upon religion. These absolute imperatives retained their revolutionizing force and they came upon the scene with elemental vigor during almost all periods of social upheaval. They produced especially the radical pacifist sects, one of which in Pennsylvania experimented in establishing a polity that renounced violence towards the outside. This experiment took a tragic course, inasmuch as with the outbreak of the War of Independence the Quakers could not stand up arms-in-hand for their ideals, which were those of the war.

Normally, Protestantism, however, absolutely legitimated the state as a divine institution and hence violence as a means. Protestantism, especially, legitimated the authoritarian state. Luther relieved the individual of the ethical responsibility for war and transferred it to the authorities. To obey the authorities in matters other than those of faith could never constitute guilt. Calvinism in turn knew principled violence as a means of defending the faith; thus Calvinism knew the crusade, which was for Islam an element of life from the beginning. One sees that it is by no means a modern disbelief born from the hero worship of the Renaissance which poses the problem of political ethics. All religions have wrestled with it, with highly differing success, and after what has been said it could not be otherwise. It is the specific means of legitimate violence as such in the hand of human associations which determines the peculiarity of all ethical problems of politics.

Whosoever contracts with violent means for whatever ends—and every politician does—is exposed to its specific consequences. This holds especially for the crusader, religious and revolutionary alike. Let us confidently take the present as an example. He who wants to establish absolute justice on earth by force requires a following, a human "machine." He must hold out the necessary internal and external premiums, heavenly or worldly reward, to this "machine" or else the machine will not function. Under the conditions of the modern class struggle, the internal premiums consist of the satisfying of hatred and the craving for revenge; above all, resentment and the need for pseudo-ethical self-righteousness: the opponents must be slandered and accused of heresy. The external rewards are adventure, victory, booty, power, and spoils. The leader and his success are completely dependent upon the functioning of his machine and hence not on his own motives. Therefore he also depends upon whether or not the premiums can be *permanently* granted to the following, that is, to the Red Guard, the informers, the agitators, whom he needs. What he actually attains under the conditions of his work is therefore not in his hand, but is prescribed to him by the following's motives, which, if viewed ethically, are predominantly base. The following can be harnessed only so long as an honest belief in his person and his cause inspires at least part of the following, probably never on earth even the majority. This belief, even when subjectively sincere, is in a very great number of cases really no more than an ethical "legitimation" of cravings for revenge, power, booty, and spoils. We shall not be deceived about this by verbiage; the materialist interpretation of history is no cab to be taken at will; it does not stop short of the promoters of revolutions. Emotional revolutionism is followed by the traditionalist routine of everyday life; the crusading leader and the faith itself fade away, or, what is even more effective, the faith becomes part of the conventional phraseology of political Philistines and banausic technicians. This development is especially rapid with struggles of faith because they are usually led or inspired by genuine leaders, that is, prophets of revolution. For here, as with every leader's machine, one of the conditions for success is the depersonalization and routinization, in short, the psychic proletarianization, in the interests of discipline. After coming to power the following of a crusader usually degenerates very easily into a quite common stratum of spoilsmen.

Whoever wants to engage in politics at all, and especially in politics as a vocation, has to realize these ethical paradoxes. He must know that he is responsible for what may become of himself under the impact of these paradoxes. I repeat, he lets himself in for the diabolic forces lurking in all violence. The great *virtuosi* of acosmic love of humanity and goodness, whether stemming from Nazareth or Assisi or from Indian royal castles, have not operated with the political means of violence. Their kingdom was "not of this world," and yet they worked and still work in this world. The figures of Platon Karatajev and the saints of Dostoievski still remain their most adequate reconstructions. He who seeks the salvation of the soul, of his own and of others, should not seek it along the venue of politics, for the quite different tasks of politics can only be solved by violence. The genius or demon of politics lives in an inner tension with the god of love, as well as with the Christian God as expressed by the church. This tension can at any time lead to an irreconcilable conflict. Men knew this even in the times of church rule. Time and again the papal interdict was placed upon Florence and at the time it meant a far more robust power for men and their salvation of soul than (to speak with Fichte) the "cool approbation" of the Kantian ethical judgment. The burghers, however, fought the church-state. And it is with reference to such situations that Machiavelli in a beautiful passage, if I am not mistaken, of the *History of Florence*, has one of his heroes praise those citizens who deemed the greatness of their native city higher than the salvation of their souls.

If one says "the future of socialism" or "international peace," instead of native city or "fatherland" (which at present may be a dubious value to some), then you face the problem as it stands now. Everything that is striven for through political action operating with violent means and following an ethic of responsibility endangers the "salvation of the soul." If, however, one chases after the ultimate good in a war of beliefs, following a pure ethic of absolute ends, then the goals may be damaged and discredited for generations, because responsibility for *consequences* is lacking, and two diabolic forces which enter the play remain unknown to the actor. These are inexorable and produce consequences for his action and even for his inner self, to which he must helplessly submit, unless he perceives them. The sentence: "The devil is old; grow old to understand him!" does not refer to age in terms of chronological years. I have never permitted myself to lose out in a discussion through a reference to a date registered on a birth certificate; but the mere fact that someone is twenty years of age and that I am over fifty is no cause for me to think that this alone is an achievement before which I am overawed. Age is not decisive; what is decisive is the trained relentlessness in viewing the realities of life, and the ability to face such realities and to measure up to them inwardly.

Surely, politics is made with the head, but it is certainly not made with the head alone. In this the proponents of an ethic of ultimate ends are right. One cannot prescribe to anyone whether he should follow an ethic of absolute ends or an ethic of responsibility, or when the one and when the other. One can say only this much: If in these times, which, in your opinion, are not times of "sterile" excitation—excitation is not, after all, genuine passion—if now suddenly the *Weltanschauungs*-politicians crop up *en masse* and pass the watchword, "The world is stupid and base, not I," "The responsibility for the consequences does not fall upon me but upon the others whom I serve and whose stupidity or baseness I shall eradicate," then I declare frankly that I would first inquire into the degree of inner poise backing this ethic of ultimate ends. I am under the impression that in nine out of ten cases I deal with windbags who do not fully realize what they take upon themselves but who intoxicate themselves with romantic sensations. From a human point of view this is not very interesting to me, nor does it move me profoundly. However, it is immensely moving when a *mature* man—no matter whether old or young in years—is aware of a responsibility for the consequences of his conduct and really feels such responsibility with heart and soul. He then acts by following an ethic of responsibility and somewhere he reaches the point where he says: "Here I stand; I can do no other." That is something genuinely human and moving. And every one of us who is not spiritually dead must realize the possibility of finding himself at some time in that position. In so far as this is true, an ethic of ultimate ends and an ethic of responsibility are not absolute contrasts but rather supplements, which only in unison constitute a genuine man—a man who *can* have the "calling for politics."

Now then, ladies and gentlemen, let us debate this matter once more ten years from now. Unfortunately, for a whole series of reasons, I fear that by then the period of reaction will have long since broken over us. It is very probable that little of what many of you, and (I candidly confess) I too, have wished and hoped for will be fulfilled; little—perhaps not exactly nothing, but what to us at least seems little. Then, I wish I could see what has become of those of you who now feel yourselves to be genuinely "principled" politicians and who share in the intoxication signified by this revolution. It would be nice if matters turned out in such a way that Shakespeare's Sonnet 102 should hold true:

> Our love was new, and then but in the spring,
> When I was wont to greet it with my lays;
> As Philomel in summer's front doth sing,
> And stops her pipe in growth of riper days.

But such is not the case. Not summer's bloom lies ahead of us, but rather a polar night of icy darkness and hardness, no matter which group may triumph externally now. Where there is nothing, not only the Kaiser but also the proletarian has lost his rights. When this night shall have slowly receded, who of those for whom spring apparently has loomed so luxuriously will be alive? And what will have become of all of you by then? Will you be bitter or banausic? Will you simply and dully accept world and occupation? Or will the third and by no means the least frequent possibility be your lot: mystic flight from reality for those who are gifted for it, or—as is both frequent and unpleasant—for those who belabor themselves to follow this fashion? In every one of such cases, I shall draw the conclusion that they have not measured up to their own doings. They have not measured up to the world as it really is in its everyday routine. Objectively and actually, they have not experienced the vocation for politics in its deepest meaning, which they thought they had. They would have done better in simply cultivating plain brotherliness in personal relations. And for the rest—they should have gone soberly about their daily work.

Politics is a strong and slow boring of hard boards. It takes both passion and perspective. Certainly all historical experience confirms the truth—that man would not have attained the possible unless time and again he had reached out for the impossible. But to do that a man must be a leader, and not only a leader but a hero as well, in a very sober sense of the word. And even those who are neither leaders nor heroes must arm themselves with that steadfastness of heart which can brave even the crumbling of all hopes. This is necessary right now, or else men will not be able to attain even that which is possible today. Only he has the calling for politics who is sure that he shall not crumble when the world from his point of view is too stupid or too base for what he wants to offer. Only he who in the face of all this can say "In spite of all!" has the calling for politics.

# "Political Philosophies of Women's Liberation"

## *Alison Jaggar (1942–        )*

*Alison M. Jaggar is Professor of Philosophy and Women Studies at the University of Colorado at Boulder. Previously, she taught for eighteen years at the University of Cincinnati, where she was Wilson Professor of Ethics. Her books include* Feminist Politics and Human Nature, *Published in 1983 and elaborating upon the analysis of feminist politics outlined in this essay. Her current work  is* Telling Right from Wrong: Feminism and Moral Epistemology. *Jaggar is a founder member of the Society for Women in Philosophy and, until 1991, was Chair of the American Philosophical Association Committee on the Status of Women.  She is active in local feminist and peace organizations.*

*Consider the connections between the various political theories described here with reference to the political role of women and the general theories of John Locke, Alexis de Tocqueville, Karl Marx and the Socialists. Does the liberalism of Locke and Smith require a different understanding of the place of women in politics from the socialism of Marx or Webb?*

Feminists are united by a belief that the unequal and inferior social status of women is unjust and needs to be changed. But they are deeply divided about what changes are required. The deepest divisions are not differences about strategy or the kinds of tactics that will best serve women's interests; instead, they are differences about what *are* women's interests, what constitutes women's liberation.

Within the women's liberation movement, several distinct ideologies can be discerned.  All[1] believe that justice requires freedom and equality for women, but they differ on such basic philosophical questions as the proper account of freedom and equality, the functions of the state, and the notion of what constitutes human, and especially female, nature. In what follows, I shall outline the feminist ideologies which are currently most influential and show how these give rise to differences on some particular issues. Doing this will indicate why specific debates over feminist questions cannot be settled in isolation but can only be resolved in the context of a theoretical framework derived from reflection on the fundamental issues of social and political philosophy.

---

[1] All except one: as we shall see later, Lesbian separatism is evasive on the question whether men should, even ultimately, be equal with women.

## THE CONSERVATIVE VIEW

This is the position against which all feminists are in reaction. In brief, it is the view that the differential treatment of women, as a group, is not unjust. Conservatives admit, of course, that some individual women do suffer hardships, but they do not see this suffering as part of the systematic social oppression of women. Instead, the clear differences between women's and men's social roles are rationalized in one of two ways. Conservatives either claim that the female role is not inferior to that of the male, or they argue that women are inherently better adapted than men to the traditional female sex role. The former claim advocates a kind of sexual apartheid, typically described by such phrases as "complementary but equal"; the latter postulates an inherent inequality between the sexes.[2]

All feminists reject the first claim, and most feminists, historically, have rejected the second. However, it is interesting to note that, as we shall see later, some modern feminists have revived the latter claim.

Conservative views come in different varieties, but they all have certain fundamentals in common. All claim that men and women should fulfill different social functions, that these differences should be enforced by law where opinion and custom are insufficient, and that such action may be justified by reference to innate differences between men and women. Thus all sexual conservatives presuppose that men and women are inherently unequal in abilities, that the alleged difference in ability implies a difference in social function and that one of the main tasks of the state is to ensure that the individual perform his or her proper social function. Thus, they argue, social differentiation between the sexes is not unjust, since justice not only allows but requires us to treat unequals unequally.

## LIBERAL FEMINISM

In speaking of liberal feminism, I am referring to that tradition which received its classic expression in J. S. Mill's *The Subjection of Women* and which is alive today in various "moderate" groups, such as the National Organization for Women, which agitate for legal reform to improve the status of women.

The main thrust of the liberal feminist's argument is that an individual woman should be able to determine her social role with as great freedom as does a man. Though women now have the vote, the liberal sees that we are still subject to many constraints, legal as well as customary, which hinder us from success in the public worlds of politics, business and the professions. Consequently the liberal views women's liberation as the elimination of those constraints and the achievement of equal civil rights.

Underlying the liberal argument is the belief that justice requires that the criteria for allocating individuals to perform a particular social function should be grounded in the individual's ability to perform the tasks in question. The use of criteria such as "race, sex, religion, national origin or ancestry"[3] will normally not be directly relevant to most tasks. Moreover, in conformity with the traditional liberal stress on individual rights, the liberal

---

[2] The inequalities between the sexes are said to be both physical and psychological. Alleged psychological differences between the sexes include women's emotional instability, greater tolerance for boring detail, incapacity for abstract thought, and less aggression. Writers who have made such claims range from Rousseau (*Émile, or Education* [1762; translation, London: J. M. Dent, 1911]; see especially Book 5 concerning the education of "Sophie, or Woman"), through Schopenhauer (*The World As Will and Idea* and his essay "On Women"), Fichte (*The Science of Rights*), Nietzsche (*Thus Spake Zarathustra*), and Freud down to, in our own times, Steven Goldberg with *The Inevitability of Patriarchy* (New York: William Morrow, 1973–74).

[3] This is the language used by Title VII of the Civil Rights Act with Executive Order 11246, 1965, and Title IX.

feminist insists that each person should be considered separately in order that an outstanding individual should not be penalized for deficiencies that her sex as a whole might possess.[4]

This argument is buttressed by the classic liberal belief that there should be a minimum of state intervention in the affairs of the individual. Such a belief entails rejection of the paternalistic view that women's weakness requires that we be specially protected.[5] Even if relevant differences between women and men in general could be demonstrated, the existence of those differences still would not constitute a sufficient reason for allowing legal restrictions on women as a group. Even apart from the possibility of penalizing an outstanding individual, the liberal holds that women's own good sense or, in the last resort, our incapacity to do the job will render legal prohibitions unnecessary.[6]

From this sketch it is clear that the liberal feminist interprets equality to mean that each individual, regardless of sex, should have an equal opportunity to seek whatever social position she or he wishes. Freedom is primarily the absence of legal constraints to hinder women in this enterprise. However, the modern liberal feminist recognizes that equality and freedom, construed in the liberal way, may not always be compatible. Hence, the modern liberal feminist differs from the traditional one in believing not only that laws should not discriminate against women, but that they should be used to make discrimination illegal. Thus she would outlaw unequal pay scales, prejudice in the admission of women to job-training programs and professional schools, and discrimination by employers in hiring practices. She would also outlaw such things as discrimination by finance companies in the granting of loans, mortgages, and insurance to women.

In certain areas, the modern liberal even appears to advocate laws which discriminate in favor of women. For instance, she may support the preferential hiring of women over men, or alimony for women unqualified to work outside the home. She is likely to justify her apparent inconsistency by claiming that such differential treatment is necessary to remedy past inequalities—but that it is only a temporary measure. With regard to (possibly paid) maternity leaves and the employer's obligation to reemploy a woman after such a leave, the liberal argues that the bearing of children has at least as good a claim to be regarded as a social service as does a man's military or jury obligation, and that childbearing should therefore carry corresponding rights to protection. The liberal also usually advocates the repeal of laws restricting contraception and abortion, and may demand measures to encourage the establishment of private day-care centers. However, she points out that none of these demands, nor the father's payment of child support, should really be regarded as discrimination in favor of women. It is only the customary assignment of responsibility for children to their mothers which makes it possible to overlook the fact that fathers have an equal obligation to provide and care for their children. Women's traditional responsibility for child care is culturally determined, not biologically inevitable—except for breast-feeding, which is now optional. Thus the liberal argues that if women are to participate in the world outside the home on equal terms with men, not only must our reproductive capacity come under our own control but, if we have children, we must be able to share the responsibility for raising them. In return, as an extension of the same principle of equal responsibility, the modern liberal supports compulsory military service for women so long as it is obligatory for men.

Rather than assuming that every apparent difference in interests and abilities between the sexes is innate, the liberal recognizes that such differences, if they do not result entirely from our education, are at least greatly exaggerated by it. By giving both sexes the same education, whether it be cooking or carpentry, the liberal claims that she is providing the only environment in which individual potentialities (and, indeed, genuine sexual differences) can emerge. She gives little weight to the possible charge that in doing this she is not liberating women but only

---

[4] J. S. Mill, *The Subjection of Women* (1869; reprint ed., London: J. M. Dent, 1965), p. 236.

[5] *Ibid.*, p. 243.

[6] *Ibid.*, p. 235.

imposing a different kind of conditioning. At the root of the liberal tradition is a deep faith in the autonomy of the individual which is incapable of being challenged within that framework.

In summary, then, the liberal views liberation for women as the freedom to determine our own social role and to compete with men on terms that are as equal as possible. She sees every individual as being engaged in constant competition with every other in order to maximize her or his own self-interest, and she claims that the function of the state is to see that such competition is fair by enforcing "equality of opportunity." The liberal does not believe that it is necessary to change the whole existing social structure in order to achieve women's liberation. Nor does she see it as being achieved simultaneously for all women; she believes that individual women may liberate themselves long before their condition is attained by all. Finally, the liberal claims that her concept of women's liberation also involves liberation for men, since men are not only removed from a privileged position but they are also freed from having to accept the entire responsibility for such things as the support of their families and the defense of their country.

### CLASSICAL MARXIST FEMINISM

On the classical Marxist view, the oppression of women is, historically and currently, a direct result of the institution of private property; therefore, it can only be ended by the abolition of that institution. Consequently, feminism must be seen as part of a broader struggle to achieve a communist society. Feminism is one reason for communism. The long-term interests of women are those of the working class.

For Marxists, everyone is oppressed by living in a society where a small class of individuals owns the means of production and hence is enabled to dominate the lives of the majority who are forced to sell their labor power in order to survive. Women have an equal interest with men in eliminating such a class society. However, Marxists also recognize that women suffer special forms of oppression to which men are *not* subject, and hence, insofar as this oppression is rooted in capitalism, women have additional reasons for the overthrow of that economic system.

Classical Marxists believe that the special oppression of women results primarily from our traditional position in the family. This excludes women from participation in "public" production and relegates us to domestic work in the "private" world of the home. From its inception right up to the present day, monogamous marriage was designed to perpetuate the consolidation of wealth in the hands of a few. Those few are men. Thus, for Marxists, an analysis of the family brings out the inseparability of class society from male supremacy. From the very beginning of surplus production, "the sole exclusive aims of monogamous marriage were to make the man supreme in the family, and to propagate, as the future heirs to his wealth, children indisputably his own."[7] Such marriage is "founded on the open or concealed domestic slavery of the wife,"[8] and is characterized by the familiar double standard which requires sexual fidelity from the woman but not from the man.

Marxists do not claim, of course, that women's oppression is a creation of capitalism. But they do argue that the advent of capitalism intensified the degradation of women and that the continuation of capitalism requires the perpetuation of this degradation. Capitalism and male supremacy each reinforce the other. Among the ways in which sexism benefits the capitalist system are: by providing a supply of cheap labor for industry and hence exerting a downward pressure on all wages; by increasing the demand for the consumption goods on which women are conditioned to depend; and by allocating to women, for no direct pay, the performance of such

---

[7] Friedrich Engels, *The Origin of the Family, Private Property and the State* (1884; reprint ed., New York: International Publishers, 1942), pp. 57–58.

[8] *Ibid*., p. 65.

socially necessary but unprofitable tasks as food preparation, domestic maintenance and the care of the children, the sick and the old.[9]

This analysis indicates the directions in which classical Marxists believe that women must move. "The first condition for the liberation of the wife is to bring the whole female sex back into public industry."[10] Only then will a wife cease to be economically dependent on her husband. But for woman's entry into public industry to be possible, fundamental social changes are necessary: all the work which women presently do—food preparation, child care, nursing, etc.—must come within the sphere of public production. Thus, whereas the liberal feminist advocates an egalitarian marriage, with each spouse shouldering equal responsibility for domestic work and economic support, the classical Marxist feminist believes that the liberation of women requires a more radical change in the family. Primarily, women's liberation requires that the economic functions performed by the family should be undertaken by the state. Thus the state should provide child care centers, public eating places, hospital facilities, etc. But all this, of course, could happen only under socialism. Hence it is only under socialism that married women will be able to participate fully in public life and end the situation where "within the family [the husband] is the bourgeois and the wife represents the proletariat."[11]

It should be noted that "the abolition of the monogamous family as the economic unit of society"[12] does not necessitate its disappearance as a social unit. Since "sexual love is by its nature exclusive,"[13] marriage will continue, but now it will no longer resemble an economic contract, as it has done hitherto in the property-owning classes. Instead, it will be based solely on "mutual inclination"[14] between a woman and a man who are now in reality, and not just formally, free and equal.

It is clear that classical Marxist feminism is based on very different philosophical presuppositions from those of liberal feminism. Freedom is viewed not just as the absence of discrimination against women but rather as freedom from the coercion of economic necessity. Similarly, equality demands not mere equality of opportunity to compete against other individuals but rather approximate equality in the satisfaction of material needs. Hence, the classical Marxist feminist's view of the function of the state is very different from the view of the liberal feminist. Ultimately, the Marxist pays at least lip service to the belief that the state is an instrument of class oppression which eventually will wither away. In the meantime, she believes that it should undertake far more than the minimal liberal function of setting up fair rules for the economic race. Instead, it should take over the means of production and also assume those economic responsibilities that capitalism assigned to the individual family and that placed that woman in a position of dependence on the man. This view of the state presupposes a very different account of human nature from that held by the liberal. Instead of seeing the individual as fundamentally concerned with the maximization of her or his own self-interest, the classical Marxist feminist believes that the selfish and competitive aspects of our natures are the result of their systematic perversion in an acquisitive society. Viewing human nature as flexible and as reflecting the economic organization of society, she argues that it is necessary for women (indeed for everybody) to be comprehensively reeducated, and to learn that ultimately individuals have common rather than competing goals and interests.

Since she sees woman's oppression as a function of the larger socioeconomic system, the classical Marxist feminist denies the possibility, envisaged by the liberal, of liberation for a few

---

[9] This is, of course, very far from being a complete account of the ways in which Marxists believe that capitalism benefits from sexism.

[10] Engels, *op. cit.*, p. 66.

[11] *Ibid.*, pp. 65–66.

[12] *Ibid.*, p. 66.

[13] *Ibid.*, p. 72.

[14] *Ibid.*

women on an individual level. However, she does agree with the liberal that women's liberation would bring liberation for men, too. Men's liberation would now be enlarged to include freedom from class oppression and from the man's traditional responsibility to "provide" for his family, a burden that under liberalism the man merely lightens by sharing it with his wife.

## *RADICAL FEMINISM*

Radical Feminism is a recent attempt to create a new conceptual model for understanding the many different forms of the social phenomenon of oppression in terms of the basic concept of sexual oppression. It is formulated by such writers as Ti-Grace Atkinson and Shulamith Firestone.[15]

Radical feminism denies the liberal claim that the basis of women's oppression consists in our lack of political or civil rights; similarly, it rejects the classical Marxist belief that basically women are oppressed because they live in a class society. Instead, in what seems to be a startling regression to conservatism, the radical feminist claims that the roots of women's oppression are biological. She believes that the origin of women's subjection lies in the fact that, as a result of the weakness caused by childbearing, we became dependent on men for physical survival. Thus she speaks of the origin of the family in apparently conservative terms as being primarily a biological rather than a social or economic organization.[16] The radical feminist believes that the physical subjection of women by men was historically the most basic form of oppression, prior rather than secondary to the institution of private property and its corollary, class oppression.[17] Moreover, she believes that the power relationships which develop within the biological family provide a model for understanding all other types of oppression such as racism and class society. Thus she reverses the emphasis of the classical Marxist feminist by explaining the development of class society in terms of the biological family rather than explaining the development of the family in terms of class society. She believes that the battles against capitalism and against racism are both subsidiary to the more fundamental struggle against sexism.

Since she believes that the oppression of women is basically biological, the radical feminist concludes that our liberation requires a biological revolution. She believes that only now, for the first time in history, is technology making it possible for women to be liberated from the "fundamental inequality of the bearing and raising of children." It is achieving this through the development of techniques of artificial reproduction and the consequent possibility of diffusing the childbearing and childraising role throughout society as a whole. Such a biological revolution is basic to the achievement of those important but secondary changes in our political, social and economic systems which will make possible the other prerequisites for women's liberation. As the radical feminist sees them, those other prerequisites are: the full self-determination, including economic independence, of women (and children); the total integration of women (and children)

---

[15] Ti-Grace Atkinson, "Radical Feminism" and "The Institution of Sexual Intercourse" in *Notes from the Second Year: Major Writings of the Radical Feminists*, ed. S. Firestone (N.Y., 1970); and Shulamith Firestone, *The Dialectic of Sex: The Case for Feminist Revolution* (N.Y.: Bantam Books; 1970).

[16] Engels recognizes that early forms of the family were based on what he calls "natural" conditions, which presumably included the biological, but he claims that monogamy "was the first form of the family to be based, not on natural, but on economic conditions—on the victory of private property over primitive, natural communal property." Engels, *op. cit.*, p. 57.

[17] Atkinson and Firestone do talk of women as a "political class," but not in Marx's classic sense where the criterion of an individual's class membership is her/his relationship to the means of production. Atkinson defines a class more broadly as a group treated in some special manner by other groups: in the case of women, the radical feminists believe that women are defined as a "class" in virtue of our childbearing capacity. "Radical Feminism," *op. cit.*, p. 24.

into all aspects of the larger society; and the freedom of all women (and children) to do whatever they wish to do sexually.[18]

Not only will technology snap the link between sex and reproduction and thus liberate women from our childbearing and child-raising function; the radical feminist believes that ultimately technology will liberate both sexes from the necessity to work. Individual economic burdens and dependencies will thereby be eliminated, along with the justification for compelling children to attend school. So both the biological and economic bases of the family will be removed by technology. The family's consequent disappearance will abolish the prototype of the social "role system,"[19] the most basic form, both historically and conceptually, of oppressive and authoritarian relationships. Thus, the radical feminist does not claim that women should be free to determine their own social roles: she believes instead that the whole "role system" must be abolished, even in its biological aspects.

The end of the biological family will also eliminate the need for sexual repression. Male homosexuality, lesbianism, and extramarital sexual intercourse will no longer be viewed in the liberal way as alternative options, outside the range of state regulation, in which the individual may or may not choose to participate. Nor will they be viewed, in the classical Marxist way, as unnatural vices, perversions resulting from the degrading influence of capitalist society.[20] Instead, even the categories of homosexuality and heterosexuality will be abandoned; the very "institution of sexual intercourse," where male and female each play a well-defined role, will disappear.[21] "Humanity could finally revert to its natural 'polymorphously perverse' sexuality."[22]

For the radical feminist, as for other feminists, justice requires freedom and equality for women. But for the radical feminist "equality" means not just equality under the law nor even equality in satisfaction of basic needs: rather, it means that women, like men, should not have to bear children. Correspondingly, the radical feminist conception of freedom requires not just that women should be free to compete, nor even that we should be free from material want and economic dependence on men; rather, freedom for women means that any woman is free to have close relationships with children without having to give birth to them. Politically, the radical feminist envisions an eventual "communistic anarchy,"[23] an ultimate abolition of the state. This will be achieved gradually, through an intermediate state of "cybernetic socialism" with household licenses to raise children and a guaranteed income for all. Perhaps surprisingly, in view of Freud's reputation among many feminists, the radical feminist conception of human nature is neo-Freudian. Firestone believes, with Freud, that "the crucial problem of modern life [is] sexuality."[24] Individuals are psychologically formed through their experience in the family, a family whose power relationships reflect the underlying biological realities of female (and childhood) dependence. But technology will smash the universality of Freudian psychology. The destruction of the biological family, never envisioned by Freud, will allow the emergence of new women and men, different from any people who have previously existed.

The radical feminist theory contains many interesting claims. Some of these look almost factual in character: they include the belief that pregnancy and childbirth are painful and unpleasant experiences, that sexuality is not naturally genital and heterosexual, and that technology may be controlled by men and women without leading to totalitarianism. Other

---

[18] These conditions are listed and explained in *The Dialectic of Sex*, pp. 206–9.

[19] "Radical Feminism," *op. cit.*, p. 36.

[20] Engels often expresses an extreme sexual puritanism in *The Origin of the Family, Private Property and the State*. We have already seen his claim that "sexual love is by its nature exclusive." Elsewhere (p. 57) he talks about "the abominable practice of sodomy." Lenin is well known for the expression of similar views.

[21] "The Institution of Sexual Intercourse," *op. cit.*

[22] *The Dialectic of Sex*, p. 209.

[23] *Ibid.*, final chart, pp. 244–45.

[24] *Ibid.*, p. 43.

presuppositions are more clearly normative: among them are the beliefs that technology should be used to eliminate all kinds of pain, that hard work is not in itself a virtue, that sexuality ought not to be institutionalized and, perhaps most controversial of all, that children have the same rights to self-determination as adults.

Like the other theories we have considered, radical feminism believes that women's liberation will bring benefits for men. According to this concept of women's liberation, not only will men be freed from the role of provider, but they will also participate on a completely equal basis in childbearing as well as child-rearing. Radical feminism, however, is the only theory which argues explicitly that women's liberation also necessitates children's liberation. Firestone explains that this is because "The heart of woman's oppression is her childbearing and child-rearing roles. And in turn children are defined in relation to this role and are psychologically formed by it; what they become as adults and the sorts of relationships they are able to form determine the society they will ultimately build."[25]

## NEW DIRECTIONS

Although the wave of excitement about women's liberation which arose in the late '60s has now subsided, the theoretical activity of feminists has continued. Since about 1970, it has advanced in two main directions: lesbian separatism and socialist feminism.

*Lesbian separatism* is less a coherent and developed ideology than an emerging movement, like the broader feminist movement, within which different ideological strains can be detected. All lesbian separatists believe that the present situation of male supremacy requires that women should refrain from heterosexual relationships. But for some lesbian separatists, this is just a temporary necessity, whereas for others, lesbianism will always be required.

Needless to say, all lesbian separatists reject the liberal and the classical Marxist beliefs about sexual preferences; but some accept the radical feminist contention that ultimately it is unimportant whether one's sexual partner be male or female.[26] However, in the immediate context of a male-supremacist society, the lesbian separatist believes that one's sexual choice attains tremendous political significance. Lesbianism becomes a way of combating the overwhelming heterosexual ideology that perpetuates male supremacy.

> Women . . . become defined as appendages to men so that there is a coherent ideological framework which says it is natural for women to create the surplus to take care of men and that men will do other things. Reproduction itself did not have to determine that. The fact that male supremacy developed the way it has and was institutionalized is an ideological creation. The ideology of heterosexuality, not the simple act of intercourse, is the whole set of assumptions which maintains the ideological power of men over women.[27]

Although this writer favors an ultimate de-institutionalization of sexual activity, her rejection of the claim that reproduction as such does not determine the inferior status of women clearly places her outside the radical feminist framework; indeed, she would identify her methodological approach as broadly Marxist. Some lesbian separatists are more radical, however. They argue

---

[25] *Ibid.*, p. 72.

[26] "In a world devoid of male power and, therefore, sex roles, who you lived with, loved, slept with and were committed to would be irrelevant. All of us would be equal and have equal determination over the society and how it met our needs. Until this happens, how we use our sexuality and our bodies is just as relevant to our liberation as how we use our minds and time." Coletta Reid, "Coming Out in the Women's Movement," in *Lesbianism and the Women's Movement*, ed. Nancy Myron and Charlotte Buch (Baltimore: Diana Press, 1975), p. 103.

[27] Margaret Small, "Lesbians and the Class Position of Women," in *Lesbianism and the Women's Movement*, p. 58.

explicitly for a matriarchal society which is "an affirmation of the power of female consciousness of the Mother."[28] Such matriarchists talk longingly about ancient matriarchal societies where women were supposed to have been physically strong, adept at self-defense, and the originators of such cultural advances as: the wheel, pottery, industry, leather working, metal working, fire, agriculture, animal husbandry, architecture, cities, decorative art, music, weaving, medicine, communal child care, dance, poetry, song, etc.[29] They claim that men were virtually excluded from these societies. Women's culture is compared favorably with later patriarchal cultures as being peaceful, egalitarian, vegetarian, and intellectually advanced. Matriarchal lesbian separatists would like to re-create a similar culture which would probably imitate the earlier ones in its exclusion of men as full members. Matriarchal lesbian separatists do not claim unequivocally that "men are genetically predisposed towards destruction and dominance,"[30] but, especially given the present research on the behavioral effects of the male hormone testosterone,[31] they think it is a possibility that lesbians must keep in mind.

*Socialist feminists* believe that classical Marxism and radical feminism each have both insights and deficiencies. The task of socialist feminism is to construct a theory that avoids the weaknesses of each but incorporates its (and other) insights. There is space here for only a brief account of some of the main points of this developing theory.

Socialist feminists reject the basic radical feminist contention that liberation for women requires the abolition of childbirth. Firestone's view is criticized as ahistorical, anti-dialectical, and utopian. Instead, socialist feminists accept the classical Marxist contention that socialism is the main precondition for women's liberation. But though socialism is necessary, socialist feminists do not believe that it is sufficient. Sexism can continue to exist despite public ownership of the means of production. The conclusion that socialist feminists draw is that it is necessary to resort to direct cultural action in order to develop a specifically feminist consciousness in addition to transforming the economic base. Thus their vision is totalistic, requiring "transformation of the entire fabric of social relationships."[32]

In rejecting the radical feminist view that the family is based on biological conditions, socialist feminists turn toward the classical Marxist account of monogamy as being based "not on natural but on economic conditions."[33] But they view the classical Marxist account as inadequate, overly simple. Juliet Mitchell[34] argues that the family should be analyzed in a more detailed, sophisticated, and historically specific way in terms of the separate, though interrelated, functions that women perform within it: production, reproduction, sexuality, and the socialization of the young.

Socialist feminists agree with classical Marxists that women's liberation requires the entry of women into public production. But this in itself is not sufficient. It is also necessary that women have access to the more prestigious and less deadening jobs and to supervisory and administrative positions. There should be no "women's work" within public industry.[35]

---

[28] Jane Alpert, "Mother Right: A New Feminist Theory," *Ms.*, August 1973, p. 94.

[29] Alice, Gordon, Debbie, and Mary, *Lesbian Separatism: An Amazon Analysis*, typescript, 1973, p. 5. (To be published by Diana Press, Baltimore.)

[30] *Ibid.*, p. 23.

[31] It is interesting that this is the same research on which Steven Goldberg grounds his thesis of "the inevitability of patriarchy"; see note 2 above.

[32] Barbara Ehrenreich, "Socialist/Feminism and Revolution" (unpublished paper presented to the National Socialist-Feminist Conference, Antioch College, Ohio, July 1975), p. 1.

[33] Engels, *op. cit.*, p. 57.

[34] Juliet Mitchell, *Woman's Estate* (New York: Random House, 1971). Lively discussion of Mitchell's work continues among socialist feminists.

[35] For one socialist feminist account of women's work in public industry see Sheila Rowbotham, *Woman's Consciousness, Man's World* (Baltimore: Penguin Books, 1973), Chap. 6, "Sitting Next to Nellie."

In classical Marxist theory, "productive labor" is viewed as the production of goods and services within the market economy. Some socialist feminists believe that this account of productiveness obscures the socially vital character of the labor that women perform in the home. They argue that, since it is clearly impossible under capitalism to bring all women into public production, individuals (at least as an interim measure) should be paid a wage for domestic work. This reform would dignify the position of housewives, reduce their dependence on their husbands and make plain their objective position, minimized by classical Marxists, as an integral part of the working class.[36] Not all socialist feminists accept this position, however, and the issue is extremely controversial at the time of this writing.

One of the main insights of the feminist movement has been that "the personal is political." Socialist feminists are sensitive to the power relations involved in male/female interaction and believe that it is both possible and necessary to begin changing these, even before the occurrence of a revolution in the ownership of the means of production. Thus, socialist feminists recognize the importance of a "subjective factor" in revolutionary change and reject the rigid economic determinism that has characterized many classical Marxists. They are sympathetic to attempts by individuals to change their life styles and to share responsibility for each other's lives, even though they recognize that such attempts can never be entirely successful within a capitalist context. They also reject the sexual puritanism inherent in classical Marxism, moving closer to the radical feminist position in this regard.

Clearly there are sharp differences between socialist feminism and most forms of lesbian separatism. The two have been dealt with together in this section only because each is still a developing theory and because it is not yet clear how far either represents the creation of a new ideology and how far it is simply an extension of an existing ideology. One suspects that at least the matriarchal version of lesbian separatism may be viewed as a new ideology: after all, the interpretation of "freedom" to mean "freedom from men" is certainly new, as is the suggestion that women are innately superior to men. Socialist feminism, however, should probably be seen as an extension of classical Marxism, using essentially similar notions of human nature, of freedom and equality, and of the role of the state, but attempting to show that women's situation and the sphere of personal relations in general need more careful analysis by Marxists.[37]

This sketch of some new directions in feminism completes my outline of the main contemporary positions on women's liberation. I hope that I have made clearer the ideological presuppositions at the root of many feminist claims and also shed some light on the philosophical problems that one needs to resolve in order to formulate one's own position and decide on a basis for action. Many of these philosophical questions, such as the nature of the just society, the proper account of freedom and equality, the functions of the state and the relation between the individual and society, are traditional problems which now arise in a new context; others, such as the role of technology in human liberation, are of more recent origin. In either case, feminism adds a fresh dimension to our discussion of the issues and points to the need for the so-called philosophy of man to be transformed into a comprehensive philosophy of women and men and their social relations.

---

[36] One influential exponent of wages for housework is Mariarosa Dalla Costa, *The Power of Women and the Subversion of Community* (Bristol, England: Falling Wall Press, 1973).

[37] Since I wrote this section, I have learned of some recent work by socialist feminists which seems to provide an excitingly new theoretical underpinning for much socialist feminist practice. An excellent account of these ideas is given by Gayle Rubin in "The Traffic in Women: Notes on the 'Political Economy' of Sex." This paper appears in *Toward an Anthropology of Women*, ed. Rayna R. Reiter (New York: Monthly Review Press, 1975). If something like Rubin's account is accepted by socialist feminists, it will be a difficult and important question to work out just how far they have moved from traditional Marxism and how much they still share with it.

# "Ethics and Politics: The American Way"

## Martin Diamond (1919–1977)

*Martin Diamond illustrates the possibilities of self-education. Though he never completed an undergraduate degree, he was admitted to graduate study at the University of Chicago on the basis of his own studies and his service in the U.S. Merchant Marine during World War II. His distinguished teaching career was spent in the study of American political institutions and their foundations in the Declaration of Independence and the Constitution. As an advisor to prominent political figures, he was described by Senator Daniel Patrick Moynihan as "almost single-handedly establish[ing] the relevance of the thought and doings of the Founding Fathers for this generation."*

*Consider the connections Diamond draws between the Aristotelean regime and the American way of life, principally through the* Federalist. *Would Aristotle view a nation whose political rulers' vices are checked by the vices of their fellow rulers and those of the citizens as ethically sound? Even if Diamond's interpretation is correct, should the American people be bound by an understanding of their political arrangements held 200 years ago? Would the United States be benefited by a move toward a more egalitarian and more openly moralistic politics? What would be gained? What might be lost?*

All men have some notion of what we may call the universal aspect of the relationship between ethics and politics, a notion of what the relationship would be for men at their very best. The unqualified phrase in the title of this essay—"Ethics and Politics"—points to that universal aspect, to the idea of an ethics proper to man as such and to the political ordering appropriate to that ethics. But the qualification—"The American Way"—reminds that ethics and politics always and everywhere form a particular relationship, a distinctive way in which each people organizes its humanness. The whole title together indicates the intention of this essay: while taking our bearings from the universal relationship of ethics and politics, we will examine the special "American way" in which ethics and politics are related to each other here.

## I

The "American way of life" is a familiar phrase that nicely captures the notion that the relationship of ethics and politics has everywhere a unique manifestation. Yet familiar as the phrase is to us, we Americans characteristically overlook that notion when we think about ethics and politics. Instead, more than most other people, we tend to consider the relationship of ethics and politics in universal terms. Perhaps this is because we have been shaped to such a great extent by the principles of the Declaration of Independence, which of course addresses itself to all mankind and conceives political life in terms of rights to which all men are by nature entitled. Our tendency to understand moral principles in universal terms may also be furthered by the lingering influence of the Biblical heritage, which lays down moral principles applicable to all men in all countries. To the extent that Americans continue to be guided by the Biblical outlook, their disposition to understand the relationship between ethics and politics in universal terms is reinforced. This propensity is perhaps also furthered by a tendency of democracy described by Tocqueville. He observed that democratic people, because of their extreme love of equality, tend to abstract from human differences and thus to think of man with a capital *M*—that is to say, in generic terms—rather than in terms of the many subtle gradations of human experience. Whatever the reasons, the familiar fact is that Americans generally think about politics in terms of a universal morality and, therefore, to view the relationship of ethics and politics almost exclusively in its universal aspect.

Oddly enough, in always thinking about ethics and politics in terms applicable to all men everywhere, we have in fact narrowed the idea of ethics. Today we think of ethics, not in the broad sense in which it was understood by classical political philosophy, but rather in the much narrower sense now conveyed by the word *morality*. Our word *morality* was originally derived from Cicero's Latin rendering of the Greek word for ethics, but it gradually acquired a quite different and narrower meaning. We think of ethics or morality today primarily in the limited, negative sense of "thou shall nots," as Puritanical or Victorian "no-no's." Ethics or morality thus narrowed down to a number of prohibitions has indeed a universal status; all men *are* under the same obligation not to murder, steal, bear false witness, and the like. Since morality thus conceived applies to all men as men, all regimes are deemed as obliged to honor it; hence the relationship of ethics and politics comes to be seen only in its universal aspect. The same narrowing effect on the idea of ethics is also produced by the modern theory of natural rights. That is, in this view of civil society, the politically relevant aspect of morality or ethics is similarly reduced to negative prohibitions on what governments and men may do. And this narrowing also has the effect of making political morality universally obligatory in the same way upon all regimes.

But morality thus universally conceived hampers our understanding of the particular relationship of ethics and politics within each political order or regime. To recover this understanding and apply it to the American case, we have to recapture something of the original broad meaning of ethics as it presented itself in classic Greek political philosophy. For that purpose Aristotle's *Ethics* will suffice. Aristotle deals of course with such universal prohibitions as those against murder, theft, and lying. However, Aristotle's understanding of ethics is not chiefly concerned with such prohibitions, but, much more importantly, with positive human excellences or virtues in the broadest sense. Notice well: excellences or virtues. Aristotle's word *arete* is usually and properly translated as *virtue*. But because the word *virtue* is now understood in the same narrow and negative sense as morality, it is important to associate with it the positive word, excellence, in order to bring out the positive implications of Aristotle's ethical teaching.

For example, the very first virtue that Aristotle discusses is courage; while late in his discussion he includes as a minor ethical virtue or excellence the quality of affability. Today we would hardly consider either courage (as Aristotle meant it, namely, the kind demanded in military combat) or affability as belonging to a discussion of virtue or morality. They might be regarded as useful or even admirable qualities, but surely not as virtuous or moral qualities; they simply do not fit our modern conception. In contrast to our narrow view, Aristotle meant by the virtues all those qualities required for the full development of humanness, that is, all those qualities that comprise the health or completion of human character. This is the key: the very word *ethics* literally meant *character* to the Greeks, and the idea of character formation is the foundation of the ancient idea of ethics. When ethics is thus understood as being concerned with the formation and perfection of human character, we may more readily understand not only why ethics and politics have a universal relationship proper to man as man, but also why a unique relationship between ethics and politics is necessarily formed within each particular political order.

This necessity is made clearer by reference to a Greek word that is still familiar to us in the English use we make of it—namely, *ethos*; indeed, this is the Greek word from which our word *ethics* derives. A given pattern of ethics forms, as it were, an *ethos*. Like the Greeks, we still mean by ethos that a group or other entity possesses certain fundamental features that form its distinctive character. Something like this is what we mean when we speak, say, of "the ethos of Chaplin's films" or "the ethos of poverty." Ethics understood in this old, broad sense, as forming an ethos, helps to make clear why there is a distinctive relationship of ethics and politics in every regime. In all political communities, humanity manifests itself in some particular way, in the formation of a distinctive character or characters. It is the distinctive human types nurtured in each regime that manifest the ethos of that regime. This is not, of course, to say that any such community is formed of identical human types; much human variety can be found in any complex society. But still we know that something is at work that makes a certain kind of human character more likely to occur in one setting and among one people, rather than another. We would be surprised, for example, to find Cotton Mather fully formed and flourishing in the Berlin of the 1920s. We would be surprised to find a full-fledged, homegrown Oscar Wilde in old Dodge City. It is likewise most unlikely that George Babbitt would have turned up in the early Roman republic; he belongs to Zenith, the fastest growing town in the Middle West. Such distinctive human characters are the nurture of a particular *ethos* so to speak.

How can we account for the fact that each country forms its own peculiar ethos? We know that differing physical circumstances have something to do with the matter. The character of a people permanently settled on rich agricultural land and earning its living by farming will differ from that of a tribe of desert nomads who eke out an uncertain existence from their flocks and herds as they move from oasis to oasis. Each people will tend by virtue of its circumstances to value different human qualities and to nurture them. Technological development, "modes of production," and other such factors all have similar effects in the production of modal human types. But greater than the effect of all such material factors is the effect on human development of mores and laws, that is, of the political order or the regime. The difference of human characters in the various regimes is above all the product of the distinctive relationship between ethics and politics within each regime. Each political regime is, so to speak, in the business of handicrafting distinctive human characters. Indeed, each political order is literally constituted by the kind of human character it aims at and tends to form.

We may explore the meaning of this by considering Aristotle's well-known argument regarding the way political communities come into being. The lesser forms of human association—the family, tribe, and village—do not suffice for the fulfillment of man's nature; for that purpose, Aristotle argues, the form of human association must reach to the level of the *polis*, the political community. This is because the prepolitical associations serve largely for the mere preservation of life; they correspond in some respects to the hives or herds through which other social animals, such as bees and elephants, preserve themselves. These primary and rudimentary associations are adequate for bees and elephants because mere preservation of life is all that their beings require.

But the full development of man's being requires something more. He has an ethical need, a need that follows from his possession of *logos*, his unique faculty for speaking-reasoning, the faculty that defines man and distinguishes him from all other creatures. It is this faculty that enables and impels man to ponder "the advantageous and the harmful, and therefore also the just and the unjust."[1] Man's ethical need consists precisely in his capacity to reason out a view of the

---

[1] Aristotle, *Politics*, 1253a15 *et seq*. The translation here, and elsewhere in this essay, is that of Professor Lawrence Berns, who has kindly given permission to quote from a translation of the *Politics* that he is now preparing.

"advantageous and the just" and to organize his character and his life upon that basis. Because of this inherent capacity, this need for the formation of his full human character, man is ultimately impelled toward the formation of the polis. The subpolitical associations of the family, the tribe, and the village do not form a sufficient habitat for the full development of humanness. The polis is then, above all, understood by Aristotle as an association for the formation of character. It is a partnership within which the character of citizens is formed in accordance with some shared view of "the advantageous and the harmful" for man.

From this it followed for Aristotle that the very best polis would be that one partnership which, because it was based on the true view of what is "advantageous and just," would generate the highest human character. This idea of the "best regime" in which the best human character would be formed represents the Aristotelian understanding of the universal aspect of the relationship between ethics and politics. In this Aristotle differs, of course, from the modern approach which, as we have seen, makes the universal aspect of the ethics-politics relationship that which can be demanded and actualized everywhere. In contrast, the ancient approach was paradigmatic only; the universal aspect for Aristotle consists in a model of the one best character-forming regime, a model that serves as a standard for understanding and dealing with the enormous variety of actual, imperfect character-forming regimes. As measured against that model of the best regime, all other regimes would be understood as based on varyingly imperfect views of what is advantageous and just, and all would differ accordingly in the human characters they produced. In this particular regime, courage would be nurtured to a fault, there piety, here the love of honor, there domination, here commercial daring, and so forth through all the shadings and combinations of the possible human qualities. This is the exact sense in which it may be said that each polis actualized human character in a particular way and hence that in each polis there is a unique relationship of ethics and politics.

On the basis of this analysis of the polis as a character-forming association, Aristotle might well have denied that most contemporary "states" are genuine political communities. In any event, he does explicitly deny the status of political community to certain aggregations of people whose arrangements sound suspiciously like our own. That is, he explicitly characterizes as subpolitical those mere alliances or contractual arrangements for the sake of commerce, and even those arrangements that, somewhat more broadly, seek to prevent fellow residents from being "unjust to one another." Societies based on such arrangements may have a thriving commerce, life in them may be secure and tranquil, and they might appear to Americans to be adequate political societies. But for Aristotle they still would lack the crucial political desideratum—namely, a "concern with what the qualities of the others are," that is, a concern for the development among fellow citizens of certain common ethical excellences and hence a common character.[2]

For Aristotle, the formation of this common character is what makes an association political, and the question of how these character-forming ethical excellences are to be developed in man is what links ethics and politics. Indeed, this is literally the link between Aristotle's two great practical works, the *Ethics* and the *Politics*.[3] At the end of the *Ethics*, when he has finished his account of the excellences that perfect the human character, Aristotle says that it will now be necessary to turn to the study of politics. This is because human nature does not find it readily pleasant to acquire and persist in the character-forming excellences. To say the least, the idea of the good is not of itself sufficiently compelling to regulate behavior. Hence men will not be perfected merely by precept and exhortation, and not even by paternal authority. Human character, Aristotle argues, can be perfected only within a comprehensive system of character-forming conditions and constraints—in short, within the political community. Only within the political community, and through what it alone can supply, namely, good laws "with teeth in

---

[2] *Ibid*., 1280a34 *et seq*.

[3] Aristotle, *Ethics*, 1179a33 *et seq*. (Loeb Classical Library ed.).

them," can men in fact raise their characters above the merely necessitous life, or above a life of mere passional indulgence.

In the ancient view, then, political life had the immensely important ethical function of providing the way through which man could complete or perfect this humanness. No wonder then that the laws, by means of which human character was to be formed, had to have teeth in them. So comprehensive and elevated an end made extraordinarily strenuous demands upon the political art. The classical political teaching took its bearings from the highest potentialities of human nature. Making no egalitarian presuppositions, it did not believe that all human beings or, indeed, even most human beings, could be perfected. But it thought it right and necessary that every resource of the political art be employed to realize the highest potential of the few, while providing as just a political order as was possible for those many others whose potentialities or circumstances precluded the highest development. This helps us to understand something of the harsh demands of the classical teaching: the general sternness of the laws; the emphasis placed on rigorous and comprehensive programs of education; the strict regulation of much that we now deem "private"; the necessity of civic piety; the extremely limited size of the polis; and the severe restrictions on private economic activity. These and other stern and strenuous measures were necessitated by the height of the human excellence that the classic political teaching sought to produce. An unceasingly demanding and powerful political art was required if men were to be raised so high against the downward pulls of ease, creature comfort, and the lower pleasures.

## II

In the light of all the foregoing, how might Aristotle rank America? Would he characterize it as a genuine political community, one with its own special moral foundation, or only as "an association of place and of not acting unjustly to one another and for the sake of trade"? Would he find it a place where law is only "a compact, just as Lycophron the Sophist said, a guarantor for one another of the just things, but not able to make the citizens good and just,"[4] —that is, good and just in the way their characters were formed and not merely in conformity to a compact? Or might he conclude that there is indeed an American political ethos, a unique character-forming mix of ethics and politics? In short, is there an "American way" by which this republic nurtures in its citizens certain ethical excellences upon the basis of some particular view of what is advantageous and just?

If the answer proves to be that somehow America is an authentic political community, that there is in fact an "American way" of political-ethical character formation, it will surely not be in the classical way but in a distinctively modern way. This is because America was formed on the basis of that modern political thought that waged so successful a war against the political outlook of antiquity. The classical understanding of the proper relationship between ethics and politics dominated the Western world for nearly two millennia, as did classical political philosophy generally, albeit modified by Christianity. But the great traditions of classical and Christian political philosophy came under trenchant attack during the sixteenth and seventeenth centuries by such political philosophers as Machiavelli, Bacon, Hobbes, and Locke.[5] These proponents of a "new science of politics" charged that classical and Christian political philosophy had been both misguided and ineffective, in a word, "utopian." They observed that, during some two thousand years of this elevated political and religious teaching, man's lot on this earth had remained miserable; his estate had not been relieved. Greed and vainglory ruled under the guise of virtue

---

[4] *Politics*, 1280b10 *et seq.*

[5] Acknowledgment is gladly made of my indebtedness here and throughout to the late Professor Leo Strauss, whose instructive account of the "battle of the books," ancient and modern, has done so much to restore the meaning of the modern enterprise and to renew our grasp of the ancient alternative.

or piety, and the religious tyrannies and wars of the sixteenth and seventeenth centuries had but climaxed two millennia of the failure of the old, utopian political science.

Blaming classical and medieval thought for adhering to dangerous illusions regarding the way men *ought* to live, that is, for trying to shape human character by misleading and unachievable standards of perfection, the new, or modern, political philosophers purported to base their views and recommendations upon the character of man "as he actually *is*." In place of the lofty and seemingly unrealistic virtues demanded by classical and Christian political philosophy, the moderns accepted as irremediably dominant in human nature the self-interestedness and passions displayed by men everywhere. But precisely on that realistic basis, they argued, workable solutions could at last be found to hitherto unresolved political problems. This meant, as opposed to ancient and medieval exhortation and compulsion of man to high virtue, a lowering of the aims and expectations of political life, perhaps of human life generally. As it were, the new political science gave a primacy to the efficacy of means rather than to the nobility of ends: The ends of political life were reduced to a commensurability with the human means readily and universally available. In place of the utopian end postulated by the ancients, the forced elevation of human character, the moderns substituted a lowered political end, namely, human comfort and security. This lowered end was more realistic, they argued, because it could be achieved by taking human character much as actually found everywhere, or by molding it on a less demanding model than that of the premodern understanding.

This removal of the task of character formation from its previously preeminent place on the agenda of politics had an immense consequence for the relationship of ethics and politics in modern regimes. The hallmark of the traditional ethics-politics relationship has been those harsh and comprehensive laws by means of which the ancient philosophers had sought to "high-tone" human character. But now, because character formation was no longer the direct end of politics, the new science of politics could dispense with those laws and, for the achievement of its lowered ends, could rely largely instead upon shrewd institutional arrangements of the powerful human passions and interests. Not to instruct and to transcend these passions and interests, but rather to channel and to use them became the hallmark of modern politics. Politics could now concentrate upon the "realistic" task of directing man's passions and interests toward the achievement of those solid goods this earth has to offer: self-preservation and the protection of those individual liberties which are an integral part of that preservation and which make it decent and agreeable.

One has only to call to mind the Declaration of Independence to see that such commodious self-preservation and its corollary individual liberties came to be viewed as the sole legitimate objects of government. In short, whatever the modern perspective may leave of the traditional lofty virtues for men to seek in their private capacities, it drastically reduces or limits the legitimate scope of government. Indeed, the very idea of *government*—as distinguished from the old, more encompassing idea of *polity* or *regime*—was a response to this restriction in the scope of the political. In the old, broader view, "government" was inextricably linked with "society." Since it was the task of the laws to create a way of life or to nurture among citizens certain qualities of character, then the laws necessarily had to penetrate every aspect of a community's life; there could be no separation of state or government and society, and no limitation of the former with respect to the latter. But under the new liberal doctrine, with its substantive withdrawal of the character-forming function from the domain of the political, it became natural to think of state and society as separated, and of government as limited to the protection of individual life, liberty, property, and the private pursuit of happiness. It became both possible and reasonable to depoliticize political life as previously conceived, and that is precisely what happened wherever the new view came to prevail. Perhaps above all, religion was depoliticized; belief and practice regarding the gods, which classical political philosophy had held to be centrally within the purview of the political community, was largely relegated to private discretion. Similarly depoliticized were many other traditional political matters such as education, poetry and the arts, family mores, and many of the activities we now lump under the term "economics." In the premodern understanding, these were precisely the matters that had to be regulated by "laws with teeth in them," because they were the essential means by which a regime could form human characters in its own particular mold.

With the removal or reduction from political life of what had for two thousand years been regarded as its chief function, namely, ethical character formation based on some elevated view of the "advantageous and just," what, then, became that chief function of politics in the new understanding? A striking and explicit answer to this question is to be found in James Madison's *Federalist* 10, perhaps the most remarkable single American expression of the "improved" or new science of politics. At the end of the famous paragraph in which he argues that the latent causes of faction are ineradicably sown in human nature, Madison sketches the "most common and durable" of those ineradicable causes, namely, the diversity of economic interests. He then states one of the most important conclusions of his essay: "The regulation of these various and interfering interests forms the principal task of modern legislation and involves the spirit of party and faction in the necessary and ordinary operations of government." Notice: "the principal task of *modern* legislation"; Madison is acutely aware of the modernity of his political analyses and solutions. He does not tell us what the premodern principal task was, and we may not put words in his mouth; but we will see how his principal modern task becomes intelligible precisely when contradistinguished from the principal task of the premodern political art as that has been presented in this essay. Bringing that modern task clearly to light may teach us something about the "American way" regarding the relationship of ethics and politics.

## III

Madison announces his theoretical intention: "To secure the public good and private rights. . . and at the same time to preserve the spirit and form of popular government, is then the great object to which our inquiries are directed." Only by a showing that popular government can now avoid committing those injuries to the public good and private rights, which have hitherto proved its undoing, can this form of government "be rescued from the opprobrium under which it has so long labored." Taken as a whole, then, James Madison's "inquiries" provide a comprehensive statement of the way political science should address the pathology of democracy. In *Federalist* 10, Madison outlines that part of his political science upon the basis of which the gravest imperfection of popular government may be guarded against, namely, the propensity of that form of government to "the violence of faction." In examining his argument regarding the problem of faction, we want to pay particular attention to the way Madison deals with the problem of *opinion*. It is through Madison's discussion of the nature of opinion in general and its particular status in American political life, that we will learn most about what is uniquely modern in that "principal task of modern legislation."

Madison argues that all earlier democracies have "been spectacles of turbulence and contention . . . as short in their lives as they have been violent in their deaths." This was because, as he observes in *Federalist* 14, all earlier democracies had been too small in scale; they had been founded on "the error which limits republican government to a narrow district." Built on the scale of the ancient polis, these republics had been utterly unable to deal with the pathogenic element of democracy, namely, majority faction. Madison's novel but now familiar conclusion was that the hitherto fatal effects of majority factiousness could be controlled only in a republic organized on a sufficiently large scale. In the course of this general argument, Madison is obliged to analyze in detail the various causes of faction, and it is this detailed analysis that brings to the fore his treatment of the problem of opinion.

Madison's first step is to identify the nature of faction. The precise statement of the elements that constitute faction prepares the way, first, for his diagnosis of how different kinds of faction come into being and, later, for his novel solution to the problem. Here is his famous definition: "a number of citizens, whether amounting to a majority or minority of the whole, who are united and actuated by some common impulse of passion, or of interest, adverse to the rights of other citizens, or to the permanent and aggregate interests of the community." We must notice the two-fold "normative" character of this definition. The generating impulse to faction is dubious or low; faction is "united and actuated" by passion or interest and not by reason. But this is not enough to denominate a group a faction. After all, not every passion or interest need impel toward policies inimical to society; although motivated by passion or interest, a group might yet seek policies that are perfectly compatible with the rights of others and the interests of the community. It is therefore further necessary that a group be following an oppressive or dangerous course of action. But this is to say in effect, as indeed becomes explicit in the very next step in the argument, that the group is possessed of an oppressive or dangerous opinion. From his definition, then, Madison's task becomes clear: to show how the conjunction of a "common impulse" of passion or interest and an "adverse" opinion in a majority may be averted or rendered unlikely.

Madison turns to the ways this may be done. "There are two methods of curing the mischiefs of faction: the one, by removing its causes; the other by controlling its effects." As to removing the causes, Madison says that there are likewise two possibilities. The first, which is to destroy the liberty essential to the existence of factions, Madison quickly rejects as a remedy worse than the disease. He then examines at length, as we must also, the remaining possible way to remove the causes of faction, which is to give to "every citizen the same opinions, the same passions, and the same interests." Opinion, passion, and interest: Madison's comprehensive theoretical statement of the causes of faction; these are the three independent generating sources of factional behavior. If all citizens have the same impulse of passion or interest, they would have no motivation to divide into oppressive or dangerous factions. And whatever the status of the passional or interested motivations, if all citizens were agreed on the same opinions, there could be no oppressive or dangerous division of the society with respect to public policy. Unanimity of impulse and opinion would of necessity extinguish the possibility of faction.

But Madison, of course, proceeds to demonstrate that such unanimity of opinion, passion, and interest is utterly "impracticable." He deals first with the irreducible diversity of opinion. "As long as the reason of man continues fallible, and he is at liberty to exercise it, different opinions will be formed." Notice: self-originated, self-formed opinion; opinion, so to speak, is an independent variable. That is to say, these are *not* opinions whose content is determined by underlying causes—not opinions as mere rationalization of underlying passion or interest, as we now typically conceive opinions to be—but rather opinions whose content is determined by the *autonomous operation of the opining faculty itself*. Thus, quite apart from the diversity or uniformity of the human passions and interests, political opinions will inevitably vary, simply as a function of man's fallible reasoning, or opining, faculty and his natural need to exercise it on political subjects. In this respect we may say that Madison is at one with Aristotle in recognizing the power and autonomy of the speaking-reasoning or opining capacity of man. But as to what should be done with that capacity, the difference between them, as we shall see, is the difference between modernity and antiquity.

Having demonstrated that all men cannot be given the same opinions, Madison proceeds to demonstrate that the passions and interests of mankind likewise cannot be reduced to uniformity; like opinion, they irremovably exert a divisive factious influence upon political behavior. The details of his argument need not detain us. It suffices here simply to state the conclusion Madison reaches at this stage of his argument: The problem of faction cannot be solved by removing its causes because "the latent causes of faction are . . . sown in the nature of man."

Still, this is no cause for despair because there remains the possibility of "controlling the effects of faction." Madison reminds us that, while the latent causes of faction are ineradicably universal, particular factions are "brought into different degrees of activity according to the different circumstances of civil society." Which kinds of factions will be brought into a high degree of "activity" and which into a low degree all depends on the circumstances of the particular society. It is in the manipulation of these "different circumstances" that Madison's novel prescription of a "cure" is to be found. By such circumstances Madison clearly includes the extent or scale of the political community and the constitutional structure and processes of government, and also apparently such things as the kind of economy to be fostered and the beliefs citizens are encouraged to hold. All such circumstances affect the operation of the universal "latent causes of faction" and thereby determine what the actual pattern of factionalism will be in any given society.

It is with precisely these circumstances that founders must deal. Armed with the proper science of politics, a founder can choose what kinds of factions to avoid and, since factionalism is inevitable, what kinds to encourage. Accordingly, in order to discover how to do the avoiding and encouraging, Madison elaborates his threefold typology of factions. He again deals first with man's natural inclination to opining, that is, with his "zeal for different opinions concerning religion, concerning government, and many other points, as well of speculation as of practice." These opinions, to repeat, are not merely rationalizations of prior passion or interest, but rather are the autonomous product of the high human need and capacity to opine about such elevated matters as, say, what is advantageous and just. Now, Aristotelian political science, as we noted earlier, takes its bearing from just this high human capacity. From the classic perspective, *the political task is to refine and improve a regime's opinion of what is advantageous and just* and to help thereby to improve the human characters formed by that regime. But Madison instead turns away almost in horror from the human "zeal for different opinions concerning religion, concerning government."[6] He is only too aware that such opining has rendered mankind "much more disposed to vex and oppress each other than to co-operate for their common good." From the perspective of the new political science, it is apparently too risky to rely on refining and improving a society's opinions. The statesmanly task, rather, is to mute as much as possible the force of religious and political opining as a cause of faction. Such opinion is not so much to be improved as tamed or devitalized. If America is to avoid the "violence of faction" that commonly destroyed earlier popular governments, "circumstances" must be so arranged that factionalism deriving from the operation of opinion must not reach to a high "degree of activity."

Madison comes to a similar conclusion regarding factions that derive directly from the human passions. These are factions caused by "an attachment to different leaders ambitiously contending for pre-eminence and power; or to persons of other descriptions whose fortunes have been interesting to the human passions." Notice that these are not the factional passions that build up around a preexisting interest or opinion; that happens commonly enough. Rather, Madison is talking here about those factions that have their genesis directly and solely in the passions themselves. He is talking about passion as an "independent variable," just as he treated opinion as such and will shortly be seen to treat "interest" in the same manner. Moreover, he is not talking about the whole range of human passions that affect political behavior. He is talking here only about that single specific passion that by itself can be the direct cause of a faction. He means that particular passion—empathy is a useful word to recall here—by force of which humans have a natural political readiness to love and hate, a kind of spiritedness that is evoked by, or reaches out to, exceptional leaders. By force of this passion, masses of men, without any reason of interest or opinion, simply are "turned on" by dazzlingly attractive leaders.

The attachments based on such loves and hates are by no means contemptible; indeed, they may well be the means by which great virtues—courage, eloquence, rectitude, wisdom—communicate their political force and charm to human beings who might otherwise never be

---

[6] As Douglass Adair's essay on Hume and Madison has shown, further light on Madison's view of factionalism may be sought in Hume's essay "Of Parties in General." Hume warns against "parties from principle, especially abstract speculative principle," and warns also that "in modern times parties of religion are more furious and enraged than the most cruel factions that ever arose from interest and ambition." Hume suggests that interest-based faction, low though it may be, is less cruel than faction based on principle or opinion.

drawn upward to such qualities of character. Nevertheless, Madison concludes that on balance such attachments are too dangerous; they generate factions that torment and destroy society and hence must somehow be avoided. What Madison is in effect saying is: no Savonarolas or Cromwells or extraordinarily "interesting" figures, thank you; what is wanted generally are men of lesser but safer political ambition and religious appeal. The thrust of the American political order must be somehow to diminish the readiness of ordinary Americans to respond to leaders who generate faction, as it were, simply out of their own "charisma."

The bold and novel requirement of Madison's political science and of the American political order, then, is to mute or attenuate the age-old kinds of political behavior that derive from two of the fundamental causes of faction. But there is also the political behavior that derives from the third fundamental cause of faction, namely, interest: "the most common and durable source of factions has been the various and unequal distribution of property." Madison is far from seeking to diminish the efficacy of this cause, as he is of the other two. On the contrary, his intention is precisely the opposite: He wishes to magnify its operation, because therein lies the new cure of the "mischiefs of faction." To anticipate the conclusion of his argument: if Americans can be made to divide themselves according to their narrow and particularized economic interests, they will avoid the fatal factionalism that opinion and passion generate. By contrast, the relatively tranquil kind of factionalism resulting from economic interests makes possible a stable and decent democracy. But this does not mean economic-based faction in general. Madison distinguishes between two kinds of economic faction, one resulting from the "unequal distribution of property" and one from its various distribution. Faction based on property inequality, like faction based on opinion and passion, also leads to the fatal factionalism that destroyed earlier popular governments—specifically, to the perennial struggle of the many poor with the few rich, fighting under the banners of grandly conflicting ideas of justice. The American polity looks to replace this struggle over the *inequality* of property by causing to flourish a new kind of economic faction derived from the *variety* of property. It is on this basis that there can arise a tranquil, modern politics of interest groups, as distinct from a politics of class struggle. This is the meaning and intention of Madison's famous "multiplicity of interests" and of democratic government based upon the "coalition[s] of a majority" that rise out of that multiplicity.

But whence derives the "multiplicity" that makes it all possible? What are the civil "circumstances" that bring the right kind of economic-based faction into a high "degree of activity"? This new, salutary multiplicity of economic factions is uniquely the product of a large modern commercial society. For millennia the mass of men had been poor in but a handful of ways, toilers little differentiated in their class-poverty by the ways they eked out their existences; the rich likewise have gained their wealth in but a handful of ways that little differentiated their common oligarchic impulses and interests. Only the modern commercial spirit flourishing in a large, complex, modern economy can supply the faction-differentiating division of labor and the great economic diversity that directs the attention of all to the moderating private pursuit of individual economic happiness.[7] "Extend the sphere" of a republic, Madison said, "and you take in a greater variety of parties and interests; you make it less probable that a majority of the whole will have a common motive to invade the rights of other citizens." But it is only in an extended *commercial* republic that men are thus moderatingly fragmented into that "greater variety" of economic activities from which alone develops the necessary variety of economic interests. In

---

[7] Cf. Alexander Hamilton in *Federalist* 12 on how the "prosperity of commerce" entices and activates "human avarice and enterprise." But this leads to a result that Hamilton regards with satisfaction. "The assiduous merchant, the laborious husbandman, the active mechanic, and the industrious manufacturer—all orders of men look forward with eager expectation and growing alacrity to this pleasing reward of their toils." We will consider later a passage in Montesquieu, on a "democracy founded on commerce," which makes a similar point. And we will in that context suggest that the "avarice" of which Hamilton speaks may better be understood as "acquisitiveness."

such a society men will tend to think in terms of their various immediate economic interests, that is, to think as members of an "interest group" rather than of a class or sect. They will then tend to form political opinions in defense of those interests and then jockey frenetically, but ultimately tamely, for group and party advantage on the basis of those interests.

Madison's search for a solution to the democratic problem thus led him to envisage and help found the extended, commercial, democratic republic. Always before the politics of democracy had flowed naturally into the fatal factionalism deriving from opinion, passion, and class interest; the democratic mass of men had always turned to opinionated politics (or, as we might say now, to ideology) or to opinionated piety, or had followed some impassioning leader, or had fought the battle of the poor against the rich and had brought their democratic governments down in ruin. Employing the "new science of politics," Madison had discovered in "interest" its latent possibility, that is, a novel way of channeling the stream of politics away from these natural directions and toward that kind of factionalism with which a democracy could cope, namely, a politics of "various and interfering interests." Such is our political world—the modern world, the substratum of which consists of these narrowed, fragmented, unleashed interests—in which the "principal task" does indeed become what Madison stated it to be: "The regulation of these various and interfering interests forms the principal task of modern legislation and involves the spirit of party and faction in the necessary and ordinary operations of government."

## IV

The American political order was deliberately tilted to resist, so to speak, the upward gravitational pull of politics toward the grand, dramatic, character-ennobling but society-wracking opinions about justice and virtue. Opinion was now to be ballasted against its dangerous tendency toward destructive zealotry, or, to change the nautical figure, to be moored solidly in the principle of commodious self-preservation and economic self-interest. As much as possible, opinion was to be kept from reaching upward to broad considerations of the advantageous and the just by being made more nearly into a reflection of "the sentiments and views of the respective proprietors" of the various kinds of property. (Is this not precisely what came to be a distinctive aspect of opinion-formation in American political life—indeed, so much so that contemporary American political science has been beguiled, as it were, into forgetting what virile autonomous opinion is really like?) In thus seeking to tame opinion, Madison was following the general tendency of modern political thought to solve the problems of politics by reducing the scope of politics. As we saw earlier, by abstracting from politics the broad ethical function of character formation, modern political thought had begun a kind of depoliticizing of politics in general. Now Madison, as it were, depoliticized political opinion in particular.

Madison's strategy for solving the democratic problem of faction—not by trying to make opinion more disinterestedly virtuous but by reducing it to a safe reflection of diverse interests—helps to illuminate, and may be understood as part of the famous general policy of opposite and rival interests that Madison derived from the new science of politics. His general strategy for moderating democracy and thus making it commendable to the "esteem and adoption of mankind" is nowhere stated more thoughtfully, nor more chillingly, than in *Federalist* 51. He is explaining why the powers formally separated under the Constitution will remain so in practice, despite a despotizing tendency for them to become concentrated in one or another of the branches of government. "The great security against a gradual concentration of the several powers in the same department," he states, "consists in giving to those who administer each department the necessary constitutional means and personal motives to resist the encroachments of the others. Ambition must be made to counteract ambition. The interest of the man must be connected with the constitutional rights of the place." This all sounds sensible, even common-place, to present-day Americans, who are habituated to the moral horizon of the American political system. But Madison was writing when the new science of politics was still unhackneyed, and he knew that there was something novel and shocking in his acceptance and counterpoised use of ambitious interest as the principal security for the public good; it smacked much of "private vice, public good."

He thus pauses immediately to apologize, in a way, for such a cool recommendation, admitting it to be "a reflection on human nature that such devices should be necessary," but justifying them as necessitated by the weakness of that nature. He then boldly and comprehensively states the general principle underlying such "devices": "This policy of supplying, by opposite and rival interests, the defect of better motives, might be traced through the whole system of human affairs, private as well as public." Restated very plainly, Madison is saying this: Human nature is such that there just are not enough "better motives" to go around, not enough citizens and politicians who will be animated by motives that rise above self-interestedness and the gratification of their own passions so as to get the work of government and society done. But again there is no reason for despair because we can "supply the defect," that is, make up for the insufficiency of "better motives" with "personal motives," that is, by means of a shrewdly arranged system of opposite and rival personal interests. We cannot here trace the "policy" through the whole system of the Constitution; it suffices for our purposes to return to the question of opinion and the problem of faction. As we saw in our analysis of *Federalist* 10, this "policy" was precisely the basis of the scheme whereby the "multiplicity of interests" solves the problem of faction. We may paraphrase Madison's language: the defect of better opinions is supplied by the system of "various and interfering interests."

Now, Aristotle and ancient political science had no illusions about the quantity of "better motives" available; Aristotle thought them to be in as short supply as is supposed by modern political thought. The difference between the ancients and the moderns consists in the way each addressed the problem of the "defect," and the costs of their respective solutions. For the ancients, since improving those motives—or virtues, we may say in this context—was the end of political life, there was no alternative but to try to increase or improve the stock of "better motives" or virtues. These virtues were not merely instrumental in achieving certain governmental or societal goals; they *were* the goals. Hence in the premodern perspective there was no way to conceive that the defect could be supplied by any substitute. But for modern political thought—because making the motives better, that is, forming the human excellences, was no longer the primary end of politics—a different prospect was opened. The chief political end had become commodious self-preservation, with the higher human matters left to the workings of society. It thus became possible to conceive of interested behavior as a general substitute for the too-hard-to-come-by "better motives."

With respect to the quality of opinion in particular, the answer is the same. For the ancients, since the opinions of society so decisively influence the character of citizens, the formation of which was the end of politics, there was no alternative but to arrange the polis so as to "high tone" the opinions of the citizens as much as possible in the circumstances. For the moderns, however, there is no such necessity; indeed, it is not too much to say that opinion must literally be toned down in order that democratic factionalism not rip society apart.

That raises the question of costs. The moderns say, and with some justification, that ancient and medieval political *practice* had not vindicated the high aims and claims of premodern *thought*; the cost of a political philosophy that aimed too high, we have heard them argue, was to perpetuate in practice a vast human misery. But what of the modern costs and, in particular, what of the cost of the "American way"?

In the public realm, as we saw regarding the separation of powers, Madison's policy condones and even encourages hitherto reprobated interests like self-serving political ambition. In the private realm of the "various and interfering interests," this policy not only accepts but also necessarily encourages perspectives and activities that had hitherto been ethically censored and politically constrained, namely, the aggressive private pursuit by all of immediate personal interests. The very qualities that the classical and Christian teachings had sought to subdue so that those with "better motives" could be brought to attain their full natural height, the new science of politics emancipates and actively employs. This means nothing less than to whet democratically the appetites of all, to emancipate acquisitiveness and its attendant qualities, and to create the matrix—the large commercial democratic republic—within which such appetites and acquisitive aims can be excited and sufficiently satisfied. Put bluntly, this means that in order to defuse the dangerous factional force of opinion, passion, and class interest, Madison's policy deliberately risks magnifying and multiplying in American life the selfish, the interested, the narrow, the vulgar, and the crassly economic. That is the substratum on which our political system was intended to rest and where it rests still. It is a cost of Madison's policy, the price to be paid in order to enjoy its many blessings.

From the point of view of the generality of mankind, the new policy delivered on its promises. In comparison with the premodern achievement, it raised to unprecedented heights the benefits, the freedom, and the dignity enjoyed by the great many. But the cost must be recognized, precisely in order to continue to enjoy the blessings. Again in comparison with the premodern perspective, that cost is the solid but low foundation of American political life. And *foundation* must be understood quite literally: American institutions rest upon it. Those who wish to improve American life—specifically, those who would improve the relationship between ethics and politics in America—must base such improvement upon the American foundation; and this means to come to terms with the "policy" that is an essential part of that foundation. Revolution or transformation, that is something else. But if the aim is improvement, it must be improvement that accepts the limits imposed by the "genius" of the particular political order; it must be improvement that makes America her better self, but still her own self.

Yet it is just this foundation that has baffled or immoderately repelled many contemporary students of American political life and history. This is the case with what is perhaps the most influential, and very likely the most widely read, scholarly statement on the American Founding, Richard Hofstadter's *The American Political Tradition*. Hofstadter's book is an especially revealing example of a work that cannot abide the Madisonian reliance upon, and deliberate encouragement of, the system of opposite and rival interests. By seeing that system in the light of Hofstadter's rejection of it, we will further our own effort to understand it. Perhaps we will enlarge our understanding of the American political order by seeing how it can be defended from Hofstadter's attack.

In the spirit of Charles Beard, Hofstadter admires the Founders' republican decency and "realism," but at the same time severely rebukes that realism because it antiquatedly restricts the moral possibilities of American democracy. The Founders, he claims, "did not believe in man." They had "a distrust of man [which] was first and foremost a distrust of the common man and democratic rule." Consequently, the political system they devised was aimed at "cribbing and confining the popular spirit." Notice that Hofstadter does not merely make an interpretive claim as to how the Constitution should be understood; most American disputation has been of that sort, a kind of "quarrel among the heirs" as to the precise meaning of the political heritage. Rather, Hofstadter challenges the worth of the heritage itself. He is not concerned with particular shortcomings in American institutions but with the foundation upon which the entire structure of American politics rests. In short, his criticism goes to the Founders' idea of human nature, of its possibilities and limitations with respect to human excellence. Thus Hofstadter's chapter on the Founders opens with a critical characterization of their idea of man as Calvinist in its sense of evil, and as Hobbesian in its view of man as selfish and contentious. The chapter closes with a long final paragraph that strongly condemns this idea of man and his ethical potential. It is a condemnation that is implicit in many other contemporary rejections of the American political-ethical presuppositions and rewards careful examination.

Hofstadter writes that "from a humanistic standpoint there is a serious dilemma in the philosophy of the Fathers, which derives from their conception of man." The dilemma is this: while the founders were not full-blooded Hobbesians, still they had not advanced sufficiently beyond Hobbes to be satisfactory from "a humanistic standpoint." They had at least advanced beyond Hobbes in that, while they accepted his view of man as murderously self-interested, "they were in no mood to follow Hobbes to his conclusion," namely, to the absolute Leviathan state that Hobbes deemed necessary to restrain natural, anarchic man. Rather, despite their Hobbesian view of man, the Founders nonetheless "wanted him to be free—free, in essence, to contend, to be engaged in an umpired strife." But such freedom, while an improvement on Hobbesian absolutism, is still unsatisfactory because it does not succeed in putting an end to "the Hobbesian war of each against all." Indeed, the Founders did not even have such an intention; they wanted "merely to stabilize it and make it less murderous." The crucial defect of the American Founding, then, is that the Founders "had no hope and they offered none for any ultimate organic change in the way men conduct themselves. The result was that while they thought self-interest the most dangerous and unbrookable quality of man, they necessarily underwrote it in trying to control it." And, Hofstadter continues, things have worked out exactly as the founders intended; the American political system has provided just the sort of "stable and acceptable medium" for "grasping and contending interests" that the founders had in mind.

Such a political system, and the ideas that shaped and inspirited it, cannot apparently be recommended from the "humanistic standpoint." Especially the Founders' chief idea, the idea of an unchanging human nature characterized by rapacious self-interestedness, is humanistically indefensible: "No man who is as well abreast of modern science as the Fathers were of eighteenth-century science believes any longer in unchanging human nature. Modern humanistic thinkers who seek for a means by which society may transcend eternal conflict and rigid adherence to property rights as its integrating principles can expect no answer in the philosophy of balanced government as it was set down by the Constitution-makers of 1787." The implications are unmistakably harsh: "Modern humanistic thinkers" must turn away from the American idea of man and the political system based on it; those who want society to "transcend eternal conflict" must look elsewhere if they are to achieve their humanistic goals.[8]

At first blush, one might think that Hofstadter reaches this conclusion from something akin to the Aristotelian perspective. Hofstadter says more or less accurately that, rather than expecting "that vice could be checked by virtue," the American founders "relied instead upon checking vice with vice." This might suggest that Hofstadter takes his stand with the ancients in accepting the tension in human nature between virtue and vice and that he prefers, along with them, to make the difficult effort to help virtue to prevail over vice. But Hofstadter in fact sees no intrinsic difficulty in causing virtue to triumph, and this reveals how much he differs from both the ancients and an early modern thinker like Madison.

Both Aristotle and Madison agree that political life confronts a fundamental and ineradicable difficulty: human nature is unchanging, and there is a shortage in it of virtue or the "better motives." As we have seen, they disagree over what to do about this perennial difficulty; Aristotle sees in politics the necessity to "high tone" virtue as much as possible in any given circumstances, while Madison chooses the moderating system of opposite and rival interests. But against both of them Hofstadter believes that the perennial "defect" of virtue can simply be overcome by an "organic change" in human nature, which is promised in an unspecified way by "modern science." Hofstadter's entire criticism of the American Founding rests upon his apparent certainty that it is going to be possible "to change the nature of man to conform with a more ideal system." On the basis of what can only be called this utopian expectation, Hofstadter rejects both the Aristotelian and Madisonian views. Or, rather, one might speculate that he

---

[8] To "transcend eternal conflict" means to end it, which means to solve all those human problems that have hitherto led to conflict. This is not humanism but utopianism, and it must not be permitted that humanism should thus be subsumed under the utopian perspective. Rather, it may be suggested, humanism means precisely to recognize as perennial those human sources of conflict and to face them reflectively and nobly.

implicitly combines them, heedless of their irreconcilabilities. He seems to take from the Aristotelian enterprise something of the elevation to which virtue is thought capable of reaching but strips it of its corollary severity and inegalitarianism; and this "high toned" expectation regarding virtue he apparently combines with the democracy and commodious well-being of Madison's enterprise, but strips it of *its* corollary, the foundation in the system of opposite and rival interests. Such complacent synthesizing or combining of irreconcilables is the hallmark of contemporary utopianism.

## V

Hofstadter's characterization of the Founders' view of human nature, and of its potential for virtue, is of course not without justification. The political science of the American Founding does indeed have roots in the new political science of Hobbes, and it does seek to "check interest with interest . . . [and] faction with faction." And if that were the whole story—if Madison's "policy" were all that there is to the American political order, and all that there is to his political science— it would be difficult to defend the Founding from Hofstadter's harsh conclusions. We might still have to opt for Madison's apparently amoral "policy" against Hofstadter's utopian alternative, but it would be a most melancholy choice. Or to state this in a way that returns us to our main concerns: if this were all there is to the American political order, we might well have to conclude that, judging by Aristotelian standards, America is not a genuine political community. That is, in the light only of what we have said about the Madisonian foundation, America would seem to be little more than a clever new social arrangement, "an association of place and of not acting unjustly to one another, and for the sake of trade" among fellow residents, but not a regime that forms a common character among fellow citizens. Yet we all know in our bones that somehow there is more to the "American way" than that, that somehow we are fellow citizens within a political order, but one of a special kind. Whether what we feel in our bones is truly so is what we must now consider.

Since a regime reveals itself in the characters it forms, we must consider the American virtues or excellences, that is to say, the particular kind of human character formed among Americans. Now, the interesting thing is that however much we are not a regime in the ordinarily recognizable Aristotelian sense, we are emphatically so in one regard: We form a distinctive being, the American, as recognizably distinctive a human product as that of perhaps any regime in history. Something here turns out humanness in a peculiar American shape. What are those American virtues or excellences and how are they generated? While never forgetting its mooring in the Madisonian base, we may now consider briefly the height to which the formation of character in America reaches. This means, of course, to conclude our consideration of the particular American relationship of ethics and politics.

While the American Founders turned away from the classic enterprise regarding virtue, they did not thereby abandon the pursuit of virtue or excellence in all other possible ways. In fact, the American political order rises respectably high enough above the vulgar level of mere self-interest in the direction of virtue—if not to the highest reaches of the ancient perspective, still toward positive human decencies or excellences. Indeed, the prospect of excellences is opened up even within the very commercial interests, the unleashing of which is requisite to Madison's scheme. To see this, it is necessary to distinguish greed, or avarice, on the one hand, and acquisitiveness, on the other. The commercial society unleashes acquisitiveness; but this is by no means the same thing as to give vent to the avarice or covetousness that, traditionally, all philosophies and religious creeds have condemned. Both modern acquisitiveness and traditional avarice have perhaps the same source, namely, the desire, even an inordinate desire, for bodily things. But, as the roots of the two words suggest, in age-old avarice the emphasis is on the passion of *having*, whereas in modern acquisitiveness the emphasis is on the *getting*. Avarice is a passion centered on the things themselves, a narrow clutching to one's self of money or possessions; it has no built-in need for any limitation of itself, no need for moderation or for the cultivation of any virtues as instrumental to the satisfaction of the avaricious passion. But acquisitiveness teaches a form of moderation to the desiring passions from which it derives, because to acquire is not primarily to have and to hold but to get and to earn, and, moreover, to earn justly, at least to the extent that the acquisition must be the fruit of one's own exertions or qualities. This requires the acquisitive man to cultivate certain excellences, minimal ones perhaps from the classical perspective, but excellences nonetheless, as means to achieve his ends. He wants enlargement and increase and these require of him at least venturesomeness, and hard work, and the ability to still his immediate passions so as to allow time for the ripening of his acquisitive plans and measures. In short, acquisitive man, unlike avaricious man, is likely to have what we call the bourgeois virtues.

It is in this context that we must understand Hamilton's observation that a commercial society nurtures "the assiduous merchant, the laborious husbandman, the active mechanic, and the industrious manufacturer." Avarice, strictly understood, has no such salutary effects; acquisitiveness does. And it is not only excellences like assiduity, labor, activity, and industry that a commercial society nurtures. "Honesty is the best policy" is not acceptable prudence to the avaricious man, but it is almost natural law to the "assiduous merchant." Acquisitiveness may not be the highest motive for honesty, but if it produces something like the habit of honesty in great numbers, is not that a prodigious accomplishment? Similarly, the notion that "it takes money to make money," a maxim familiar to the acquisitive man, bears at least a relation to the ancient virtue of liberality; but the avaricious man simply cannot let loose his money to the extent that the commercial principle makes common practice. Scrooge was surely not less successful as a merchant after he acquired the liberal spirit of Christmas; indeed, the old Scrooge belonged to an older world of avarice, while the new Scrooge would perhaps be more at home in a modern commercial society. Finally, the acquisitive man is plunged by his passion into the give-and-take of society and must thus learn to accommodate himself to the interests of others. In this he is at least pointed toward something like justice. But the avaricious man is drawn by his passion wholly within the confines of his own narrow soul.

When Madison's "policy of opposite and rival interests" is understood in the light of this distinction between avarice and acquisitiveness, we can begin to see the ground for some of the excellences we all know to be characteristic of American life. We can then avoid thinking, as many have, that the vice of avarice peculiarly flourishes in America. On the contrary, we can claim that avarice here is peculiarly blunted by the supervening force of acquisitiveness and its attendant valuable qualities. No one understood this possibility more profoundly than Montesquieu, who argued that "frugality, economy, moderation, labor, prudence, tranquility, order, and rule" are virtues or excellences that are naturally generated in a "democracy founded on commerce."[9] These may be put down as merely "bourgeois virtues," but they are virtues, or human excellences, nonetheless. They reach at least to decency if not to nobility; they make life at least possible under the circumstances of modern mass society and seem more useful and attractive than ever now that they are in diminishing supply.

Tocqueville, who learned from Montesquieu, also teaches virtue in the same spirit but still more hopefully, and with him we may see a higher level to which the formation of American character reaches. The foundation, Tocqueville understands as does Montesquieu, is an acquisitive commercial order in which self-interest must be allowed to flourish; Tocqueville coolly accepts that it cannot be suppressed or transcended. Whatever might have been possible in earlier aristocratic ages, when men had perhaps been able to sacrifice self-interest for the "beauty of virtue," this is now impossible. In the modern age of equality, "private interest will more than ever become the chief if not the only driving force behind all behavior." But this is not cause for despair; if there is no hope of transcending private interest, still much depends on how "each

---

[9] Montesquieu, *The Spirit of the Laws*, Book 5, chap. 6.

man will interpret his private interest."[10] What is necessary is that men learn to follow the "principle of self-interest properly understood." The Americans, Tocqueville says, have "universally accepted" that principle and have made it the root of all their actions: "The Americans enjoy explaining almost every act of their lives on the principle of self-interest properly understood. It gives them pleasure to point out how an enlightened self-love continually leads them to help one another and disposes them freely to give part of their time and wealth for the good of the state."

Oddly, and in a manner reminiscent of Madison in *Federalist* 51, Tocqueville interrupts his presentation at this point as if wishing to draw a veil over the harsh foundation of this "principle." But he forces himself, as it were, to a full statement of its implications.

> Self-interest properly understood is not at all a sublime doctrine. . . . It does not attempt to reach great aims, but it does . . . achieve all it sets out to do. Being within the scope of everybody's understanding, everyone grasps it and has no trouble bearing it in mind. It is wonderfully agreeable to human weaknesses and so easily wins great sway. It has no difficulty in keeping its power, for it turns private interest against itself and uses the same goad which excites them to direct the passions.

> The doctrine of self-interest properly understood does not inspire great sacrifices, but every day it prompts some small ones; by itself it cannot make a man virtuous, but its discipline shapes a lot of orderly, temperate, moderate, careful, and self-controlled citizens. If it does not lead the will directly to virtue, it establishes habits which unconsciously turn it that way.

One element in Tocqueville's account of these "habits," which are the common stuff of American political life, is especially worth noting. Not only does "self-interest properly understood" cause Americans to acquire certain personal excellences, and not only does it lead them regularly to help one another in their private capacities, but it also "disposes them freely to give part of their time and wealth for the good of the state." By this Tocqueville refers to the extraordinary extent to which Americans actually govern themselves; from the habit and practice of self-government, American character reaches up to the republican virtues. The imposing extent of American self-governance, and hence its character-forming significance, has been obscured in recent years because observers have brought to the question a utopian expectation that degraded the reality. But Tocqueville, by making realistic comparisons and taking his bearings from the nature of things, was able to appreciate the astonishing degree in America of self-governing and self-directing activity in all spheres of life. In fact, he warns his readers that, while they could very well conceive all other aspects of America, "the political activity prevailing in the United States is something one could never understand unless one has seen it. No sooner do you set foot on American soil than you find yourself in a sort of tumult; a confused clamor rises on every side, and a thousand voices are heard at once, each expressing some social requirements."[11] This tumult, this clamor, is the sound of men and women governing themselves. And in presupposing and summoning forth the capacity of a people to govern themselves, the American political order advances beyond mere self-interest toward that full self-governance which is the very idea of virtue.

We may very briefly note two further aspects of American life which are, in a way, at the peak of the "ascent" we are sketching. First, American democracy as understood by its Founders, whether in the Declaration of Independence or the Constitution, made only a modest claim. It never denied the unequal existence of human virtues or excellences; it only denied the ancient claim of excellence to *rule as a matter of right*. Now this denial is of immense importance because, in contrast with the ancient justification of the political claims of the few, it deeply popularizes

---

[10]Alexis de Tocqueville, *Democracy in America*, trans. George Lawrence (New York: Harper & Row, 1966). Unless otherwise noted, all references are to pp. 497–99.

[11]*Ibid*., p. 233.

the very foundation of political life. But the American political order nonetheless still presupposed that an inequality of virtues and abilities was rooted in human nature and that this inequality would manifest itself and flourish in the private realm of society. The original American democratic idea thus still deferred to a relatively high idea of virtue, the while denying its claim to rule *save by popular consent*. Indeed, not only was the idea of unequal excellence acknowledged and expected to flourish privately, but it was the proud claim of American democracy to be the political system in which merit, incarnated in Jefferson's "natural aristocracy," was likeliest to be rewarded with public office, in contrast with the way "artificial aristocracy" flourished corruptly in other systems. Nothing is more dangerous in modern America than those subverting conceptions of human nature or of justice that deny that there are men and women who deserve deference, or deny democracy its aspiration to be that political system which best defers to the truly deserving.

Finally, and with a brevity disproportionate to importance, one should also note gratefully that the American political order, with its heterogeneous and fluctuating majorities and with its principle of liberty, supplies a not inhospitable home to the love of learning. This is at a respectable distance indeed from its foundation in a "policy of opposite and rival interests."

## VI

We have examined the "policy" that is the restraining or ballasting base of the "American way," and now we have some idea of what are the distinctive and respectable American virtues or excellences that rise on and above the base. In the light of those distinctive virtues, we can claim that America manifestly qualifies as an authentically political community or regime, at least with regard to the production of an ethos, or of a distinctive human character or characters. But we still have not gotten a satisfactory handle on the political side of the ethics-politics relationship here: while American character is as much our distinctive ethical nurture as is the human character formed in any other regime, it still remains a puzzle as to how that character is politically generated here.

We cannot hope to explicate the matter fully, but it will help to recur to the Aristotelian understanding of a regime. In Aristotle's view, three elements together make a community authentically political rather than merely a social arrangement that lacks a regard for "what the qualities of the others are." A community is a political regime when: (1) it forms itself upon some particular idea of what is "advantageous and just" for human beings; (2) its citizens are molded into a particular human character on the pattern of that idea; and when (3) this is done by means of vigorous, comprehensive, and penetrating laws, that is, by means of a political art that regulates—not just Madison's "various and interfering interests," but religion, education, family life, mores generally, economic behavior, and whatever helps bring into being the kind or kinds of human being contemplated by the central idea of the particular regime.

The puzzle in the American case is the discrepancy between the way we fully qualify as a regime regarding the second requirement, the forming of distinctive virtues or characters, but emphatically do not qualify regarding the last requirement, namely, the use of governmental authority to form those virtues. It is in this respect, in the absence of the censorious and sumptuary laws and institutions characteristic of ancient political science, that America is most unlike an Aristotelian regime. As we saw earlier, this removal of government from the business of directly superintending the formation of character is central to the "new science of politics," on the basis of which the American republic was largely founded. And this narrowing of the range of political authority, we also saw, resulted from a lowering of the aims of political life. This meant a lowering of the idea of the "advantageous and the just." It is likely, then, that the explanation of the puzzling American discrepancy—character formation, but not by use of the laws—will be found in the status in America of the first of Aristotle's three regime requisites, that is, in the American idea of what is advantageous and right for humans.

By the "American idea" of the advantageous and just, we mean here the idea contained in the Declaration of Independence and the Constitution, the two linked founding documents of the American republic. This is not to deny that many other elements form part of the American idea in practice—elements like the Anti-Federalist "virtuous republic" tradition, or Puritanism with its original high-pitched piety, or the high-toned Anglicanism that long persisted in this country, or vestiges of the English aristocratic tradition, or, more recently, elements derived from powerful intellectual currents in the contemporary world, or from the many other possibilities that crowd into a particular national "idea" in practice. All of these elements must be given their due weight in a full account of the American relationship of ethics and politics. But they all become most intelligible in their operation when they are seen in tension with the central American idea, the idea derived from the new science of politics, the idea decisively embodied in the "frame" of the republic, that is, in the principles, institutions, and processes of the Constitution.

The central American idea of what is advantageous and just for humans, as we have seen, is clearly less elevated than that of the classical teaching. The ethical aim of the American political order being less lofty, the kinds of human characters to be politically formed are likewise less lofty and, hence, less difficult of formation. Such human beings may be produced by softer means, subterranean in their operation and indirect, thereby rendering unnecessary the strenuous and penetrating political authority characteristic of the ancient regime. It has in fact proved possible to raise human character to the American height in this gentler, less demanding fashion.

Consider what we have called the "bourgeois virtues." As Montesquieu observed, the "spirit of commerce" of itself entices these modest excellences into being. Their formation does not require the severity and constant statesmanship of the classical political outlook; it suffices that a modern regime generate that "spirit" and then the desired virtues tend naturally to form themselves. This fundamental difference is revealed in a superficial similarity between the ancient and modern ways of generating their respectively required virtues. In one interesting respect, the modern bourgeois virtues are formed politically the same way that the ancient teaching prescribed regarding its virtues, namely, by a decision regarding the size of the political community. The decisions are, of course, exactly opposite: The classical ethical-political teaching requires the small scale of the polis; the Madisonian "policy" with its attendant "bourgeois virtues" requires the scale of a very large republic. For the ancients, the polis had to be small so as to provide a constraining environment for the appetites; for the moderns, the republic had to be large so as to excite the acquisitive appetites whence the spirit of commerce arises. But for the ancients the size of the polis of itself accomplishes little regarding the right character formation; the polis was simply the requisite setting within which a high political art could be employed to generate the appropriate virtues. But once the modern republic has been organized on a large enough scale and, of course, once its fundamental laws have established the framework for the life of commerce, government need not be used thereafter closely to superintend the formation of the bourgeois character. The appropriate ethical consequences may be expected to flow. In this respect, the relationship of ethics and politics in America is more the work of the original Founding than of a demanding statesmanship thereafter; appropriate characters are formed by force of the original political direction of the passions and interests.

We have also pointed to the American republican virtues that arise from the habit and practice of self-government. Like the bourgeois virtues, these too are formed in the milder modern way. The American republican virtues arise primarily from political arrangements that accept and seek to channel the force of human passion and interest rather than to suppress or transcend them. And these republican virtues likewise arise primarily from the original Founding and not from subsequent statesmanship shaping the character of the citizenry. The Constitution, and, thanks to federalism, the state constitutions as well, establish a basic framework of institutions that elicit ethical qualities of citizenship such as independence, initiative, a capacity for cooperation and patriotism. Tocqueville teaches us the way these qualities are formed in the American character. He shows how, by means of administrative decentralization, the jury system, voluntary associations, and the like, self-interest is "unconsciously" drawn in the direction of republican virtue. Like the bourgeois virtues, these republican decencies in the American character do not depend decisively upon constant constraint or encouragement by statesmanship but tend to flow from the operation of the political institutions as originally founded. James Madison also teaches us about the character-forming possibility of the Founding, for example, in his understanding of the Bill of Rights. Madison justified the addition of the Bill of Rights to the Constitution in part on "declaratory" grounds. "The political truths declared in that solemn manner," he said, "acquire by degrees the character of fundamental maxims for free Government, and as they become incorporated with the national sentiment, counteract the impulses of interest and passion."[12] In this sense, the Founding becomes more than an arrangement of the passions and interests; when "venerated" by the people, it can serve as an ethical admonition to the people, teaching them to subdue dangerous impulses of passion and interest. This goes far in the direction of genuine republican virtue, but it still rests on the mild and merely declaratory tutelage of the Founding, not on the sterner stuff of ancient political science.

Finally, the American Founders seem simply to have taken for granted that the full range of the higher human virtues would have suitable opportunity to flourish, so to speak, privately. They presumed that man's nature included a perhaps weak but nonetheless natural inclination to certain virtues. Although they did not rely upon these "better motives," as we have here called them, as the basis for the political order, they were apparently confident that, privately and without political tutelage in the ancient mode, these higher virtues would develop from religion, education, family upbringing, and simply out of the natural yearnings of human nature. Indeed, they even accorded to these higher excellences a quasi-public status in the expectation mentioned earlier, that American democracy would seek out and reward the "natural aristocracy" with public trust. Whether these expectations of the Founders were reasonable then or remain so now is a grave matter for inquiry, but an inquiry beyond the scope of this essay.

We have suggested here a way through which Americans should inquire into, and go about, the ethical enterprise of politics. We have argued that there is a distinctive American way respecting the relationship of ethics and politics; and hence, while taking our bearings from the universal commands of the highest ethics, we must as political beings seek to achieve politically only that excellence of character that, to adapt a phrase from Tocqueville, "is proper to ourselves." That character largely remains the product of the subtle strategy of the American Founders, the understanding of which thus remains indispensable to us. We must accept that their political order had its foundation in the human interests and passions; but we must appreciate also that their political order presupposes certain enduring qualities that can and should be achieved in the American character. The preservation of that foundation and at the same time the nurturing of the appropriate ethical excellences remains the compound political task of enlightened American statesmen and citizens. The easy error is to deal with only one side of that compound task. On the one hand, it is easy to be concerned only with the foundation and to settle for a form of liberty that consists only in the free play of raw self-interest. But this is to ignore the subtle ethical demands of the American political order. On the other hand, it is even easier today to make utopian demands upon the political system for unrealizable ethical perfections. But this is to ignore the limiting requisites of the unique American ethos, namely, the foundation in the passions and interests upon which it rests. Moreover, such utopianizing has the tendency inexcusably to ignore or depreciate the liberty and decencies which the American political order, resting on that foundation, continues to secure in an ever more dangerous world.

---

[12] Madison to Jefferson, Oct. 17, 1788, in *Writings of James Madison* (New York: Putnam's, 1904), 5:273. I am indebted to my wife, Ann Stuart Diamond, for calling to my attention the appositeness of this passage to my purposes. Madison's view of how the Bill of Rights can acquire "the character of fundamental maxims of free Government" should be considered in connection with his discussion of "veneration" and public opinion in *Federalist* 49.

In contrast to both these one-sided approaches, it is intellectually and ethically rewarding to grasp the compound ethical-political demands of the "American Way" and to seek within each day's budget of troubles "to attain that form of greatness . . . which is proper to ourselves" and even enclaves of other greatnesses as well.[13]

---

[13] Tocqueville, *Democracy in America*, p. 679.

# "Truth and Freedom: A Reply to Thomas McCarthy"

## Richard Rorty (1931–      )

*Educated at the University of Chicago and Yale University, Richard Rorty became the Vienan Professor of Humanities at the University of Virginia in 1982. He has been called "the most influential contemporary American philosopher," yet his view, articulated during the last two decades, is that philosophy is inferior to novels in analyzing the world and its meanings. This position has been seen to link him with the post-modernists. Arguing in this essay and elsewhere that philosophical argument cannot enlighten political decisions, Rorty seeks other grounds for his affinity for liberal and democratic political arrangements, such as individual freedom, in a notion of self-creation.*

*Consider Rorty's point that principles present a serious problem for achieving a decent politics. Can Rorty endorse free, open, and imaginative discussion without recourse to principles? Do you think that, as Rorty says, "there is no way to 'refute' a sophisticated, consistent, passionate" Nazi?*

## I

Thomas McCarthy is remarkably good at seeing the interconnections between theorists' ideas, at explaining why they say the odd things they do, and at helping them out of the holes they dig themselves into. When I feel baffled by something Jürgen Habermas is saying, I read McCarthy on Habermas and things clear up. I am very flattered that he has taken the time to write about my stuff. I got the same benefits out of reading him on myself as I have gotten from reading him on Habermas and on Michel Foucault. He writes about me with great understanding and sympathy, and helps me understand my own twists, turns, and predicaments better than I had before. . . .

Generalizing from the case of Putnam, I would reply to McCarthy by urging that when we look for regulative ideals, we stick to freedom and forget about truth and rationality. We can safely do this because, whatever else truth may be, it is something we are more likely to get as a result of free and open encounters than anything else. Whatever else rationality may be, it is something that obtains when persuasion is substituted for force. So what is really important to think about is what makes an encounter free from the influence of force. As I have urged elsewhere, if we take care of political and cultural freedom, truth and rationality will take care of themselves.[1] Since I regard modern philosophy as having centered around a discussion of truth, I regard philosophy as not very useful in the pursuit of such freedoms, as having become largely a distraction from that pursuit. That is why I say things that surprise and distress McCarthy—for instance, that philosophers should not expect to be the avant-garde of political movements.

McCarthy thinks truth more important than I do. Specifically, he thinks that "'truth' . . . functions as an 'idea of reason' with respect to which we can criticize not only particular claims within our language but the very standards of truth we have inherited" (p. 369). By contrast, I think that what enables us to make such criticisms is concrete alternative suggestions— suggestions about how to redescribe what we are talking about. Some examples are Galileo's suggestions about how to redescribe the Aristotelian universe, Marx's suggestions about how to redescribe the nineteenth century, Heidegger's suggestions about how to redescribe the West as a whole, Dickens's suggestions about how to redescribe chancery law, Rabelais's suggestions about how to redescribe monastaries, Virginia Woolf's suggestions about how to redescribe women writing.

Such fresh descriptions, such new suggestions of things to say, sentences to consider, vocabularies to employ, are what do the work. All that the idea of truth does is to say, "Bethink yourself that you might be mistaken; remember that your beliefs may be justified by your other beliefs in the area, but that the whole kit and kaboodle might be misguided, and in particular that you might be using the wrong *words* for your purpose." But this admonition is empty and powerless without some concrete suggestion of an alternative set of beliefs, or of words. Moreover, if you have such suggestion, you do not need the admonition. The *only* cash value of this regulative idea is to commend fallibilism, to remind us that lots of people have been as certain of, and as justified in believing, things that turned out to be false as we are certain of, and justified in holding, our present views. It is not, as McCarthy says, a "moment of unconditionality that opens us up to criticism from other points of view" (p. 370). It is the particular attractions of those other points of view.

For example: my awareness that my beliefs "'may turn out to be false after all'" (p. 369) does not open me up to criticism from the poor lost souls who write me abusive twelve-page single-spaced letters, replete with diagrams exhibiting the nature of the universe. I *am* opened up to criticism by critics like Habermas, McCarthy, Nancy Fraser, and others, because they are able to redescribe my own position in terms that make me say, "Gee, there might be something to that; when so described, I *do* look pretty bad." The "moment of unconditionality" is, in Ludwig Wittgenstein's phrase, "a wheel that can be turned though nothing else moves with it, . . . not part of the mechanism."[2] "Idealizing elements" do *nothing* to help me sort out the nut cases from the people to whom it pays to listen.

Concrete suggestions are a necessary condition of intellectual and moral progress, but not, of course, sufficient. Good luck is another necessary condition, and political and cultural freedom are others. Here is another area of disagreement between McCarthy and myself. McCarthy thinks that the ideals of political and cultural freedom are linked, in our culture, to "transcultural notions of validity." He says that our culture is "everywhere structured around" such notions (p. 361). Maybe so, but maybe the temptation to believe that it is so structured is just a professional deformation of us philosophy professors. My own hunch, or at least hope, is that our culture is gradually coming to be structured around the idea of freedom—of leaving people alone to dream

---

[1] See Rorty, "The Priority of Democracy to Philosophy," in *The Virginia Statute for Religious Freedom: Its Evolution and Consequences in American History*, ed. Merrill D. Peterson and Robert C. Vaughan, Cambridge Studies in Religion and American Public Life (Cambridge, 1988), pp. 257-288.

[2] Ludwig Wittgenstein, *Philosophical Investigations*, 3d ed., trans. G. E. M. Anscombe (New York, 1958), § 271.

and think and live as they please, so long as they do not hurt other people—and that this idea provides as viscous a social glue as that of unconditional validity.[3]

McCarthy, however, thinks that the question "Is the proposition 'freedom is a good thing' true in an unconditional sense?" is still one our culture is moved to ask. By contrast, I argue against Putnam that when we gave up on God, we tacitly and gradually began giving up on "true in an unconditional sense." I think that we may have moved on, or may at least be in the process of moving on, to a culture in which freedom can stand on its own feet. By contrast, McCarthy and Jacques Derrida are at one in believing that the entire culture of the West, right down to our own day, is permeated and structured by Greek metaphysics—by an aspiration toward something transcendent, beyond historical and cultural change, toward what Derrida calls "a reassuring certitude, which is itself beyond the reach of play."[4]

I have to admit that this claim has some plausibility. Perhaps the best evidence for it is that we philosophers are still called on to "answer Hitler," and abused if we confess our inability to do so. We are supposed to prove Hitler wrong by finding something beyond him and us—something unconditional—that agrees with us and not with him. It might well be said that a culture in which such demands are incessant is still structured by metaphysical ways of thinking, and that in such a culture one cannot responsibly decline the task McCarthy assigns the philosopher—the task of "recogniz[ing] the idealizing elements intrinsic to social practices and build[ing] on them" (p. 370).

Like Habermas and Karl-Otto Apel, McCarthy sees my refusal to take on the job of answering Hitler as a sign of irresponsible "decisionism" or "relativism."[5] But I have always (well, not always, but for the last twenty years or so) been puzzled about what was supposed to count as a knockdown answer to Hitler. Would it answer him to tell him that there was a God in Heaven who was on our side? How do we reply to him when he asks for evidence for this claim? Would it answer him to say that his views are incompatible with the construction of a society in which communication is undistorted, and that his refusal of a voice to his opponents contradicts the presupposition of his own communicative acts? What if Hitler rejoins that to interpret truth as a product of free and open encounters rather than as what emerges from the genius of a destined leader begs the question against him? (What if, in other words, he goes Heideggerian on us?) Richard Hare's view that there is no way to "refute" a sophisticated, consistent, passionate psychopath—for example, a Nazi who would favor his own elimination if he himself turned out to be Jewish—seems to me right, but to show more about the idea of "refutation" than about Nazism.[6]

If I were assigned the task not of refuting or answering but of *converting* a Nazi (one a bit more sane and conversable than Hitler himself), I would have some idea of how to set to work. I could show him how nice things can be in free societies, how horrible things are in the Nazi camps, how his Führer can plausibly be redescribed as an ignorant paranoid rather than as an inspired prophet, how the Treaty of Versailles can be redescribed as a reasonable compromise rather than as a vendetta, and so on. These tactics might or might not work, but at least they would not be an intellectual exercise in what Apel calls *Letztbegründung*.[7] They would be the sort of thing that sometimes actually changes people's minds. By contrast, attempts at showing the

---

[3] I discuss the question of the strength of this social glue in my *Contingency, Irony, and Solidarity* (Cambridge, 1989), pp. 82-88.

[4] Jacques Derrida, *Writing and Difference*, trans. Alan Bass (Chicago, 1978), p. 279. I have previously criticized Derrida's claim that this characteristically metaphysical urge is central to our culture, particularly in "Deconstruction and Circumvention," *Critical Inquiry* 11 (Sept. 1984) : 1 23, esp. pp. 19-21.

[5] See Karl-Otto Apel, *Diskurs und Verantwortung: Das Problem des Übergangs zur postkonventionellen Moral* (Frankfurt am Main, 1988), esp. pp. 399-425.

[6] See R. M. Hare, "Toleration and Fanaticism," *Freedom and Reason* (Oxford, 1963), pp. 157-85.

[7] See Apel, *Diskurs und Verantwortung*, pp. 406ff.

philosophically sophisticated Nazi that he is caught in a logical or pragmatic self-contradiction will simply impel him to construct invidious redescriptions of the presuppositions of the charge of contradiction (the sort of redescriptions Heidegger put at the Nazis' disposal).

Like a lot of other people who wind up teaching philosophy, I, too, got into the business because, having read some Plato, I thought I could use my budding dialectical talents to *demonstrate* that the bad guys were bad and the good guys good—to do to contemporary bad guys (for example, the bullies who used to beat me up in high school) what Socrates thought he was doing to Thrasymachus, Gorgias, and others. But, some twenty years back, I finally decided that this project was not going to pan out—that "demonstration" was just not available in this area, that a theoretically sophisticated bully and I would always reach an argumentative standoff. McCarthy, Apel, and Habermas still see some hope for the Socratic project. Since I do not, I decline the assignment McCarthy offers the philosopher and try to redescribe my own job. I redescribe it as picking and choosing among the elements in our culture, playing up some and playing down others.

In the light of this redescription, I can formulate the gist of my reply to McCarthy by saying: there are traditions within our culture that stand over and against the one you take as central, and these are the ones I want to encourage. I am not caught in the trap you describe, of being unable to "appeal to peer agreement, established norms, or anything of the sort" because I do not, in fact, find myself in a culture "everywhere structured around transcultural notions of validity" (p. 361). It is, fortunately, not so structured *everywhere*, just in some places. So I can appeal to things that are said and done in the other places. I can play off some elements in our culture against others (thus doing, I think, the same thing that Socrates and Plato did, no matter what they described themselves as doing). We live in a culture that has been nurtured not just on "the Bible, on Socrates and Plato, on the Enlightenment" (p. 365), but on, for example, Rabelais, Montaigne, Sterne, Hogarth, and Mark Twain.

The novel is just one of the elements in our culture that I should argue is *not* structured around transcultural notions of validity. But it is perhaps the clearest case, so I happily join Milan Kundera in appealing to the novel against philosophy. In his *Art of the Novel*, currently one of my favorite books, Kundera says:

> As God slowly departed from the seat whence he had directed the universe and its order of values, distinguished good from evil, and endowed each thing with meaning, Don Quixote set forth from his house into a world he could no longer recognize. In the absence of the Supreme Judge, the world suddenly appeared in its fearsome ambiguity; the single divine Truth decomposed into myriad relative truths parceled out by men. Thus was born the world of the Modern Era, and with it the novel, the image and model of that world. . . .
>
> Man desires a world where good and evil can be clearly distinguished, for he has an innate and irrepressible desire to judge before he understands. Religions and ideologies are founded on this desire. They can cope with the novel only by translating its language of relativity and ambiguity into their own apodictic and dogmatic discourse. They require that someone be right: either Anna Karenina is the victim of a narrow-minded tyrant, or Karenin is the victim of an immoral woman; either K. is an innocent man crushed by an unjust Court, or the Court represents divine justice and K. is guilty.[8]

Focusing more closely on the opposition between the "idealizing elements" in our culture and the elements that represent what he calls "the wisdom of the novel," Kundera says:

> Rabelais' erudition, great as it is, has another meaning than Descartes'. The novel's wisdom is different from that of philosophy. The novel is born not of the theoretical spirit but of the spirit of humor. One of Europe's major failures is that it never understood the most European of the arts—

---

[8] Milan Kundera, *The Art of the Novel*, trans. Linda Asher (New York, 1988), pp. 6-7.

the novel; neither its spirit, nor its great knowledge and discoveries, nor the autonomy of its history. The art inspired by God's laughter does not by nature serve ideological certitudes, it contradicts them. Like Penelope, it undoes each night the tapestry that the theologians, philosophers, and learned men have woven the day before.[9]

This undoing is effected by redescription, by proffering a vocabulary for talking about some particular person, situation, or event that cuts across the vocabulary we have so far used in our moral and political deliberations. The novel does not offer an argument within the same dialectical space we have previously been occupying, but rather the glimpse of other such spaces. The urge to redescribe, cultivated by reading novels, is different from the urge to demonstrate, cultivated by reading metaphysics. Kundera's "wisdom of the novel" has no use for McCarthy's "moment of unconditionality." The closest it can come to this is the regulative ideal of All Possible Novels—every redescription from every possible angle, all available at once. But this is not very close. For the realm of possibility is not something with fixed limits; rather, it expands continually, as ingenious new redescriptions suggest even more ingenious re-redescriptions. Every purported glimpse of the boundaries of this realm is in fact an expansion of those boundaries.

Does this mean that the wisdom of the novel encompasses a sense of how Hitler might be seen as in the right and the Jews in the wrong? Yes, I am afraid that it does. Someday somebody will write a novel about Hitler that will portray him as he saw himself, one that will, momentarily, make its readers feel that the poor man was much misunderstood. (A. J. P. Taylor's *Origins of the Second World War* can be viewed as a sketch for certain chapters of that novel.)[10] Someday somebody will write a novel about Stalin as Good Old Uncle Joe. I hope nobody writes either very soon, because reading such a novel seems too much for the remaining victims of either murderer to have to bear. But such novels will someday be written. If we are to be faithful to the wisdom of the novel, they *must* be written.

This ability to adopt every possible point of view is the aspect of the novel that is hardest for us to take, the ability that made Plato turn away in revulsion from the poets and attempt to invent a less flexible genre, one that had more in common with geometry. But, as I suggested above, the poet's flexibility turned out to be matched by the ability of Plato's heirs to formulate axioms from which to deduce, and vocabularies in which to phrase, an apologia for anything you please (slavery, the Inquisition, bourgeois democracy, the Nazis, the Cultural Revolution). This is the aspect of philosophy that is hardest for us to take, and that has, in recent times, made many poets and novelists turn from it in revulsion.

The impulse that leads us to reject instruments (the philosophical system, the novel) that can be turned to any and every purpose is that we *know* that we are the good guys and the Nazis are the bad guys. We should like to find some way of making this knowledge as clear to *everyone* as it is to us—to exhibit what McCarthy calls its "transcultural . . . validity" (p. 361). The trouble is, of course, that this same sort of knowledge-claim is made, in all sincerity, by the bad guys, and that we shall never have any resources available that will not be equally available to them. Talk of a "moment of unconditionality" does nothing, as far as I can see, to get us out of this predicament. That is why I can only suggest we cease to feel it as a predicament—that we cease to want something we have learned we cannot have, that we give up on "transcultural validity." This amounts to giving up on what so-called postmodernists call "logocentrism." That renunciation seems to me what pragmatism and "postmodernism" have in common. Where the latter goes off the rails is, as McCarthy nicely puts it, in "inflating the overcoming of metaphysics into a substitute for politics" (p. 363). So I do not see myself as, in McCarthy's words, "attempt[ing] to

---

[9] Ibid., p. 160.
[10] See A.J.P. Taylor, *The Origins of the Second World War* (1963; Harmondsworth, 1977).

neutralize the political implications" of postmodernist theorizing (p. 367). What's to neutralize? I do not see that there are any such implications.[11]

As long as one thinks of "reason" as the name for a faculty capable of attaining transcultural validity, one will want a theory of the nature of rationality. But if one gives up on transcultural validity, then one will suspect that we have said enough about rationality when we say that any fool thing can be made to seem rational by being set in an appropriate context, surrounded by a set of beliefs and desires with which it coheres. The interesting question is not whether a claim can be "rationally defended" but whether it can be made to cohere with a sufficient number of *our* beliefs and desires.[12] My suspicion of theories of rationality, and of grand social theory generally, is not, however, offered as a result of a philosophical demonstration. That would, indeed, be self-referentially inconsistent in just the way McCarthy suspects I am inconsistent. I would defend this suspicion, instead, by pointing to the track record of the journalists, novelists, and anthropologists—the people who bring lots of sordid details to our attention—and arguing that the utility of their contributions has been much greater than that of the theorists. They seem to me to be the people who lately have been most efficient at doing social good, in regulating and criticizing our political activities. My attitude is not "theory is dead," but rather "as things have been going, it looks as if we could use a bit less theory and a bit more reportage." I am not saying that the idea of truth is "invalid" or "untenable," nor that it "deconstructs itself," but simply that for our present purposes there are more useful ideas (for example, freedom).

. . . Don't assume that because we are philosophers we can be of any special use, in our professional capacity, to struggles against imperialism, or racism. Don't assume, because Lenin wrote about Berkeley and Mach, that all revolutionaries need to be briefed on such topics. Don't assume that the Marxists were right that a correct theoretical analysis of the situation will be indispensable for getting rid of the local oligarch, or the CIA, or the KGB. Don't assume that, because the leader of Sendero Luminoso wrote his dissertation on Kant, he has a clearer view of Peru's problems, or a clearer vision of a possible future for his country, than the relatively uneducated woman trying to organize a food cooperative in the shantytowns outside of Lima.

McCarthy finds it ironic that an "absolute split between a depoliticized theory and a detheorized politics should be the final outcome of a project that understands itself as a pragmatic attempt to overcome the dichotomy between theory and practice" (pp. 366–67). But the only reason I speak of "depoliticized theory" is to take note of the fact that the most original theorists of recent times (for example, Heidegger, Derrida) do not give liberals like McCarthy and me any useful new tools.[13] As to "the dichotomy between theory and practice," this seems to me overcome as soon as we follow Alexander Bain and C.S. Peirce in thinking of our beliefs as rules for action—tools for getting what we want—rather than as accurate or inaccurate representations of reality, or as candidates for unconditional validity. Thinking of belief in this way, as McCarthy rightly says, "amounts to flattening out our notions of reason and truth by removing any air of transcendence from them" (p. 360). But once this flattening is accomplished, the question of

---

[11] See, on this point, my "Two Cheers for the Cultural Left," *South Atlantic Quarterly* (forthcoming). McCarthy shares some of my doubts on this point, as when he criticizes Derrida's attempt to "be postmetaphysical in thinking about ethics, law, and politics" and says that "a better way of being postmetaphysical in ethics, law, and politics is to stop doing metaphysics, even of a negative sort, when thinking about them" (McCarthy, "On the Margins of Politics," *Journal of Philosophy* 85 [Nov. 1988]: 645, 648.) More generally, McCarthy tends to agree with Jürgen Habermas's criticisms of the political utility of Derrida and Foucault in Habermas, *The Philosophical Discourse of Modernity: Twelve Lectures*, trans. Frederick Lawerence (Cambridge, Mass., 1987); as do I, with the reservations expressed in Rorty, *Contingency, Irony, and Solidarity*, pp. 61-69.

[12] For a defense of this brand of ethnocentrism, see my "Solidarity or Objectivity," in *Post Analytic Philosophy*, ed. John Rajchman and Cornel West (New York, 1985), pp. 3-19, and also my "On Ethnocentrism: A Reply to Clifford Geertz," *Michigan Quarterly Review* 25 (Summer 1986): 525-534.

[13] On this point, see Rorty, *Contingency, Irony and Solidarity*, pp. 91-95.

which tools are best suited to achieve which ends remains as salient as ever. That question can only be answered experimentally—by reference to local conditions, the situation in which alternative tools are proffered. A fortiori, the question of how much theorizing political deliberation needs at any given point can only be answered in this way. This is what I meant by saying that "we should think of politics as one of the experimental rather than of the theoretical disciplines."[14]

So when McCarthy says that my view prevents us "from even thinking, in any theoretically informed way, the thought that the basic structures of society might be inherently unjust in some way, that they might work to the systematic disadvantage of certain social groups" (p. 367), all the burden falls on "basic" and on "in any theoretically informed way." There is nothing in my view that hinders our noticing the misery and hopelessness of inner-city American blacks or Latin American slum-dwellers or Cambodian peasants. Nor is there anything that suggests such misery and hopelessness is irremediable. There is only the suggestion that we already have as much theory as we need, and that what we need now are concrete utopias, and concrete proposals about how to get to those utopias from where we are now.

That the middle class of the United States, as of South Africa, is unwilling to pay the taxes necessary to give poor blacks a decent education and a chance in life seems to me a fact we need no fancier theoretical notions than "greed," "selfishness," and "racial prejudice" to explain. That successive American presidents have ordered or allowed the CIA to make it as difficult as possible to depose Latin American oligarchies seems another such well-known fact, whose explanation is to be found on the level of details about the activities of, for example, the United Fruit Company and Anaconda Copper in Washington's corridors of power. When I am told that to appreciate the significance of these facts I need a deeper understanding of, for example, the discourses of power characteristic of late capitalism, I am incredulous.

Maybe I have not been reading the right theorists, but I really have no clear idea what it means to say that "the basic structures of society" (capitalist society, presumably) are responsible for these facts, any more than to say that other "basic structures" (those of noncapitalist societies) are responsible for the plight of the Romanians or the Tibetans. I am not sure what a "theoretically informed way" to think about these matters would be, as opposed to a historically and journalistically informed way. I can happily agree that philosophers and social theorists have, in the past, done a lot of good by giving us ways to put in words our vague sense that something has gone terribly wrong. Notions like "the rights of man," "surplus value," "the new class," and the like have been indispensable for moral and political progress. But I am not convinced that we are currently in need of new notions of this sort. A lot of social theory nowadays seems to me just putting overelaborate icing on cakes historians, journalists, economic statisticians, anthropologists, and others have already baked.

It seems to me that people who believe in "a moment of unconditionality" and in intercultural validity are still prone to think that there is an activity called "radical reconceptualization" that might tear the scales from our eyes and let us see what is *really* going on—see things as God sees them. Even though McCarthy and Putnam claim to have renounced the idea of a God's-eye point of view, their faith in theory and for the idea of truth seems to me to reflect a nostalgia for the logocentrist's unveiling-reality model of inquiry as opposed to the pragmatist's invention-of-new-tools model. For if one uses the latter model, the notion "basic structure of society" will fade out in favor of notions like "malleable social structure," "pressure point for initiating structural change." The question "What is the truth about our society?" fades out in favor of questions like "What would let more people in this society get more freedom?" "What will it take to elect a left-wing Democratic (Labor, SPD) government?" and "Is there anything except coca paste that Peru could produce and export in quantities sufficient to

[14] Rorty, "From Logic to Language to Play: A Plenary Address to the Inter-American Congress," *Proceedings and Addresses of the American Philosophical Association* 59 (1986): 752-53.

significantly raise the Peruvian standard of living?" The question "Is this value interculturally valid?" fades out in favor of questions like "Do you have any better values to suggest?" The question "How can you be sure your values are unconditionally valid?" fades out in favor of the question "How can we be sure that discussion of alternative values is as free, open, and imaginative as possible?" Social theorists and philosophers deserve a hearing in such discussion, for, like everybody else, they may have something imaginative to say. But there is no guarantee that they will, and no reason to view them as indispensable.